ENGLAND ON EDGE

England on Edge
Crisis and Revolution
1640–1642

DAVID CRESSY

OXFORD
UNIVERSITY PRESS

OXFORD

UNIVERSITY PRESS

Great Clarendon Street, Oxford OX2 6DP

Oxford University Press is a department of the University of Oxford.
It furthers the University's objective of excellence in research, scholarship,
and education by publishing worldwide in

Oxford New York

Auckland Cape Town Dar es Salaam Hong Kong Karachi
Kuala Lumpur Madrid Melbourne Mexico City Nairobi
New Delhi Shanghai Taipei Toronto

With offices in

Argentina Austria Brazil Chile Czech Republic France Greece
Guatemala Hungary Italy Japan Poland Portugal Singapore
South Korea Switzerland Thailand Turkey Ukraine Vietnam

Oxford is a registered trade mark of Oxford University Press
in the UK and in certain other countries

Published in the United States
by Oxford University Press Inc., New York

First published 2006
First published in paperback 2007

British Library Cataloguing in Publication Data

Data available

Library of Congress Cataloging in Publication Data

Data available

Typeset by Laserwords Private Limited, Chennai, India
Printed in Great Britain
on acid-free paper by
Biddles Ltd., King's Lynn, Norfolk

ISBN 978-0-19-928090-2 (Hbk)   978-0-19-923763-0 (Pbk)

1 3 5 7 9 10 8 6 4 2

'Here's fine Revolution, if we had the trick to see it.'
—William Shakespeare, *Hamlet*, V. i.

Contents

PART IV. THE ONSET OF CIVIL WAR

List of Illustrations

List of Maps and Figures

Preliminaries

Introduction

This book deals with the collapse of the government of Charles I, the disintegration of the Church of England, and the accompanying panic that swept through much of the country on the eve of the English civil war. Focused on the years 1640 to 1642, it examines stresses and fractures in political and religious culture and disturbances to customary social relationships in the opening stages of the English revolution. The shock and magnitude of these changes is made more apparent by reference to the conditions, practices, and arrangements that came before, as a peaceable and orderly kingdom descended into turmoil and confusion.

Like all my work, this book is concerned with the relationships between governors and governed, centre and periphery, elite and popular, high culture and low. Hundreds of people not normally seen in historical surveys make appearances here, in a drama much larger than the struggle of king and parliament. Historians commonly assert that royalists and parliamentarians parted company over issues of principle, constitutional scruples, and religious belief, and that remains true enough. However, a more complex picture emerges when we explore the historical experience of anxiety, mistrust, and fear.

When I started work on this project my English friends enquired, 'What are you trying to find out?' while my American colleagues asked me, 'What are you going to argue?' The two questions expose different approaches to historiographical discourse and different traditions of rhetoric and research, and each deserves an answer. I began by trying to discover as much as possible about the social and religious condition of England at the time of its most acute domestic crisis. Combining manuscript and printed sources, I set out to discover the pulse of the nation and the temper of the times in the sixteenth and seventeenth years of the reign of Charles I, between the spring of 1640 and the summer of 1642. I wanted to understand how people in various circumstances coped with the ordeal of the kingdom amidst the shattering of the church, the breakdown of the government, and the descent into civil war. The archives have told me more than I ever thought possible about challenges in churches, collisions between soldiers and civilians, and the deployment of rhetoric and texts. However, they have also given me an argument.

Put simply, my argument here is that England in 1641 was in the throes of a revolution with political, constitutional, religious, cultural, and social dimensions. The strains of this revolution, reactions against it, and the inability of the political elite to harness or contain it best explains why civil war broke out in the summer of 1642. It was the revolution that caused the war, not the war that caused the revolution. Contemporaries found the crisis of 1640–2 to be profoundly disturbing. Their reactions ranged from exhilaration to perplexity and dread. The upheavals of these years led important people to make bad decisions—to practice a politics of anxiety and misperception—that hampered efforts to avoid a war that was by no means inevitable.

Rather than seeing the revolutionary transformation of religious and political culture as products of the civil war, as has been common among historians, I find the world turned upside down in the two years preceding the outbreak of hostilities. The humbling of Charles I, the erosion of the royal prerogative, and the rise of an executive parliament were central features of the revolutionary drama of 1640–2. The collapse of the Laudian ascendancy, the splintering of the Church of England, the rise of radical sectarianism, and the emergence of a conservative Anglican resistance, all took place in these two years before the outbreak of civil war. The world of public discourse became rapidly energized and expanded, in counterpoint with an exuberantly unfettered press and a deeply traumatized state. This study is an attempt to tell that story.

Sources

The following discussion draws on a wide range of manuscript and printed sources. I have tried to read as much as possible of the surviving correspondence, memoranda, accounts, reports, and publications of the two years immediately preceding the civil war. No single study can claim to be exhaustive, but this rests on as broad a substructure of evidence as can be amassed.

Manuscript sources include the records of central and local government, the processes of secular and ecclesiastical courts, parish registers and account books, petitions, diaries, note-books, memoranda, and letters. Although most of this material was generated by the literate and prosperous it sometimes includes sayings of the humble and poor. Depositions, examinations, and other court records include versions of conversations in alehouses and disputes in private houses, as well as statements before magistrates. Letter collections include transcripts of libels and verses that originally circulated in the streets. Echoes and traces of many of the voices of the tumults and tensions of 1640–2 survive in the documentary record. Much of this is well known and has long been available to scholars. But I was moved by the county archivist who produced some quarter sessions records with the comment, 'I don't remember anyone ever looking at these before.' I have used this material to capture the immediacy of the crisis for those who lived through it, while acknowledging inevitable mediations, shadings, and distortions.

Printed sources for this period are especially rich and abundant. No previous moment in British history produced so much from the press. Modern bibliographical analysis finds over 800 published items from 1640, more than 2,000 from 1641, and in excess of 4,000 from 1642. There were probably several hundred more printed products that have vanished. The period 1640–2 was exceptional for the number and diversity of its printed publications, and not until the eighteenth century would this peak be surpassed. I have made extensive use of rare book collections in Britain and the United States, and occasional use of Early English Books On-Line, guided by the online English Short-Title Catalogue. Full references appear in my notes.

Acknowledgements

I have accumulated many scholarly debts while researching and writing this book. Other historians have been generous with their comments on my work-in-progress and presentations at seminars and conferences. I am fortunate to have been working at a time when the boundaries between social, cultural, and political history have been dissolved or transcended. These acknowledgements are insufficient and incomplete, but I am particularly grateful to the following for their inspiration, criticism, and advice: T. H. Breen, Charles Carlton, Tom Cogswell, David Como, Robert Davis, Barbara Donagan, Lori Anne Ferrell, Charles Mark Fissel, Mark Goldie, Christopher Haigh, Tim Harris, Clive Holmes, Peter Lake, Sears McGee, John Morrill, Geoffrey Parker, Carla Pestana, Kevin Sharpe, Alexandra Shepard, Keith Thomas, Alexandra Walsham, Michelle Wolfe, Andy Wood, and Keith Wrightson. I am also indebted to literary scholars who have helped to sharpen my analysis, especially Sharon Achenstein, Cyndia Clegg, Jean Howard, Paulina Kewes, and Debora Shuger. It is a pleasure to record that our work is collaborative as well as competitive, in the common pursuit of the early modern past. Valerie Cressy checked my writing and accompanied me on many journeys, not all of them academic. The design and execution of this project, however, is mine alone, and I am responsible for any remaining errors.

Among various agencies and institutions, my greatest debt is to the Department of History and the College of Humanities at the Ohio State University for their continuing support of my research. I am grateful to the Master and Fellows of Churchill College, Cambridge, for an Overseas Fellowship in 2000–1 that enabled me to lay the archival foundations for this study. In a year marked by petrol shortages, railway disasters, cattle disease, countryside closures, and exceptional flooding, I worked my way around forty-five English archives and record offices, whose staffs were professional and accommodating. I am grateful to the Huntington Library, San Marino, California, for the opportunity to deliver the Homer D. Crotty Lecture in 2002, and to the editors of *Past and Present* for publishing a version of that lecture as 'Revolutionary England, 1640–1642' (*Past and Present*, no. 191, November 2003), and for allowing me to incorporate parts of it in this book. I extend thanks to the Rockefeller Foundation for a memorable month at their Conference and Study Center at Bellagio, Italy, in the late spring of 2003. And thanks again to the President, Director, and staff at the Huntington for the award of the Fletcher Jones Distinguished Fellowship during 2003–4, when the bulk of this study was written. I wish to acknowledge the support of the National Endowment for the Humanities for funding a summer institute at the Folger Shakespeare Library in Washington, DC, in 2003 on the theme of 'Cultural Stress from Reformation to Revolution,' in which I was as much a learner as teacher, and for the award of a Fellowship in 2004 that enabled me to bring this project to conclusion.

In works cited the place of publication is London unless otherwise indicated. Spelling and punctuation have been modernized, except in the titles of publications. I retain, however, the usage 'mechanick' to refer to artisan preachers. Dates are given old style, except that the year is taken to have begun on 1 January. Among standard abbreviations, *CSPD* represents *Calendar of State Papers, Domestic*, HMC is Historical Manuscripts Commission, and PRO is Public Record Office, Kew, now known as the British National Archives.

MAP 1. Map of England

PART I

CAROLINE DISTEMPERS

1

Crisis and Revolution

Charles I's reign ended in catastrophe for his supporters, his family, and his kingdoms. The general history of this unravelling is very well known, though some of the sources and some of the observations presented here may be unfamiliar. A brief review of the Caroline crisis will provide a framework for the discussion that follows. The developments mentioned here were among the most noteworthy of the era, but, as this book relates, there were many subsidiary narratives. This chapter begins with an historical sketch of the years before the civil war, and then attempts to situate the current study historiographically. It turns next to the ways in which the history of this period was handled by historians who lived through it, and examines some of the changing analyses of the later seventeenth century. It concludes with a review of the language commentators used to describe these developments, in particular their use of the word 'revolution.'

STRESSES AND FRACTURES

Early Stuart England coped with a series of stresses, both structural and contingent. Some were deep-rooted, stretching back to the cultural and religious changes of the Reformation, but others were recently inflicted or exacerbated by the rigidities of the Caroline regime. By 1640 the government of Charles I had managed to alienate a high proportion of those subjects who might otherwise have been the most fervent supporters of the Crown.

For the gentry the principal issues of contention included ship money, forest laws, and fines in distraint of knighthood, involving the allegedly arbitrary exercise of royal prerogative power. Some religious activists were alarmed that England's foreign policy showed insufficient support for embattled international protestantism, and many more feared that the churchmanship favoured by the King and Archbishop Laud was leading England back towards Rome. The parliamentary politics of the later 1620s had soured over constitutional and religious issues, and many grievances festered in the eleven-year period in which there was no Parliament to redress them. The fiscal, political, religious, and cultural problems of the 1630s were not unmanageable, but they belied the conceit, promoted by court conservatives, that these were England's Halcyon Days. Apologists for the personal rule of Charles I frequently asserted that England was the most fortunate of kingdoms, but this was a blinkered perception, or pride before a fall.

The Caroline regime's imposition of a ceremonialist prayer book on presbyterian Scotland in 1637 destabilized the politics of both north and south Britain. England's peaceable kingdom—once the envy of war-torn Europe—became embroiled in a British rebellion. The Bishops' Wars of 1638 to 1640 drained its coffers. Political and religious grievances that were previously subject to containment began, by the end of the decade, to overwhelm the traditional confessional state.

Determined to take his war to the enemy in Scotland, and with no other apparent financial recourse, King Charles reluctantly called a parliament to meet in April 1640. This so-called Short Parliament, the first to meet in eleven years, produced nothing but bitterness, and its dissolution after just three weeks precipitated outbreaks of unrest. Later that summer England's ill-prepared army crumbled under Scottish pressure at the battle of Newburn (28 August 1640), allowing the Scots to occupy north-east England with its important reserves of coal. The Stuart regime was dishonoured, the Crown's weakness was exposed, and the personal rule of Charles I was falling apart.

A new parliament in November raised hopes of a settlement for both kingdoms. Urged on by the Scots, some members seized the opportunity to plunge into religious reform, and some directly challenged the authority of the Stuart ancien regime. The arrest of the Earl of Strafford (11 November) and the impeachment of the Archbishop of Canterbury (18 December) left the government reeling and altered the dynamics of power. By the end of the year the church, the court, the crown, and the law—the customary structures of the constitution, religion, and society—were all in a state of flux. Soldiers threatened mutiny, citizens threatened insurrection, and sectaries set about to overthrow Babylon. Enthusiasts anticipated a godly reformation, though many among the ruling elite feared slippage into chaos.

The year 1641 saw crisis compound into revolution. The King let his prerogative unravel, submitting to triennial and semi-permanent parliaments (16 February and 10 May), permitting the execution of the Earl of Strafford (12 May), and allowing the abolition of such powerful prerogative instruments as the courts of Star Chamber and High Commission (5 July). Episcopal authority crumbled, ecclesiastical discipline ceased to operate, and a variety of radical ideas and practices clamoured for attention. Before the year was out the King's main advisors were humiliated or imprisoned, exiled or executed. Most of the bishops were discredited or impeached. Half the circuit judges were disabled and could no longer ride to assizes. Hundreds of parishes were in uproar. There was a massive settling of scores, as victims of Laudian discipline were rehabilitated and agents of the hardline policy of 'Thorough' were brought to book.

Traditional social and political hierarchies were challenged, in the course of this revolutionary ferment, as broadening sectors of the populace joined arguments and demonstrations. Subjects and citizens began to behave as if they had the right to engage boisterously in the kingdom's public affairs. Press licensing and censorship collapsed, sectaries and satirists were sharpening their pens, and people throughout the country discovered unrestrained appetites for news and opinion.

Many supporters of the parliamentary programme expressed pride in their achievements by the time of the peace treaty with Scotland in September 1641, although some worried that religious radicalism was growing out of control. But all grounds for optimism were crushed by news of the Irish uprising in late October. Reports of atrocities inflicted on Protestants, anxiety about continued popish plotting, and realization that a new army would be required to put down the rebellion transformed the political environment at Westminster. Parliamentary politics became further embittered in November as members divided over the Grand Remonstrance, a catalogue of grievances against the Caroline regime. Popular agitation against bishops and Catholics, and violent demonstrations in London and Westminster, made for a memorably disorderly Christmas season.

In 1642 it only got worse. When King Charles attempted to arrest parliamentary leaders in January 1642 and failed in this coup, the outrage against him drove the King and his family from London. He was further humiliated in April when he was denied admission to the royal garrison town of Hull. Political and religious fracturing intensified in the spring of 1642 as Parliament assumed authority to raise troops for Ireland and religious radicals battled conservatives in the parishes. Uncertainty, alarm, anxiety, and fear coloured the national conversation. Political factions slowly mutated into opposing armies, and local competition to control weapons and resources led to clashes between proto-Roundheads and Cavaliers. The summer of 1642 saw a national competition for allegiance, as supporters mobilized on behalf of the parliamentary Militia Ordinance (5 March) and the King's Commission of Array (11 June). Against a background of polarization and panic, amidst a forlorn debate about the urgency of accommodation, the polity blundered into civil war.

By September 1642 the rival forces were manoeuvring for military advantage, wondering whether they would have to fight. By 1643 the casualty count was already in the thousands. By 1646 the King was a prisoner. By 1649 he was dead, his royal office abolished. England would undergo a further decade of constitutional experiment, religious exploration, and military rule before embracing, or succumbing to, the counter-revolution of the Restoration.

HISTORIES AND HISTORIANS

This well-known history of the collapse of the Caroline regime and the undermining of the Tudor–Stuart state commands formidable scholarly attention. The English Revolution is widely regarded as a 'world-historical' event, notwithstanding the efforts of revisionists to cut it down to size. Casting long shadows from the seventeenth century, the entanglements of 1640–2 and the eighteen years that followed belong to an enduring historiographical conundrum, alongside such classics as the nature of the Reformation, the French Revolution, and the origins of the First World War. Explanation of the causes of the English Revolution has become a holy grail for early modern scholars; royalists and revisionists, Marxists and Whigs, neo-Marxists and post-revisionists, all have had their stir of the pot.[1] Literary scholars have also been drawn to this terrain, exploring subaltern poetic voices, the dying gasps of the early-Stuart drama, and the polemical rhetoric of Milton's early prose.[2] Social scientists have been especially willing to see revolutionary England as a font or forcing house of modernity. If they

---

[1] The debate is summarized and advanced in Jack A. Goldstone, *Revolution and Rebellion in the Early Modern World* (Berkeley and London, 1991); Ann Hughes, *The Causes of the English Civil War* (1991); R. C. Richardson, *The Debate on the English Revolution* (3rd edn., Manchester, 1998); and John Morrill, *Revolt in the Provinces: The People of England and the Tragedies of War 1630–1648* (2nd edn., 1999). See also Barry Coward, 'Was There an English Revolution in the Middle of the Seventeenth Century?', in Colin Jones, Malyn Newitt, and Stephen Roberts (eds.), *Politics and People in Revolutionary England* (Oxford, 1986), 9–39; Alastair MacLachlan, *The Rise and Fall of Revolutionary England: An Essay on the Fabrication of Seventeenth-Century History* (New York, 1996); and James Holstun, *Ehud's Dagger: Class Struggle in the English Revolution* (London and New York, 2000).

[2] See especially Sharon Achinstein, 'The Politics of Babel in the English Revolution', in James Holstun (ed.), *Pamphlet Wars: Prose in the English Revolution* (1992), 14–44; idem., 'Texts in Conflict: The Press and the Civil War', in N. H. Keeble (ed.), *The Cambridge Companion to the Writing of the English Revolution* (Cambridge, 2001), 50–68; idem., *Literature and Dissent in Milton's England* (Cambridge, 2003); David Norbrook, *Writing the English Republic: Poetry, Rhetoric, and Politics, 1627–1660* (Cambridge, 1999); Nigel Smith, *Perfection Proclaimed: Language and Literature in English Radical Religion, 1640–1660* (Oxford, 1989); idem., *Literature and Revolution in England, 1640–1660* (New Haven, 1994); Susan Wiseman, *Drama and Politics in the English Civil War* (Cambridge, 1998).

no longer see the English Revolution as a classic case of class conflict they are nonetheless inclined to champion its alleged fostering of democracy, liberty, citizenship, religious toleration, pluralism, and the expanded public sphere.[3]

Enormous effort has gone into characterizing the English Revolution and anatomizing its origins, although there is no consensus about its nature, its timing, its meaning, or its consequences. Questions continue to be raised about the structural and circumstantial factors that led to the breakdown, the passions that fuelled the conflict, and the blame to be assigned for successive failures of accommodation. The years 1640–2 in particular are among the most intensively examined in British history. Generations of historians have grappled with the foundering of the government of Charles I, the rise of a revolutionary Parliament, the fragmentation of the Church of England, and the descent into civil war. The international research bibliography in this area is vast, contentious, and ever-growing. This is blood-stained historiographical terrain.

Recent contributions to the debate have emphasized both its ideological and geographical dimensions. The 'puritan revolution' has yielded to 'England's wars of religion.' The 'revolt of the provinces' has expanded into 'the wars of the three kingdoms'. The revolution, if such it was, is now properly seen to be British as well as English, inexplicable without its Scottish and Irish components. Charles I's problems, like those of Protector Cromwell, are understood in terms of the management of complex international territories with competing religious and constitutional traditions. Some scholars find even this archipelagian approach too narrow, and emphasize instead the European or even global compass. Jonathan Scott has relocated 'England's troubles' within the larger context of European political instability, whereas Geoffrey Parker sees these local disturbances as part of the larger 'world crisis' of the seventeenth century, tied to global cooling and demographic stress.[4]

Dating the revolution proves notoriously tricky. By some accounts the revolution did not happen before the autumn of 1648 and was probably all over by the following spring. Others allow it a longer period of vitality, perhaps from 1647 to 1658 or from the Scottish wars of the late 1630s to the Restoration reaction of 1662. The most fruitful approach seems to be to

---

[3] For a selection, see Barrington Moore, *Social Origins of Dictatorship and Democracy: Lord and Peasant in the Making of the Modern World* (Boston, 1966, reprinted 1993); Conal Condren, *The Language of Politics in Seventeenth-Century England* (Basingstoke and New York, 1994); David Zaret, *Origins of Democratic Culture: Printing, Petitions, and the Public Sphere in Early-Modern England* (Princeton, 2000).

[4] Morrill, *Revolt in the Provinces*; Conrad Russell, *The Fall of the British Monarchies 1637–1642* (Oxford, 1991); Jonathan Scott, *England's Troubles: Seventeenth-Century English Political Instability in European Context* (Cambridge, 2000); Geoffrey Parker, *The World Crisis, 1635–1665* (forthcoming).

consider the revolution as a process rather than a moment, an evolution rather than an event, involving a series of crashes and crises between 1640 and 1660, with reverberations that went on even longer. Regis Debray's concept of 'revolution within the revolution' proves helpful in this regard, while Christopher Haigh's emphatic plural in *English Reformations* provides another descriptive model. There are many answers to the essential question, 'What was revolutionary about "England's age of revolution"?'[5]

Some scholars have been reluctant to countenance an English Revolution at all. Eyeing structural and demographic continuities across the early modern era, the pioneering social historian Peter Laslett found no trace of an English Revolution and called for the phrase to be 'expunged' or 'entombed'.[6] Theorists equipped with a model of revolutionary change based on France in 1789 or Russia in 1917 likewise judged the seventeenth-century English case unrealized, its revolutionary status overclaimed.[7] Determined to distance themselves from Whiggish and Marxist excesses, high political revisionists of the 1980s also set their face against the notion that anything earth-shattering took place in the seventeenth century, except perhaps the killing of the King. Some argued that the last thing to expect in the reign of Charles I was civil war or revolution, and if they attempted to explain the former it was often by denying the latter. Conrad Russell, for example, scrupulously eschewed the word 'revolution', and titled his essays on the pre-war period *Unrevolutionary England*.[8] Reactions to these assaults temporarily stunned some scholars into silence, although like the historiographical undead the English Revolution keeps getting up and pulling the stake from its heart.

Most scholars who recognize an English Revolution take it to have embraced a transformed political environment, profound constitutional upheaval, a shattered religious culture, and a spate of radical ideas. However, too often these developments are located *after* 1642, as if they were products or consequences of the civil war. Alan G. R. Smith, in an influential survey, locates the radicalization of political, religious, and social attitudes 'in the years

---

[5] Regis Debray, *Revolution in the Revolution* (Harmondsworth, 1967), 127, concerns the Cuban revolution and its export to Latin America. It argues that not even Marxist revolutions need to adhere to the classic communist model: 'In a given historical situation there may be a thousand ways to speak of the revolution', Christopher Haigh, *English Reformations: Religion, Politics, and Society under the Tudors* (Oxford, 1993). Cf. Christopher Hill, *The Century of Revolution, 1603–1714* (1962); proceedings of a conference at the University of Chicago on 'England's Age of Revolution', November 2001.

[6] Peter Laslett, *The World We Have Lost* (1965), 150–8; idem, *The World We Have Lost— Further Explored* (1983), 182–206.

[7] Theda Skocpol, *States and Social Revolutions* (Cambridge, 1979); Charles Tilly, *From Mobilization to Revolution* (Reading, Mass., 1978); Goldstone, *Revolution and Rebellion*.

[8] Conrad Russell, *Unrevolutionary England, 1603–1642* (1990); idem, *The Causes of the English Civil War* (Oxford, 1990), 8–9.

after 1642'.[9] Kevin Sharpe finds the world turned upside down after 1642, when the civil war 'produced' a burgeoning pamphlet literature and an expanded public sphere.[10] John Morrill similarly presents the English Revolution as 'the product of the traumas of civil war'. The regicide was the crucial event, though there is some doubt whether this represented an end or a beginning.[11] In Mark Kishlansky's pithy characterization, 'the English Revolution was born of the axe' in 1649 and died with the death of Oliver Cromwell.[12]

However, this is to miss the moment and invert the sequence, by leaping over the transformations that occurred in the two years immediately before the war. Much of England's world turned upside *before* the outbreak of hostilities, between 1640 and 1642. The collapse of the Laudian ascendancy, the humbling of Charles I, the splintering of the Church of England, and a transformation of the social circumstances for public debate, all took place before the outbreak of war, against the background of an exuberantly unfettered press and a deeply traumatized state. The twenty-four months between the failure of the Short Parliament in the spring of 1640 and the beginnings of armed mobilization in the spring of 1642 saw the Elizabethan confessional state disintegrate and the Stuart ancien regime fall apart. Although there would be further revolutions within the revolution, involving Levellers, Quakers, regicide, republicanism, and constitutions backed by military rule, the fundamental shifts occurred in the sixteenth and seventeenth years of the reign of Charles I.[13]

This early dating of the revolution used to be more common, but was swamped by the revisionist tide. Christopher Hill commented on the 'revolutionary innovation' of the legislation of 1641, whereas Perez Zagorin opined that 'the revolution began with the opening of the Long Parliament at Westminster on November 3, 1640'.[14] H. R. Trevor Roper characterized 'the

---

[9] Alan G. R. Smith, *The Emergence of a Nation State: The Commonwealth of England, 1529–1660* (London and New York, 2nd edn., 1997), 296.

[10] Kevin Sharpe, *Remapping Early Modern England: The Culture of Seventeenth-Century Politics* (Cambridge, 2000), 22, 115.

[11] John Morrill, *The Nature of the English Revolution* (1993), 17, 23–4; idem, 'The Causes and Course of the British Civil Wars,' in Keeble (ed.), *Cambridge Companion to Writing of the English Revolution*, 29–30.

[12] Mark Kishlansky, *A Monarchy Transformed: Britain 1603–1714* (1996), 186, 189, 191.

[13] This is the view sketched out in David Cressy, 'Revolutionary England 1640–1642', *Past and Present*, 181 (2003), 35–71. Cf. James Harrington's remark in the preliminaries to *Oceana* [1656] that 'the dissolution of this government caused the war, not the war the dissolution of this government', in J. G. A. Pocock (ed.), *The Political Works of James Harrington* (Cambridge, 1977), 198.

[14] Hill, *Century of Revolution*, 111; Perez Zagorin, *Rebels and Rulers, 1500–1660* (2 vols., Cambridge, 1982), ii. 13; idem, *The Court and the Country: The Beginning of the English Revolution* (New York, 1969).

excitement, the exhilaration and expectancy' of mid-1641, as 'a revolution, or the beginning of a revolution, of vast, even cosmic proportions'.[15] This was also the view of some of the earliest historians of England's troubles, who similarly dated the core of the crisis to 1641.[16]

MYTHS AND MEMORIES

The battle to control the meaning and memory of the English Revolution began even as its earliest episodes were unfolding. The reiteration of recent historical developments enabled contemporaries to make sense of the disturbances of their age. The writing of history imposed narrative order and thematic coherence on a bewildering clutter of confusions. History, then as now, allowed participants to understand their place in time.

Sermons, tracts, remonstrances, and petitions employed historical framing to justify grievances, to proclaim their righteousness, and to promote their points of view. Parliamentary speech-makers, pamphleteers, and propagandists similarly deployed and invoked the past. Some looked back over a century to the beginnings of the Tudor Reformation, but most dwelt mainly on the past few months or years. Whether supportive or critical of the King, favourable or antagonistic to Parliament, or hostile or enthusiastic for religious reform, they all attempted to harness history to their present partisan concerns. A few engaged in counterfactual speculation, ruefully considering how crucial episodes might have turned out differently if providence or policy had been otherwise.

Two principal stories emerged from contemporary historical writing. One told of the imperilment of the Protestant Reformation, especially in the 1630s, under a malignant and ill-advised regime, and then the providential resumption of reform after 1640 that was tested to extremes by civil war. The other told how King Charles's 'fortunate islands' fell into 'horrid distempers', how 'England the glory of all islands...one of the most puissant and flourishing monarchies in the world' was overwhelmed by unexpected catastrophe.[17] One was a story of darkness followed by light, the other of

---

[15] H. R. Trevor Roper, *Catholics, Anglicans and Puritans: 17th Century Essays* (Chicago, 1988), 250.

[16] Edward Hyde, Earl of Clarendon, *The History of the Rebellion and Civil Wars in England Begun in the Year 1641*, ed. W. Dunn Macray (6 vols., Oxford, 1888); [Edward Howard], *Caroloiades, Or, The Rebellion of Forty One* (1689); *A Discourse Discovering Some Mysteries of Our New State...ab anno illo infortunato, 1641* (Oxford, 1645).

[17] [James Howell], *The True Informer...of the Sad Distempers in Great Britanny and Ireland* (1643), 4; *The Weekly Discovery of the Mystery of Iniquity in The Rise, Growth, Methods and Ends of the Late Unnatural Rebellion in England, Anno 1641* (1681), broadside, 30 parts, no. 1; [Howard], *Caroloiades*, 3–4.

sunshine extinguished by storms. Parliamentary puritans told the first story, conservative royalists told the second. Between them they gave shape to three and a half centuries of commentary and interpretation: Roundhead and Cavalier, Whig and Tory, liberal and revisionist, post revisionist and neo-ironic.

Parliamentary propagandists of the early 1640s typically cast their exhortations in historical terms, reviewing the 'ebbings and flowings in matters of religion' since the Tudor Reformation. They adhered to a standard historical narrative in which Henry VIII threw out the pope, Edward VI threw out popery, and the Marian popish frenzy was ended by the providential accession of Queen Elizabeth. Elizabeth made English Protestantism secure, though not without concessions to conservatives. King James held the church steady, in line with international Calvinism, but under his son the church was once more at risk. By some accounts the Church of England was the most fortunate and best governed in Christendom, but others feared that it had fallen into idolatry and superstition and was in need of a vigorous reformation.[18] The theme of Edmund Calamy's history was 'the ruin and repair of kingdoms', and his call to the 'worthies of Israel' in the light of this history was 'to reform the reformation itself'.[19] John Vicars wrote similarly of a 'tottering state', overflowing with fears, that could only be cured by a godly reforming Parliament.[20]

The London petition of December 1640, known since the nineteenth century as 'the root and branch petition', listed 'the manifold evils, pressures and grievances, caused, practiced and occasioned by the prelates', during the archiepiscopate of William Laud.[21] Parliament's articles of impeachment against the Archbishop cited his policies and dealings to prove that he had 'traitorously laboured to subvert the fundamental laws and government of the kingdom', had gone about 'to subvert religion established in this kingdom, and to set up papistry and superstition in the church', and had caused 'a bloody war' between England and Scotland.[22] The petition used recent history to argue for the dismantling of the entire episcopal hierarchy. The impeachment articles cited the history of the same few years to justify the

[18] Cornelius Burges, *The First Sermon, Preached to the Honourable House of Commons...Novemb. 17. 1640* (1641), 49; Stephen Marshall, *A Sermon Preached before the Honourable House of Commons...November 17. 1640* (1641); Henry Burton, *Englands Bondage and Hope of Deliverance* (1641).

[19] Edmund Calamy, *Englands Looking-Glasse* (1642), sig. A2, 46. Cf. [John Milton], *Of Reformation Touching Church-Discipline in England: And the Causes that hitherto have hindered it* (1641), 8–22, and John Vicars, *God in the Mount. Or, Englands Remembrancer* (1641), 5.

[20] Vicars, *God in the* Mount, 6–7.

[21] *The First and Large Petition of the Citie of London* (1641), 3.

[22] *Articles Exhibited in Parliament against William Archbishop of Canterbury* (1640), 1, 3, 4; *The Speech or Declaration of John Pymm...against William Laud* (1641). See also *Articles of Impeachment...against Matthew Wren* (1641).

punishment of a principal offender. Petitions and charges against so-called 'scandalous' ministers were often cast as micro-historical dramas, citing particular 'innovations, usurpations, vexations, and wrongs' that mirrored the oppressions of the kingdom.[23]

The articles of accusation and impeachment against Lord Keeper Finch, submitted to the House of Commons in December 1640, built an historical case to prove that Finch and others had 'traitorously and wickedly endeavoured to subvert the fundamental laws and established government of the realm of England'. The Lord Keeper's treason, proved by his legal opinions and decisions across the 1630s, served 'to alienate the hearts of his majesty's liege people from his majesty, and to set a division between them, to ruin his majesty's realm of England'.[24] So too, the Earl of Strafford's traitorous intention 'to introduce an arbitrary and tyrannical government' and 'to ruin and destroy his majesty's kingdoms' was declared by his actions as a royal councillor and Lord Deputy in Ireland from the seventh to the sixteenth years of the reign of Charles I. The articles of impeachment against Strafford, and the Earl's point-by-point defence, had elements of an historical debate on the government of Ireland, fiscal policy in England, and the conduct of the recent Scottish war.[25] The detailed case against these disgraced government ministers supported parliamentary efforts to bring them to justice. The public rehearsal of this embittered history helped justify the extraordinary action of instituting trienniel parliaments and dismantling the apparatus of the royal prerogative courts.

Parliament's controversial *Remonstrance of the State of the Kingdom* (1641), known since Victorian times as the 'Grand Remonstrance', set out to show 'the root...growth...maturity and ripeness' of the various 'miseries and calamities...distempers and disorders' that afflicted the kingdom since the accession of Charles I, and the progress towards their 'extirpations' in the last twelve months.[26] Its procedure was essentially historical, employing narrative, chronology, and analysis to explain the course of the crisis. It reported the unremitting labour of papists and prelates, courtiers and

---

[23] For example, *The Articles and Charge Proved in Parliament against Doctor Walton, Minister of St. Martin Orgars* (1641), 13; *Articles Exhibited in Parliament, against Master Iohn Squire, Viccar of Saint Leonard Shoreditch* (1641); *The Petition and Articles Exhibited in Parliament against Doctor Heywood* (1641); *The Petition and Articles Exhibited in Parliament against Iohn Pocklington* (1641).

[24] *The Accusation and Impeachment of Iohn Lord Finch* (1640), 1, 9. Finch fled to France on 22 December 1640. See also *Articles of Accusation Exhibited By the House of Commons* [against six judges] (1641).

[25] Articles of Impeachment, with Strafford's responses, in Maija Jansson (ed.), *Proceedings in the Opening Session of the Long Parliament...Volume 3: 22 March–17 April 1641* (Rochester, NY, 2001), 8–48.

[26] *A Remonstrance of the State of the Kingdom* (1641), 3, 4.

councillors, to subvert the fundamental principles of government and to deliver English religion into anti-Protestant hands. And it used this highly partisan history to justify a revolutionary constitutional change that would subject government appointments and policies to parliamentary approval.

'After the breach of the parliament in the fourth year of his majesty (1629), injustice, oppression, and violence broke in upon us, without any restraint or moderation.' The regime imposed fines for default of knighthood, forest fines, ship money, and monopolies, among various vexatious and illegal measures. 'The Court of Star Chamber hath abounded in extravagant censures...fines, imprisonments, stigmatizings, mutilations, whippings, pillories, gags, confinements, banishments', and 'other English courts have been grievous in exceeding their jurisdiction.' The ecclesiastical courts inflicted miseries, while 'the High Commission grew to such excess of sharpness and severity as was not much less than the Romish Inquisition.'[27]

The Remonstrance identified the Archbishop of Canterbury and the Earl of Strafford as leaders of 'the malignant party' who drew the King into an unfortunate war with Scotland, and 'wickedly advised' him to break off the Short Parliament. 'The popish party' was said to have enjoyed privileges and exemptions while 'the people languished under grief and fear'. However, the tables turned later in 1640 with the Scottish occupation of Newcastle and the calling of the November Parliament, allowing good men to tackle 'the multiplied evils and corruption of sixteen years'.[28]

Parliamentary preachers and propagandists repeatedly recited this story and identified 1641 as the 'golden year' in which 'God's mercies to England' were revealed.[29] The London schoolmaster John Vicars constituted himself as remembrancer in chief, chronicling all the 'mercies' that had befallen the nation 'in her years of jubilee, 1641 and 1642'. His principal purpose was to construct an 'historical narration' designed to 'tell our souls, our wives, children and friends, yea and teach our children to tell their posterity after us, how great and good things the lord our God hath done for us.' Ship money was abolished, monopolies were suppressed, and the courts of Star Chamber and High Commission were put down; Archbishop Laud was imprisoned, the Earl of Strafford executed, and peace made with Scotland; Parliament was made secure by the Triennial Act and the Act for Parliamentary Continuance; church reformation was in hand, scandalous priests were 'discountenanced', and the printing presses were set open.[30] This became a canonical list of accomplishments, and its reiteration gave strength and

[27] Ibid., 12–15, 16, 18, 20.   [28] Ibid., 25–7, 30–4.
[29] J.L., *Englands Doxologie* (1641), 9, 11–12; George Hughes, *The Art of Embalming Dead Saints* (1642), 48.   [30] Vicars, *God in the Mount*, title page, sig. A4, 5, 109.

confidence to the discouraged. 'Are not the righteous delivered and the wicked brought into their places', asked the London preacher Thomas Case in 1642, reciting a similar catalogue of England's 'seasonable mercies'.[31]

Whereas parliamentary reformers regarded 1641 as their '*annus mirabilis*', royalist historians looked back at a time of disaster and betrayal. They told of a successful and satisfied society under Charles I that was cruelly sabotaged and taken by surprise. The governing tone of their history was lamentation for a golden age that turned into 'an age of scarlet calamities'. Theirs was a tragic tale of declension, in which a 'land flowing with milk and honey', once 'the envy of all Europe', fell into 'horrid distempers'.[32] This motif was well established early in the civil war, was elaborated during the dark days of the interregnum, and was further polished amidst the renewed partisan politics of the reign of Charles II. 'Behold, consider, and look back, and see how we have been put to the rack', invited a Restoration verse review of 'the remarkable passages that have happened to this land from the year 1640 to the year 1660'.[33]

Royalists often argued that King Charles's golden days were ended, not by any fault of the monarch, but by the perversity and perfidy of his subjects. 'How is it possible . . . that the best of princes should meet with the worst of subjects', asked the Restoration historian Sir Roger Manley.[34] Whereas reformers invoked a Providence that seemed to be on their side, conservatives used historical writing as a device for assigning blame. Writing in 1643, in the midst of the civil war, the royalist James Howell blamed the disaster on 'a pack of perverse people, composed for the most part of the scummy and simplest sort', who were opposed to hierarchy and monarchy.[35] Others placed all the blame on treasonable parliamentarians who had stirred up faction and tumults in pursuit of their 'design for altering the government in the church and state'.[36]

Charles I himself was found guiltless in these proto-revisionist accounts. Rather than seeing any folly or clumsiness in his dealings with Scotland, or any flaws in his religious policies or kingcraft, apologists saw only the King's 'holy and pious inclinations endeavouring to advance the protestant religion

---

[31] Thomas Case, *Gods Waiting to be Gracious Unto his People* (1642), 72, 96, 115. The quote is based on Proverbs 11: 8.

[32] [Howell], *True Informer*, 4; John Harris, *Englands Out-Cry, for the sad distractions now lying upon the Church and State* (1644), 1.

[33] *Arbitrary Government Display'd . . . And A Compendious History of those Times* (1683), 210.

[34] Sir Roger Manley, *The History of the Rebellions in England, Scotland, and Ireland* (1691), 2.

[35] [Howell], *True Informer*, 5, 21–2.

[36] *An orderly and plaine Narration of the Beginnings and Causes of this Warre* (Bristol?, 1644), 17, 5.

by promoting unity and purity in the holy church'. Here was a king more sinned against than sinning.[37]

Seventeenth-century historians, like their modern successors, were interested in causes and explanations, and sought to understand the origins of the national crisis. Few on the royalist side looked further back than 1637. It was in Scotland, wrote James Howell, that 'the cloud began to condense first...here began the storm'.[38] 'Here you have the beginning of our woeful troubles', and 'the true source of our miseries', concluded other historians of his persuasion, who traced the powder trail back to Edinburgh's High Kirk of St Giles.[39] The rebellious Scots were held accountable, although their English puritan allies shared some of the blame for the combustion of the three kingdoms. Much of the terminology of the crisis, including 'malignants' and 'incendiaries', came directly from the north. Although the Scots were the initial cause of trouble, they were 'instigated to it by the English puritans', explained Sir Roger Manley.[40] 'If the flint and steel had not struck fire in England, the tinder had never took fire in Scotland, nor had the flame ever gone over to Ireland to increase the fire', claimed a royalist assessment published in 1645.[41]

One incisive analysis, written on the eve of the civil war, found the cause of Britain's troubles by reference to the difficulty of governing composite kingdoms. Like the contemporary problems of Catalonia, Portugal, and Spain, or of Transylvania, Walachia, and Moldavia, Britain's crisis erupted 'because there was not heretofore a perfect union twixt England and Scotland'. The crisis was a consequence of the dynastic union of 1603, though it was the Bishops' Wars and their aftermath that caused 'the present malady'.[42] Conrad Russell more recently developed this insight, with extensive documentation.[43]

The dissolution of the Short Parliament, most contemporary analysts agreed, was an ill-judged move that cost the King dearly. In breaking the parliament in May 1640 King Charles lost the chance to deal with a relatively moderate assembly containing 'many wise gentlemen...well inclined for his and the public good', so one of those wise gentlemen later opined.[44] In the

---

[37] *The Grand Rebels Detected. Or, the Presbyter unmasked. Shewing to all loyal hearts who were the first founders of the Kings Majesties ruine, and Englands misery* (1660), 2. Cf. the apologetic tenor of Mark A. Kishlansky and John Morrill, 'Charles I (1600–1649)', *Oxford Dictionary of National Biography* (Oxford, 2004).   [38] [Howell], *True Informer*, 7–8.

[39] *Grand Rebels Detected*, 2; Manley, *History of the Rebellions*, 7.

[40] Manley, *History of the Rebellions*, 11,

[41] *A Discourse Discovering Some Mysteries of Our New State and Remembering Some Fatal Daies...Shewing the Rise and Progresse of England's Unhappinesse, Ab Anno illo infortunato, 1641* (Oxford, 1645), 15.   [42] *The Times Dissected* (1642), sig. A2v.

[43] Russell, *The Causes of the English Civil War*; idem., *Fall of the British Monarchies*.

[44] Jack Binns (ed.), *The Memoirs and Memorials of Sir Hugh Cholmley of Whitby 1600–1657*, Yorkshire Archaeological Society Record Series (2000), cliii. 99. Cholmley was an opponent of Strafford and ship money who ultimately sided with the King.

view of Hamon L'Estrange, writing in the 1650s, 'this still-born parliament' might have had 'power and probably will enough to impede the torrent of the late civil war'.[45] Sir Edward Walker agreed that this Short Parliament was 'unhappily dissolved, because some conclude had they sat longer they would have been more tractable'.[46] This was one of many occasions when royalists wondered wistfully what might have happened if history had taken a different course.

Royalist and Restoration historians described the Long Parliament that assembled in November 1640 as the 'fatal parliament' that 'confirmed the Commons with strength and power ... and utterly disabled the king'.[47] This was said to be a 'Scotified' assembly that was precipitated and driven by the Scots,[48] and its leaders, royalists insisted, were 'zealous fomenters of the rebellion' who 'made use of the holy scripture to stir up the king's subjects against him'.[49] Sir Roger Manley characterized the Long Parliament as 'that fatal convention' that ended 'by ruining the most apostolic church under heaven, and murdering the best prince that ever swayed the English sceptre'.[50] Sir Edward Walker invited more counter-factual speculation when he reflected that 'if many of [the Lords and Commons] had not so violently gone with the tide at first as they did ... the miseries many of them after felt might have been prevented.'[51]

The core of the crisis, for most seventeenth-century analysts, lay in 1641. It was in that year that grievances crystalized into rebellion. A royalist historical survey published in 1645 attempted to show how the rebellion 'was conceived, born and nursed', and located its origins '*Ab Anno illo infortunato, 1641*'. All the miseries since the start of the civil war, it claimed, 'were hatched in the year 1641'.[52] Dozens of subsequent histories memorialized the spirit or spectre of '41, making that year a code-phrase or symbol for the start of England's troubles.

Although the political culture of Restoration England was based in part on oblivion, it could not escape the entanglements of memory and history. The partisan politics of the reign of Charles II fanned memories of the reign of Charles I, and identified its turning point in 1641. John Tatham's tragedy, *The Distracted State*, about a polity ruined by ambitious politicians and an

---

[45] [Hamon L'Estrange], *The Reign of King Charles. An History Disposed into Annals ... with a reply to some late observations* (1656), 188.
[46] Sir Edward Walker, 'A Short Review of the Life of King Charles' [1655], in his *Historical Discourses upon Several Occasions* (1705), 367.
[47] Walker, *Historical Discourses upon Several Occasions*, 356, 368.
[48] *Grand Rebels Detected*, 3; [Howell], *True Informer*, 11–12.
[49] *Grand Rebels Detected*, 5.   [50] Manley, *History of the Rebellions*, 14.
[51] Walker, *Historical Discourses upon Several Occasions*, 356–7.
[52] *Discourse Discovering Some Mysteries of Our New State*, title page, 3.

'easily corrupted multitude', claimed to have been 'written in the year 1641', although it was more likely a product of 1650.[53] The Earl of Clarendon's influential *History* found the beginning of the rebellion in 1641, and expressed amazement that a 'universal apostasy in the whole nation from their religion and allegiance could, in so short a time, have produced such a total and prodigious alteration and confusion over the whole kingdom.'[54]

Among a spate of historical treatises prompted by the political crisis of 1679–81, *The Weekly Discovery of the Mystery of Iniquity in The Rise, Growth, Methods and Ends of the Late Unnatural Rebellion in England, Anno 1641* reviewed 'the horrid revolutions which happened in twenty years in our English world'.[55] At greater length, though with no greater skill, a heroic poem of the late 1680s entitled *Caroloiades* traced England's 'late unhappy times' to 'the rebellion of forty one'. 'Unhappy war began in forty one', it trumpeted, 'nourished by pasquils, libels, threats, demands' and an 'all-daring vulgar rage'. This account, like many others, held King Charles blameless as his kingdom was rocked by 'unthought storms'. The people, not their sovereign, were held responsible for the tragedy, and their fury first showed itself in 1641.[56] Among the ephemeral publications of this period was *The Whig's Exaltation; A Pleasant New Song*, set to 'an old tune of 41'. Its refrain repeated the revolutionary vaunt of the early 1640s, 'hey boys up go we'.[57] The year 1641 was when the music started.

REVOLUTION

Nobody before the civil war used the word 'revolution' to explain what had happened in England, although several preachers and commentators visualized a God who was turning a revolutionary wheel. Following the ascendancy of 'the ill affected party' in the 1630s, explained the Presbyterian Edmund Calamy, 'Almighty God' had lifted our 'grievous yokes' and 'made a blessed turn of things for the better'. This was God's nature, his divine

---

[53] John Tatham, *The Distracted State, A Tragedy* (1651), title page, 3.

[54] Clarendon, *History of the Rebellion*, i. 1.

[55] *Weekly Discovery of the Mystery of Iniquity*, no. 1, broadside. Gilbert Burnet wrote of the crisis of 1679 that 'nothing was so common in their mouths as the year 41, in which the late wars begun, and which seemed now to be near the being acted over again.' Osmund Airy (ed.), *Burnet's History of My Own Time* (2 vols., Oxford, 1897–1900), ii. 221.

[56] [Howard], *Caroloiades*, 1, 22. See also the early eighteenth-century song, 'the trimming parson', akin to 'The Vicar of Bray', which opens with the line, 'I loved no king in forty one when prelacy went down' (Bodleian Library, Ms. Rawlinson D. 383, f. 115).

[57] *The Whig's Exaltation; A Pleasant New Song* (1682). See also *The Whig Rampant; Or, Exaltation* (1682), which used the same chorus to satirize 'the good old cause'.

prerogative, for, Calamy observed, he 'can build and plant a nation, and he can pluck up, pull down and destroy a nation. And when a kingdom is in the depth of misery, he can in an instant, if he but speak the word, raise it up to the top of happiness; and when it is in the height and zenith of happiness, he can in another instant speak a word and throw it down again into an abyss of misery.'[58] This was a Christian providential version of the old wheel of fortune, whose revolutions governed the rise and fall of princes and kingdoms. The drama and intensity of these particular revolutions hastened the emergence of a new vocabulary that would soon refer more directly to 'the revolutions of the times.' By the mid-1640s the word 'revolution' had acquired new political and constitutional shadings, and was frequently so employed in the 1650s.

Something of a myth has arisen that mid-Stuart Englishmen did not know a revolution when they saw one, or if they did, their vocabulary was deficient in this regard. The word 'revolution', we have been told, applied primarily to celestial mechanics, and its figurative use extended no further than the idea of cyclical recurrence or periodic return.[59] If used at all, it had a 'mainly non-political meaning'. Rooted in cyclical rather than linear views of history, revolutions are said to have been both rotational and conservative, returning to their point of beginning. Dictionary-makers and lexicographers continued to read 'revolution' in astronomical and scientific terms.[60]

However, that is not what 'revolution' meant in England in the 1640s and 1650s. The dictionary-makers were out of touch. In the course of the mid-seventeenth century, under the pressure of events, the word 'revolution' acquired new meaning and entered into more frequent use. Writers employed

[58] Edmund Calamy, *Gods Free Mercy to England* (1642), 5–6; idem, *England's Looking-Glasse, Presented in a Sermon* (1642), 2. See also Stephen Marshall, *Reformation and Desolation* (1642), 10, 47.

[59] Copernicus, *De Revolutionibus Orbium Caelestium* (Nuremberg, 1543). See also Robert Pont, *A new treatise of the right reckoning of years . . . concerning courses of times and revolutions of the heaven* (Edinburgh, 1599); Leonard Digges, *A prognostication euerlasting of right good effect . . . to iudge the weather by the sunne, moone, starres, cometes, rainebow, thunder, clouds* (1605).

[60] Perez Zagorin, *The Court and the Country: The Beginning of the English Revolution* (New York, 1969, 1971 edn.), 13. The argument seems to be that historians can refer to an English Revolution, but those who lived through it could not. MacLachlan, *Rise and Fall of Revolutionary England*, 8, implies that the word 'revolution' was rarely used by seventeenth-century Englishmen. For classic statements see Vernon F. Snow, 'The Concept of Revolution in Seventeenth-Century England,' *Historical Journal*, 5 (1962), 167–74; Christopher Hill, 'The Word "Revolution" in Seventeenth-Century England', in Richard Ollard and Pamela Tudor-Craig (eds.), *For Veronica Wedgwood These Studies in Seventeenth-Century History* (1986), 134–51. For an important addition to the debates, see Ilan Rachum, 'The Meaning of "Revolution" in the English Revolution (1648–1660)', *Journal of the History of Ideas*, 56 (1995), 195–215.

the word metaphorically to signify a sudden and dramatic change, or significant and abrupt turnover in the politics and religion of the state. Although some authors retained the old astronomical usage, contemporaries became increasingly aware that revolutions could happen in kingdoms as well as planets.

Commentators talked increasingly of 'our late revolutions' in the same way as they spoke of 'our late unhappy troubles', referring to recent history. By the time of the Restoration (also a revolution in these terms), there were histories of 'the general revolutions [in England] since 1639 to 1660'.[61] Without this expanded usage the so-called 'glorious revolution' of 1689 could not have been so quickly and confidently named.

Astrologers were especially important in linking the two usages together, coupling the revolutions of the heavens to the revolutionary transformation of terrestial political affairs. George Naworth's almanac for 1642 predicted that the eclipses in 'this year's revolution' would bring forth 'fevers, war, famine, pestilence, house-burnings, rapes, depopulations, manslaughters, secret seditions, banishments, imprisonments, violent and unexpected deaths, robberies, thefts, and piratical invasions'.[62] Using the same phrase in 1649, another astrologer linked 'this year's revolution' to the sad misfortunes of the English commonwealth, although he was unable to anticipate the execution of the King. Rotations and revolutions within the three-dimensional geometry of the heavens were understood to be responsible for the 'changes and alterations' in the religion and politics of the kingdom. Another publication of this sort in 1649 was *Speculum Anni, or A Glasse in whch you may behold the revolution of the yeare*.[63]

The 1640s saw a rapid evolution in the usage and connotations of the word 'revolution'. It began to appear in all sorts of publications, both learned and popular. One of the characters in a dialogue of 1641 considers 'the vicissitudes and revolution of the states and conditions of men in these last days of the world'.[64] Another publication describes the English soldiers

---

[61] For example, *A Lively Pourtraict of our New-Cavaliers, Commonly Called Presbyterians...In a Compendious Narrative of our late Revolutions* (1661); David Lloyd, *Modern Policy Completed...under the general Revolutions since 1639, to 1660* (1660); idem, *Never Faile, or, That sure way of thriving under all Revolutions...From 1639. to 1661* (1663); James Howell, *Twelve Several Treatises, of the Late Revolutions in These Three Kingdoms* (1661), 116.

[62] George Naworth, *A New Almanacke and Prognostication for...the Year of our Lord God 1642* (1642), sigs. Cv, C2.

[63] Vincent Wing, *A Dreadfull Prognostication, or An Astrological Prediction of several Contingencies incident to all Europe* (1649), 30–43; William Leybourne, *Speculum Anni, or A Glasse in whch you may behold the revolution of the yeare* (1649).

[64] *The Brothers of the Blade: Answerable to the Sisters of the Scaberd* (1641), 3.

assembled for war against the Scots as 'mere atheist and barbarian in these revolutions'.[65] A popular pamphlet of 1642 described the wheel of fortune as 'an emblem of the revolution and change of these present times', with reference to the downfall of the bishops.[66] Thereafter the word entered general parlance to describe abrupt and profound alterations in religion and government. Yoking together the astronomical and political meanings of the word in his letter to the Earl of Dorset in 1646, James Howell thought he had lived through 'the strangest revolutions and horridest things... not only in Europe but all the world' that had happened 'in so short a revolution of time'.[67]

A quick and crude measure of this change of usage may be found in the titles of publications contained in the online English Short Title Catalogue, which includes full titles for every published work that survives from the period. A more nuanced but less systematic reading may be obtained through tracking references to 'revolution' or 'revolutions' in manuscripts and printed texts. Besides a few early summaries of Copernicus, not a single publication before 1642 featured 'revolution' or 'revolutions' on its title page. Between 1642 and 1649 the word made ten such appearances, and the number rose to 54 in the 1650s, 25 in the 1660s, 36 in the 1670s, 90 in the 1680s, and 115 in the 1690s.[68]

John Fenwicke's meditation on *Zions Ioy in Her King*, published in 1643, offered serious commentary on the Psalms, such 'as the weight of the subject and the revolutions of the times required'. The Bible, to this author, was a book of revolutions as well as revelations, in which God raised his people from their 'lowest and deepest extremity' to their 'height of... transcendent joy'. The final revolution would occur, Fenwicke predicted, 'when the Lord shall roar out of Zion', betokening a 'wonderful change' that would shake 'the old rotten foundations of the world and all things in it, both in religion and governments'.[69] That would be a revolution indeed.

A more pessimistic view of revolutions appeared in *A Looking-Glas for the Presbytary Government*, another publication of 1643, subtitled *A Declaration of the Revolution of the times*. The revolution in question was the adoption of the Solemn League and Covenant and the end of the

---

[65] *The Scots Scouts Discoveries* (1642, probably written 1640), quoted in C. H. Firth, 'Ballads on the Bishops' Wars, 1638–40', *Scottish Historical Review*, 3 (1906), 259.

[66] [Henry Peacham], *Sqvare-Caps Turned into Rovnd-Heads* (1642), 2.

[67] James Howell, *Familiar Letters*, quoted in Snow, 'Concept of Revolution', 169.

[68] My calculations from ESTC online, September 2004. The still-incomplete Early English Books Online Text Creation Partnership yields 76 examples from publications of 1640–50, 133 for 1650–60, 132 for 1660–70, 153 for 1670–80, 217 for 1680–90, and 350 for 1690–1700, results from January 2005.

[69] John Fenwicke, *Ioy in Her King, Coming in his Glory* (1643), title page, 2, 137.

Elizabethan religious settlement, an evil, thought this author, 'not to be parallelled amongst all the distempers and revolutions of times, since Christianity first entered this island'.[70]

Comments like these advanced the notion that English history, like Biblical history, was a history of revolutions. 'Revolution' became a term of choice for the confusions and changes of the times. The new usage was apparently well established by 1648 when a broadsheet attacking the Long Parliament cited William Prynne as 'a restless stickler in all those revolutions'.[71] And Prynne himself, in his history of England, came to describe almost any shift of power, usurpation, or coup at home or abroad as a revolution.

After the royalist defeat Anthony Ascham, tutor to the duke of York, produced *A Discourse, Wherein is examined, What is particularly lawful during the Confusions and Revolutions of Government*, which used both English and Roman history to assess the subject's obligations to a victorious but illegitimate regime. In 1649, after the execution of the King, Ascham expanded his tract and re-titled it *Of the Confusions and Revolutions of Governments*. Ascham's career as a theorist was cut short by his assassination by royalist fanatics, but his *Discourse*, in various editions, helped to imprint the concept of revolution as an abrupt and forceful reallocation of power.[72] Accounts from abroad of 'the late revolutions' in Naples and Catalonia in the late 1640s further associated the term with popular insurrection and radical political change.[73] This political meaning was also prominent in *Notable Revolutions: Being a True Relation of What Happened in the United Provinces* (1653).[74]

By 1650 such phrases as 'the late revolution of government' had general currency. William Beech used it in *A View of Englands Present Distempers. Occasioned by the late Revolution of Government in this Nation*, without having to explain that he was referring to the execution of the King and the creation of an English republic.[75] Henceforth, any dramatic shift of power,

---

[70] *A Looking-Glas for the Presbytary Government, Establishing the Church of England. Or, A Declaration of the Revolution of the times* (1643), title page, 12. George Thomason's copy is dated 23 December and has the year amended to 1644, British Library, E.21 (40).

[71] *A more Exact and Necessary Catalogue of Pensioners in the Long Parliament* (1648).

[72] Anthony Ascham, *A Discourse, Wherein is examined, What is particularly lawful during the Confusions and Revolutions of Government* (1648), preface, sigs. *2v, *3, 25, 86–7; idem, *Of the Confusions and Revolutions of Governments* (1649). Ascham was murdered in Spain by exiled royalists in 1650.

[73] Alessandro Giraffi, *Le Rivolutioni di Napoli* (Venice, 1647); idem, *An Exact Historie of the Late Revolutions in Naples* (1650); Luca Assarino, *Le Rivolutioni di Catalogna* (Bologna, 1648).   [74] Cited in Hill, 'The Word "Revolution"', 143.

[75] [William Beech], *A View of Englands Present Distempers. Occasioned by the late Revolution of Government in this Nation* (1650). The epistle dates the writing to 4 June 1649. On the title page Beech pressed three assertions: 'That the present powers are to be

usurpation, or coup at home or abroad could be designated a revolution. The term would be applied to the convolutions of the Cromwellian protectorate, the restoration of kingship in 1660, and the further (and ultimately 'glorious') revolution of 1688–9. Unpublished correspondence as well as printed texts referred almost casually to 'these late revolutions', 'the great revolutions of this kingdom', and 'the revolutions of the times'. The plural usage outweighed the singular, suggesting that revolution was a process as well as an event.[76]

Oliver Cromwell spoke in 1653 of 'this revolution of affairs', and in 1655 he lectured Parliament on his own role in 'these great revolutions'.[77] Cromwell's imposition of a 'new test and engagement' on his elected assembly in 1654 occasioned *A Declaration…touching the late Change and Revolution in Parliament*.[78] Later that year a royalist prophet predicted 'great changes and revolutions' in government, including the rise of a magistrate 'whose royal style and dignity will cause England to rejoice and sing'. Another in 1655 referred to 'the intended revolution of government to his majesty's advantage'.[79] What is significant is not that authors from this time anticipated the Restoration by half a decade, but that they referred to such changes as revolutions.

John Warren wrote in 1656 of 'the amazing changes and revolutions which our eyes have seen', and attributed them to 'a grand design of God'.[80] God was also the maker of revolutions in William Prynne's monumental history. 'Crowns and kingdoms have their periods and revolutions', observed Prynne, 'and that by the secret justice and wise disposing providence of God, who disposeth, translateth, dissipateth, dissolveth kingdoms at his pleasure, and giveth them to whomsoever he pleaseth.' This was Prynne's conclusion to his history of Anglo-Saxon England, published in 1657, which treated 'the public revolutions of state' before the Norman conquest as products of the will of God. This theory of revolution applied as much to Prynne's own time as to the time of King Aethelred, and it helped him make sense of the sufferings of 'our unsettled distracted English nation'.[81]

---

obeyed. That Parliaments are the powers of God. That the generality of God's enemies are the Parliament's enemies.'

[76] Hill, 'The Word "Revolution"', 144–5.

[77] Quoted in Rachum, 'Meaning of "Revolution"', 205–6.

[78] *A Declaration of The Proceedings of His Highness the Lord Protector; And His Reasons touching the late Change and Revolution in Parliament* (1654). Thomason's copy is dated 14 September 1654, British Library, E.811 (6).

[79] *The Royall Merlin; or, Great Brittains Loyal Observator…Denoting also, the time and year of the great Changes and Revolutions* (1655). Thomason's copy is dated 4 December 1654, British Library, E.818 (12); C. H. Firth (ed.), *The Clarke Papers. Selections from the Papers of William Clarke, Secretary to the Council of the Army, 1647–1649* (Camden Society, new series, vol. lxii, 1901), 303.   [80] John Warren, *Man's Fury* (1656), 31.

[81] William Prynne, *The Third Part of a Seasonable, Legal and Historical Vindication of the good old Fundamental Liberties…of all English Freemen* (1657), title page, preface, 398–9.

A tract of 1659 blamed the army for 'our late and present revolutions', and for bringing the country to ruin. The army, in this view, was 'the primum mobile of all our state and present motions, commotions, ringing the changes in our churches, kingdoms, parliaments, governments and religion, modelling and unmodelling, chopping, changing, altering, building them up and pulling them down.' These were revolutions without purpose or direction, in a nation 'addicted to changes, unstable, variable, unconstant, mutable, tossed to and fro, backward forward, upward and downward, this way and that, like children, fools, reeds, vanes, weather-cocks, empty clouds, wandering stars, the restless sea.'[82] There was nothing triumphant in this view of revolution, but rather a view that Babylon had given way to Babel in a world turned upside down.

Revolutions happened, explained Robert Fitz-Brian, when states and governments became corrupt and when God helped men bring about change. A die-hard radical defending 'the good old cause' against the hopelessness and cynicism at the end of the Protectorate, Fitz-Brian provided 'a short and sober narrative of the great revolutions of affairs in these later times'. Not unlike some modern historians, he located 'the true sources of our late revolutions' in the reign of Charles I. Passionate and partisan, Fitz-Brian's history was a series of 'great revolutions' in the 1640s and 1650s that had by no means come to an end.[83]

It should come as no surprise, then, to find Charles II referring to 'great revolutions' in his Declaration of Breda of April 1660.[84] Royalists were not alone in regarding the Restoration as a revolution, though this appellation did not endure for long in the history books. James Howell, now 'his majesty's historiographer royal', offered *Twelve Several Treatises, of the Late Revolutions in These Three Kingdoms* in 1661, though he adopted the counter-revolutionary view that the kingdoms for most of the past twenty years had been in 'rebellion'. Other Restoration writers turned their backs on the term.[85]

A generation later contemporaries had no doubt that a 'revolution' had taken place in the change from James II to William and Mary. John Evelyn concluded on 2 December 1688, 'it looks like a revolution', and he offered

---

[82] *Twelve Seasonable Quaeries Proposed to all True Zealous Protestants and English Free-men: Occasioned by our late and present Revolutions* (1659), 1, 5, 6.

[83] R. Fitz-Brian, *The Good Old Cause Dress'd in its Primitive Lustre* (1659), title page, 2, 4–6, 10, 12, 15. Thomason's copy is dated 16 February 1658 [i.e., 1659], British Library, E.969 (6).

[84] Declaration of Breda, in J. P. Kenyon (ed.), *The Stuart Constitution* (2nd edn., Cambridge, 1986), 332.

[85] Howell, *Twelve Several Treatises, of the Late Revolutions*, 116; Rachum, 'Meaning of "Revolution"', 214–15.

Samuel Pepys his services 'in this prodigious revolution'. Indeed, the immediate adoption and enduring attachment of the world 'revolution' to describe the events of 1688–9 owed much to increased familiarization with the term over the preceding forty years.[86]

Back in 1641, when a truly significant revolution was happening, there was no 'revolutionary' vocabulary to describe it. However, there was no mistaking the earthquake or watershed, the cleavage in time, the radical transformation of political and religious culture, that took place between the opening of the Long Parliament and the start of the civil war.

---

[86] E. S. De Beer (ed.), *The Diary of John Evelyn* (6 vols., Oxford, 1955), iv. 609; Richard Lord Braybrooke (ed.), *Diary and Correspondence of Samuel Pepys* (4 vols., 1876), iv. 244. See also Nathaniel Crouch, *The Extraordinary Adventures and Discoveries of several Famous Men...Being and Account of a Multitude of Stupendous Revolutions, Accidents, and Observable Matters in many Kingdomes, States and Provinces* (1685); Gilbert Burnet, *Reflections on Mr. Varilla's History of The Revolutions that have happened in Europe in Matters of Religion* (1689).

2

The Pulse of the Kingdom: Distempers of the Times

A great fear descended over Caroline England in the two years before the civil war. Many among the governing class were gripped by a formless and unfocused dread.

The political nation had lost its bearings, and events seemed out of control. Contemporaries were shocked by the disruption of cultural and political landmarks, and bewildered what would happen next. Frightening disturbances in religion and politics threatened their security and peace. Most of the people who expressed these fears in writing belonged to the propertied elite, who had most at stake and most to lose. Others were swept along by the panic. Correspondence and commentary reveals swings of despondency and surges of pessimism, with moments of hope dashed by waves of alarm and despair. Local administrative records show a similar pattern, as authorities translated their anxieties into preparations for defence.

This chapter examines reactions to England's crisis from the spring of 1640 to the summer of 1642. It follows the unfolding national drama through the sometimes-tortured rhetoric of letters, diaries, and contemporary commentary. It also makes use of local records to show how magistrates, town governments, and some gentle households responded to alarms and braced themselves for trouble. Hardly anyone before 1642 contemplated the possibility of civil war, although many thought catastrophe of some sort was upon them. Threats and enemies abounded, but few in England imagined they would have to fight each other.

HALCYON DAYS

The distempers of the 1640s shattered the complacency of a proud and satisfied elite. The court of Charles I had fostered the belief that England was uniquely fortunate in its government and church, and uniquely blessed by tranquillity and peace. King Charles played the role of arbiter and conciliator in the mythic golden world of the masque.[1] 'Never did this or any nation enjoy more blessings and happiness than hath been by all his majesty's subjects enjoyed ever since his majesty's access to the crown, nor did this kingdom ever so flourish in trade and commerce as at this present, or partake of more peace and plenty in all kinds whatsoever', proclaimed Lord Keeper Finch at the dissolution of the Short Parliament in May 1640.[2] Supporters of the regime frequently aired such sentiments, though by the time of the war with Scotland they seemed increasingly strained. A proclamation of June 1640 reminded the King's subjects that they lived 'in plenty and tranquillity all the time of his majesty's blessed reign'.[3] Country correspondents shared this view that King Charles had enjoyed 'long happiness in the quiet of his kingdoms', and had governed 'so flourishing a kingdom, of which the whole world grew jealous daily', though sentiments of this sort were already tinged with nostalgia.[4]

It had been a commonplace of English national congratulation that 'amidst the distraction of foreign nations, we only have sat under the shadow of our vines, and drank the wines of our own vintage.' No matter that English vines were as rare as figs and olives, for observations of this sort likened England more to the land of Canaan than to a storm-tossed Atlantic archipelago.[5] The author of *Englands Doxologie* in 1641 reminded readers that 'there is no nation under heaven that hath received more temporal and spiritual favours from almighty God than this kingdom of England.' While European neighbours suffered 'havoc and desolation', England uniquely was free from wars. 'Other great kingdoms have lamentably suffered, only this little island

---

[1] See, for example, [Thomas Carew], *Coelum Britanicum: A Masque at White-Hall* (1634); Murray Lefkowitz (ed.), *Trois Masques a la Cour de Charles Ier D'Angleterre* (Paris, 1970); Martin Butler, 'Reform or Reverence? The Politics of the Caroline Masque', in J. R. Mulryne and Margaret Shewring (eds.), *Theatre and Government under the Early Stuarts* (Cambridge, 1993), 118–53.

[2] *His Majesties Declaration: To All His Loving Subjects, Of the causes which moved him to dissolve the last Parliament* (1640), 50–1. On Finch's authorship, see Esther S. Cope, 'The King's Declaration Concerning the Dissolution of the Short Parliament of 1640: An Unsuccessful Attempt at Public Relations', *Huntington Library Quarterly*, 40 (1977), 325–31. For a more sympathetic view of Caroline political culture see Kevin Sharpe, *The Personal Rule of Charles I* (1992).

[3] James F. Larkin (ed.), *Stuart Royal Proclamations ... 1625–1646* (Oxford, 1983), 714.

[4] Mary Anne Everett Green (ed.), *The Diary of John Rous ... 1625 to 1642* (Camden Society, London, 1856), 92; Dorothy Gardiner (ed.), *The Oxinden Letters 1607–1642* (1933), 173.

[5] *Mr. Speakers Speech, Before the King, in the Lords House of Parliament, July the third, 1641* (1641), 2.

is secure.'[6] Comforting assessments like these had to be abandoned by 1642 when God's most favoured nation was plunged into storms and troubles.

TUMULTUOUS AND DISJOINTED TIMES

From 1640 to 1642 the horizon became clouded with dangers. The subjects of Charles I faced myriad fears and alarms from enemies who were menacing, immeasurable, or imagined. At first the Scots posed the most pressing problem. The danger was compounded because an unknown number of Englishmen actively sympathized with the rebels. But neither the capability nor the intentions of the Scottish forces were fully understood. Before the battle of Newburn in August 1640 the Scots might be reckoned as a horde of redshanks and blue bonnets, with a few canny leaders, who were unlikely to cross into England. However, once Newcastle, Northumberland, and Durham fell to a disciplined Covenanter army there was no telling what further damage they might inflict. Ripples of fear ran from Yorkshire to Sussex, spreading rumours that the Scots were again on the march. Scottish forces remained in northern England through much of the following year, only withdrawing after the peace treaty of September 1641.

Other rumours persisted that the French were massing forces or readying a fleet to take advantage of England's distractions. The French, of course, were ancient allies of the Scots, and had been England's adversary since medieval times. King Charles had a French queen, and a French-Italian mother-in-law, and it was not far-fetched to imagine that Louis XIII had designs on England. Nor were the French the only foreign forces thought likely to intervene. The Spanish were not forgotten, though their power had waned since the days of the Armada. Some people feared the Danes, the King's cousins, as if an Elsinore auxiliary might enter the Humber or the Thames. There was even talk of the Tangiers fleet or Barbary pirates coming up river to London.

Reports spread in 1640 of 'the mighty Spanish fleet now preparing', and of French designs on the Channel Islands while the English were distracted in the north.[7] The gentry of Cornwall secured gunpowder in 1641 in case of 'a sudden surprise of a foreign enemy'.[8] In Oxfordshire Thomas Wyatt

---

[6] J.L., *Englands Doxologie* (1641), 1–4. For similar sentiments see Nathaniel Richards, *Poems Sacred and Satyricall* (1641), 2

[7] *Vox Borealis, or The Northern Discoverie* (1641), not paginated.

[8] R. N. Worth (ed.), *The Buller Papers. A Series of Historical Documents Selected from the Family Records of the Bullers of Shillingham and Morval in the County of Cornwall* (privately printed, 1895), 46.

recorded 'fear that some in France should come against England'.[9] Sir Simonds D'Ewes warned in Parliament in April 1641 that 'the French had a great navy ready, that we had just occasion to fear the worst.'[10] Sir Edward Dering wrote in May 1641 of French intentions against Kent,[11] and word spread in Devonshire of 'provision of men and ships from France against England'.[12] Thomas Smith wrote from Dover on 10 May 1641 of 'approaching dangers' from across the Channel.[13]

Writing from Chester in January 1642, John Ogle reported the fear that the King would seek support from overseas, inviting a French army into the kingdom.[14] A Huntingdonshire gentleman believed that a French force of 10,000 men would make the King 'hardy enough for the parliament'.[15] Rumours swept through the crowds at Westminster early in 1642 that a force of 15,000 Frenchmen 'should soon come...upon our backs', a number that swelled to 30,000 in subsequent tellings.[16] Other rumours held that Spanish, French, or Danish forces were preparing to enter England.[17] One writer in Staffordshire expressed relief in April 1642 that 'nothing appears yet, either from France or Denmark'.[18] What were the Danes up to at the end of May when they put one hundred ships to sea? The answer was that they had gone to fetch salt, though why they needed light horse for that purpose was not clear.[19]

Ireland, of course, posed perennial problems. Charles I's Lord Deputy Strafford had kept a tight grip on the island, and had readied an army that some feared could be deployed against Edinburgh or London. Cartloads of weapons and mysterious assemblies of horsemen were believed to be trafficking between Ireland and England, in preparation for an uprising. Fears

[9] Diary of Thomas Wyatt, Bodleian Library, Ms. Top. Oxon. C. 378, 325.
[10] Maija Jansson (ed.), *Proceedings in the Opening Session of the Long Parliament...Volume 3: 22 March–17 April 1641* (Rochester, NY, 2001), 585.
[11] Sir Edward Dering to his wife, 2 May 1641, British Library, Add. Ms. 26786, f. 36.
[12] Devonshire Record Office, Chronicle of John White of Exeter, Ms. 73/15, 113.
[13] Bodleian Library, Oxford, Tanner Ms. 66, f. 88.
[14] Bodleian Library, Carte Ms. 2, f. 298.
[15] Willson H. Coates, Anne Steele Young, and Vernon F. Snow (eds.), *The Private Journals of the Long Parliament 3 January to 5 March 1642* (New Haven and London, 1982), 101.
[16] Willson Havelock Coates (ed.), *The Journal of Sir Simonds D'Ewes From the First Recess of the Long Parliament to the Withdrawal of the King from London* (New Haven and London, 1942), 360; Coates, Young, and Snow (eds.), *Private Journals of the Long Parliament 3 January to 5 March 1642*, 112.
[17] Gardiner (ed.), *Oxinden Letters 1607–1642*, 286; *A Letter from Mercurius Civicus to Mercurius Rusticus* (Oxford?, 1643), 10; Bodleian Library, Oxford, Tanner Ms. 66, f. 252.
[18] Staffordshire Record Office, Leveson Letter Book, D. 868/2/32.
[19] *A Letter Sent by a Yorkshire Gentleman, to a friend in London* (1642), 7. For more on the Danish threat, see *The King of Denmarks Resolution Concerning Charles King of Great Britain* (1642); *Journals of the House of Commons*, ii. 484, 535.

abounded that Ireland would become a springboard for a foreign Catholic invasion, and these fears intensified after the Irish rebellion in autumn 1641.[20]

Many in England believed that the greatest danger was in their midst, from armed Catholic recusants who were waiting their moment to arise. Memories of the Gunpowder Plot were ritually reinforced by annual commemorations on 5 November. English anti-popery had deep roots, periodically nourished by renewed scares. Although there is no evidence of any concerted Catholic plotting, it was widely believed, from the alehouse to the House of Commons, that recusants were stashing weapons and were only awaiting the word—from the Irish, the Pope, the Spanish, the French, the bishops, or perhaps even the King—before slaughtering good Protestants in their beds.[21] Papers allegedly found by a maidservant in Gray's Inn fields in late May 1640 claimed that popish conspirators intended to blow up the City.[22] A year later they were still expected to strike. Fear of the popish plot was a key element in John Pym's grip on the House of Commons.[23] Few Protestants would have disagreed with the remark attributed to Sir Nathaniel Coppinger in October 1641 that 'the papists have been always mortal enemies to our state, and especially to our religion'.[24]

In some quarters the English army assembled to fight the Scots seemed more a menace than an instrument of national security (see Chapter 4). The conscripted soldiers were notoriously disorderly, and intimidated many of the communities through which they marched. Deserters and veterans made further disruptions. Elements in the army had Catholic sympathies, and supporters of Parliament came to believe, perhaps not without cause, that the King might use the army to retrieve his prerogative power.

By the end of 1641 another home-grown menace gave cause for alarm. The rise of radical sectarianism and the erosion of social discipline convinced many in the gentle elite that a levelling disorder was about to set in. The heirs of John Ball and Wat Tyler had no armed capability, no organizational

[20] *CSPD 1640*, 342; *CSPD 1640–41*, 76; PRO, SP16/458/12 and 13. Diary of Thomas Wyatt, Bodleian Library, Ms. Top. Oxon. C. 378, 325.

[21] Caroline Hibbard, *Charles I and the Popish Plot* (Chapel Hill, 1983); David Cressy, *Bonfires and Bells: National Memory and the Protestant Calendar in Elizabethan and Stuart England* (1989); Peter Lake, 'Anti-popery: The Structure of a Prejudice', in Richard Cust and Ann Hughes (eds.), *The English Civil War* (1997), 181–211.

[22] *CSPD 1640*, 231. The libel, exhibited on 28 May, named Thomas Heywood, the Laudian rector of St Giles in the Fields, as one of the master plotters.

[23] Conrad Russell, *The Fall of the British Monarchies 1637–1642* (Oxford, 1991); Hibbard, *Charles I and the Popish Plot*.

[24] Nathaniel Coppinger, *A Seasonable Speech by Sir Nathaniel Coppinger, Spoken in the High Court of Parliament. October 24, 1641* (1641), sig. A2v. This is a fabricated speech, for no such member is known to have existed.

coherence, but they thrived in every county and threatened general chaos, at least in the imaginations of nervous landowners.

Finally, every community faced everyday hazards, which seemed to loom larger in times of uncertainty. Towns and cities braced themselves against fire and contagion, catastrophe and loss. Local authorities set watch against suspected plague carriers, and tried to ward off vagabonds and beggars. The plague returned in 1640 and 1641, at a time when there seemed to be many more wanderers on the roads. Even the weather appeared to conspire against England, with a miserably cold and wet 1640 followed by 'hideous and violent' storms in 1641. The entire world was afflicted by meteorological distress, though contemporaries could not have known the extent of environmental change.[25]

THE STATE LAY SICK

As England's crisis worsened between 1640 and 1642 authors and correspondents wrote despairingly of a slide towards chaos. They used the language of pathology and medicine to describe a body politic wracked by fever and distemper, or imagery from seamanship and meteorology to picture a ship of state beset by tempestuous winds. In some accounts the pulse of the kingdom weakened or quickened, or its mind was beset by distraction; in others its steering gear was overwhelmed and its foretops fractured as the vessel slipped onto the rocks. The dominant discourse was of crisis and wreckage, in contrast to the courtly complacency of the previous decade.

A common theme here was confusion, bewilderment, and uncertainty. Correspondents wrote of being lost in a wood or a labyrinth, disordered, adrift, bereft. They used images of fire and conflagration, and references to infestation by insects and vermin. Religious writers evoked the plagues of Egypt and other biblical torments to describe the unfolding ordeal of the kingdom, and some saw signs of millennial catastrophe, the last days of the world. Very few, however, attributed England's troubles to malign supernatural intervention. Though God was omnipresent in contemporary discourse, the Devil was rarely mentioned, and witchcraft was almost entirely absent. There were enough home-grown troubles to avoid invoking the nether world.

'The state lay sick', sang balladeers in 1640, imagining a country in need of enemas and purges. England's humoral balance was awry, suffering fever, surfeit, and consumption; the patient might respond to glisters and phlebotomy,

---

[25] Geoffrey Parker, *The World Crisis, 1635–1665* (forthcoming).

if only the physicians could agree on a diagnosis and procedure.[26] Political commentators, like disputing doctors, would argue about the nature of the ailment, the specifics of the affliction, and the remedies that might effect a cure.

Acute symptoms appeared at the time of the Scottish wars, when legal, fiscal, and religious problems produced division and dissent. Manuscript libels posted on churches imagined 'John of the commonwealth . . . sick of the Scotch disease', and looked for a remedy in Parliament.[27] 'What will be the event of this burning fever no mortal man can make any certain prognostics', wrote John Castle to the Earl of Bridgewater in March 1640.[28]

Many looked to Parliament for an overdue dose of physic. Members of Parliament likened themselves to 'skillful physicians' addressing the 'danger which so much concerns the welfare of the body politic'. It now fell to 'the doctors of state' to deal with the kingdom's 'disease', wrote one commentator on the Scottish wars.[29] It was Parliament's task, wrote another, 'to recover the kingdom of its heartsick disease and otherwise-incurable mortal wounds'.[30] Speaking of England's ills in April 1641, Sir Harbottle Grimston told the House of Commons that 'it is impossible to cure an ulcerous body unless you first cleanse the veins and purge the body from these obstructions and pestilential humours that surcharge nature, and being once done the blotches, blains and scabs which grow upon the superficies and outside of the body dry up, shed, and fall away of themselves. . . . The diseases and distempers that are now in our body are grown to that height that they pray for and importune a cure.'[31] England's ailments included prerogative taxation, ship money, forest laws, Sunday sports, altar rails, busy bishops, deficient preachers, and court monopolies, as well as hardships and irregularities associated with the raising of the army for the north. However, 'over-strong purgations' might weaken the state, some critics of Parliament cautioned, and 'instead of restoring it to its primitive vigour and health, must needs drive it to a fatal period'.[32] The royalist post-mortem would say, that is exactly what happened.

---

[26] PRO, SP16/473/25. Another manuscript version entitled 'A Satyre upon the state of things this Parliament' is in British Library, Thomason Tracts, E. 205 (3).

[27] Cambridge University Library, Ms. Mn. 1. 45 (Baker transcripts), 29. One such libel appeared at St Mary Woolnoth, London, where Josias Shute was rector. Another was posted at Royston, Cambridgeshire, when the King went by in March 1639. Green (ed.), *Diary of John Rous*, 87–8; D.L., *The Scots Scouts Discoveries by their London Intelligencer* (1642), 23.

[28] Huntington Library, Ms. El. 7828, 25 March 1640. Castle wrote weekly news letters from London under the pen name Desacro Bosco.

[29] Folger Shakespeare Library, Ms. G.a.11.

[30] John Vicars, *God in the Mount. Or, Englands Remembrancer* (1641), 27.

[31] Esther S. Cope and Willson H. Coates (eds.), *Proceedings of the Short Parliament of 1640* (Camden Society 4th ser., vol. xix, 1977), 135, 137.

[32] *A Declaration, or Resolution of the County of Hereford* (1642), broadsheet.

Following the failure of the Short Parliament and the subsequent social disturbances around Lambeth, John Castle wrote of 'a stifling at heart and distemper in the head' in the environs of Westminster. 'There is cause to fear that almost generally through the kingdom the common people are sick of those parts. They labour of a suffocation of their hearts in the duty and obedience they owe to his majesty's service and commands, and they are struck in the head that they rave and utter they know not what against his majesty's government and proceedings.'[33] England was afflicted with a widespread political sickness, he reported, and the patient's prognosis was not good. Maintaining the medical metaphor a few months later, Castle again attempted to diagnose the condition of the kingdom when the Scots, he thought, sought to take advantage of 'the present distempers of our people, whose humours are *in moto fluido*, apt for change and easily running to a part affected *sub ratione similitudinis*, as they surmise, though falsely.'[34] Writing in August 1640, when the reappearance of plague compounded the problems of the kingdom, Castle wished Lord Bridgewater 'safety and health in these valetudinary times when all is sick and ill at ease'.[35]

The prospect of another Parliament in the autumn produced widespread hopes that the 'present distractions and distempers' would be brought to an end.[36] It would be time, thought Sir Kenelm Digby, for the King to 'administer nothing but balm and healing medicaments'.[37] In the first week of the Long Parliament in November 1640 his kinsman Lord George Digby quoted Hippocrates to the effect that 'bodies thoroughly purged must have their humours made fluid and moveable'. Other members called for a purging or scouring against the bishops.[38] Even Archdeacon Thomas Marler, who had much to fear from religious reformers, hoped 'that we shall be blessed with another golden age after the parliament hath purged out all the corrupt humours of the state'.[39]

Sir John Wray told the Commons that though the kingdom was 'dislocated... out of joint', it 'may be well set by the skilful surgeons of this

---

[33] Huntington Library, Ms. El. 7838, 23 June 1640.

[34] Huntington Library, Ms. El. 7847, 8 August 1640.

[35] Huntington Library, Ms. El. 7846, 4 August 1640. A valetudinary condition was one of infirm or invalid health.

[36] Huntington Library, Ms. El. 7864, copying Lord Mayor's letter of 25 September 1640.

[37] Lismore Mss., vol. xxi, National Register of Archives, vol. 20594/15, 865.

[38] Maija Jansson (ed.), *Proceedings in the Opening Session of the Long Parliament.... Volume 1: 3 November–19 December 1640* (Rochester, NY, 2000), 83.

[39] Bodleian Library, Ms. Clarendon 20, no. 1503, Marler to Hyde, January 1641. Praising the 'great achievements' of Parliament in January 1641, John Bampfield wrote to Edward Seymour, 'we dream now of nothing more than of a golden age'. HMC, *Fifteenth Report, Appendix, Part VII. The Manuscripts of the Duke of Somerset* (1898), 64.

honourable House'. In his view the 'body politic' was afflicted by '*mal caducus*, or falling sickness', brought on by the falling out of England and Scotland. The remedy, he told Parliament in January 1641, was to 'find out the boutefeu [firebrand] of this prelatical war, and make them pay the shot for their labour'. It was, in other words, to proceed firmly against the Earl of Strafford and Archbishop Laud, cast here as pathogens as well as evil advisors. By taking 'the recipe with all the ingredients without any scruple of distaste', Wray was 'confident the recovery will be perfect and the whole of Great Britain safe and sound'.[40]

Popular authors latched onto this medical imagery, offering 'potions' to cure the commonwealth of its 'dangerous disease' and 'great distemper'. They recommended 'cordials, potions, electuaries, syrups, plasters, unguents, glisters, vomits, baths, suppositories', as well as 'pills, lozenges, oils…and such like', to purge the ecclesiastical hierarchy of its corporeal corruption. Parliament would play the doctor, to help void or evacuate 'several raw humours and unwholesome things' associated with the Laudian religious regime.[41] John Milton called more forcefully in his pamphlet *Of Reformation* (1641) for surgeons to 'cut away from the public body the noisome and diseased tumor of prelacy'.[42]

Amidst the confusions of 1641, Thomas Jordan offered 'a medicine for the times, or an antidote against faction', including cures for 'obstinacy', 'impatience', and 'a factious spirit'.[43] The pamphleteer John Taylor followed by listing 'the immedicable tumor of faction, the strange diffusion of Brownianism, the stupendous inundation of heresy, the desperate swelling of obstinacy, the dangerous disease of feminine divinity, the aspiring ambition of presumption, the audacious height of disobedience, [and] the painted deceitfulness of hypocrisy' among 'the diseases of the times or, the distempers of the commonwealth'.[44] By this diagnosis the body politic suffered from a complex of malignancies, newly arisen, and mostly rooted in its lower members.

Although some enthusiasts in 1641 thanked Parliament for bringing 'the balm of Gilead to our diseased nation',[45] others doubted that the sickness

---

[40] John Morrill, *The Nature of the English Revolution* (1993), 45; Maija Jansson (ed.), *Proceedings in the Opening Session of the Long Parliament….Volume 2: 21 December 1640–20 March 1641* (Rochester, NY, 2000), 240–1.

[41] *Saint Pauls Potion, Prescribed by Doctor Commons* (1641), sig. A2; *Canterburies Potion* (1641), sigs. A2, A2v–A4.; *The Bishops Potion* (1641), 1, 3–4.

[42] [John Milton], *Of Reformation* (1641), 70. Thomas Edwards would later employ this powerful imagery in *Gangraena* (1646).

[43] T.J. [Thomas Jordan], *A Medicine for the Times. Or, an Antidote against Faction* (1641), title page.

[44] [John Taylor], *The Diseases of the Times or, The Distempers of the Common-wealth* (1641?), title page. [45] *Canterburies Amazement* (1641), sig. A4v.

had been reversed. Alarmed by the growth of 'all-daring liberty' and 'lewd licentiousness' in the spring of 1641, Sir Edward Dering began to fear that, unless cured quickly, 'the disease will be above the cure'.[46] 'Sects in the body and factions in the head are dangerous diseases, and do desperately threaten the dissolution of a well-governed state', wrote William Montague in December.[47]

Political diagnosis in the following year pointed to 'the common and epidemical disease wherein this kingdom at this time lies now gasping under, being filled with nothing but fears, jealousies and perplexities'.[48] Despairing that civil war now seemed inevitable, Thomas Knyvett in May 1642 could foresee 'nothing but a public phlebotomy, if God in mercy doth not in time cast out these evil spirits amongst us'. He sent pamphlets home to Norfolk with the comment, 'out of these prints you may feel how the pulse of the king and kingdom beats, both highly distempered.'[49]

The ancient image of the ship of state helped several commentators describe the crisis. Writing to the Earl of Bridgewater after the dissolution of the Short Parliament, John Castle envisaged the vessel adrift in dangerous waters: 'God I trust will guide the rudder of this ship, and give you a healthful body to support the concussions and tossings of these stormy times.' Following the commotions of May 1640 he observed, 'into what a wide sea this poor ship is driven, which God inspire his majesty to guide into a quiet and safe harbour.' Writing again in July, Castle prayed God to 'defend this great ship from breaking upon these rocks'.[50] The terrestrial helmsmen, it seemed, were confused and negligent, and only God could protect the commonwealth from sinking.

Making similar use of this venerable metaphor, Thomas White offered assistance to the government in September 1640 when he relayed some 'general murmurs collected out of the public discourse' to Secretary Windebank: 'I am one of the mean ones carried in the public bark, now in a most impetuous tempest, where I aspire not to steer, but would not be wanting in my labours at the pump, or any other office befitting my condition, for shipwreck is imminent.'[51] White was, apparently, a minor gentleman or former official from that class on the edge of the traditional political nation

---

[46] National Library of Wales, Ms. 17091E/87.

[47] HMC, *Report on the Manuscripts of the Duke of Buccleuch and Queensberry…at Montague House* (1899), 287.

[48] *An Appeale to the World in These Times of Extreame Danger* (1642), 1.

[49] Bertram Schofield (ed.), *The Knyvett Letters (1620–1644)* (Norfolk Record Society, 1949), 105, 107.

[50] Huntington Library, Mss. El. 7832, 11 May 1640; El. 7833, 12 May 1640; El. 7841, 1 July 1640.   [51] *CSPD 1640–41*, 66.

that was now being drawn headlong into revolutionary public affairs. His letter suggests that the English ship of state depended increasingly on the humbler members of its crew.

In yet another deployment of this rhetoric, John Milton in 1641 pondered 'how to stop a leak, how to keep up the carcass of a crazy and diseased monarchy or state', and blamed the foundering of the commonwealth vessel on the 'timpany of Spaniolized bishops swaggering in the fore-top of the state'.[52] Adrift 'in the ocean of divers factions', the kingdom was battered by 'this deluge of distempers', observed Edward Reynolds early in 1642. His analysis of 'Great Britain's distractions' was one of several to include illustrations of the ship or shipwreck of state and its foundering between Scylla and Charibdis.[53]

Meteorological imagery conveyed similar concerns. 'I pray God the violent turning of the tide do not make an inundation', wrote Thomas Knyvett in November 1640.[54] 'I profess to see a great tempest hanging over the kingdom', wrote Sir Roger Twysden the following summer.[55] Others anticipated 'sharp storms' or 'a deluge of the whole kingdom'.[56] 'Tis to be feared this threatening storm will not be allayed without some showers (I pray God not a deluge) of blood', Thomas Knyvett told his wife in April 1642.[57] John Ogle referred early in 1642 to the 'unmusical discord of this kingdom', amidst increasingly jarring disharmony.[58]

Participants in this crisis repeatedly called on God to 'bring good out of all these trouble and fears', and to 'send us a quiet and untroubled kingdom'.[59] 'The God of heaven send us better days', implored Sir Thomas Jermyn in September 1640.[60] 'God send us peace and deliver us from our divisions and distractions', wrote Secretary Henry Vane.[61] 'God put an end to these distractions', prayed John Hampden.[62] A constant refrain in contemporary correspondence was 'God send a good end', 'God send good issue', and

---

[52] [John Milton], *Of Reformation* (1641), 43, 59.
[53] Edward Reynolds, *Evgenia's Teares for great Brittaynes Distractions* (1642), 2, 8, 20, 36. See also Thomas Stirry, *A Rot Amongst the Bishops, Or, A Terrible Tempest in the Sea of Canterbury* (1641).
[54] HMC, *Report on Manuscripts in Various Collections*, (1903), ii. 259.
[55] 'Sir Roger Twysden's Journal', *Archaeologia Cantiana*, 2 (1859), 176.
[56] *CSPD 1641–43*, 126; HMC, *14th Report, Appendix, part IV, The Manuscripts of Lord Kenyon* (1894), 59, 60.   [57] Schofield (ed.), *Knyvett Letters (1620–1644)*, 101–3.
[58] Bodleian Library, Carte Ms. 2, f. 298.
[59] Woodford's diary, New College, Oxford, Ms. 9502, 11 May, 16 May 1640; Centre for Kentish Studies, Maidstone, U350/C2/77, Henry Hammond to Sir Edward Dering, 16 May 1640.
[60] Bodleian Library, Oxford, Tanner Ms. 65, f. 35v.   [61] *CSPD 1641–43*, 17.
[62] University of Hull, Brynmor Jones Library, Hotham Papers, DDHO/1/2, John Hampden to Sir John Hotham, 17 May [1642, year inferred].

'Lord have mercy upon us.'[63] 'In these distracted times', wrote George Henley, there was no alternative but 'to depend upon the lord and make him your hiding place.'[64] It seemed, wrote John Merrill, 'that the Lord hath decreed to afflict and scourge this nation for the manifold sins thereof.'[65]

POOR ENGLAND

Correspondents feared that the times were out of joint, as they responded to menaces and threats. The country was on edge, its nerves ajar, as enemies threatened within and without. Urban authorities responded by ordering emergency measures, securing gates and bridges, stockpiling gunpowder, readying weapons, and watching out for trouble. These nervous preparations only added to the climate of unease.

A sense of dread accompanied the approaching war with Scotland. 'God grant peace in our days', wrote Lord Montague in February 1639, 'If we should once fall to blows, it would be the heaviest plague that ever fell upon England.'[66] 'The times in the apprehension of all seem to be very doubtful, and many fears we have of dangerous plots by French and papists', worried the Northampton steward Robert Woodford in March 1639.[67] 'What will become of us belongs to astrology', wrote Lord John Poulett in April.[68] 'All things are like to go off in perplexity and trouble', John Castle judged in October 1639. Referring presciently to dealings with Scotland, he concluded that 'surely things are likely to grow worse and worse'.[69]

Gloom and frustration was widespread by the spring of 1640. Dealings with the Scots were at a critical phase. A parliament was about to meet for the first time in eleven years, and nobody could predict the course of relations between the kingdoms or within them. Observers in London could see 'no

---

[63] Cambridge University Library, Ms. Dd. 3. 68, no. 10, f. 30; British Library, Add. Ms. 26786, f. 36; Bodleian Library, Oxford, Tanner Ms. 65, ff. 2, 35v; HMC, *Report on the Manuscripts of the Earl of Egmont* (i. part 1, 1905), 120; *CSPD 1641–43*, 126; PRO, C115/109/8897; Gardiner (ed.), *Oxinden Letters 1607–1642*, 248–9; British Library, Nicholas Papers, Egerton Ms. 2533, f. 141; HMC, *12th Report. The Manuscripts of the Earl Cowper...Preserved at Melbourne Hall, Derbyshire* (1888), ii. 286; Huntington Library, Ms. Stowe-Temple Correspondence, STT 2225.

[64] Cambridge University Library, Ms. Dd. 3. 68, no. 10, f. 34.

[65] County Record Office, Huntingdon, Manchester papers, Acc. 1983/6.

[66] HMC, *Report on the Manuscripts of the Duke of Buccleuch and Queensberry* (The Montague papers, 2nd series, 1926), iii. 380.

[67] Woodford's diary, New College, Oxford, Ms. 9502, 22 March 1639.

[68] J. H. Bettey (ed.), *Calendar of the Correspondence of the Smyth Family of Ashton Court 1548–1642* (Bristol Record Society, vol. xxxv, 1982), 142.

[69] Huntington Library, Ms. El. 7809, 24 October 1639.

hope of peace, but the whole sky of the court disposed to the tempest of a bloody war'.[70] These were 'troublesome and hostile times', declared the mayor of Hastings.[71] 'There are certain disastrous comets in Scotland represented to his majesty, but even the last day, which foretell of war and invasion', wrote Thomas Morton, Bishop of Durham, on 9 April 1640.[72] The Bristol landowner George Wyllys wrote that 'the times are so ill and things so unsettled in the commonwealth' and all was 'very dangerous and unsettled', though the prospects of a parliament raised hopes of 'better times'.[73]

It was hard to see the dissolution of the Short Parliament as anything but catastrophic. Commentators reflected on the compounding crisis, war with Scotland, a broken parliament, a failing economy, a weakened government, an undisciplined soldiery, and rioting apprentices. 'Oh lord God, bring good out of all these troubles and fears for the lord's sake', wrote Robert Woodford on 11 May. A few days later he prayed again, 'Oh lord bring good out of all these evils, and peace and quietness out of these distempers'.[74] This was a sentiment echoed throughout the elite, as Henry Hammond wrote to Sir Edward Dering in May, 'God send us a quiet and untroubled kingdom'.[75] Sir Thomas Peyton's view was bleak when he observed on 14 May 1640 that 'death's harbinger, the sword, famine and other plagues that hang over us are ready to swallow up the wicked age...in this fiery declination of the world.'[76]

The Scots were not the only source of danger. The social disturbances following the failure of the Short Parliament led some officials to fear 'mutiny' or 'insurrection' from discontented citizens. Following the Lambeth riots of May 1640 (discussed in Chapter 5) the authorities imposed 'a substantial double watch' on 'gates and landing places' around London and set guard against 'tumultuous assemblies'.[77] Further precautions followed including day and night watches against 'insolencies' and 'the like tumults and disorders'.[78]

The summer of 1640 was a season of disturbance and distress, climaxing in the Scottish victory at Newburn on 28 August. Adding to the chorus of despair the Earl of Northumberland remarked in June that 'so general

---

[70] Huntington Library, Mss. El. 7828, 25 March 1640; El. 7829, 28 March 1640.

[71] *CSPD 1640*, 35.

[72] Lincolnshire Archives, Ancaster Mss., 10 ANC/388, Morton to Lord Willoughby.

[73] *The Wyllys Papers* (Collections of the Connecticut Historical Society, vol. xxi, Hartford, Conn., 1924), 9, 11.

[74] Woodford's diary, New College, Oxford, Ms. 9502, 11 May, 16 May 1640.

[75] Centre for Kentish Studies, Maidstone, U350/C2/77, Hammond to Dering, 16 May 1640.

[76] Gardiner (ed.), *Oxinden Letters 1607–1642*, 174.

[77] Huntington Library, Ms. El. 7835, 18 May 1640; *CSPD 1640*, 250.

[78] *Privy Council Registers* (facsimile of PRO, PC2/53) (1968), xii. 36, 42.

a defection in this kingdom hath not been known in the memory of any'.[79] The Somerset squire Edward Phelips wrote in August 1640, 'now things are in a desperate condition, and there is no probable way but by prayer to bring this to a good end.'[80] 'All things stand in a doubtful condition', concurred William Hawkins, writing to the Earl of Leicester that month.[81] A correspondent of the Archbishop of Canterbury summed up a widespread perception, 'the times look very black'.[82]

The unexpected reversals of the Bishops' Wars turned a punitive expedition against rebels into a potential siege of the homeland. The King's strategy had been to take the war to the Scots, but by the summer of 1640 many feared that the Scots or their allies were coming to them. There was no telling at this time whether rebel sympathizers, seditious saboteurs, armed recusants, or foreign armies were the greatest or most immediate threat. Fear that the war against Scotland was going badly wrong led towns as far south as Sussex to take military precautions. The enemy might strike from the north, from the sea, or from within. The trained bands of Rye and the other Cinque Ports were made ready at twenty-four hours notice in August 1640, 'either for defence of the ports or for the public safety of the realm'.[83]

In the aftermath of the Scottish victory at Newburn the government began to strengthen its garrison defences. Secretary Windebank was among those who feared that the Scots might come further, urging the King to prepare Portsmouth as a south-coast bolt hole in case matters came to the worst. The Channel port was designated as a final refuge that might in extremis be resupplied from France.[84] 'The danger is greater than any since the [Norman] Conquest', Windebank advised Sir Anthony Hopton on 5 September.[85] The Scots themselves expected England to break out in revolt, and Secretary Vane acknowledged that 'the matter grow[s] very combustible and universal. . . . God send us but hearts and hands to stand our ground.'[86] News from the north was 'very uncertain' following the fall of Newcastle, and 'what the event will be the Lord alone knoweth', wrote Robert Woodford.[87] London was shaken with 'fears and distractions' after the defeat at Newburn and the loss of Newcastle.[88]

[79] Centre for Kentish Studies, Maidstone, U 1475/C85/16, Algernon Percy to Earl of Leicester, 4 June 1640 (National Register of Archives transcript).
[80] Bettey (ed.), *Calendar of the Correspondence of the Smyth Family of Ashton Court*, 159.
[81] HMC, *Report on the Manuscripts of the Right Honourable Viscount De L'Isle . . . Vol. VI. Sidney Papers, 1626–1698* (1966), 315.
[82] HMC, *9th Report* (1884), Part II, Appendix, 432.
[83] East Sussex Record Office, Rye Letters, 47/133.   [84] *CSPD 1640–41*, 9.
[85] O. Ogle and W. H. Bliss (eds.), *Calendar of the Clarendon State Papers Preserved in the Bodleian Library* (Oxford, 1872), i. 204.   [86] *CSPD 1640–41*, 15.
[87] Woodford's diary, New College, Oxford, Ms. 9502, 8 September 1640.
[88] HMC, *Report on the Manuscripts of the Right Honourable Viscount De L'Isle*, 323.

York, the main garrison town in the north, set repeated watches on walls and bars and ordered the north postern gate that faced towards the Scots to be shut both day and night.[89] Other cities looked urgently to their defences. The strategically important city of Chester repaired its gates in September 1640 and mounted a night-time watch.[90] Reviewing their stock of weapons 'in these warlike and dangerous times', the authorities at Chester found seventy-eight muskets were available, and urged citizens to obtain more 'for the better safeguard of themselves and the city'.[91] Military defences in Wales were hastily made ready in the face of 'dangerous and perillous times'.[92] London strengthened its watch, readied its munitions, and secured its gates and chains 'for the better defence of this city'.[93] Fearful that a Scottish military success would trigger rebellion in London, the Constable of the Tower had 'orders from the king that in case of a rising he is to raise platforms of earthworks in the Tower and take steps to command the city with guns'.[94] Another plan called for the gunpowder stored at the Tower to be moved to the south side of the Thames to deny it to any advancing enemy.[95]

The English governing class was gripped by panic. Some rushed to arm themselves against 'the great and approaching disaster', while others were paralysed with fear.[96] The King himself chastized his ministers at York on 7 September, 'I see ye are all so frighted, ye can resolve nothing.'[97] Some of those closest to the King had lost their nerve. Observing the Great Council at York, Lord Willoughby remarked, 'we are in a wood, knowing not well where we are.'[98] A northern newswriter lamented on 7 September 1640, 'O pitiful case, that so flourishing a church and state should, by our own distractions and the ambition of our discontented and schismatical neighbours, be thus in danger of ruin.'[99] Edmund Percival wrote from Hampshire that month, 'we live in as doleful and fearful conditions as any nation doth in the world, if God of his great mercy doth not suddenly stop the current of evils now upon us.... Every man may write over his own door, "Lord have mercy upon us".'[100]

---

[89] York City Archives, Corporation House Book, 1638–50, B/36, ff. 44–9.

[90] Cheshire Record Office, Chester Assembly Book 1624–84, Z.AB2, ff. 52v.

[91] Ibid., ff. 52v–53.

[92] National Library of Wales, Llanfair-Brynodel letters, C28 and 29, 7 September and 31 October 1640.

[93] Corporation of London Record Office, Repertories of the Court of Aldermen, Repertory 54, ff. 271v, 277v, 283v, 303v.

[94] Edward Razell and Peter Razell (eds.), *The English Civil War. A Contemporary Account. Volume 2: 1640–1642* (1996), 27.   [95] *CSPD 1640–41*, 2, 4, 6, 9.

[96] Ibid., 16.   [97] Ogle and Bliss (eds.), *Calendar of the Clarendon State Papers*, i. 205.

[98] HMC, *The Manuscripts of His Grace the Duke of Rutland, G.C.B., Preserved at Belvoir Castle* (1888), i. 523.

[99] Staffordshire Record Office, Notebook of Richard Dyott, D.661/11/1/5.

[100] HMC, *Report on the Manuscripts of the Earl of Egmont* (vol. 1, part 1, 1905), 120.

The Lords who called upon Charles in September to call a new parliament pointed to 'the great distempers and damages now threatening the church, the state, and your royal person', and warned that 'your whole kingdom falls of fears and discontents'.[101] Sir Humphrey Mildmay noted on 16 September 1640, 'the news vulgar of his majesty is not good, God almighty help him and us.'[102] John Cosin wrote on 21 September, 'these times are exceeding bad…I beseech God to send us better times.'[103] John Castle wrote grimly to the Earl of Bridgewater of 'these intestine troubles and dangers that threaten us at home'.[104]

The prospect of a new parliament produced swellings of optimism. Lord Goring's letters to his wife in late September 1640 were 'full of good news and great hopes of a speedy conclusion of all things'.[105] 'The news of a parliament is most acceptably welcome in all these parts, and a strong expectation of much ensuing good has possessed every man', wrote Francis Read to his cousin in early October.[106] Writing from York on 9 October, George Ravenscroft looked forward to promising political developments. 'God prosper this good beginning, and send a successful parliament which, by God's assistance, will put life into us all', he wrote.[107] 'God grant a blessing', echoed the Suffolk clergyman John Rous.[108] William Saville expressed his belief that 'this will be a very free parliament and his majesty will be apt to hearken to the desires of his people'.[109] The King, thought Sir Kenelm Digby, would now administer 'balm and healing'.[110] John White, the member-elect for Rye, hoped 'that God may so unite the hearts of king and people that this may be truly styled the blessed parliament'.[111] John Amye prayed that the November parliament would 'hold and set all things straight and right'.[112] But nobody believed that England's distempers were in remission. Endymion Porter wrote in October 1640 that the insolence of the Scots and the malice of the English were such 'that a general ruin is to be feared with the overthrow of a tottering monarchy'.[113] 'An unfortunate planet hangs over this country', lamented Edward Phelips.[114]

---

[101] Huntington Library, Ms. El. 7872, 10 September 1640.
[102] British Library, Harleian Ms. 454, f. 35.   [103] *CSPD 1640–41*, 82.
[104] Huntington Library, Ms. El. 7858, 26 September 1640.
[105] Lismore Mss., vol. xxi, National Register of Archives, vol. 20594/15, 864.
[106] *CSPD 1640–41*, 139.
[107] Cheshire Record Office, Chester Z ML/2, Mayor's Letter Book, 1599–1650, 281.
[108] Green (ed.), *Diary of John Rous…1625 to 1642*, 98.
[109] HMC, *Report on Various Collections* (1914), vii. 425, checked against University of Nottingham Library, Clifton Papers, CL/C 617, William Saville to Sir Gervase Clifton.
[110] Lismore Mss., vol. xxi, National Register of Archives, vol. 20594/15, 865.
[111] East Sussex Record Office, Lewes, Rye Letters, 47/133 (1640).
[112] HMC, *The Manuscripts of His Grace the Duke of Rutland, G.C.B.*, 524.
[113] Lismore Mss., vol. xxi, National Register of Archives, vol. 20594/15, 866, Endymion Porter to the Earl of Cork, 7 October 1640,
[114] Bristol Record Office, Smyth Papers, AC/C/58/5.

Correspondents wrote of 'great matters' and 'happy issue', and many looked forward to 'a settlement both of our religion and peace', as the parliament began its work.[115] William Wynn wrote in November of 'great hopes that all the grievances of this kingdom shall be redressed in this parliament.'[116] Robert Woodford expressed a 'very great rejoicing'.[117] 'Huge things are here in working', declared Robert Baillie, there was 'never such a parliament in England ... God is making here a new world.'[118] 'Every week will now bring forth remarkable things, and we pray that all may end well', wrote William Hawkins in mid-November, 'there was never, I dare say, so busy a time in England.' In January 1641 Hawkins still expected 'a possibility of reformation, so that we all hope for good days hereafter if there be but a good success to these earnest beginnings'.[119]

Some commentators were exhilarated by the parliament's apparent successes, though others were more wary of setbacks. 'God ... hath done wonderful things among us already, and gives us hope of more', wrote the godly Ann Temple in January 1641.[120] Edmund Percival expressed his hope in March that the parliament, which 'hath hitherto prosperously gone on, will in some years make again a flourishing kingdom'.[121] When 'a stork was seen to sit upon the House of Commons' on the last Monday in May 1641 it was 'taken for a presage of much peace, and quick, Amen.'[122]

Several writers dubbed 1641 their '*annus mirabilis*', 'a wonderful year of God's mercies to England'.[123] Writing to Sir Robert Harley at midsummer in that '*anno renovationis*', John Hall enthused that a miracle had been accomplished. 'How many mouths have you opened that were sealed up, yea many spirits have you enlarged that was straightened, yea many congregations give abundant thanks to God on your behalf.'[124] The Puritan Robert Woodford praised God in July 1641, 'oh lord, what great things hast thou done for this kingdom', and spoke optimistically about a godly 'triumph'.[125]

---

[115] HMC, *14th Report, Appendix, part IV, The Manuscripts of Lord Kenyon* (1894), 59, 60, letters of Alexander Rigby.

[116] National Library of Wales, Wynn Papers, no. 1672 (microfilm). William Wynn, 28 November 1640.

[117] Woodford's diary, New College, Oxford, Ms. 9502, 31 August 1637, 28 November 1640.

[118] David Laing (ed.), *The Letters and Journals of Robert Baillie* (3 vols., Edinburgh, 1841), i. 274, 278, 280, 283.

[119] HMC, *Report on the Manuscripts of the Right Honourable Viscount De L'Isle*, 341, 352, 359.   [120] East Sussex Record Office, Lewes, Dunn Ms. 51/54 (microfilm XA 73/11).

[121] HMC, *Report on the Manuscripts of the Earl of Egmont*, 128.

[122] Bedfordshire and Luton Archives, Bedford, St John Papers, J. 1382.

[123] George Hughes, *The Art of Embalming Dead Saints* (1642), 48.

[124] British Library, Add. Ms. 70003, f. 111.

[125] Woodford's diary, New College, Oxford, Ms. 9502, 29 July 1641.

Anti-puritans, not surprisingly, were less hopeful. The times for them were 'black' or 'doubtful' or, in Thomas Knyvett's phrase, 'this whipping time'.[126] John Farmer of Cookham vented his frustration in June 1641 about 'this awful parliament', and lamented 'the resentments of these sad times'.[127] Isaac Basire's correspondents early in 1642 wrote of 'these tumultuous and disjointed times' and of 'times of contradiction'.[128] Others wished the parliament well, but despaired of difficulties. 'These are dangerous times, I pray God deliver us all', wrote Thomas Temple in March 1641, as 'bitter' and 'underhand' dealings soured local and national relations.[129] Sir John Temple wrote that month of 'an universal disorder in all the affairs of all the three kingdoms'.[130] Writing from Oxford later in March, Edward Perkins remarked, 'we are sick with expectations what will be the issue of the present grave business.'[131]

Anxieties were widespread in the spring of 1641. God seemed to withhold his blessings from England, as the Scottish business was unresolved, the trial of Strafford dragged on, the streets were wild with tumults, and rumours of anti-parliamentary plotting abounded. The Earl of Bridgewater wished in April that 'things were in a better temper'.[132] Brilliana Harley despaired that month 'that things are now in such a condition that if the Lord does not put forth his helping hand his poor children will be brought low.'[133] Sir Thomas Peyton concurred that 'all things are in an ill condition and nothing has yet succeeded according to the hope and expectation of men.'[134]

Still in control, or at least acting as if they were still in control, the Privy Council instructed the London and Middlesex authorities in the spring of 1641 to set up watches and to muster the trained bands against Shrovetide and May Day disturbances. They feared, not unreasonably, the 'confluence together' of apprentices, discharged soldiers, and other 'loose and dissolute persons' on those days of traditionally licensed disorder.[135] Customary spring rowdiness combined with the novel energies of 1641 to form a volatile grenade, but it was not entirely clear who was protecting what from whom.

---

[126] Schofield (ed.), *Knyvett Letters (1620–1644)*, 96.

[127] Huntington Library, STT 748, Farmer to his kinsman Sir Peter Temple.

[128] W. N. Darnell (ed.), *The Correspondence of Isaac Basire, D.D.* (1831), 40; Durham University Library, Special Collections, 'John Cosin Letterbook', 1A/31.

[129] Huntington Library, Ms. Stowe–Temple Correspondence, STT 2225.

[130] HMC, *Report on the Manuscripts of the Right Honourable Viscount De L'Isle*, 393.

[131] HMC, *14th Report, The Manuscripts of His Grace the Duke of Portland* (1894), iii. 75.

[132] Huntington Library, Ms. El. 7333, Bridgewater to his steward Henry Ecclestone.

[133] British Library, Add. Ms. 70110, f. 60.

[134] HMC, *10th Report* (1887), Appendix, part 6, 86. Sir Thomas Peyton, MP for Sandwich, 29 April 1641.

[135] *Privy Council Registers* (facsimile of PRO PC2/53) (1968), xii. 105, 125–6.

Worried lest disorderly elements engaged in 'riots and tumults' during the trial of the Earl of Strafford, the Council attempted to put London under curfew. Servants and apprentices were supposed to be kept indoors, while the trained bands were ordered to take up strategic positions.[136] Amongst other precautions, they established strong watches day and night throughout the liberty of Westminster, 'and especially towards Hyde Park and other places near the king's palace'.[137]

By May 1641, however, some people feared that a greater danger came from the papists, the army, and the court than from a politically aroused citizenry. News and rumour fed fears of popish plotting, with repeated warnings that the recusants were about to rise.[138] Reports came from Lichfield early in 1641 'concerning hatchets and such instruments of death prepared for mischief' by papists and their supporters. Fears spread that the Catholics would rise and massacre the godly on one of their Wednesday fast days.[139] Rumour told that Strafford was about to be freed, that the French were coming, that the army would strike against the City, that the Commons house would be set on fire, and that all the achievements of the past six months were in peril.[140] 'We have an overwhelming of our hopes', wrote George Wyllys, junior, on hearing that the King had declared that 'the Earl of Strafford ... shall not die.'[141] The Venetian ambassador fanned the flames by reporting 'fears that if the fire of these differences is not extinguished by the more prudent, it will finally break out in a terrible civil war.'[142]

These fears were not entirely groundless, for several army officers were heard speaking recklessly 'in commendation of the Earl of Strafford' and proclaiming that the citizens 'deserved to have the city fired about their ears'. Richard Neville, a commander of troops in Berkshire, boasted how easy it would be to set fires and take plunder, though his defenders said in mitigation that he 'spoke in a light way'.[143] Correspondents were abuzz with 'strange plots and stratagems' concerning a military threat to the parliament.[144]

---

[136] Ibid., 108, 109.

[137] London Metropolitan Archives, Sessions Books, MJ/SBB/18 (calendar 10360.t.1, 72).

[138] Jansson (ed.), *Proceedings in the Opening Session of the Long Parliament ... Volume 1*, 60, 68, 99, 110, 352, 435; British Library, Add. Ms. 70002, ff. 315, 353 (Gower to Harley, 9 November and 12 December 1640).

[139] HMC, *9th Report* (1884), Part II, Appendix, 391.

[140] For fears of the French, see Sir Edward Dering to his wife, 2 May 1641, British Library, Add. Ms. 26786, f. 36.   [141] *Wyllys Papers*, 17.

[142] Razell and Razell (eds.), *English Civil War. A Contemporary Account. Vol. 2*, 73–4.

[143] Bodleian Library, Nalson Ms. 13/19, 20.

[144] National Library of Wales, Pitchford Mss. Correspondence C/1/97, Richard Browne to Sir Francis Ottley, 11 May 1641.

'God send good issue', prayed Edward Dering at the beginning of May 1641, 'my despairs begin to go above my faith.' By this time Dering could see nothing ahead but 'confusion'.[145] Anticipating a violent outcome, George Wyllys wrote from Bristol on 6 May, 'we may be all in a hurly-burly ere long'.[146]

The Protestation, a pledge to defend English protestantism against all popery and popish innovations, directly addressed these concerns.[147] Parliament also took practical precautions. Fearful of a recusant rising combined with a military coup, the House of Commons on 5 May 1641 instructed all counties, cities, and boroughs to make sure that their arms and ammunition were in serviceable condition.[148] Dozens of constituencies reported back on their stocks of weapons. The borough of Leicester assured its members of Parliament that they had 'munition and arms . . . in readiness'. The town could put forty muskets and corslets into immediate use, and controlled a share of the powder in the county magazine.[149] Staffordshire had four barrels of powder on hand, which 'cost very dear and was procured with a great deal of trouble . . . in regard of the scarceness at that time.'[150] The Cinque Port of Rye reported a variety of ordnance, two demy calverins, two sacres, two brass minions, and two mortar pieces, but no carriage for them.[151] Oxford provided 'a barrel or two of powder . . . at the city's charge'.[152]

Gentry families also put themselves on a martial footing. Expecting 'stirs' in Herefordshire earlier in the spring, Lady Brilliana Harley had already begun to prepare the defences of her house.[153] In April 1641 the Wynn family in north Wales secured powder, muskets, pikes, head-pieces, swords, and bows and arrows for their defence in case 'the times prove bad'.[154] The times were 'more dangerous . . . than ever', reported Robert Wynne to his kinsmen, 'but I hope in God it will be otherwise, and we shall have peace'.[155]

---

[145] British Library, Add. Ms. 26786, f. 36; Lambert B. Larking (ed.), *Proceedings, Principally in the County of Kent, in Connection with the Parliaments Called in 1640* (Camden Society, first series, vol. lxxx, 1862), 46.   [146] *Wyllys Papers*, 18, 38.

[147] Conrad Russell, 'The First Army Plot of 1641', in his *Unrevolutionary England, 1603–16, 1603–1642* (1990), 281–302; David Cressy, 'The Protestation Protested, 1641 and 1642', *Historical Journal*, 45 (2002), 251–79.

[148] Bedfordshire and Luton Archives, St John Papers, J. 1381.

[149] Helen Stocks and W. H. Stevenson (eds.), *Records of the Borough of Leicestershire . . . 1603–1688* (Cambridge, 1923), 307.

[150] Staffordshire Record Office, Q/SR/245/1, Thomas Davenport's account, 13 January 1641. The gunpowder cost 21d. a pound, almost £9 a barrel.

[151] East Sussex Record Office, Rye Letters, 47/133 (1641).

[152] M. G. Hobson and H. E. Salter (eds.), *Oxford Council Acts 1626–1665* (Oxford Historical Society, vol. xcv, Oxford, 1933), 99.

[153] HMC, *14th Report, The Manuscripts of His Grace the Duke of Portland*, iii. 75.

[154] National Library of Wales, Wynn Papers, no. 1683 (microfilm).

[155] National Library of Wales, Llanfair-Brynodel letters, C34, Robert Wynne to Richard Griffith, 19 March 1642.

George Wyllys of Bristol told his father in Connecticut that he had spent £3.9s. for 'three muskets bought to send to New England, but in respect of the dangerous times I have kept and have them still by me, being firelocks.'[156]

'Distractions and fears here do daily increase', wrote Robert Slingsby in June 1641, in a sentence that could serve as the motto for the times.[157] 'Every day will now produce a new treason', wrote the lawyer Roger Hill in June, 'there will be no rest among these wasps that are now stirred. We find new mercies every morning and have still sad resolutions to devour us, were we not seamed by a divine providence.'[158] 'I much fear a great calamity to fall upon this land', wrote Sir John Temple, 'the preparations are laid, the way is open, and unless it please God to bless the king and his people to superinduce a good understanding betwixt them, we must look for a greater concussion than this nation hath for many years endured.'[159] 'We are here still in the labyrinth and cannot get out', wrote Secretary Vane on 18 June. 'God send us peace and deliver us from our divisions and distractions.'[160] John Milton wrote similarly in 1641 of 'those mazes and labyrinths of dreadful and hideous thoughts', in which England had lost its direction.[161]

Anxieties intensified over the summer. 'We are here in very unstable and uncertain condition, expecting every day some alteration in the government or amongst the governors', wrote Edward Nicholas at the beginning of July. A few days later he despaired, 'I see nothing hereabout that may give a rational and moderate man any measure of content or hope for good.'[162] The following month Nicholas found Parliament 'full of jealousies and apprehensions', and feared 'we shall suddenly come into a great confusion'.[163] 'The times are so perplexed that there is no resolving of anything', complained James Duport that summer.[164] 'We were never fuller of jealousies than we are at present, nor less hopeful of avoiding confusion,' wrote the Earl of Northumberland in August.[165] 'I pray God . . . that there be not at this time a general assize and judgement intended upon the kingdom', wrote the Earl of Holland.[166] The danger from the north appeared to have receded, to be overtaken by domestic in-fighting, schism, and popish plotting.

---

[156] *Wyllys Papers*, 18, 38.　　[157] *CSPD 1641–43*, 7.
[158] Buckinghamshire Record Office, Hill Family Letters (Transcripts), D 192/8/1b.
[159] HMC, *12th Report, The Manuscripts of the Earl Cowper . . . Preserved at Melbourne Hall, Derbyshire* (1888), ii. 286. Sir John Temple to Sir John Cook, 28 June 1641.
[160] *CSPD 1641–43*, 17.　　[161] [John Milton], *Of Reformation* (1641), 86.
[162] *CSPD 1641–43*, 38, 41.
[163] British Library, Nicholas Papers, Egerton Ms. 2533, ff. 143v, 157v.
[164] Barrington Papers, British Library, Egerton Ms. 2646, f. 161.
[165] *CSPD 1641–43*, 104.　　[166] British Library, Nicholas Papers, Egerton Ms. 2533, f. 141.

While arming themselves, Protestant gentlemen were concerned to remove dangerous weapons from the hands of potential enemies. Some engaged in periodic and panicky attempts to disarm papists, citing the Jacobean statute made following the Gunpowder Plot. Justices in Devonshire, for example, made repeated searches for all arms, muskets, gunpowder, pikes, corselets, 'or other munition of war' in Roman Catholic hands.[167] Lancashire magistrates confiscated pistols, muskets, corselets, breastplates, and gorgets from Catholic households and absorbed this equipment into their own armory.[168] Yorkshire magistrates undertook similar searches and confiscations.[169] In Essex Harbottle Grimston raided more than two dozen recusants' houses in August 1641, searching for arms, powder, and ammunition, and transferring weaponry from 'popish' to 'safe' hands. 'We took from Mr. White of Mountnazing one musket with the appurtenances complete, which we placed in the custody of Mr. Carrier, High Constable of Chelmsford Hundred, left for the defence of the house two birding pieces.... We took from Lady Garrard of Brentwood one new pike and corslet complete.'[170] Scant evidence emerged of real popish plotting, but the fears continued to fester all summer and autumn. Rumours persisted 'that secret forces were ready in some places and secret meetings had been had in Hampshire by sundry great recusants, which might justly give us occasion to conceive that some wicked designs were still in hatching.'[171]

Men of action proposed active preparations. In August 1641 Parliament instructed the Constable of the Tower to take up residence, along with forty extra soldiers to reinforce the London garrison.[172] 'Hull is by order from both houses to be secured from a surprisal, Portsmouth is to be reinforced with men and ammunition, the papists generally will be disarmed', wrote the Northamptonshire MP Sir Gilbert Pickering on 19 August.[173] All highways within twenty miles of London were to be watched for 'loose and disorderly persons' including wandering soldiers.[174]

The settlement of peace with Scotland in September 1641 lifted spirits and gave renewed ground for optimism. It produced, wrote chroniclers, 'a general

---

[167] Devon Record Office, Quarter Sessions Order Book 1640–51, Q/S 1/8, nf. Their statutory authority came from 3 Jac. c. 5, and repeated proclamations and orders from Quarter Sessions.

[168] Lancashire Record Office, QSB/1/246/40, /60–62, QSO2/17.

[169] John Lister (ed.), *West Riding Sessions Records. Vol. II. Orders, 1611–1642. Indictments, 1637–1642* (Yorkshire Archaeological Society, vol. liii, 1915), 359; York City Archives, Corporation House Book, 1638–1650, B/36, ff. 57v, 68.

[170] Bodleian Library, Nalson Ms. 13/26.

[171] Coates (ed.), *Journal of Sir Simonds D'Ewes from the First Recess of the Long Parliament to the Withdrawal of the King from London*, 58.

[172] British Library, Nicholas Papers, Egerton Ms. 2533, f. 157v.

[173] Bedfordshire and Luton Archives, St John Papers, J. 1387.

[174] House of Lords order of 21 September 1641, *Lords Journal*, iv. 397.

thanksgiving through England, with sermons and feasting and bonfires and ringing of bells, the king joyfully received by the Londoners at his return' in November.[175] The return of the King was the return of sunshine, wrote loyal versifiers.[176] 'He's come to salve this kingdom's discontents, | To cure all wrenches, fractions, sprains and rents', trilled John Taylor at the King's re-entry into London.[177] But optimism was neither universal nor long lasting. Endymion Porter, who had accompanied the King to Scotland, saw nothing to celebrate in the Treaty of Edinburgh. 'I fear this island before it be long will be a theatre of distractions', he prophesied on 11 September 1641, 'for we are like to see lamentable times.'[178] Edward Reed wrote similarly from London in September that 'affairs here...are in a distempered way'. The 'distemper' would grow, he feared, unless control was exercised over 'the soldiers and over-busy men in the affairs of the church'.[179]

News of the Irish rebellion, which spread rapidly in the first week of November, jolted people into urgent reappraisal of their danger. It confirmed and reinforced all recent fears. Sir Henry Vane, who was among the first to hear of the uprising, recognized at once that it would 'cause a great distraction'.[180] Thomas Barrow reported 'very ill news from Ireland. I pray God in his good time in mercy to look upon us.'[181] The plots and conspiracies that Pym had so relentlessly forecast seemed indeed to be coming to fruition. John Scudamore wrote from Sussex that the news of the Irish rebellion 'makes our puritans in this county buy powder and arms for fear. God send us peace in the three kingdoms.'[182]

Responding to the crisis in November, 'in regard of these dangerous times', the authorities at Dorchester ordered bars and covers for the shire hall windows, and mounted 'a constant watch...every night' until further notice. The governors were so nervous that they ordered the townsmen 'to provide all their arms in readiness for defence', and set an additional watchman at the top of St Peter's church tower to 'view the country round about' during service time.[183] The Wiltshire borough of Devizes repaired the town muskets early in November 1641, and purchased supplies of powder and

---

[175] The Chester Chronicle, British Library, Harleian Ms. 2125, f. 65.
[176] *Ovatio Carolina: The Triumph of King Charles...Upon his Safe and Happy Return from Scotland* (1641); *Evcharistica Oxoniensia* (Oxford, 1641).
[177] John Taylor, *Englands Comfort and Londons Joy* (1641), 5, 7.
[178] British Library, Nicholas Papers, Egerton Ms. 2533, f. 207.
[179] HMC, *12th Report, The Manuscripts of the Earl Cowper*, ii. 291, 293.
[180] British Library, Nicholas Papers, Egerton Ms. 2533, ff. 246, 252.
[181] Gardiner (ed.), *Oxinden Letters 1607–1642*, 248–9.   [182] PRO, C115/109/8897.
[183] Charles Herbert Mayo (ed.), *The Municipal Records of the Borough of Dorchester, Dorset* (Exeter, 1908), 508–9.

match, belts, and bandoliers 'for the town's use'.[184] Frodsham beacon in Cheshire was hastily repaired at a cost of twenty nobles, while other signal beacons throughout the north were put in readiness.[185] Not since 1588 had so much of England been placed on an armed defensive footing. The previously desultory inventorying of arms became a matter of urgency, driving up the price of gunpowder and weapons.

On 17 November 1641 (the anniversary of Queen Elizabeth's accession), an excited Sir Robert Harley urged the citizens of Ludlow to 'look well to your town, for the papists are discovered to have a bloody design in general, as well against this kingdom as elsewhere'. Reporting the resultant 'stir' to the Earl of Bridgewater a few days later, Henry Ecclestone added, 'the same news it seems came to Bewdley and caused them all in the town to be up in arms with watch all night in very great fear, and here the town hath kept watch ever since; and at Brampton Bryan they were all in arms upon the tops of Sir Robert's castle and took up provisions thither with them and in great fear, all which put the country in a great amaze.'[186] Lady Brilliana Harley assured her husband on 20 November that she had 'caused a good provision of bullets to be made, and the pieces charged', but planned to take refuge in Shrewsbury 'if the papists should rise or any commotion should be'. Ned Harley thought that papists lacked the strength to do damage, but Brilliana told her husband, 'I think he is much mistaken.'[187]

At Bridgenorth on 19 November 'a strong watch was kept in the town, upon information from Kidderminster of a sudden insurrection and rising of the papists that night in the kingdom.' Several shillings were spent on burnt sack and beer to cheer the watchers, and a 'great fire' was kept all night at the town cross.[188] In Lancashire on 23 November 1641 the magistrates ordered the trained bands into a state of heightened preparedness of watch and ward, having first made sure that no Catholics had infiltrated the force. All soldiers and officers were required to subscribe to the Oath of Allegiance, and to 'be in a readiness as occasion shall answer', with powder, bullets, and match. The watch was specifically instructed to stay all known Catholics and to search for 'unlawful assemblies or tumults' at recusants' houses.[189] More 'strict watches' with 'musters and training' were ordered elsewhere in

---

[184] Wiltshire Record Office, Devizes General Entry Book, 1572–1660, f. 151.

[185] Cheshire Record Office, QJB 1/6, f 50v; Martyn Bennett, *The Civil Wars Experienced: Britain and Ireland, 1638–1661* (2000), 17–18.

[186] Huntington Library, Ms. El. 7352; HMC, *11th Report* (1888), Appendix, Part VII, 147.

[187] British Library, Add. Ms. 70003, ff. 172–172v; HMC, *14th Report, The Manuscripts of His Grace the Duke of Portland*, iii. 81–2.

[188] HMC, *Tenth Report, Appendix, Part IV* (1885, reissued 1906), 434.

[189] Lancashire Record Office, Kenyon Papers, DDF/2437/90.

response to the apparent popish threat.[190] At Exeter the authorities ordered that 'the inhabitants of this city shall hold a club or some other weapon in readiness for the preservation of the peace.'[191]

The onset of winter brought a crescendo of troubles, with the widening breach between King and Parliament. Gentry papers point to a further disintegration of morale. William Drake wrote in his journal in December 1641 that 'these troubles that now distract us would be like the travails of childbirth and produce either a monstrous frenzy or an absolute tyranny, if a potent and prudent prince had the managing of them.'[192] *Utinam*, as the Latinists said, if only that were so. 'We are running to ruin', wrote William Montague to his father on 2 December, 'there is scarce any hopes of better.'[193] 'We hope and pray for a better unity', Thomas Stockdale wrote on 10 December 1641, as 'astonishment and fears' seemed to change 'our happy peace . . . into a chaos of miseries'.[194]

Guy Molesworth wrote to Sir John Pennington on 16 December, 'all things grow daily into a more dangerous expectation'.[195] 'I doubt we are not far from ruin', Thomas Wiseman concluded that same day, 'unless God in mercy unite the hearts of the parliament to the king and people.'[196] On 17 December Thomas Smith reported, 'much discourse in court, Parliament and city, nay, and country too, and much discontent in all of them; factions increasing as men's humours vary, most men governing themselves rather by passion than judgement, and few regarding either religion or honesty in their censures of affairs of state.'[197] 'Poor England, in what a miserable estate art thou, groaning under the burden of so many divisions', lamented a pamphlet of this time.[198] 'If things may not proceed in order', opined another pamphleteer, 'a commonwealth will quickly prove a heap of ruins, and resolve, as the world must at the general doom, to its first chaos.'[199] The lights were not yet extinguished, but it was getting darker by the hour.

Commentary became even more doom-laden in the opening months of 1642, although Lady Brilliana Harley was persuaded 'that this is the time that the Lord will set up his kingdom in glory. . . . I trust he will bring his own work to a glorious end.'[200] Few correspondents shared her eschatological enthusiasm.

---

[190] G. W. Johnson (ed.), *The Fairfax Correspondence. Memoirs of the Reign of Charles the First* (2 vols., 1848), ii. 290.

[191] Devon Record Office, Exeter Chamber Act Book, 1634–47, 253.

[192] William Drake's Journal, Huntington Library Ms., HM 55603, f. 38.

[193] HMC, *Report on the Manuscripts of the Duke of Buccleuch and Queensberry*, 287.

[194] Johnson (ed.), *Fairfax Correspondence*, ii. 291–2.   [195] *CSPD 1641–43*, 203.

[196] Ibid., 202   [197] Ibid., 206.

[198] *Lucifers Lackey, or, The Devils new Creature* (1641), sig. A2.

[199] T.J. [Thomas Jordan], *A Medicine for the Times*, sig. A4.

[200] British Library, Add. Ms. 70003, f. 192.

Most reacted with 'great fear and sadness' to the 'heavy news' of the King's failed coup against Parliament on 4 January, and his subsequent departure from London.[201] This was an especially tense time around Westminster and Whitehall, with 'everyone possessed with strange fears and imaginations'.[202] One of Sir John Pennington's correspondents wrote on 6 January that 'all things are now in so great distraction here that there is no thinking of doing anything, but everybody are providing for their own safety, as if everything were inclinable to ruin.'[203] Thomas Coke wrote to his family in Derbyshire a few days later, 'I fear God hath some heavy judgement to execute upon this nation. Every hour here threatens public insurrection and confusion.'[204] In Kent a Mr Cecil Cave spread alarm 'that blood should be sold as cheap as milk'.[205] John Price, a citizen of London, wrote that 'we live in a kind of twilight, a cloudy and foggy clime of sadness and uncertainty.'[206]

Nobody knew what would happen. Many feared for the worst. Threats abounded from 'papists and their adherents', who now included the Cavalier gentlemen gathering about the King. King Charles himself believed he was facing rebellion. 'We all fear some secret machination to disturb the peace of the land and to divert the courses of the parliament', wrote Thomas Stockdale in February.[207] 'Prayers and tears are the best arms we can use', wrote Will Sancroft to his father in early April, 'I pray God we may stay there and take up no other.'[208]

When the King attempted to enter Hull in April and was rebuffed by the parliamentary governor, the register of alarm moved even higher. There followed a season of deepening menace and gathering gloom, as bloodshed seemed increasingly likely. (See Chapter 18 for these crucial months.) When civil war finally broke out, it began, like many wars, in a muddle of fear and misapprehension. Writing from the royalist camp in 1643, when the outcome of the conflict was still uncertain, James Howell recalled its recent origins, when 'the huge bug-bear Danger was like a monster of many heads', and a host of irrational fears made people 'simple and sottish'.[209] 'Thus into war we scared ourselves', with 'strange wild fears' and fancies, wrote the poet Abraham Cowley that same year, in a sad and unfinished history.[210]

---

[201] Johnson (ed.), *Fairfax Correspondence*, ii. 297.
[202] *CSPD 1641–43*, 244; Coates (ed.), *Journal of Sir Simonds D'Ewes from the First Recess of the Long Parliament to the Withdrawal of the King from London*, 392.
[203] *CSPD 1641–43*, 241.
[204] HMC, *12th Report, The Manuscripts of the Earl Cowper*, ii. 303.
[205] *Commons Journal*, ii. 373.
[206] [John Price], *Some Few and Short Considerations on the Present Distempers* (1642), 6.
[207] Johnson (ed.), *Fairfax Correspondence*, ii. 347, 374.
[208] Bodleian Library, Oxford, Tanner Ms. 63, f. 3.
[209] [James Howell], *The True Informer…of the Sad Distempers in Great Britanny and Ireland* (1643), 5, 21–2.
[210] *Abraham Cowley. The Civil War*, ed. Allan Pritchard (Toronto, 1973), 76.

3

⌘

Life and Death Amidst Distraction
and Fears

On the brink of civil war, amidst acute political and religious distempers, the English people experienced unprecedented cultural and constitutional disruption. Over two years of crisis they witnessed the beginning of a revolution in which many of the traditional landmarks of church and state were overturned. Yet not all eyes were on the nation's troubles, at least not all the time. Many of the structures, patterns, and routines of life continued uninterrupted, as people went about their ordinary business. The rhythms of birth, marriage, and death were largely insulated from political history, and so too were the everyday rounds of recreation and pleasure. Our perspective on the crisis is broadened when we take note of these less sensational concerns.

LIFE GOES ON

One would not know from Henry Best's diary for 1640 and 1641 that the nation was gripped by turmoil. It is hard to imagine that the affairs of the kingdom failed to touch this East Riding farmer, but they left no trace in his records. Instead he documents a routine of payments to servants and shepherds, consideration of tithes, and the wintering of ewes and hogs.[1] Country work continued, even if the Scots were over the horizon, even if an English army was manoeuvring nearby. Economic and agrarian work went on because it had to, even if times were tough. There was no abrogation of the cycle of the seasons, no cancelling of appetites or the distributive arrangements of markets and fairs.[2]

---

[1] Donald Woodward (ed.), *The Farming and Memorandum Books of Henry Best of Elmswell, 1642*, (1984), 192–3.

[2] Only in August 1642 was the mayor's feast at Evesham cancelled 'in respect of the trouble and distraction of these present times' (Stephen K. Roberts (ed.), *Evesham Borough Records of*

In Buckinghamshire the politically astute lawyer Roger Hill, who was closely involved in the prosecution of Archbishop Laud, found time during the crisis to win and wed a new wife. Hill's letters to his beloved Abigail mix reports of business in Parliament with affectionate intimate yearnings.[3] And why should they not? Public and personal life did not cancel each other out, but rather commingled or occupied adjacent compartments. So too the Northamptonshire puritan Robert Woodford was passionately concerned for God's people during the crisis of 1640 and 1641, and his diary shows him to have been an attentive observer of public events. Yet a parallel domestic drama unfolds in Woodford's pages, as he monitored his wife's pregnancies and childbearing, and his family's difficulty with debts.[4]

With much more money and leisure, the Essex landowner Sir Humphrey Mildmay sought amusement and distraction in the midst of the revolutionary crisis. Mildmay was in London during the opening week of the Long Parliament, but his diary records merely that on 6 and 9 November 1640 he spent the afternoons at a play. Mildmay took a passing interest in public events, but seems to have regarded Strafford's passage to the Tower and the homecoming of Bastwick, Burton, and Prynne as spectacles for a gentle loiterer rather than episodes in the trauma of a kingdom. He had much to tell his Essex neighbours after each trip to the metropolis, but he gave more attention to merry-making than to politics. Again, we may ask, why should one not? Mildmay was in London again on 26 May 1641, at a time of high political drama, but he seems to have been more concerned with his pleasures than with the tumults taking place around him. His diary for that day records that he 'rambled about but to small purpose, doing no more than before, and supped with the dean of Peterborough and came home late to bed'. One wonders what the table talk was with his dinner companion, the controversial and embattled ceremonialist John Cosin. Another of Mildmay's dinners was spoiled on 3 January 1642 by 'the bugbear news at London', but his pursuit of merriment continued unabated.[5] Similarly the young John Evelyn spent the critical period from January to March 1642 'studying a little, but dancing and fooling much', if his memoir is to be believed.[6]

the Seventeenth Century, 1605–1687 (Worcester Historical Society, new series, vol. xiv, 1994), 42). This 'time of distraction' prevented the churchwardens and parishioners of St Mary Crypt, Gloucester, from conducting their normal business 'without danger', so the existing parish officers served an extra year (Gloucestershire Record Office, P 154/11/CW2/1).

[3] Buckinghamshire Record Office, Hill Family Letters (Transcripts and copies), D 192/8 and 9.
[4] Robert Woodford's diary, New College, Oxford, Ms. 9502, passim.
[5] British Library, Harleian Ms. 454, ff. 36v, 37, 41, 46v.
[6] William Bray (ed.), *The Diary of John Evelyn* (1879), i. 38.

Nor did the panic and confusion in the capital stand in the way of Henry Oxinden's country pursuits in Kent. His usual round of fox-hunting, match-making, and local and familial aggrandizement continued in May 1641, under the shadow of the national crisis. Yet intimations of doom were unavoidable. Early in February 1642 Oxinden reported that 'great matches are easily to be had now in London, for certain great heirs are afraid the world is almost at an end, or that ere long they shall be killed, and would gladly have some sport before they die; and can you blame them, sith they believe when they are gone all the world is gone with them.'[7] John Gage of Northamptonshire was too 'depressed with grief and sorrow' at the death of his son to pay close attention to national affairs in February 1641. Yet private and public sorrows were linked, he thought, 'considering Satan by his wretched ministers who are executors of his most damnable will did never more reign than in these our latter days'.[8]

County and local government continued to operate, and their courts still met on schedule, even as the crisis developed. Borough sessions concerned themselves as ever with the measurement of ale, the assize of bread, the maintenance of bastards, relief of the poor, and keeping of the peace.[9] Leet courts still went about their business of abating nuisances, curbing encroachments, and generally maintaining the fabric of urban life, as shown by the example of Hereford. There may have been more defaulters than usual, greater resistance to orderly discipline, perhaps a higher level of disrepair, but at least the officials went about their tasks and still sought sanctions for anti-social behaviour.[10] The Norwich and London Bridewells continued to duck scolds, and set offenders in the pillories or stocks.[11]

Quarter Sessions still met quarterly, following established procedures. Crime too took no holiday. The magistrates coped as usual with the picking of pockets, stealing of clothes and chickens, and receiving of stolen goods, and issued citations for selling short measure or butchering unwholesome meat. Most of the disorders they dealt with were only tangentially related to the contemporary emergencies at Westminster.

In Wiltshire, for example, the Quarter Sessions in January 1641 handled business from the previous summer, when the young men and women of Broad Chalk entertained themselves with 'a dancing match' and an all-night

---

[7] Dorothy Gardiner (ed.), *The Oxinden Letters 1607–1642* (1933), 196–7, 283.

[8] John Gage to Sir Roland St John, 20 February 1640/1, Bedfordshire and Luton Archives, St John Papers, J.1377.

[9] Shropshire Record Office, Shrewsbury Borough Records, 3365/2238–41, Quarter Sessions Rolls, 1639–43. [10] Herefordshire Record Office, Tourn Book 1625–42, BG 11/4/5.

[11] Norfolk Record Office, Norwich Mayor's Court Book, 1634–46; Corporation of London Record Office, Bridewell and Bethlem, Court of Governors Minutes, 1640–42.

party at the mill on St John's night. One of the villagers, the aptly named Thomas Wild, 'termed himself to be the bishop' and touched young women in the dark. Catherine Sanger of Knoyle 'was set upon her head and was bishopped, but by whom it was done she knoweth not'. Far from the root and branch movement that was stirring in the capital, and remote from the episcopal palaces at Salisbury and Wells, this Wiltshire 'bishop' was akin to a midsummer lord of misrule. The magistrates who admonished him included veterans of campaigns for the reformation of manners—puritans as well as Laudians—who saw the 'dancing match' as an affront to ecclesiastical and godly authority.[12]

Also in January 1641, while Parliament was debating religious reform, the Exeter Quarter Sessions dealt with the case of Margaret Paul, 'a neger (sic) born and a servant unto the Lord Bishop of Exeter', who had been 'unlawfully begotten with child' by a fellow servant 'in a hayloft of the said Lord Bishop'. Besides revealing the presence of a black female servant in Devonshire, and the apparent moral laxity of some episcopal households, the record shows the secular court engaged in the routine disciplining of offences of the kind previously the preserve of the church courts. Three months later the magistrates learned that the alleged father of the child had moved to Essex, where he was known as a yeoman, but they still held him liable for the maintenance of Margaret Paul's child, and ordered him to pay sixpence a week for the next eight years.[13]

On Trinity Sunday in June 1641, when Londoners were taking the Protestation and godly ministers elsewhere were urging reformation, the inhabitants of Malmesbury and Long Newnton, Wiltshire, engaged in a festive battle for a garland. This was rough sport, of a kind not even countenanced by the King's book of recreations, involving rival teams of forty to eighty men, accompanied by hobby horses, bells, and drums. The battle went on all afternoon with such cries as 'we will have the garland' and 'win it and wear it, come three score of you, you are but boys to we'. Many of the combatants were armed with sticks and cudgels, and several were left bleeding and 'quaking' on the ground. The combat belonged to an ancient tradition of communal rivalry and village revels, rather than the new polarities beginning to divide England. However, fought on the Cotswold edge of north Wiltshire, the ritual battle for the garland had elements of chalk versus cheese and might be imagined as a surrogate prefiguring of Roundheads versus Cavaliers. Magistrates termed it 'an unlawful assembly', and six months later they were still proceeding against some participants for actions for 'riot and battery'.

---

[12] Wiltshire Record Office, Quarter Sessions Great Roll, A1/110 Hilary 1641, 149.
[13] Devon Record Office, Exeter Quarter Sessions Order Book, 1630–42, ff. 343, 355.

The hobby horse and bells appear to have been lain aside in 1642 when villagers had less playful combat on their minds.[14]

In May 1641, on the day that the House of Commons adopted the Protestation, the magistrates of East Sussex were dealing with bastard births and unauthorized cottages, and were setting the wage rates for servants and labourers.[15] In February 1642, when neighbours were arguing about the Protestation, the Exeter woollen-draper William Pennye was more concerned about the theft of nineteen yards of grey frieze.[16] Uppermost on the Earl of Bridgewater's mind in mid-July 1641 was the six thousand pounds in part payment due for the marriage portion of Lady Elizabeth Cavendish, daughter of the Earl of Newcastle.[17] A temporary distraction from the trial of Strafford and the rumours of plotting was the royal wedding on 2 May 1641 of the Princess Mary and Prince William of Orange.

Antiquarians and academics, as usual, pursued their scholarly pre-occupations, concerned with antiquity as well as the distractions of the present. But the present impinged too much on their projects. Distracted from his study of Anglo-Saxon manuscripts, Abraham Wheelock wrote from Cambridge soon after the Scottish seizure of Newcastle in 1640, 'I fear Leslie will set fire on these rare monuments, far more precious than all the treasure he (I hope) shall get in England.' He implored Sir Simonds D'Ewes, 'if you hear that they come this way, to direct us where to hide under ground these reverend Saxon sermons' for posterity.[18]

Also anxious about the fate of his ancient manuscripts, Archbishop Laud completed the transfer of his collection of Arabic and Hebrew texts to Oxford University on 6 November 1640, three days after the opening of the parliament that threatened his ruin, because 'they are not safe in his own house these perilous times'.[19] The antiquarian William Dugdale commenced his survey of cathedral monuments in September 1641, beginning with St Paul's in London, 'to the end that by ink and paper the shadows of them, with their inscriptions, might be preserved for posterity, forasmuch as the things themselves were so near unto ruin.'[20] In the spring of 1642, while many

---

[14] Wiltshire Record Office, Quarter Sessions Great Roll, A1/110 Trinity 1641, 183–5; A1/110 Hilary 1642, 128; David Underdown, *Revel, Riot and Rebellion: Popular Politics and Culture in England 1603–1660* (Oxford, 1985), 96.   [15] East Sussex Record Office, QR/E/52/149.

[16] Devon Record Office, Exeter Quarter Sessions Book, 1630–42, f. 394.

[17] Nottingham University Library, Portland Papers, PW 1/628.

[18] British Library, Harley Ms. 374, f. 144. I am grateful to Sears McGee for this reference.

[19] O. Ogle and W. H. Bliss (eds.), *Calendar of the Clarendon State Papers Preserved in the Bodleian Library* (Oxford, 1872), i. 210; William Laud, *The Works of the Most Reverend Father in God, William Laud, D.D.*, ed. W. Scott and J. Bliss (7 vols., Oxford, 1847–60), v. 293–4. The collection included 34 Arabic manuscripts, 11 in Greek, and 6 in Hebrew; the donation had been months in the planning.

[20] William Dugdale, *The History of St. Pauls Cathedral* (1658), sig. A3v.

of their countrymen were preparing for war, John Selden and Bryan Twyse were immersed in a project to transcribe the Arabic canons of the Council of Nicea.[21]

ECONOMIC WOES

It was a perennial complaint among farmers and traders that times were tough and cash was scarce. The English economy in the 1630s was already disrupted by the Thirty Years War, which led to recessions in the cloth industry.[22] The country also suffered from the deteriorating global climate, with shorter growing seasons, reduced crop yields, and volatile agricultural prices in the 'little ice age'.[23] Grants of monopolies skewed the economy, aggravating complaints that commodities were overpriced.[24]

Businessmen complained of the slowdown of trade and the scarcity of money, as confidence in the economy crumbled. Londoners protested in May 1641 that the political crisis hindered the trade of the city and the kingdom. The 'multitudes of the city' complained, Bishop John Warner reported, 'that their trade was lost and they undone, no man would pay or part with money till they saw justice done upon the lord Strafford, the other incendiaries, and great offenders.'[25] 'The English trade, by reason of our general distractions and fears, is so much decayed that country tradesmen cannot pay their debts in London as formerly', claimed citizen petitioners.[26] In December 1641 Londoners complained again that 'the trading of the city and kingdom is much more of late decayed than it hath been for many years past, no man following his trade cheerfully whilst the lives of himself and family and the public safety of the kingdom are in danger.'[27]

Comments in gentle correspondence suggest that the flow of cash was severely constricted. 'The times are so ill and things so unsettled in the

---

[21] Bodleian Library, Ms. Selden Supra, 109, f. 278.

[22] Cf. the complaint to Parliament in December 1640 of 'the decay of our kingdom's commodities, and especially the wools of this kingdom of late years much decayed in price' (Ralph Maddison, *Englands Looking In and Out* (1640), sig. A3).

[23] Brian M. Fagan, *The Little Ice Age: How Climate Made History, 1300–1850* (New York, 2001).

[24] *An Humble Petition and Remonstrance . . . Concerning the insupportable grievance of the Transportation of Leather* (1641),

[25] 'A Diary of ye Lords in Parliament' [Bishop Warner], Hertfordshire Record Office, XII.B.37, f. 65.

[26] *The Petition of the Citizens of London . . . with their desires for Iustice to be executed upon the Earle of Strafford* (1641).

[27] *The Citizens of London's Humble Petition* (1641), sig. A3.

commonwealth' that it was impossible to sell any land 'except for an extreme under value', wrote George Wyllys at the time of the Short Parliament.[28] 'Here is no money stirring, all things are at a miserable damp', wrote Edmund Percival from Hampshire in September 1640.[29] 'The want of money is such a disease', it was said of some gentlemen, that they could scarce afford to come to London 'to petition for their grievances'.[30] An agent for the Earl of Worcester explained his tightness of wallet in October 1641, when 'of late my lord hath been somewhat reserved, scarce parting with his money in any kind in regard of the times'.[31]

By 1642 the political and economic crises were inseparable. Sir Simonds D'Ewes remarked in January 1642 'that all men are put into such a general distraction and fear by the present jealousies between his majesty and the parliament that there is neither buying nor selling nor almost any commerce or trade.'[32] Economic woes sharpened and compounded all other distresses and problems. Writing in February 1642, Henry Oxinden remarked on the economic impact of the 'great distractions' of the realm. 'The poor handi-craftsmen are already driven to miserable want in all countries and especially in [London]; it is said that they are risen in Essex, and it is feared they will do so in all parts else . . . There were petitioning women of a great number last Tuesday at the parliament, and so far as I could learn their great and old grievance was want of trading.'[33] His kinsman Adam Oxinden, a London apprentice, told his mother in March 1642 that 'times being so dangerous and so uncertain it gives very little encouragement to shopkeepers.'[34] A destitute Norfolk labourer, Henry Rowlands, blamed his own troubles in April 1642 on 'the deadness of the times and want of employment'.[35]

SEA COAL EXCEEDING DEAR

The unexpected reverses of the Bishops' Wars caused economic dislocations as well as widespread panic. The Scottish occupation of Newcastle from the end of August 1640 was not just a strategic disaster and a blow to England's honour. It also curtailed the nation's supply of coal. Early Stuart London

---

[28] *The Wyllys Papers* (Collections of the Connecticut Historical Society, vol. xxi: Hartford, Conn., 1924), 9, 11.

[29] HMC, *Report on the Manuscripts of the Earl of Egmont* (vol. 1, part 1, 1905), 120.

[30] *The Distractions of Our Times* (1642), 4.

[31] National Library of Wales, Ms. 17091E/3.

[32] Willson H. Coates, Anne Steele Young, and Vernon F. Snow (eds.), *The Private Journals of the Long Parliament 3 January to 5 March 1642* (New Haven and London, 1982), 112–13.

[33] Dorothy Gardiner (ed.), *The Oxinden Letters 1607–1642* (1933), 285.   [34] Ibid., 300.

[35] Norfolk Record Office, Quarter Sessions Rolls, C/S3/33.

had become heavily dependent on coal from Newcastle, burning it by the shipload in domestic fires, industrial hearths, furnaces, kilns, and ovens. 'Vaporous soot-faced sea coal' was already a controversial contaminant of the metropolitan air.[36] Dozens of towns and parishes purchased coal as a winter dole to the poor, to make up for dwindling supplies of firewood.[37]

After their victory at Newburn the Scots had 'the honour and the coal of the kingdom in their possession'.[38] The entire Tyneside coal industry came to a halt as mines, staithes, and colliers came under Scottish control. Their stranglehold on London's energy supply gave the Scots a powerful bargaining counter. When digging and shipping resumed, at a reduced level, the Scots threatened to favour the Flemish market rather than London. A widely circulated letter from Newcastle reported the Scots' intention 'to ship away all the coals already digged', and the fear that 'they will send them abroad in Flemish vessels and make themselves a revenue by a custom and imposition they mean to lay upon them'.[39] Charles I's income shrank further as he lost the lucrative coal levy, and fuel was in short supply.

The course of the coal crisis can be traced in contemporary correspondence. Roger Holland reported to Lord Bridgewater on 10 September 1640 that the Scots 'have the profit of the coal pits and salt pits' at Shields and Sunderland, as well as command of the Tyne.[40] Secretary Windebank complained on 24 September that 'the rebels make vast profits of the Newcastle collieries, and intend by manning the colliers to grow powerful by sea'.[41] Edward Rossingham informed Viscount Scudamore on 29 September that the Newcastle coal trade was 'much impaired, by reason the workmen which wrought in those mines quit their works at what time the Scots took the town, and in their absence the sea broke into the coalpits'.[42] Local officials thought the region had been set back twenty years, and advised Parliament in January 1641 'that the coal mines of Newcastle will not be set right again for

---

[36] *Sea-Coale, Char-Coale, and Small-Coale* (1643), 7.

[37] J. U. Nef, *The Rise of the British Coal Industry* (2 vols., 1932, 1966 reprint); John Hatcher, *The History of the British Coal Industry. Vol. 1, Before 1700: Towards the Age of Coal* (Oxford, 1993).

[38] Edward Hyde, Earl of Clarendon, *The History of the Rebellion and Civil Wars in England Begun in the Year 1641*, ed. W. Dunn Macray (6 vols., Oxford, 1888), i. 189; John Rushworth, *Historical Collections of Private Proceedings of State* (8 vols., 1680–1701), iii. 1239; Roger Howell, Jr., *Newcastle upon Tyne and the Puritan Revolution* (Oxford, 1967), 130–2.

[39] Berkshire Record Office, microfilm 605 (Trumbull Mss. Miscellaneous Correspondence, vol. xx); Huntington Library, Ms. El. 7859, 8 September 1640; Richard Welford, *History of Newcastle and Gateshead* (3 vols., 1887), iii. 3, 394; Maija Jansson (ed.), *Proceedings in the Opening Session of the Long Parliament . . . Volume 1: 3 November–19 December 1640* (Rochester, NY, 2000), 80.   [40] Huntington Library, Ms. El. 7872.

[41] Ogle and Bliss (eds.), *Calendar of the Clarendon State Papers*, i. 207.

[42] British Library, Add. Ms. 11045, vol. v., f. 119v.

£100,000'.[43] A committee of the House of Lords met several times with the Lord Mayor, sheriffs, and justices of Middlesex and Westminster early in 1641 to discuss the fuel emergency and 'the great and excessive prices' of sea coal.[44]

In the short run London's lime kilns, glass furnaces, and brick works all faced cutbacks due to this war-induced energy crisis. The saltpetre men, essential to the supply of gunpowder, reported a lack of fuel in late September 1640.[45] Although Bristol was locally supplied with coal from Kingswood, there was distress in the city in 1641 when the Newcastle problem caused a rise in coal prices. The corporation was forced to import Welsh coal from Swansea to meet its obligations to the poor.[46]

Constricted supplies led inevitably to rising prices. Dr William Roane remarked on the increased cost of coal at Cambridge as early as 2 September 1640.[47] 'We here already quake for want of coals', wrote the Cambridge divine Abraham Wheelock to Simonds D'Ewes.[48] Coal that cost 16s. 6d. a ton in London in the spring of 1640 cost 22s. 6d. a ton by the end of September. By early October 1640 George Gerrard was grumbling of 'the dearness of sea coal' in Middlesex, while John Amye complained that 'coal is almost thirty shillings a cauldron, and is thought it will be three pounds before winter be done.' In the parish of St Margaret, Westminster, which provided fuel for the hospital children, sea coal that cost 17s. 6d. per cauldron in the 1630s cost 24s. in 1641.[49] At least two contemporary publications claimed to be 'printed in the year that sea coal was exceeding dear'.[50]

Modern analyses show that coal prices at Kings Lynn, Cambridge, and London hit record levels in 1641, a third or more higher than in any previous year. Coal prices in London in the 1640s were generally 25% higher than in the previous decade.[51]

---

[43] Maija Jansson (ed.), *Proceedings in the Opening Session of the Long Parliament . . . Volume 2: 21 December 1640–20 March 1641* (Rochester, NY, 2000), 240.

[44] HMC, *Report on the Manuscripts of the Duke of Buccleuch and Queensberry* (The Montague papers, 2nd series, 1926), iii. 406–7; *Lords Journal*, iv. 131.

[45] *CSPD 1640–41*, 56, 65, 79.

[46] John Latimer, *The Annals of Bristol in the Seventeenth Century* (Bristol, 1900), 154.

[47] *CSPD 1640–41*, 6.   [48] British Library, Harley Ms. 374, f. 144.

[49] *CSPD 1640–41*, 145; HMC, *The Manuscripts of His Grace the Duke of Rutland, G.C.B., Preserved at Belvoir Castle* (1888), i. 524; Westminster Archives, St Margaret, Westminster, churchwardens' accounts, E18, E23.

[50] *The Iury of Inquisition. De Iure Divino. Whether by Divine Right it is Lawfull to Inflict Punishment upon the Offending Lordly Bishops* (1640); *A Brief Discourse, Concerning the Power of the Peeres, and Commons in Parliament* (1640).

[51] Nef, *Rise of the British Coal Industry*, ii. 403, 405; Hatcher, *History of the British Coal Industry*, 582; Jeremy Boulton, 'Food Prices and the Standard of Living in London in the "Century of Revolution", 1580–1700', *Economic History Review*, 53 (2000), 488.

THE RETURN OF THE PLAGUE

Prophets and pessimists found no shortage of evidence that God was chastising a sinful nation. On top of everything else—rebellion, war, hardship, religious schism, social insubordination, and political revolution—England faced the return of the plague. Periodically recurrent since the fourteenth century, the bubonic plague flared up again in 1640 to add to the nation's miseries. Other illnesses came in waves, mixed with smallpox and forms of malaria, which contemporaries referred to generically as 'the sickness'.

The sicknesses of 1640–2 were by no means the worst of the seventeenth century, or even the worst in the reign of Charles I, but they added to strains in a system already under stress.

Moralists often argued that the pestilence was sent from God, and 'unless we speedily repent, worse things will happen to us'.[52] 'Death's harbinger, the sword, famine and other plagues that hang over us are ready to swallow up the wicked age', wrote Thomas Peyton to Henry Oxinden in May 1640.[53] The plague was God's sword, sent as punishment for 'the multitude of our sins', proclaimed a pamphleteer of 1641. 'The sign of the red cross' on plague victims' doors was but a reminder of our 'red crimson sins', the anonymous author continued, for 'God has sent his angel of wrath, and nothing can appease him but prayers'.[54] 'God hath three shafts in the quiver of his justice', wrote another popular writer, 'famine, plague, and war. These sharp arrows this great archer usually shoots at a nation in his anger and indignation, being provoked thereunto by their grievous and crying sins.'[55]

Sir Robert Harley's friend the Herefordshire minister Stanley Gower offered special prayers in August 1641, 'because we understand God's arrows of pestilence, pox and spotted fever are flying about you'. These arrows were flying, Gower suggested, because the Gospel had not yet penetrated the dark corners of the land, episcopacy had not yet been abolished, and Archbishop Laud had not yet been brought to trial.[56] Henry Burton preached in October 1641 on 'the necessity of self-denial and humiliation, by prayer and fasting before the lord, in regard of the present plague we now lie under.' Perversely, the plague could even be interpreted as a hopeful sign, Burton suggested, for 'the nearer we come to Christ, the more we must look for persecution', with the plague 'so hot amongst us'.[57] Edmund Calamy preached similarly in

---

[52] *The Atachment Examination and Confession of a French-man upon Christmas day* (1641), sig. A3.   [53] Gardiner (ed.), *Oxinden Letters 1607–1642*, 174.
[54] *Londons Lamentation. Or a fit admonishment for City and Countrey* (1641), 1, 3, 4.
[55] J.L., *Englands Doxologie* (1641), 8, 9. Cf. William Gouge, *Gods Three Arrows: Plague, Famine, Sword* (1631).   [56] British Library, Add. Ms. 70003, f. 152.
[57] Henry Burton, *A Most Godly Sermon: Preached at St. Albons in Woodstreet* (1641), title page, sigs. A5–A5v.

December on 'the ruin and repair of kingdoms and nations', explaining the plague as a consequence of neglecting 'the reformation of the church'.[58]

Contemporary references allow us to plot the course of plague morbidity against the chronology of the political crisis. They show the sickness to have been a terror, but not an unfamiliar enemy against which people were powerless to act. The disease showed up in May 1640, when Elias Ashmole's maid 'fell sick of the plague, but escaped'.[59] That month the sickness grew 'somewhat hot in St Martin's parish', where several died, and the next month was said to be 'increasing'.[60] By June 1640 magistrates at the Essex Quarter Sessions were reprimanding villagers who sheltered suspected carriers, 'to the great danger of infecting divers inhabitants there with the plague and other deadly contagions'.[61]

The government declared a day of general prayer and fasting on Wednesday, 8 July, 'for averting the heavy calamities of sickness and war' and 'for the averting of the plague and other judgements of God from this kingdom'.[62] In the first week of July 1640 the Oxfordshire minister Thomas Wyatt 'heard that fifty died of the plague in London'.[63] Attempts to raise troops in Somerset that month were handicapped because 'parts in and about Taunton' were 'so dangerously infected with the plague'.[64]

'The sickness increaseth, and is much in Westminster', wrote William Hawkins at the end of July 1640. In August John Castle wrote from Westminster, 'the contagion spreadeth hereabouts very dangerously', affecting 'two of the queen's coachmen two days since, their houses shut up in the mews'.[65] Within a week it had spread to Windsor, where plague was found among the King's servants, and to Hampton Court, where 'three houses at the very gate' were infected and 'one of the king's coachmen dead'.[66] Further up the Thames Valley, 'visited people' were locked in the pest house at Reading.[67] Lord Keeper Finch withdrew from London, citing 'the increase of sickness'

---

[58] Edmund Calamy, *England's Looking-Glasse* (1642), sig. A2v, 17–18, 45–6, 49, 51. See also Edmund Calamy, *Gods Free Mercy to England* (1642).

[59] C. H. Josten (ed.), *Elias Ashmole (1617–1692) His Autobiographical and Historical Notes* (Oxford, 1966), ii. 335.

[60] HMC, *Report on the Manuscripts of the Right Honourable Viscount De L'Isle . . . Vol. VI. Sidney Papers, 1626–1698* (1966), 276, 282.   [61] Essex Record Office, Q/SR/310/10.

[62] James F. Larkin (ed.), *Stuart Royal Proclamations, vol. II. Royal Proclamations of King Charles I, 1625–1646* (Oxford, 1983), 714–15. Purchases of these prayers sometimes appear in churchwardens' accounts.

[63] HMC, *Report on the Manuscripts of the Right Honourable Viscount De L'Isle*, 286; John Burghall, 'Providence Improved', in J. Hall (ed.), *Memorials of the Civil War in Cheshire* (Lancashire and Cheshire Record Society, vol. xix, 1889), 17; Diary of Thomas Wyatt, Bodleian Library, Ms. Top. Oxon. C. 378, 309.   [64] *CSPD 1640*, 436.

[65] HMC, *Report on the Manuscripts of the Right Honourable Viscount De L'Isle*, 309; Huntington Library, Ms. El. 7845, 1 August 1640.

[66] HMC, *9th Report* (1884), Part II, Appendix, 432.

[67] Berkshire Record Office, Reading Corporation Minutes 1636–1761, 126.

and its proximity to his residence.[68] The royal children were removed for safety to Woodstock, while common sufferers 'were removed to the pest house at London, being servants of mean place and quality'.[69] The sickness appeared at Oatlands and Lincoln's Inn.[70] 'Three of the king's servants are dead of the sickness', Francis Sawle reported on 18 August, 'it follows the court much; there died of the sickness this week 89' in London.[71] Chroniclers claimed that 'there died of the plague in London towards the latter end of summer 1000 some weeks, and some weeks 1200 or more. So that God this year punished the land with three of his sore judgements, sword, plague, and unseasonable weather which threatened famine.'[72]

On 11 September 1640 the London theatres were closed because of the infection.[73] *The Stage-Players Complaint* of the following year deplored 'their sad and solitary conditions for want of employment in this heavy and contagious time of the plague in London'.[74] The philosopher Thomas Hobbes feared that he had been exposed to infection at this time. 'It was my fortune to go into a shop in Fleet Street', he wrote, 'the master whereof, I not knowing it, lay then sick and died the next day of the plague.' The experience cost him six weeks of precautionary isolation.[75]

Plague was still present in October 1640, when plans were advanced for the calling of Parliament, and it had already infected both the English and the Scots armies in the north.[76] If fear of the plague had prompted King Charles to postpone the opening of the autumn parliament, or to hold it in another location such as Oxford, the political history of the 1640s may well have been very different. Hearing 'that divers places are infected with the plague and that divers wander from the said places of their abode whereby there is danger of further infection', magistrates in Devon set up a special watch that autumn 'to apprehend all suspicious and wandering persons'. They set a Colyton man in the stocks in October 1640 'for going abroad from his house being shut for fear of the plague'.[77]

[68] *CSPD 1640*, 547.   [69] Huntington Library, Ms. El. 7846, 4 August 1640.
[70] Huntington Library, Ms. El. 7847, 8 August 1640; W. C. Trevelyan and C. E. Trevelyan (eds.), *The Trevelyan Papers, Part III* (Camden Society, no. 105, 1872), 193; Bodleian Library, Oxford, Tanner Ms. 65, f. 154.
[71] Cornwall Record Office, DD R(S)/1/140, Francis Sawle to Jonathan Rashleigh, 18 August 1640.
[72] Burghall, 'Providence Improved', in Hall (ed.), *Memorials of the Civil War in Cheshire*, 18.
[73] *CSPD 1640–41*, 46. After reopening, the theatres were closed permanently in September 1642.
[74] *The Stage-Players Complaint* (1641), title page.
[75] Perez Zagorin, 'Thomas Hobbes's Departure from England in 1640: An Unpublished Letter', *The Historical Journal*, 21 (1978), 159.
[76] Huntington Library, Ms. El. 6578, 6580; *CSPD 1640–41*, 129; HMC, *7th Report* (1879), 434.
[77] Devon Record Office, Quarter Session Order Book 1640–1651, Q/S 1/8.

When Parliament eventually assembled in November 1640 there was some doubt whether to admit the member from Taunton, 'a town in Somerset much visited by the sickness'.[78] One of its first actions was to arrange for another day of prayer and fasting 'to implore the divine mercy in removing the pestilence, war, and other signs of God's anger'. London and Westminster would observe the fast on 17 November, the anniversary of Queen Elizabeth's accession, while the rest of the country would meet in prayer on 8 December.[79]

By this time the plague was abating, though it never entirely vanished. The 'heavy visitation of the plague' continued in Yorkshire into January 1641, and magistrates adopted the usual quarantine to prevent it spreading.[80] The sickness recurred in the spring, though its incidence was lighter than the previous year. Somerset was afflicted again in 1641, with particularly severe outbreaks at Langport and Taunton lasting all spring and summer.[81] Exeter, Dorchester, and Bristol mounted special watches at their gates to keep out travellers from the infected parts.[82]

Anxiety about infection added to the tensions surrounding the trial of the Earl of Strafford in spring 1641.[83] More London houses were hit in April and May, and the annual outing of the Bridewell apprentices was cancelled for fear of dispersing the disease.[84] 'The smallpox is very common and more mortal than usual; few or none do escape', the Cornish member of Parliament Sir Bevil Grenville warned his wife.[85] 'The worst news here is that the sickness increases', Sir John Coke wrote from London in May 1641.[86] 'The sickness and smallpox increaseth much here', wrote Sir Edward Nicholas from the metropolis towards the end of the month. By June it had reached King Street, causing Edward

---

[78] *Journals of the House of Commons 1640*, 21; Jansson (ed.), *Proceedings in the Opening Session of the Long Parliament . . . Volume 1*, 19. See also Helen Stocks and W. H. Stevenson (eds.), *Records of the Borough of Leicestershire . . . 1603–1688* (Cambridge, 1923), 301.

[79] *CSPD 1640–41*, 255; Larkin (ed.), *Stuart Royal Proclamations, vol. II*, 734–6. For local participation in these prayers, see Charles Herbert Mayo (ed.), *The Municipal Records of the Borough of Dorchester, Dorset* (Exeter, 1908), 535.

[80] John Lister (ed.), *West Riding Sessions Records. Vol. II. Orders, 1611–1642. Indictments, 1637–1642* (Yorkshire Archaeological Society, vol. liii, 1915), 260–1.

[81] J. S. Cockburn (ed.), *Western Circuit Assize Orders 1629–1648: A Calendar* (Camden Society, 4th series, 17, 1976), 214, 221; idem., *Somerset Assize Orders 1640–1659* (Somerset Record Society, vol. lxxi, 1971), 3, 4, 6.

[82] Devon Record Office, Exeter Chamber Act Book, 1634–47, 237, 241, 248; Mayo (ed.), *Municipal Records of the Borough of Dorchester*, 535; Latimer, *Annals of Bristol in the Seventeenth Century*, 153.

[83] National Library of Wales, Wynn Papers, no. 1680 (microfilm).

[84] Corporation of London, Bridewell, and Bethlem, Court of Governors' Minutes, 24 April 1641.   [85] Roger Granville, *The History of the Granville Family* (Exeter, 1895), 242.

[86] HMC, *12th Report, The Manuscripts of the Earl Cowper . . . Preserved at Melbourne Hall, Derbyshire* (1888), ii. 283.

Montague to remove to safer lodgings in the Temple.[87] 'I have no desire to stay any longer, in regard the sickness and other diseases do daily increase,' Maurice Wynn told his brother on 8 June, 'God preserve us all.'[88]

Chester had the plague in July 1641.[89] Reading had it in August.[90] One hundred and forty families were put out of work at Witham, Essex, when the community was visited 'with the dangerous and infectious disease of the plague'.[91] In Northamptonshire Robert Woodford changed his travel plans that summer 'in regard of the sickness raging at Stony Stratford'.[92] High status was not necessarily a safeguard, for Sir George Hastings, brother of the Earl of Huntingdon, was 'dead of the plague' in July 1641.[93] Even in Parliament, 'some members died and others were in danger'.[94]

Once again, the plague had political consequences. Fear of the sickness inhibited both King and Parliament from meeting 'to compose the great distempers imminent to church and people' because London and Westminster were so dangerous during the summer.[95] Attendance in both Houses grew thin in late August and early September when both plague and smallpox threatened.[96] The Venetian ambassador reported that much of London was shut up, as people fled the city and all the other ambassadors were gone.[97] The peak of morbidity coincided with the King's absence in Scotland. Thomas Wyatt remarked on the 'great fear of the plague in Oxford' when several houses were 'shut up'.[98] Cambridge took special precautions to examine college bedding, and the vice-chancellor ordered college gates to be shut during the fourteen days of Stourbridge fair in an attempt to keep out the disease.[99] There was alarm in September 1641 with the discovery of plague at the Rose Inn at Cambridge, and the town's Michaelmas feast was set aside.[100]

[87] HMC, *Report on the Manuscripts of Lord Montague of Beaulieu* (1900), 130.

[88] National Library of Wales, Wynn Papers, no. 1686 (microfilm). See also National Library of Wales, Llanfair-Brynodel letters, C33, William Thomas to Richard Griffith, 4 September 1641, on plague deaths in London.

[89] PRO, SP16/482/10; Cheshire Record Office, QJB 1/6, f. 49.

[90] J. M. Guilding (ed.), *Reading Records. Diary of the Corporation, Vol. IV (1641–1654)* (1896), 21.

[91] Essex Record Office, Q/Sba2/43, /45. For similar problems in the north-west, see Lancashire Record Office, QSB/1/253/38.

[92] Robert Woodford's diary, New College, Oxford, Ms. 9502, 22 July 1641. See also Diary of Thomas Wyatt, Bodleian Library, Ms. Top. Oxon. C. 378, 323.

[93] HMC, *12th Report, The Manuscripts of the Earl Cowper*, ii. 289.

[94] Clarendon, *History of the Rebellion*, i. 381; British Library, Nicholas Papers, Egerton Ms. 2533, f. 192; *CSPD 1641–43, 115*.

[95] Thomas Wiseman to Sir John Pennington, 30 September 1641; *CSPD 1641–43, 128*.

[96] *CSPD 1641–43*, 105; *CSP Venetian, 1640–42*, 213.   [97] *CSP Venetian, 1640–42*, 210.

[98] Diary of Thomas Wyatt , Bodleian Library, Ms. Top. Oxon. C. 378, 322.

[99] Cambridge University Archives, V.C. Ct. I 12, f. 12.

[100] Cambridgeshire Record Office, Cambridge Corporation Common Day Book, (1610–46), vii. 347.

Because 'divers places upon the roadway from London are infected with the plague and therefore may prove dangerous to this city', the authorities at Gloucester mounted a day and night watch in September against 'suspicious persons'.[101]

Disease hung over the Thanksgiving for peace with Scotland, planned for 7 September, when one diarist noted, 'the Commons solemnized the gratulation at Lincoln's Inn, the reason guessed to be in regard of the sickness increasing in Westminster'.[102] The authorities were alarmed that disbanded soldiers and wandering beggars might exacerbate the capital's problems 'during this time of infection'.[103] Then on 9 September, to the relief of most members, Parliament recessed for over a month.[104]

Plague deaths continued to mount all autumn, as the disease spread along the Thames Valley from London to Richmond.[105] 'The sickness increased the last week, and of the plague died within a few of 200 and almost as many of the smallpox', wrote Edward Reed from London on 5 September 1641. Citing the City bills of mortality, Philip Morgan reported on 14 September, 'there died the last week of the plague 212'. Thomas Wyatt noted 230 London plague deaths in the last week of September. John Mostyn cited weekly mortality of 239 at the beginning of October. By 9 November the weekly toll was 118, reducing to 67 in the week of 18 November and down to 15 by 10 December.[106]

Yorkshire reported scattered outbreaks in October, when disbanded soldiers risked carrying the disease to their home parishes.[107] Lancashire ordered 'watch and ward' throughout the hundred of Salford, 'by reason of the infection which has now dispersed in every part of the country'.[108] Essex had renewed fears of 'the infection still increasing and likely to spread'.[109] There were infected houses in Westminster Palace Yard, and the sickness was keeping members away from Parliament. One of the lawyers in Parliament was said to have sat in the House on a Thursday and 'died of the plague' the Saturday following. John Evelyn was among those who kept his distance from the Inns

---

[101] Gloucestershire Record Office, Sessions Orders 1633–71, GBR/G3/SO2.

[102] Diary of Thomas Wyatt, Bodleian Library, Ms. Top. Oxon. C. 378, 323. The House of Lords issued precautionary orders regarding the plague on 8 September 1641, *Lords Journal*, iv. 391.

[103] *Privy Council Registers* (1968), xii. 190; *CSPD 1641–43*, 141; PRO, SP/16/484/15.

[104] PRO, SP16/484/16 and 20.

[105] HMC, *12th Report, The Manuscripts of the Earl Cowper*, ii. 291; *CSPD 1641–43*, 120, 126.

[106] British Library, Add. Ms. 33936, ff. 246, 249, 250, 252; Diary of Thomas Wyatt, Bodleian Library, Ms. Top. Oxon. C. 378, 323; National Library of Wales, Wynn Papers, no. 1692 (microfilm). See also John Bell, *Londons Remembrancer: or, A True Account of Every Particular Weeks Christnings and Mortality* (1665), sig. C2v.

[107] Lister (ed.), *West Riding Sessions Records, Vol. II*, 321, 328, 336, 350.

[108] Lancashire Record Office, QSO/2/16.   [109] Essex Record Office, Q/Sba2/43.

of Court in October 1641, 'by reason of the contagion then in London'.[110]
Bedding despatched from London to the Earl of Cork in October 1641
'required a certificate that it came not from an infected house'.[111] Among the
autumn plague victims were the churchwarden of Lambeth, whose 'accounts
could not be found',[112] and 'William Staines, a minister who died . . . in
Fetter Lane'.[113]

Bubonic plague appeared dramatically in Parliament on 25 October 1641
when John Pym unwrapped a package containing 'a contagious plaster of a
plague sore'. This was the seventeenth-century version of a biological
weapon or letter-bomb, designed to spread terror if not death. It was delivered
by an unsuspecting porter, who had it from a 'wretched fellow' distinguished
only by a wart on his nose and a red ribbon around his arm. Pym and his
associates interpreted the package as 'a damnable treason', an assassination
attempt by popish malignants, though some might wonder whether the incident
was staged to give credence to the much-discussed Catholic conspiracy.[114]
Continuing reports of plague about Westminster led some members to propose
moving the annual Gunpowder Treason observance to Lincoln's Inn or
Temple church as a precaution.[115] Sickness and anxiety formed part of the
back-drop to discussions of the Grand Remonstrance.

Once again the plague abated as the weather cooled, but it flared up again
the following spring.[116] Among its winter victims were the separatists
Richard Farnham and John Bull, who 'died of the plague in a house where
they usually met in Rosemary Lane' in January 1642.[117]

Fortunately the sickness of 1642 was relatively mild. According to a
pamphlet published that summer the only plague was 'that plague of
plagues, want of trading'.[118] Parts of Wiltshire suffered badly in June as 'the
infection . . . spread further abroad'.[119] Cambridge was visited again in June,

---

[110] HMC, *Report on the Manuscripts of Lord Montague of Beaulieu*, 132; HMC, *12th
Report, The Manuscripts of the Earl Cowper*, ii. 293–4; William Bray (ed.), *The Diary of John
Evelyn* (1879), i. 38.

[111] Lismore Mss., vol. xxi; National Register of Archives, vol. 20594/15, 904.

[112] Charles Drew (ed.), *Lambeth Churchwardens' Accounts 1504–1645* (Surrey Record
Society, vol. xx, 1950), 162.   [113] Guildhall Library, Ms. 2968/3.

[114] *A Damnable Treason, By a Contagious Plaster of a Plague Sore* (1641), title page, sigs.
A2v, A3; Willson Havelock Coates (ed.), *The Journal of Sir Simonds D'Ewes from the First
Recess of the Long Parliament to the Withdrawal of King Charles from London* (New Haven
and London, 1942), 37.

[115] Coates (ed.), *Journal of Sir Simonds D'Ewes from the First Recess of the Long
Parliament to the Withdrawal of King Charles from London*, 81. The service went ahead at
St Margaret's as planned.

[116] PRO C115/107/85421; British Library, Add. Ms. 70003, f. 173v; HMC, *5th Report*,
Part 1, 22.   [117] *False Prophets Discovered* (1642), title page.

[118] *St. Hillaries Teare. Shed Upon all Professions* (1642), sig. A2.

[119] Wiltshire Record Office, Quarter Sessions Great Roll, A1/110 Trinity, 1642, 166.

necessitating the suspension of university sermons and lectures.[120] Cambridge authorities feared 'some new danger of the sickness likely to break forth', and were particularly alarmed in July 'lest in the dog days of this hot and intemperate month the sickness may be dispersed by much conversing together and public thronging of people at great meetings'.[121] Magistrates in Suffolk ordered the scrutiny of all travellers because 'the contagious infection of the plague is lately happened in the town of Cambridge'.[122] The excited discourse in the expanded public sphere had become a health hazard. But by this time the familiar arrow of plague was overshadowed by the unimaginable horror of civil war.

[120] Charles Henry Cooper, *Annals of Cambridge* (4 vols, Cambridge, 1842–52), iii. 325.
[121] Cambridge University Archives, CUR 54.2, f. 374. See also Suffolk Record Office, B 105/2/1, f. 49.   [122] Suffolk Record Office, B 105/2/1, f. 49.

4

⚔

Insolencies of the Army:
Soldiers and Civilians, 1640–1642

This chapter examines interactions between soldiers and civilians from the time of the Short Parliament to the outbreak of the civil war. It traces the build-up of Charles I's northern army in the spring and summer of 1640, its humiliation at the battle of Newburn at the end of August, and the costly endgame in 1641 when English troops were languishing in Yorkshire while the Scots occupied Northumberland and Durham. Against the background of the second Bishops' War and the military stasis that followed, it shows how problems of recruitment and impressment, discipline and disorder, and the difficulties facing discharged veterans and their dependents compounded the distempers of the times.

Soldiers are often seen as central to the English Revolution. Were it not for his failed campaign against Scotland and the inadequacies of his northern army, Charles I might not have needed to face the Long Parliament in November 1640. Were it not for the necessity to send soldiers to subdue Ireland a year later, Parliament might not have needed to assume command of the militia. Disorderly soldiers added to the confusions of 1640 and 1641, and were actively engaged in religious iconoclasm. Conservative senior officers were behind the army plot of May 1641 to free the Earl of Strafford and to undo the work of Parliament, to which the Protestation was an immediate response. Well before the civil war, and long before the rise of Oliver Cromwell, the army imprinted itself on English public life.

It is often said that the civil war turned soldiers into citizens, making them politically aware and teaching them to demand their rights; but the case can just as well be made that the war turned citizens into soldiers. Following the collapse of censorship at the beginning of the Long Parliament, and the accelerated circulation of news and opinion, many of the recruits who joined both sides in 1642 were already politically engaged and informed. It was clear from the outset, as some of them later claimed, that they were no mere mercenary army. Revolution and war engulfed subjects and citizens, soldiers and civilians, who were already drawn into an expanding public sphere.

The armies of the 1640s caused social, financial, and administrative problems, not only for the central governments responsible for their deployment and pay, but also for the local communities from which they were recruited, through which they marched, and where they campaigned. The 'insolencies of the army' in 1640 and 1641 provided chilling examples of a collapse of deference, a degrading of hierarchy, and a spread of insubordination that seemed to be contagious among both military and civilian populations. The disruptive mobility and mixing of the civil war armies was anticipated in the Bishops' Wars, when the world began to turn upside down.[1]

The military equation changed again in the autumn of 1641 with the conclusion of peace with Scotland and the outbreak of rebellion in Ireland. One army disbanded and another was summoned to action. The drift towards civil war in the summer of 1642 produced very different mobilizations, as Parliament's Militia Ordinance and the King's Commissions of Array re-recruited recent veterans and turned thousands more civilians into soldiers. Throughout this time, in addition to all other troubles, English society suffered the social and economic costs of militarization. The Scottish wars disrupted community life from Cornwall to Cumberland, and gave a new and dangerous edge to insubordination. People of all sorts, from county gentry to village maidens, became caught up in 'the insolencies of the army', as soldiers were marched from their homes to the war zones and back again.

THE BISHOPS' WARS

Charles I's misguided attempt to impose prayer-book uniformity on Presbyterian Scotland precipitated the events that led to revolution and civil war. His blind pursuit of conformity proved disastrous for his family, his church, and his realm. The first public reading of the prayer book in Edinburgh in July 1637 led to riots and a widespread rejection of royal ecclesiastical authority. In February 1638 the Scots subscribed their national Covenant, and soon were in open rebellion. No king could tolerate such a challenge, and Charles decided, following reason and tradition, to restore his authority and his honour by force.[2]

---

[1] Christopher Hill, *The World Turned Upside Down: Radical Ideas during the English Revolution* (1972), 306: 'the mixing, the cross-fertilization, must have been immense'.

[2] Scholarly accounts of these developments include David Stevenson, *The Scottish Revolution, 1637–1644: The Triumph of the Convenanters* (Newton Abbot and New York, 1973); Anthony Fletcher, *The Outbreak of the English Civil War* (1981); Peter Donald, *An*

By the spring of 1639 the King was ready to take the battle to the Scots. Every effort was made to divide or intimidate his enemies and to force them into submission. The Council planned to raise 30,000 men, and a royal army approaching 20,000 strong was assembled in Yorkshire and directed towards the north. The garrisons at Carlisle and Berwick were strengthened. Plans were made for a sea-borne assault on Scotland's east coast, to be coordinated with attacks on the west from Ireland, in support of a main thrust towards Edinburgh. This was the largest military mobilization in English living memory—there had been nothing on this scale since 1588—and it put extraordinary strain on local administrative systems.[3] But the campaign of March to June 1639 ended in indecisive action and humiliating withdrawal. The Scottish Covenanter forces proved sharper and more flexible, with better intelligence and more imaginative commanders. The English were handicapped by logistics, bogged down by bad weather, and troubled by constant bickering along the lines of command. The trained bands were reluctant to serve so far from home, and some questioned the propriety of invading Protestant Scotland. Pay was scarce, morale was low, and the King's standard bearer, Sir Edmund Verney, observed that he never seen 'so raw, so unskillful, and so unwilling an army brought to fight'.[4]

After much marching but little combat, the first Bishops' War of 1639 concluded with the pacification of Berwick. This represented an armed stalemate, a temporary peace, which allowed both sides to attend to their resources and to reconsider their strategies. The armies were disbanded and most of the soldiers on both sides returned to their civilian lives. But Scotland was still in rebellion, and Charles was still determined to act as a warrior monarch. The Covenanters would never accept episcopacy and the prayer book in Scotland, and Charles I would never permit his subjects to decide for themselves about the organization of religion. There was little likelihood of negotiation, and apparently no way out but capitulation or war.

For the next campaign the King dismissed his humbled commanders, the Earls of Arundel and Holland (Thomas Howard and Henry Rich), and relied

---

Uncounselled King: Charles I and the Scottish Troubles, 1637–1641 (Cambridge, 1990); Conrad Russell, *The Fall of the British Monarchies 1637–1642* (Oxford, 1991), 45–146; Kevin Sharpe, *The Personal Rule of Charles I* (New Haven and London, 1992), 769–824, 885–921; Mark Charles Fissel, *The Bishops' Wars: Charles I's Campaigns against Scotland, 1638–1640* (Cambridge, 1994). I am grateful to Mark Fissel for discussion of the sources that underpin his book.

[3] The campaigns of the 1620s had raised approximately 12,000 men for Count Mansfeldt and 10,000 each for the expeditions to Rhé and Cadiz.

[4] Russell, *Fall of the British Monarchies*, 55–89; Fissel, *Bishops' Wars*, 3–39; Victor L. Stater, 'The Lord Lieutenancy on the Eve of the Civil Wars: The Impressment of George Plowwright', *Historical Journal*, 29 (1986), 279–96; H. Verney (ed.), *Letters and Papers of the Verney Family* (Camden Society, vol. lvi, 1853), 228.

more heavily for advice on Thomas Wentworth (made Earl of Strafford in January 1640) and Archbishop Laud. The Earl of Northumberland (Algernon Percy) became Lord General, and directed the campaign from London until he became too ill to act. Viscount Edward Conway was made commander of the King's forces in the north, with responsibility for carrying the war against the Scots. Sir Jacob Astley, an able soldier with Dutch and Danish experience, served as sergeant major general in charge of the rendezvous in Yorkshire.

The plan was to mobilize another army and to repeat the strategy of 1639 with greater hopes of success. A new force of 20,000 foot and 3,000 horse would rendezvous in Yorkshire before being thrust against the Scots. Its goal was to take Edinburgh, reduce lowland Scotland, and crush the Covenanter revolt. Strafford promised 8,000 Irish troops (many of them Catholics) who would bolster the attack.[5]

Military campaigns by this time had become ruinously expensive, with untold social and political costs. The early modern 'military revolution' raised both the cost and the killing power of national armies.[6] But Charles was determined that war must be waged, whatever the impact on his coffers. Councillors estimated that a million pounds would be needed to renew the campaign against Scotland in 1640, and the raising of such sums by taxation would necessitate the calling of a parliament. By April 1640 the army was costing the government £100,000 a month.[7] The royal treasury was exhausted, the King's credit anaemic, and neither loans nor ship money would supply the need.

King Charles expected the parliament that met on 13 April to vote subsidies and to mobilize support for the campaign against Scotland. But many of the members wanted first to discuss grievances that had accumulated over the previous eleven years. Some sought the abolition of ship money, others argued against Laudian religious policies or recent judicial decisions. Several members made common cause with their religious brethren, the Presbyterian Scots, and may have deliberately sabotaged the voting of supply. Some openly questioned the legality of impressment for military service in the north. Rancorous debate took precedence to the King's financial and military necessities.

A frustrated Charles I dissolved this 'Short Parliament' after three weeks on 5 May 1640, with disastrous consequences for his regime.[8] (The popular

---

[5] 'The chaos of summer 1640 makes ascertaining actual troop strength exceedingly difficult.' Mark Charles Fissel, *English Warfare, 1511–1642* (2001), 279, 359.

[6] Geoffrey Parker, *The Military Revolution: Military Innovation and the Rise of the West, 1500–1800* (Cambridge, 1996).

[7] Russell, *Fall of the British Monarchies*, 92; Esther S. Cope and Willson H. Coates (eds.), *Proceedings of the Short Parliament of 1640* (Camden Society 4th ser., vol. xix, 1977), 165, 207.

[8] Russell, *Fall of the British Monarchies*, 90–123; Mark Charles Fissel, 'Scottish War and English Money: The Short Parliament of 1640', in idem (ed.), *War and Government in Britain, 1598–1650* (Manchester and New York, 1991), 193–223; *CSPD 1640*, 153.

reaction in London is discussed in Chapter 5.) When news of the dissolution reached Dorset, a company of newly recruited soldiers stopped their march, 'and steadily refused to serve against that people', the Scots.[9] Despite official declarations, there were many who disputed that the 'blue bonnets' were enemies or rebels, and were willing to sing ballads, 'gramercie good Scot'.[10] The Scots had never been popular in England, but some disaffected gentry were willing to make common cause with them in 1640 to advance their religious and political agenda.[11]

Despite Parliament's refusal to provide supply, and notwithstanding the Crown's overstretched financial condition, Charles persisted in his campaign against Scotland. As Strafford forcefully reminded him, on the very day of the dissolution of Parliament, the 'honour and reputation' of the King and the kingdom were at stake.[12] The King seemed unmoved by the evident lack of money, but his officers wondered how success could be achieved without it. The Lord General, the Earl of Northumberland, complained privately to friends that without proper funding the campaign was likely to fail.[13]

Mobilization proceeded throughout the spring and summer of 1640, though never as speedily or effectively as hoped. With 30,000 men needed to take the war to the Scots, every county was supposed to provide its share.[14] Everything went wrong. Prospective soldiers proved hard to find, pressed men proved unamenable to military discipline, pay and provisions were desperately short. The high command was indecisive and plagued by ill health.[15] Sympathy for the Scottish cause further undercut morale. The English were

---

[9] Edward Razell and Peter Razell (eds.), *The English Civil War. A Contemporary Account. Volume 2: 1640–1642* (1996), 15.

[10] James F. Larkin (ed.), *Stuart Royal Proclamations, vol. II. Royal Proclamations of King Charles I, 1625–1646* (Oxford, 1983), 726–8; *CSPD 1640*, 493; Staffordshire Record Office, Correspondence of Bishop Bridgeman, D.1287/18/2, f. 183; R. N. Worth (ed.), *The Buller Papers. A Series of Historical Documents Selected from the Family Records of the Bullers of Shillingham and Morval in the County of Cornwall* (privately printed, 1895), 27. For ballads, *The Subiects Thankfulnesse: or, God-a-mercie good Scot* (1640); C. H. Firth, 'Ballads on the Bishops' Wars, 1638–40', *Scottish Historical Review*, 3 (1906), 258–9; Folger Ms. V.b. 303, p. 315; British Library, Harley Ms. 4931, ff. 80–1; Durham University Library, Special Collections, Mickleton-Spearman Ms. MSP/9, ii. 195–6; Mary Anne Everett Green (ed.), *The Diary of John Rous...1625 to 1642* (Camden Society, London, 1856), 110–11. The Scottish commissioner Robert Baillie also took note of these ballads; David Laing (ed.), *The Letters and Journals of Robert Baillie* (3 vols., Edinburgh, 1841), i. 282.

[11] David Scott, ' "Hannibal at our Gates": Loyalists and Fifth-columnists during the Bishops' Wars—the Case of Yorkshire', *Historical Research*, 70 (1997), 269–93.

[12] PRO, SP16/452/31; Fissel, *Bishops' Wars*, 48–9.

[13] Northumberland to Leicester and Conway, quoted in Sharpe, *Personal Rule*, 887.

[14] *CSPD 1640*, 98. For county quotas see the table in this chapter and PRO, PC2/52, ff. 230v, 232, 257v.

[15] Both Northumberland and Strafford were 'very sick' in August 1640. Cornwall Record Office, DD R(S)/1/140, Francis Sawle to Jonathan Rashleigh, 18 August 1640.

surprised in August 1640 when the Scots crossed the Tweed, shocked when they took possession of Newcastle and most of Northumberland and Durham. A weakened and dishonoured king was forced to call another parliament, and this time he faced not criticism but revolution. The second Bishops' War proved a military disaster, a political catastrophe, a financial sink, with destructive results for the King and both kingdoms.[16]

RECRUITS

Because there was no standing army in early Stuart England the Crown had to assemble a fresh fighting force each time it faced a military emergency. It was both a demonstration and a test of royal authority to put an army in the field. The trained bands and county militias had been mobilized for the first Bishops' War of 1638–9, but when the war against Scotland resumed in 1640 the royal ranks were largely filled by impressment. Many of those men were of dubious military quality. Rather than being rate-payers, substantial parishioners, and members of the trained bands, they more often included marginal men, strangers, dependents, poor men, and even criminals. A 'substitution clause' allowed militia men, who were unwilling to serve outside their county, to send untrained men in their stead. The very men best prepared for military service against Scotland considered themselves exempt.[17] The task of filling the ranks was made more than usually difficult by the government's lack of money.

Funds were inadequate, equipment was deficient, and the men were unreliable. Recruitment was sluggish, capricious, and inefficient. The troops at Berwick were reported restless, and discipline at Newcastle was disrupted by grievances about money.[18] The army was short of gunpowder, Lord Conway wrote in April, and the soldiers had 'no flasks nor horns' to carry it. 'Whereas there should be 700 spades there are only 300.' Crucial equipment failed to reach the north. When firearms reached Newcastle in May many were defective, 'hardly any of the pistols sound, divers of the barrels are without touch holes', their metalwork too thin. When troops finally arrived in Yorkshire the sergeant major general found them 'very ill clothed, most wanting shoes and stockings'.[19] Of 13,000 men sent north from Selby to face

---

[16] Russell, *Fall of the British Monarchies*, 123–46; Fissel, *Bishops' Wars*, 39–61; Stevenson, *Scottish Revolution 1637–1644*.

[17] The substitution clause is discussed in Fissel, *Bishops' Wars*, 206–13.

[18] *CSPD 1640*, 73.

[19] Ibid., 43, 190. *An Humble Petition and Remonstrance . . . Concerning the insupportable grievance of the Transportation of Leather* (1641), 5, asserted that 'in all places in the north the last year the soldiers could scarcely get shoes for money, many went barefoot'.

the Scots in August, 3,000 were 'not armed', reported a frustrated Sir Jacob Astley.[20]

The piecemeal assembling of Charles I's army in the spring and summer of 1640 took place during some of the foulest weather in memory. Conductors responsible for the movement of men and weapons, horses and carts, had to contend with flooded rivers and sodden roads. At Gloucester they faced 'abundance of rain' and 'inundations of the water', which flooded the river Severn.[21] The men were supposed to make fifteen miles a day, but were sometimes lucky to travel ten. The recruiting was also done in a plague season, though not in the worst afflicted areas. There was always the risk that pressed men might be infectious, and that the disease could be spread along the line of march. In Somerset the deputy lieutenants reported the parts around Taunton 'so dangerously infected with plague' in July 1640 'that we fear to call any companies together'.[22] Most of the pressed men from Devon and Cornwall had to pass through this area, putting several thousand soldiers at risk. Once they were on the move their captains or 'conductors' were supposed to keep them 'from straggling and pilfering of the country as they go'.[23]

All over England the officials charged with raising and equipping the army complained of refractoriness, recalcitrance, and lack of cooperation. The nobles entrusted with command complained endlessly about the 'slender preparation for an army' as they mobilized to face the Scots.[24] The Council badgered county lieutenants about 'delays and difficulties' in the national military effort.[25] During April and May many deputy lieutenants and colonels were preoccupied with parliamentary business, and the men from their counties would not march without leaders they knew and trusted. Many resented the demands of 1640 after their efforts of the previous year had been squandered. Militia companies from Dorset to Northamptonshire claimed exemption from impressment and exemption from service outside their local areas.[26] The Hertfordshire trained bands, while expressing 'from the bottom of our hearts' their loyalty to the King and kingdom, firmly resisted impressment for service in the north. 'We, the yeomanry, are as freeborn as any of the gentry of this kingdom, and in this respect we know no privilege they have

[20] *CSPD 1640*, 574.
[21] Gloucestershire Record Office, City of Gloucester Sessions, GBR/G3/So4.
[22] *CSPD 1640*, 436–7.   [23] PRO, PC2/52, ff. 257v, 324v.
[24] HMC, *Report on the Manuscripts of the Duke of Buccleuch and Queensberry...at Montague House* (1899), 280–2.
[25] PRO, PC2/52, f. 266v; Hampshire Record Office, Jervoise of Herriard Ms. 44 M69/G5/45/1/2.
[26] Christopher A. Markham and J. Charles Cox (eds.), *The Records of the Borough of Northampton* (2 vols., Northampton, 1898), ii. 437; *CSPD 1640*, 35, 44, 55; Scott, ' "Hannibal at our Gates" ', 272.

above us', they asserted, in what the Council regarded as a 'scandalous petition'.[27] The mobilization slackened around Bristol when 'a press [went] out for land soldiers which . . . all fear are speedily intended against Scotland'.[28]

Local officials and property-owners frustrated the work of recruitment as much as they facilitated it. Many set local privileges or protection of their pockets above the needs of the nation. The recruiting effort was severely prejudiced in Kent because the constables responsible for 'raising men for the northern army' had not been reimbursed for their outlays. Vespasian Harris, late a constable in Canterbury and 'a man of a cross grain and contentious' according to Kentish magistrates, sued the city for his costs, and others refused to cooperate until the suit was settled. The Canterbury justices were concerned not just that King Charles might be denied his army, but that 'turbulent spirits may not be animated to disobey their superiors'. They were faced, they thought, with social and civil indiscipline as well as military emergency, amidst a clamour of mutiny and insurrection.[29]

Recruiting in Cornwall was held up by 'refractaries, as refuse to pay their rates towards this service'.[30] Similar problems beset the raising of troops in Wales.[31] The Cinque Ports faced 'great charge and trouble' with concerns that the raising of men undercut their privileges.[32] In London 'the victuallers refuse to victual the [transport] fleet without ready money'.[33] In Worcestershire the Rector of Birlingham, Henry Whittington, was called a liar, a knave, and a 'pilled priest' for his efforts in setting men forth 'about the time when the soldiers were first impressed for the northern expedition' around Easter 1640.[34] In Berkshire, when four men of Cookham were committed at the midsummer Assizes 'for refusing press money' they were merely bound over to appear, and 'little or nothing was said to them'. But the justices who charged these reluctant soldiers were themselves fined on a technicality of law. The outraged magistrates wrote to the attorney general that this 'was a great disservice to his majesty, for some of the constables have since told us, they dare not offer press money to any'.[35]

Even after impressment, people with sufficient resources could buy their way out of military service. In Essex in May officials reported, 'divers able

[27] *CSPD 1640*, 95–6, 120.

[28] *The Wyllys Papers* (Collections of the Connecticut Historical Society, vol. xxi: Hartford, Conn., 1924), 11.   [29] Bodleian Library, Ms. Bankes 65/2, f. 124.

[30] Charles Trevanion to the Earl of Pembroke, 17 May 1640, quoted in Anne Duffin, *Faction and Faith: Politics and Religion of the Cornish Gentry before the Civil War* (Exeter, 1996), 173.

[31] National Library of Wales, Wynn Papers, no. 1668 (microfilm).

[32] East Kent Archives, Sandwich Borough Muniments, Mayor's Letter Book 1639–44, Sa/C1, ff. 24v, 26v, 27.   [33] Huntington Library, Ms. El. 7837, 9 June 1640.

[34] Worcestershire Record Office, BA 2102/9, pp. 416, 419, 422.

[35] Bodleian Library, Ms. Bankes 65/2, f. 133.

men who were to be employed in this expedition to the north' paid up to five pounds to be discharged.[36] Another report in July cited sums from twenty shillings to thirty pounds paid to free men from the army. Some of those released had been pressed while travelling on the highway on business, but at least one was a notorious cutpurse.[37]

The following table shows the Council's county-by-county requirement of recruits.[38] Actual numbers raised fell somewhat short. The northern counties were omitted because they were expected to deploy their locally-raised trained bands (in the case of Yorkshire, 13,000 men).[39] Midland counties made considerable use of their militia, but numbers from the south were mostly made up through impressment. The main line of march drew huge concentrations of troops through the south-west and central counties on their way to the north. The heartland from Oxfordshire to south Yorkshire was especially exposed to military traffic.

Bedfordshire	400 via Yarmouth
Berkshire	600
Bristol	200
Buckinghamshire	500 via Harwich
Cambridgeshire	300 via Yarmouth
Cheshire	500
Cinque Ports	300 via Gravesend
Cornwall	1,600
Derbyshire	400 via Grimsby
Devon	2,000
Dorset	600
Essex	700 via Harwich
Gloucestershire	500
Hampshire	1,300
Herefordshire	300
Hertfordshire	650 via Harwich
Huntingdonshire	400 via Yarmouth
Kent	700 via Gravesend
Leicestershire	400
Lincolnshire	200 via Grimsby
London	4,000

[36] *CSPD 1640*, 224.   [37] PRO, SP16/461/102.

[38] PRO, PC2/52, ff. 230v, 232, 257v, Privy Council orders of 3, 6, and 31 May 1640 for general rendezvous at Newcastle in June. See also *A List of the Colonels as also of the Severall Counties ovt of which they are to Raise their Men* (1640).

[39] Scott, ' "Hannibal at our Gates" ', 269.

Middlesex	1,200 via Harwich
Norfolk	750 via Yarmouth
Northants.	550
Nottinghams.	300 via Grimsby
Oxfordshire	600
Rutland	60
Shropshire	500
Somerset	2,000
Staffords.	300
Suffolk	600 via Yarmouth
Surrey	800 via Gravesend
Sussex	600 via Gravesend
Warwicks.	500
Worcesters.	600
Wiltshire	1,300
Total England	**27,210**
Brecknock	200
Cardigan	150
Carmarthen	250
Caernarvon	160
Denbigh	200
Glamorgan	200
Flints.	80
Merioneth	100
Montgomery	200
Monmouth	250
Pembroke	300
Radnor	100
Total Wales	**2,190**

Total England and Wales   29,400

Exempt Cumberland, Durham, Lancashire, Northumberland, Westmorland, Yorkshire

Suitable soldiers proved very hard to find. Under pressure from London to meet their quotas, county officials vented their frustration in correspondence. In Hampshire at the beginning of May the deputy lieutenants 'found a great proportion wanting, by reason that many are run away out of the county upon the noise of the impress, and divers of those brought before us by the captains were so unfit that we refused them.... Those already impressed we retain with much difficulty for want of money to pay them.'[40] 'Poor fellows' in Herefordshire 'hid themselves for fear' until the press men went away.[41]

Recruitment and retention became even more difficult later in May as reports of the Lambeth disturbances echoed across England. Warning of 'a great blemish and disadvantage to the king's service', Hampshire officials thought it likely that 'for want of pay the soldiers will be hardly kept from mutiny'.[42]

The lieutenants of Lincolnshire complained that 'the constables . . . think to satisfy us with lame, sick and unserviceable men, and report that all other men more able in their townships do forsake their habitation, fly into the woods, and there arm themselves with pitchforks and other weapons in order to defend themselves.'[43] Likewise in Berkshire, 'divers men fittest to serve, when they hear of a press, run away and hide in the woods and other places, and are cherished by their parents or masters until the press is passed.'[44] Young men escaping impressment in other parts of England added to the disorderliness of the capital by 'lurking . . . in and about the city of London'.[45]

The first batch of recruits from London included 'idle persons that were to be found in taverns, inns and alehouses'.[46] The Council instructed the Lord Mayor to do better to take 'an especial care . . . in the choice of men, that they be of able bodies and of years meet for this employment'. But none were to be taken from the city's trained bands, who were needed to protect the capital after the recent Lambeth riots.[47] Impressment continued apace throughout the summer 'in all counties, and in every street of London', as the likelihood of a Scottish invasion intensified.[48]

Local court records expose some of the problems in recruiting soldiers and setting them forth.[49] A London feltmaker, Joseph Braine of St Andrew Holborne, was charged at the Middlesex Quarter Sessions in August 1640 with 'beating Robert Watts, constable, and hindering [him] from the executing of his office in pressing of soldiers for his majesty's service', almost on the eve of the Scots entry into England.[50] Another Londoner took the King's shilling, 'notwithstanding he was impressed before', and reviled the headborough, 'saying that he scorned to give him any obedience'.[51] While drinking at

---

[40] *CSPD 1640*, 123, report dated 6 May.
[41] Thomas Taylor Lewis (ed.), *Letters of the Lady Brilliana Harley* (Camden Society, vol. lviii, 1854), 91.   [42] *CSPD 1640*, 151, report dated 12 May.
[43] Ibid., 197, report dated 21 May.   [44] Ibid., 490.   [45] Ibid., 250.   [46] Ibid., 7.
[47] PRO, PC2/52, f. 257v.
[48] HMC, *Report on the Manuscripts of the Right Honourable Viscount De L'Isle . . . Vol. VI. Sidney Papers, 1626–1698* (1966), 301.
[49] Bristol Record Office, Quarter Sessions Minute Book 1634–47, JQS/M/3, f. 142v; Cheshire Record Office, Quarter Session Rolls, QJF 69/3, f. 12.
[50] London Metropolitan Archives, MJ/SBB/878/46.
[51] London Metropolitan Archives, MJ/SBB/882/109.

the Dolphin tavern in Sandwich in July 1640, a Kentish soldier, Robert Vicars, spoke 'dangerous words concerning the king and his privy council' (though unfortunately his exact words are nor recorded). The mayor and jurats of Sandwich had the offender imprisoned, but the warden of the Cinque Ports thought Vicars more useful in the ranks and petitioned for his release.[52]

Using military service as an alternative punishment, the Hertfordshire sessions committed Richard Powers to the house of correction 'on suspicion of stealing a silver spoon', then ordered him to be 'sent away for a soldier'.[53] A night-time wanderer with 'no habitation and can give no account of his life' chose to 'go for a soldier' in June 1640 as an alternative to commitment to Bridewell.[54] Two offenders bound over to appear at the summer sessions at Gloucester in 1640 failed to appear because they were 'pressed and gone for his majesty's service'.[55] In Norfolk in January 1642, two condemned felons were similarly 'reprieved in gaols to the intent that they shall be sent into Ireland when a press come for soldiers'.[56] When Worcestershire church officials sought to impose a sentence of excommunication on Richard Faukes they found him 'pressed out of Leigh for a soldier and is gone for Scotland'.[57]

Recruitment for the army disrupted hundreds of families and communities. At Otterbourne, Hampshire, 'a poor friendless child' had to be cared for by the parish after his father, 'being a stranger, was lately taken and thence impressed for a soldier in the service against the Scots'.[58] A poor Middlesex woman described herself in June 1640 as 'in the nature of a widow, her husband being in the service of his majesty' as a trooper in the north.[59] At Ipswich the children of John Brett, tailor, became dependent on poor-relief, 'he being run away or pressed for a soldier', and an apprentice had to be provided for, 'his master being pressed away for a soldier'.[60]

The result was a ramshackle motley army, able-bodied but disorderly minded and notoriously averse to authority.[61] These soldiers *were* civilians until they accepted the King's shilling, and their entry into military service caused untold problems for their neighbours and kin. Few of them absorbed military values before they reached the rendezvous in the north, and many wore their association with the army lightly. A pamphlet criticizing the English soldiers assembled for the Scottish war claimed that they 'care not who lose, so they get, being mere atheists and barbarous in their resolutions; and indeed

---

[52] East Kent Archives, Sandwich Borough Muniments, Mayor's Letter Book 1639–44, Sa/C1, ff. 29–29v.   [53] Hertfordshire Record Office, QSB 2B, f. 15v.
[54] Corporation of London, Bridewell and Bethlem, Court of Governors' Minutes, 5 June 1640.
[55] Gloucestershire Record Office, Recognizances and Orders 1639–1647, GBR/G3/SO4.
[56] Norfolk Record Office, C/S1/6.   [57] Worcestershire Record Office, BA 2302/3, no. 864.
[58] Hampshire Record Office, Q1/2, 194.   [59] PRO, SP16/457/3.
[60] Suffolk Record Office, C/5/3/2/3/1 (St Mary at Elms).   [61] *CSPD 1640*, 502.

they are the very scum of the kingdom.'[62] Scum or not, the soldiers who moved north in the summer of 1640 included some of the most marginal members of their communities. Lord Conway thought his troops at Newcastle more 'fit for Bedlam and Bridewell' than for military service, including many who 'never kept any law either of God or the king'.[63]

Rarely has an English army been so disparaged by those responsible for putting it into the field. The Lord General, the Earl of Northumberland, considered his forces in 'most miserable' condition, and opined on 21 May 1640 that it 'must needs bring us into contempt abroad and into disorders at home'. Three weeks later he remarked that 'the men that are pressed run so fast away and are so mutinous, that I doubt we shall want a very great part of our number, and those that remain will be readier to draw their swords upon their officers than against the Scots'.[64] At the end of May Northumberland complained to the Earl of Leicester that 'both our men and money are so unready that it will be near the middle of August before we shall be in the field.' On 25 June he confided again to Leicester that 'we are in a most wretched and beggarly condition'. A month later, when the Scots were advancing towards England and the kingdom as well as the campaign was in peril, Northumberland feared that his army would have to be dissolved for want of pay. On 6 August he wrote in desperation to Leicester, 'the straits we are in are not to be imagined'.[65] The west-country gentleman Edward Phelips wrote in August 1640 that the army was so unprepared and disordered that there was no means 'but by prayer to bring this to a good end'.[66] 'Our war seems to go backward', wrote a despairing Robert Crane.[67]

DESERTERS

Raising the army was slow and frustrating, and many of the men impressed or recruited for service in the north failed to reach their rendezvous. The deputy lieutenants of almost every county complained of numbers that were 'wanting' and of companies that were 'weak and unserviceable', as men ran away or failed to appear.[68] Every early modern army faced similar problems,

---

[62] D.L., *The Scots Scouts Discoveries by Their London Intelligencer* (1642), 42.
[63] *CSPD 1640*, 231, Conway to the Countess of Devonshire, 28 May 1640.
[64] HMC, *Report on the Manuscripts of the Right Honourable Viscount De L'Isle*, 270, 285.
[65] HMC, *3rd Report* (1872), 81–2.
[66] J.H. Bettey (ed.), *Calendar of the Correspondence of the Smyth Family of Ashton Court 1548–1642* (Bristol Record Society, vol. xxxv, 1982), 159.
[67] Bodleian Library, Oxford, Tanner Ms. 65, f. 78.
[68] *CSPD 1640*, 219, 27, 440; PRO, SP2/52, f. 289v.

but rarely on the scale of the northern expedition of 1640.[69] None of the recruits assembled against the Scots could be guaranteed to buckle to military discipline.

Despite the legally binding obligations of impressment,[70] many recruits treated press money as drinking money, and regarded their season of soldiering as little more than a summer spree. Many deserted at the earliest opportunity. The diarist Thomas Wyatt noted 'many soldiers pressed' at Oxford and Abingdon in June 1640, and seven pressed from his own parish of Ducklington. These soldiers 'did much hurt in many places, went not forward but some went and some returned home.' Few of them saw service against the Scots.[71]

The troops 'run away so fast that scarce half the number will appear at the rendezvous in the north', Northumberland complained to Conway in mid-June.[72] 'The regiments are so weak that some of them must needs be cast to complete the others', Northumberland despaired on the eve of the Scottish incursion.[73] 'Very many' of the troops raised in Hampshire returned home, some claiming certificates of discharge and 'some followed by hue and cry'. 'Very many' from Devon likewise 'disbanded themselves in a tumultuous manner'.[74] Of two hundred men pressed in London to go to Scotland in April, sixty mutinied and fled the night before setting sail.[75] Another column of 534 marching north in July lost 82 men on the way.[76] Losses of twenty to thirty per cent were not uncommon, though this did not prevent conductors from claiming the absconded men's pay.

The problems faced by the Northamptonshire lieutenancy may have been typical. Local constables were uncooperative in attending meetings and executing warrants, and proved sluggish or deficient in pressing men and raising money for their 'coat and conduct'. Recruits were unruly and unreliable, and their numbers tended to shrink 'in regard of the long stay betwixt their pressing and setting forward'. More than ten per cent of the '240 able and serviceable men for the war' supposed to be delivered to Stamford Baron failed to make the rendezvous. Another contingent bound towards Newcastle lost more than forty of its members to straggling and desertion. Thirty-four of a troop of sixty marching through Abingdon simply went missing.[77]

---

[69] Fissel, *English Warfare 1511–1642*, 108.

[70] By law, 'if a man take press money willingly he has contracted with the king and is bound to stand to his contract under the pain of felony.' Maija Jansson (ed.), *Proceedings in the Opening Session of the Long Parliament . . . Volume 2: 21 December 1640–20 March 1641* (Rochester, NY, 2000), 163.

[71] Diary of Thomas Wyatt, Bodleian Library, Ms. Top. Oxon. C. 378, 308–9.

[72] *CSPD 1640*, 306.   [73] Ibid., 573.   [74] Ibid., 440, 485.   [75] Ibid., 19.

[76] Ibid., 543.

[77] Bedfordshire and Luton Archives, St John Papers, J.1412, J.1414; *CSPD 1640*, 509.

The county of Somerset, originally charged with raising 2,000 soldiers, had its quota adjusted to 1,200 but could find no more that 833 when their orders came to march in mid-June.[78] By the time they reached Yorkshire on 7 July they were down to 640 men. Their leader, Lieutenant Colonel Thomas Lunsford, had fought with them all the way. These were the men who later bore the brunt of the Scottish cannonry at Newburn, and whose failure in battle perhaps cost Charles I his kingdom.[79]

Two of the Somerset men, the aptly named John Silly and William Witts, were arrested in Wiltshire in July 1640 for feloniously running away from their captain, but were treated leniently by the local courts. By their own account they had started off 'with a full purpose and settled resolution to follow their colours and leaders'. But Silly fell sick 'of the moass or measles and thereby so weakened that he could not make more speed'. Straggling through Wiltshire, the pair were apprehended as deserters, but were able to secure letters of support from their home parish of Lymington seeking 'all lawful favour' on their behalf.[80] Another prisoner in Wiltshire was 'accused to have received press money and clothes to serve his majesty in the late expedition, and running away with his clothes and money not being lawfully discharged'. This unnamed deserter was said to have 'repented him he had not killed the first officer that laid hands on him'.[81]

Discipline would be enhanced, thought Sir Thomas Jermyn, if 'example be made of some runaways'. He gave Secretary Vane a detailed account of continuing troubles in Suffolk, where 'disbanded soldiers...had forsaken their commanders and without leave straggled about the country'.[82] Similarly in Cheshire several pressed men faced charges at the autumn assize for departing from their captains 'without licence or pass'.[83]

DISORDERS

While the high command struggled with strategy, money, and logistics, the common soldiers and the civilians with whom they mingled experienced a deterioration of order. Swathes of the English countryside were exposed to haphazard violence and pilferage as the troops languished in billets or made their way north. From recruitment and impressment, through passage and service, to their eventual demobilization, underpaid soldiers were prone to disorder at every stage of their military careers.

[78] *CSPD 1640*, 318; PRO, PC2.52, f. 278v.   [79] *CSPD 1640*, 462.
[80] Wiltshire Record Office, Quarter Sessions Great Roll, A1/110 Hilary 1641, 168, 173, 206.
[81] Wiltshire Record Office, A1/110, Hilary 1641, 206, name torn away.
[82] PRO, SP16/458/18.   [83] Public Record Office, CHES 24/125/4.

Civilian grievances about billeting were nothing new, and had poisoned politics after Charles I's campaigns of the 1620s.[84] Complaints were renewed and amplified in the spring and summer of 1640, when the scale of the problem was expanded. Delays in the mobilization of troops caused additional hardships to communities charged with their billeting, as the general rendezvous was repeatedly postponed from May to June then July.[85] With hundreds of men stalled in Somerset in May 1640, the areas around Bruton and Wincanton were 'harder pressed with the lodging of the soldiers than the country can well bear'.[86] Householders were particularly averse to outsiders who might be touched by the plague.

When 100 'especially ungovernable' soldiers from Sussex and another 150 from Kent were billeted at Rochester in July 1640, the Council feared for the safety of the nearby naval stores.[87] In Essex, where similar concentrations of troops awaited shipment to the north, officials worried that 'so many being billeted together gives them power to commit incredible villainies'.[88] The Lord Lieutenant of Essex complained to the Council on 22 July of the 'many great outrages committed by soldiers in those places where they are billeted, which daily increase the longer they stay'.[89] Soldiers at Oxford occasioned 'a very mutinous quarrel in their drink' and fought with the university scholars.[90] In Wiltshire, John Nicholas complained, thieving soldiers 'took all they could catch in their way, and being resisted by their owners . . . beat many very sorely'. It was, he concluded, 'an ill beginning'.[91]

At Norwich too the impressed men caused repeated problems with violence, drunkenness, and petty theft. Some of them took to showing off their weapons at night, walking the streets with their matches lit. One member of the Norwich watch was sent to Bridewell in May 1640 for encouraging disorderly soldiers instead of apprehending them.[92] These Norfolk men refused to be transported by sea, citing 'the hardships, miseries and deaths' of their counterparts who had been shipped north the previous year.[93]

It became a common conceit that England suffered more from its own army than it was likely to endure from the Scots. In Yorkshire, most heavily burdened with soldiers, some 'feared they will ruin the country worse than the Scots'.[94] The Scots, many believed, would pay for their provisions, whereas

---

[84] Fissel, *English Warfare 1511–1642*, 112; Thomas Cogswell, *The Blessed Revolution: English Politics and the Coming of War, 1621–1624* (Cambridge, 1989); Conrad Russell, *Parliaments and English Politics, 1621–1629* (Oxford, 1979).   [85] *CSPD 1640*, 210.
[86] Ibid., 221.   [87] PRO, PC2/52, f. 324; *CSPD 1640*, 541.   [88] *CSPD 1640*, 371.
[89] Ibid., 500.
[90] William Laud, *The Works of . . . the Most Reverend Father in God, William Laud, D.D.*, ed. W. Scott and J. Bliss (7 vols., Oxford, 1847–60), v. 271, 282.   [91] *CSPD 1640*, 258.
[92] Norfolk Record Office, Norwich Mayor's Court Book, 1639–1644, NCR/16a/20, ff. 282–4.
[93] *CSPD 1640*, 161.   [94] Ibid., 571.

the English were billeted 'at the country's cost' on unreliable credit.[95] Yorkshire was sick of soldiers and petitioned to be rid of them, but their commander, Lord Conway, dismissed complaints of rapes and robberies as 'but the tricks of the soldiers', as if no better could be expected.[96] In Monmouthshire a deputy lieutenant felt so menaced by 'pressed soldiers who threatened him particularly', that he set out by night to escape, only to die of misadventure.[97]

Newsletters and correspondence reverberated with complaints about 'the stubbornness and unwillingness of the soldiers' and the 'outrages and cruelties' they committed against local civilians. 'Insolencies' and 'abuses' became indelibly associated with the army of 1640.[98] Edward Rossingham's newsletter of 14 April 1640 reported desertions by English troops at Berwick.[99] The author of 'Pigg's Corranto', a mock-newsletter of mid-1640, said of the troops bound for York that he could not tell 'what religion or what side they would be of till they come there, nor how many be valiant before they be drunk, nor how many will fight without money'.[100] The newswriter William Hawkins observed that the pressed men marching to their rendezvous 'make many broils with their commanders and conductors'.[101]

News reached the capital in May 1640 of 'foul misdemeanours committed by the troops', including the burning of houses, the ravishing of maidens, and the theft of private property along their line of march. Reports of disaffection, desertion, and indiscipline in the army added to the anxieties raised by rebellious insurrections in the City and suburbs, where billeted soldiers engaged in night-time brawls with local artisans.[102]

Writing to a kinsman in Cornwall in August, Francis Sawle reported that the pressed men in the north were so ill-behaved, 'that they are fain to have the train bands always in arms to keep them in good order; they are so unruly that they dare not to give them arms, and it is feared that divers of our soldiers will go to the Scots. . . . Our own soldiers have done much harm abroad in the country, great complaints we hear every day of them, some almost half undone by them.'[103] John Burghall's chronicle recorded 'many outrages' by

---

[95] *CSPD 1640*, 586, 600,

[96] HMC, *Report on the Manuscripts of the Right Honourable Viscount De L'Isle*, 311; Lismore Mss., vol. xxi, National Register of Archives, vol. 20594/15, 859.

[97] PRO, C115/99/7265, John Scudamore to Viscount Scudamore, 3 August 1640.

[98] Huntington Library, Ms. El. 7868, Roger Holland to Earl of Bridgewater, 8 August 1640; El. 7847, John Castle to Earl of Bridgewater, 8 August 1640; El. 7849, 15 August 1640.

[99] Rossingham newsletter, British Library, Add. Ms. 11045, vol. v., f. 110.

[100] Durham University Library, Special Collections, Mickleton-Spearman Ms. MSP/9, ii. 139; PRO, SP16/475/16.

[101] HMC, *Report on the Manuscripts of the Right Honourable Viscount De L'Isle*, 286.

[102] *CSPD 1640*, 156, 190, 196; London Metropolitan Archives, Sessions Roll, MJ/SR/882/16.

[103] Cornwall Record Office, DD R(S)/1/140, Francis Sawle to Jonathan Rashleigh, 18 August 1640.

the soldiers, 'pilfering and stealing what they could get, robbing men by the highways, killing some of their captains, pulling down houses, and ravishing women'.[104] Sir Thomas Colepepper wrote about the 'great disorders done by the soldiers', and the difficulty in conducting them to Stamford.[105] Walter Yonge made note of the 'many insolencies' committed by these soldiers.[106] The diarist Robert Woodford also observed that the soldiers 'will scarce be ruled by their captains'.[107]

Magistrates complained that soldiers 'have done many more mischiefs, and do rob all men they meet as they go straggling through the country without any order or command, to the great disturbance of his majesty's peace and the danger of the country, threatening to burn towns in their return.' Local justices referred the worst crimes to the assizes and quarter sessions, but by the time the courts met the troops were usually long gone.[108]

Soldiers inevitably attracted camp followers. A ragtag of prostitutes, laundry women, and wives accompanied the soldiers towards the north.[109] Two women from Surrey, Mary Jones and Catherine Pell of Epsom, were whipped and sent home in July 1640 after Essex magistrates found them full of drink in company with the impressed men at Great Waltham.[110] Two Kentish women 'travelling to their husbands, being in the king's service', received charitable relief from constables in Nottinghamshire.[111] A Devon woman, Ann Williams, followed her soldier husband all the way to Northumberland, where Scottish cannonry made her a widow. Ann and her child drifted south again over the next few months, needing a cart to carry them through Lancashire, 'she being lame'.[112] Mary Dibben, arrested in London as 'a common night walker', told the Bridewell court that 'her husband is a trooper and she hath no course of life'.[113]

Shocking reports circulated in August 1640 of 'the ravishing of a woman by eight several soldiers near Kings Norton in Gloucestershire'.[114] Dozens of

---

[104] John Burghall, 'Providence Improved', in J. Hall (ed.), *Memorials of the Civil War in Cheshire* (Lancashire and Cheshire Record Society, vol. xix, 1889), 16.

[105] HMC, *Report on Various Collections* (1914), vii. 424.

[106] Diary of Walter Yonge, British Library, Add. Ms. 35,331, f. 77.

[107] British Library, Sloane Ms. 1457, ff. 60, 63; New College, Oxford, Ms. 9502.

[108] *CSPD 1640*, 449–50; HMC, *12th Report, The Manuscripts of the Earl Cowper... Preserved at Melbourne Hall, Derbyshire* (1888), ii. 256–8, 282.

[109] Durham University Library, Special Collections, Mickleton-Spearman Ms. MSP/9 ii. 133–9.   [110] Essex Record Office, Quarter Sessions Rolls, Q/SR/311/14.

[111] Martyn Bennett (ed.), *A Nottinghamshire Village in War and Peace: The Accounts of the Constables of Upton 1640–1660* (Thoroton Society Record Series, vol. xxxix, Nottingham, 1995), 2.

[112] J. P. Earwaker (ed.), *The Constables' Accounts of the Manor of Manchester* (3 vols., Manchester, 1892), ii. 87.

[113] Corporation of London, Bridewell, and Bethlem, Court of Governors' Minutes, 22 September 1641.   [114] Huntington Library, Ms. El. 7868, 8 August 1640.

local girls were left carrying the children of anonymous soldiers. A Somerset woman 'great with child in fornication' confessed in February 1641 that 'when the soldiers went towards the north [a stranger] lay in bed with her and begot her with child'.[115] Several women in Nottinghamshire and Yorkshire were cited in 1641 'for fornication with a soldier' or 'incontinency with a soldier, as the common fame goeth'.[116] Finding two or three soldiers dallying with his teenage female servants, John Skinner of Worcester declared angrily about midsummer 1640, 'I will have no whorish tricks played in my house.'[117] John Welsh, one of four 'dangerous fellows' apprehended in Devon in October 1640, justified his attempt on the chastity of Adriana Dare of Seaton 'because he was a soldier and therefore must be relieved'.[118] A local man, Albert Weymouth, thought he would try this trick, demanding food and drink 'in a terrifying gesture and manner', and 'pretending himself to be a soldier'.[119] In 1641 it was 'merry news' for some 'that the Yorkshire maids have put down many of your gallants with their own weapons, and that there are more wenches with child than ever was known in those countries'.[120]

MUTINIES

Disorderly troops did not just disturb the civilian population but turned violently against their own officers. In extreme cases mutiny extended to murder, like the practice known in America's Vietnam war as 'fragging' (from fragmentation grenades). At least four officers in the campaign of 1640 died from sword-cuts or cudgels at their own men's hands, and their story grew in the telling. Like comments comparing the depredations of English soldiers to the more benign reputation of the Scots, it was commonly remarked that the officers risked more from their own recruits than from any opposing forces.

The violence worsened as the weather warmed up, after the Maytide disturbances in London and when the men were on the march. On 21 May 1640 the deputy lieutenants of Lincolnshire warned of the 'distempers and distraction' in their forces, and the 'mutinous and rebellious' condition of the men already pressed.[121] By 30 May some officers in Lincolnshire were calling

---

[115] Somerset Record Office, D/D/Ca 334, f. 123v.
[116] Nottingham University Library, Manuscripts and Special Collections, AN/A48, ff. 17v, 18; Borthwick Institute, York, C/V/CB3, ff. 77v, 84v, 85v, 87, 92.
[117] Worcestershire Record Office, BA 2102/9, p. 321.
[118] Devon Record Office, Q/SB/43/15.   [119] Ibid., Q/SB/46/9.
[120] *A Remonstrance of Londons Occurrences* (1641), sig. A3v.
[121] *CSPD 1640*, 196. See also Lewis (ed.), *Letters of the Lady Brilliana Harley*, 95, for a rumoured mutiny in Herefordshire.

for exemplary executions lest the 'distempers' of the soldiers erupt into violence.[122] In Suffolk, the deputy lieutenants reported, 'the soldiers are so mutinous they refuse to obey us or their commanders.... What they will do when they meet altogether is to be feared.' At Bungay on 12 June, 'the soldiers mutinied, threatening our deaths...and waylaid us to that we were forced to keep our chambers.... They are as saucy with the officers as with us.'[123] Cheshire officials dared not arm and exercise their five hundred recruits, 'lest they fall to be mutinous and disordered'.[124]

One of the most disturbing incidents involved a troop of some six hundred pressed men from Dorset who turned violently against the officers who were leading them towards the north. By 17 June they had got as far as Farringdon, Berkshire, when 'a most insolent and desperate mutiny' occurred. The soldiers murdered their Lieutenant Mohun, who they believed to be a papist, and 'dragged him at a horse tail and then hung him upon the pillory'. According to Rossingham's newsletter, when three officers were trapped in the upper room of an inn Mohun tried to escape through the window, climbed out onto the inn sign, and was beaten down and pelted with stones before being dragged through the mire and left for dead in a ditch. On recovering, he was beaten again and killed, and his body was paraded through the town and set up on display. Not surprisingly, the entire company of soldiers disbanded and fled.[125] In response to this outrage the government issued a proclamation, 'for the finding out and apprehending of the principal actors and abettors of the said mutiny and murder'. Three of the mutineers were captured by 1 July, and warrants sought to arrest ten more 'movers and actors in the same mutiny and murder'. By the time two of the ringleaders were hanged at the Abingdon summer assizes, most of their fellows had melted away into the south-west.[126]

News of the murder of Lieutenant Mohun spread rapidly around the country, further undermining discipline and fanning fears. 'People are strangely disaffected and untoward', wrote Sir Kenelm Digby.[127] Commanders became alarmed 'that the soldiers had resolved to kill all of their officers in their march', and some captains were 'so fearful of their soldiers they dare not march with them'.[128] Other companies became 'refractory' and began to disband. The sheriff of Berkshire feared that 'the soldiers being now at liberty...will

---

[122] *CSPD 1640*, 247.   [123] Ibid., 275, 291.   [124] Ibid., 212.

[125] Ibid., 316, 323–4; HMC, *Report on the Manuscripts of the Right Honourable Viscount De L'Isle*, 290; John Rushworth, *Historical Collections of Private Proceedings of State* (8 vols., 1680–1701), iii. 1190, 1193; Fissel, *Bishops' Wars*, 278–80.

[126] PRO, PC2/52, ff. 278v, 279v, 289v; Larkin (ed.), *Stuart Royal Proclamations...1625–1646*, 718–20; Marjorie Maslen (ed.), *Woodstock Chamberlain's Accounts, 1609–50* (Oxfordshire Record Society, vol. lviii, 1993), 185.   [127] *CSPD 1640*, 333.

[128] Larkin (ed.), *Stuart Royal Proclamations...1625–1646*, 723n; Diary of Thomas Wyatt, Bodleian Library, Ms. Top. Oxon. C. 378, 308; *CSPD 1640*, 492.

endanger the town and country adjoining'. Oxford, seventeen miles from the mutiny, mounted precautionary watches, especially 'towards Farringdon where the late rebellion was'.[129]

Five days after the mutiny of the Dorset men Colonel Lunsford wrote to Northumberland from Warwick, 'I find my regiment in the greatest disorder, divers of them in troops returned home, all are forward to disband and the countries rather inclined to foment their dislikes than assist in punishment or persuasions.' The Council in London shared this view that local magistrates seemed 'rather to foment' the disorders 'than to endeavour the[ir] suppressing and reformation'. Without recourse to martial law it was hard to punish the deserters or to reduce them 'to conformity and obedience'.[130] A proclamation of 1 July directed local authorities to apprehend all runaway soldiers, to suppress all mutinies, and to quell 'other insolencies and disorders' emanating from the army. Another of the same date offered pardon to those of the Farringdon mutineers who surrendered, except for named 'principal movers and actors'.[131] Sensing a link between military and religious disorders, Archbishop Laud enquired whether separatist conventiclers were present at Farringdon that summer.[132]

Ripples of disturbance spread to East Anglia, where soldiers refused to embark for the north. 'About Newmarket', it was reported, 'the men of Cambridgeshire have very lately fallen upon their officers and beaten them', and gained possession of the trained band's arms.[133] Early in July the newswriter John Castle reported more 'very bad news out of Essex, where it is said the soldiers have slain some of their officers and beaten a deputy lieutenant'.[134] The Council authorized judges to try soldiers around Chelmsford involved in this 'mutiny and tumult', and to bring them to 'speedy and exemplary punishment'.[135] Similar instructions went to the assize judges in Herefordshire after a battle between soldiers and civilians left several slain, many hurt, and many of the pressed men missing.[136]

Another notorious incident occurred on Sunday 8 July when a company of one hundred and sixty pressed men from Devon, pausing at Wellington, Somerset, fell on one of their officers, Lieutenant Compton Euers, dragged him through the streets and killed him with his own sword. Like Lieutenant Mohun, who was murdered two weeks earlier, Euers was suspected of being

[129] *CSPD 1640*, 316, 341; Laud, *The Works of . . . William Laud*, v. 274–5.
[130] *CSPD 1640*, 327; Rushworth, *Historical Collections of Private Proceedings of State*, iii. 1191; PRO PC2/52, f. 288v.
[131] Larkin (ed.), *Stuart Royal Proclamations . . . 1625–1646*, 716–20.
[132] Roger Quatermayne, *Qvatermayns Conqvest Over Canterbvries Covrt* (1642), 22.
[133] Huntington Library, Ms. El. 7838, 23 June 1640; *CSPD 1640*, 336.
[134] Huntington Library, Ms. El. 7642, 6 July 1640.   [135] PRO, PC2/52, f. 303v.
[136] Ibid., f. 306.

a papist. One of the pressed men, Hannibal Pounceford, formerly a butcher, took 'a crucifix tied in a ribbon' from the slain officer's neck, while others rifled his pockets. Most of the company took flight, scattering westward, though several were arrested for murdering the lieutenant. A proclamation of 24 July sought the speedy apprehension and punishment of the others.[137] The Council expressed surprise that local civil authorities had been so easily over-awed by the soldiers, and several inhabitants of Wellington were later fined at the Western Assizes for failing to hold the suspected killers.[138]

The problem was compounded by uncertainty about the powers of the military courts. Legal opinion held that 'martial law cannot be executed legally and justifiably in England but where an army is in a body drawn together and near an enemy'.[139] It therefore did not apply to recent recruits or troops on the march. Lord Conway forced leaders of a minor mutiny at Newcastle to cast dice to see which one of them should face a firing squad. The loser was shot, Conway told Laud on 20 May, 'because I could not get any to hang him'. He was not sure whether he had overstepped his authority.[140] In the face of mounting disorders, Conway complained that commanders still had no commission for the execution of martial law, but fortunately, the troops did not know this. 'If the soldiers do know that it is questioned they will decide by their disobedience, as the country doth for the Ship Money, and with far more dangerous consequence; for the soldier may bring the country to reason, but who shall compel the soldier?'[141] Writing in July 1640, Conway had articulated a crucial question that would trouble a militarized England for the next twenty years.

News from all parts about 'the great disturbance of the country' eventually moved the regime to action.[142] Shaken by reports of the 'notorious and foul outrages' of his soldiers, the King finally authorized martial law on 15 July. Northumberland commented wryly to Conway, 'you may now hang with more authority'.[143] Writing a week later from Yorkshire, Sir Jacob Astley let it be known 'that for the remainder of those at the rendezvous that are not run away, he dares not arm them; and for the safety of his own person he is driven to keep a double guard about him.'[144] But using his new legal powers

---

[137] *CSPD 1640*, 476, 494, 496, 506, 579; PRO, SP16/463/88; Larkin (ed.), *Stuart Royal Proclamations . . . 1625–1646*, 722–4.
[138] PRO, PC2/52, f. 338; J. S. Cockburn (ed.), *Western Circuit Assize Orders 1629–1648: A Calendar* (Camden Society, 4th series, 17, 1976), 222; Fissel, *Bishops' Wars*, 281–4.
[139] *CSPD 1640*, 355, Conway to Strafford, 28 June 1640, citing 'all the lawyers and judges'.
[140] *CSPD 1640*, 189. Execution under martial law was still a matter of controversy at Strafford's trial in March 1641 (Maija Jansson (ed.), *Proceedings in the Opening Session of the Long Parliament . . . Volume 3: 22 March–17 April 1641* (Rochester, NY, 2001), 167).
[141] Lambeth Palace Library, Ms. Misc. 943, 696, 701.   [142] *CSPD 1640*, 475.
[143] Ibid., 477, 514.   [144] Huntington Library, Ms. El. 7844, 25 July 1640.

early in August, Astley dealt firmly with disorderly soldiers from Dorset by executing their ringleader. 'We arquebused him in the sight of the rest, some 340, whereupon they were all quiet.'[145]

REGULATORS

The 'insolencies of the army' were not all directed against officers, nor were they confined to acts of random violence. Some of the soldiers of 1640 distinguished themselves through behaviour with a reformist or regulatory air. They seem to have adopted an informal agenda of retribution, imposing a rough moral discipline on some of the communities through which they passed. Collectively the soldiers acted as if they were outside the law, and sometimes as its instruments. Unstable and undisciplined transients with weapons, they reacted against authority of all kinds, social, military, and religious. In Derbyshire, wrote Edward Rossingham, 'as they pass they inquire where they may do mischief, and as people inform them, so they are ready to do prejudice more or less upon such as the people complain of.'[146]

In Suffolk, Rossingham reported in June, the soldiers 'have been very unruly . . . and have kept commissaries' courts and have done justice upon a man and a wench that were taken in their sin; many mad pranks they have played which are not fit to be written.'[147] Other correspondents commented on the 'insolent behaviour' and 'mad and base pranks' of these enlistees.[148] Referring to 'what the soldiers had done to the supposed witch', without saying exactly what it was, Sir Thomas Jermyn implied that these troops in Suffolk had exercised a form of vigilante justice, rough enough to land one of them before the summer assizes.[149]

Often enough the troops took sides in agrarian disputes and troubles relating to forests and common land. When Colonel Lunsford's West Country men reached Derbyshire in July they took to pulling down enclosures and burning fences. Urged on by disgruntled local tenants, they broke down rails, destroyed a mill belonging to Sir John Coke, and killed some of the Earl of Huntingdon's deer.[150] Soldiers in Staffordshire similarly levelled and burned 'the lofts and rails of certain enclosed grounds called Uttoxter wood'.[151] Shaken by reports of the soldiers' 'insolency' and 'mischief', the Worcestershire diarist Henry Townsend worried that his own orchards and fences might be molested next.[152]

---

[145] *CSPD 1640*, 559.   [146] Ibid., 450.   [147] Ibid., 336.
[148] William Bagnall to John Hobart on 29 June 1640, Bodleian Library, Oxford, Tanner Ms. 65, f. 91.   [149] PRO, SP16/458/18.
[150] *CSPD 1640*, 450.   [151] PRO, PC2/52, f. 338v; *CSPD 1640*, 477.
[152] British Library, Add. Ms. 38, 490, 4, 5.

Marching through Derbyshire and Yorkshire, soldiers opened prisons and freed debtors and deserters. Sir Jacob Astley observed in June, 'they break open all prisons and ... do great mischief in the country'.[153] In July they broke windows and smashed tools at the Wakefield house of correction.[154] They seem to have engaged in a campaign against confinement of all sorts, opening gaols that confined men, demolishing fences that enclosed commons, and pulling down rails that distanced communion tables from parishioners.

RELIGION

Around midsummer 1640 the soldiers discovered religion. While outrages and disorders continued, they were increasingly directed against religious targets or acquired a religious dimension. Mutinous troops displayed a boisterous anti-Catholicism, targeting known recusants and suspected papists. Some of them engaged in violent iconoclasm, pulling up altar rails and attacking the accoutrements of Laudian ceremonialism. In some areas soldiers and civilians joined together to express contempt for recent religious innovations. (See Chapter 7.)

Although it is impossible to characterize with any accuracy the religious persuasions of the recruits, they seem to have exhibited the proclivities of a rough mainstream Protestantism, perhaps even popular Puritanism. The Presbyterian propagandist John Vicars called them 'rude reformers' and interpreted their actions against altars as 'a special hand of divine providence'.[155] They attended church, received communion, heard sermons, and joined in the singing of psalms. Soldiers at Marlborough listened approvingly in July to a sermon 'tending to commendation of the Scots in point of religion'.[156] Some of the troops in Essex possessed religious tracts against the war that they had been recruited to fight.[157]

Many of the soldiers refused to serve under officers who they suspected of Roman Catholicism. Troops in Berkshire, for example, objected to Captain Andrews 'in respect he is a recusant, as they say'.[158] Wiltshire recruits told one of their officers 'that if he would not receive the communion and pray with them, they would not fight under him, and so they cashiered their captain.'[159]

---

[153] *CSPD 1640*, 365.

[154] John Lister (ed.), *West Riding Sessions Records. Vol. II. Orders, 1611–1642. Indictments, 1637–1642* (Yorkshire Archaeological Society, vol. liii, 1915), 227.

[155] John Vicars, *God in the Mount. Or, Englands Remembrancer* (1641), 23.

[156] *CSPD 1640*, 493. The preacher was a Mr Barnard, who travelled for that purpose to the camp.   [157] *CSPD 1640*, 622, 635, 638; PRO, SP16/465/43.

[158] *CSPD 1640*, 219.   [159] Ibid., 281.

Passing through Daventry, Northamptonshire, in July 1640 some of the West Country troops 'began to mutiny and would go no further, some alleging they would not fight against the Gospel, and others that they were to be shipped and commanded by papists'. This particular mutiny did not lead to violence, but hundreds 'forsook their officers' and went their own way.[160] The Earl of Warwick found the soldiers 'very jealous in point of religion, they having often moved me that their officers might receive the communion with them'.[161] The murders of lieutenants Eures and Mohun resulted from taking this prejudice to extremes. Nor were civilian Catholics any safer. At Cirencester in July soldiers 'forced two recusants to church in a most tumultuous manner'.[162] In Essex in August they looted a house where the wife was a recusant.[163]

Engaged in a British war of religion, a war between episcopacy and Presbyterianism, some of the soldiers turned violently against the Laudian Church of England. From south to north, in an unofficial crusade of reformation, they taunted conformist clerics, tore up surplices, ripped Books of Common Prayer, and pulled down communion rails.[164] Laud himself knew exactly what they were about: 'the soldiers are very unruly and now begin to pull up the rails in churches, and in a manner to say they will reform since the laws everywhere broken'.[165] Nehemiah Wallington marvelled at the iconoclasm of soldiers in Essex and Berkshire who desecrated churches and pulled down communion rails[166] (Plate 1).

Lord William Maynard wrote from Essex in late July that the soldiers 'have now within these few days taken upon them to reform churches'. They had begun intimidating ultra-conformist ministers and had pulled down the rails around communion tables.[167] At Braintree, 'seeing the communion table railed about, they cried out, it was not fit the table should be impounded.' At Radwinter, 'they took away the statue of our saviour, with some cherubim and seraphim, and carried them to Maldon, where they burned them.'[168]

All over East Anglia the soldiers engaged in a frenzied destruction of communion rails and religious imagery, as military discipline gave way to 'tumult and uproar'. One of the ringleaders in Essex, Edward Aylee, a former glazier, was said to have pulled down seventeen altar rails 'with his own hands'. Another, William Bates, foolishly claimed licence from the Earl of Warwick who was 'a king in Essex'.[169] At Saffron Walden churchwardens paid for 'work done in the church to make the doors fast when the soldiers

---

[160] *CSPD 1640*, 476–7.   [161] Ibid., 517.   [162] Ibid., 497.   [163] Ibid., 551
[164] HMC, *Report on the Manuscripts of the Right Honourable Viscount De L'Isle*, 318; Fissel, *Bishops' Wars*, 268–9.   [165] *CSPD 1640*, 432.
[166] British Library, Add. Ms. 21935, ff. 86–90.   [167] *CSPD 1640*, 517.   [168] Ibid., 522.
[169] Rushworth, *Historical Collections of Private Proceedings of State*, iii. 1192, 1194–5; PRO, SP16/466/23; *CSPD 1640*, 517–18, 522, 555.

that lay in town did attempt to break in the church' in the summer of 1640.[170]
An inventory of church goods at Waltham Holy Cross a year later noted that
'the service books was torn by soldiers'.[171]

Early in August Lord Salisbury reported from Hertfordshire, 'the soldiers
here begin to follow the example of those of Essex in pulling down communion
rails'. At Hadham, Hertfordshire, where the soldiers also destroyed a stained-
glass window, 'it is very likely the people of the town set them on'.[172] As iconoclastic avengers, as well as scourges of enclosures, the soldiers were able to
perform deeds that the more settled civilian population would not dare.
'Vagabond soldiers' continued to smash rails and desecrate churches in
Hertfordshire in late August.[173] A Hertfordshire magistrate, Sir John Jennings,
later came in for reproach from the Council for his 'great remissness' regarding
the soldiers who 'committed great profanity and riot in churches'.[174]

At Ashford, Kent, in August 1640 a soldier by the name of Bishop was
induced 'to put on a gown and a pair of white sleeves, and being brought to
the pillory by the rabble he was by them accused of being cause of a great
many disorders'. This outdoor theatre was quickly broken up by the officers
who 'marred their play', and the soldier Bishop was beaten 'for his roguerie'.[175]
But it revealed a hostility to episcopal authority among many of those mobilized for 'this prelatical war'.[176] It was a warning that the Laudian ascendancy
was in trouble.

AFTER NEWBURN

Most of these soldiers never saw battle. The northern campaign was over
much quicker than anyone expected because of the speed and surprise of the
Scottish victory. The English commanders persistently underestimated the
strength of Scottish forces and their willingness to engage in combat.[177] When
the crucial moment arrived the King's Englishmen were found wanting.

Viscount Conway spent most of the summer of 1640 believing that 'the
Scots will not come into England'.[178] As late as 19 August the governor of
Berwick could write that 'they will not come over at all', convinced that the

---

[170] Essex Record Office, mf. T/A599/1.   [171] Essex Record Office, D/P75/5/1.
[172] *CSPD 1640*, 580.   [173] *CSPD 1640–41*, 70; PRO, SP16/467/79.
[174] PRO, PC2/52, f. 355v.   [175] Huntington Library, Ms. El. 7856, 29 August 1640.
[176] Jansson (ed.), *Proceedings in the Opening Session of the Long Parliament . . . Vol. 2*, 241.
The phrase was used by Sir John Wray in January 1641.
[177] *CSPD 1640*, 81–2, 28, 311, 347, 446, 478.
[178] Conway to Laud, 6 July 1640, Lambeth Palace Library, Ms. Misc. 943, 695; *CSPD 1640*,
483, 516, 526, 562, 608. Contrast the rumours reported on 8 and 15 August 'of the Scottish
army marching toward our parts'. Huntington Library, Ms. El. 7868; El. 7869.

Scots intended not to invade but to stir up revolt in England.[179] Within twenty-four hours they would be proven wrong. The Earl of Strafford, weak, sick, and removed from the action, but still capable of martial bluster, railed against the futile commanders. On 27 August he told Conway that 'all men' at York were 'extreme ill satisfied' with his generalship, and urged him to take 'some noble action to put yourself from under the weight of ill tongues'.[180] But by this time it was too late.

The Scots crossed the border on 20 August 1640, meeting no resistance for almost a week. To the amazement of all observers, their passage from the Tweed to the Tyne was 'without any hostile act or spoil in the country as they passed'.[181] In a masterpiece of military theatre, the Scots presented themselves more like solemn petitioners than an invading army.[182] The contrast between England's ill-governed military rabble and the disciplined and purposeful Covenanters could not have been more pointed. Trailing pikes with black ribbons, the Scottish soldiers were accompanied by trumpeters dressed in mourning, gentlemen carrying white roses, and ministers carrying Bibles and dispersing books.[183] At Haddon on the Wall, one of the incoming Scots recalled, 'old mistress Finnick came out and met us, and burst out and said, "And is it not so, that Jesus Christ will not come to England for reforming of abuses, but with an army of 22,000 men at his back?" '[184]

At Newburn, west of Newcastle, the Scots routed Conway's troops on 28 August, and entered Newcastle without resistance two days later. The Scots were as surprised as anyone at the ease with which they established their control of Northumberland and Durham. The English forces retreated in panic, leaving wagons, horses, and equipment behind them.[185] Civilians too experienced 'horrible confusion', with 'riding and running and routing beyond expression, for we expected the Scots would presently come on in pursuit of our army', wrote one Durham cleric who managed to escape south to York.[186]

---

[179] Sir John Conyers to Secretary Windebank, 19 August 1640, *CSPD 1640*, 606–7.

[180] Sheffield Archives, Wentworth Woodhouse Muniments, Strafford Papers 21/204.

[181] Bodleian Library, Ms. Rawlinson D. 141 ('England's Memorable Accidents'), 6.

[182] 'Informations from the Scottish Nation, to all the true English, concerning the present expedition', Bodleian Library, Oxford, Tanner Ms. 65, f. 41.

[183] William Perkins to the Earl of Cork, 25 August 1640, Lismore Mss. vol. xxi, National Register of Archives, vol. 20594/15, 858–9; Huntington Library, Ms. El. 7852, 22 August 1640; John Livingston, *A Brief Historical Relation, of the Life of Mr. John Livingston* (1727), 24–5.

[184] Livingston, *Brief Historical Relation*, 25.

[185] PRO, C115/99/7267, Barnabas Scudamore to Viscount Scudamore, 8 September 1640; Stevenson, *Scottish Revolution 1637–1644*, 207–11; Roger Howell, Jr., *Newcastle upon Tyne and the Puritan Revolution* (Oxford, 1967), 120–4.

[186] Cambridge University Library, Ms. Mn. 1. 45 (Baker transcripts), 107, 'A paper of intelligence sent to my Lord Bishop of Ely Dr. Wren from York', 24 September 1640, perhaps written by Dr Eleazar Duncan, rector of Houghton and prebendary of Durham.

Commentators were at first more inclined to blame the common soldiers than the generals for the English military collapse. One report 'from the northern parts' at the end of August insisted, 'our gentlemen behaved themselves right valiantly, and if they had not been basely forsaken by the ordinary troopers in likelihood had won the day.'[187] Another 'intelligence' reaching Cambridge in September compared 'the commanders and gentlemen' who did their part 'manfully' to 'our ordinary troopers' who fled in disgrace.[188] Our foot soldiers 'did us no great stead', said another letter, citing Secretary Vane's remark that had the men been well seconded, 'it would have been easy to have driven the Scots back across the river'.[189] 'The greater part of our common troops shamefully ran away, scattering their arms and leaving their commanders to charge alone', so it was reported in London. Faced with Scottish gunnery, the young soldiers 'quitted work and ran away in great confusion'.[190] 'Never so many ran from so few with less ado' was Thomas Gower's pre-Churchillian comment on the decisive battle of Newburn.[191]

Strafford's analysis was deeply pessimistic. 'Pity me', he wrote to Sir George Radcliffe on 1 September, 'for never came any man to so mightily a lost business.' The army was 'altogether unexercised and unprovided of all necessaries', and the troops straggling southward were 'the worst I ever saw'. This was a rout, 'our horse all cowardly, the country from Berwick to York in the power of the Scot, a universal affright in all men, a general disaffection to the king's service, none sensible of his dishonour.'[192]

A muster after the battle showed that Charles had 17,383 men still in arms. Although desertion and disbandment took their toll, fresh troops continued to arrive, and the army remained close to this strength well into 1641.[193] It seemed likely that they would still be needed, for as Strafford insisted, 'it was not for the king's honour to treat with rebels'.[194] Some in the royal camp recommended a counterattack, on the grounds that they would 'rather venture our profit than willfully yield up our honour'.[195] Courtiers still

---

[187] Staffordshire Record Office, Notebook of Richard Dyott, D.661/11/1/5.

[188] Cambridge University Library, Ms. Mn. 1. 45 (Baker transcripts), 99.

[189] HMC, *10th Report, Appendix, Part IV* (1885, reissued 1906), 393.

[190] HMC, *Report on Manuscripts in Various Collections* (1903), ii. 256; Berkshire Record Office, microfilm 605 (Trumbull Mss. Miscellaneous Correspondence, vol. xx, John Thorogood to George Rudolph Weckherlin, 8 September 1640).

[191] HMC, *The Manuscripts of His Grace the Duke of Rutland, G.C.B., Preserved at Belvoir Castle* (1888), i. 523.

[192] Bodleian Library, Additional Ms. C. 259, f. 149 (Beaumont letters, transcribed 1801).

[193] Rushworth, *Historical Collections of Private Proceedings of State*, iii. 1241–52; *CSPD 1640–41*, 438, 513; Jansson (ed.), *Proceedings in the Opening Session of the Long Parliament . . . Vol. 3*, 416.

[194] Lismore Mss., vol. xxi, National Register of Archives, vol. 20594/15, 861.

[195] Cambridge University Library, Ms. Mn. 1. 45 (Baker transcripts), 107.

believed that the King was 'resolved to give [the Scots] battle before they came to York'.[196]

Fears abounded in England that the Covenanters had not finished their advance, that they might soon enter Yorkshire, and might even strike south against the capital.[197] A second Scottish army was said to be massing to enter Westmorland and Cumberland.[198] England needed to be ready 'in case of disaster', wrote Secretary Windebank on 1 September, as if there had not been disaster enough. Yorkshire was braced for conflict, and Bishop Towers of Peterborough fretted that his see was in the Scottish line of march: 'We are here in their road if God be not pleased to put his hook in their nostrils.'[199] Hull was to be strengthened against Scottish attack, and Windebank proposed moving the gunpowder stored in the Tower to the south side of the Thames to protect it in case the Scots reached London. Anticipating the worst, plans were even afoot to prepare Portsmouth, on the Channel coast, as a final defensive refuge for the King, with links by sea to France.[200] However, with 'an army of 50,000 in Artois and Picady, and a fleet not far off', some thought the French more likely to invade than to provide succour.[201] The trained bands of the Cinque Ports were put on alert, 'either for defence of the ports or for the public safety of the realm'.[202] Military defences in Wales were hastily made ready in the face of 'dangerous and perillous times'.[203] The Scots with their 'great and puissant army' had already subjugated north-east England, 'and intend without all doubt to march forward until they shall be repelled', so the Earl of Arundel wrote to the Cinque Ports on 22 September.[204] Only with the Treaty of Ripon (21 October 1640) were these fears allayed, when the Scots were promised £850 a day until their armies could be sent home.

---

[196] Sir Thomas Jermyn to Sir Robert Crane, Bodleian Library, Oxford, Tanner Ms. 65, f. 35.

[197] Huntington Library, Ms. El. 7860, 24 September 1640; HMC, *10th Report, Appendix, Part VI* (1887), 137; Jack Binns (ed.), *The Memoirs and Memorials of Sir Hugh Cholmley of Whitby 1600–1657* (Yorkshire Archaeological Society Record Series, vol. cliii, 2000), 103.

[198] Staffordshire Record Office, Notebook of Richard Dyott, D.661/11/1/5.

[199] Bishop Towers to Sir John Lambe, 2 September 1640, *CSPD 1640–41*, 6. Cf. 2 Kings 19: 28 and Isaiah 37: 29, 'Because thy rage against me and thy tumult is come up into mine ears, therefore I will put my hook in thy nose, and my bridle in thy lips, and I will turn thee back by the way by which thou camest.'   [200] *CSPD 1640–41*, 2, 4, 6, 9.

[201] HMC, *10th Report, Appendix, Part IV*, 393.

[202] East Sussex Record Office, Rye Letters, 47/133; East Kent Archives, Sandwich Borough Muniments, Mayor's Letter Book 1639–44, Sa/C1, ff. 36v–37.

[203] National Library of Wales, Llanfair-Brynodel letters, C28 and 29, 7 September and 31 October 1640.

[204] East Kent Archives, Sandwich Borough Muniments, Mayor's Letter Book 1639–44, Sa/C1, f. 37.

WOE TO YORKSHIRE

After the turning point of Newburn the English troops were no better organized or disciplined than before. Describing their condition in mid-September, Thomas Gower found 'no real preparation that I can see'.[205] More troops were mustered in Leicestershire in September, 'to prevent the malice and ill intentions of such rebels as are entered into this kingdom'.[206] The men of the Cumberland trained bands were summoned to a general muster at Carlisle, instructed to bring digging tools as well as weapons.[207] As if to emphasize the continuing military emergency, Sir Jacob Astley ordered a month of live-fire exercises in Yorkshire that coincided with the opening of the Long Parliament. One wonders who was most impressed: the soldiers themselves or their Yorkshire neighbours, the Scots commissioners heading south, or the political grandees gathering at Westminster?[208]

For the next ten months the King's army remained languishing in Yorkshire, waiting for redeployment, waiting to be demobilized, and waiting to get paid. With the Scots occupying the northeast, there were 'two armies in the very bosom of this kingdom', as the King himself reminded Parliament in January 1641.[209] Bills for their maintenance came to £50,000 a month.[210] The troops were in 'a miserable condition of want', complained Sir Thomas Roe in November 1640, with little to eat besides bread and water. Observers feared 'misdemeanours' from an army whose morale was lower than ever. 'They have had no pay and are enforced to commit insolencies', reported Sir John Hotham later in the month.[211] By December it was said that Yorkshire 'had suffered more by the insolencies of the king's army' than Durham under occupation by the Scots.[212]

Newswriters reported of the army, 'that they commit many spoils and disorders about the city of York.'[213] Yorkshire parishes complained again about the burden of provisioning.[214] The village of Fountains, by the abbey,

---

[205] HMC, *Manuscripts of His Grace the Duke of Rutland*, i. 523.

[206] Helen Stocks and W. H. Stevenson (eds.), *Records of the Borough of Leicestershire...* *1603–1688* (Cambridge, 1923), 300.

[207] HMC, *10th Report, Appendix, Part IV*, 274–5.

[208] Staffordshire Record Office, Dartmouth Papers, cited in Peter Edwards, *Dealing in Death: The Arms Trade and the British Civil Wars, 1638–52* (Stroud, Gloucestershire, 2000), 91.

[209] Jansson (ed.), *Proceedings in the Opening Session of the Long Parliament... Vol. 2*, 264.

[210] Jansson (ed.), *Proceeding in the Opening Session of the Long Parliament... Vol. 1*, 133.

[211] Ibid., 216, 218, 26, 277, 279.

[212] Ibid., 459; 'Answers to the complaynt and grievances given in by the Bishoprick and County of Durham, County of Northumberland and some of Newcastle alleaged committedd by ye Scottish army. 5 October 1640', Northamptonshire Record Office, Finch-Hatton Ms. FH 581 (another copy in Huntington Library Ms. El. 7742).

[213] Huntington Library, Ms. El. 7860, 24 September 1640. [214] HMC, *3rd Report*, 83.

billeted nine soldiers, four in the constable's house.[215] The garrison port of Hull complained repeatedly of the 'great ruins' caused by billeted regiments.[216] Communities were expected to find not just food and shelter for the soldiers but also blankets and sheets.[217] Writing from Yorkshire in January 1641, Edward Verney feared that 'unless there be some speedy course taken for payment, you may well expect to hear that all our soldiers are in a mutiny, to the ruin of the country, for they are notable sheep stealers already.' Hungry, cold, angry, and unpaid, the troops were ready to mutiny, 'and then woe be to the poor county of Yorkshire'.[218] On 7 January Lord General Northumberland warned fellow peers that 'some ill consequence' might befall among the army in the north for want of pay.[219]

A new year's brawl among soldiers at York resulted in Sgt. James Pilbean's death from a sword.[220] A widely circulated 'letter from York to a friend at London', which survives in Nehemiah Wallington's compendium, blamed the soldiers for 'most fearful blasphemies, horrible thefts, and most barbarous and invidious adulteries and ravishings'.[221] So disruptive was 'the great disorder' of soldiers billeted around Helmesley in January 1641 that the North Riding Quarter Sessions had to be postponed.[222] Other crimes committed by soldiers were referred to the Northern Assizes.[223] Commanders reported on 'the calamitous condition of those parts'.[224] But such insolencies could only be expected of 'an army neither paid nor punished', declared their treasurer Sir William Uvedale.[225]

Poor Yorkshire groaned under the burden of an abusive soldiery for most of 1641. Observers wrote of the English army as 'a threatening cloud' and 'a charge and terror to this kingdom'.[226] Thomas Stockdale complained to Lord Ferdinando Fairfax on 5 March 1641 that 'the insolency of the soldiers is such as

---

[215] Martyn Bennett, *The Civil Wars Experienced: Britain and Ireland, 1638–1661* (2000), 20.

[216] I. E. Ryder, 'The Seizure of Hull and its Magazine, January 1642', *Yorkshire Archaeological Journal*, 61 (1989), 141–2.

[217] Jansson (ed.), *Proceedings in the Opening Session of the Long Parliament . . . Vol. 1*, 463.

[218] Edmund Verney to Ralph Verney, 15 and 24 January 1640/1, HMC, *7th Report* (1879), 435. See also Ronan Bennett, 'War and Disorder: Policing the Soldiery in Civil War Yorkshire', in Fissel (ed.), *War and Government in Britain, 1598–1650*, 251–3.

[219] HMC, *Report on the Manuscripts of the Duke of Buccleuch and Queensberry*, (The Montague papers, 2nd series, 1926), iii. 406; Jansson (ed.), *Proceedings in the Opening Session of the Long Parliament . . . Volume 2*, 33.   [220] PRO, ASSI 45/1/3/9 and 10.

[221] British Library, Sloan Ms. 922, f. 129.

[222] J. C. Atkinson (ed.), *Quarter Sessions Records [1634–47]* (North Riding Record Society, vol. iv, 1886), 187.   [223] PRO, ASSI 45/1/3/12, /15, /25, /42.

[224] Jansson (ed.), *Proceedings in the Opening Session of the Long Parliament . . . Vol. 2*, 409.   [225] *CSPD 1640–41*, 417.

[226] Willson Havelock Coates (ed.), *The Journal of Sir Simonds D'Ewes from the First Recess of the Long Parliament to the Withdrawal of the King from London* (New Haven and London, 1942), 34.

they do not only abusively use all persons whatsoever, and beat, affront and vilify them; but also by stealth and by open force and robbery they take all men's goods and consume them as they please.'[227] Pamphlets spoke of the pillage of poultry, food, and cattle, and abuse of the countrymen's daughters, servants, and wives.[228] One group of soldiers attached themselves to a renegade cleric, Christopher Fisher, and violently rescued him on his way to York castle. Fisher exhibited further contempt for the law when he told the magistrate, Charles Tankerd, 'that he was more fitter for a swine-herd than for a justice of peace'.[229]

Reports from the north spoke repeatedly of disorders amongst the military. 'The insolencies of the army daily increase', said a communiqué of February 1641. 'The foot officers are discontented', warned another in April.[230] English soldiers at Berwick were said to be 'dangerous and desperate', protesting, 'we will not be slaves to serve, but will be maintained like men.'[231] The 'want and distress' of the army portended 'misery and distraction' to the kingdom, Francis Gamull warned his father-in-law in May.[232] 'The unruly soldiers' of Yorkshire cried, 'from the parliament and the devil deliver us', and threatened 'money or mutiny', according to Thomas Gower.[233] There was 'great confusion' in the army in June 1641 when yet another captain was 'barbarously murdered'.[234] Soldiers in Sir Thomas Glemham's regiment hacked one of their officers to pieces 'and would not let him be buried', resisting attempts to control them by martial law.[235]

For much of this time 'An act for the relief of the king's army in the northern parts' was working its way through Parliament. Its passage was accompanied by reports of 'distress' and 'disorder', 'miseries' and 'discontent'.[236] In January 1641 the money was eight weeks late. Some funds arrived in March, but by the time that the legislation was almost complete in June army pay was five months in arrears.[237] Money from the new poll tax of 1641 was

---

[227] G. W. Johnson (ed.), *The Fairfax Correspondence. Memoirs of the Reign of Charles the First* (2 vols., 1848), i. 203; British Library, Add. Ms. 18979, f. 36.

[228] *Newes from the North. Or, A Dialogue betwixt David Dammeeslash a Souldier, and Walter Wheeler, a rich Northerne Farmer* (1641).

[229] Atkinson (ed.), *Quarter Sessions Records [1634–47]*, 204.

[230] *CSPD 1640–41*, 473, 531. See also Bodleian Library, Oxford, Tanner Ms. 65, f. 283; Tanner Ms. 66, ff. 55, 63.

[231] Maija Jansson (ed.), *Proceedings in the Opening Session of the Long Parliament ... Volume 4: 19 April–5 June 1641* (Rochester, NY, 2003), 68–70.

[232] British Library, Harley Ms. 2081, f. 94.

[233] Cambridge University Library, Ms. Mn. 1. 45 (Baker transcripts), 33.

[234] *CSPD 1641–43*, 8.

[235] Cambridge University Library, Ms. Mn. 1. 45 (Baker transcripts), 33.

[236] Jansson (ed.), *Proceedings in the Opening Session of the Long Parliament ... Vol. 2*, 78, 99, 140, 230, 613, 629.

[237] Ibid., 229, 828; 'A Diary of ye Lords in Parliament' [Bishop Warner], Hertfordshire Record Office, XII.B.37, f. 5; *CSPD 1640–41*, 440, 499, 502; *CSPD 1641–43*, 22.

specifically intended 'for disbanding the armies and settling the peace of the two kingdoms, England and Scotland'.[238] Sir Gilbert Pickering remarked that the soldiers were 'unwilling to disband any till they have a considerable sum', predicting that the attendant financial strain 'will in a short snap lay a burden upon this kingdom which it must needs sink under'.[239] The Scots themselves threatened to move further south if they were not given their share of the money.[240]

Idle, ill-disciplined, and unpaid, the army in Yorkshire seemed ready to turn against its southern masters. In March 1641 alarming reports reached London of 'disturbance in our army in the north for want of pay'. Thomas Knyvett commented, 'this is feared will be great affliction to the country, for soldiers will not starve'.[241] The army was said to be suffering from 'great necessity and want' that caused 'tumultuous and mutinous disorders'.[242] In April 'certain reformados in the king's army in the north' petitioned Parliament for four months arrears. (Reformados were officers without command, whose company had been disbanded or reformed.) Thomas Stockdale explained that the troops were 'all fearful of disbanding without pay'. John Barry warned, 'we shall have trouble at home, our own army is ready to mutiny'.[243]

Many of these problems could be solved by money. Thomas Stockdale told Lord Fairfax on 10 April that news that Parliament had raised £120,000 for military arrears 'hath settled those fluent humours of the soldiery, and dispersed those mists which the country feared would have fallen upon them in bitter showers. For certainly, this kingdom is yet of such a frame and constitution as cannot admit of armies nor war within it, without hazard of destruction.'[244] Yet there were renewed reasons to fear 'the present inclination of the soldiery' and their readiness to interfere in politics. Stockdale warned Fairfax on 30 April 1641 that 'every day their affection to the Lord Strafford's deliverance and safety doth appear most evidently; and it is the more remarkable because it is not many months since he was scarcely beloved or valued by any of them.'[245] Here, perhaps, were seeds of the Army Plots, as well as the process that turned some of the nation's iconoclastic soldiers into the King's Cavaliers.

---

[238] PRO, SP16/481/70. [239] Bedfordshire and Luton Archives, St John Papers, J. 1387.
[240] National Library of Wales, Wynn Papers, no. 1682 (microfilm), Maurice Wynn to Owen Wynn, 27 April 1641, reporting that the Scots were scouting a passage into Yorkshire.
[241] HMC, *Report on Manuscripts in Various Collections* (1903), ii. 262.
[242] House of Lords Record Office, Main Papers, 22 March 1641.
[243] Jansson (ed.), *Proceedings in the Opening Session of the Long Parliament . . . Vol. 3*, 547; British Library, Add. Ms. 11045, vol. v., f . 138; Johnson (ed.), *Fairfax Correspondence*, ii. 112; HMC, *Report on the Manuscripts of the Earl of Egmont* (i. part 1, 1905), 132.
[244] Johnson (ed.), *Fairfax Correspondence*, ii. 101, 102.
[245] British Library, Add. Ms. 18979, f. 76.

It was in these months of languor, rather than earlier on the march, when recruits and pressed men became more thoroughly acculturated to army life. Arrayed in regiments rather than travelling companies, and subject to training and discipline, they began to absorb military values. But they did not necessarily become more tractable. Anticipating some of the problems of 1647, when another idle army turned against its masters, the soldiers of 1641 were also frustrated, disaffected, and potentially dangerous. They were by no means insulated from the political crisis in London, and could not be counted upon to follow directives from Westminster. Although some of them had shown hostility to popish officers, and had acted violently against communion rails, their religious propensities were largely unknown and unstable. Some were Cavaliers in the making, and a few of their officers had opened dangerous lines of communication with the court, which would come to light in the Army Plots.[246]

The House of Commons received intelligence at the beginning of May 1641 that 'a bad understanding of the parliament [was] bred in our English army', and that its officers were ready to rise in arms against them.[247] In June several officers were examined 'for suspicion of high treason as having a design to bring up our army southward, to have mastered us here'.[248] Colonel Goring confessed to some knowledge of 'a design against the parliament, by working the army against it', but deemed such plotting unlawful because 'it belongs to an army to maintain, not to contrive acts of state'.[249] Some members of Parliament feared that the Queen might become the focus for 'persons ill affected and discontented, who may have some plot to make use of the soldiers now to be disbanded'.[250] Even before the civil war, the civil authorities had created a military monster that they did not know how to tame.

Disorders within the army continued to cause alarm throughout the spring and summer of 1641, with more reports of attacks against officers. A pamphlet entitled *An Uprore in the North* described a military 'rebellion' at Hull in which Captain Edward Walbrucke was killed by his men because 'he exercised tyranny over them, and they inhumanity over him'.[251] Thomas Stockdale reported in June that dissident soldiers 'have murdered captain Wythers at Hull and taken the block-house to secure themselves till they constrain a pardon for their barbarous fact'. Elements of Lord Newport's regiment

---

[246] Conrad Russell, 'The First Army Plot of 1641', in idem, *Unrevolutionary England, 1603–1642* (1990), 281–302; Fissel, *English Warfare 1511–1642*, 295.

[247] 'A Diary of ye Lords in Parliament' [Bishop Warner], Hertfordshire Record Office, XII.B.37, f. 68.   [248] Buckinghamshire Record Office, Hill Family Letters (Transcripts) D 192/8/1b.

[249] [George Goring], *The Declaration of Colonel Goring Upon his Examination, touching the late intended Conspiracies against the State* (1641), 3, 6.

[250] 'A Diary of ye Lords in Parliament' [Bishop Warner], Hertfordshire Record Office, XII.B.37, f. 97.   [251] H.T., *An Uprore in the North, At Hvll* (1641), title page, 4.

threatened 'they would come and pull down the town' unless they were paid.[252] Parliament was in receipt of 'a menacing letter' from some in the army, 'full of mutinous, discontented and obscure language', prompting Lord Saville to call its authors 'a rabble of the base multitude'. More soberly, Thomas Jenyson reported to Sir Roland St John, 'the House of Commons thought it derogatory from the honour of the parliament that the representative body of the commonwealth should fear the menacing threats of any army.'[253] Such sentiments would be aired again in 1647, and in many of the years that followed.

The formal peace treaty with Scotland in September 1641 finally allowed the troops to be stood down. Their numbers had been shrinking over the summer as various regiments were disbanded, but the process went on slowly 'for want of money'.[254] A correspondent at York opined that if only the money arrived the army could be discharged and 'all manner of doubts and fears will be taken away'.[255] Assize judges had orders 'to prevent and suppress any disorders or outrages of the soldiers which might otherwise happen upon their disbanding', while local officials were reminded 'to punish wandering soldiers'.[256] Rather belatedly on 22 October the Crown issued a proclamation 'for the securing of the peace and safety of his majesty's subjects against outrages and disorders by any that were soldiers of his majesty's army, lately disbanded'.[257]

The roads south from Yorkshire were filled with discharged soldiers, stragglers, and deserters. Along the way they begged and stole, or turned to local authorities for relief. The constables of Upton, Nottinghamshire, for example, gave travelling soldiers twopence apiece so long as they were well behaved.[258] Leicestershire braced for the southward flow in August 1641, taking 'special care to prevent and suppress any disorders or outrages of the soldiers which might otherwise happen upon their disbanding'. Justices and constables were ordered to set 'sufficient watches' to contain 'any such disorders or violations of the public peace of the realm'.[259] Cornish soldiers making their way home from 'the northern peaceable wars' once again distinguished themselves

---

[252] Johnson (ed.), *Fairfax Correspondence* ii. 112.
[253] Bedfordshire and Luton Archives, St John Papers, J. 1384.
[254] *Calendar of Wynne Papers*, 273; Staffordshire Record Office, Leveson Letter Book, D.868/2/31; Bennett, *Civil Wars Experienced*, 21.
[255] University of Hull, Brynmor Jones Library, Hotham Papers, DDHO/1/6, Arthur Ingram to Sir John Hotham, 9 September 1641.
[256] *Privy Council Registers* (1968), xii. f. 179, August 1641; British Library, Nicholas Papers, Egerton Ms. 2533, f. 129.
[257] Larkin (ed.), *Stuart Royal Proclamations . . . 1625–1646*, 750–1.
[258] Bennett (ed.), *A Nottinghamshire Village in War and Peace*, 2–5.
[259] Leicestershire Record Office, Borough Hall Papers, 1640–1645, BR II/18/22/87.

by despoiling church fonts and organs, 'with many other disorders'. The Cornish magistrate Sir William Courtney thought that 'the honour of the state is engaged to see those bold disorders punished, or else greater oppression will certainly follow on men of the best ranks if it be not prevented in time, for I have seen the disposition of men that have arms and strength that the many times makes themselves master of their officers.'[260]

VETERANS

Considerable political and financial effort had gone into assembling and organizing the army. But there were also significant costs associated with its disbandment. Distressed veterans needed relief, and maimed soldiers and their dependents demanded pensions. Charles I's northern wars incurred substantial social costs, not all of which could be met by money. Even at the best of times the resettlement of an army caused hardship and confusion, but both the scale and the circumstances of the demobilization of 1641 brought additional problems.

The soldiers were released from military service into a society embroiled in a revolution. In the year following the defeat at Newburn, England's political and religious environment had been transformed. Parliament had accomplished a constitutional coup, while the traditional authority of the Crown was in tatters. The Earl of Strafford was executed, the Archbishop of Canterbury imprisoned. Episcopacy was embattled, the prayer book was openly disparaged. The Act of Uniformity had become unenforceable, and radical sectarians had found their voice. The collapse of press censorship allowed unprecedented numbers of texts onto the market, and radical conversations were in the air. Army veterans who returned to their homes might find their parishes in uproar, their communities divided, their families impoverished, and themselves no longer welcome. Demobilized veterans, hardened and embittered after long months in camp, and perhaps also possessed of dangerous ideas, caused almost as much trouble as soldiers in arms.

After the army was disbanded most of the soldiers set out for home. Some returned late, with physical or psychological scars, and some never came back at all. Eleanor Vaure told Shrewsbury magistrates in October 1641 that she was married to John Davis two years earlier, but 'knoweth not whether he be living or not because he went for a pressed soldier the last press and not returned'.[261]

---

[260] Worth (ed.), *The Buller Papers*, 48.
[261] Shropshire Record Office, Shrewsbury Borough Records, 3365/2240, no. 33.

Since a goodly proportion of the pressed men were marginal to begin with, and may have been dispatched by their communities to be rid of them, their former neighbours were not all overjoyed to see them again. Returning servicemen faced exclusion because they placed a burden on parish resources, and perhaps also because they were thought to have been degraded by their recent military experience. In the West Riding of Yorkshire, for example, John Wilson of Rastrick claimed that after his time in the army his former neighbours 'do refuse to let [him] inhabit and continue in that township, contrary to equity and conscience'.[262] William Wright and his wife lost their settlement rights at Rockliffe, 'he being a soldier in this last expedition into the north'.[263] John Stringer of Woodlesford told the court that he was 'a poor impotent man, and having been impressed for his majesty's service, hath received divers hurts, insomuch that he is past all labour or getting his living'.[264] The magistrates intervened to order the parish authorities to grant these men residence, to find them work or supply relief, or to help them find or build a house.

Similarly in Hampshire, George Elderfield of Bentworth, pressed in 1640 to serve 'in the northern parts of this kingdom', returned to his wife's home at Herriard, where he was considered likely to be a charge on the rates. Neither parish wanted him, but the Hampshire sessions decided in October 1641 that he should be settled at Bentworth.[265]

The Nottinghamshire sessions ordered the parish of Mysall to provide habitation and work for Isabel Chamberlain after her husband was pressed for a soldier 'in the north parts'. Isabel had followed her husband, journeying into Yorkshire to see him, only to discover on her return that the parish denied her residence. She was forced to wander and beg, she said, until the court intervened to secure her right of settlement.[266] Veterans who were denied settlement and denied relief joined the army of vagrants and beggars, like Robert Vickers, who was cited before the Middlesex magistrates in August 1641 'for begging money of divers persons as a soldier'.[267]

Claims and orders for disability pensions became a common feature of quarter sessions records on the eve of the English civil war. Every county had its treasurer for maimed soldiers, and the campaigns of 1640 and 1641 brought increasing pressure upon the public purse.[268] The courts heard many haunting

[262] Barber (ed.), 'West Riding Sessions Rolls', 396.   [263] Ibid., 398.

[264] Ibid., 397. For more examples see Bennett, *Civil Wars Experienced*, 19–20.

[265] Hampshire Record Office, Q1/2, 208.

[266] Nottinghamshire Archives, C/QSMI/11 (January 1641).

[267] London Metropolitan Archives, MJ/SR/902.

[268] Staffordshire Record Office, Q/SO/5, 80; Cheshire Record Office, Quarter Sessions Books 1640–1643, QJB 1/6, f. 23v; Quarter Sessions Rolls, QJF/70/1, f. 21

stories. Thomas Maris of Salford, Warwickshire, for example, was pressed for the northern service and 'lost his thumb and forefinger in the discharging of a musket', thereby becoming a burden on local ratepayers.[269] In Sussex, the magistrates authorized forty shillings a year for John Kemp, 'a maimed soldier heretofore pressed out of this county'.[270]

Certificates of discharge in the files of the Wiltshire quarter sessions describe severely wounded soldiers 'altogether disabled for further service'. One of them, Thomas Snooke, a tradesman's son, was 'pressed for a soldier for service in the northern parts against the Scots', and was so badly wounded that part of his skull was removed. Discharged as 'insufficient for his majesty's service', he sought relief at the Wiltshire Sessions in January 1641. Another, John Blundell, told the court in May that he 'was pressed as a soldier...and served under Sir William Ogle, colonel, in his majesty's service against the Scots, where in a skirmish about Newcastle [he] received a great hurt in his right leg, whereupon he is utterly disabled to serve any longer.' Now, 'in great want, need, and misery', he petitioned for public assistance.[271]

In July 1641 Devon magistrates awarded forty shillings a year to Ellis Boyse who 'being pressed for his majesty's service in the north...received a lame hip in the said service'.[272] In October the Cheshire quarter sessions heard requests from Ralph Jackson, pressed from Macclesfield, who was wounded in the knee, and from John Moore of Sale, who had been made lame by a musket. Each had hungry dependents, and neither was fit for work. Richard Marron, once a labourer at Winham, was impressed for the Scottish war and lost a hand at Carlisle, becoming unable to live without relief.[273] John Griffith of Pattingham, Staffordshire, had been a servant when he was impressed as a waggoner 'to carry ammunition for the northern expedition' where, unfortunately, he was lamed in the leg 'by a stroke of a trooper's horse'. He lived, he told the court, 'in great misery, languishing in pain and penury', and in April 1642 was awarded five pounds from the county funds.[274] Seeking to avail himself of resources of this kind, Randall Mees, 'a wandering person' from London, was gaoled at Exeter in June 1641 for 'pretending himself to be a maimed soldier'.[275]

---

[269] S. C. Ratcliff and H. C. Johnson (eds.), *Warwick County Records, Vol. II. Quarter Sessions Order Book, Michaelmas, 1637, to Epiphany, 1650* (Warwick, 1936), 104.

[270] East Sussex Record Office, QR/E/53/132.

[271] B. Howard Cunnington (ed.), *Records of the County of Wilts. Being Extracts from the Quarter Sessions Great Rolls of the Seventeenth Century* (Devizes, 1932), 322–3; Wiltshire Record Office, Quarter Sessions Great Roll, A1/110 Easter 1641, 188; A1/110 Trinity 1641, 208.

[272] Devon Record Office, Quarter Session Order Book 1640–1651, Q/S 1/8, nf.

[273] Cheshire Record Office, QJF 70/3, ff. 25, 33; QJF 71/1, f. 26.

[274] Staffordshire Record Office, Q/SO/5, 117; Q/SR/250, 11.

[275] Devon Record Office, Exeter Quarter Sessions Order Book, 1630–1642, f. 365v.

London became a magnet for wanderers from the army, where 'disorderly persons and disbanded soldiers' added to the volatile social mix. Beggars on the streets of the capital included newcomers purporting to be army veterans.[276] Others straggled into London, 'pretending that they have not had their pay, which the officers affirm the contrary'.[277] Members of Parliament became concerned that 'the confluence of soldiers...about this town' would add to the urban tumults, and there were many reports of 'dispersed persons' the worse for drink who were making play with their swords.[278]

Popular pamphlets satirized the soldiers 'late-coming to London...from the camp in the north, at the disbanding of the army' as penniless rogues, bent only on drinking, whoring, and petty crime. One publication of 1641 entitled *The Brothers of the Blade: Answerable to the Sisters of the Scaberd, Or, A Dialogue betweene two Hot-spurres of the Times* featured Sergeant Sliceman, who had served in the Low Countries, in discourse with Corporal Dammee, a veteran of the northern campaign.[279] Another pamphlet associated the returning soldier with pimps and pickpockets, imagining him turning 'ballad singer, which I am informed is at this present a very thriving trade'.[280] A third reported 'robberies' and 'other outrages' committed by lately discharged troopers who had turned highway-men.[281]

A proclamation of 22 October 1641 noted the 'insolencies and outrages' done by disbanded soldiers around London and Westminster, and directed them to return to their home parishes and lawful vocations. Rather than this having its desired effect, it is likely that ex-servicemen added force to the politicized mobs of November and December 1641 who were radicalizing the revolution. Office-holders from mayors and sheriffs down to constables and headboroughs attempted to move the veterans on, but many simply disregarded the authorities.[282] Without employment or strong ties in their home communities, there was little motivation and scant reward for these former pressed men to follow the law. As William Drake warned, in a speech prepared for Parliament, their experience of 'rapine and spoil' made many of these

---

[276] London Metropolitan Archives, Sessions Roll, MJ/SR/902/59.

[277] HMC, *12th Report, Manuscripts of the Earl Cowper*, ii. 293.

[278] Coates (ed.), *Journal of Sir Simonds D'Ewes from the first Recess of the Long Parliament to the Withdrawal of the King from London*, 12, 34.

[279] *The Brothers of the Blade: Answerable to the Sisters of the Scaberd, Or, A Dialogue betweene two Hot-spurres of the Times* (1641), title page.

[280] *Newes from the North*, sigs. A4–A4v.

[281] *A Discovery of many, great, and Bloudy Robberies: Committed of Late by Disolute and Evill affected Troopers* (1641), sigs. A2–A4. For the robbery of the post in October 1641, see *CSPD 1641–43*, 134 and *Privy Council Registers*, xii. 183, 189.

[282] Larkin (ed.), *Stuart Royal Proclamations...1625–1646*, 750–1.

soldiers 'unwilling...to tie themselves to order and industry'.[283] An unknown number of veterans were reabsorbed into the new armies prepared to put down the Irish rebellion. And many more, along with thousands more civilians, were swept up in the rival mobilizations of 1642 as the King and Parliament readied for civil war.

CAVALIERS

Opportunist adventurers and veterans of the European wars began showing up in London at the end of the 1630s 'in hope of warlike employment' in Charles I's British campaigns.[284] In social rank and military experience, these officers were very different from the militia men and pressed recruits who made up the rank and file. Some were professional soldiers with experience in Irish and continental campaigns. Some, like the ill-fated lieutenants Mohun and Eures, were Roman Catholics. Many were younger sons of gentlemen. Even before there were 'roundheads' to oppose them, some of these men became known as 'cavaliers'. In April 1639, as the first Bishops' War gathered momentum, Lord John Poulett told his Bristol kinsman that the streets of York were 'full of cavaliers'.[285] Sir John Suckling repeated Lord Loudon's self-definition, 'that they were cavaliers that studied not the cause, but came for honour and love to the king'.[286] The word still had positive connotations, as in Baynham Throckmorton's commendation of Sir James Thynne in February 1640 for behaving himself 'like a cavalier and a man of honour'.[287]

To their detriment, Cavalier officers also became known as swash-buckling braggarts and anti-puritan bullies. They included the likes of Captain Watts, who pledged the honour of the King and railed against 'puritans' in the Green Dragon tavern in Bishopsgate in August 1640. Tankards flew and Watts drew his sword after telling the company 'he had that day seen the king and kissed his hand', and accusing less respectful diners of being 'puritans'.[288] An engraving of 1641 depicted overdressed wastrel officers as 'roaring boys' and 'hot-spur cavaliers'.[289] By 1642 Cavaliers were reputed as 'nothing but

---

[283] Huntington Library, Ms. HM 55603, 'William Drake's Journal, 1631–42', f. 42.
[284] *CSPD 1640*, 92.
[285] J. H. Bettey (ed.), *Calendar of the Correspondence of the Smyth Family of Ashton Court 1548–1642* (Bristol Record Society, vol. xxxv, 1982), 145.
[286] HMC, *4th Report* (1874), Appendix, 294.
[287] Bettey (ed.), *Calendar of the Correspondence of the Smyth Family of Ashton Court 1548–1642*, 152.   [288] PRO, SP16/466/116.
[289] *The Sucklington Faction* (1641).

the desperate sons of furious faction and fawning favour', most 'busy and daring' in the north.[290] Anyone in London 'with a tilting feather, a flaunting periwig, buff doublet, scarlet hose, and a sword as big as a lath', who 'looked as like a Dammee newly come out of the north as could be imagined', might be taken to be a Cavalier.[291]

An archetypal Cavalier was Col. Thomas Lunsford, who led the Somerset men in the second Bishops' War. Described by Lord Dorset as 'a young out-law' and a 'swaggering ruffian', Lunsford was aged thirty in 1640. Following a disorderly march north, in which he was said to have killed men in self-defence, he gave distinguished service at the battle of Newburn when he tried to keep discipline under fire. He became Charles I's controversial lieutenant of the Tower in December 1641, and almost started the civil war in January 1642 by trying to rally forces for the King at Kingston.[292] Another was 'young Mr. Sawyer', one of the King's guard when he came to arrest the five mem-bers, who recommended Catholicism to a London citizen at the point of a knife.[293]

Towards the end of 1641 a volunteer Cavalier militia began to gather about the King as 'many officers of the late-disbanded army . . . offered themselves for a guard to his majesty's person'.[294] Observers remarked around the turn of the year on 'the multitude of gentry and soldiers who flock to the court . . . armed with swords and pistols'.[295] It was these men who encouraged the King against Parliament, and some of them accompanied him on his failed attempt to arrest the five members. (See Chapters 17 and 18.)

By the spring of 1642 Charles I's peripatetic court was attracting a following of Cavaliers who were lobbying for places and commissions.[296] At York they included 'two hundred blue ribbons' (not to be confused with the Scottish 'blue bonnets') who used their muscle to intimidate local puritans. Collisions between Cavaliers and Roundheads became common, anticipating and per-haps even precipitating the hostilities of the civil war.[297] 'If this be the begin-ning of their behaviour before they can be sure of the event, man may easily

---

[290] *A Remonstrance of Londons Occurrences* (1642), sigs. A2–A2v.

[291] *Old Newes Newly Revived* (1641), sig. A3. See also 'Agamemnon Shaglock VanDammee', *The Speech of a Cavaleere to his Comrades* (1642); *The Wicked Resolution of the Cavaliers* (1642); and [George Lawrence], *The Debauched Cavalier: or the English Midianite* (1642).

[292] Basil Morgan, 'Lunsford, Sir Thomas', *Oxford Dictionary of National Biography* (Oxford, 2004).

[293] HMC, *Report on the Manuscripts of Lord Montague of Beaulieu* (1900), 141, 147.

[294] Edward Hyde, Earl of Clarendon, *The History of the Rebellion and Civil Wars in England Begun in the Year 1641*, ed. W. Dunn Macray (6 vols., Oxford, 1888) i. 456, 485.

[295] *CSPD 1641–43*, 242.

[296] John Ward to William Morton, 14 February 1641/2, British Library, Add. Ms. 33936, f. 261.

[297] Johnson (ed.), *Fairfax Correspondence*, ii. 375, 390, 391.

judge what the end will be if they prevail', wrote John Hampden of the King's adherents in July 1642.[298] The following months saw many more diatribes against 'those malignant and blood-sucking cannibals, the cavaliers . . . whose name is more cause of quarrel for us than the people themselves'.[299] Charles I's peaceable kingdom had become horribly warlike, with standing, contending, and barely controllable armies.

[298] University of Hull, Brynmor Jones Library, Hotham Papers, DDHO/1/7, John Hampden to Sir John Hotham, 18 July 1642.
[299] *Nocturnall Occurrences Or, Deeds of Darknesse: Committed, By the Caveleers* (1642), sigs. A2–A2v.

5

The People's Fury, the Lambeth Disturbances, and the Insurrection of May 1640

The parliament that met on 13 April 1640 was the first to sit since March 1629. Its dissolution three weeks later on 5 May made it one of the shortest on record. The dissolution triggered a shockwave of disturbances and recriminations, focused, perhaps unfairly, on the figure of Archbishop William Laud. Laud was blamed for the Scottish war, which necessitated the parliament, and was widely regarded as 'the prime cause on earth' of the compounding distemper of the kingdom.[1]

The high political history of this episode has been intensively studied, though questions remain about the roles of the Archbishop of Canterbury and the Earl of Strafford, as well as the King and the Queen. My purpose in this chapter is to examine the immediate consequences of the dissolution, particularly in the area around London.[2] The events of May 1640 stretched the sinews of the Caroline regime, and showed the body politic beset by distractions and distempers. Wise men knew from recent experience that 'breakings of parliaments makes dangerous wounds in the body politic, and if these splinters be not pulled out with a gentle hand we may hereafter despair of cure'.[3]

---

[1] Huntington Library, Ms. El. 7001; Bodleian Library, Carte Ms. 1, f. 288v.

[2] Conrad Russell, *The Fall of the British Monarchies 1637–1642* (Oxford, 1991), 90–123. Russell gives just one paragraph to the Lambeth riots, ibid. 129–30. See also Valerie Pearl, *London and the Outbreak of the Puritan Revolution: City Government and National Politics, 1625–1643* (Oxford, 1961), 107–9; Keith Lindley, *Popular Politics and Religion in Civil War London* (Aldershot, 1997), 4–35; and Austin Woolrych, *Britain in Revolution 1625–1660* (Oxford, 2002), 129–40.

[3] Sir Benjamin Rudyard's speech, 16 April 1640, in Esther S. Cope and Willson H. Coates (eds.), *Proceedings of the Short Parliament of 1640* (Camden Society, 4th ser., vol. xix, 1977), 139, 249.

The Short Parliament of spring 1640 solved none of the problems of the King or the kingdom, and its precipitous dissolution only made matters worse. The meeting raised expectations, then swept them cruelly aside. The King had felt compelled to summon the two Houses, for the first time in eleven years, to seek financial and political support for his war with Scotland. When neither money nor concord proved forthcoming he brought the parliament to an end.[4] While the King blamed the failure on 'the malicious cunning of some few seditiously-affected men',[5] many in the nation at large attached blame to a government that appeared haughty, misguided, and unyielding.

At the beginning there were high hopes that a parliament would relieve the 'perplexity and trouble' of the kingdom. News of its calling was 'joyful tidings'.[6] 'John of the commonwealth' lay 'sick of the Scottish disease', according to a widely distributed libel, but Parliament, 'the great physician of the kingdom', would 'cure their infinite infirmities'.[7] 'A godly new song... on the occasion of the parliament' promised 'we shall be eased from priests and ship money.'[8] Although the nation's affairs were 'very dangerous and unsettled', observers hoped that the parliament would bring about 'better times and a thorough settlement of peace with the Scots'.[9] The exceptionally large number of seats that were contested that spring—two to three times the number in Jacobean parliaments—points to heightened interest and expectations.[10]

[4] Cope and Coates (eds.), *Proceedings of the Short Parliament of 1640*; Judith D. Maltby (ed.), *The Short Parliament (1640) Diary of Sir Thomas Aston* (Camden Society, 4th ser., vol. xxxv, 1988); Mark Charles Fissel, 'Scottish War and English Money: The Short Parliament of 1640', in idem (ed.), *War and Government in Britain, 1598–1650* (Manchester and New York, 1991), 193–223.

[5] *His Majesties Declaration: To All His Loving Subjects, Of the causes which moved him to dissolve the last Parliament* (1640), 46. See also Esther S. Cope, 'The King's Declaration Concerning the Dissolution of the Short Parliament of 1640: An Unsuccessful Attempt at Public Relations', *Huntington Library Quarterly*, 40 (1977), 325–32.

[6] Huntington Library, Mss. El. 7809, 24 October 1639; El. 7814, 6 December 1639.

[7] D.L., *The Scots Scouts Discoverie by Their London Intelligencer* (1642), 23; Cambridge University Library, Ms. Mn. 1. 45 (Baker transcripts), 29; Mary Anne Everett Green (ed.), *Diary of John Rous, Incumbent of Santon Downham, Suffolk, from 1625 to 1642* (Camden Society, 1856), 88.   [8] British Library, Harley Ms. 4931, f. 39.

[9] *The Wyllys Papers* (Collections of the Connecticut Historical Society, vol. xxi, Hartford, Conn., 1924), 9.

[10] Derek Hirst, *The Representative of the People? Votes and Voting in England under the Early Stuarts* (Cambridge, 1975), 111; Mark Kishlansky, *Parliamentary Selection: Social and Political Choice in Early Modern England* (Cambridge, 1986), 108–11; P. A. Slack, 'An Election to the Short Parliament', *Bulletin of the Institute of Historical Research*, 46 (1973), 108–14; J. K. Gruenfelder, 'The Election to the Short Parliament, 1640', in H. S. Reinmuth (ed.), *Early Stuart Studies: Essays in Honour of D. H. Willson* (Minneapolis, 1970), 180–230. At least 62 elections were contested in spring 1640, compared to 20 to 40 in the 1620s and only a dozen or so in the early Jacobean parliaments.

Whereas the King expected a supply of money and a loyal mobilization for his war, others seized the opportunity to address long-festering concerns. It was customary, they argued, to discuss grievances before voting supply. 'We had many thorns to pull out', some said, 'before we were able to serve the king.' Freeholders from Northamptonshire looked to Westminster to rectify 'innovation in religion, exactions in spiritual courts, molestations of our most godly and learned ministers, ship money, monopolies, undue impositions, army money, wagon money, horse money, conduct money, and enlarging the forest beyond the ancient bounds.'[11] After three weeks of fruitless wrangling the King brought discussion to an end.

King Charles may have imagined he could wage war through alternative means, perhaps using soldiers from Ireland. He may have thought he could sustain his war by the exercise of prerogative power. He seems to have wanted to continue his personal rule, without having to deal with grievances about ship money or religion. Whatever the reason, it proved an expensive miscalculation. The dismissal of the long-awaited parliament was a fatal move, driving a deepening wedge between the Crown and nation. Desperate for money, the King requested £200,000 from the City of London, but squandered all hope of cooperation by imprisoning four aldermen who refused to return the names of men thought capable of contributing to the loan. Their imprisonment from 7 to 15 May coincided with the Maytide disturbances, and was one of its contributory causes.[12] Many people remained unconvinced that the Scots were actually their enemies, and located the cause of their troubles at Lambeth or Whitehall rather than Edinburgh.

The dissolution of Parliament came 'suddenly and unexpectedly' on 5 May 1640, dashing all hopes of a national political settlement. As Clarendon wrote in his *History*, 'there could not a greater damp have seized upon the spirits of the whole nation than this dissolution caused.'[13] From this point onwards many commentators registered a gathering sense of gloom. Correspondence and newsletters that had previously focused on court appointments and intrigues became increasingly concerned with the developing crisis of the kingdom.

---

[11] Cope and Coates (eds.), *Proceedings of the Short Parliament of 1640*, 170, 275; *CSPD 1640*, 7. See also the Essex and Hertfordshire petitions in British Library, Harley Ms. 4931.

[12] The aldermen were Nicholas Rainton, John Gayre, Thomas Soame, and Thomas Atkins. Reginald R. Sharpe, *London and the Kingdom* (3 vols., 1894), ii. 123–5; Huntington Library, Mss. El. 7832, 7833, 11 and 12 May 1640; *CSPD 1640*, 142–3. They were imprisoned in the Gatehouse, the Fleet, the Marshalsea, and the King's Bench prison, but when rioters offered to set them free the aldermen refused.

[13] Edward Hyde, Earl of Clarendon, *The History of the Rebellion and Civil Wars in England Begun in the Year 1641*, ed. W. Dunn Macray (6 vols., Oxford, 1888), i. 183.

To Robert Griffith the dissolution of Parliament was 'the worst news that could, I think, befall this kingdom'. Grievances had been aired but not answered, tempers had been raised but not cooled, and the nation's business was patently unfinished. The failure to address the national emergency left parties on all sides frustrated with 'great displeasure on all hands'.[14] Laud's own comment on the parliament was 'nothing done'.[15]

Christopher Wandesford, Strafford's deputy in Ireland, judged the dissolution 'unfortunate, fatal I wish I might not call it', and feared that 'mischief' would follow.[16] Sir Thomas Peyton told Henry Oxinden on 6 May that 'every hour seemed ready to bring forth some strange matter', and judged the dissolution to reflect badly on the royal and national honour: 'neighbouring princes... may privately rejoice to see distractions breed in so flourishing a kingdom'.[17] The ship of state was heading into dangerous waters, wrote John Castle to the Earl of Bridgewater, 'God I trust will guide the rudder of this ship, and give you a healthful body to support the concussions and tossings of these stormy times.'[18]

Correspondence from London spread the news of Parliament's failure to every shire and borough, and even to Englishmen abroad. There would be no concerted reaction, but rather a widespread sighing of despair. It 'makes us all amazed', wrote Thomas Hamilton on 5 May, suggesting that one would be better off dead 'than we who are here in the conjected miseries that are likely to follow'.[19] Sir Humphrey Mildmay in Essex recorded 'the dissolving of the parliament, to the much sorrow of all good men'.[20] In Worcestershire Henry Townsend noted 'the infinite dislike, distaste and repining of the commons, that their just complaints be without redress'.[21] In Northamptonshire the diarist Robert Woodford found 'the hearts of good people were much dejected' by the news from Westminster.[22] 'Lord fit us for the worst times', wrote William Bisbey to a kinsman in New England, 'bad times we have

---

[14] HMC, *14th Report, The Manuscripts of His Grace the Duke of Portland* (1894), iii. 63; William Bray (ed.), *The Diary of John Evelyn* (1879), i. 10.

[15] William Laud, 'Devotions, Diary and History', in *The Works of the Most Reverend Father in God, William Laud, D.D.*, ed. James Bliss and William Scott (7 vols., Oxford, 1847–60), iii. 234.

[16] John Burghall, 'Providence Improved', in J. Hall (ed.), *Memorials of the Civil War in Cheshire* (Lancashire and Cheshire Record Society, vol. xix, 1889), 15; HMC, *Report on Various Collections* (1914), vii. 423.

[17] Dorothy Gardiner (ed.), *The Oxinden Letters 1607–1642* (1933), 173, 172.

[18] Huntington Library, Ms. El. 7832, 11 May 1640.

[19] *CSPD 1640*, 119, Thomas Hamilton at Whitehall to Patrick Hamilton in Edinburgh, 5 May 1640.

[20] Diary of Sir Humphrey Mildmay, British Library, Harleian Ms. 454, f. 31v.

[21] Diary of Henry Townsend, British Library, Add. Ms. 38490, f. 1.

[22] New College, Oxford, Ms. 9502, Robert Woodford's diary, 5 May 1640.

cause to expect; here was a parliament called but dissolved and nothing done; we are full of fears generally.'[23]

The gentry and townsmen of the political class, men with a stake in the parliamentary process, were by no means alone in their frustration. Soldiers, artisans, and apprentices also had hopes for the parliament and expressed outrage when the assembly was dismissed. While the gentry grumbled and fretted, commoners took their anger to the streets. The spring of 1640 saw a widening political involvement, an expanding interest in public affairs, and an increase of popular militancy. The social and political disturbances of May took place amidst a national mobilization for war, marked by non-cooperation among civilians and 'distempers and distraction' among 'mutinous and rebellious' troops.[24]

Londoners looking for the cause of their distress found it in the Archbishop of Canterbury. Laud, they believed, was the architect of the religious policy that precipitated the Scottish troubles, and was 'the chief cause of breaking the parliament'.[25] Critics commonly referred to Laud as 'the pope of Lambeth' and some wished to see him hanged. One drinker in Southwark proclaimed that 'the pope of Lambeth . . . doth pluck the royal crown off his majesty's head and trample it under his feet, and did whip his majesty's arse with his own rod.' Another offered that 'if nobody would cut off the lord of Canterbury's head he would do it himself.'[26] Popular anger at the dissolution focused on William Laud and crystallized into an assault against the Archbishop's palace.

Even before 5 May 'flying speeches' around London warned 'that if the parliament should be dissolved . . . his grace's house of Canterbury at Lambeth should be fired, and that they would keep his lordship in until he should be burnt, and that thousands would say as much.' Parties to these discussions included a skinner, a tailor, and Chancery clerks dining at Symon's Inn. Reports of their remarks spread as far as Northamptonshire and Warwickshire. One reported 'that Blackhall would be fired', citing the popular name for the Archbishop's residence across the Thames from Whitehall. It was only appropriate, some thought, that the leading 'incendiary' should be the first to feel the fire.[27]

Although the press remained under tight control, with a government lock on licensing, oral and scribal communication proved effective in mobilizing a crowd. 'Libels spread about London daily', complaining of innovations in religion and breaches of the privileges of Parliament. Contemporary

---

[23] *Wyllys Papers*, 12.   [24] *CSPD 1640*, 196, 247.
[25] Gardiner (ed.), *Oxinden Letters 1607–1642*, 174.
[26] Lambeth Palace Library, Ms. Misc. 943, 717, 721, 725; PRO, SP16/248/93; 250/58; 327/140; 372/109.   [27] *CSPD 1640*, 88; PRO, SP16/451/81.

correspondents were impressed by the proliferation of 'scandalous and seditious libels' and the cascade of 'bills cast abroad in London'.[28] Clarendon recalled that 'cheap, senseless libels were scattered about the city and fixed upon gates and public remarkable places, traducing some and proscribing others'.[29] John Evelyn blamed the stirring up the 'rude rabble' on the 'many scandalous libels and invectives scattered about the streets'.[30] Placards and 'pasquils' appeared all through the weekend following the dissolution calling for a rally against the Archbishop and a hunt for 'William the Fox'. Many repeated the belief that Laud was turned papist, with 'a crucifix on his altar and on his breast'.[31] On Saturday, 9 May, Laud noted in his diary, libels were 'continually set up in all places of note in the city', including 'a paper posted upon the old Exchange, animating 'prentices to sack my house upon the Monday following.'[32] One slogan written on the Exchange simply said 'bishops devils', while another more politely invited 'all gentlemen 'prentices that desire to kill the bishops' to 'repair to St George's fields on Monday morning... *vivat rex*'.[33]

One handwritten libel, satirically announcing itself as 'published by authority', called on Londoners to 'destroy this subtle fox and hunt this ravening wolf out of his den which daily plotteth mischief and seeks to bring this whole land to destruction by his popish inventions. Canterbury we mean who savours of nothing but superstition and idolatry and daily more and more infecteth the flock of Christ. So odious is he grown in the eyes of all men that we believe he stinketh in the nostrils of almighty God.' It ended with the hope that 'all his greatness and magnificence will shortly be laid in the dust'. Laud himself acquired a copy of this libel and filed it with his papers.[34]

Libels and placards had appeared before in moments of crisis and controversy, and were familiar vehicles for deriding or attacking powerful enemies. Some of the most vicious libels of the 1620s had been directed against the Duke of Buckingham and others at the early Stuart court.[35] But the outpouring of agitational writing in May 1640 was remarkable for its

[28] William Hawkins to the Earl of Leicester, 14 May 1640, HMC, *Report on the Manuscripts of the Right Honourable Viscount De L'Isle... Vol. VI. Sidney Papers, 1626–1698* (1966), 267; Diary of Walter Yonge, British Library, Add., Ms. 35331, f. 77; John Castle's newsletter, Huntington Library, Ms. El. 7833, 12 May 1640.

[29] Clarendon, *History of the Rebellion*, i. 188.

[30] Bray (ed.), *Diary of John Evelyn*, i. 11.

[31] Diary of Henry Townsend, 2; *CSPD 1640*, 174, 272.

[32] Laud, 'Diary', in *The Works of... William Laud*, ed. Bliss and Scott, iii. 234–5; Bulstrode Whitelocke, *Memorials of the English Affairs* (4 vols., Oxford, 1853), i. 99.

[33] British Library, Harley Ms. 4931, f. 8.

[34] Lambeth Palace Library, Ms. Misc. 943, 717.

[35] The tradition is examined in Alastair Bellany, ' "Rayling Rymes and Vaunting Verse": Libellous Politics in Early Stuart England, 1603–1628', in Kevin Sharpe and Peter Lake (eds.),

volume and venom. Fuelled by frustrations following the failure of Parliament, and taking advantage of London's literacy, the libelling campaign seized the initiative for the artisans and apprentices and redirected the political agenda out of doors. As the Scots in the north had shaken the regime from its complacency, so the young men of London shocked the capital to attention. 'We hear of divers other libels, and the state of things in the kingdom is very doubtful and uncertain', wrote the Northamptonshire diarist Robert Woodford on 12 May.[36]

The French diplomat M. de Montereul captured some of the drama of these 'evenements de Mai' in his dispatches to Paris. All talk in London, he reported, was 'de billets sédicieux jettés, d'affiches injurieuses attachés aux places publiques, de dispositions du peuple a quelques soulevements, enfin de touttes choses forts estranges, en etat paisible comme celuy d' Angleterre.'[37] The Venetian ambassador remarked on 'the murmurs of the people, who felt certain that England will not see parliament for a long while', and wrote of two thousand armed men at Lambeth and another seven thousand menacing the Archbishop's palace at Croydon.[38] 'Oh unheard of malicious disobedience! The vile rabble of prentices and other discontented scum of the people in and about London passed by the court gates and made horns with their fingers, with other rude and base gestures of disgrace', complained one of the Cambridge clerics associated with Bishop Matthew Wren.[39]

Conservative correspondents wrote of a 'rude rabble', 'a furious multitude', or a 'disorderly rout',[40] but the demonstrators who responded to the libels were broadly representative of the metropolitan male population. Their social range is indicated by subsequent indictments at the Middlesex

---

Culture and Politics in Early Stuart England (1994), 285–310; Alastair Bellany, 'Libels in Action: Ritual, Subversion and the English Literary Underground, 1603–1642', in Tim Harris (ed.), *The Politics of the Excluded, 1500–1850* (Basingstoke, 2001), 99–124; Thomas Cogswell, 'Underground Verse and the Transformation of Early Stuart Political Culture', in Susan Amussen and Mark A. Kishlansky (eds.), *Political Culture and Cultural Politics in Early Modern Europe* (Manchester, 1995), 277–300; Pauline Croft, 'Libels, Popular Literacy and Public Opinion in Early Modern England', *Historical Research*, 68 (1995), 266–85; Adam Fox, 'Ballads, Libels and Popular Ridicule in Jacobean England', *Past and Present*, 145 (November 1994), 47–83; and Andrew McRae, 'The Literary Culture of Early Stuart Libelling', *Modern Philology*, 97 (2000), 364–392; idem, *Literature, Satire and the Early Stuart State* (Cambridge, 2004).

[36]   New College, Oxford, Ms. 9502, Woodford's diary, 12 May 1640.

[37]   PRO, PRO 31/3/72.

[38]   Edward Razell and Peter Razell (eds.), *The English Civil War. A Contemporary Account. Volume 2: 1640–1642* (1996), 13, 14, 16.

[39]   Cambridge University Library, Ms. Mn. 1. 45 (Baker transcripts), 36. The entry is undated as well as unattributed, but it appears to refer to the events of May 1640.

[40]   Bray (ed.), *Diary of John Evelyn*, i. 11; Gardiner (ed.), *Oxinden Letters 1607–1642*, 174; Rossingham newsletter, British Library, Add. Ms. 11045, vol. v., f. 117; Bodleian Library, Oxford, Tanner Ms. 65, f. 78.

sessions when some of those unlucky enough to be arrested were brought to book. William Harris, a weaver of St Botolph's, Aldgate, was indicted for his part in 'the dispersing of scandalous libels and setting them over the doors of divers his majesties subjects, whereby much mischief hath arisen'.[41] Various artisans faced charges of assault on the constables and 'riotous contempt against the watch'. So too did three young gentlemen of Gray's Inn who were training to be lawyers.[42] Francis Lee, a forty-five-year-old wool-comber, was imprisoned at the White Lion for his part in the riots, and was among those who subsequently escaped. Others included the poulterer, George Sears, the glover John Archer, the shoemaker William Saltrum, and a glazier, a perfumer, a pin-maker, and a blacksmith. The majority of the crowd may have been apprentices, but most of those identified as ringleaders were established tradesmen and craftsmen. One apothecary's apprentice gave evidence about plans to pull down buildings.[43] A woodmonger's apprentice from Whitefriars refused instructions to serve on the watch, threatening, 'if I will be forced to watch I will turn rebel with the rest of my fellow apprentices.'[44] It was most likely a mariner's apprentice, the sixteen-year-old Thomas Bensted, who carried the rioters' drum.[45]

Most members of the crowd belonged to those strata below the 'political nation' whose occupations, youth, or dependent status denied them a political voice. But in May 1640 these young men determined that their voices would be heard. Their placards and libels called for a public protest against one of the highest men in the land, in a season traditionally marked by licensed misrule. Apprentices who customarily marked Maytide with carousing, and whose Shrovetide antics featured attacks on houses of ill repute, would now descend on the home of a prelate who some considered to be an agent of the Whore of Babylon. Indeed, making light of these May disorders, Viscount Conway affirmed, 'I believe the apprentices will make but a Shrove Tuesday business of it.'[46]

---

[41] London Metropolitan Archives, Sessions Roll, MJ/SR/878/61.

[42] Ibid., MJ/SR/875/55–7.

[43] Essex Record Office, Colchester, Book of Examinations and Depositions, 1619–1645, D/5/Sb2/7, 281v; *CSPD 1640*, 174–5; Lindley, *Popular Politics and Religion*, 27.

[44] London Metropolitan Archives, Sessions Roll, MJ/SR/877/2. At the summer assizes in 1641 Judge Edward Reeve refused to proceed against one of those indicted for the previous year's Lambeth riot, saying 'that he would have no hand in any man's blood', Green (ed.), *Diary of John Rous*, 101.

[45] Bensted has been variously identified as a tailor, a cobbler, and an apprentice sailor from Rochester, and his age given as 16 and 19. Lindley, *Popular Politics and Religion*, 8, 27.

[46] *CSPD 1640*, 190; HMC, *14th Report, The Manuscripts of His Grace the Duke of Portland* (1894), iii. 64. For an attack on bawdy houses, only loosely related to the political troubles, see *CSPD 1640*, 221 and PRO SP16/455/7. A similar attack occurred the following year: London Metropolitan Archives, Sessions Roll, MJ/SR/891/2.

Robert Woodford noted that the apprentices' plan was not just to invest Lambeth House but to try to pull it down. Some of the libels threatened to set it afire. Walter Yonge thought they intended to capture the Archbishop, while Clarendon said that the 'rabble' intended 'to tear him to pieces'. What else did hounds do when they cornered a fox? Laud himself worried for his safety and did all that was possible to fortify his home and safeguard his treasure. Lambeth House was hastily prepared for a siege, with the mounting of ordnance on the roof, prompting bad puns about canons and cannons. However, Laud himself would not be present. At the last minute, with great indignity, the Archbishop 'was compelled to take a gray cloak, as was said, and escape over the Thames'. Warned that the apprentices were coming, 'before about eleven of the clock at night [he] took a pair of oars and got into Whitehall and so escaped them'.[47] (See Plate 2.)

Estimates of the size of the crowd that gathered on 11 May range from several hundred to several thousand. Laud himself put the number of 'rascal routers' at his door as five hundred, and thanked God for his safe 'deliverance'.[48] The 'unruly multitude' that gathered at Lambeth that Monday was not intimidated by the presence of justices and constables, nor by the trained bands held in reserve in St George's Field. Normal deferential and disciplinary restraints seemed not to apply. The authorities found the insolence and bravado of the apprentices deeply disturbing. According to the newswriter John Castle, 'there did assemble this night at my lord of Canterbury's gate well near twelve hundred 'prentices and others, who knocking at the gate said they must needs speak with his grace, of whom they would ask, as they termed it, but one civil question; and it was, who was the cause of breaking up the parliament.' Armed with clubs and led by drums, they 'came thither about twelve o'clock in night, and stayed there till about half an hour past two', and only dispersed when they were satisfied that Laud 'lodged not there, but at Whitehall'. The apprentices left promising that they would speak with the Archbishop, 'by hook or by crook, sooner or later'. As for the target of this noisy assembly, now enjoying the King's protection on the opposite side of the river, it was reported, 'his grace . . . intendeth to keep at Whitehall till the tempest of the people's fury be evaporated and quite over'.[49]

[47] Robert Woodford's Diary, 9 May 1640, 11 May 1640; Diary of Walter Yonge, British Library, Add. Ms. 35331, f. 77; Clarendon, *History*, i. 188; Laud, 'Diary', in *The Works of . . . William Laud*, ed. Bliss and Scott, iii. 234–5; John Rushworth, *Historical Collections of Private Proceedings of State* (8 vols., 1680–1701), iii. 1085.

[48] Laud, 'Diary', in *The Works of . . . William Laud*, ed. Bliss and Scott, iii. 236.

[49] Huntington Library, Ms. El. 7833, 12 May 1640. See also John Vicars, *Jehovah-Jireh. God in the Movnt. Or, Englands Parliamentarie-Chronicle* (1644), 17.

During the next few days 'the people's fury' grew rather than abated when the authorities tried to crack down on the apprentices' leaders. It was reported that 'some of them are taken and will be made exemplary', but this did not bring a restoration of calm. The nights were filled with noise and threats, directed against the Earl of Strafford and the Bishop of Ely as well as the Archbishop of Canterbury. An apothecary's apprentice, Richard Beaumont, told of threats to pull down 'houses of popery', including the Queen Mother's house, the chapel at Somerset House, and the home of the Earl of Arundel. Another apprentice, Edmund Wilson, said that if the apprentices did not pull down the bishop's house on Thursday they would do it in the Whitsun holidays.[50] On 14 May William Hawkins wrote to the Earl of Leicester, 'these beginnings make all men fear what the success will be. I never knew the subjects of England so much out of order, what with the disorders of some and the fears of the rest.'[51]

Angry and energetic, the mob was not easily overawed. The detention of a few ringleaders or scapegoats at the White Lion prison provided another focus for the crowd until the prisoners managed to escape. John Castle observed, 'I do not find that the taking and committing of so many of the rebellious rabble that...beset Lambeth House on Monday night, nor the putting the trained bands yesterday into the Field, neither the armed watches that have been placed both here and at Lambeth...have struck any great terror into them, or procured any great security in the places near abouts.' The sturdy Endymion Porter stood guard with a hundred men, but this did not stop the apprentices gathering reinforcements. Following leaders named 'Captain Club' and 'Captain Mend-all', they returned in greater force. 'Three thousand of the mutineers came up to the town in the night, where they stayed very little. But in their return they assaulted and brake down the gates and windows of the prison of the White Lion, where they took their drummer and one other that had been committed there, and set free all the rest of the prisoners. It is said that one of the assailants was killed upon the place by a shot that was made from within by the keeper, and two more hurt. They give out that they will not give over until they have caught the fox and the little birds.... The king I am told is extremely troubled both of this and other insolences and outrages committed daily in the country by the troops and others.'[52]

Faced with the loss of control, the authorities spoke not just of 'insolencies' but of mutiny and insurrection. The commotions of 1381, 1450,

---

[50] *CSPD 140*, 174–5. Beaumont later apologized for his words and advised that 'those were wisest who stayed home', (ibid., 188).

[51] HMC, *Report on the Manuscripts of the Right Honourable Viscount De L'Isle*, 267.

[52] Huntington Library, Ms. El. 7834, 15 May 1640. For Captains Club and Mend-all, see British Library, Add. Ms. 11045, vol. v., f. 117v.

and 1549 came ominously to mind. The Privy Council blamed 'lewd and base persons' for 'the late traitorous and rebellious assemblies' and 'the many insolencies and disorders lately committed' about Lambeth.[53] Laud himself affected nothing but contempt for 'these mutinous people' and 'their fellows' who had exposed his person and his office to such dishonour and derision.[54] But the newswriter Edward Rossingham warned that the 'unruly rogues' involved in this 'disorderly rout' might soon be joined by thousands more supporters from the country. The government too believed that the crowds of apprentices and workers were thickened with runaway soldiers and other 'base' and 'loose' persons who thrived in the anonymity of early Stuart London.[55] Disorders in the army, the city, and the country fed into each other, turning a local protest into a national emergency.

To counter the perceived threat Whitehall was hastily supplied with three hundred arms from the Tower, 'which were bestowed in the room under the masquing house', and two hundred more weapons were brought to St James's where the Queen Mother had lodgings. The delapidated drawbridge on London Bridge was readied for repair in case it needed to be raised. Boats were readied along the Thames 'for the better suppressing of such disorders and tumults as may happen'. 'Gates and landing places' were protected by 'a substantial double watch'. A special guard was placed on the royal children at Richmond. In a show of force, the trained bands of Middlesex, Surrey, Kent, and Essex were mobilized for assembly at Blackheath, a traditional rallying point for rebels, and their commander, Sir Jacob Astley, had orders 'to suppress any insurrection'.[56] The state's forces were armed and exercised, 'to suppress any disorderly, riotous and like tumultuous meetings which might happen'. The churchwardens of Lambeth contributed a pound 'for training when the mutiny was...against the archbishop'. Some people believed that the army mobilized for Scotland would have to be redeployed to quell disturbances in London, and rumour to that effect circulated in the provinces.[57] A provost marshal was appointed to combat 'tumultuous assemblies' within twenty miles compass of the City, and Captain Davies was authorized to sweep the metropolis for military deserters.[58]

A proclamation of 15 May sought punishment for the leaders of 'the late rebellious and traitorous assemblies'. Its references to treason and rebellion

[53] PRO, PC2/52, ff. 236v, 241, 242, 254v.
[54] Laud, 'Diary', in *The Works of... William Laud*, ed. Bliss and Scott, iii. 236.
[55] British Library, Add. Ms. 11045, vol. v., f. 117.
[56] Huntington Library, Ms. El. 7835, 18 May 1640.
[57] Ibid.; Corporation of London Record Office, Repertories of the Court of Aldermen, Repertory 54, ff. 180–1v; Charles Drew (ed.), *Lambeth Churchwardens' Accounts 1504–1645* (Surrey Record Society, vol. xx, 1950), 157; PRO, PC 2/52, ff. 236v, 237, 240v, 241, 242, 254; *CSPD 1640*, 150, 167, 184, 190; PRO, SP16/458/110.   [58] *CSPD 1640*, 250.

reflected official perceptions of the seriousness of the situation. All those who had assembled 'in a warlike manner' in Lambeth and Southwark to invest the Archbishop's palace and to assault the White Lion prison were deemed 'guilty of high treason', as were any who aided or abetted them. The rebels were clearly guilty of treason 'because they had a drum which beat up before them' in martial manner. A drum, everyone knew, was an instrument of war. Archer the glover, Sears the poulterer, and Saltrum the shoemaker, who had escaped from the White Lion, were identified as the 'principal actors in the said traitorous and rebellious assemblies', and were particularly wanted for apprehension. That these alleged ringleaders were adult artisans rather than youthful apprentices reinforced the authorities' belief that they were facing not just disorder but insurrection.[59]

By 21 May the panic had subsided, the insurrection had come to nought. William Hawkins wrote to the Earl of Leicester that 'we have had a time full of fears ever since the parliament brake up, but I hope things will amend.'[60] The streets of London and Westminster grew relatively quiet, the provinces appeared relatively calm. 'I hope all the noise and rumours are past with you, as our great thunder did with us', wrote Sir William Croft in Herefordshire, adding 'we are now in possession again of a fair, quiet season, which God continue'.[61] 'Dangerous and desperate libels' were still 'scattered and set up in the town and suburbs', but renewed 'tumultuous assemblies' failed to appear.[62] There was no apparent panic later in the month when a libel allegedly found by a maidservant in Gray's Inn fields claimed that popish conspirators intended to blow up the city.[63]

Two of the White Lion escapees, William Saltrum and John Archer, were recaptured and tried for treason. Drinkers at the King's Head tavern celebrated the shoemaker and his fellows as plebian heroes, crediting them with anti-authoritarian exploits, even after they had suffered at the hands of the law.[64] Archer was put to the rack at the Tower, the warrant written in the King's own hand, in the last recorded instance of judicial torture in England.[65]

---

[59] Ibid., 167; James F. Larkin (ed.), *Stuart Royal Proclamations, vol. II. Royal Proclamations of King Charles I, 1625–1646* (Oxford, 1983), 710–11; Whitelocke, *Memorials*, i. 99. A verse libel of 1641 reminded Laud, 'when the young lads did to you come you knew their meaning by their drum', Huntington Library, Ms. HM 39466.

[60] HMC, *Report on the Manuscripts of the Right Honourable Viscount De L'Isle*, 267.

[61] Ibid., 269.   [62] *CSPD 1640*, 219, 231; British Library, Add. Ms. 11045, vol. v., f. 117.

[63] *CSPD 1640*, 231. The libel implausibly named Thomas Heywood, the Laudian rector of St Giles in the Fields, as one of the plotters.   [64] PRO, SP16/455/7.

[65] *CSPD 1640*, 192; PRO, SP16/454/39. Larkin (ed.), *Stuart Royal Proclamations... 1625–1646*, 711n, reports that both Archer and Saltrum were executed. Lindley, *Popular Politics and Religion*, 27, finds Archer surviving the rack and in November 1640 receiving a special pardon. On the end of judicial torture, see L. A. Parry, *The History of Torture in England* (1933), 60; James Heath, *Torture and English Law: An Administrative and Legal History from the Plantagenets to the Stuarts* (Westport, Conn., 1982), 154–5, 234–5.

Another prominent rioter, the teenage apprentice Thomas Bensted who had carried a drum at the siege of Lambeth, was judged guilty of treason on 21 May and was hung and quartered two days later, allegedly at Laud's insistence, as a chilling example to the others.[66] His body parts were distributed on London bridge. The savagery of official reaction seems to indicate that Laud and the King were deeply rattled. Months later Bensted's ghost was said to torment the sleepless Archbishop. 'Since the uproar at the dissolution of the last parliament', it was said, Laud no longer visited St George's Fields to take the air, but 'was afraid of the ghost of him he set upon the City gates to keep watch.'[67]

'All tumults are well quieted since the man was drawn, hanged and quartered', wrote William Hawkins with some relief. On 27 May John Castle reported that the Archbishop lodged at Lambeth 'the first time . . . since the rabble assailed it . . . his house being guarded with many gentlemen of the court'.[68] And in case this show of state power was insufficient it was said that the Lieutenant of the Tower was furnishing a thousand horse to overawe the people.[69]

London may have been subdued, but outbreaks of insubordination and unrest continued across southern and central England. News travelled fast, and many in the country shared the apprentices' frustration. Much of their anger was focused on Laud and his associates, but other streams of dissatisfaction fed into the mix. Disorderly soldiers and reluctant recruits added to the late-spring fevers. It could not help that the season saw 'lamentable wet weather, as if the heavens had mourned with continual rain', followed by 'violent and sudden' flooding.[70] The rebels in Scotland were said to 'brag much since they have heard of the disorders there are at London', and took it as a sign that the English would not fight seriously against them.[71] Tempers were up and social civilities were down, prompting Sir Kenelm Digby to remark that the 'people are strangely disaffected and untoward'.[72]

---

[66] Laud, 'Diary', in *The Works of . . . William Laud*, ed. Bliss and Scott, iii. 236; Whitelock, *Memorials of the English Affairs* (1682), 33.

[67] *Canterburies Amazement* (1641), title page; *Old News Newly Revived* (1641), sig. A2v. In 1641 the House of Commons re-examined the evidence and the jury directions that led to Bensted's execution. Maija Jansson (ed.), *Proceedings in the Opening Session of the Long Parliament . . . Volume 4: 19 April–5 June 1641* (Rochester, NY, 2003), 5, 11, 12.

[68] HMC, *Report on the Manuscripts of the Right Honourable Viscount De L'Isle*, 276; Huntington Library, Ms. El. 7836, 27 May 1640.

[69] Huntington Library, Ms. El. 7841, 1 July 1640.

[70] *Vox Borealis, or The Northern Discoverie* (1641), sig. C2.; Woodford's diary, New College, Oxford, Ms. 9502, 1 April, 8 April 1640; Diary of Thomas Wyatt, Bodleian Library, Ms. Top. Oxon. C. 378, 306.   [71] *CSPD 1640*, 207.

[72] Ibid., 333.

Rumours swept the court in the days after the Lambeth disturbances that in Norfolk the people are ready to run and stir, and like the sea will surely rise upon the first wind that blows upon them; and the same ill news are come likewise from the western parts, where the clothiers have in many parts discharged their workfolks because they cannot vent their cloth hereabout. The ball of wildfire that is kindled hereabout will fly and burn, it is feared, a great way off, where there will not be so good means to quench it as here under the king's window, where his person strikes more terror than the train band with their arms.[73]

There were riots in the fen country, mutinies in the army, and disturbances in more than a dozen counties. Seven or eight thousand insurgents were said to be gathering to descend on Blackheath but, as the newswriter Rossingham laconically reported, 'it proved otherwise'.[74]

In Kent, 'the rumour and noise in the country was great and the fear of the people far greater'.[75] In Lincolnshire 'mutinous and rebellious and ill-affected people' added to 'the distemper and distraction at this time'.[76] A husbandman in Berkshire 'heard that the apprentices did rise in London and would have destroyed the bishop', a sentiment he evidently approved.[77] 'Flying speech' against the Archbishop of Canterbury reverberated similarly in Northamptonshire and Warwickshire.[78] Rumour persisted—none of it true—that the papists were rising in Essex, that Irish infiltrators were about to burn English towns, and that bishops Laud and Wren had joined up with assemblies of armed Roman Catholics.[79]

At Shelley in Essex Edward Neale attempted to arouse his neighbours by declaring before morning prayer, 'that the apprentices were up in arms in London already, and it may be they will arise as well in the country shortly, which if they do, I will acquaint them with our parson, Mr. [Edward] Greene, for taking the archbishop of Canterbury's part as much as he doth.' This would have been on 17 May, the Sunday after the Lambeth uprising. One witness recalled Neale saying, 'if they did rise in the country that they would pull down the houses of all those that were [Laud's] favourites and begin with them first.' Another quoted him to the effect that if the trained bands came out 'the soldiers would fall upon them that took the bishops' part'. A third repeated Neale's words, 'that they would rise in the country, and that there was no laws now'. This was revolutionary rhetoric that shocked the Privy Council when it took up Neale's case in September. It was as if the social compact was broken, order inverted, and the apprentices were agents of an

---

[73] Huntington Library, Ms. El. 7835, 18 May 1640.
[74] British Library, Add. Ms. 11045, vol. v., f. 117.   [75] *CSPD 1640*, 228.
[76] Ibid., 196.   [77] PRO, SP16/561/46.   [78] PRO, SP16/451/81.
[79] *CSPD 1640*, 336.

alternative retribution. It was stunning claim, a portent of revolutionary antinomianism, that 'there was no laws now'.[80]

Another dangerous mobilization occurred not far away at Colchester where a group of 'gentlemen apprentices' resisted the authority of the mayor and defied the trained bands. Led by a drummer, like the rioting apprentices in London, they gathered in the fields outside the city in a scene blending festivity with insurrection. By one account, they were drawn from church by the prospect of intercepting Bishop Wren and a party of suspicious armed men at the house of a local recusant. By another, they had simply gone out 'to play a match at football'.[81] This would not be the first or last time that football provided cover for disorderly conduct or politicized rioting.[82]

Magistrates and commentators commonly referred to the apprentices' actions as 'an insurrection'.[83] Though overshadowed by subsequent developments, the disorders of May 1640 reveal many of the fissures that would open within the next two years. It was as if a crack had appeared in the edifice of social and political control, and a subtle shift in its foundations. It was not for nothing that William Hawkins wrote presciently of 'these beginnings',[84] or that John Evelyn recognized in the 'frequent disorders and great insolences' of 1640 'the fermentation of our since distractions'.[85] The compilers of the Grand Remonstrance credited 'the tumultuous rising in Southwark and about Lambeth' with distracting the Caroline regime from taking even 'harsher courses' after the dissolution of the Short Parliament.[86] But only hindsight allows us to see the attack on Lambeth House as the first violent stirring of the English Revolution.

So, what did it all amount to? Should we see these events as a coda to the personal rule of Charles I or as a harbinger of future distractions? What do they have to tell us about the vitality, or pathology, of the early Stuart regime?

---

[80]   PRO, SP16/454/37, SP16/468/139.

[81]   Essex Record Office, Colchester, Book of Examinations and Recognizances, 1619–1645, D/5/Sb2/7, ff. 277v–278; PRO, SP16/459/12 and 13.

[82]   In April 1640, on the eve of the Short Parliament, the vice-chancellor of Cambridge, John Cosin, rebuked a total of forty-five university men 'for playing at football in the castle yard . . . and for fighting with townsmen there' (Cambridge University Library, Peterborough Dean and Chapter Ms. 20, f. 33). In the Lincolnshire fenlands in April 1642, 'sundry are gathered together to a great number, who throwing out a football and playing at it, drive it against a new house set up in the drained fens, and be it stood in their way pulled it down (as the relation is) and so have pulled down many, and will not be appeased by justices nor by any sheriff' (Bodleian Library, Oxford, Tanner Ms. 63, f. 17).

[83]   Green (ed.), *Diary of John Rous*, 88, 90; Burghall, 'Providence Improved', 15–16; Diary of Henry Townsend, 2.

[84]   HMC, *Report on the Manuscripts of the Right Honourable Viscount De L'Isle*, 267.

[85]   Bray (ed.), *Diary of John Evelyn*, i. 11.

[86]   *A Remonstrance of the State of the Kingdom* (1641), 28.

Driven by anger at the dissolution, and spurred on by libels against Laud, the Maytide disturbances drew together grievances about the parliament, the church, Catholic recusants, and the war with Scotland. Economic problems also lay close to the surface, as many of those involved in the disturbances had been hurt by a slowdown of trade. Londoners simply could not accept the government's claim that no nation enjoyed 'more blessings and happiness . . . nor did . . . so flourish in trade and commerce'.[87] Archbishop Laud's hand could be seen in all these areas, so he became the lightning rod for popular hostilities. It was his house that was targeted, his reputation and comfort that were disturbed.

Although the crowd included established artisans and a sprinkling of adventurous clerks, it lacked links to the gentry or parliamentary elite. Unlike the politicized crowds that would emerge six months later, the militants of May were relatively amorphous and undirected. Nor was there any discernible religious element in the London and Lambeth riots. The crowd responded more to anti-popery than to calls for puritan reform, and its anger was directed against the Archbishop's person rather than his office. There was as yet no 'root and branch' movement against episcopacy, no popular challenge to the Church of England. The press was still tightly controlled, and the riots were not accompanied by a spate of pamphleteering, as they would be within a year. Though battered and troubled, the regime remained intact, at least for the moment.

In the midst of the crisis Viscount Conway counselled Archbishop Laud not to bow down or be despondent. 'The mutinies of the base multitude are not to be feared, nor to be neglected [he wrote]. The chief inciters are to be castigated, and that quickly. If there were persons fitting to be heads to a discontented multitude there were some danger if those men could not be secured; but he that fears any head that can be given to a discontented body here in England will be afraid like boys and women of a turnip cut like a death's head with a candle in it. All these accidents must be overcome with patience, dexterity, and courage.'[88] Laud and the Privy Council reacted exactly as Conway recommended, by cracking down on ringleaders and tightening security, and Laud himself took an active role in punishing offenders. The state apparatus proved adequate to the crisis, customary containment mechanisms proved effective, as order, law, and authority were restored.

---

[87] *His Majesties Declaration: To All His Loving Subjects, Of the Causes which moved him to dissolve the last Parliament* (1640), 50–1. There were economic grievances against Archbishop Laud too for his monopoly patent on tobacco.

[88] PRO, SP16/456/58; *CSPD 1640*, 277; Lambeth Palace Library, Ms. Misc. 943, 697.

By the summer of 1640 the Lambeth events were a receding memory. Archbishop Laud 'stood overwhelmed with an extraordinary multitude of most important business', promulgating the new church canons and attending to the Scottish campaign.[89] Although Laud's dignity was diminished by the events of May 1640, his authority was not seriously undermined. King and council continue to govern, cracking down on seditious publications at home and projecting military force against the enemy to the north. Six months later Laud was still smarting under the 'causeless malignity' that led to 'the tumult that lately beset my house'.[90]

'The rising of prentices and seamen on Southwark side to assault the archbishop of Canterbury's house at Lambeth' was one of the 'memorable and wonder-striking' incidents of contemporary history graphically depicted in a compendium published in 1642.[91] Looking back from the 1650s, the historian Hamon L'Estrange referred to the uprising at Lambeth as 'our first probationary tumult', a practice for others that followed.[92]

Clarendon in his *History* downplayed the significance of 'this infamous, scandalous, headless insurrection' because it was not 'contrived or fomented by any persons of quality'.[93] But it was a mark of a changing world that 'persons of quality' no longer monopolized the political arena. The events of May 1640 demonstrated that the political domain now encompassed the streets of the metropolis, suburban taverns, country churchyards, toll booths, and markets, where commoners took issue with the affairs of the kingdom. The emergence of Captain Club and Captain Mend-all suggests that the demonstrators were not quite headless, and their use of placards and libels showed them capable of sustaining and directing a crowd, even without the aid of the press. One could glimpse in these sites and activities if not the makings of a revolution, at least the mobilization of popular political culture, a flexing of agitational muscle, and the energizing of a public sphere. If the May events were not an insurrection, they were a rehearsal for something more shocking, something for which historians are still trying to find the appropriate name.

---

[89] Huntington Library, Ms. Hastings Irish Papers, HA 15859, James Usher to John Bramhall, 29 July 1640.

[90] Laud to Mayor of Reading, 13 November 1640, in John Bruce (ed.), *Original Letters, and Other Documents Relating to the Benefactions of William Laud, Archbishop of Canterbury, to the County of Berks.* (Berkshire Ashmolean Society, London, 1841), 34.

[91] *All the memorable and wonder-striking Parliamentary Mercies effected & afforded unto this our English Nation within the space of less then 2 yeares past A 1641 & 1642* (1642).

[92] [Hamon L'Estrange], *The Reign of King Charles. An History Disposed into Annals . . . with a reply to some late observations* (1656), 191.

[93] Clarendon, *History of the Rebellion*, i. 188.

PART II

THE GREAT AFFAIRS OF THE CHURCH

6

The Laudian Ascendancy

In order to comprehend the novelty and profundity of the religious revolution of the early 1640s we need to take the measure of English religious culture on the eve of the Long Parliament. Until the later months of 1640 the Church of England seemed impregnable; its domination by ceremonialists and disciplinarians appeared deeply entrenched. Two years later the unity of the church was shattered, its leaders discredited, its discipline and worship in disarray. The disintegration of the Church of England was one of the most startling and disturbing features of the English Revolution. The rapidity of its collapse was shocking. Radical reformers revelled in the collapse of episcopacy and the undermining of the Book of Common Prayer, while conservatives looked on these developments with alarm and despair.

Although the terms 'radical' and 'conservative' are strictly anachronistic, belonging more to the nineteenth than the seventeenth century, they are not out of place in this discussion. 'Radical' refers here to those godly reformers who pressed to the root of the problem, and who sought to achieve fundamental change, root and branch. 'Conservative' covers those who opposed the radicals, and who clung to the established religious order. Even Laudian innovators could regard themselves as 'conservative', as could more moderate conformists attached to the prayer book and to the established structures of the church.

It would, of course, be anachronistic to speak of 'left wing' radicals or 'right wing' conservatives, since labelling of this sort is usually taken to post-date the French Revolution. However, observers of the early 1640s used similar language to thread their way between opposing extremes. The standard catechism warned against deviation from the word of God, 'either to the right hand or the left'.[1] Thomas Edwards, a Presbyterian writing in 1641, contrasted the 'errors of the left hand' associated with popery and

---

[1] *A Catechism Written in Latin By Alexander Nowell . . . Translated into English by Thomas Norton* [1570], ed. G. E. Corrie (Parker Society, Cambridge, 1853), 115. For a critique of the word 'radical' see Conal Condren, *The Language of Politics in Seventeenth-Century England* (1994), 140–68.

superstition, and the 'errors on the right hand' brought on by Anabaptism and Brownism.[2] The classically minded could talk of Scylla and Charybdis, or imagine England tossed between the vortex of idolatry and the dangerous rock of schism, between popery and Anabaptism.[3]

ESTABLISHED RELIGION

By the time of Charles I the Church of England was a venerable institution, three to four generations old. Its origins lay beyond recall of living memory. Founded on Henry VIII's break with Rome, it followed a liturgy based on Edward VI's Books of Common Prayer, a theology encapsulated in the Elizabethan 39 Articles, and a disciplinary apparatus codified in the Jacobean church canons. The English church was unique in Christendom, with its hierarchical but anti-papal episcopal organization, a reformed Protestant theology imbued with Calvinism, and a standardized ceremonial worship that retained elements of pre-Reformation practice. Royal, national, inclusive, and compulsory, its legal status was enshrined in the Act of Uniformity of 1559. Eighty years later the Church of England was somewhat calcified, its members habituated to its customs and procedures.

To its many champions the Church of England was especially favoured of God. One Gloucestershire gentleman called it, 'the best constituted that any kingdom hath been blessed withal since the Apostles' times'.[4] It was, thought the moderate Thomas Warmstry, 'the pattern of the world.... If ever any church hath taken the living water clearly and purely from the fountain, it is the Church of England.'[5]

Occupying the balanced mean between profanity and superstition, the English church had shed the corruptions of Rome while retaining the vigour of early Christianity. Self-satisfied histories told how King Henry had thrown out the pope, brought in the Bible, and established the royal supremacy; how Edward made the Church of England Protestant and equipped it with the Book of Common Prayer; how Mary launched a popish fury and reopened the door to Antichrist; and how Elizabeth had restored her brother's church

---

[2] Thomas Edwards, *Reasons against the Independent Government of Particular Congregations* (1641), sigs. *v, *2.

[3] Edward Reynolds, *Eugenia's Teares for Great Brittaynes Distractions* (1642), title page, 22; [Joseph Hall], *A Survay of That Foolish, Seditious, Scandalous, Prophane Libell, The Protestation Protested* (1641), 5.

[4] Gloucestershire Record Office, D2510/14, Letters of John Smyth of Nibley.

[5] Thomas Warmstry, *A Convocation Speech ... Against Images, Altars, Crosses, the new Canons and the Oath, etc.* (1641), 2, 10. See also *A Defensive Vindication of the Publike Liturgy, Established Ceremonies, and Settled Patrimony, of the Church of England* (1641).

and furnished it with the Articles of true religion. God's blessings on the English church could be seen in a sequence of providential deliverances, most notably the defeat of the Spanish Armada and the discovery of the Gunpowder Plot. Almanacs listed the years that had passed since these crucial events, so that readers could see how far they were in time from the expulsion of the pope, the dissolution of the monasteries, the reign of Queen Elizabeth, or the accession of the present monarch.[6]

Within this framework of law and authority the church harboured critical voices and dissenting traditions. Catholic recusants were outside the fold, while so-called church papists conformed only superficially. Puritans of various sorts argued that the task of reformation was incomplete, and pressed for more committed godliness. A few radical sectarians sought paths of separation. Like Elizabeth and James before him, Charles I considered it his duty as supreme governor of the church to quash religious contentions and preserve 'that circle of order' against 'unquiet and restless spirits'. A proclamation early in Charles's reign warned subjects, especially churchmen, 'that neither by writing, preaching, printing, conferences or otherwise, they raise any doubts, or publish or maintain any new inventions or opinions concerning religion, than such as are clearly grounded or warranted by the doctrine and discipline of the Church of England.'[7]

Dozens of points of contention remained in the 1630s, though none of them seriously threatened the peace of the church or the security of the kingdom. Some of the issues were puritan perennials, echoing the concerns of Elizabethan and Jacobean reformers. Others, however, were new, responding to shifts in power and policy that originated in the reign of Charles I. Although the Laudian church laid claims to ancientry, drawing authority from the Tudors and even earlier, its critics charged it with innovation. Many of the disputes of the era hinged on interpretations of church history, among heirs and contestants for the legacies of Elizabeth and James. Activists could not agree whether the Church of England was perfectly reformed, half-reformed, or excessively reformed to the point of deformation. Controversy was exacerbated in the 1630s when the Caroline regime favoured a high ceremonialist style of churchmanship with anti-Calvinist leanings, backed by hardline episcopal discipline.

The issues that disturbed the church were theological, ecclesiological, liturgical, and disciplinary. Some were confined to clerical academics while others impinged on the beliefs and practices of the laity. Debate in these areas

---

[6] A. G. Dickens and John Tonkin, *The Reformation in Historical Thought* (Cambridge, Mass., 1985); David Cressy, *Bonfires and Bells: National Memory and the Protestant Calendar in Tudor and Stuart England* (1989).

[7] James F. Larkin (ed.), *Stuart Royal Proclamations . . . 1625–1646* (Oxford, 1983), 92–3.

waxed and waned, and the elements were variously combined. It was not necessarily 'puritan' to adopt contentious opinions, nor would all puritans agree on the same array of issues. The church was buffeted by a host of stresses, but most of these stresses could be contained. Nobody could predict at the beginning of 1640 that the stresses would become fractures, or that the Church of England would soon be facing disintegration.

The mature Elizabethan church had adopted a Calvinist theology, and its Jacobean successor had a broad Calvinist mainstream. At the heart of this theology lay belief in the sinfulness and depravity of man, and his utter dependence on the grace and providence of God. Salvation depended on predestination, the elect being predestined to heaven and the reprobate to hell. Life was a struggle to identify and conform to God's intentions.

Challenges to this theology had begun at the universities, and coalesced in the movement known as Arminianism (after the Dutch theologian Jacob Arminius who died in 1609). Arminians gave greater emphasis to man's free will, and denied the rigidities of predestination. Taken to extremes, this seemed to threaten the fundamentals of reformed Protestantism and open the way towards rapprochement with the church of Rome. Adherents of this position stressed good works and free will as means to salvation; some claimed a proper sacrifice was present in the Lord's Supper, and preached that penance was satisfactory before God; some countenanced prayer for the dead, and a few went so far as to deny original sin. These were all anti-Calvinist doctrines that were hard to reconcile with reformed Protestantism.[8]

The Arminian controversy peaked in the 1620s when members of Parliament objected to the writings of Richard Montague and his supporters. Calvinist traditionalists expressed alarm at a rising cadre of clerical intellectuals who were advancing dangerous ideas. The 'Arminianism', they protested, was as much a bugbear as a firm position, and its adherents were hard to pin down. They included John Cosin and his circle at Durham and rising stars at Oxford and Cambridge, and extended, at least by association, to Bishop William Laud. The power of the Arminians lay as much in the patronage they enjoyed as in the theology they advanced, and under Charles I a growing number of anti-Calvinists secured key appointments in the hierarchy. The old joke was 'what do the Arminians hold? Answer: all the best bishoprics and deaneries.' By the late 1630s many of the most valuable rectories, prebendaries, chaplaincies, and university positions were held by clerics who had moved away from Calvinism. Old time Calvinists, who had dominated religious culture just a generation earlier, naturally felt aggrieved, but many

---

[8] *A Copie of the Proceedings of some Worthy and Learned Divines Appointed by the Lords to meet at the Bishop of Lincolnes in Westminster, Touching Innovations in the Doctrine and Discipline of the Church of England* (1641, reprinted 1660).

of them were deeply worried by a theological reorientation that appeared to be taking the church in the wrong direction.[9]

Another topic of concern among controversialists, though probably of limited interest at the parish level, was the relation of the Church of England to other Christian communities. Most English Protestants recognized Roman Catholicism as an implacable enemy, and many identified the pope as the Antichrist. However, there were powerful voices under the protection of Charles I who were willing to acknowledge Rome as a true church, albeit erroneous, and the Caroline regime extended diplomatic recognition to agents of the papal curia. Catholicism appeared to be making headway at court, where the queen and her associates were permitted to hear mass, and a series of high-level conversions fed fears of a popish conspiracy. It was not hard to believe that the Catholics aimed to achieve by subtlety and stealth what they had failed to achieve by gunpowder or invasion. To those who believed such things, a benign or accommodating relationship to Rome endangered England's liberty and God's true religion.[10] International and inter-confessional concerns fed currents of popular anti-popery that periodically led to a frenzy.

A connected though subordinate issue concerned England's relationship to other reformed churches. What kind of fellowship should link English Protestants to Swedish and German Lutherans, Dutch, Swiss, or central European Calvinists, Huguenots in France and in exile, and Calvinist Presbyterians in Scotland? Some puritans looked abroad for models of 'the best reformed churches', while others in the episcopal hierarchy regarded their continental co-religionists with distaste. Catholic advances in the Thirty Years War prompted calls for international Protestant solidarity, though few were willing to act on those sentiments. The struggle between the Caroline regime and the Church of Scotland, which broke out in 1637, further divided English Protestants, with consequences discussed elsewhere in this book.

THE TRIBE OF LEVI

The 1630s saw relatively little argument about the organization of the church, but much more dispute about its ceremonies and discipline. Most

[9] Nicholas Tyacke, *Anti-Calvinists: The Rise of English Arminianism, c.1590–1640* (Oxford, 1987).

[10] Caroline Hibbard, *Charles I and the Popish Plot* (Chapel Hill, 1983); Anthony Milton, *Catholic and Reformed: The Roman and Protestant Churches in English Protestant Thought, 1600–1640* (Cambridge, 1995); Peter Lake and Michael Questier (eds.), *Conformity and Orthodoxy in the English Church, c.1560–1660* (Woodbridge, Suffolk, and Rochester, NY, 2000).

controversialists took the hierarchical structure of the Church of England for granted, and many looked enviously on its system of patronage and rewards. The two Provinces of Canterbury and York encompassed twenty-seven bishoprics, each with its subdivisions of archdeaconries, deaneries, cathedral chapters, and peculiar jurisdictions, and each with a panoply of ecclesiastical courts. By the reign of Charles I the Elizabethan Presbyterian movement had long since dissipated, leaving activists to argue over particular episcopal policies rather than the institution of episcopacy itself. Charles I's bishops promoted the idea that episcopacy was *jure divino*, that the structure of the Church of England was ordained by God, not simply an organizational convenience devised by human hands. In overstating their case they exposed its weaknesses, preparing the ground for the 'root and branch' movement that erupted in late 1640.

The clerical profession in the 1630s had some twelve to fourteen thousand members. Not all were beneficed, though most were based in England's nine and half thousand parishes. In their own eyes they were 'the tribe of Levi', separated from the laity by their training, ordination, and function. Laymen sometimes derisively called them blackbirds, jackdaws, or magpies after their black clerical garb. The clergy alone could conduct public religious services, and they alone could offer the sacrament of Holy Communion. Baptisms, weddings, and burials were formally confined to their hands. The Book of Common Prayer prescribed their offices, while the ecclesiastical canons set forth the clergy's duties and privileges. Lay participation in religious services was mostly passive, though householders assumed religious leadership at home.

Strains developed in Caroline England over the status and role of the clergy as well as the power of the bishops. Charles I's bishops had an elevated estimation of the clerical and episcopal estates, advancing policies that might be termed sacerdotalist. Archbishop Laud's programme was especially protective of clerical privileges, resources, incomes, and honour. Puritan ministers might not subscribe to the Laudian enshrinement of episcopacy but they were inclined to share pride in their clerical profession. Only a fine line divided Laudian high sacerdotalism from proto-Presbyterian ministerial self-esteem. The term 'Laudian' is used here to signify the people and programmes associated with the Archbishop, including the clergy he favoured and promoted.[11] Not all Laudians were bishops, nor were all bishops Laudians.

---

[11] Peter Lake, 'The Laudian Style: Order, Uniformity and the Pursuit of the Beauty of Holiness in the 1630s', in Kennneth Fincham (ed.), *The Early Stuart Church, 1603–1642* (1993), 161–86; Anthony Milton, 'The Creation of Laudianism: A New Approach', in Thomas Cogswell, Richard Cust, and Peter Lake (eds.), *Politics, Religion and Popularity in Early Stuart Britain* (Cambridge, 2002), 162–84.

Early Stuart clerics commonly identified themselves as God's ambassadors, his husbandmen and builders, the Lord's soldiers and captains. 'Watchmen we are, to promote the good and to give warning against the evils of the land', declared the Exeter Puritan John Bond who included himself in the company of 'conscientious and powerful ministers'.[12] Calvinists and Arminians shared this opinion of the clerical estate, even if they were inclined to express their views in somewhat different language. 'You are the salt of the earth, the lights of the world', Bishop Montague reminded his Norwich diocesan clergy in 1638.[13] 'Our God will have us reputed as his ambassadors, and as shining stars, yea, as angels', preached the Laudian conformist William Hardwick to a visitation assembly in Surrey.[14] Preachers and ministers of the Gospel were 'the stars in the right hand of Christ', according to the Sussex minister Richard Bayly.[15] Humphrey Sydenham preached on 'the sacredness of priesthood', and made heavy use of the text from Psalms, 'touch not mine annointed, and do my prophets no harm', a text that would reverberate in 1642 with special reference to the King.[16] Adherents of this position became outraged when laymen disparaged clerical authority and undercut their priestly dignity. Presbyterian ministers a few years later would express similar alarm when lay sectarians stepped out of bounds.

Parish sacerdotalists reinforced the distinction between clergy and laity by elaboration of clerical vestments and more formal demarcation of sacred space. There were many different registers of engagement and distance between parishioners and priests. Whereas puritans were inclined to neglect or reject the surplice (which was required by the prayer book and canons), their arch-conformist counterparts luxuriated in ecclesiastical costume. While some parish ministers brought the sacrament down into the body of the church to give the bread and wine to communicants, the high ceremonialists of the 1630s increasingly withdrew behind steps and rails to a sanctified sanctuary where laymen were forbidden to tread. Hyper-conformist ceremonialists directed their service to God rather than to the congregation.

---

[12] John Bond, *A Doore of Hope, also Holy and Loyall Activity* (1641), sigs. H, L3.

[13] Richard Montague, *Articles of Enquiry and Direction for the Diocese of Norwich ... 1638* (1638). For similar assertions by Jacobean clerics, see George Downame, *Two Sermons, The One Commending the Ministerie in Generall: The Other Defending the Office of Bishops* (1608); Samuel Crooke, *The Ministeriall Husbandry and Building* (1615); Charles Richardson, *A Workeman That Needeth Not to be Ashamed: Or the Faithfull Steward of Gods House* (1616); and Richard Bernard, *The Faithfull Shepherd* (1621).

[14] William Hardwick, *Conformity with Piety, Requisite in God's Service* (1638), 8. For a recent study of clerical claims, see Andrew Foster, 'The Clerical Estate Revitalised', in K. Fincham (ed.), *Early Stuart Church, 1603–1642*, 139–60.

[15] Richard Bayly, *The Shepheards Starre, or the Ministers Guide* (1640), 5.

[16] Humphrey Sydenham, *Moses and Aaron, or The Affinitie of Civil or Ecclesiastick Power* (1636) in his *Five Sermons* (1637), 141; *The Soveraignty of Kings* (1642).

Another area dividing them was the name for their calling or office. Most clerics since the Elizabethan era had been content with the title of minister or parson, regardless of whether they served as rectors, vicars, or curates. Increasingly from the 1620s the clergy associated with ceremonialism and Arminianism self-consciously adopted the pre-Reformation term 'priest'. Whereas a 'minister' was the servant and guardian of his flock and the interpreter of God's word, the word 'priest' conjured up a sacramental officiant, reminiscent of the days of popery.[17]

During this period clerical power expanded into other areas of public life in ways not known since the Reformation.[18] Not since Cardinal Wolsey's days had prelates exercised so much political authority. (John Williams, Bishop of Lincoln, became Lord Keeper in 1621 but surrendered his office soon after the accession of Charles I.) Richard Neile (later Archbishop of York) and William Laud (later Archbishop of Canterbury) became privy councillors in 1627. When William Juxon, Bishop of London, joined the council in 1636 it put three senior clerics at the centre of government. Laud was appointed Lord Treasurer in 1635, before turning the office over to Juxon the following year. In 1639 it was rumoured that 'Wren [Bishop of Ely] and Warner [Bishop of Rochester] should have the keeping of the great and little seals, and . . . the clergy will have a golden time of it.'[19]

An increasing number of lesser clergymen acquired administrative and judicial office, serving as magistrates on county commissions of the peace. By the late 1620s almost every county had clerical justices of the peace. Those with doctorates outranked lay gentlemen and esquires. Their rate of appointment peaked during Bishop Williams's tenure as Lord Keeper, slackened somewhat under Sir Thomas Coventry's administration, and picked up again in the late 1630s. Roughly one in twenty of all Caroline justices were men in clerical orders.[20] They included such controversial high Laudians as John Pocklington, the Arminian prebendary of Windsor, on the Bedfordshire commission of the peace; Christopher Wren, Bishop Wren's brother, appointed to Berkshire; and the anti-puritan Christopher Dow, among the justices for Sussex.

Criticism of this practice was mute at the time, but would develop in 1641 and 1642 into legislation designed to bar clerics from secular office or appointments and to exclude bishops from the House of Lords. A bill 'for the disenabling of the clergy to exercise any temporal or lay office or commission

---

[17] See, for example, Jasper Fisher, *The Priest's Duty and Dignity* (1636).

[18] Foster, 'Clerical Estate Revitalised', in Fincham (ed.), *Early Stuart Church*, 148–58.

[19] D.L., *The Scots Scouts Discoverie by Their London Intelligencer* (1642), 28.

[20] Christopher Haigh and Alison Wall, 'Clergy JPs in England and Wales, 1590–1640', *The Historical Journal*, 47 (2004), 233–59.

in his majesty's courts of justice' was working its way through Parliament in the spring of 1641 and received the royal assent in February 1642.[21]

COMMON PRAYER

Every clergyman in England used the Book of Common Prayer, though not all followed it to the letter. Disputes in the 1630s turned not on whether to employ the prayer book but rather how exactly its rubric should be followed and how much flexibility the minister was permitted. There was no chorus of demand for its abolition. Some Jacobean clerics had cut corners or adapted the rubric to their own taste and convenience, a practice that conformists thought slovenly and disobedient. Puritans since the sixteenth century had criticized elements of the Book of Common Prayer, which they thought tinged with popery and superstition. Elizabethan reformers had called the prayer book a mingle-mangle, culled and picked from the popish dunghill.[22] Moderate Jacobean puritans were particularly averse to the sign of the cross in baptism and the use of the ring in marriage. Friction continued under Charles I when ministers fell short of full compliance with prescribed readings, rubrics, ceremonies, and calendars.

The official position, endorsed by John Swan, curate of Duxford, Cambridgeshire, was that the Book of Common Prayer 'contains the services of the living God' and 'nothing contrary to his holy word'.[23] Episcopal visitations exposed clerical shortcomings and violations, and the ecclesiastical courts imposed sanctions on offenders. In some areas the ceremonialists went *beyond* the requirement of the prayer book, demanding that women at their churchings wear veils and that the area before the Communion table be railed.[24]

The most divisive controversies in Caroline parish life concerned arrangements for Holy Communion or the Lord's Supper. Communicants were expected to take the sacrament during the major festivals of Easter, Whitsun, and Christmas, but some parishes instituted monthly Communions.

[21] Maija Jansson (ed.), *Proceedings in the Opening Session of the Long Parliament . . . Volume 2: 21 December 1640–20 March 1641* (Rochester, NY, 2000), 594, 595; HMC, *5th Report*, Part I (1876), 7; *Statutes of the Realm*, 17 Car. I. c. 27.

[22] 'A View of Popish Abuses yet Remaining in the English Church', in *An Admonition to the Parliament* (Hemel Hempstead?, 1572).

[23] John Swan, *Redde Debitum. Or, A Discovrse in defence of three chiefe Fatherhoods* (1640), 137.

[24] Martin Ingram, *Church Courts, Sex, and Marriage in England, 1570–1640* (Cambridge, 1987); David Cressy, *Birth, Marriage and Death: Ritual, Religion and the Life Cycle in Tudor and Stuart England* (Oxford, 1997), 197–229.

Hundreds of arguments broke out about the location and furnishing of the Communion table; whether communicants should be sitting, standing, or kneeling before altar rails; and whether the elements should be reserved for those who were spiritually prepared or open to all in the parish. Many of these matters were governed by local custom and convenience, but during the 1630s they became tests of obedience to authority. Services became soured as parishioners begrudgingly accommodated themselves to episcopal discipline. What should have been a joyful and comforting ceremony of Holy Communion became marred in many places with sullenness, discord, and confrontation.[25]

Laudian ceremonialists preferred the table to stand altarwise, north–south against the eastern wall of the church, rather than lengthwise in the chancel or in the body of the church. By the mid 1630s they were insisting that the chancel be separated from the nave by rails, and approached by an ascent of three steps. The piecemeal imposition of this policy produced local outbreaks of opposition, as well as expressions of support, but by the end of the decade the rearrangement of sacramental space was almost complete.[26] Most tables had been moved to the east, and most churches sprouted rails. The ceremonialist wing of the church was clearly dominant, if not triumphant, as recalcitrant parishes were brought into line.

Some ceremonialist churchmen, including many who preferred the term priest, chose to call the Communion table an altar. The term had never been excised from English Protestant usage, but it had strong popish and pre-Reformation connotations. Bishop Richard Montague made this explicit in his 1638 articles for the diocese of Norwich, acknowledging that 'it offendeth many, that we sometimes call the Lord's Table an Altar, and dispose of it Altar-wise'. As far as he was concerned, this usage followed 'the Ancient, Primitive, Apostolical Church [so] we ought not to traduce or be offended at the name, thing, or use of Altar, whereat manifold Sacrifice is offered to God.' The ceremonialist tendency produced a proliferation of candlesticks, crucifixes, images, and altar decorations.[27]

By the late 1630s the Laudian refashioning of the church was almost complete. It was not done without bruises, but the relatively slack Jacobean

---

[25] Arnold Hunt, 'The Lord's Supper in Early Modern England', *Past and Present*, 161 (November 1998), 39–83; Christopher Haigh, 'Communion and Community: Exclusion from Communion in Post-Reformation England', *Journal of Ecclesiastical History*, 51 (2000), 699–720.

[26] David Cressy, *Travesties and Transgressions in Tudor and Stuart England* (Oxford, 2000), 186–212; Kenneth Fincham, 'The Restoration of Altars in the 1630s', *The Historical Journal*, 44 (2001), 919–40.

[27] Montague, *Articles of Enquiry and Direction for the Diocese of Norwich . . . 1638*; *A Copie of the Proceedings of some Worthy and Learned Divines.*

church was stiffened with a strict ceremonialist style and a hardline episcopal discipline. The initiative and momentum lay with Canterbury and Lambeth, and with the lesser Laudians in the provinces. Puritan objectors had been mostly muted or marginalized. Evangelical Calvinist writing had difficulty getting to the press. Vigorous visitation and energetic use of the ecclesiastical courts ensured a carapace of conformity, although it also generated waves of resentment. Thousands of laymen suffered harassment, hundreds suffered excommunication, and some of the most troublesome activists had removed themselves to New England. The most outspoken clerical critics of Laudian ceremony had been sanctioned, suspended, or deprived of their livings. The savage punishments of Burton, Bastwick, and Prynne in 1637 had a chilling inhibiting effect. Local reactions to the Laudian programme ranged from joyful acceptance through grudging accommodation, to obstinate recalcitrance and outright defiance.

Archbishop Laud and his associates worked hard to restore order, conformity, and reverence to the Church of England. Their aim was to enhance God's honour and the dignity of those who served him through heightened respect for God's house, the Lord's Table, and his ministers. As sacerdotalists they sought the augmentation of clerical incomes and the proper payment of tithes. As champions of 'the beauty of holiness' they promoted the ornamentation of churches and demarcation of sacred space. The high ceremonialists among them encouraged a devotional athletics of bowing, kneeling, and standing, and sometimes ostentatious gestures with the sign of the cross. Puritans thought it stank of popery, though conformists claimed they were merely giving God his due.[28]

Parish churches like Barking and Radwinter in Essex, or St Giles in the Fields in Middlesex, became showcases for the high-ceremonial style. Much of what we know about them comes from petitions and pamphlets opposed to their ornamentation, but churchwardens' accounts provide ample corroboration of the ostentatious Laudian refurbishment. Hundreds of churches remained poor and bare, but the 1630s saw major investment in decorations, remodelling, and repair. There was a widespread re-decking of the altars, a flourishing of velvet and gilt, as parishes made up for earlier neglect.

St Giles in the Fields was a rich metropolitan church frequented by members of the nobility. Archbishop Laud particularly commended the rector, Dr William Heywood, for being 'very diligent for a long time to bring his parishioners to decency of behaviour in the church'.[29] The Northamptonshire

---

[28] John Swan, *Profano-Mastix. Or, a Briefe and Necessarie direction concerning the respects which wee owe to God, and his house* (1639); D.C., *Superstitio Svperstes: Or, The Reliques of Superstition newly Revived* (1641).   [29] *CSPD 1640*, 280.

puritan Robert Woodford attended a service at St Giles during Christmas 1637 and wrote disapprovingly of 'a superstitious altar'.[30] Benefactors had invested heavily in the ornamentation of the church, including luxurious blue silk taffeta curtains. The rector officiated within a 'sanctum sanctorum' separated from the rest of the chancel by a large screen carved with pillars and statues in the latest baroque fashion. 'On the one side is Paul with his sword, on the other Barnabas with his book, and over them Peter with the keys; they are set above with winged cherubims, and beneath supported with lions.' The area before the east end altar was covered with 'a fair wrought carpet', while the minister's desk was draped with 'purple velvet, which hath a great gold and silk fringe round about'. The altar itself had 'a double covering, one of tapestry, and upon that a long fine lawn cloth with a very rich bone lace.' Communion accoutrements included 'a fine linen cloth' with 'the corners laid in the figure of a cross', which the priest laid over the bread and the wine in the fashion of a Catholic corporal cloth. Heywood's worship included devotional gestures and genuflections that his critics described as 'beckings, bowings and bendings'.[31]

At Barking, Essex, Dr Edward Layfield had instituted a similar high-ceremonialist regime within a lavishly ornamented church. He had not only set the Communion table altarwise behind rails, in compliance with diocesan policy, but had ornamented the ensemble with holy images. 'He hath caused I.H.S. to be set up in golden letters upon the table, and forty places besides', justifying this by declaring, 'heretofore we saw Christ by faith, but now by our fleshly eyes we see him in the sacrament.' (I.H.S. was a monogram for Jesus, and was especially controversial because of its adoption by Counter-Reformation Jesuits.) Critical parishioners were neither pleased nor persuaded, but Layfield charged them with sacrilege when they sought to have the images removed.[32]

Deeper into rural Essex at Radwinter, the vicar, Richard Drake, not only complied enthusiastically with Laudian policy but spent thirty pounds of his own money erecting elaborate images and altar rails. Drake was an arch-ceremonialist and a stickler for discipline, devoted to the beauty of holiness.

---

[30] New College Oxford, Ms. 9502, 'Robert Woodford's Diary', 25 December 1637.

[31] *The Petition and Articles Exhibited in Parliament against Doctor Heywood* (1641), 1, 2, 5–7; A. G. Matthews, *Walker Revised. Being a Revision of John Walker's Sufferings of the Clergy during the Grand Rebellion 1642–60* (Oxford, 1948), 50. The church goods and furnishings are listed in Holborn Central Library, P/GF/M/1, Vestry minutes of St Giles in the Fields 1618–1719, and P/GF/CW/1, Churchwardens' Accounts of St Giles in the Fields, 1640–1694.

[32] John Rushworth, *Historical Collections of Private Proceedings of State* (8 vols., 1680–1701), iv. 58–9. The parish was in uproar, even before the opening of the Long Parliament, with the vicar denouncing his critics as 'spotted toads and venemous toads . . . that were in the state of damnation', Matthews, *Walker Revised*, 53.

He was not content with an ordinary surplice, which he wore on all church occasions, but had his embroiderd with a cross and the emblem I.H.S. His preaching gave traditional Protestants pause when he taught that Christ was upon the altar, and that the dead might pray for the living.[33]

Others of this ilk included John Duncan of Stoke by Ipswich, Suffolk, one of Bishop Wren's chaplains, who 'maintained that there was a relative holiness in the communion table, in the timber of the church, and in the surplice';[34] Nicholas Felton of Stretham in the Isle of Ely, who 'caused his parishioners to expend twelve pounds to rail in the communion table with wainscot and rails and make new steps up to the altar';[35] and Emanuel Uty, of Chigwell, Essex, notorious for his 'frequent and offensive bowing and cringing' before the altar, which he kissed 'three times in one day'.[36]

These were among the lesser Laudians, not episcopal timber but essential to the construction of the ceremonialist edifice. All were comfortable incumbents until late in 1640, and all were to suffer the humiliation of petitioning, investigation, and parliamentary sanction when the tide turned unexpectedly against them.[37] (See Chapter 11.)

PURITANS AT BAY

Where were the puritans during this time of hyperconformity? What happened to the godly when the Laudians ruled the roost? Before venturing an answer we need to re-examine the usage of the term during periods of heightened religious contest. Puritans had been visible since the early Elizabethan era, but there had been major modulations in their character, aims, and strength.

The word 'puritan' was abused as much by early Stuart contemporaries as by modern historians. It could attach to opponents of prayer-book

---

[33] Bodleian Library, Rawlinson Ms. D 158, ff. 43–55. In the summer of 1640 iconoclastic soldiers pulled down Drake's precious rails and whipped and burned his holy images. When the soldiers could not find the vicar himself 'they caught a duck and pulled off her head and hurled it into the church', saying that 'they would serve the Drake so if they could catch him.' British Library, Sloan Ms. 1457, f. 60; Matthews, *Walker Revised*, 150.

[34] Jansson (ed.), *Proceedings in the Opening Session of the Long Parliament . . . Vol. 2*, 301; Matthews, *Walker Revised*, 151.   [35] Bodleian Library, Ms. Rawlinson D. 924, f. 177.

[36] *To the Right Honourable The Knights, Citizens and Burgesses . . . The Humble Petition of Some of the Parishioners of the Parish of Chigwell* (1641), broadsheet; Matthews, *Walker Revised*, 166.

[37] Heywood was petitioned against in 1641 and imprisoned in 1642; Layfield was one of the first 'scandalous ministers' to be examined by the House of Commons Committee on Religion; Drake faced repeated charges from 1641 and was imprisoned in 1643; Duncan was petitioned against in 1640; Felton was sequestered in 1644; Uty was declared unworthy to hold any benefice in May 1641; Matthews, *Walker Revised*, 50, 53, 150, 151, 79, 166.

ceremonies and critics of episcopal authority as well as to advocates of moral rectitude and Protestant piety. It could indicate a zealous Calvinism, even if no liturgical nonconformity was suspected. It also applied to radicals on the verge of separation.

Laudian conformists branded their opponents 'with the nicknames of puritan, Brownist, schismatic, and precise fellow', as if these words were interchangeable.[38] They used the word puritan promiscuously to denigrate or to demonize their opponents. Puritans, in Laudian usage, were also 'the factious party... the precise tribe... begetters of schisms... disturbers of the peace... hypocritical professors... the counterfeit elect'.[39] They were 'the refractory brethren', 'spirit-mongers, puritans and people of fanatical spirits', and even 'our Jews'.[40] 'Puritanism' was 'the root of rebellions and disobedient intractableness in parliaments, etc., and all schism and sauciness in the country, nay in the church itself', wrote the master of Trinity College, Cambridge, to Archbishop Laud in 1630.[41] 'Separatists alias puritans' refused to kneel for the sacrament and went 'walking after the imaginations of their own hearts', claimed the gentleman controversialist John Harris.[42] Parishioners who refused to receive Communion at the newly installed rails, though their conformity was otherwise unexceptional, were 'puritans, itching puritans', according to the Kentish Laudian Jeffery Amherst.[43]

By 1640 the term puritan had become 'an epithet of reproach which rash or malicious men do cast upon many persons who do strive to live in God's fear'. It was 'likewise a name which covers a great deal of craft and villany, under the veil and vizard of hypocritical sincerity', wrote the pamphleteer John Taylor.[44] Alehouse arguments could descend into violence if one drinker called the other puritan. Parish meetings could collapse in disarray when one faction called the other 'puritan dogs'.[45] We even find a Middlesex shopkeeper berating female neighbours as 'puritan whores'.[46] Marauding

---

[38] *Canterburies Tooles* (1641), 6.

[39] Such usage is common in clerical correspondence and polemical writing. Most of these terms appear in Huntington Library, Ms. HM 6066, 'A new ballad called the Northamptonshire high constable,' c.1638, which tells the story of a puritan minister hung for murder.

[40] *CSPD 1641–43*, 131; British Library, Add. Ms. 5829, f. 9; John Harris, *The Pvritanes Impvritie: Ot the Anatomie of a Puritane or Seperatist* (1641), 1–5.

[41] Samuel Brooke to William Laud, 15 December 1630, quoted in Stephen Foster, *Notes from the Caroline Underground: Alexander Leighton, the Puritan Triumvirate, and the Laudian Reaction to Nonconformity* (Hamden, Conn., 1978), 29.

[42] Harris, *Pvritanes Impvritie*, 2, 4.

[43] Lambert B. Larking (ed.), *Proceedings, Principally in the County of Kent* (Camden Society, first series, vol. lxxx, 1862), 183.

[44] John Taylor, *A Cluster of Coxcombes* (1642), 6.

[45] *CSPD 1640–41*, 36; PRO, SP16/467, 14 and 15.

[46] London Metropolitan Archives, Sessions Roll, MJ/SR/904/72.

Cavaliers used the same abusive language in August 1642 against the wife of a godly Yorkshire gentleman.[47] By this time, when emergent sectarians had complicated the picture and other vituperative insults were available, the word puritan was more often used to mean Presbyterian.[48]

This broad, loose, and largely hostile usage brought some unlikely characters under the puritan label. During the elections for the Short Parliament in April 1640 some people accused Sir Edward Dering of being a puritan, and claimed 'he is none of our church' for refusing to go up to the rails to receive Communion. His conformist rival Sir Roger Twysden wrote reassuringly to Dering, 'all the world knows you were no puritan', although doubts would recur when Dering introduced a bill for the reduction of episcopacy.[49] Later that year the Earl of Leicester defended himself against Sir Kenelm Digby's accusation of being a puritan by saying, 'I do not perfectly know what it is to be one.'[50]

So-called puritans rarely adopted the term for themselves. They were more likely to think of themselves as the godly, professors of truth, or 'true protestants'. If Nehemiah Wallington is a reliable guide, the godly adopted the identity of 'the holy people of the lord', 'the dear children of the most high God', 'god's saints and servants', 'holy and faithful ministers', true Christians.[51] According to the Cheshire minister John Ley, puritans were 'men of strict life and precise opinions, which cannot be hated for anything but their singularity in zeal and piety'. The damage came when 'anti-puritans... accuse all good men for precisians, and all precise men for puritans, and all puritans for the only firebrands of the world.'[52]

The puritans of the 1620s and 1630s were the godly, the zealous, the precise—both clerical and lay—more likely to be identified as puritans by their enemies than by themselves. They tended to define themselves against the failings or shortcomings of a church that they otherwise loved and served. Only the most extreme became sectarians or went into exile, and in doing so

---

[47] *A Full Relation of all the late proceedings of his majesties Army in the County of Yorke* (1642), sig. A2v.

[48] *The Divisions of the Church in England* (1642), sig. A3v; *Religions Lotterie, or the Churches Amazement* (1642), sig. A4.   [49] British Library, Stowe Ms. 184, f. 10.

[50] HMC, *Report on the Manuscripts of the Right Honourable Viscount De L'Isle... Vol. VI. Sidney Papers, 1626–1698* (1966), 356. Some believed puritans held 'dangerous and seditious positions, because Buchanan and, as they say, one Parsons did so, who peradventure may have been called puritans'. As for himself, Leicester assured the King, he 'never had a thought of disobedience or unconformity to any ordinance of the Church of England' (ibid., 356–7).

[51] Nehemiah Wallington, *Historical Notices* (2 vols., 1869), i. 8, 9, 20, 24, 25, 26, 61, 72, 130, 139, 148.

[52] [John Ley], *A Discourse concerning Puritans. Tending to a Vindication of those who unjustly suffer by the mistake, abuse, and misapplication of that Name* (1641), 11, 16.

they removed themselves to the margins. In other circumstances, some of the leading puritan moderates might even have become bishops, but under Charles I the flow of patronage became blocked, and in 1640 the 'roots and branches' movement made the mitre untenable.

By the late 1630s the puritans were on the defensive. Rather than pushing the Reformation forward, they were struggling to prevent Laudians and Arminians from rolling it back. The moderate London minister George Walker, for example, struggled against 'the increase of Arminians and popish reconcilers in the city', who he believed to be 'enemies and underminers of the true religion'.[53] The old puritan issues of the surplice and the cross in baptism had not disappeared, but they were swamped by the pressures of conformist discipline and ceremonialist innovation. The Laudian ascendancy was a disaster for puritans, as Laud and his associates intended. Doctrinaire Calvinists, the hotter sorts of Protestants, heirs to the Jacobean godly tradition, watched in alarm as their church appeared to embark on an alternative direction. The most prescient or paranoid among them feared it was heading towards Rome.

In some areas the godly were energized and aroused by the Laudian campaign, but more often they were battered into silence. There were a few notable confrontations, but most commonly the episcopal authorities prevailed. If ministers persisted in nonconformity they were likely to be cited, suspended, or in extreme cases deprived of their livings. If parishioners resisted the new rules for the churching of women (with veils), or the new enforcement of kneeling for Communion (at rails), they too faced sanctions, including excommunication. Puritans may have loathed the new liturgical deckings, just as they were averse to paying for them, but there was little anyone could do against an incumbent who insisted on beautifying his church.

Meeting at the summer assizes in 1639 the leading gentry of Northamptonshire expressed their 'general readiness...to conform to the government of the church, and to observe all the right and ceremonies thereof', provided the bishop would moderate his 'strict and unusual' visitation articles and cease 'to press new things to be practiced in the worship and service of God which are not enjoyed by the rubric and canons.'[54] If these were puritans, they were puritans of the most moderate sort, content to operate within the law. Their initiative was couched in respectful language, though the ecclesiastical authorities would see it as a provocation. Fifteen months later all chance of compromise was lost, all moderation set aside.

A survey of the puritan movement at the end of the 1630s would find that many of the godly had become silent and subdued, focused more on private

---

[53] PRO, SP16/472/37.   [54] Bedfordshire and Luton Archives, St John Papers, J.1361.

prayer than public activism. Hundreds had gone abroad to the Low Countries or New England, while many more had withdrawn to a kind of internal exile, nourishing their faith or licking their wounds. Nonconformity attracted unfavourable attention, especially in areas with busy bishops or aggressive archdeacons. Begrudging acquiescence was the better part of valour. 'Oh lord, look upon us in mercy, it is an evil time and the prudent hold their peace', the Northamptonshire puritan Robert Woodford confided to his diary in August 1637.[55] The times were bleak for the godly, who had to endure 'sinful innovations', 'debauched courses', and 'superstition'.[56]

Some stalwart Calvinists still preached, but their sermons taught fortitude and endurance, appropriate lessons for the times. Woodford heard John Stoughton preach 'very boldly' in London in February 1638, giving 'comfort against times of sufferings'. The diarist was moved to pray God 'to uphold him and suffer not his malicious enemies to prevail'.[57] Later in the year Woodford heard Thomas Ball preach at Northampton, encouraging 'God's people to wait on God for deliverance and to live by faith.'[58]

Calvinist teaching and biblical precept prepared the godly for 'times of sufferings'. Predestination to election did not guarantee comfort or security on earth. Some puritans found solace in scripture and in Christian fellowship with each other. Some collected examples of divine providence, featuring judgements on sinners who flaunted their profanity on the sabbath or were crushed while dancing round holiday maypoles.[59]

Some puritans met privately in each other's houses to study the scriptures and to seek the Lord. The authorities were inclined to label such gatherings as 'conventicles' and sometimes secured their suppression. These prayer and discussion groups were not sectarian assemblies, although they prepared some laymen for spiritual leadership and may have sowed the seeds of separation. In October 1640 Roger Quatermayne, a godly gentleman, attempted to assure the High Commission that nothing illegal was taking place. 'We pray, and we read the scriptures, and as well as we are able find out the meaning of the Holy Ghost therein, and what we understand of the word we impart to our company.... It is nothing but godly conference, which every Christian man is bound to do and perform; for it is our duty to edify and build up one another in our most holy faith.'[60]

---

[55] New College, Oxford, Ms. 9502, Woodford's diary, 31 August 1637.
[56] Ibid., 14 April, 16 May, 10 July 1639.   [57] Ibid., 2 February 1638.
[58] Ibid., 5 November 1638.
[59] Nehemiah Wallington notebook, British Library, Sloane Ms. 1457, ff. 13–15v; Henry Burton, *A Divine Tragedie Lately Enacted* (1636). See also Alexandra Walsham, *Providence in Early Modern England* (Oxford, 1999).
[60] Roger Quatermayne, *Qvatermayns Conqvest Over Canterbvries Covrt* (1642), 28.

Radical separatists were few and their meetings secret and intermittent during the Laudian ascendancy. Both ecclesiastical and secular authorities sought their suppression, so sectaries endeavoured to stay out of sight. They seemed to have become bolder in the spring of 1640, and by the autumn were gathering strength. As Chapter 10 will show, the year 1641 saw a separatist explosion, and fear of religious extremism fed the cultural panic that gave rise to the civil war.

RELIGIOUS TEMPERAMENTS

The period from 1640 to 1642 saw a hardening of temperament and a sharpening of divisions as the established religious culture fell apart. It was a bad time for moderation. Neglected, disrespected, shamed, and defamed, the poor Church of England was 'nigh torn to pieces', wrote the poet George Wither in 1641.[61] Uniformity yielded to a confusing diversity, '*quot homines, tot sententiae*, so many men, so many minds'.[62] Ideals of order, orthodoxy, harmony, and discipline all were overturned. This was no time for the Christianity of meekness, pacification, or turning the other cheek.

Among the casualties of this transformation were the irenic temperament, the willingness to wink, accommodation, consensus, and the ability of Protestants of varying persuasions to live peaceably together. Dozens of observers remarked on the inflammation of religious passions and the rousing of religious zeal, as 'heat and acrimony' supplanted charity and moderation.[63] There was 'no place left for a moderate neutrality', lamented an anonymous pamphleteer of 1641,[64] 'no middle betwixt the extremes' of popery and Anabaptism, worried the judicious Joseph Hall.[65] 'Alas, we cannot keep the middle way', Sir Nathaniel Coppinger told Parliament in October 1641.[66]

Activists of all sorts rejected the spirit of accommodation, which compromised strict principles or did less than justice to God. The Laodicians, condemned in the book of Revelation for being 'lukewarm, and neither hot or cold', were attacked from every side.[67] Preaching at Oxford in

---

[61] George Wither, *A Prophesie Written Long Since for the Yeare 1641* (1641), 26.

[62] *The Anatomy of the Separatists, alias Brownists, the factious Brethren in these Times* (1642), 2.   [63] [Ley], *Discourse concerning Puritans*, 'to the puritan reader'.

[64] *Complaints concerning corruptions and Grievances in Church-Government* (1641), 3–4.

[65] [Joseph Hall], *A Survay of That Foolish, Seditious, Scandalous, Prophane Libell, The Protestation Protested* (1641), 5.

[66] Nathaniel Coppinger, *A Seasonable Speech by Sir Nathaniel Coppinger, Spoken in the High Court of Parliament. October 24, 1641* (1641), sig. A3.   [67] Revelation 3: 16.

September 1640, Henry Wilkinson condemned the lukewarm temper, the Laodician approach, the middle way, claiming that anything but 'ardent zeal' would display contempt for God. For 'he that is not with me, saith Christ, he is against me.' Only 'a most masculine . . . courageous nature, free from all base and servile fears', would serve the Christian soldier henceforth. Marking its approval of these uncompromising sentiments, the House of Commons in November 1640 ordered Wilkinson's sermon to be printed.[68] Thomas Wilson preached a similar message before Parliament in April 1641, insisting, 'it is irreligious to be lukewarm, neuters, time servers, indifferent men'.[69] The land was 'guilty of much lukewarmness . . . too much slackness in perfecting the work of reformation', Cornelius Burges told the House of Commons in March 1642.[70] Yorkshire petitioners in February 1642 declared themselves 'against the church of the Loadician, for their lukewarmness in religion' and 'against the church of Thyatira, for keeping seducers', but rather 'resolved to live and die in the protestant religion', under God and the King.[71]

Pamphlet writers repeated the warning that God would spew out the neuter, like the lukewarm Christians of Laodicea. They attacked 'Jack a both sides, lukewarm Laodicians', who had not striven hard enough against Laudian innovations.[72] 'Neuters are enemies in Christ's catalogue', charged the London lecturer Thomas Case.[73] Enthusiasts condemned 'lukewarmness, that odious and nauseous bane of religion', and charged men of moderate opinion with being 'ambidexter' or 'neuter'.[74] John Milton excoriated 'that queasy temper of lukewarmness that gives a vomit to God himself'.[75] Self-styled 'moderate and peace-desiring ministers', who sought the 'happy and certain reconciling' of church differences, found themselves upstaged by 'the giddy sons of Apollo, who would set the whole world on fire'.[76] The following chapters show this temperament at work in the unravelling of Laudianism, renewed attempts at Reformation, the rise of sectarianism, and conservative reaction up to the outbreak of civil war.

---

[68] Henry Wilkinson, *A Sermon Against Lukwarmenesse in Religion* (1641), 4, 5, 7, 20, 23, 38, 39.

[69] Thomas Wilson, *Davids Zeal for Zion* (1641), 15. See also Stephen Marshall, *A Sermon Preached before the Honourable House of Commons . . . November 17 1640* (1641), sig. A3.

[70] Cornelius Burges, *Two Sermons Preached to the Honourable House of Commons* (1645), 45.

[71] House of Lords Record Office, Main Papers, 10 February 1642. Revelation 1: 11, 2: 18.

[72] *Mercuries Message Defended* (1641?), 2.

[73] Thomas Case, *Gods Waiting to be Gracious Unto his People* (1642), sig. A2v.

[74] [Ley], *Discourse concerning Puritans*, 'to the puritan reader'.

[75] [John Milton], *Of Reformation* (1641), 13.   [76] *Vnitie, Trvth and Reason* (1641), 6.

What was the cause of England's 'distemper'? According to the manuscript 'Pigg's Corranto' there was blame enough to go round, but most fingers pointed to religion.

One honest man puts it upon another, the papist on the protestant, the protestant on the Jesuits, the Jesuits on the puritan, the puritan on the Brownist, the Brownist on the Family of Love, the Family of Love on the sincere hypocrite, he upon the pastors, and they upon the laymen, who rumble the question amongst the schoolmen, till at last it comes to the logicians, where another believes he could make two eggs three, and he ends the brabble with a fine distinction and concludes that religion by what name or title soever it be called *est causa sine qua non*, but Pigg is of another opinion, he believes as the kirk believes.[77]

An appropriate image for the times, repeated in woodcut engravings, was the turmoil of religion tossed in a blanket.[78]

---

[77] Durham University Library, Special Collections, Mickleton-Spearman Ms. MSP/9, ii. 137; PRO, SP16/475/16.

[78] *A Whip for the back of a backsliding Brownist* (1640?); John Taylor, *Religions Enemies. With a Brief and Ingenious Relation, as by Anabaptists, Brownists, Papists, Familists, Atheists, and Foolists, sawcily presuming to tosse Religion in a Blanquet* (1641).

7

Laudian Authority Undermined

The Laudian ascendancy was beginning to crumble even before the Long Parliament assembled in November 1640. Even at the height of its power, as Convocation passed the new ecclesiastical canons in May, the authority and hegemony of the Laudian episcopal regime was being undermined. The war with Scotland generated waves of resentment against the bishops, who were widely blamed for the conflict. Scottish Covenanter propaganda circulated clandestinely in England, building pockets of sympathy for the Presbyterian cause. The dissolution of the Short Parliament in May 1640 created widespread anger and frustration, much of it directed against the Archbishop and his associates. There were signs that the ceremonialist-sacerdotalist wing of the church had overreached itself, and the entire religious hierarchy bore the cost.

Laudian religious conformity faced challenges from several directions. Principled godly clergy, who were generally persuadable towards orthodoxy, baulked at provisions in the 1640 canons, especially the controversial new 'etcetera' oath. Intended to elevate episcopal authority and to strengthen religious conformity, the canons had the opposite effect of reinvigorating the puritan cause. Objectors became more outspoken against ceremonialist innovations, and some parishioners took part in iconoclastic assaults against images and altar rails. Soldiers recruited for the war with Scotland served as shock troops for the anti-ceremonialist campaign. Local Laudian incumbents faced rising levels of irreverence, hostility, and non-cooperation. Dissenters of all types became emboldened, and sectarian conventicles reportedly emerged into view. Although the established Church of England still commanded general loyalty, and its disciplinary apparatus still functioned, the Laudian regime showed symptoms of mounting stress from the spring to the autumn of 1640.

MONSTROUS, MENSTRUOUS CANONS

The *Constitutions and Canons Ecclesiastical* that emerged from Convocation in May 1640 were the high water mark of Laudian self-confidence, and they contributed to the downfall of the church. Adopted, their authors asserted, to secure 'unity of practice in the outward worship and service of God', the new canons triggered a backlash that helped to destroy the regime.[1] Their apparent intent was to consolidate the Laudian arrangements and make permanent the innovations of the past few years. The most conscientious parishes paid sixpence, tenpence, or more 'for a book called the Canons Constitutions', only to find them contested and annulled within a few months.[2] William Heywood's parish of St Giles in the Fields spent two shillings and eightpence on 'four books of new orders made by the convocation house'.[3]

Laudian clergy promoted the new canons as timely, necessary, and godly. John Manby, the rector of Cottenham, Cambridgeshire, 'read the late new canons and exhorted the people to receive and observe them as scripture, affirming them to be drawn out of scripture'.[4] Others insisted that 'there was nothing to be disliked in the new canons', and that the Convocation that made them had 'more force and authority than all parliaments'.[5]

A polarizing preface by the King excoriated 'pretence of zeal... brain-sick jealousies... counterfeit holiness' and any who 'cast these devilish aspersions and jealousies upon our royal and godly proceedings'. The canons required every parish minister to 'audibly read' an assertion of divine right kingship and to secure diligent observance of the anniversary of the King's accession. They tightened restrictions on popish recusants, and took up arms against 'the damnable and cursed heresy of Socinianism' (denial of the divinity of Christ, not a widely held view). The canons took a strong stand against sectaries, especially 'anabaptists, Brownists, separatists, familists, or other' who endeavoured 'the subversion both of the doctrine and discipline of the Church of England'. Targets for correction included 'factious people, despisers and depravers of the Book of Common Prayer', who sought out sermons beyond their parish or otherwise neglected 'the service of God'.[6] In both tenor and substance the canons marked the closure of consensus and signalled the determination of the regime to impose discipline.

---

[1] *Constitutions and Canons Ecclesiasticall... 1640* (1640), sig. E3. The bishops ordered 17,500 copies to be printed. PRO, SP16/455/138.

[2] Devon Record Office, 540 A/PW/1. Other examples include Saffron Waldon, Essex Record Office, mf. T/A599/1; Westminster Archives, B10 (St Clement Danes), V22 (St Mary le Strand); East Sussex Record Office, 415/9/1a (St Thomas Cliffe, Lewes).

[3] Holborn Central Library, P/GF/CW/1.

[4] John White, *The First Century of Scandalous, Malignant Priests* (1643), 20.

[5] A. G. Matthews, *Walker Revised. Being a Revision of John Walker's Sufferings of the Clergy during the Grand Rebellion 1642–60* (Oxford, 1948), 363; White, *First Century of Scandalous, Malignant Priests*, 23.

[6] *Constitutions and Canons Ecclesiasticall... 1640*, 4–5, sigs. B4, C2v, C3v, D3, E.

At the heart of the new canons was a new oath that required every minister to swear before 2 November that the doctrine and discipline of the Church of England contained 'all things necessary to salvation', and that they would never consent 'to alter the government of this church by archbishops, bishops, deans and archdeacons, etc. as it stands now established'. Quite what the 'etcetera' covered was unclear, though Bishop Juxon of London glossed it to cover 'the rest that bear office' in the church. The new oath was in addition to the oath ex officio that already drove a wedge between puritans and conformists. The canons further mandated that tables or altars stand sideways under the east window of every chancel or chapel, insisted that they be railed to protect them from abuses, legitimized reference to Communion tables as 'altars', and required communicants to 'approach to the holy table, there to receive the divine mysteries' on their knees. All these provisions were intended, said their framers, for 'the honour of God, the peace of the church, [and] the tranquillity of the kingdom'.[7] Almost immediately they had the opposite effect.

The Laudian attempt to impose even stricter conformity was mistimed and ill-judged. The new canons proved vastly unpopular, especially among conscientious churchmen, and provoked a puritan reaction. Like the King's earlier *Book of Sports* (1633), the canons helped turn moderate godly ministers into rebels. Clerical opposition concentrated on the 'etcetera' oath, which raised a wave of queries and objections. Protesters complained that although the Church of England's doctrine contained 'all things necessary to salvation', the same could not be said of its organization and discipline.[8]

James Usher, Archbishop of Armagh, warned his colleague John Bramhall about the oath: 'I see great trouble is like to rise from hence, which God knows this time had little need of.'[9] In Oxfordshire the rector of Ducklington, Thomas Wyatt, wrote in his diary that the new oath 'caused exceeding much trouble and none would take it'.[10] A correspondent of the Earl of Rutland predicted in August 1640 'that you will find many thousands [of ministers] will rather out of their livings than take it'.[11] A widely circulated manuscript described the oath as 'a strange mis-shapen monster' and an aspect of Antichrist.[12] An illicit

---

[7] Ibid., sigs. E 2, E3v–E4, G3v; William Juxon, *Articles to be Enquired of Within the Diocesse of London* (1640), sig. A3v.

[8] Bodleian Library, Rawlinson Ms. C 785, C 262; British Library, Harley Ms. 4931, ff. 52–62.

[9] Huntington Library, Ms. Hastings Irish Papers, HM 15959.

[10] Bodleian Library, Ms. Top. Oxon, c. 378, 310.

[11] HMC, *The Manuscripts of His Grace the Duke of Rutland, G.C.B., Preserved at Belvoir Castle*, (1888), i. 522.

[12] 'A dialogue of two zealots concerning the oath in the last book of canons', in Mary Anne Everett Green (ed.), *The Diary of John Rous...1625 to 1642* (Camden Society, 1856), 102; Durham University Library, Special Collections, Mickleton-Spearman Ms. MSP/9, ii. 192.

publication of 1640 entitled *Englands Complaint to Iesus Christ Against the Bishops Canons* described them as products of a 'sinful synod, a seditious conventicle...a traiterous conspiracy'.[13] To Nehemiah Wallington the 'cursed book of canons' was 'a most grievous cunning snare...with a filthy execrable oath'.[14] Other critics seethed at 'those monstrous, Babylonish, menstruous canons'.[15] Satirists punned on the link between the canons of convocation and the explosive cannons of the Scots. The bishops themselves would be brought down by 'the discharging of their roaring canons, overladen with an oath of an unreasonable size, and rammed up to the very mouth with a voluminous etcetera.'[16] (See Plate 3.)

Hearing 'the buzz' against the new canons, the Lincolnshire minister Robert Sanderson warned Archbishop Laud in September 1640 that not only 'the preciser sort' but also 'such as are otherwise every way conformable will utterly refuse to take the oath'. Sanderson continued, with extraordinary foresight, 'the peace of this church is apparently in danger to be more disquieted, though there be little cause, by this one occasion than by anything that has happened in our memories.'[17]

As soon as Parliament met in November there were demands that the *Book of Canons* should be burned.[18] In December 1640, after considerable debate, the Commons condemned the canons as 'contrary to the king's prerogative, to the fundamental laws and statutes of the realm, to the rights of parliament, to the property and liberty of the subject, and matters tending to sedition and of dangerous consequence.'[19] Twelve bishops were impeached in 1641 for their part in making the hated canons.[20]

---

[13] *Englands Complaint to Iesus Christ, against the Bishops Canons* (Amsterdam?, 1640), 'title page. See also *Certaine Questions Propounded to Archbishops, Bishops, Archdeacons...and other audacious usurpers* (1640); 'Samoth Yarb' [Thomas Bray], *The Anatomy of et caetera. Or the Unfolding of that Dangerous Oath* (1641).

[14] British Library, Add. Ms. 21935, f. 11v.

[15] *The True Character of an Untrue Bishop* (1641), 3.

[16] Thomas Case, *Gods Waiting to be Gracious Unto his* People (1642), 109. See the engraving (Plate 3) by Wenceslaus Hollar (1640), 'This canons seal'd', British Museum, Satirical Prints and Drawings: Political and Personal, no. 148.

[17] *CSPD 1640–41*, 57. Sanderson, a member of the 1640 Convocation, became Bishop of Lincoln after the Restoration.

[18] Maija Jansson (ed.), *Proceedings in the Opening Session of the Long Parliament.... Volume 1: 3 November–19 December 1640* (Rochester, NY, 2000), 81, 82, 85. The call to burn the canons came from Sir Henry Anderson, burgess for Newcastle, which was still under Scottish occupation. Anti-episcopal petitions of 1641 reiterated the call for the burning of the new canons. Maija Jansson (ed.), *Proceedings in the Opening Session of the Long Parliament.... Volume 4: 19 April–5 June 1641* (Rochester, NY, 2003), 17.

[19] Jansson (ed.), *Proceedings in the Opening Session of the Long Parliament...Vol. 1*, 619.

[20] *Commons Journal*, ii. 235.

IRREVERENCE AND ICONOCLASM

The spring and summer of 1640 saw increasing numbers of local religious disturbances as parishioners revolted against high-ceremonial discipline. Acts of iconoclasm were widely reported, prompting discussion, condemnation, or emulation. Before 1640, laymen who were unhappy with local liturgical arrangements might protest in a passive way, by refusing to stand or kneel when requested, by ostentatiously wearing their hats in church, or by grumbling against the incumbent. Rarely did their disaffection extend to direct action. But beginning in spring 1640 the records are filled with reports of outrages in churches, attacks on altar rails, invective against ministers, and iconoclastic action against vestments and images. Disorderly religious conduct was not unprecedented, but none could recall such concentrations of irreverence and insubordination.

Conservatives used words such as 'sacrilege' and 'outrage' to refer to these episodes, and described them as 'mutiny' or 'riots'. But the iconoclastic action of 1640 was not a general assault on the Church of England. It was, rather, an opportunist effort by members of the laity to reverse the Laudian altar policy and to rid the church of ceremonial innovations. The strains in religious culture would intensify during the coming months, when it became hard to tell 'reformation' from 'insurrection'.

Hostility to Laud and the leading Laudians grew with the dissolution of the Short Parliament and the continuing war with Scotland, both of which were commonly blamed on the bishops. Activists took exception to the tenor as well as the substance of the new Laudian canons, and some became dangerously outspoken. Magistrates in Berkshire in July 1640 examined a husbandman who blamed Laud for raising the army, said the King was ruled by him, and claimed that the Archbishop was turned papist. Drinkers at the Three Cranes in Chancery Lane in the same month drank healths to the destruction and confusion of the Archbishop.[21] Card players in a private house in London reportedly used 'disloyal and abusive language' when one laid two knaves on the table and another 'said they wanted but a third, the archbishop of Canterbury'.[22] More slanders against the Archbishop were reported at the Somerset spring assize.[23]

Laud himself was aware of this vilification, which he took to be one of the crosses that went with his office. He reportedly said in a sermon that 'it was a

---

[21] *CSPD 1640*, 474, 487, 522.   [22] *CSPD 1640–41*, 169.
[23] J. S. Cockburn (ed.), *Western Circuit Assize Orders 1629–1648: A Calendar* (Camden Society, 4th series, vol. xvii, 1976), 197.

fortune that followeth all men in high places and authority to be evil spoken of'.[24] On 22 August 1640 the Archbishop recorded in his diary, 'a vile libel brought me, found in Covent Garden, animating the apprentices and soldiers to fall upon me in the king's absence'. A month later he received a letter from Durham reporting that the Scots 'inveigh and rail at me exceedingly' and hoped to see him slain.[25] Country correspondents repeated the persistent rumour that Laud had gone over to Rome.[26]

The Scots had no difficulty identifying Archbishop Laud as the architect of their troubles. It was his influence on the King, his innovations in religion, that led to the present 'commotions' and 'combustions'. Scottish demands in September 1640 identified both Laud and Strafford as 'the common incendiaries who have been the authors of this combustion'.[27] Matthew Wren too, who had imposed discipline and ceremony on the diocese of Norwich and was intrusively busy as Bishop of Ely, attracted similar slurs and threats. September 1640 brought news from Essex that the Bishop of Ely 'was beset with an unruly company that had sworn to kill him, but having six good horses in his coach he escaped'.[28]

The lesser Laudians, local representatives of sacerdotal authority, encountered a quickening pulse of hostility. In Dorset, for example, a tailor, Walter Bayley, called the rector of Bridport, 'a base knave, a dangerous knave, a base rogue, a dangerous rogue, [who] sought the blood of honest people'.[29] Richard Bond of Chard, Somerset, unleashed a torrent of abuse at one of the bishop's apparitors, calling him 'very base and unmannerly names in the churchyard there, viz: base knave and lying knave, and many other abusive and disgraceful terms'.[30] John Counsell of Barrow Gurney, Somerset, likewise impugned clerical dignity in October 1640 when he 'publicly laughed' at the minister who had rebuked him 'for not kneeling in the church there on both his knees'.[31] Also in October, on the eve of the assembly of Parliament, visitation proceedings at Sudbury, Suffolk, were violently disrupted by an armed 'rout of 'prentices, say-weavers, and other poor rascals' who broke down the altar rails and snatched at the visitors' books. In the

---

[24] D.L., *The Scots Scouts Discoverie by Their London Intelligencer* (1642), 33.

[25] William Laud, 'Devotions, Diary and History', in *The Works of the Most Reverend Father in God, William Laud, D.D.*, ed. James Bliss and William Scott (7 vols., Oxford, 1853), iii. 327.

[26] HMC, *14th Report, The Manuscripts of His Grace the Duke of Portland* (1894), iii. 67.

[27] Huntington Library, Ms. El. 7861, copying Scottish demands of 8 September 1640.

[28] Huntington Library, Ms El. 7872, 10 September 1640.

[29] Cockburn (ed.), *Western Circuit Assize Orders 1629–1648*, 198–9.

[30] Somerset Record Office, D/D/Ca 331, f. 82v.

[31] Somerset Record Office, D/D/Ca 333, nf.

ensuing melee one Hodgkins, keeper of the inn where the bishop's men lodged, charged one of the clerics 'with the name of knave, rogue, fool, jack-sauce' before swinging at his head with a cudgel.[32] The complaint was serious enough to come to the attention of the authorities in London, but by the autumn of 1640 episcopacy was under pressure, the ecclesiastical courts were faltering, and the government of Charles I had few remaining weapons to use against parishioners who insulted or assaulted their priests.[33]

Reports of the violent destruction of Communion rails and attacks on liturgical furnishings became increasingly common in the summer of 1640. One of the first was at Esher, Surrey, where late one night in July intruders broke into the church and destroyed the controversial altar rails.[34] A rash of similar attacks followed, mostly in East Anglia and central England, along the line of march from the recruiting grounds to the military rendezvous in the north. The assaults were often blamed on unruly soldiers, though many of the iconoclasts were supported by local civilians.[35]

Late in July 1640 the Earl of Warwick wrote to Secretary Vane about the insolencies of Captain Rolleston's company in Essex, 'caused by a barrel of beer and fifty shillings in money sent them by Dr. [John] Barkham, parson of Bocking, of whose kindness it seems they took too much; for I found them much disordered by drink that day, and they went to his church and pulled up the rails about the communion table, and burnt them before their captain's lodgings.' A similar fate befell the Communion rails at churches along the Stour Valley between Suffolk and Essex. One of the soldiers derisively adopted the *nom de guerre* of 'Bishop Wren'.[36]

At Radwinter, Essex, where the arch-ceremonialist Richard Drake had spent thirty pounds of his own money erecting elaborate images and altar rails, iconoclastic soldiers invaded the church and pulled down the ceremonial accoutrements. They burned the rails and subjected the images to a whipping. When the soldiers could not find the vicar himself 'they caught a duck and pulled off her head and hurled it into the church', saying that 'they would serve the Drake so if they could catch him'. One section of the parish commiserated with the minister for this affront to his dignity and the violation of his chancel, while another gloated at the parson's distress.

[32] *CSPD 1640–41*, 105.   [33] PRO, SP16/470/55.   [34] *CSPD 1640*, 486.
[35] John Walter, 'Popular Iconoclasm and the Politics of the Parish in Eastern England, 1640–1642', *Historical Journal*, 47 (2004), 261–90; idem, ' "Abolishing Superstition with Sedition"? The Politics of Popular Iconoclasm in England 1640–1642', *Past and Present*, 183 (2004), 89–123.
[36] *CSPD 1640*, 517, 522; PRO, SP16/463/27; Tom Webster, *Godly Clergy in Early Stuart England, c.1620–1643* (Cambridge, 1997), 213; Mark Charles Fissel, *The Bishops' Wars: Charles I's Campaigns against Scotland, 1638–1640* (Cambridge, 1994), 264–9.

Drake himself was convinced that the soldiers 'were invited to the fact, they were but instrumental', urged on by disaffected parishioners.[37]

The iconoclasts did not have to be soldiers. In August 1640 a mob made up of labourers, husbandmen, weavers, carpenters, cordwainers, clothiers, and a blacksmith, 'violently and in a warlike manner entered the chancel of the parish church of Kelveden, Bradford-iuxta-Coggeshall, and Great Braxted, and riotously and unlawfully broke and carried off the rails enclosing the communion table into the churchyard'. Another group similarly entered churches in eastern Essex 'and forcibly broke and carried off the rails and burned them'.[38]

More attacks took place in Hertfordshire, where the Earl of Salisbury reported in August 1640 that 'the soldiers here begin to follow the example of those of Essex in pulling down communion rails, and at Hadham in Hertfordshire, where Dr. [Thomas] Paske is incumbent, they have pulled down a window lately built by him. . . . It is very likely the people of the town set them on.' In fact 'this sacrilegious act' (as the incumbent called it) was performed by young men of the parish, with some of their elders offering money for them to complete the destruction of the rails. Some asked scathingly 'what the doctor would bow to now, the rails being broken, and whether he would bow to the holes'.[39]

William Hawkins similarly reported to the Earl of Leicester, 'Our soldiers in divers places commit great disorders, even in our churches, pulling down the rail about the communion table in a strange manner.'[40] Urged on by radicals, fuelled by drink, and excited, perhaps, by the pleasure of smashing things, the iconoclasts tore down the rails in at least seventeen churches in Hertfordshire. The season was memorialized in later chronicles as the time when 'the soldiers in their passage to York turn reformers, pull down popish pictures, break down rails, turn altars into tables.'[41]

One of the most disturbing outrages occurred at King's Walden where two dozen soldiers entered the church during Sunday service. They 'sat in the chancel till the sermon was ended, and then, before all the congregation, they tore down the rails and defaced the wainscot which adorned the chancel,

---

[37] Bodleian Library, Rawlinson Ms. D.158, ff. 43–55; British Library, Sloan Ms. 1457, f. 60.

[38] Essex Record Office, Quarter Sessions Rolls, Q/SR/311/46–51. The rioters were identified as residents of a dozen local parishes.

[39] *CSPD 1640*, 580; Hertfordshire Record Office, QSR 5/78, /82, /83, /141; William Le Hardy (ed.), *Hertfordshire County Records. Calendar to the Sessions Books . . . 1619 to 1657* (Hertford, 1928), v. 68. The Arminian Dr Paske was absentee Master of Clare Hall, Cambridge, spending much of his time as a prebendary of Canterbury.

[40] HMC, *Report on the Manuscripts of the Right Honourable Viscount De L'Isle . . . Vol. VI. Sidney Papers, 1626–1698* (1966), 318.

[41] John Vicars, *A Sight of ye Trans-actions of these latter yeares* (1646), 6, 7, and illustration.

invited themselves to the churchwardens to dinner, exacted money from the minister, brought an excommunicated person into the church and forced the minister to read evening prayer in his presence.' Here as elsewhere, the soldiers seem to have behaved more like Protestant vigilantes than a disorderly mob, driven more by a corrective religious agenda than an appetite for destruction. The authorities were unable to identify those responsible among the 'servants, labourers and tradesmen' impressed for military service, but rather thought the iconoclasts to be 'vagabonds . . . whom neither the house of correction nor any other punishment will reform of their roguish life'. The Council demanded the names of the 'countenancers and abettors' of the rioters, but to little avail.[42]

Pressured from London, county magistrates attempted to stem these religious disorders and to punish the culprits. Although local people might be suspected of encouraging the iconoclasts, their involvement in attacks on Communion rails was difficult to prove. Reputable parishioners often seemed content to have the controversial rails demolished, but were uneasy with the violence of their destruction. Hertfordshire magistrates identified Edward Aylee of Bishop's Stortford, glazier, a local man impressed for military service, as the ringleader in pulling down the altar rails at Rickmansworth. Aylee confessed his crime, and also acknowledged defacing the cover of the font, but insisted 'that he was not hired nor entreated by anybody to do the same'. Further charged with speaking in favour of the Scots, against whom he was supposed to march as a soldier, he said 'that if he did speak any such words it was in heat of drink, and not out of any ill purpose or intent.'[43] Richard Mose, blacksmith, told the Hertfordshire Quarter Sessions that he only joined in the defacement of the chancel at Much Hadham after other men promised him money and urged him on.[44]

Another rash of rail-breaking broke out in the autumn in some of the same areas that had experienced the summer iconoclasm. Early in October 1640 'unruly people' committed 'a notorious misdemeanour' against a church near Reading, Berkshire, breaking in at night and smashing the organs and breaking down the Communion rails. More rails fell in Suffolk, Essex, and Buckinghamshire, in the weeks before Parliament assembled.[45]

---

[42] *CSPD 1640–41*, 69–70, 140; PRO, SP16/467/79 (2, 4, 7, and 17 September 1640).

[43] *CSPD 1640*, 7, 12, 22; PRO, SP16/466/23, ff. 67–73. For the bitter background to the battle of the altar rails at Rickmansworth, see Nehemiah Wallington, *Historical Notices* (2 vols., 1869), i. 70–1.

[44] W. J. Hardy (ed.), *Hertford County Records. Notes and Extracts from the Sessions Rolls 1581 to 1698* (Hertford, 1905), 64–5.

[45] British Library, Add. Ms. 11045, vol. v., f. 125v; PRO, SP16/470/55; Mary Anne Everett Green (ed.), *The Diary of John Rous, Incumbent of Santon Downham, Suffolk, from 1625 to 1642* (Camden Society, 1856), 99; Wallington, *Historical Notices*, i. 123–6.

THE DUCK'S CORANTO

London had been relatively quiet since the springtime disturbances at Lambeth but a new round of disorder broke out in the autumn of 1640. Bishop William Juxon's attempt to conduct a routine visitation of his diocese produced waves of hostility and derision. Much of this focused on Dr Arthur Duck, the Bishop of London's chancellor who was also vicar general to the Archbishop of Canterbury, and whose unfortunate name invited relentless punning. According to 'the Duck's Coranto', a verse account of this failed visitation, 'there was never poor Duck met so with her mate since ducks began to quack'.[46]

In his visitation articles Juxon invoked the authority of the recently adopted canons, as well as the legacy of Queen Elizabeth, when he insisted that all parishes should have 'a comely partition betwixt your chancel and the body of the church', an 'ascent or steps' before the holy table, and the table itself to be 'set as is directed in the queen's Injunctions and as appointed by the canon made in the Synod held at London, anno 1640.' By this time most parishes had moved their tables to an east-end altarwise position, and many had installed rails, steps, and screens, often at considerable cost of coin and controversy. Juxon also insisted that churchwardens report criticism of the Book of Common Prayer 'or any part of the government or discipline of the Church of England now established', so that puritans or dissidents could be punished.[47]

As the visitation was beginning in early September 'a seditious paper was put on the standard in Cheapside requesting apprentices and all other brave spirits (as they are termed) to meet in Moorfield that night for the reformation of religion.'[48] Their target this time was not the house of the bishop or archbishop but the hierarchy and ceremonies they represented. Dr Duck provided a convenient surrogate as he set off to inspect the diocese, which encompassed Middlesex and Essex, and a strip of Hertfordshire, as well as the city of London.

In the leading towns of Essex, from Chelmsford to Dunmow, the episcopal entourage met obstacles and objections. Villages in this area had already experienced waves of religious iconoclasm and disturbances involving men and women. At Halsted, as 'Duck's Coranto' relates, they were beset by 'amazons' who made off with their books. Back in London at the end

---

[46] British Library, Harley Ms. 4931, f. 63.
[47] William Juxon, *Articles to be Enquired of Within the Diocese of London* (1640), sigs. A3, A3v.   [48] HMC, *Report on Manuscripts in Various Collections* (1903), ii. 258–9.

of September they faced jostling, jeering, and prolonged cries of 'no oath' against the Laudian canons.[49] The episode can be pieced together from newsletters, correspondence, diaries, registers, and occasional writings.

Ignoring or misjudging the mood in the parishes, the diocesan authorities held firm to Laudian policy and demanded that churchwardens swear to the controversial articles. There were 'great stirs...in London about the taking of an oath by the churchwardens to present according to the new church canons'. Visitation assemblies in the churches of St Lawrence and St Magnus broke up in disorder as dozens of churchwardens refused to take the oath. The chant rang out again, 'no oath, no oath'. One of the apparitors (a lay official of the court) accused the recalcitrant churchwardens of being 'puritans, which word occasioned such a hurly-burly in the church among the multitude that the sheriff was fain to be sent for, and the officers were all in danger that attended the court.' The disturbance was widely reported, some accounts claiming that the apparitor maligned the churchwardens as 'all puritan curs' or 'a company of puritan dogs'. The result was a melee, with hissing, pinching, and punching. Someone shouted that 'a mad ox' or 'a mad bull' was loose in the church, and further 'uproar' followed. The hapless Arthur Duck, one of the most senior ecclesiastical judges in England, 'was afraid of his life' and was forced 'to run to save himself, and the sheriffs made way for his escape to the waterside'. 'In great confusion up they rise | And out of church the Duck she flies. | Lets hunt the Duck the people cries, | And shoos her out of place,' so versifies 'Duck's Coranto'. By some accounts Dr Duck was lucky to get out with little more damage than the loss of his hat. He was rowed across the Thames towards the Archbishop's house at Lambeth, 'some boats following him', amidst a hail of stones, the inevitable quacking noises, and cries of 'a Duck, a Duck'.[50] It was only four months since Archbishop Laud had been forced to escape by water in the opposite direction.

A few weeks later the church sought justice against those who had challenged its authority, using the prerogative power of the Court of High Commission. But rather than restoring ecclesiastical discipline, the authorities became subject to further scorn. Instead of proceeding against the taunting crowd, lay officials associated with the Sheriff of London threatened Dr Duck's apparitor with prison for calling the churchwardens puritan dogs.

[49] British Library, Harley Ms. 4931, ff. 63–63v.

[50] HMC, *Report on the Manuscripts of the Right Honourable Viscount De L'Isle...Vol. VI*, 333; HMC, *Report on the Manuscripts of Lord Montague of Beaulieu* (1900), 129; HMC, *The Manuscripts of His Grace the Duke of Rutland, G.C.B., Preserved at Belvoir Castle*, i. 524; Dorothy Gardiner (ed.), *The Oxinden Letters 1607–1642* (1933), 182–3; Rossingham newsletter, British Library, Add. Ms. 11045, vol. v., f. 122–122v; British Library, Harley Ms. 4931, f. 63v; Diary of Walter Yonge, British Library, Add. Ms. 35331, f. 78v.

Most citizen parishioners were resistant to innovation, but their experience in 1640 may have inclined them more towards radicalism.

The meeting of the Court of High Commission in the Convocation House at St Paul's Cathedral on Thursday, 22 October, degenerated into a brawl, its business halted by an angry mob. 'Unruly fellows' asked derisively after the bishops, saying, 'they dare not come; but where is Wren, said some of them, without any other title but plain Wren.' The newswriter Edward Rossingham was quick to note the subversiveness of this casual usage that denied the bishop his customary dignity.[51] Laymen crowded the court making 'a hemming, hooting and shouting', and began to throw cushions at the commissioners.[52] Poor Chancellor Duck suffered further humiliation, his dignity and his robes in tatters for the second time in a month. A correspondent reported to Sir John Coke, 'the common people crowding in did force Dr. Duck out at a hole in a window when, as I am informed, he lost some part of his garment and got to his house with some difficulty.'[53] The people followed him, 'hooting as birds at an owl' and making the usual duck noises.[54] A contemporary satire memorialized this assault on 'the inquisition' at St Paul's when 'a ragged regiment of mad souls...would have devoured a Duck and a Lamb'[55] (referring to the ecclesiastical lawyer Sir John Lambe, Dean of the Court of Arches and a member of the High Commission).

Relishing the chancellor's discomfort, hostile cartoonists took to depicting Dr Duck with wings, alongside other Caroline clerics and courtiers with avian names like Drake, Finch, and Wren. One pamphlet of 1641 recalled 'when Dr. Duck was hunted dry foot into the water, where had he not dived, the spaniels would have tore him in pieces.'[56] Another depicted the chancellor among the 'hell-born crew' of the High Commission, as 'the Duck takes wings' above the bishops.[57] Another pamphlet of 1641 concocted a mocking recipe including 'a Lambe's tongue...Duck's feathers...the white of a Duck egg' as part of a purgative against idolatry.[58] 'Quack, quack, quoth all the ducks', recited another printed attack on the ecclesiastical hierarchy.[59]

---

[51] British Library, Add. Ms. 11045, vol. v., f. 127v.

[52] Roger Quatermayne, *Qvatermayns Conqvest Over Canterbvries Covrt* (1642), 26–7.

[53] HMC, *12th Report, The Manuscripts of the Earl Cowper...Preserved at Melbourne Hall, Derbyshire*, (1888), ii. 262.

[54] Quatermayne, *Qvatermayns Conqvest Over Canterbvries Covrt*, 27.

[55] Huntington Library, Ms. El. 8847; British Library E.205 (3), 'A satyre upon the state of things this Parliament'.

[56] *The Spirituall Courts epitomized* (1641), 5, and illustrated title page.

[57] Thomas Stirry, *A Rot Amongst the Bishops, or, A Terrible Tempest in the Sea of Canterbury* (1641), 1–2.   [58] *Saint Pauls Potion, Prescribed by Doctor Commons* (1641), sig. A4.

[59] *The Decoy Duck* (1642), sig. A3v. See also *The Wrens-nest defiled* (1640 and 1641).

The disruption of the High Commission was more than a disturbance, it was another sign of a faltering and weakening regime. The Venetian ambassador wrote of an 'uproar' and a 'rising' by the 'libertine people' of London.[60] Already there were indications that the soon-to-assemble Parliament would be boisterous, and rumours of 'root and branch' petitions were in the air. The stresses in England's religious culture were becoming more acute, as some parishes sponsored prayer meetings and others were drawn to iconoclasm. As William Hawkins observed to the Earl of Leicester at the beginning of November, 'our clergy begin to apprehend some danger, seeing the people are so much bent against them, and such insolencies committed against the chancellors of bishops and officers of the High Commission.'[61] The Laudian regime had made heavy use of the court of High Commission to discipline religious offenders, and mockery of its officers demeaned both church and state. But the Privy Council proved powerless to discover the authorship of 'the late tumultuous riot and outrage', and could not guarantee that 'the late insolencies . . . and seditious tumults' would not break out again.[62]

Archbishop Laud called the outrage at St Paul's a 'mutiny', and blamed the disturbance on 'near two thousand Brownists' who 'made a tumult at the end of the court, tore down all the benches in the consistory, and cried out they would have no bishop nor no High Commission'.[63] Several of the newswriters also blamed the uproar on 'separatists'.[64] The assaults were especially galling for an archbishop who had worked so hard to restore the fabric of St Paul's Cathedral, who placed such a high value on the solemnity of ecclesiastical proceedings, and who put so much effort into the elevation of clerical dignity and the hallowing of holy space. Whether the crowd was really composed of Brownists or separatists, and whether two thousand of that sort could so readily be mobilized in October 1640, is open to question. Certainly there were sectarian and anticlerical elements in London, and since May their numbers had been growing. But Laud was prone to labelling, if not libelling, his opponents, and was ready to see separatists where there were merely angry adherents of a fractious Church of England. The composition

---

[60] Edward Razell and Peter Razell (eds.), *The English Civil War. A Contemporary Account. Volume 2: 1640–1642* (1996), 41.

[61] HMC, *Report on the Manuscripts of the Right Honourable Viscount De L'Isle . . . Vol. VI*, 339. By the time the news reached Robert Baillie, the Scottish commissioner, it was of 'the prentices pulling down of the High-Commission house of London' (David Laing (ed.), *The Letters and Journals of Robert Baillie* (3 vols., Edinburgh, 1841), i. 269).

[62] *Privy Council Registers* (facsimile of PRO, PC2/53) (1968), xii. 36, 42.

[63] Quatermayne, *Qvatermayns Conqvest Over Canterbvries Covrt*, 23; Laud, 'Diary' in *The Works of . . . William Laud*, ed. Bliss and Scott, iii. 237.

[64] British Library, Add. Ms. 11045, vol. v. f. 129.

of the crowd was most likely similar to the one that invested Lambeth house earlier in the year.

A section of the mob returned to St Paul's on the following Sunday at morning-prayer time, and 'broke into the round house where the records of the High Commission are kept, and tore them all to pieces'.[65] They subjected the proctors and other officers to 'beating and evil handling', while they ripped their way through boxes of irreplaceable court papers. The mob action partially explains why the surviving archive of the Court of High Commission is so fragmentary for the reign of Charles I. Faced with this 'new insolency and seditious tumult' the Privy Council ordered another fruitless enquiry to discover and punish the offenders.[66] But the politics of religion were changing rapidly, and by the time of the Council meeting on 5 November Parliament was already assembled, and the Laudian ascendancy was coming to an end.

GODLY MEETINGS

Popular challenges to episcopal authority could be quiet and private as well as public and violent. The frequent reference to prayer meetings and conventicles in the middle months of 1640 suggests either that such unauthorized gatherings became more common or that the authorities became increasingly alert to them. The evidence suggests that growing numbers of parishioners sought religious fulfilment beyond the routine services of their parish, while the episcopal authorities and magistrates intensified their effort to stamp such assemblies out.

In April 1640, on the eve of the first parliament to be held in eleven years, London authorities raided a house in the parish of St Botolph's Aldgate where they found a dozen workmen 'exercising the holy duty of prayer and hearing the scriptures expounded by men of the laity'. The offenders at this 'unlawful assembly or conventicle' included feltmakers, tailors, merchants, and yeomen from London, the Tower liberties, and Southwark.[67]

Early in May, while London was in uproar over the dissolution of the Short Parliament, the Court of High Commission examined James Hunt of Sevenoaks, Kent, described as 'a fanatic and frantic person, a husbandman

---

[65] HMC, *12th Report, The Manuscripts of the Earl Cowper*, ii. 262; HMC, *Report on the Manuscripts of the Right Honourable Viscount De L'Isle . . . Vol. VI*, 339; British Library, Add. Ms. 11045, vol. 16, f. 131.

[66] *Privy Council Registers* (facsimile of PRO, PC2/53) (1968), xii. 47.

[67] London Metropolitan Archives, Sessions Roll, MJ/SR/873/49–54.

and altogether illiterate, who took upon him to preach and expound the scriptures, and was lately taken absurdly preaching on a stone in St Paul's churchyard.' The location of this outrage, next to the official sermon venue of Paul's Cross, in an area surrounded by book-stalls, was highly public and highly symbolic. Hunt must have been mad, the authorities decided, and committed him to Bridewell.[68] The episode became fixed in the popular imagination over the next year and a half, when a spate of anti-puritan controversialists ridiculed 'Prophet Hunt' or 'Hunt the farmer' as the archetype of lay sectarian preachers.[69]

Elsewhere in London huge audiences gathered in the summer to hear the extempore preaching of Samuel How, a cobbler, at the Nag's Head tavern in the parish of St Stephen Coleman Street. How mounted a barrel or tub for a pulpit, and preached to crowds who pressed against the window. Dying excommunicate in September 1640, he was buried in the highway near Shoreditch instead of in consecrated ground. But How's memory lived on among his followers and in the world of anti-separatist print.[70]

Essex authorities uncovered an active conventicle at Colchester at the house of John Pirkis in East Street. Participants gathered to hear the preaching of another layman, Richard Lee, a forty-year-old tailor, and were able to attract a cross section of the Colchester artisan population. About twenty men and women were present when the meeting was raided on Wednesday, 29 July. Some of those present claimed only to have gone out of curiosity, though one or two had recently embraced Anabaptism. Among the group was Francis Lee, a comber, aged forty-five, perhaps a kinsman of the preacher, who had just arrived in Colchester from London. Francis Lee had been one of the artisans committed to the White Lion prison in Southwark earlier in May for his part in the assault on Archbishop Laud's palace, and was among those who managed to escape. He served now to link the forces of insurrectionary agitation and radical religious sectarianism between the Stour Valley and the Thames. There was much talk at this time of the episcopal 'incendiaries' who had fomented the war with Scotland, but there were other incendiaries like the Lees who fanned the flames of disaffection.[71]

---

[68] *CSPD 1640*, 415.

[69] *A Curb for Sectaries and Bold Propheciers* (1641), title page; *The Sermon and Prophecie of Mr. James Hunt* (1641), with a title-page illustration of Hunt preaching from a barrel. For more on Hunt and other lay preachers, see, Chapter 10.

[70] *The Coblers threed is cut* (1640), broadsheet; *The Vindication of the Cobler* (1640), broadsheet; Murray Tolmie, *The Triumph of the Saints: The Separate Churches of London 1616–1649* (Cambridge, 1977), 17, 36.

[71] Essex Record Office, Colchester, Book of Examinations and Depositions, 1619–1645, D/5/Sb2/7, ff. 281–281v.

Other religious assemblies were more benign, but nonetheless attracted suspicion. A London gentleman, Roger Quatermayne, was called before the High Commission four times between May and October 1640 for allegedly promoting conventicles. Archbishop Laud branded Quatermayne 'the ringleader of all the separatists', and wanted him punished. But Quatermayne produced evidence that he was 'conformable to the doctrine, discipline, and all holy orders and constitutions of our church, save only he maketh some scruple in taking the oath *ex officio*', and claimed only to have engaged in 'godly conference'. Godly conference, the authorities feared, contained the seeds of religious rebellion, and led to the flouting of ecclesiastical discipline. The Archbishop judged Quatermayne to be a casuistic Nicodemite familist, but he may simply have been a godly layman who attracted hostile attention.[72]

STRANGE UNLICENSED PREACHERS

'Strange unlicensed preachers' gatecrashed pulpits in dozens of parishes during the weeks before and after Parliament met on 3 November. If parishioners permitted the intruders to speak, there was little that incumbents or churchwardens could do to keep them out. The authorities proved powerless to prevent puritans or schismatics from preaching, and ineffective in meting out punishment after the event.

In one such episode the charismatic William Erbery, a suspended Nonconformist from south Wales, took the area south of Bristol by storm. Erbery had been vicar of St Mary's, Cardiff, and was admonished in 1634 for refusing to read the *Book of Sports*. In 1638 the High Commission removed him from his post for preaching they deemed dangerous and schismatical. Erbery's book *The Great Mystery of Godliness* preceded him to Bristol, and gave a foretaste of his radical opinions. It was filled with references to fusion with Christ and the spiritual blessings of redemption but did not overtly challenge the established church.[73]

---

[72] Quatermayne, *Qvatermayns Conqvest Over Canterbvries Covrt*, 13, 19, 23, 24, 28. Quatermayne appeared before the High Commission in April, May, June, and October 1640, and was then examined before the Privy Council. A London court acquitted him on 26 October 1640, just a week before the opening of Parliament.

[73] William Erbery, *The Great Mystery of Godliness* (1639 and 1640), was an above-board publication entered in the Stationers' register and openly printed for Robert Milbourne. As a work of Christian mysticism it was somewhat removed from the Calvinist and puritan opinions that troubled Laudian licensers. For Erbery's career, see Stephen K. Roberts, 'Erbery [Erbury], William (1604/5–1654)', *Oxford Dictionary of National Biography* (Oxford, 2004), and Richard L. Greaves and Robert Zaller (eds.), *Biographical Dictionary of British Radicals in the Seventeenth Century* (3 vols., 1982).

At Burrington, Somerset, to the disquiet of officials, and perhaps to the exhaustion of his auditors, Erbery preached for two hours both morning and afternoon on 25 and 28 October 1640. This was a major undertaking of both voice and spirit. Besides local residents the congregation included more than forty 'strangers' from Bristol, Chew Stoke, and elsewhere, who spread reports of the performance.[74] When one of the Burrington churchwardens, William Gregory, did his duty in asking to see Erbery's licence to preach, the visitor answered, 'he was not like a shepherd that did carry his tar box on his back'. The churchwarden reported that when Erbery took to the pulpit, disregarding custom, he 'did neither pray for his majesty or any archbishop of bishop...neither at the end of his prayer did he rehearse the Lord's Prayer'. Other parishioners were apparently well pleased, for after the sermon a group of them accompanied Erbery to William Luff's house in Burrington, though what they did there the churchwarden could not tell.[75]

On Sunday, 1 November, three days before the opening of Parliament, Erbery preached again at Chew Stoke, Somerset, at the invitation of the newly radicalized minister William Legg. He declaimed from nine in the morning until one in the afternoon, took a short break while the congregation sang psalms, then returned to preach two hours more. An informer reported to the Bishop of Bath and Wells that Erbery 'publicly spake and preached against the government of the Church of England as it is now established and against the authority of bishops'. He further preached 'that any person that could preach might as lawfully preach as the bishop of the diocese or any bishop in England'. This was seditious as well as schismatical, but the authorities were unable to stop him. Remaining in the pulpit, Erbery then 'publicly asked some of the company present...what they had learned out of his sermon, and they publicly answered him in the church'. The people of Chew Stoke were joined by visitors from Burrington, Chew Magna, and Bristol, and 'the church was so full that divers stood in the churchyard'.[76]

One of these auditors, John Cole of Chew Magna, explained how he came to be present at Erbery's sermon instead of attending his own church on 1 November. He had been in Bristol the day before, he said, when he learned 'that there would be a sermon tomorrow at Stoke.' Everyone was talking about Mr Erbery and said he was 'an extraordinary preacher'. The opportunity was not to be missed, so Cole went to Chew Stoke, 'but not out of any factious humour or dislike of the minister of Chew Magna', he

---

[74] Somerset Record Office, D/D/Ca 333, f. 83v.
[75] Somerset Record Office, D/D/Ca 334, ff. 109–10.   [76] Ibid., ff. 94–5.

insisted. Cole, who took notes on Erbery's sermon, was astonished by what he heard:

Amongst other things preached by him, he desired the congregation to pray to God that they might have a Christian church here in England. And further he said that a Christian church did consist in these three particulars: the members, the pastors, and the administration of God's ordinances. For the first, the members, he said they must be saints by calling. The pastors, he said, must be chosen by the members. And the administration of God's ordinances, these must be administered to none but those that were saints by calling.[77]

Another witness, Samuel Gutch, had been on his way to his own church that Sunday when he encountered his landlord who invited him to hear preach 'a man of great esteem and note'. He too took notes on Erbery's sermon, and repeated the business about the members, the pastors, and the administration. By this account Erbery not only prayed for a Christian church in England but prayed 'that Jesus Christ might reign among them, and for the destruction of that anti-Christian synagogue'.[78]

These were scandalous words, subverting the authority, overturning the liturgy, and undermining the teaching of the Church of England. They were preached from the pulpit in open church by a renegade minister with no authorization, except what he claimed from God. Nobody was punished for these irregularities, though a few churchwardens and parishioners gave accounts of themselves before the diocesan court, before that court itself guttered to a halt. Erbery himself after his triumph moved in radical godly circles between England and Wales. The new House of Commons evidently had confidence in him in January 1641 to name William Erbery among a dozen ministers granted 'liberty . . . to preach in Wales where [preaching] was wanting'.[79] Erbery later earned fame as a Seeker, even gaining credit for converting Oliver Cromwell's daughter, though one of his opponents would declare that Erbery's 'new light was no light but blackness of darkness'.[80] Erbery's exploit in Somerset on the eve of the opening of Parliament was a foretaste of challenges and confrontations that would become more frequent and more virulent in the following year and a half as English religious culture fell into confusion. The Laudian ascendancy abrubtly ended in November 1640, and the Church of England teetered on the brink of destruction.

---

[77] Somerset Record Office, D/D/Ca 334, ff. 103v–104v.   [78] Ibid., ff. 104v–105v.
[79] British Library, Harley Ms. 4931, f. 90.
[80] Henry Nicols, *The Shield Single Against the Sword Doubled* (1653), title page.

8

Babylon is Fallen

'Reformation goes on again as hot as toast', observed Thomas Knyvett in November 1640, 'I pray god the violent turning of the tide do not make an inundation.'[1] This cautious Norfolk gentleman, a moderate Protestant conformist, found himself caught up in a revolution. Like many of his contemporaries, he was not sure whether to run for shelter or to praise the Lord.

The parliament that met in November 1640 exhibited a euphoric sense of possibilities, portending changes in policy and power whereby the proud would be humbled and the righteous would rise. Encouraged and pressured by the Scots, Parliament sought to dismantle the policies of 'Thorough' that had sustained the personal rule of Charles I, and to punish the promoters of the recent Bishops' Wars. Members would seek satisfaction for a wide accumulation of grievances, from ship money to monopolies to abuse of the prerogative courts. This chapter examines aspirations for religious reformation at this time among the parliamentary elite and in the country at large.

Parliamentary leaders pursued three principal religious objectives: first, to change the face of the Caroline church, to reverse the innovations of the Laudian ascendancy, and to eradicate the errors and excesses of ceremonialism, sacerdotalism, and Arminianism. This was partly a programme of cleansing, partly a programme of salvage and restoration. It aimed to purge liturgical excrescences, and by removing such impositions as altars and kneeling rails to return to the early Jacobean status quo. The second policy, closely related, was to punish the perpetrators of the Laudian campaign, and to rehabilitate or promote its victims. This was a programme of personnel measures, encouraging and answering parishioners' complaints about innovations, targeting 'malignants' and 'incendiaries', and pointedly rehabilitating those who had been suspended, excluded, or imprisoned over the previous few years. The third policy was more visionary, and therefore harder to achieve.

[1] Thomas Knyvett to John Buxton, 24 November 1640, HMC, *Report on Manuscripts in Various Collections* (1903), ii. 259.

It was to embark on a true reformation of religion, to pick up where the Tudor reformers had stopped, to repair the damage done by back-sliding, and to perfect a church that would be truly pleasing to God. Militants believed they had the best opportunity in a hundred years to pursue religious reformation. It was also a matter of urgency, some thought, to remove the impurities that threatened England with the wrath of an angry God.[2]

These policies occupied Parliament intermittently throughout the 1640s. And, like most programmes driven by righteousness, anger, and zeal, they had unintended consequences. Reformers were unable to prevent religious life in many parishes from degenerating into disorder. They could not control the surge of religious energies released in radical sectarianism. Nor could they forestall a reactive surge of sympathy for the traditional Church of England. The turning of the tide threatened the inundation of both church and state, releasing the torrents that led to civil war.

GOD PROSPER THIS GOOD BEGINNING

The calling of a parliament in the autumn of 1640 produced expectations of a providential transformation of fortune. Godly observers, who just a few months earlier had prayed for relief from their Egyptian or Babylonian captivity, now expected 'a settlement both of our religion and peace, with the punishment of offenders and reformation of grievances, which had almost made a deluge of the whole kingdom.'[3] Godly diarists, who had earlier despaired about 'sinful innovations' and 'debauched courses', now expressed delight in the 'blessed news' and 'good hopes' of 'the sweetest goings on of the parliament'.[4] A correspondent wrote confidently to the mayor of Chester about the coming reckoning, 'God prosper this good beginning and send a successful parliament, which by God's assistance will put life into us all. Guilty and obnoxious men do tremble and wax pale since the report of a parliament.'[5] Indeed, Laudian and ceremonialist clergy were already commiserating, 'the times look very black'. John Cosin wrote to Archbishop Laud, 'these times are exceeding bad. . . . God send us better times', as they braced for attack by

[2] The best introduction to this topic is still John Morrill, 'The Attack on the Church of England in the Long Parliament, 1640–1642', in Derek Beales and Geoffrey Best (eds.), *History, Society and the Churches: Essays in Honour of Owen Chadwick* (Cambridge, 1985), 105–24.

[3] Alexander Rigby to his brother in Lancashire, HMC, *14th Report, Appendix, part IV, The Manuscripts of Lord Kenyon* (1894), 59, 60.

[4] New College, Oxford, Ms. 9502, Robert Woodford's diary, April–July 1639, November–December 1640.

[5] Cheshire Record Office, Mayor's Letter Book, Z. ML/2, f. 281.

people they deemed 'the malignant enemies of the church'.[6] Expecting 'a stirring parliament', William Hawkins observed that 'our clergy begin to apprehend some danger, seeing the people are so much bent against them.'[7] William Barret prayed for the new parliament to have 'zeal, courage, and boldness for God and his truth, and to fight it out against the Goliaths of these times'.[8]

The collapse of the Laudian ascendancy was one of the earliest and most obvious signs of revolution. Priests and prelates who had only a few months earlier gathered in convocation to draft new canons were now shaken, humbled, or disgraced. The leading bishops were impeached or imperilled, the Arminian avant-garde faced parliamentary investigation. Petitions from 'we the distressed throughout the land' sought relief and revenge, as ceremonialists and disciplinarians were called to account at Westminster and were pilloried in the newly unfettered press.[9]

Until the opening of the Long Parliament, Laudians and Arminians had enjoyed the favour of the episcopal hierarchy and the disciplinary backing of the ecclesiastical courts. After November 1640 they found themselves under attack from a hostile parliament and press. Until November 1640 ministers were likely to be censured by the ecclesiastical authorities if they failed to read the King's *Book of Sports* from their pulpits. Under the auspices of the Long Parliament they were likely to be singled out for scrutiny if they did.[10] The installers of altars and Communion rails, who had earlier basked in the approbation of the bishops, now found themselves answerable as 'delinquents'.[11] The humiliation and degradation was particularly acute for those priests who had claimed that 'God will have us reputed as his ambassadors, and as shining stars, yea, as angels'.[12]

The Wiltshire minister Thomas Marler, Archdeacon of Salisbury and a correspondent of Edward Hyde, sensed a 'violent feeling' against the clergy,

---

[6] HMC, *9th Report* (1884), Part II, Appendix, 432; *CSPD 1640–41*, 82.

[7] HMC, *Report on the Manuscripts of the Right Honourable Viscount De L'Isle . . . Vol. VI. Sidney Papers, 1626–1698* (1966), 356, 337, 339.

[8] William Barret to Sir Edward Dering, 2 November 1640, in Lambert B. Larking (ed.), *Proceedings, Principally in the County of Kent, in Connection with the Parliaments Called in 1640* (Camden Society, first series, vol. lxxx, 1862), 21.

[9] Richard Bernard, *A Short View of the Praelaticall Church of England* (1641), title page.

[10] British Library, Add. Ms. 26786, ff. 7v, 8, 8v, 9v; Maija Jansson (ed.), *Proceedings in the Opening Session of the Long Parliament . . . Volume 1: 3 November–19 December 1640* (Rochester, NY, 2000), 368, 372, 377. The King's declaration was variously referred to as 'the book for recreations,' 'the book of liberty,' and 'the morris book' for its advocacy of morris dancing.

[11] J. H. Bettey (ed.), *Calendar of the Correspondence of the Smyth Family of Ashton Court 1548–1642* (Bristol Record Society, vol. xxxv, 1982), 164.

[12] William Hardwick, *Conformity with Piety, Requisite in God's Service* (1638), 8.

especially in Parliament, and wrote in January 1641 that 'all the clergy look for a doom as well as the metropolitan' [Archbishop Laud].[13] High-fliers and over-reachers like John Pocklington and William Heywood found their careers in tatters, their parishes against them, their books publicly burnt.[14] 'Here's like to be such a purgation of black-coats', wrote Thomas Knyvett in January 1641, 'as if the parliament entertains all the complaints of the brethren, I know not where they will find new ones to put in.... The country is now full of warrants for certificates against bishop Wren.'[15]

A subversive pamphlet of the time entitled *Fortunes Tennis-Ball* admonished 'all those that are elevated to take heed of falling'. It warned the Caroline elite of courtiers, judges, and, above all, prelates that their 'pride will have a fall'. Substituting the bouncing ball for the classic revolutionary wheel of fortune, it predicted that those who 'soar aloft' would surely fall, and that 'Fortune' would humble the mighty and 'kick [them] down below'.[16] Popular songs echoed this sentiment with lines like 'down go they' and 'up go we'.[17] A mocking pamphlet of 1641 depicted the rise and fall of the prelates who, 'when they have gotten to the height of pride' are suddenly 'pulled from state' and 'at the last they ever tumble down'.[18] With somewhat more polish Henry Burton told the House of Commons, 'When the enemies of God are advanced to the height and to the pitch of all their pride and all their cruelty, then this is a time that doth fore-run their destruction.'[19] It was another way of saying 'down go they' and 'up go we'.

The new political circumstances produced a dramatic realignment of career paths, with altered opportunities for publishing, patronage, and preferment. Clergy who had been silenced, suspended, or inhibited now commanded the most prominent pulpits, while their Laudian adversaries fell from favour. The choice of parliamentary preachers reflected the abrupt reversal of fortunes. Many of the ministers selected to preach at Westminster had previously experienced trouble with the authorities. Stephen Marshall, for example, had been reported as 'dangerous' in 1637 and had been investigated for 'want of conformity'. Cornelius Burges had faced interrogation before the High Commission, and as recently as September 1640 his house had been

---

[13] O. Ogle and W. H. Bliss (eds.), *Calendar of the Clarendon State Papers Preserved in the Bodleian Library* (Oxford, 1872), i. 211, 217.

[14] House of Lords Record Office, Main Papers, 13 January 1641; John Rushworth, *Historical Collections of Private Proceedings of State* (8 vols., 1680–1701), iv. 188; HMC, *14th Report, The Manuscripts of His Grace the Duke of Portland* (1894), iii. 75.

[15] Bertram Schofield (ed.), *The Knyvett Letters (1620–1644)* (Norfolk Record Society, 1949), 98–9.   [16] *Fortunes Tennis-Ball* (1640), 1–4.

[17] For example, 'The Roundheads Race', in *The Distraction of Our Times* (1642), 7–8.

[18] *A Second Message to William Laud* (1641), sigs. A2v–A3.

[19] Henry Burton, *Englands Bondage and Hope of Deliverance* (1641), 1, 9.

searched for incriminating writings.[20] In November Marshall and Burges not only preached before the House of Commons but had their sermons recommended for printing.[21] Henry Burton recalled a more dramatic change of fortune when he preached before Parliament in June 1641, 'this very month four years ago when God called me to preach in another kind of pulpit [the pillory], not far from this place'. Formerly, said Burton, 'many mouths were stopped, many shut up', but now 'parliament hath opened their mouths... it has opened the prisons'.[22]

The new parliamentary preaching was inspirational, electric, a summons to activism and zeal. It affected people in the country as well as at Westminster, as manuscript reports preceded printed copies. Writing to Viscount Scudamore in late November 1640, Edward Rossingham remarked that the sermons were 'delivered in such a manner as was not safe to have been done of late days, but now the truth is, all the pulpits do now ring of the disorders of the clergy both in doctrine and discipline.'[23] Robert Baillie reported back to Scotland that 'many ministers used greater freedom than ever was heard of. Episcopacy itself beginning to be cried down and [the] Covenant cried up, and the liturgy to be scorned.'[24]

The Northamptonshire steward Robert Woodford, who was in London on the fast day of 17 November, could barely restrain his enthusiasm. 'I was in Aldermanbury church about fourteen hours together, where three ministers prayed and preached one after another, Mr. Calamy and two strangers', he wrote in his diary. The Westminster preachers Marshall and Burges 'delivered glorious things with extraordinary zeal and fervour. This hath been a heavenly day, Lord hear the prayers of your people, work a holy reformation, and make this nation to praise.'[25]

Woodford's prayers appeared to be answered, and he was soon thanking God for letting him see the light of a new era. Early in December 1640 Woodford registered 'good hopes of good from God by means of this parliament'. On 11 December he recorded 'blessed news from London of the sweetest going on of the parliament'. By 26 December he could point to significant steps towards reformation: 'the Lieutenant of Ireland is in the Tower, the archbishop of Canterbury under the Black Rod, the Lord Keeper

---

[20] PRO, PC2/52, f. 369.

[21] Cornelius Burges, *The First Sermon, Preached to the Honorable House of Commons, now assembled in Parliament at the Publique Fast. Novemb. 17. 1640* (1641); Stephen Marshall, *A Sermon Preached before the Honourable House Of Commons...November 17 1640* (1641). [22] Burton, *Englands Bondage*, 1, 9, 14.

[23] British Library, Add. Ms. 1045, vol. v., f.144v.

[24] David Laing (ed.), *The Letters and Journals of Robert Baillie* (3 vols., Edinburgh, 1841), i. 273.

[25] Robert Woodford's diary, New College, Oxford, Ms. 9502, 17 November 1640.

run away, bishop Wren bound to appear, and six judges.'[26] In July 1641 he looked back in gratitude, 'oh Lord, what great things hast thou done for this kingdom, thou hast made the cursed bishops and their clergy which were the head to be now at the tail, and thy faithful and godly ministers and people to triumph.'[27]

William Hawkins likewise enthused about the 'remarkable things' done in Parliament, observing in December, 'there was never, I dare say, so busy a time in England'. Affairs continued well into January 1641, with 'a possibility or reformation, so that we all hope for good days hereafter if there be but a good success to these earnest beginnings'.[28] The godly Ann Temple expressed similar enthusiasm. 'God . . . hath done wonderful things among us already, and gives us hope of more', she wrote to her daughter on 16 January, 'let us labour to be thankful and continue in our prayers.'[29] There had been a sea change, a seismic shift, the beginning of a world turned upside down.

THIS GOLDEN YEAR

Many members of the godly community looked back on November 1640 as a hinge-point in time, the beginning of an almost cosmic divide. Dozens of contemporary observers contrasted 'then' with 'now', and remarked on the miracles that had happened in England 'of late'. An era of 'great affliction' gave way to one of 'seasonable mercies'.[30] (In stark contrast, conservative historians of the 1640s and later looked back on the 1630s as England's Halycon days, and dated the distempers from 1641, '*ab anno illo infortunato*'.)[31]

Formerly, observed the London wood-turner Nehemiah Wallington, 'the whole land was overrun with idolatry and popery and all manner of abominations', but latterly 'the lord's hand is open and giving', with 'mercies . . . so exceeding great and many that I know not where to begin or where to end'.[32] In another notebook he wrote emphatically, 'Oh remember, remember, and let it never be out of your mind, that the year 1640 was a praying year', and that the prayers of 'the poor people of god' were answered. 'Tell it to your children,' Wallington continued, 'that they may show it to their children and they to the next generation, that in the year 1640 when the people of God did humble themselves in fasting and prayer, God did then hear them and . . . sent

---

[26] Woodford's diary, 2, 11, 26 December 1640.   [27] Ibid., 29 July 1641.
[28] HMC, *Report on the Manuscripts of the Right Honourable Viscount De L'Isle . . . Vol. VI*, 341, 352, 359.
[29] East Sussex Record Office, Lewes, Dunn Ms. 51/54 (microfilm XA 73/11).
[30] Thomas Case, *Gods Waiting to be Gracious Unto his People* (1642), 96.
[31] *A Discourse Discovering Some Mysteries of our New State* (Oxford, 1645), title page.
[32] British Library, Sloan Ms. 922, ff. 105–105v.

his mercies to come flowing in amain among us.'[33] 'There is a time when Babylon must down, and the bishops who are but whelps of that whore's litter must down before her, and why may not the time be now?' reasoned the Scots-leaning 'northern scout'.[34]

By the middle of 1641 some writers were dating their letters '*annus mirabilis*' or '*anno renovationis*', as if they knew themselves to be in the midst of something strange and special.[35] To the Cornish minister William Crompton it was '*annus mirabilis* 1641 . . . a wonderful year of God's mercies to England'.[36] They were 'now *in loco et tempore mutationis*', Lord Saye proclaimed in March 1641.[37] A publication entitled *Englands Reioycing*, celebrating 'God's goodness and mercy to England in delivering them from the cruel tyranny of blood-thirsty prelates', was printed, so it proudly proclaimed, 'in the year of the downfall of the prelates, 1641'.[38] Another pamphlet of 1641, *Englands Doxologie*, applauded the members of Parliament, 'those illustrious worthies of the world', and their work '*hoc anno aureo*, this golden year'. They have restored 'religious Christians' and 'silenced scandalous priests'. They have imprisoned the Archbishop and 'quelled all the Canturburian faction'. They have dismounted the canons, cut off the Deputy of Ireland, and enacted a triennial parliament. 'They have damned ship-money . . . taxed monopolists . . . displaced pluralists . . . extirpated innovations', and confirmed a peace with Scotland. They have, in short, 'righted the wronged, eased the oppressed [and] punished the . . . delinquent.'[39] In a similar catalogue of achievements Thomas Mocket gave thanks for those who had 'taken away arbitrary government . . . quelled evil councillors . . . settled a triennial parliament . . . put down the High Commission . . . damned the oath *ex officio* . . . punished (the) authors of innovations . . . recalled the banished exiles', and so on. Righteousness had been delivered, Israel had been restored, and Parliament had secured 'the glory, safety and sinews of our nation'.[40]

'Those who did strive to trample o'er the crown | By your true justice are all tumbled down', declaimed the poet John Bond in praise of the parliament in October 1641. 'Behold', he continued, 'papists tremble . . . Arminians tumble'

[33] British Library, Add. Ms. 21935, ff. 94–94v.
[34] *The Second Discovery by the Northern Scout* (1642), 16. This pamphlet is mostly concerned with events of 1640.
[35] John Hall to Sir Robert Harley, 21 June 1641, HMC *14th Report, The Manuscripts of His Grace the Duke of Portland*, iii. 77; British Library, Add. Ms. 70003, f.111.
[36] George Hughes, *The Art of Embalming Dead Saints* (1642), 48.
[37] W. A. Shaw, *A History of the English Church 1640–1660* (2 vols., 1900), i. 65.
[38] *Englands Reioycing at the Prelats Downfall* (1641), title page.
[39] J.L., *Englands Doxologie* (1641), 9, 11–12.
[40] Thomas Mocket, *The National Covenant* (1642), sigs. A, Av, A2v, 13.

and 'the priests of Baal ... lament their fortunes'. England was never happier or more secure, for 'Thus do all things by you securely stand, | And thus all things do flourish in our land'.[41] Another pamphleteer of 1641 celebrated 'the happy deliverance of this land' from ambitious prelates, popish plots, surplices, organs, and altars.[42] It was one more case of 'down go they' and 'up go we'.

Preachers commonly adopted triumphant, biblical, even mystical, terms to describe the transformation. The text from Revelation, 'Babylon is fallen, is fallen', inspired countless sermons in the winter of 1640 and the spring of 1641, as preachers associated the late Caroline religious regime with Babylon, and its downfall with the judgement of the Lord.[43] Cornelius Burges's fast-day sermon on 17 November 1640 set the tone. The 'Babylonish captivity' was over, Babylon was confounded, and the people of God were 'returning to Zion'. It was only a beginning, he warned, and dangers abounded, but England was poised at last to complete the Reformation.[44] William Bridge, who titled his parliamentary sermon *Babylons Downfall*, urged auditors and readers towards 'full and perfect' reformation so that 'Babylon shall fall ... down with it, down with it, even to the ground. ... How else shall Sion rise, if Babylon do not fall?'[45] A year later Burges made a congratulatory progress report when he told members of Parliament that they had saved 'our religion from corruption in doctrine, from pollution in worship, from superstition in ceremonies, from exhorbitancy and tyranny in ecclesiastical government and discipline'.[46]

Lecturers like John Bond of Exeter exalted in the astonishing change of circumstances, almost a reordering of time, as England was delivered from its 'Babylonish captivity' and returned to the task of building the temple:

Hast thou an estate or lands or houses, go home and new date thy leases, let them all run from the year 1640. I say again, one thousand six hundred and forty, for then was thy term renewed ... hast thou a wife, children, yea a life of thine own to lose, I tell thee ... all these are new given thee too, in the same year 1640.[47]

'It is the regeneration of a nation', exulted John Geree in May 1641.[48] The church of God was delivered 'from bondage, and from the Babylonian

---

[41] John Bond, *Englands reiocying for the Parliaments Retvrne* (1641), 4–6.

[42] *A Rent in the Lawn Sleeves or Episcopacy Eclypsed* (1641), title page, 1, 4.

[43] Revelation 14: 8.

[44] Cornelius Burges, *The First Sermon, Preached to the Honorable House of Commons Novemb. 17. 1640*, 8.

[45] William Bridge, *Babylons Downfall. A Sermon Lately Preached at Westminster Before Sundry of the Honourable House of Commons* (1641), 1, 10, 23, 28.

[46] Cornelius Burges, *Another Sermon Preached to the Honourable House of Commons now assembled in Parliament, November the fifth, 1641* (1641), preface.

[47] John Bond, *A Doore of Hope, also Holy and Loyall Activity* (1641), sigs. B, Bv, G3, 10, 23, 45.

[48] John Geree, *Iudah's Ioy at the Oath* (1641), sig. B4.

captivity', claimed Henry Burton in June.[49] The world had changed from confinement to liberty, from night to day, from darkness to light.

It became a common device in parliamentary preaching to compare the world before 1640 with the new world that was now being born. 'It was not long since that God called us to mourning and weeping... darkness surrounded us. But now behold, the Lamb stands upon Mount Sion', preached Jeremiah Burroughs in September 1641. 'This is the year of mercies', Burroughs told the House of Commons, 'this year is the *mirabilis annus*, in that it is such a resemblance of the day of judgement; we see now the goats stand on the left hand and the sheep on the right.' As it was said of the Armada year, '*octogessimus octavus mirabilis annus*, much more may it be said of this, *quadragessimus primus mirabilis ille annus*.' Only recently God's worship was oppressed, but now those who vilified the saints were themselves made vile. 'Religion is maintained... prelatical tyranny banished', and liberties secured through triennial parliaments. 'Babylon is fallen, it is fallen,' Burroughs enthused, and characterized this change of affairs as 'the miracle of our age'. God's hand was evident in this revolutionary change of fortune, for 'scarce ever was there a more sudden turn of the face of things in a kingdom since the world began'.[50]

Stephen Marshall likewise waxed lyrical about 'this one year, this wonderful year, wherein God hath done more for us... than in four score years before.' This year, Marshall continued, 'have we seen broken the yokes which lay upon our estates, liberties, religion and conscience; the intolerable yokes of Star Chamber and terrible High Commission and their appendances, unsufferable pressures to many thousands, all eased, removed, broken and swept away.' Looking back from September 1641, ignorant of the disasters about to befall, Marshall thanked God for 'this one year, this wonderful year', with its 'hopes and beginnings of a very jubilee and resurrection both of church and state'. 'Oh wonderful year', he expostulated, all the more remarkable comparing England's experience to that of neighbouring countries like Germany that were drenched in blood.[51]

Marshall's colleague Edmund Calamy shared this sense of living through a special moment in history. Preaching in February 1642, when the revolution was already losing direction, he reminded members that 'the mercies of these

---

[49] Burton, *Englands Bondage*, 14.

[50] Jeremiah Burroughs, *Sions Ioy. A Sermon Preached to the Honourable House of Commons* (1641), 3, 23–5, 33, 44, 48.

[51] Stephen Marshall, *A Peace-Offering to God* (1641), 40, 45–6. John Vicars also saw 1641 as a year of jubilee, a year of memorable mercies, *God in the Mount* (1641), title page, 5. Enthusiasm of this sort was hard to sustain after the outbreak of the Irish rebellion and the sharp break between King and Parliament.

last two years do far exceed all the mercies that ever this nation did receive since the first reformation.' Members would recall a time when

> pits were digged for the righteous, gallows provided for Mordecai because he would not bow to Haman, dens of lions for Daniel because he would not leave praying, fiery furnaces for the three children because they would not worship the golden image, dungeons for Jeremiah because he would preach the truth in boldness. We were like firebrands in the fire, like birds in the snare.

Then came the change, the turn.

> God almighty hath made a blessed turn for the better. . . . The enemies of the church hang down their heads and the godly begin to lift them up. . . . The winter is past, the rain is over and gone, the flowers appear on the earth, the time of the singing of birds is come.[52]

PETITIONS FROM WE THE DISTRESSED

The opening of a parliament friendly to religious reform stimulated a nation-wide surge of letters and petitions denouncing scandalous and inadequate ministers. Hundreds of petitioners excoriated the Laudian regime and called for redress and renewal. The process of petitioning and denunciation that began in November 1640 continued up to the outbreak of civil war, and would not be complete until the purging of 'scandalous and malignant' ministers in the mid-1640s. County petitions for and against episcopacy added to the pressure from the provinces.

The Commons created a Grand Committee for Religion with a subcommittee specifically charged to receive parish petitions. Part of its brief was to enquire into the scarcity of preaching ministers throughout the kingdom, and to consider ways of removing 'persecuting, innovating or scandalous ministers' and putting others in their place. The committee was empowered to send for witnesses and to examine all relevant writings and records.[53] The chairman, Sir Edward Dering, was particularly energetic in gathering information from Kent, but members from every constituency and 'all ingenuous persons in every county' were invited to contribute to

---

[52] Edmund Calamy, *Gods Free Mercy to England* (1642), sigs. A3, A4v, 4–6, quoting Canticles 2: 11. Haman had sought to destroy the Jews, but was hanged on the gallows he had prepared for Mordecai (Esther 7: 10). For another ecstatic review of the achievements of 1641 see Thomas Case, *Gods Waiting to be Gracious Unto his People* (1642), 114–16.

[53] Jansson (ed.), *Proceedings in the Opening Session of the Long Parliament . . . Vol.1*, 156; British Library, Harley Ms. 4931, f. 100; Larking (ed.), *Proceedings, Principally in the County of Kent*, 80–100; Bedfordshire and Luton Archives, St John Papers, J. 1365.

the effort.[54] This was a recipe for trouble, for it stirred up local discontents, further stimulated the submission of petitions, and encouraged parishioners who felt aggrieved to seek revenge.

Parliamentary business was almost overwhelmed by the inflow of paper from the country. 'There is working in all parts, petition upon petition', wrote William Bedford at the end of November 1640.[55] John Pym observed in December that there were 'divers hundred complaints there depending in the House against scandalous ministers, and yet (I believe) the hundredth part of them is not yet brought in.'[56] 'Here are divers petitions already come up, and more are daily expected', wrote Charles Howard in January 1641. Most of these petitions targeted particular incumbents, but many added the plea 'that episcopacy may be utterly abolished'.[57] Another wave of parish petitions came in May, perhaps stimulated by discussion of the Protestation. By the summer of 1641 Parliament had received approximately nine hundred petitions, representing roughly one in ten of England's parishes.[58]

Some of the resulting letters and petitions survive among the records of Parliament, and many more can be found in local and family archives. Sometimes the files include written responses from the ministers concerned, with answers and explanations that tell different sides of the story. High-profile cases appeared in print, no doubt prompting other parishes to rat on their troublesome priests.[59]

Historians may exploit this body of material in various ways. They can use it, most fruitfully, to show how the Laudian ceremonialist programme of the 1630s had been locally implemented, and how it had been received. The

---

[54] Mary Anne Everett Green (ed.), *Diary of John Rous, Incumbent of Santon Downham, Suffolk, from 1625 to 1642* (Camden Society, 1856) 112; British Library, Add. Ms. 26786, passim; Larking (ed.), *Proceedings, Principally in the County of Kent*, 101–240.

[55] Bodleian Library, Oxford, Tanner Ms. 65, f. 209.

[56] *The Speech or Declaration of John Pymm, Esquire, To the Lords . . . Against William Laud* (1641), 28.

[57] Bettey (ed.), *Calendar of the Correspondence of the Smyth Family of Ashton Court*, 168.

[58] Maija Jansson (ed.), *Proceedings in the Opening Session of the Long Parliament . . . Volume 4: 19 April–5 June 1641* (Rochester, NY, 2003), 421; Shaw, *History of the English Church, 1640–1660*, i. 14.

[59] House of Lords Record Office, Main Papers, 1640–2. See also *Articles Exhibited in the Parliament Against William Beale, Doctor of Divinity, and Master of St. Johns Colledge in the Vniversity of Cambridge* (1641); *The Petition and Articles of severall Charge exhibited in Parliament against Edward Finch* (1641); *The Petition of the Inhabitants of Istleworth in the County of Middlesex against William Grant* (1641); *Articles Exhibited in Parliament against Master Iohn Squire, Vicar of Saint Leonard in Shoreditch* (1641). Others under investigation included William Fuller of Ely; Phillip Gray of Pont Island, Northumberland; William Heywood of St Giles in the Fields; Timothy Hutton of St Giles Cripplegate; William Lang of Bradworthy, Devon; John Pocklington of Yelden, Bedfordshire; and Benjamin Spencer of Southwark.

letters and petitions shed light on the introduction and impact of liturgical accoutrements like altars and rails, and the ceremonialist practice of kneeling and bowing. Their information about the elaboration of vestments and church furnishings is invaluable. Though hostile and biased, and designed to settle scores, the parish petitions expose strained relations between clergy and laity during Charles I's personal rule. They also reveal how rapidly the religious environment was changing after November 1640, amidst calls for far-reaching reform.

By no means were all the reports bad. Many parishioners were satisfied with their clergy, especially those who practiced good neighbourliness and peace. The parishioners of Hinxhill, Kent, for example, certified their minister, Elias Wood, to be 'a diligent and faithful preacher of the word of God every Lord's day, orthodox in doctrine, and of godly life and conversation, but his living is a very small parsonage not above forty pounds per annum.'[60] Kentish magistrates reported that George Stancombe, curate of Birchington in the Isle of Thanet, 'hath for divers years past . . . civilly, peaceably, and fairly demeaned and deported himself towards us and his neighbours, and thereby gained their good esteem and opinion.'[61] By contrast, there were dozens of alleged womanizers and drunkards, back-biters and bullies, as well as proponents of Arminian theology and Laudian innovations, who needed to be reformed or removed.

Testimony poured into Parliament of the malignancy affecting the clerical establishment, and the apparent penetration of idolatry and superstition. The episcopal licensing chaplains were revealed to be hostile to godliness and friendly to Arminianism.[62] Parish Laudians were denounced as 'the gall and wormwood of the episcopal government', and as 'vermin' who defiled the church.[63] Reports of their 'popish' practices fed puritan fears of a drift towards Rome. Much of this was exaggerated, of course, but it fuelled the conviction that the church was contaminated, and that drastic remedies were required.

By the close of 1640 Parliament had acted against scandalous or malignant clergymen from Buckinghamshire, Essex, Northamptonshire, Oxfordshire, Somerset, Suffolk, and Surrey, with many more awaiting review.[64] The most common complaints concerned ostentatious veneration of the altar and

---

[60] British Library, Add. Ms. 26786, f. 135;. Larking (ed.), *Proceedings, Principally in the County of Kent*, 173.

[61] British Library, Add. Ms. 26785, f. 141; Larking (ed.), *Proceedings, Principally in the County of Kent*, 180. Stancombe became a notable collector of parliamentary pamphlets, many of which survive in North American libraries.   [62] See Chapter 12.

[63] John White, *The First Century of Scandalous, Malignant Priests* (1643), sig. A2.

[64] Shaw, *History of the English Church, 1640–1660*, ii. 295–9.

denial of Communion to parishioners who would not kneel at the rail. Most of these ministers had embraced the Laudian innovations, engaged in ceremonial posturing, and embellished their churches with 'superstitious' images. Many were negligent or contentious preachers as well as sticklers for ceremonial discipline. Emanuel Uty of Chigwell, Essex, for example, practised 'frequent and offensive bowing and cringing' before the altar, and allegedly told parishioners that 'if the bishops command he ought to obey, and that he might be as well damned for not obeying the bishops' laws as God's laws.'[65] John Duncan of Stoke near Ipswich, Suffolk, allegedly 'maintained that there was a relative holiness in the communion table, in the timber of the church, and in the surplice'.[66] Thomas Vahan of Chatham, Kent, not only promoted bowing at the name of Jesus but cursed refusers, 'that their bowels might drop out that did not observe it'.[67] Ministers given the chance to rebut such allegations attempted to expose their inconsistency and error.[68]

Some of the rancor and enmity that went into this process may be gauged from the papers from Huntingdonshire, where earlier anodyne estimations were revised to make them much more critical. Initially, in response to solicitations from Westminster, the officers of each hundred or division prepared certificates identifying most of their ministers as 'painful' in their calling and adequate in their preaching. This was rather like churchwardens at a visitation responding '*omnia bene*'. The worst they could say of the Laudian John Pocklington, pluralist vicar of Waresley and author of controversial works about sabbaths and altars, was 'for his life his parishioners find no fault, though some think there be much cause'. But when the returns from the four divisions were revised they said nothing about 'painful' and well-intentioned curates. Now the county appeared to be riddled with unworthy hunters and tipplers and Arminians enmired in religious error. Pocklington was now described as 'non-resident, defamed for a superstitious Arminian, and no friend of preaching'. Others were attacked as 'drones, given to the world only, and rich'. The 'certificate of unworthy ministers in the county of Huntingdon' submitted to Parliament in January 1641 was a hatchet job, feeding a reformist frenzy.[69]

---

[65] *To the Right Honovrable The Knights, Citizens and Bvrgesses . . . The Humble Petition of Some of the Parishioners of the Parish of Chigwell* (1641), broadsheet; British Library, Add. Ms. 21935, f. 113.

[66] Maija Jansson (ed.), *Proceedings in the Opening Session of the Long Parliament . . . Volume 2: 21 December 1640–20 March 1641* (Rochester, NY, 2000), 301; A. G. Matthews, *Walker Revised. Being a Revision of John Walker's Sufferings of the Clergy during the Grand Rebellion 1642–60* (Oxford, 1948), 151.

[67] Larking (ed.), *Proceedings, Principally in the County of Kent*, 227.

[68] Bodleian Library, J. Walker Ms. c. 11; Daniel Whitby, *The Vindication of a True Protestant* (Oxford, 1644).   [69] Bodleian Library, Carte Ms. 103, ff. 58–65.

PARLIAMENTARY PROCEEDINGS

It became clear from its opening session that the new parliament was bent on reform. Almost immediately the Commons accepted petitions on behalf of Burton, Bastwick, and Prynne, and released Alexander Leighton, John Lilburne, and Peter Smart from prison. All had clashed with the Laudian authorities, and their rehabilitation signalled a new dispensation. The favourable treatment of parish petitions also promised change. Another signal was sent on Sunday, 22 November, when 'the parliament men would not receive the communion at St Margaret's church in Westminster . . . before the rails were pulled down and the communion table was removed into the middle of the chancel.' This was a vivid indication that the Laudian altar policy was ended, and an incitement to other parishes to take similar initiatives of their own.[70]

Over the next eighteen months the signals became more confusing. While some members wished to plunge into religious reform, others enjoined caution or delay. Some favoured moderate adjustments to the established discipline and worship, whereas others wanted radical pruning, 'root and branch'. The House of Lords was always more conservative than the Commons, and 1641 saw sharpening polarization within each House as well as divisions between them. The pronouncements, orders, remonstrances, and protestations that emerged from Westminster on the subject of religion were inconsistent and ambiguous, and none commanded the force of law.[71] Local reactions to these mixed signals are discussed in the following chapter.

Alarmed by reports of religious disturbances, the Lords issued an order on 16 January 1641 'that the divine service be performed as it is appointed by the Acts of Parliament of this realm', and that all clergy 'shall forbear to introduce any rites or ceremonies that may give offence otherwise than those which are established by the laws of the land.' This attempt to stabilize the established order was originally intended for churches within the London area, but it was seized on by conformists nationwide.[72]

A radically different proposal emerged from the House of Commons a week later on 23 January, 'concerning commissions to be sent into all counties for the defacing, demolishing, and quite taking away of all images, altars or tables turned altarwise, crucifixes, superstitious pictures, monuments, and

---

[70] *Commons Journal*, ii. 32; HMC, *Report on Manuscripts in Various Collections* (1903), ii. 259. [71] Shaw, *History of the English Church, 1640–1660*, i. 103–10.

[72] *Journals of the House of Lords*, iv. 134, 395; *Die Sabbati 16. Januarii. 1640. It is this day ordered* (1641), broadsheet (printed pursuant to order of 9 September).

relics of idolatry out of all churches or chapels.'[73] Parliamentary reformers envisaged an orderly reversal of Laudian arrangements and a systematic undoing of ceremonial innovations under the guidance of local authorities; but activists in some parishes took this proposal as a licence for iconoclasm and freelance reformation.

Parliament's Protestation of 5 May 1641 upheld 'the true reformed protestant religion, expressed in the doctrine of the Church of England, against all popery and popish innovations.' This was a unifying declaration to which almost everyone could subscribe, although the words were susceptible to various interpretations. The Commons quickly added a clarification declaring that the Protestation extended only to 'the public doctrine professed in the said church, and that the words are not to be extended to the maintaining of any form of worship, discipline or government, nor of rites or ceremonies.' By inviting laymen throughout England to set their hands against 'popish innovations', and by stimulating discussion about the potential meanings of this phrase, the Protestation triggered rancorous debate about religious discipline and practice.[74]

Reformers in Parliament continued to lend their authority to efforts to purge the church of Laudian innovations and popish remnants. On 8 August 1641 the Commons passed an order *permitting* churchwardens to remove Communion rails and to reposition tables.[75] Three weeks later on 1 September 1641 they prepared an ordinance, to be read in all counties, cities, and boroughs, *instructing* churchwardens to restore Communion tables to their pre-Laudian positions, to remove the rails, and level the chancels, 'as they were before the late innovations'. The order furthermore outlawed crucifixes and scandalous pictures and images, forbade all corporal bowing at the name of Jesus or bowing towards the altar, and enjoined a more disciplined observance of the sabbath without Sunday dancing or sports.[76]

Invited on 8 September to endorse this measure, the Lords instead ordered the printing of their conservative resolution of the previous January that upheld the established form of worship and forbade any changes that might give offence. This was a snub to the lower house, who responded on 9 September by ordering that their own declaration against innovations

---

[73] Jansson (ed.), *Proceedings in the Opening Session of the Long Parliament . . . Vol. 2*, 258.

[74] *Commons Journal* ii. 132; PRO, SP16/480/6; Rushworth, *Historical Collections*, iv. 273; Denzil Holles, *A True Copie of the Speech, made by the Honourable Denzell Holles . . . Concerning the Protestation . . . With an Explanation Upon some Doubts made upon the said Protestation* (1641), 8. This clarification was repeated in the bill 'for the securing of the true religion' read on 24 July (HMC, House of Lords, Addenda 1517–1714, 278). See also David Cressy, 'The Protestation Protested, 1641 and 1642', *The Historical Journal*, 45 (2002), 251–79.   [75] *Commons Journal*, ii. 246.

[76] Ibid., ii. 279.

be printed.[77] Both Houses utilized the press to publicize their positions, presenting parishioners with alternative justifications for action or inaction.

The King too contributed to the religious debate on behalf of the established church. On 10 December 1641, amid mounting 'division, separation and disorder', the Crown issued 'a proclamation for obedience to the laws ordained for establishing of the true religion in this kingdom of England', enjoining clergy to introduce no rite or ceremony 'other than those which are established by the laws and statutes of the land'. This was a comfort to some, a rebuke to others. Although everyone sought 'the very essence and substance of true religion', as the proclamation put it, few could agree what 'true religion' looked like or how it should be achieved.[78] The arrival of the proclamation at Dover 'caused much rejoicing', according to Anthony Percival, 'the people crying "God bless his majesty, we shall have our old religion again".'[79] Other conservatives took comfort in the King's assertion 'that he is resolved to live and die in the protestant religion, already established by the laws',[80] and in his charge to the judges in July 1642 'to give a stop to the over-hasty growth of anabaptism and other schisms' and to uphold 'the true protestant religion, established by law in this church of England'.[81]

A wide range of opinion agreed that religion was out of order and desperately needed to be settled, but there was no consensus how that should be achieved. Sir Simonds D'Ewes expressed the view, no doubt shared by many, that 'the settling of the matter of religion will be as a salve to cure all our sores'.[82] Parliament continued to struggle with the religious problem while petitions piled up, asking for 'a thorough reformation' or 'a happy reformation' of the church, or for the work of reformation to be perfected.[83]

---

[77] *Commons Journal*, ii. 287; *Lords Journal*, iv. 392, 395. HMC, *Report on the Manuscripts of the Duke of Buccleuch and Queensberry* (The Montague papers, 2nd series, 1926), iii. 413; British Library, Harleian Ms. 6424, f. 95, diary of John Warner, 8 September 1641. In response to these orders, the minister and churchwardens of Little Ravely, Huntingdonshire, duly certified that 'our communion table is removed from the east end of the chancel, the rails are taken away, our chancel is level', that 'corporal bowing at the name of Jesus is forborne', and 'the Lord's day is duly observed and sanctified' (Bodleian Library, Carte Ms. 228, f. 74).

[78] James F. Larkin (ed.), *Stuart Royal Proclamations, vol. II. Royal Proclamations of King Charles I, 1625–1646* (Oxford, 1983), 752–4.

[79] *CSPD 1641–43*, 207, Anthony Percival to Sir John Pennington, 18 December 1641.

[80] Ibid., 212, Thomas Wiseman to Sir John Pennington, 23 December 1641.

[81] *The Kings Maiesties Charge Sent to all the Judges of England* (1642), 2.

[82] Willson Havelock Coates (ed.), *The Journal of Sir Simonds D'Ewes from the First Recess of the Long Parliament to the Withdrawal of the King from London* (New Haven and London, 1942), 13.   [83] HMC, *5th Report*, Part 1 (1876), 7–10.

THE ASSAULT ON EPISCOPACY

Before the autumn of 1640 there was little support for the abolition of episcopacy. Puritans had been harassed by individual bishops and thwarted by particular policies, but only extremists imagined a dismantling of the entire episcopal order. The anger directed against Laud and Wren had been personal rather than institutional, and hostility to hardline Arminians and disciplinarians did not generally translate into calls for Presbyterianism or Independency. Common complaints addressed the cruelty and pride of the prelates, not the unlawfulness of their function. Learned disputants challenged the assertion that epsicopacy was *jure divino*, mandated by the law of God, but generally conceded its appropriateness for the government of the Church of England.

By the end of the year, however, episcopacy was in trouble. Anti-episcopal polemic became more strident in pulpits and pamphlets and in the street. The bishops were blamed for misleading the church, for the offensive new canons, and for the failings of the northern war. The triumphant Scots sought not only the punishment of the principal 'incendiaries' (especially Archbishop Laud), but also a restructuring of the Church of England along Presbyterian lines. Although this had never been an indigenous English priority, it gained support in the House of Commons and among some puritan militants. Archbishop Laud was impeached, other bishops faced investigation, and every mitre was at risk.

A growing number of reformers identified the bishops as the root cause of England's troubles and came to see the institution of episcopacy as an obstacle to further reformation. One member of the Commons wrote in November 1640, 'the hierarchy shakes, and if this parliament continue, they are gone root and branch'.[84]

Ten thousand Londoners subscribed a petition to Parliament demanding that episcopal government 'with all its dependencies, roots and branches, may be abolished'. Fifteen hundred reputable citizens delivered the petition to Westminster on 11 December 1640, and the House of Commons somewhat uneasily took it under consideration. Referred to by contemporaries as 'the city petition', but known to posterity by its most famous phrase as 'the root and branch petition', it served as the model for subsequent anti-episcopal petitions from the counties. Its opening assertion, that 'the government of archbishops, and lord bishops, deans, and archdeacons, etc. . . . . hath

---

[84] Quoted in Conrad Russell, *The Fall of the British Monarchies 1637–1642* (Oxford, 1991), 222, where the words are tentatively attributed to Francis Rous.

proved prejudicial and very dangerous both to the church and commonwealth', echoed and inverted the infamous 'etc.' clause of the 1640 canons.[85]
Conservatives were scandalized by the content of the petition and by the
manner of its presentation. A satirical 'ballad against the city petitions'
enjoyed wide manuscript circulation, deriding the petitioners for their
humble social position and ridiculing the naïveté of their religious
demands.[86]

The London petition directly inspired a similar effort from Kent, which Sir
Edward Dering commended to Parliament in January 1641.[87] Cheshire,
Nottinghamshire and Lincolnshire followed suit, and by the end of the year
some twenty county petitions against episcopacy had been brought to
Westminster.[88] The anti-episcopal petitions typically asked Parliament to
'remove our lordly prelates, the sole authors of all our present miseries', and
argued that although many grievances had 'issued immediately from the
personal evils of particular governors', the fundamental problem lay with
'the form or constitution' of episcopacy itself.[89] Inevitably, these petitions
were countered by others in favour of episcopacy and the Book of Common
Prayer.[90]

Reporting from London in November 1640 the Scot Robert Baillie
observed that 'many ministers used greater freedom than ever was heard of.
Episcopacy itself beginning to be cried down and Covenant cried up, and the
liturgy to be scorned.'[91] At the beginning of December Baillie observed, 'the
courage of this people grows daily, and the number, not only of people but of
preachers, who are rooting out of episcopacy'.[92] Gentlemen who gave no
thought to 'root and branch' reform before November 1640 became converted
within six months to the view that bishops should go, 'since now there is no
other remedy for cure of the disease'.[93] Conservatives complained of radical

---

[85] Jansson (ed.), *Proceedings in the Opening Session of the Long Parliament . . . Vol. 1*, 1,
564, 568, 571–5; Jansson (ed.), *Proceedings in the Opening Session of the Long
Parliament . . . Vol. 2*, 389, 390, 398; *The First and Large Petition of the Citie of London and
Other Inhabitants Thereabouts: For a Reformation in Church-Government* (1641).
[86] PRO, SP16/473/48; Folger Shakespeare Library, Folger Ms. X. d. 20; Northamptonshire
Record Office, Finch-Hatton Ms. FH 593. The ballad is discussed in Chapter 15.
[87] Larking (ed.), *Proceedings, Principally in the County of Kent*, 25–38.
[88] Jansson (ed.), *Proceedings in the Opening Session of the Long Parliament . . .
Vol. 4*, 14–18, 46–7, 611; Anthony Fletcher, *The Outbreak of the English Civil War* (1985),
191–227.
[89] Jansson (ed.), *Proceedings in the Opening Session of the Long Parliament . . . Vol. 4*, 15, 47.
[90] Judith Maltby, *Prayer Book and People in Elizabethan and Early Stuart England*
(Cambridge, 1998), 83–180.
[91] Laing (ed.), *Letters and Journals of Robert Baillie*, i. 273.   [92] Ibid., i. 275.
[93] Bettey (ed.), *Calendar of the Correspondence of the Smyth Family of Ashton
Court*, 172.

preachers and returners from New England who 'railed most damnably against all church government as it is established'.[94]

Hostility to episcopacy produced vitriolic language. John Bond of Exeter blamed the bishops for 'a kind of murrain and rot of soul' and preached vehemently against 'these gangrenes and pests of the church'.[95] John Milton similarly saw 'an universal rottenness and gangrene in the whole function' of episcopacy.[96] To Nehemiah Wallington the bishops were 'ravening wolves and cunning foxes' that have ravaged 'God's flock'. They were 'the very limbs of antichrist', the cause of 'all those miseries in church and commonwealth', and were 'odious and stink in the nostrils of all good men that love God'.[97] Thomas Constable, a wooden heel maker of Winwick, Lancashire, called the bishops 'the very scum of our country' and 'an accursed hierarchy', for which words and other irregularities he was summoned before the May 1641 Quarter Sessions.[98] It was shocking, though perhaps not surprising, that revellers at a bonfire celebrating the passage of the Triennial Bill in February 1641 'dressed a puppet like a bishop, and so flung him into the fire and burnt him'.[99]

A spate of anti-episcopal writing raised the rhetorical temperature by likening the bishops to vermin or beasts of prey. Archbishop Laud's enemies called him an 'arch-tyrant', 'the orc of Canterbury', and the *'primum mobile'* of the 'mischievous designs' of the prelates.[100] Harbottle Grimston called Laud 'the sty of all pestilent filth that hath infected the state and government of the church and commonwealth' and 'the corrupt fountain that hath infected all the streams'.[101] Another author denouncing the lordly prelates hoped 'to see these cockatrice eggs crushed to pieces'.[102] Lady Brilliana Harley wished the downfall of the bishops to be 'as it was with Haman', the Old Testament official who was hanged on his own gallows.[103] With words like these in their ears, members of Parliament worked intermittently on two bills on episcopacy, one to limit the bishops' authority in secular matters, the other to

---

[94] *CSPD 1641–43*, 77. Samuel Eaton returned from New England in 1640 and preached against episcopacy in Cheshire. Thomas Weld and Hugh Peter arrived back in England in September 1641 and galvanized congregations in the north and west.

[95] John Bond, *A Doore of Hope, also Holy and Loyall Activity* (1641), sigs. Cv, E2v, P3v–P4v, A3.   [96] [John Milton], *Of Reformation* (1641), 15.

[97] British Library, Add. Ms. 21935, f. 95; Sloan Ms. 922, f. 133v.

[98] Lancashire Record Office, QSB/1/246/30–2.

[99] Cambridge University Library, Ms. Mm. 1. 45 (Baker transcripts), 31.

[100] Ibid., 30; *Canterburies Pilgrimage* (1641), title page, sigs. A2, A2v; *The Bishops Mittimvs to goe to Bedlam* (1641), 4. See also *The Bishops Downefall or, The Prelates Snare* (1642).

[101] *Mr Grymstons Speech in Parliament Upon the Accusation and Impeachment of William Laud* (1641), 2, 5.   [102] *The Iyry of Inquisition De Jure Divino* (1641), 3.

[103] Thomas Taylor Lewis (ed.), *Letters of the Lady Brilliana Harley* (Camden Society, vol. lviii, 1854), 119; Esther 7: 10.

abolish them altogether. Both bills made progress in the Commons but were blocked in the House of Lords.[104]

As debate proceeded, against increasingly raucous extra-parliamentary clamours, some members adopted cautious reformist positions. Their hostility to prelatical sacerdotalism, they explained, did not necessarily make them supporters of root and branch. To the contrary, some of the most vigorous critics of Archbishop Laud stood up for the institution of episcopacy. Sir Benjamin Rudyerd told the Commons in February 1641 that he was opposed to the 'Roman ambition' of bishops who would have a 'pompous, sumptuous religion with additionals of temporal greatness'. But rather than overturning episcopacy he wished to amend it, to 'reduce and reform the calling for better men hereafter'.[105] Warning of the danger of 'sudden and great change' in religion, he advised his parliamentary colleagues to 'beware we bring not in the greatest innovation that ever was in England'.[106] Rudyerd's speech was widely reported, and helped shape some of the moderate pro-episcopal petitions.

Lay supporters of episcopacy were not only persuaded by the attractions of an ancient form of church government or arguments from scripture. They were also driven by fear of the alternative, 'an anarchy . . . which must necessarily produce an extermination of nobility, gentry, and order, if not of religion'. Some even feared that incest, adultery, and fornication would grow unchecked if the authority of the episcopal courts was not upheld.[107]

The main debate took place on 27 May 1641 on 'an act for the utter abolishing and taking away of all archbishops, bishops, their chancellors and commissaries, deans, deans and chapters, archdeacons, prebendaries, chanters, and canons, and other under-officers, out of the Church of England.' Sir Edward Dering introduced the bill, saying that 'his vote should ever have gone for the eclipsing of [bishops'] power, but not for the utter extirpating of them', but now he favoured 'a more sharper judgement'. It required some subtlety a few months later to explain that he was not against 'pure' episcopacy but only its recent corrupted form.[108] Sharp exchanges followed, in which William Pleydell wished the bill 'might be committed to the fire', and Sir Simonds D'Ewes retorted that Pleydell's previously published speech in support

---

[104] Jansson (ed.), *Proceedings in the Opening Session of the Long Parliament . . . Vol. 2*, 693, 700–3; Jansson (ed.), *Proceedings in the Opening Session of the Long Parliament . . . Vol. 4*, 74, 76, 158, 160, 163, 605.

[105] British Library, Harley Ms. 4931, ff. 103–103v.

[106] Northamptonshire Record Office, Finch-Hatton Mss., FH 3699.

[107] Sir Thomas Aston (ed.), *A Collection of Sundry Petitions Presented to the King's Most excellent Majestie* (1642), 3 (from the Cheshire petition), 34 (from the Kent petition).

[108] Jansson (ed.), *Proceedings in the Opening Session of the Long Parliament . . . Vol. 4*, 602, 613–14, 617–18; [Sir Edward Dering], *A Collection of Speeches* (1642), 64–5, 69, 70, 77.

of episcopacy 'might be better burnt than this bill'.[109] Sir John Wray said that everything possible had been done to reform episcopal government, without success, 'and now this bill is a vomit to them'. William Cages agreed with some of the county petitioners 'that bishops were the cause of all our miseries, and he feared God was angry with us for neglecting his service so long'.[110] Edmund Waller thought that 'episcopacy and the evils thereof are mingled like water and oil', but urged that the institution be reformed, not abolished. Episcopacy he held to be 'a counter-scarf or outwork', a bulwark against the 'assault of the people', which had to be held if property, hierarchy, and other 'things temporal' were to be protected.[111] The bill passed in the Commons by a vote of 139 to 108, but died when it reached the House of Lords.[112] Episcopacy remained legally intact for several more years, although attacks continued from many parts of the kingdom.

Observers remarked on the fluidity and uncertainty of the situation. 'Bishops or no bishops, 'tis not yet known which way the scales will go, but deans and chapters are in a swoon, and 'tis thought they will never be more', John Turbeville reported in June 1641, 'what the parliament will do next the lord knows'.[113] The authority of the Church of England was unravelling, ancient institutional structures were falling apart, and nobody could tell how far the attack might go. Pamphleteers punned about a tempest in the see of Canterbury and published woodcut caricatures of bishops toppling upside down.[114] (See Plates 4–7.)

The long sitting of Parliament kept bishops from attending to business in their sees. Diocesan administration ground to a halt across England as the bishops were buffeted by the political storm. Most of the diocesan courts lost business or guttered to a standstill between 1641 and 1642. Their authority was further weakened by the abolition of the Court of High Commission in July 1641. Consistory and archidiaconal courts continued to meet in some dioceses, but the heart had gone out of them. The 'office' side of their work, proceeding against moral and religious offenders, virtually vanished, leaving only a dribble of 'instance' business, mostly in testamentary matters. Churchwardens were no longer compelled to present local offenders or answer to diocesan officials.[115]

[109] Jansson (ed.), *Proceedings in the Opening Session of the Long Parliament . . . Vol. 4*, 606–7.
[110] Ibid., 615.   [111] Edmund Waller, *A Speech . . . Concerning Episcopacie* (1641), 4–5.
[112] Jansson (ed.), *Proceedings in the Opening Session of the Long Parliament . . . Vol. 4*, 602, 611.
[113] W. C. Trevelyan and C. E. Trevelyan (eds.), *The Trevelyan Papers, Part III* (Camden Society, no. 105, 1872), 211.
[114] See, for example, Thomas Stirry, *A Rot Amongst the Bishops, or, A Terrible Tempest in the Sea of Canterbury* (1641); [Alexander Leighton], *A Decade of Grievances* (1641).
[115] For the diocese of Winchester, Hampshire Record Office, 21 M 65/B1/34, 21 M 65/C2/71; for Bath and Wells, Somerset Record Office, D/D/Ca 331, 333, and 334, D/D/Cd 80; for

Opponents gloated that those who 'got their livings by citing, presenting, informing, suspending, excommunicating and molesting many of the best ministers and people' were now out of work, and that ecclesiastical 'judges, vicar-generals, chancellors, commissaries, archdeacons, deans and chapters, and their surrogates, and also... registrars, deputy registrars, proctors, examiners, and public notaries... pursuivants, apparators, promoters, etc.' went down with Doctors Commons.[116] The Bishop of Lincoln, John Williams, himself a victim of Laudian censure, was observed in the autumn of 1641, 'alone of all the bishops, a stout defender of his order and discipline, not without the envy, hatred and broad censures of the people'.[117]

The impeachment of Archbishop Laud in December 1640 was quickly followed by charges against Matthew Wren of Ely and William Piers of Bath and Wells. More charges followed in August 1641 against the episcopal authors of the recent hated canons.[118] At the end of December 1641 the House of Commons charged a dozen bishops with high treason for protesting against parliamentary business done without them. A satiric woodcut shows the bishops signing their fatal Protestation, then taking flight like birds into the Tower[119] (see Plate 8). 'Thus was the parliament most happily freed of twelve of them at one clap', wrote the anti-episcopal chronicler John Vicars.[120]

Joining Archbishop Laud in the Tower were George Coke of Hereford, Godfrey Goodman of Gloucester, Joseph Hall of Norwich, John Owen of

---

Chichester, West Sussex Record Office, Ep 1/17/28, Ep 1/10/45, Ep 1/11/16; for Gloucester, Gloucestershire Record Office, GDR 202, 203, 205, and 206, GDR 142 A (Institution Book 1620–1673); for Worcester, Worcestershire Record Office, BA 2513/17, BA 2302/3; for Exeter, Devon Record Office, Ms. Chanter 812, 813, and 866, CC 7, CC 180; for Peterborough, Northamptonshire Record Office, Visitation Book 8a, f. 40v; for Lichfield and Coventry, Lichfield Record Office, B/C/2/73, B/C/3/17, B/C/5; for London, London Metropolitan Archives, DL/C/30, DL/C/90, DL/C/322; Guildhall Library, Ms. 9064/21, Ms. 9065A/7, Ms. 9065H/5 and 6, Ms. 9168D/2; Essex Record Office, Chelmsford, D/AB/A9, D/AB/C7, D/AB/D8, D/AC/A54, D/AE/A42, D/AE/D8; Hertfordshire Record Office, AHH/17; for Norwich, Norfolk Record Office, DN/ACT/69B and C, DN/DEP/45. Archdeaconry visitors in some areas still went through the motions, but with little cooperation or enthusiasm.

[116] *Canterburies Tooles* (1641), 1 (attributed to William Prynne); *The Late Will and Testament of the Doctors Commons* (1641), broadsheet. See also *The Proctor and Parator their Mourning* (1641).

[117] W. N. Darnell (ed.), *The Correspondence of Isaac Basire, D.D.* (1831), 39.

[118] Jansson (ed.), *Proceedings in the Opening Session of the Long Parliament ... Vol. 1*, 656; Jansson (ed.), *Proceedings in the Opening Session of the Long Parliament ... Vol. 2*, 48; *Commons Journals*, ii. 235; Peter King, 'The Episcopate during the Civil Wars, 1642–1649', *English Historical Review*, 83 (1968), 523–6; *The Wrens Nest Defild, or, Bishop Wren Anatomiz'd, his Life and Actions dissected and laid open* (1641); *Articles of Impeachment ... Against Matthew Wren* (1641).   [119] *The Decoy Duck* (1642), title page.

[120] John Vicars, *God in the Mount. Or, Englands Remembrancer* (1641), 69.

St Asaph's, Morgan Owen of Llandaff, William Piers of Bath and Wells, Robert Skinner of Oxford, John Towers of Peterborough, John Williams of York, and Matthew Wren of Ely. Thomas Morton of Durham and Robert Wright of Lichfield and Coventry, who were elderly and infirm, were taken into custody by the Usher of the Black Rod. Not until March 1642 were these two given 'liberty to take the air in the company of the gentleman usher'.[121] William Juxon, Brian Duppa, and John Warner were among the few senior prelates remaining at large. One observer thought the bishops lucky to be in the Tower, for otherwise the apprentices would tear 'those magpies' in pieces.[122] Laud stayed in the Tower until his execution in 1645. Following a brief release on bail, Wren remained in custody until the Restoration.

Six bishops died during this period of revolutionary turmoil: Richard Neile of York in October 1640, John Bancroft of Oxford in February 1641, Richard Montague of Norwich and John Davenant of Salisbury in April, John Thornburgh of Worcester in July 1641, and Barnaby Potter of Carlisle in January 1642. It took an average of seven and a half months for their successors to be installed (though this was not unusual). The dioceses of Bristol, Chichester, Exeter, and Lincoln suffered temporary disruption as their bishops were translated to some of the vacant sees. The diocese of Gloucester also experienced difficulties after Bishop Godfrey Goodman, a suspected Catholic convert, was suspended in 1640 for objecting to the new Laudian canons. When the new Bishop of Chichester, Henry King, attempted to preach in St Olave's Church, London, in May 1642 he was shouted out of the pulpit by a hundred 'rude rascals' crying, 'a pope, a pope, a pope'.[123]

Despite their political losses, and the cost to their esteem and coffers, the bishops still retained some of their spiritual authority. Royalists and conformists continued to acknowledge their position. Even while imprisoned in the Tower in the early stages of the civil war, Matthew Wren was able to fulfil some of his episcopal functions.[124] The business of ordaining and instituting ministers continued during 1641 and 1642, at least where there were bishops to perform it, and the episcopal registers of most dioceses show this activity continuing into the mid-1640s.[125] The number of ordinations, however, was severely reduced, and was often performed by surrogates. The Church of England no longer offered attractive career prospects, and sectarians allowed no role to bishops in the making of ministers.

---

[121] Copy of Commons order in Lichfield Record Office, B/C/5 1641/2.
[122] *The Bishops Downefall or, The Prelates Snare*, 3; *The Bishops Last Good-Night* (1642).
[123] *The Anatomy of the Separatists, alias, Brownists, the factious Brethren in these Times* (1642), 6.   [124] Folger Shakespeare Library, Folger Ms. X. d. 460.
[125] David M. Smith, *Guide to the Bishops' Registers of England and Wales* (1981).

By the beginning of 1642 the bishops had been hobbled but the episcopal structure of the Church of England remained intact. After a year of 'root and branch' agitation for the abolition of their office, and a prolonged parliamentary campaign to exclude them from the House of Lords, the bishops lost their votes in the upper house in February 1642.[126] The London parish of St Botolph without Bishopsgate paid a shilling and sixpence for celebratory bellringing that month 'when the bishops were rooted out of the House of Lords'.[127] Only in 1646 was the title and authority of bishops abolished by parliamentary ordinance.

THE NEW REFORMATION

Although Babylon had apparently fallen, reformation had yet to be accomplished. It proved much easier to bring down Babylon than to raise the temple. As distractions and distempers compounded, preachers spoke with increasing desperation about the urgency of fundamental change. Altar rails and images, bishops, and the Book of Common Prayer were only part of the problem for reformers who hoped to bring English culture closer to God. John Bankes, the Kentish minister who described himself as 'a watchman for Israel, zealous of the glory of my maker', called in January 1641 for a reformation of manners as well as reformation of the church, to counter 'the divorcing sin of idolatry and the building of temples for Baal' in an England 'overgrown with . . . drunkenness, swearing, whoredom and debate'.[128] Other reformers sought to discern God's will, to better understand the present, the future, and the past.

Preaching before the Commons in December 1641, Edmund Calamy laid England's crisis to 'the great demur and delay of the reformation of the church'. Rebellion in Ireland, faction at Westminster, and even the return of the plague had crept in through Parliament's neglect of its fundamental mission. 'There must be a court reformation, a country reformation, a city reformation, a general reformation', Calamy thundered, as well as a reformation of manners. There must be thorough repentance, and a ridding of the pollutions, innovations, and defilements that still stained the church, 'a national reformation' that would deliver England 'from everlasting

---

[126] *Statutes of the Realm*, 17 Car. I., c. 27, 'An act for disenabling all persons in holy orders to exercise any temporal jurisdiction or authority.'

[127] Guildhall Library, Ms. 4524/2, f. 64.

[128] Centre for Kentish Studies, Maidstone, Dering. Mss. U.350/C2/88, Bankes to Dering, 16 January 1641.

misery'. It fell to Parliament, 'the representative body of this nation', to move this reformation forward.[129]

Cornelius Burges warned the House in March 1642 that it was dangerous 'for a people to trifle with God by an halting Reformation'. Evidence could be found in the ancient sufferings of Israel and the recent sufferings of England. God's people had sought the Lord, Burges claimed, but 'a great work came to nothing'. The rottenness of the people's hearts, long accustomed to idolatry and all manner of wickedness, was such as would admit no cure. The reformation Burges wanted was a reformation of the spirit, a reformation of the heart, a reformation of manners, as well as a reformation of the structures of religion. 'Are we not a sinful, leprous people?' Burges asked, and his answer of course was affirmative. The way forward, the way out of England's dangerous confusions, was not for Parliament and the King to seek accommodation. It was instead to seek God's blessings by addressing the core problem of religious corruption. Parliament needed to purge people of 'their idolatries and superstitions, their oaths and blasphemies, their drunkenness and uncleanness, their lying and oppressions'. The land was 'guilty of much lukewarmness and tolerating of much superstition and idolatry, by too much slackness in perfecting the work of reformation, especially in worship, government and discipline of the church'.[130] The problem, of course, was the impossibility of agreeing what 'a perfect reformation' might look like, as well as how to achieve it. The religious revolution had moved out of Parliament's control, beyond anyone's imagining, into the realms of chaos.

---

[129] Edmund Calamy, *England's Looking-Glasse* (1642), 17–18, 45–6, 49, 51. See also Edmund Calamy, *Gods Free Mercy to England* (1642).

[130] Cornelius Burges, 'The necessity and benefit of washing the heart', [1642] in *Two Sermons Preached to the Honourable House of Commons* (1645), 2, 36, 37, 45–6, 50. See also Mathew Newcomen, *The Craft and Cruelty of the Churches Adversaries* (1643).

9

Parish Turmoils

The pressures on Parliament for the reformation of religion came from a variety of sources, English and Scottish, metropolitan and provincial, clerical and lay. While the most notorious Laudian clerics came under attack, the self-styled godly took advantage of the collapse of episcopal discipline to change the face of the church. Some parishioners took their cues from Westminster, but others acted independently without tarrying for the magistrate. By the summer of 1641 the puritans in Parliament had lost control of their allies in many localities. Agitation for reform increasingly gave way to direct action, as 'the common people...without authority, order or decency' disrupted church services, ripped prayer books, and tore up surplices.[1] Some simply stopped coming to church. The records reveal a shifting balance of advantage and initiative as clergy and laity, conformists and reformers, struggled to shape the religious culture of revolutionary England. This chapter examines these local struggles against the background of the drama at the centre.

VEXATIONS AND REFORMS

Scores of parishes had already been traumatized by attacks on images and altar rails during the summer of 1640. Many more were inspired by the November parliament to remove Laudian accoutrements or to impose less ritualized forms of worship. Sometimes it was the minister himself who took the initiative, moving the Communion table, shedding his surplice, or experimenting with extempore prayers. Often it was a faction within the parish or a particularly zealous inhabitant who took down Communion rails, removed 'superstitious' windows, or led the assault on the Book of Common Prayer.

[1] Thomas May, *The History of the Parliament of England which began November the third, MDCXL* (1647), 113.

Orderly services gave way to shouting and shoving, amidst contests for control of the pulpit and the reading desk. Report of such disruptions fed the fear that an 'insolent zeal and ungoverned fury' was ultimately leading to chaos.[2]

Within a week of the opening of the Long Parliament the churchwardens of Minehead, Somerset, took it upon themselves to install a lecturer, Mr Whitehorne, to supplement the teaching of their Laudian vicar, Robert Knolles. Furthermore, diocesan authorities learned, they had 'permitted a stranger called Mr Gwynn to preach in their church upon a Sunday before noon, which Gwynn the Saturday before publicly went up and down the town like a layman with a sword by his side and in grey clothes.'[3] The parish was clearly slipping out of the incumbent's control, and out of the control of the bishop, with parishioners deciding for themselves who should occupy the pulpit. Still banking on its disciplinary power, the diocesan court repeatedly called Whitehorne to appear 'for preaching a public lecture within the parish church of Minehead without any lawful authority to do it', but the delinquent simply ignored the summons. After several weeks of turmoil, including dispute about the lecturer's stipend, Whitehorne departed for Ireland. The court then attempted to punish one of the churchwardens, Simon Valentine, for permitting unlicensed strangers to preach, but was no more effective in imposing its authority.[4]

Orderly services at Brislington, Somerset, collapsed on 22 November 1640 when Robert Bacon, a suspended minister who had recently served as curate, commandeered the pulpit before evening prayer. When one of the churchwardens attempted to eject him a parishioner told him 'to hold his babbling, and bade Mr Bacon go on'. When the incumbent minister, Mr Tracy, arrived and began the formal service, Bacon 'went forth under a tree in the street' to expound, and several dozen parishioners followed him. Later in the afternoon Bacon returned to the church and preached again from the minister's pew. One of the parishioners helpfully locked the pew door so that the interloper could not easily be removed, and handed Bacon the key.[5] The bishop of Bath and Wells had suspended Bacon earlier in the year for not wearing his surplice, for baptizing without the sign of the cross, and for making up prayers of his own expounding. Bacon was moving rapidly from conformity to dissent, associating with the incipient separatist congregation at Bristol as well as emigrants to New England. At the beginning of November 1640

[2] J.W. [James Wilcock], *A Challenge Sent to Master E. B. a Semi-Separatist from the Church of England* (1641), 3.   [3] Somerset Record Office, D/D/Ca 331, f. 187v.
[4] Ibid., ff. 188, 198, 227; D/D/Ca 334, f. 106.
[5] Somerset Record Office, D/D/Ca 333, nf.

Robert Bacon was effectively a religious outlaw, but as soon as the new parliament was sitting he was able to preach with impunity.[6]

Similar divisions at Barnstable, Devon, intensified in 1641 when a vigorous local lecturer, described by opponents as 'a rigid Brownist', stole parts of the conformist vicar's congregation. Demanding a sharper separation of the sheep from the goats, the radicals complained of the 'administering of the sacrament...unto a promiscuous multitude, without putting a difference between the precious and the vile'. They also 'caused certain tickets to be thrown into men's doors with these words, take heed of your stinted morning prayer.'[7]

Goudhurst, Kent, was likewise polarized between supporters of the reforming lecturer, Edward Bright, and the conformist vicar, James Wilcock. Petitioners to Parliament described Bright as 'a faithful and able preacher', but the incumbent called him 'a wolf in the fold, busy in my flock', and 'this master B. whom my parishioners follow in swarms'.[8] In London the rector of St Bartholemew Exchange, John Grant, was 'outfaced in every corner of the church, disgracefully nicknamed, out-prated rudely and savagely', by yelling parishioners who would rather hear their lecturer, Simeon Ash.[9] Other conservative preachers experienced 'humming and hissing' as well as 'railing and reviling'.[10]

Emboldened by signals from Westminster, and freed from effective disciplinary constraints, previously conforming ministers experimented with modified services while puritans departed from the Book of Common Prayer. Conservatives complained of 'innovators who have neglected upon Sunday to read divine service at all, but entertained the people with novel exhortations and inventions of their own.'[11] Radicals dismissed the set prayer-book rituals as 'porridge'.[12]

Even before Parliament met in November 1640, James Crawford, the rector of Brockhall, Northamptonshire, was said to be preaching against ceremonies 'as confidently as though he had been in New England'.[13]

---

[6] Somerset Record Office, D/D/Ca 334, ff. 23, 47–48v; John Latimer, *The Annals of Bristol in the Seventeenth Century* (Bristol, 1900), 151; Roger Hayden (ed.), *The Records of a Church of Christ in Bristol, 1640–1687* (Bristol Record Society, vol. xxvii, 1974), 90.

[7] Bodleian Library, Ms. J. Walker c. 5, ff. 146v, 170v. I am grateful to Mark Stoyle for directing me to this manuscript.

[8] Lambert B. Larking (ed.), *Proceedings, Principally in the County of Kent, in Connection with the Parliaments Called in 1640* (Camden Society, vol. lxxx, 1862), 144–5; J.W., *A Challenge Sent to Master E. B.*, 4, 6.

[9] [John Grant], *Gods Deliverance of Man by Prayer* (1642), sigs. A2–A2v.

[10] *The Distractions of Our Times. Wherein is discovered the Generall discontent of all Estates throughout the whole Land* (1642), 5.   [11] British Library, Add. Ms. 36914, f. 224.

[12] *A Witty Answer, and Vindication To a Foolish Pamphlet* (1642), sig. A4v.

[13] *CSPD 1640*, 351.

At Hingham, Norfolk, the minister, Mr Violet, led his congregation in confession of sins, 'Oh Lord, we have offended thee in wearing the surplice, in signing with the cross, and using the ring at marriage.'[14] Other ministers berated themselves for their previous conformity, rejecting not just Laudian innovations but a range of contentious rubrics from the Book of Common Prayer.

At Leominster, Herefordshire, in December 1640, 'hearing of the proceedings in the House of Commons concerning communion tables and canons', the puritan John Tombs restored the table to its former place in the chancel, and 'began to disuse the surplice, and the cross at baptism'. The parish was in turmoil for the next twelve months as conformists resisted the changes, and enthusiasts pressed for further reform.[15]

At Cambridge John Ellis, a fellow of Catherine Hall, explained in December 1641 why he had stopped using the sign of the cross in baptism.

Formerly in my practice I have used it, but now of late many people have been so much offended at the use of the said ceremony . . . I have forborne the use of it; and the rather because I found that by the judgement of the House of Commons published September the ninth it was thought unseasonable at this time to urge the severe execution of such laws.

In September Ellis had stirred up the crowds at Sturbridge Fair, crying, 'pardon us great Lord our superstition and idolatry countenanced by authority'. In November he had 'mangled the service' at St Clement's Church, Cambridge, by leaving out crucial words. Called before the vice-chancellor's court to answer for his nonconformity, Ellis was let off with a mild rebuke and advised to be more cautious in future. In previous years, especially under John Cosin's vice-chancellorship (1639–40), he would have faced serious sanctions.[16]

Some clergy did not just modify the service book but preached vehemently against it. The Book of Common Prayer, which had governed the form of worship since the sixteenth century, became an object of contempt and derision. The book came in for physical as well as rhetorical abuse, in some places being 'trampled under foot and torn in pieces'.[17] Sacrilege of this sort may not have been common, but like flag-burning in the modern United

---

[14] Cambridge University Library, Ms. Mn. 1. 45 (Baker transcripts), 32.

[15] British Library, Add. Ms. 70003, ff. 92, 204.

[16] Cambridge University Archives, V.C. Ct. I 58, f. 115, 129v, 121; V.C. Ct. I 12, ff. 55, 58, 61–2; V.C. Ct. III 37, ff. 121–5.

[17] Willson H. Coates, Anne Steele Young, and Vernon F. Snow (eds.), *The Private Journals of the Long Parliament 3 January to 5 March 1642* (New Haven and London, 1982), 137; May, *History of the Parliament*, 113.

States, a few well-publicized incidents could produce a frenzy of righteous anxiety. The Act of Uniformity (1559) made it a crime to derogate or deprave the Book of Common Prayer, and the courts were still willing to punish offenders. Conformists believed that the prayer book contained 'the services of the living God' and 'nothing contrary to his holy word'.[18] Anyone speaking or acting against the prayer book was defying both church and state.

Some ministers made their defiance public. Edward Whale, a radical minister returned from Rotterdam, energized worship at Norwich by carrying a prayer book into the pulpit at St George's and stamping it under his feet, 'saying he came not by any prelatical popish imposition of hands but was sent from God'.[19] At Bocking, Essex, Lemuel Tuke caused controversy by preaching and speaking 'things derogatory to the Book of Common Prayer'.[20] Henry Burton, who returned not from exile but from prison, was said to have preached that the prayer book was 'framed and composed by the devil, and practised by the devil's imps or instruments'.[21]

Lay activists joined in the attack on the Book of Common Prayer. Although hundreds of parishioners expressed affection for the service book, hundreds more joined the radicals in disparaging it. Whereas some parishioners felt aggrieved if their minister failed to follow the prayer book exactly, others were furious that he used it at all. Many areas were free of trouble, but others experienced months of turmoil brought on by religious squabbles.

At Cranbrook, Kent, the moderate conformist vicar, Robert Abbott, suffered 'daily vexations' as parishioners turned against the Book of Common Prayer. It was galling, he wrote, 'to have my conscience, credit and pains trampled upon by my people, after twenty four years.' In July 1641 someone warned him that some forty of the 'middle sort of the parish' would stay away from church if he did not abandon the book. Some had attempted to persuade the churchwardens 'to take away the common prayer books out of the church, and the truth is, there is almost a general distaste of such service.' When parishioners recruited a lecturer who shared their views, Abbott resolved 'that no man shall possess my pulpit against my will.' But it would not be long, he told Sir Edward Dering, before 'I be driven through tumult to leave my station.'[22] Dering in turn took exception to the 'lewd licentiousness' in the parishes, and told Parliament in October that

<hr />

[18] John Swan, *Redde Debitum. Or, A Discovrse in defence of three chiefe Fatherhoods* (1640), 137.   [19] Cambridge University Library, Ms. Mn. 1. 45 (Baker transcripts), 31.
[20] Essex Record Office, Quarter Sessions Rolls, Q/SR/315/22. Tuke appeared to answer the indictment at the Easter 1642 sessions, Q/SR/316/79.
[21] Cambridge University Library, Ms. Mn. 1. 45 (Baker transcripts), 38.
[22] British Library, Stowe Ms. 184, ff. 43v, 44, 47, 47v.

'now infected sheep...run and straggle from [their pastors] more in these last ten months than in twenty years before.'[23]

Near riot ensued at Muggleswick, Durham, when the minister, Richard Bradley, described by parishioners as 'one of the most deboshed amongst the sons of men', pulled the coat of a visiting minister and forcefully blocked him from entering the pulpit. When the visitor persisted in preaching Bradley tried to drown his words by vigorous ringing of the bells. On one winter Sunday 'he took the lock from the church door and fastened on one of his own, so as the parishioners were forced to discharge divine duties...in cold frost and snow.' When sixty-seven parishioners refused to take Communion from their hated priest he initiated proceedings against them at the Quarter Sessions, and they in turn appealed to Parliament, calling 'help, help, help'.[24]

With the demise of the church courts the only legal remedy against derogation of the prayer book lay with the secular magistrates. The records of county and borough quarter sessions are scattered with cases of this nature. In Devonshire, for example, an Exeter cordwainer, John Vigures, allegedly claimed in March 1641 that the service used in St Peter's Church was popery, as was bowing at the name of Jesus, and that most of the church-men there were Arminians. He was later bound over 'for breaking of some glass in St Mary Arches church'.[25] Edward Williams of Marlborough was charged at the May 1641 Wiltshire Quarter Sessions with saying that 'there was base roguery' in the Book of Common Prayer, but witnesses failed to appear and the case could not go forward.[26]

Walter Wasse, a London stationer, ventured the opinion in June 1641 'that the Book of Common Prayer was no divine prayer, and that he had rather hear a sermon under a tree than out of a pulpit.'[27] William Creake, a silk-stocking weaver from Cripplegate, would no longer come to church, he told the Middlesex sessions in July 1641, because 'signing with the sign of the cross is not warranted by the word of God'.[28] Other Londoners, identified by a hostile observer as 'those who would have themselves thought to be most holy', disrupted services in the Old Jewry in September 1641, tore up the Book of Common Prayer, and committed 'misdemeanours against the

---

[23] Sir Edward Dering, *A Collection of Speeches* (1642), 93, 96–105.

[24] Durham University Library, Special Collections, Mickleton-Spearman Ms. MSP 9, ii. 238.

[25] Devon Record Office, Exeter Quarter Sessions Order Book, 1630–1642, ff. 351v, 380v.

[26] B. Howard Cunnington (ed.), *Records of the County of Wilts. Being Extracts from the Quarter Sessions Great Rolls of the Seventeenth Century* (Devizes, 1932), 140. See also London Metropolitan Archives, MJ/SR/895, MJ/SR/908; Essex Record Office, Q/SR/315/22, Q/SR/316/79; Hertfordshire Record Office, QSMB 2/410; Wiltshire Record Office, A1/110, Michaelmas 1641, 120.

[27] London Metropolitan Archives, Sessions Roll, MJ/SR/895/90.

[28] London Metropolitan Archives, MJ/SBB/22.

minister'.[29] A Scotsman who ripped leaves from the prayer book in St Olave's Church, and 'offered injustice to the very book', was bound over by the Lord Mayor to appear at the next sessions.[30]

An incident at Earls Colne, Essex, revealed a fanatical hostility to the traditional service book. Thomas Harvey, weaver, was bound over in September 1641 'for taking away the common prayer book out of the church there and abusing it'. Examined by Sir William Maxey before the Essex Quarter Sessions, Harvey confessed that on Sunday, 29 August, having heard Ralph Josselin preach, he went back into the church and took the prayer book and threw it into a nearby pond. The next day 'he went to the pond and took out the said book, cut it in pieces, part thereof he did burn, some he threw away, and some he kept in his pockets, and further he cannot say.' The incident speaks to a deeply troubled relationship to the Book of Common Prayer, which here was stolen, tortured, drowned, burned, and partially annihilated before being resuscitated by the courts.[31]

Other assaults on the prayer book were more mundane. In November 1641 Robert Farre, cutler, stopped the parish clerk of Shrewsbury from carrying the prayer book to church, declaring 'that he cared not for the Book of Common Prayer', and gave his opinion that 'it is fitter it were burnt than to be used'. Farre also disparaged the minister, calling him a 'knave', and asked rhetorically, 'what shall we do with one for a curate that speaketh like a child in the pulpit?' The artisans and shopkeepers of St Chad's parish 'had much talk about religion' and the community was deeply divided. Farre eventually faced charges at the January 1642 sessions 'for depraving the Book of Common Prayer', but most likely escaped penalty.[32] At Birmingham Joseph Baker, a saddler, said in December 1641 that the Book of Common Prayer was 'mere popery, and those that take part with it are no better than papists.' James Warton, a Southampton pewterer, was similarly brought to court for saying that the prayer book was mostly 'popery'.[33]

There seemed to be a quickening of such charges in the spring of 1642, when conformists attempted to bring enemies of the prayer book before the

[29] HMC, *12th Report, The Manuscripts of the Earl Cowper... Preserved at Melbourne Hall, Derbyshire* (1888), ii. 291. [30] *A True Relation of a Scotchman* (1641).
[31] Essex Record Office, Q/SR/314/92; Q/SB12/43. There is no reference to this in Ralph Josselin's voluminous diary. See also John Walter, '"Abolishing Superstition with Sedition"? The Politics of Popular Iconoclasm in England 1640–1642', *Past and Present*, 183 (May 2004), 91–2.
[32] Shropshire Record Office, Shrewsbury Borough Records, 3365/2240, no. 29.
[33] S. C. Ratcliff and H. C. Johnson (eds.), *Warwickshire County Records, vol. VI. Quarter Sessions Indictment Book. Easter, 1631, to Epiphany, 1674* (Warwick, 1941), 65; R. C. Anderson (ed.), *The Book of Examinations and Depositions 1622–1644* (Southampton Record Society, 1936), 38.

law. (See Chapter 11) The Hertfordshire Quarter Sessions heard in April 1642 that Henry Harlow, a tailor of Ashwell, 'spoke scandalous words...in derogation and depravation of the Book of Common Prayer and the sacraments of the Church of England', calling it 'partly God's and partly man's tradition and hotchpotch'. Harlow particularly objected when the conformist curate of Tharfield, William Turner, attempted to use the prayer book when burying the dead.[34] Two artisans from the London suburbs, Richard Bailey, a glover of Cripplegate, and William Turner, a leatherseller from Bermondsey, were similarly cited at the Middlesex sessions in April 1642 'for depraving the Book of Common Prayer, saying it is lies, and they knaves and fools that maintain it'. The charge was preferred not by the magistrates or aggrieved churchmen, but by two of Turner's neighbours, a victualler and a yeoman.[35] In most cases the offenders were bound over to keep the peace, and were required to retract their offensive words. Unrepentant offenders faced brief spells in prison, but the confusions of 1642 allowed most to escape unpunished.

DISTEMPERS AND DERISION

Some parishioners directed their anger at their minister, as well as his service book and surplice. Anti-clerical diatribes were not uncommon in early modern England, and some clerics understood abuse to be the cost of their calling.[36] But a fresh onslaught of insults between 1640 and 1642 contributed to the undermining of the church.

At Clifton, Staffordshire, a blacksmith, John Webster, poured scorn on the parish priest, Henry Gilbert, repeating thrice over that 'he did not care a fart of his arse for him'. Webster further disparaged the minister by asserting 'that he was as well bred and born as thou art, and as good a man as thyself, excepting thy cloth'.[37] In Lancashire a linen weaver and a feltmaker poured 'contemptuous and malicious' abuse on the parson of Ashton-under-Lyme in November 1641, calling him 'a goose and a popish priest, with many other unseemly terms of disgrace not fit to be given to a man of his worth and calling'.[38] A Bristol weaver, Henry Matthew, asserted that the minister, Mr Ludowicke, 'could preach no more than a black dog, and other vilifying

---

[34] Hertfordshire Record Office, QSMB 2/410.
[35] London Metropolitan Archives, Sessions Roll, MJ/SR/908/15–17.
[36] David Cressy, *Travesties and Transgressions in Tudor and Stuart England* (Oxford, 2000), 138–61.   [37] Staffordshire Record Office, Q/SR/244/30.
[38] Lancashire Record Office, QSB/1/263/65.

language'.[39] Robert Cobbet of Stepney, Middlesex, likewise called his vicar, William Stamp, a dog, and said when the vicar was in the pulpit 'that then there was a dog preaching'.[40] In London it was said that a canonically attired cleric could scarce pass through the streets in the autumn of 1641 without being taunted, 'yonder goes a Jesuit...one of Baal's priests, one of Canterbury's whelps'.[41]

Insulting language and violent behaviour often combined to bring worship to a halt. Disruption of services and destruction of liturgical furnishings were widely reported in the opening year of the Long Parliament, and each month brought news of further outrages. The circulation of these accounts contributed to the growing fear of 'miserable and remediless confusion' in religion.[42]

Reports reached the House of Lords in late November 1640 of 'notable abuses done at Halsted in Essex by a multitude of people in the church at the administration of baptism. They tore the surplice and a hood a pieces and trample[d] the service book upon the ground, saying it was a popish book.' Two of the most forward iconoclasts 'were sent for as delinquents', and proceedings commenced against them. But although their misdemeanour was proved in court, their only punishment was 'to be admonished from future disorders'.[43] Disorders of this sort continued unabated. On New Year's morning 1641 the bell ringers at Latton, Essex, decided on their own initiative to set the Communion table in the chancel 'as it had formerly stood' and to pull down and destroy the rails. One of the ringleaders explained that the rails 'gave great offence to his conscience' and 'that the placing of them was against God's laws, and the king's, as appeared by the 20th chapter of Exodus, about the 20th verse.' Some of the iconoclasts later apologized for their exploit and confessed 'it was most unadvisedly done', but others justi- fied their action, 'because the rails had been pulled down in other places without punishment therefore'.[44] Elsewhere in East Anglia the rails in St Laurence's church, Ipswich, were burnt down with broom faggots,[45] and 'young ruffians...hired with half a barrel of beer' pulled down the

[39] Bristol Record Office, Quarter Sessions Minute Book 1634–47, JQS/M/3, f. 192v.

[40] London Metropolitan Archives, Sessions Roll, MJ/SR/905/93.

[41] Thomas Cheshire, *A Sermon Preached in Saint Paules Church the tenth of October 1641* (1641), 12.

[42] I.W., *Certaine Reasons why the Book of Common-Prayer being Corrected should Continue* (1641), 'to the reader', sig. A2v.

[43] HMC, *Report on the Manuscripts of the Duke of Buccleuch and Queensberry* (The Montague papers, 2nd series, 1926), iii. 395, 398, 401.

[44] Essex Record Office, Chelmsford, Q/Sba2/41. Exodus 20: 25–6 appears to forbid hewn altars and altar steps.

[45] Cambridge University Library, Ms. Mn. 1. 45 (Baker transcripts), 31.

Communion rails at Hingham, Norfolk, and threatened to dump them in 'the parson's pond'.[46]

Ann Temple of Broughton, Warwickshire, sister of the puritan Lord Saye and Sele, expressed delight in January 1641 that 'altars begin to go down apace, and rails in many places'. Championing the 'rooters' with their 'root and branch' petitions, she hoped and prayed 'that we shall see idolatry and superstition rooted out, and God's ordinances set up'.[47] By contrast, the conservative Sir Humphrey Mildmay of Danbury, Essex, expressed dismay at disorderly excesses. In February 1641 he recorded that 'the holy wives of Sandon cut down the rails of their church and burnt them on the green, bravely like quick', adding, 'God send them a day of payment.'[48] Later in February a group of Essex villagers, both men and women, 'riotously assembled and entered the church of Great Waltham and tore in pieces the surplice worth forty shillings and the hood worth twenty shillings, being the goods and ornaments of the parish church'. It was April before they were bound over to keep the peace, and May before they appeared at the quarter sessions.[49]

In March 1641 a group of Staffordshire metal workers with their apprentices and wives—described by the authorities as 'ill-disposed and malicious persons'—made a night-time raid on the church at Wolverhampton, where they pulled down the Communion rails and moved the table back to its pre-Laudian position. One of them, Robert Ebbe, being asked to explain himself, 'answered it was an idol, and [he] would do it again if it were to do'. The iconoclasts had acted 'without any power or authority to them granted', but nobody was willing to undo their work. The ceremonialist curate of Wolverhampton, Hugh Davis, had basked in the patronage of Matthew and Christopher Wren, but now his enemies declared him 'a great scandal to our holy religion and...a great hinderer of the faithful preaching of God's word'. Invoking the punishment meted out to Burton, Bastwick, and Prynne, the puritan lawyer William Pinson said that Davis deserved to lose one of his ears.[50]

In April the Easter Communion service at Danbury, Essex, broke down in 'disorder', according to Sir Humphrey Mildmay.[51] But it was mild compared

---

[46] Ibid., 38; Walter, ' "Abolishing Superstition with Sedition"?', 84–8.

[47] East Sussex Record Office, Lewes, Dunn Ms. 51/54 (microfilm XA 73/11).

[48] British Library, Harley Ms. 454, f. 38v.

[49] Essex Record Office, Q/SR/312/58, /112, /136.

[50] Staffordshire Record Office, Q/SR/246/11–13, Q/SR/250/27. For Pinson's previous collisions with church authorities see David Cressy, 'Purification, Thanksgiving and the Churching of Women in Post-Reformation England', *Past and Present*, 141 (1993), 138–40.

[51] British Library, Harley Ms. 454, f. 40. See also Joseph Alfred Bradney (ed.), *The Diary of Walter Powell of Llantilio Crossenny in the County of Monmouth, Gentleman, 1603–1654* (Bristol, 1907), 25, for reports of 'quarrelling in the churches'.

to the scene at Neston, Cheshire, where Lady Brereton (wife of the member of Parliament) took the initiative for reform by requesting the minister 'to take down some . . . imagery which was in the glass windows' of the church. Saying that 'he knew none that took offence at them', the minister refused, whereupon Lady Brereton came to the church 'and brought a man with her who with a staff most zealously broke all the windows into fitters [fragments]'.[52] Less than a decade earlier the destruction of a stained glass window at Salisbury had brought Henry Sherfield to trial before Star Chamber.[53] Now the central government was powerless, the locality was polarized, and the iconoclasts earned both abuse and applause.

Parliament's Protestation in May 1641 triggered another round of troubles. In June, when parishioners of St Thomas the Apostle, London, gathered to subscribe the Protestation the grocer John Blackwell urged his neighbours to action, saying, 'Gentlemen, we have here made a Protestation before almighty God against all popery and popish innovations, and these rails (laying his hand upon the rails about the communion table) are popish innovations, and therefore it is fit they be pulled down, and shall be pulled down.' The Protestation was intended to unite the political nation in defence of the reformed Church of England, but here as elsewhere it served as a licence and catalyst for direct action.[54] A scuffle broke out in the church as Blackwell and his allies pulled down the rails, saying 'that Dagon being now down they would burn him'. A few enthusiasts threatened to burn the minister's surplice, and perhaps the minister too if he opposed them, in the same cleansing fire. In earlier times, in the face of such sacrilegious disorder, parish conservatives might have turned to the ecclesiastical courts for disciplinary redress; but now, with the courts in disarray and episcopacy itself in trouble, their only hope was that Parliament might punish the offenders. The rector and eight parishioners directed a petition to the House of Lords, bewailing the violence and misrule. A counter-petition to the House of Commons, subscribed by more than forty parishioners, presented the more radical point of view, blaming dissension in the parish on those who had installed the rails, not those who pulled them down.[55]

[52] British Library, Add. Ms. 36914, ff. 215–215v.
[53] *A Complete Collection of State-Trials* (6 vols., 1730), i. 377–96; Paul Slack, 'The Public Conscience of Henry Sherfield', in John Morrill, Paul Slack, and Daniel Woolf (eds.), *Public Duty and Private Conscience in Sseventeenth-Century England: Essays Presented to G. E. Aylmer* (Oxford, 1993), 151–72.
[54] House of Lords Record Office, Main Papers, Petition of 30 June 1641. The rector was William Cooper. Only one of the subscribers made a mark. For the Protestation see HMC, *5th Report* (1876), Part 1, Appendix 3.
[55] House of Lords Record Office, Main Papers, Petition of 1 July 1641. Twelve of the 41 subscribers made marks instead of signatures. On Blackwell and his son, see Keith Lindley,

Also in June 1641, one of the Southwark ministers, Oliver Whitby, had a rough time when unruly parishioners disturbed his administration of the sacrament, 'put on their hats, some crying lay hands on him, kick him out of the church, pull him by the ears, Baal's priest, bald pate, carry home your consecrated bread and your pottage.' The service degenerated into a riot because Whitby still expected parishioners to kneel for Communion. Parishioners in the gallery shouted 'pope and Baal's priest' as radicals attempted to wrench down the Communion rails, and a tussle broke out between the kneelers and the sitters.[56] In the aftermath of this disturbance the minister complained to the House of Lords, who ordered the worst offenders to perform public penance, standing on stools in Cheapside and Southwark markets, 'there to acknowledge their faults'. Others were referred to the next assizes and a few were threatened with prison. The men who had broken the rails were ordered to repair them at their own charge and to replace them, 'as they had stood, not according to the four or five last years, but thirty or forty years before'. The recent Laudian arrangements were effectively set aside in favour of those prevailing a generation earlier.[57] Thomas Jenyson, who reported these developments to Sir Roland St John, said that the Commons were displeased that the Lords committed thirty of the troublemakers to prison. One of the prime movers of the Southwark disorders, William Sheppard, was held for a month in the Fleet prison, but the House of Commons decided he had been punished enough and ordered his release.[58]

The House of Commons indicated its hostility to Communion rails through its preferred manner of taking the sacrament at Westminster, and in its motions and directives of January, August, and September 1641. But members insisted that rails should only be taken down but in an orderly manner, under parish supervision, not by hooligans with hammers. Churchwardens' accounts of 1641 often include references to this activity.[59] The accounts of

Popular Politics and Religion in Civil War London (1997), 39–40, 224; Tai Liu, *Puritan London* (Newark, Del., 1986), 134–5; Robert Brenner, *Merchants and Revolution: Commercial Change, Political Conflict, and London's Overseas Traders, 1550–1653* (Princeton, NJ, 1993), 527, 548–9.

[56] House of Lords Record Office, Main Papers, 11 June 1641, 22 July 164; John Rushworth, *Historical Collections of Private Proceedings of State* (8 vols., 1680–1701), iv. 284, 292; Bishop Warner's Diary, British Library, Harleian Ms. 6424, f. 72v–73; HMC, *7th Report* (1879), 686; Lindley, *Popular Politics and Religion*, 39–42.

[57] Rushworth, *Historical Collections*, iv. 4, 284, 292; Bishop Warner's Diary, British Library, Harleian Ms. 6424, f. 72v–73; HMC, *7th Report* (1879), 686.

[58] Bedfordshire and Luton Archives, St John Papers, J. 1386; John Nalson, *An Impartial Collection of the Great Affairs of State* (2 vols., 1683–4), ii. 328.

[59] See examples in Julie Spraggon, *Puritan Iconoclasm during the English Civil War* (2003), 100, 138–44.

St Mary le Strand, Westminster, include payments 'for taking down the rail about the communion table' and 'for removing the stone going up into the chancel'.[60] The churchwardens at St Botolph without Bishopsgate, London, spent a shilling and sixpence in June 1641 'for the taking down the rails and carrying them away'.[61] A similar task at St Botolph Billingsgate cost a shilling.[62] At St Michael Cornhill the same workmen who had set up the rails in 1638 were employed in November 1641 'for taking away the rails about the communion table' and 'for laying the pavement where the communion table stood'.[63]

The task of removing the rails cost considerably less than their installation. At Honiton, Devon, 'the taking up of the rails' in 1641 cost sixpence, whereas their erection in 1636 cost £2.8s.10d.[64] The churchwardens of Buckden, Huntingdonshire, paid one shilling and sixpence in 1641 'for removing the rails and laying down the brick in the chancel', undoing work that had cost them four pounds in 1635.[65] The rails at St Mary, Chester, had cost £2.15s. to install but only a shilling to remove.[66] At Lichfield, Staffordshire, the churchwardens of St Mary's paid sixteenpence in 1641 'for taking down the rails and levelling the ground', and sixpence more 'for the certificate of the order to the parliament'.[67] Weeks of disagreement and negotiation lay behind some of these brief financial entries. The reconfiguring of liturgical arrangements was no light matter, and was guaranteed to offend some sections of parish opinion.

Local turmoils intensified in the autumn of 1641 after the House of Commons order against Communion rails and images appeared in print. Late in September, in defiance of the ceremonialist minister but apparently in accord with directions from Westminster, one of the churchwardens at Radwinter, Essex, removed the Communion table from its east-end position 'and set it below the steps . . . and close to the north wall'. The long-suffering minister, Richard Drake, endured further affronts to his authority as the churchwarden, Richard Durden, failed to open the church, locked away the minister's surplice and hood, and refused to provide bread and wine for Communion. Other parishioners joined in the attack, shouting 'enough, enough', in the midst of Drake's prayers, leaving the church before service was ended, and interrupting worship with quacking noises and jangling of bells.[68]

---

[60] Westminster Archives, V22 (St Mary le Strand).   [61] Guildhall Library, Ms. 4524/1.
[62] Ibid., Ms. 942/1.   [63] Ibid., Ms. 4071/2.
[64] Devon Record Office, 1639A/PW/1.
[65] Huntingdonshire County Record Office, Ms. 2661/5.
[66] Cheshire Record Office, P20/13/1.   [67] Lichfield Record Office, D20/4/1.
[68] Bodleian Library, Rawlinson Ms. D. 158, ff. 43–55; Rawlinson Ms. D. 80, ff. 17–17v; British Library, Sloan Ms. 1457, f. 60.

At Packington, Leicestershire, a long-running dispute between conservatives and reformers was aggravated early in 1642 when a former churchwarden confiscated the Communion cup and utensils and prevented Thomas Pestell from performing the sacrament.[69]

News of 'Sir Robert Harley's vehement course in pulling down the cross at Wigmore [Herefordshire] the 27th September' gained wide circulation. This Puritan member of Parliament implemented the Commons order with a vengeance, causing the cross 'to be beaten in pieces, even to dust, with a sledge, and then laid it in the foot-path to be trodden on in the churchyard'. Three days later 'he pulled down the cross at Leintwardine and broke the windows in the church and chancel and beat the glass small with a hammer and threw it into [the river] Teame, in imitation of King Asa (2 Chonicles, 15 and 16) who threw the images into the brook Kydron.' According to the steward of Ludlow Castle, who reported this outrage to Lord Bridgewater, Harley also took his hammer to another nearby church 'to have done the like, but the parish and Mr Lake the minister withstood him, and so he departed for that time.'[70] But the setback was only temporary, for Sir Robert Harley invoked parliamentary authority in October 1641 to destroy the stone cross, the crucifix above the porch, the crucifixes painted in the east and west windows, and 'other scandalous pictures of the persons of the Trinity' at Leominster, Herefordshire.[71]

Lacking a member of Parliament as their leader, the activists who pulled down Isham cross in Northamptonshire faced prosecution for 'riot', despite claiming to be part of 'a lawful assembly'. At issue was whether the iconoclasts had authority for their actions. Some said 'that by order of parliament they might pull the cross down', but opponents asserted that the order was 'only for crucifixes, etc.' and that no removal should be done without the authority of the churchwardens. A spokesman for the defendants 'produced a quotation out of a remonstrance, that it was lawful to pull down superstitious monuments', and insisted to the jury that 'crosses were superstitious things, and to pull them down could be no riot'. Lord Montague received reports of this case in July 1642, but the incident at Isham apparently happened several months earlier.[72]

---

[69] Bodleian Library, J. Walker Ms. c.11, f. 14; Christopher Haigh. 'The Troubles of Thomas Pestell: Parish Squabbles and Ecclesiastical Politics in Caroline England', *Journal of British Studies*, 41 (2001), 403–28.

[70] HMC, *11th Report* (1888), Appendix, Part VII, 147; Huntington Library, Ms. El. 7350, Henry Ecclestone to Bridgewater, 25 October 1641.

[71] HMC, *14th Report, The Manuscripts of His Grace the Duke of Portland* (1894), iii. 81.

[72] HMC, *Report on the Manuscripts of the Duke of Buccleuch and Queensberry*, iii. 415–16.

The same parliamentary order that motivated Sir Robert Harley may have prompted Daniel Lane of Shenley, Hertfordshire, to 'beat down the church and chancel windows...to the great defacing of the same'.[73] It may also have stimulated the Londoners who attacked the organs and ornaments at St Paul's Cathedral later in September.[74] News spread quickly to the country 'that they pull down all the pictures in the churches about London'.[75]

The godly artisan Nehemiah Wallington noted that 'at Margaret's church in New Fish Street the scandalous pictures in the glass windows were broke to pieces, and the pictures [i.e., carvings] on the pew doors were cut off and the idolatrous brass was taken off the stones.'[76] In October 1641, he recorded,

at Leonard's Eastcheap, being our church, the idol in the wall was cut down and the superstitious pictures in the glass was broken in pieces, and the superstitious things and prayers for the dead in brass were picked up and broke, and the picture of the virgin Mary and the branch of candlesticks was broke. And some of the pieces of broken glass I have to keep for a remembrance to show to the generation to come what God hath done for us to give us such a reformation that our forefathers never saw the like.[77]

In another London church, 'in obedience to the order of the House of Commons', the puritan alderman John Warner 'pulled down all the painted glass in the windows...which some valued at £1000.' A purchaser offered forty pounds 'for the picture of Lazarus whom Christ raised from the dead, it was so very well done.'[78]

At Owlthorpe, Nottinghamshire, where the east window of the church was adorned with images of 'Christ upon the cross, the Virgin, and [Saint] John', the minister, pursuant to parliamentary directions, 'took down the heads of the images and laid them carefully in his closet', and attempted to certify that the order was fulfilled. But this was not enough for the godly John Hutchinson, who insisted on complete erasure of the 'superstitious paintings'. Previous reformations had been thwarted by churchwardens and incumbents who took such 'relics of superstition' into their custody. After much argument, in the course of which Hutchinson earned 'the name of puritan', the paintings were blotted out and the offending glass broken.

---

[73] Hertfordshire Record Office, QSB 2B, f. 28.

[74] HMC, *12th Report, The Manuscripts of the Earl Cowper*, ii. 291.

[75] National Library of Wales, Wynn Papers, no. 1692 (microfilm), John Mostyn to Owen Wynn, 5 October 1641, reporting John Griffith's news from London.

[76] British Library, Add. Ms. 21935, f. 148.   [77] Ibid.

[78] HMC, *Calendar of the Manuscripts of the Most Honourable The Marquess of Salisbury Preserved at Hatfield House, part 24, Addenda 1605–1668* (1976), 364.

This incident is recalled in Lucy Hutchinson's famous memoir of her husband, where it is intended to redound to his credit.[79]

A somewhat different construction was placed on the parish reformation at Chelmsford, Essex. According to the reactionary Bruno Ryves, 'before this parliament was called' in 1640 there was not a single man or woman at Chelmsford 'that boggled at the common prayers or refused to receive the sacrament kneeling.... But since this magnified reformation was set on foot...a third part of the people refuse to communicate in the church liturgy, and half refuse to receive the blessed sacrament unless they may receive it in what posture they please.' Ryves recalled that the chancel had 'a goodly fair window at the east end, untouched from the first foundation of the church, in which was painted the history of Christ from his conception to his ascension', ringed with the heraldic emblems of gentle benefactors. But when the Commons directive against scandalous pictures arrived in October 1641 it was the window's undoing. 'In obedience to the order the churchwardens took down the pictures of the blessed virgin, and of Christ on the cross, and supplied the places with white glass.' Not content with these half measures, a more radical group came to church on 5 November (a potent annual occasion for anti-popish agitation), 'and in a riotous manner with long poles and stones beat down and deface[d] the whole window.' Nor was that the end of the disturbance, for over the following months 'these new proselytes' reviled the minister, John Michaelson, 'for wearing the rags of Rome', called him 'Baal's priest', and claimed he had 'violated his faith engaged in the Protestation to abolish popery'.[80]

There were other disturbances that autumn in Essex and elsewhere. Faced with 'four very profane persons who do frequently misdemean themselves in the church in time of divine service', the rector of Rayleigh, Stephen Vassell, asked the quarter sessions to take 'some severe course' against the offenders, but there is no evidence that the magistrates were able to oblige.[81] At Kirmond, Lincolnshire, a group of parishioners, including a gentleman, his sons, and his servants, brought worship to a standstill in October 1641 through 'riots and outrages in the church', and poured vile contempt on the minister. At root their quarrel was more about money than religion, prompted by a dispute over tithes of sheep, but it added to the erosion of ecclesiastical discipline and the increasing tenor of disorder.[82] So too did the conduct of John Harvey, a Wiltshire clothworker, who 'did unreverently behave himself by sitting upon the communion table at Dilton in sermon time'.[83]

---

[79] Lucy Hutchinson, *Memoirs of Colonel Hutchinson*, ed. C. H. Firth (1906), 80.
[80] Bruno Ryves, *Angliae Ruina* (1647), 23–4.   [81] Essex Record Office, Q/Sba2/43.
[82] Lincolnshire Archives, LQS/A/10/106–7.
[83] Wiltshire Record Office, Quarter Sessions Great Roll, A1/110 Trinity 1642, 134.

Even the instruction to read the declaration of thanksgiving for the peace between England and Scotland in September 1641 could be a source of local conflict. Local Laudians like George Tongue, the rector of Kimcote, Leicestershire, and Hugh Barcroft in Lincolnshire had previously denounced the Scots as rebels, dogs, or 'worse than papists or barbarians'.[84] Now they had to bite their tongues or eat their words. 'What said our Arminian foul-mouthed priests to this?' asked the Presbyterian chronicler John Vicars.[85]

Christmastide services at Exeter Cathedral were disrupted in December 1641 by two young men who 'stood with their hats on their heads', demanded music for dancing, and threatened to bring in 'a company or rogues and tinkerly boys'. They laughed when a gentleman reminded them of their manners, and when someone threatened to summon the Dean, they responded by saying, 'let Mr Dean go shit'. The incident carried no particular religious message, except fondness for traditional merriments, and was certainly not part of the new reformation, but it demonstrated yet again the degree to which deference and decorum were imperilled.[86]

Other offenders were cited in court records for the disruption of divine services,[87] purloining of church fabric,[88] and 'for riotously assaulting and beating' the clerk in the chancel.[89] At All Saints upon the Pavement, York, the merchant Edward Gyllyot interrupted John Rawlinson's fast day sermon early in 1642 by shouting, 'thou art a Jew', and 'no more, no more!' When stewards hustled him out of the church, Gyllyot 'returned in again at the choir door near the pulpit', as noisy as ever, and declared 'he would stay there in despite of his teeth'.[90] In April 1642, during a service of institution, a Londoner visiting Wells Cathedral 'most maliciously threw a well-aimed stone' at the 'very fair crucifix at the upper end . . . behind the choir', and succeeding in breaking it.[91]

It is impossible to quantify such incidents or fully to explain their background. The records are too fragmentary to allow much reconstruction in depth. We cannot say for certain whether criminal greed or vestarian

---

[84] Bodleian Library, J. Walker Ms. c.11, ff. 49, 51v; J. W. F. Hill, 'The Royalist Clergy of Lincolnshire', *Lincolnshire Architectural and Archaeological Society Reports and Papers* (new series, 1940 for 1938), ii. 46.

[85] John Vicars, *God in the Mount. Or, Englands Remembrancer* (1641), 58.

[86] Devon Record Office, Exeter Quarter Sessions Book, 1630–1642, ff. 385v–387v.

[87] Wiltshire Record Office, Quarter Sessions Great Roll, A1/110 Easter 1641, 10.

[88] Public Record Office, Chester Court of Great Sessions, CHES 24/125/4; Wiltshire Record Office, Quarter Sessions Great Roll, A1/110 Hilary 1641, 206.

[89] Ratcliff and Johnson (eds.), *Warwickshire County Records, vol. VI*, 44, 67–8.

[90] York City Archives, Quarter Sessions Minute Book, 1638–62, F7, 157–8.

[91] HMC, *Calendar of the Manuscripts of the Dean and Chapter of Wells* (1914), ii. 426.

1. 'The soldiers in their passage to York turn unto reformers, pull down popish
pictures, break down rayles, turn altars into tables'
*All the memorable & wonder-strikinge, Parliamentary Mercies effected & afforded
unto this our English Nation, within this space of lesse then 2 yeares past ano.* 1641
& 1642 (1642)

2. 'The rising of Prentices and Sea-men on Southwark side to assault the Archbishops of Canterburys House at Lambeth'
*All the memorable & wonder-strikinge, Parliamentary Mercies effected & afforded
unto this our English Nation, within this space of lesse then 2 yeares past ano.* 1641
& 1642 (1642)

3. 'This canons seal'd', engraving of Archbishop Laud and bishops by Wenceslas Hollar, 1640; British Museum, Satirical Prints and Drawings: Political and Personal, no. 148

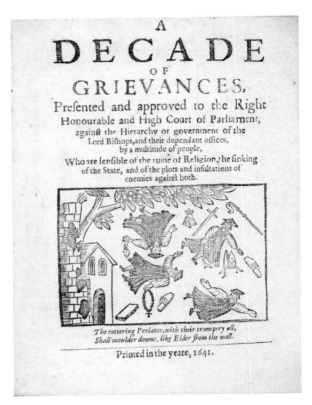

A

DECADE

OF

GRIEVANCES,

Prefented and approved to the Right Honourable and High Court of Parliament, againft the Hierarchy or government of the Lord Bifhops, and their dependant offices, by a multitude of people, Who are fenfible of the ruine of Religion, the finking of the State, and of the plots and infultations of enemies againft both.

The tottering Prelates, with their trumpery all,
Shall moulder downe, like Elder from the wall.

Printed in the yeare, 1641.

4. [Alexander Leighton], *A Decade of Grievances* (1641), title page

Canterburies Tooles:

OR,

Inftruments wherewith he hath effected many
rare feats, and egregious exploits, as is very well known,
and notorioufly manifeft to all men.

Difcovering his projects and policies, and the ends and pur-
pofes of the Prelates in effecting their facino-
rous actions and enterprifes.

EZEKIEL 34. 6, 10.

*My sheep wandered thorow all the mountains, and upon every high hill : yea my flock
was scattered upon all the face of the earth, & none did search or seek after them.
Therefore thus faith the Lord God, Behold, I am against the shepherds, and I will require my flock at their hand, and cause them to cease from feeding the flock, neither shall the shepherds feed themselves any more: for I will deliver my flocke
from their mouth, that they may not be meat for them.*

Printed in the yeere, when Prelates fall is neere, 1641.

5. *Canterburies Tooles: Or, Instruments wherewith he hath effected many rare feats*
(1641), title page

6. Thomas Stirry, *A Rot Amongst The Bishops, Or, A Terrible Tempest in the Sea of Canterbury* (1641) Emblem I: The Ship of Fools

7. Thomas Stirry, *A Rot Amongst The Bishops, Or, A Terrible Tempest in the Sea of Canterbury* (1641) Emblem II: Shipwreck

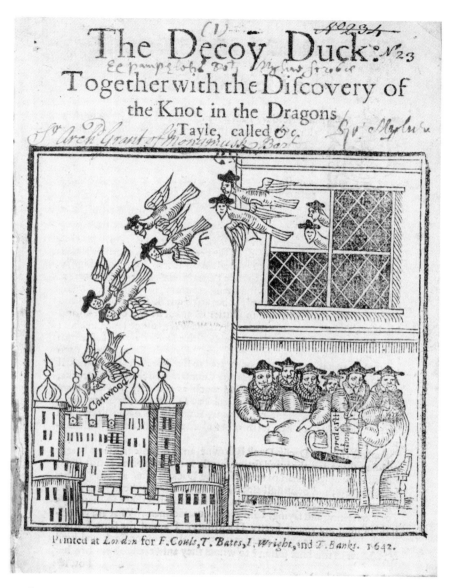

8. *The Decoy Duck: together with the Discovery of the Knot in the Dragons Tayle* (1642), title page

A TALE
In a Tub, Or a tub
LECTVRE

As it was delivered by *Mi-heele Mend-*
foale, an Infpired Brownift, and a moft upright Tranfla-
tor. *In* a mceting houfe nccre B*edlam,* the one and
twentieth of *December,* Laft, 1641.

Written by I. T.

London Pɩinted in the yeare when Brownift did
Domineare 1642

9. John Taylor, *A Tale in a Tub, Or a Tub Lecture* (1642), title page

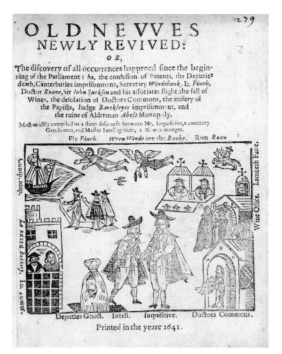

10. *Old Newes Newly Revived* (1641), title page

11. 'Colonell Lunsford assaulting the Londoners at Westminster Hall, with a great rout of ruffinly Cavaleires'
All the memorable & wonder-strikinge, Parliamentary Mercies effected & afforded unto this our English Nation, within this space of lesse then 2 yeares past ano. 1641 & 1642 (1642)

12. Edward Reynolds, *Evgenia's Teares for Great Brittaynes Distractions* (1642), title page

reformism lay behind the theft of the surplices, Communion cloths, and plate from a Cheshire church in 1640 and the stripping of the linen from a Wiltshire church in 1641.[92] Nor is it entirely clear whether financial grievances outweighed disagreements about liturgy in cases of violence against ministers. Whether the disturbers of worship were radical or conservative the impact was equally transgressive. One comment recorded at the Exeter Quarter Sessions in October 1641 appears to be both wise and prophetic. Thomas Minshall, gentleman, conversing with a Devonshire cutler, gave his opinion 'that the images and rails in the churches cost blood in setting of them up, and he did think they would cost somewhat ado before they would be pulled down.'[93]

RADWINTER TROUBLES

We will conclude this section by returning to Richard Drake's parish of Radwinter, Essex, which had been in near-perpetual turmoil since unruly soldiers attacked the images and altar rails in the summer of 1640. Drake himself had been summoned before Parliament in December and was declared unfit for the ministry, but he had not been removed from his parish. There followed a year of contest over parochial authority, ceremonial practices, the position of the Communion table, and the minister's embroidered surplice, which served as an emblem of his priesthood and his ceremonial conformity. Parishioners interrupted Drake's service by shouting, 'Are you at Mass again?' and by unseasonable and aggressive bell-ringing. Baptisms degenerated into battles, as the minister attempted to follow the prayer book while parents and godparents pulled babies back and forth to prevent them being signed with the cross.[94]

In February 1642 a Radwinter cobbler, Abraham Chapman, demanded in church that Drake hand over his surplice, threatened the minister with a 'bastinado' or cudgel, and stole the service books from the chancel. Early in March two women disfigured the precious surplice by cutting it 'about a foot deep before and behind'. Later that month, after the minister had conducted a burial in the churchyard, three women and three men 'laid violent hands on him, drew their knives, and near cut his throat, and rent off his surplice and hood in most barbarous manner before the whole congregation, and so

---

[92] PRO, Chester Court of Great Sessions, CHES 24/125/4; Wiltshire Record Office, Quarter Sessions Great Roll, A1/110 Hilary 1641, 206.

[93] Devon Record Office, Exeter Quarter Sessions Order Book, 1630–1642, ff. 380–380v.

[94] Bodleian Library, Rawlinson Ms. D. 158, ff. 43–55; British Library, Sloan Ms. 1457, f. 60.

carried away their spoils, triumphing in their victory'. On another day in March 'George Traps in service time came to the reading desk and threw to the curate a base pamphlet called *An Answer of the Roundheads to the Rattleheads*, saying, there is reading work for you, read that.'[95]

It would be hard to classify Drake's enemies as puritans or separatists; perhaps they were just ordinary parish Protestants who did not like overbearing priests. Their prolonged and inventive torment of the minister may have been associated with a puritan reaction to Laudian ceremonialism, but it also had elements of a cruel village sport. Drake fought back, bringing charges against his parishioners at the July 1642 Chelmsford assize, but to no avail. He clung to his post for the first few months of the civil war, and was eventually forced to leave in January 1643. The Radwinter troubles are particularly well documented, since Drake set forth his case at length in hope of restitution. Although the story is told from the minister's point of view, it contains intriguing echoes of the voices of his adversaries.

Taken together, the petitions, court documents, diaries, and letters point to deep rifts in local religious culture and rapidly eroding respect for the established church. They may say more about the rise of Babel than the pulling down of Babylon, more about the fracturing of community than advancement of the work of the Lord. The seamless coat of Christ was seamed and rent, so that people no longer knew what to believe. 'Oh miserable state, oh cruel fate! | I know not my religion now of late', lamented a rhymester of 1642.[96] His confusion and frustration was emblematic of the nation at large.

---

[95] Bodleian Library, Rawlinson Ms. D. 80, ff. 17–17v; Rawlinson D. 158, ff. 43–4.

[96] *Turn-over and Read, And after Reading Censure* (1642), 1, 4; *The Distractions of our Times* (1642), 2, 4.

10

Swarms of Sectaries

The puritan attack on the prayer book and episcopacy, and the sectarian exploration of unregulated gathering and worship, constituted two religious revolutions that swirled around each other. While some clerics and laymen thought themselves engaged in a rekindling of the Reformation and a blending of English life with the will of God, others concluded that all was going to the Devil. The established church was half abandoned. The Act of Uniformity, which had governed English religious life since 1559, became impossible to enforce. It was scandalously remarked in November 1640 that 'the king hath no more power in matters ecclesiastical than the boy that rubs his horse heels',[1] and events confirmed it to be true. English religious culture was irreversibly fractured, and out of the cracks crawled swarms of sectaries, from Brownists to Anabaptists to radical activist women.

That, at least, is how it seemed. But neither contemporaries nor modern historians could clearly comprehend the nature and the scale of the separatist phenomenon. Important questions about its origins and emergence, its impact and its threat remain unanswered. We would like to know more about the sociology, demography, and development of radical separatism as well as its religious aspirations. We need to know whether the 'swarms of sectaries' allegedly observed in 1641 were newly emergent, long submerged, truly rampant, or figments of an alarmed conformist imagination. Also we need to know what people thought of them as the country slipped towards civil war. The following discussion examines lay preaching and sectarian dissent through contemporary commentary and through the voices of separatists themselves.

Pamphleteers of 1641 and 1642 claimed that the sectaries were 'once a handful and then crept in corners . . . but now they are like Egyptian locusts,

---

[1] British Library, Add. Ms. 38490, 12. The remarks stem from a comment by the sacerdotalist John Cosin, widely reported late in 1640 and taken out of context. In December 1640 'Dr Cosin answered his denying the king to be head of the church thus, that he was governor, not head, inasmuch as there ought to be no visible head, which he proved out of bishop Jewell' (Will Dillingham to Will Sancroft, Bodleian Library, Oxford, Tanner Ms. 65, f. 223).

covering the whole land'.[2] Commentators reported a recent and disturbing upsurge of radical sectarian boldness that they likened to a plague of caterpillars or a swarm of locusts. The country appeared to be troubled by hosts of 'new upstart sectaries', 'mechanick preachers', lay prophets, and 'women schismatics', who avoided parish churches, despised community worship, chose their own leaders, and met in suspicious secret gatherings of the self-proclaimed elect. However, whether this amounts to the emergence into view of an existing antinomian underground amidst the distractions of the established order, or a novel radical movement made possible by the opportunities of 1641, is yet to be determined. The pamphlets rest on a core of contemporary observation, but they incorporate the concerns of religious conservatives and are prone to exaggeration and distortion. In order to make sense of the separatist phenomenon we need to integrate the evidence of court cases, print culture, correspondence, and both radical and anti-separatist writings. We need to understand why the separatist phenomenon of the early 1640s produced so much ridicule, anxiety, and fear.

THE SEPARATIST EXPLOSION

The religious fracturing tendency was as old as Christianity, indeed older, and the church had battled repeated outbreaks of heresy, disruption, and schism. Theological similarities, if not continuities, linked some of the radical explorations of the ancient world, the middle ages, and the sixteenth-century Reformation. Familist, antinomian, and Anabaptist subcurrents swirled around early modern London, with a small and shifting membership beset by internal controversies. Considerable effort has gone into tracing the genealogy of heterodox ideas in Elizabethan and early Stuart England. Their re-emergence at the time of the Long Parliament caught everyone's attention, and caught most observers by surprise.[3]

Shadowy networks of irregular godly activity persisted throughout the 1630s and continued into the civil war. Some were led by radicals who

---

[2] *Lucifers Lackey, or, The Devils new Creature* (1641), sig. A3; *The Anatomy of the Separatists, alias, Brownists, the factious Brethren of these Times* (1642), 2. Each pamphlet used almost identical words.

[3] Champlin Burrage, *The Early English Dissenters in the Light of Recent Research (1550–1641)* (2 vols., Cambridge, 1912); Geoffrey F. Nuttall, *Visible Saints: The Congregational Way 1640–1660* (Oxford, 1957); Murray Tolmie, *The Triumph of the Saints: The Separate Churches of London 1616–1649* (Cambridge, 1977); Peter Lake, *The Boxmaker's Revenge: 'Orthodoxy', 'Heterodoxy' and the Politics of the Parish in Early Stuart London* (Stanford, 2001); David Como, *Blown by the Spirit: Puritanism and the Emergence of an Antinomian Underground in Pre-Civil-War England* (Stanford, 2004).

advocated separation from the Church of England. Others included seekers and activists who steered a course between parish membership and outright schism. A fitful sectarian underworld operated in Caroline London, which left only occasional traces in the records.[4] In 1634 and again in 1636 the authorities were convinced that they faced 'sundry sorts of separatists and sectaries, as namely Brownists, Anabaptists, Arians, Thraskists, Familists, Sensualists, Antinominans, and some other sorts', though these were mainly spectres of their own conjuring and evidence of actual schismatic activity was slight.[5] Laudian episcopal vigilance was largely successful in crushing or inhibiting dangerous religious ideas.

By 1640 there was little more than a ghostly half-life to radical sectarianism. Even in London the antinomian underground was minimal and deeply buried. The pressure of Laudian discipline had taken its voice or broken its spirit. There were memories, and perhaps residues, of the separatist movement from earlier in the century. There were a few underground gatherings and deeply divided conventicles left over from the Elizabethan controversies or reinforced by books and activists from Amsterdam. But they had no oxygen, no fire. Episcopal and magisterial efforts in the later 1630s had driven most radicals into conformity or silence.[6] Of necessity they kept a low profile. Archbishop Laud himself faced 'professed separatists' in Kent, but the 'infection', as he called it, was localized and confined to mean and simple people.[7] In January 1640 Laud could inform the King that his province was generally 'quiet, uniform and conformable', though an outbreak of Brownists in Herefordshire showed 'how these schismatics increase in all parts of your dominions'.[8] They were an irritant, but no worse.

Usually when Laud and his associates spoke of 'schismatics' it was to smear adversaries who were merely moderate puritans. Conservatives branded their opponents 'with the nicknames of puritan, Brownist, schismatic, and precise fellow',[9] as if those conditions led one to another. It was

---

[4] Tolmie, *Triumph of the Saints*, 12–27.

[5] PRO, SP16/256/6, SP16/314/34. For alleged conventicles of familists in 1638 see PRO, SP16/378/24 and SP16/520/85. A visitation sermon preached at Southwark in 1635 observed that sectaries 'formerly swarmed in this our kingdom; but (God be blessed) the care of those who watch over us hath corrected the fury of their public disorder' (John Featly, *Obedience and Submission* (1636), 10).

[6] Como, *Blown by the Spirit*, 4, 22, 72, 74, 101, 393. See also Tolmie, *Triumph of the Saints*, and Lake, *Boxmaker's Revenge*.

[7] Lambeth Palace Library, Ms. Misc. 943, Reports on the Province of Canterbury 1633–39, pp. 251, 261, 267, 275, 283, 291.

[8] Ibid., 292, 295; William Laud, *The Works of the Most Reverend Father in God, William Laud, D.D.*, ed. James Bliss and William Scott (7 vols., Oxford, 1853), v. part 2, pp. 361–70.

[9] *Canterburies Tooles* (1641), 6.

'schismatical', said some Laudians, not to bow at the name of Jesus.[10] It was 'Brownist', wrote another in 1639, not to honour the beautification of churches.[11] Within a year or two they would know better. The word was used indiscriminately against all sorts of deviants, dissidents, protesters, and iconoclasts, but especially against laymen who questioned clerical discipline. Enemies of the hierarchy (like Roger Quatermayne) were liable to be labelled 'a separatist, an anabaptist, a Brownist, a Familist', without much discrimination.[12] As Lord Saye and Sele discovered, after the Archbishop charged him with being a separatist in 1640, 'the word schism, as it is now used, is a theological bug-bear' (an imaginary terror). A separatist, said Saye and Sele, was one who denied the faith of the church, and that he had never done.[13]

The attribution 'Brownist' was loosely applied to separatists, semi-separatists, and breakaway puritans, although it applied most appropriately to early Congregational Independents. The word was derived from the Elizabethan East Anglian separatist Robert Browne, who was in fact reconciled to the Church of England before the time of the Spanish Armada. According to John Taylor, whose pamphlets helped popularize the Brownist label, the eponymous Browne 'died a conformable churchman, but he hath left a most pernicious and seditious train of his sect behind him, of all trades, ages, sexes, and conditions'.[14] By 1642 the origin of the word was almost lost, with one pamphleteer explaining that separatists were called Brownists 'because they preach and teach at the backside of Browne's barn'.[15] At least forty-five publications between 1640 and 1642 had the word 'Brownist' in their title,[16] and most encouraged readers to sneer at Brownists with ridicule and contempt. William Enfield, of Nayland, Suffolk, appeared before the October 1641 quarter sessions for calling Mr Ludgatur 'anabaptist and Brownist', although the minister was neither.[17] In the spring of 1642 a Westminster yeoman was cited for calling the constable 'Brownist and crop-ear'.[18] By the summer the insult 'Roundhead' would supplant 'Brownist' in the conservative lexicon of derision.

---

[10] *Articles Exhibited in Parliament Against Master Iohn Sqvire* (1641), 2; *An Answer to a printed paper Entituled Articles Exhibited in Parliament Against Mr. John Sqvier* (1641), 3.

[11] Foulke Robarts, *Gods Holy Hovse and Service* (1639), 72–5, 98.

[12] Roger Quatermayne, *Qvatermayns Conqvest Over Canterbvries Covrt* (1642), 23.

[13] Hertfordshire Record Office, 'A Diary of ye Lords in Parliament' [Bishop Warner], XII.B.37, f. 48. On the slipperiness of religious labelling, see Peter Lake and Michael Questier (eds.), *Conformity and Orthodoxy in the English Church, c.1560–1660* (Woodbridge, 2000), pp. ix-xx.   [14] John Taylor, *A Cluster of Coxcombes* (1642), title page, 5.

[15] *The Master-piece of Roundheads* (1642), sig. A2v.

[16] My calculations from ESTC online, June 2004.

[17] Suffolk Record Office, B 105/2/1, f. 38.

[18] London Metropolitan Archives, Sessions Books, MJ/SBB/28 (calendar 10360.t.1, 119–20).

Sectaries and schismatics became increasingly visible in 1640 and 1641, not just in popular print but in observed social experience. Reports of their activity became more numerous around the time of the Short Parliament, especially in London and East Anglia. Radical religion appeared to be welling up towards the end of 1640, and by the summer of 1641 separatism had become a surging stream. By 1642, to continue the aqueous metaphor, it had become a cataract or maelstrom.

One of the early signs of sectarian behaviour was chronic absence from public worship. The Essex Quarter Sessions faced this problem in April 1640, citing as 'separatists' two weavers of Bocking who had not attended church on three successive Sundays.[19] By October 1640 there were growing numbers of Essex workmen, including a chapman and a cordwainer of Moulsham, cited 'for being separatists and absenting themselves from church'.[20] Sectarianism had become rampant by May 1641, with weavers, clothiers, tailors, and husbandmen from dozens of Essex villages detaching themselves from the customary religious life of the parish.[21] Quarter sessions in other counties faced similar problems that amounted to an artisan revolt against the structures and conventions of national communal worship.[22] The magistrates could cope with isolated outbreaks of religious insubordination, but disciplinary action proved ineffective in the face of growing sectarian dissent.

Church attendance became more sporadic in the summer and autumn of 1641, though absentees were not necessarily drawn into alternative gathered congregations. The crippled church courts could no longer enforce parish discipline, and the secular courts targeted only the most egregious offenders. Many of the labourers, artisans, and yeomen cited for absence from divine service in Hertfordshire in October 1641 had only recently stopped attending their parish church.[23] In the same month Yorkshire magistrates attempted to enforce the law requiring attendance at church, 'which law being of late time neglected . . . many persons neglect and absent themselves'.[24] The law in question, the Elizabethan Act of Uniformity on which the Church of England was founded, had apparently lost its teeth.

More indications of the sudden rise of separatism appear in court records, correspondence, and contemporary publications. The six months from autumn 1640 to the spring of 1641 saw a separatist explosion, coincident

---

[19] Essex Record Office, Q/SR/309/15. The separatists charged on 14 April 1640 were John Thorowgood and Joseph Crowe of Bocking, weavers.

[20] Essex Record Office, Q/SR/311/11.   [21] Essex Record Office, Q/SR/312/67–72.

[22] Hertfordshire Record Office, QSMB 2; Wiltshire Record Office, A1/110.

[23] Hertfordshire Record Office, QS MB 2/389, /396.

[24] John Lister (ed.), *West Riding Sessions Records. Vol. II. Orders, 1611–1642. Indictments, 1637–1642* (Yorkshire Archaeological Society, vol. liii, 1915), 317.

with the collapse of episcopal discipline. Conservative petitioners in December 1640 complained that 'schisms that for a long time slept or lurked in corners' were now emerging 'almost as publicly amongst us as the true doctrine of the Church of England', and were spreading tumults, disobedience, and sedition.[25] Conventicles were reported all over the country, mostly in towns and suburbs. 'The divisions among . . . God's people' at Nottingham, wrote a correspondent of Nehemiah Wallington, were reminiscent of splits among the early Christians. 'Some are for Paul and some are for Apollo, and so we know not what to do.'[26]

Splinter groups became loose congregations. In January 1641 it was reported, 'conventicles every night in Norwich, as publicly known as the sermons in the day-time, and they say much more frequented.'[27] And from Herefordshire later in the month came reports that 'the Brownists are very busy in meetings'.[28] A Lincolnshire minister complained of 'private and separate congregations within his parish', in which parishioners vented 'anabaptism, Brownism, and other heretical and blasphemous opinions'.[29] The evidence gives the impression of an urgent spiritual questing that could not be contained or satisfied within the established church.

By March 1641 there were 'conventicles at Nantwich', though a correspondent advised Sir Thomas Aston, 'I have so little conversation with any of that tribe that I cannot well inform myself of their privacies.'[30] This was a revealing and condescending remark, for most of the writers who reported the existence of conventicles had no idea what went on inside them. Some suggested that unregulated religious enthusiasm was bad for the economy as well as disruptive of society, for attendance at 'private meetings and conventicles' two or three days a week caused 'men and women to neglect their callings and trades' in hours of 'long and tedious tattling'.[31] But the main charge against separatist gatherings, besides their secrecy, was their destruction of religious unity.[32]

Dozens of commentators remarked on the changes affecting religious culture 'of late', as the shadowy sectarian underworld expanded. The Brownist sect was 'much increased of late' in London, according to *The Brownists Synagogue* of 1641.[33] These developments were all the more unnerving for

[25] *CSPD 1640–41*, 307; PRO, SP16/473/49.   [26] British Library, Sloan Ms. 922, f. 120.
[27] Bertram Schofield (ed.), *The Knyvett Letters (1620–1644)* (1949), 98–9.
[28] HMC, *14th Report, Manuscripts of His Grace the Duke of Portland*, iii. 73.
[29] Bodleian Library, J. Walker Ms. c.11, f. 59v, regarding Andrew Larmont's parish of Claybrooke.   [30] British Library, Add. Ms. 36914, f. 197v.
[31] *New Preachers, New* (1641), sigs. A3v, A4.
[32] [John Hales], *A Tract Concerning Schisme and Schismatiques* (Oxford, 1642), 2; Thomas Morton, *The Presentment of a Schismaticke* (1642), 20.
[33] Tolmie, *Triumph of the Saints*, 12–27; *The Brownists Synagogue or a Late Discovery Of their Conventicles, Assemblies, and places of meeting* (1641), title page.

being so recent and so volatile. The 'evils' and 'affronts' of schism were like the plague, wrote Joseph Hall in 1640, both 'very catching and do much mischief'.[34] Later in 1641 Hall complained of 'the sectaries who swell now beyond the reach of names and numbers'. A menace had become a movement, a trickle had become a flood. If left unchecked, he thought, the result would be 'chaos... anarchy, and... all imaginable ruin and confusion'.[35] The most pressing question concerned not its origin but its consequences.

Petitioners from Huntingtonshire similarly complained of the 'great increase of late of schismatics and sectaries' who 'of late' were emboldened 'to solicit and draw the people to them'. If not quickly checked, the petitioners warned, there would be 'anarchy...the utter loss of learning and laws... extermination of nobility, gentry and order, if not of all true religion'.[36] Other writers echoed this concern, associating the rise of separatism with the downfall of the entire social and religious order. The kingdom had become 'very fruitful' of new sects, reported the Venetian ambassador in July 1641, who thought they would flourish even more without the disciplinary restraint of the High Commission. England would suffer the 'pernicious consequences which usually follow in states where the exercise of religion is left to the ignorant comprehension of the common people', he predicted. Parliament led the way, the ambassador believed, encouraging confusion of opinions, so that now there were 'as many religions as there are persons'.[37]

By the autumn of 1641 alarmed observers reported that the city and suburbs 'swarm[ed]' with open condemners of the ordinance of God.[38] 'The Brownists and other sectaries make such havoc in our churches by pulling down of ancient monuments, glass windows and rails, that their madness is intolerable', wrote Thomas Wiseman in October.[39] In the same month a Lincolnshire preacher complained of 'so many covies of new doctrines sprung up', and 'more false and superstitious doctrines vented' in the past twelve months than at any time since the mid-sixteenth century.[40] 'The world is grown into a new confused chaos, full of new wine lately come from New England, a new spirit, new revelations, and new forms of prayer', pronounced another anti-separatist observer. Everything was collapsing into chaos, just as the Scriptures predicted, in 'these last and perilous days of the

---

[34] Joseph Hall, *Episcopacie by Divine Right Asserted* (1640), dedication to King Charles.

[35] [Joseph Hall], *A Survay of That Foolish, Seditious, Scandalous, Prophane Libell, The Protestation Protested* (1641), sig. A2v, 12.

[36] Northamptonshire Record Office, Finch-Hatton Ms. FH 2609.

[37] Allen B. Hinds (ed.), *Calendar of State Papers and Manuscripts Relating to English Affairs, Existing in the Archives and Collections of Venice*, Vol. 25, 1640–1642 (1924), 178, 188.

[38] Thomas Cheshire, *A True Copy of that Sermon which was preached at S. Pauls the tenth day of October last* (1641), 17.   [39] PRO, SP16/484/66.

[40] [Robert Sanderson]. *Ad Clerum. A Sermon Preached...8 Octob. 1641* (1670), 27.

world'.[41] A preacher at Southampton in February 1642 joined in protesting against the 'new upstart sectaries of this town'.[42] Replying to Parliament's Nineteen Propositions in June 1642, King Charles cited, among other ills, 'the irreverence of those many schismatics and separatists' and 'those many conventicles which have within these nineteen months begun to swarm'.[43]

Writing in November 1641, Henry Oxinden of Deane reviewed the range of religious positions that had emerged in his part of Kent.

For these parts, they are divided into so many sects and schisms that certainly it denotes the latter days to be very near at hand. Some whereof deny St Paul and upbraid him with bragging, fantastical and inconstant; others say that there is no national church, and so separate from us and the puritans as being no true church, of which kind there are a great number. There is another which preach against the keeping of holidays and Christmas day, and exhort the people to follow their vocation thereon, and in their pulpits vilify and blaspheme our saviour's name, affirming that it ought to be of no more account than Jack or Tom, and begin to deny the sacraments to noted sinners or drunkards, etc., and these are puritans. There is another and they are conformalists, and they resort most to this place; priests which must needs have a specious, pompous religion, all glorious without; bishops must continue their dignities and authorities lest despised and brought into contempt.

The author's own sympathies lay with the so-called 'puritans', who upheld the notion of a national church but wanted it radically reformed.[44]

Robert Abbott, the moderate conformist minister of Cranbrook, Kent, provided a perceptive analysis of the emerging separatist agenda. He advised Sir Edward Dering in March 1641,

these Brownists are not an inconsiderable part. They grow in many parts of the kingdom, and in your dear country among the rest. And though it were thought that the high courses of some bishops were the cause of their revolt from us, yet now they profess that were bishops removed, the common prayer book and ceremonies taken away, they would not join with us in communion. They stick not only at our bishops, service and ceremonies, but at our church. They would have every particular congregation to be independent, and neither to be kept in order by rules given by king, bishops, councils or synods. They would have the votes about every matter of jurisdiction in choice, admission of members and ministers, excommunication and absolutions, to be drawn from the whole body of the church in communion, both men and women. They would have none enter communion but by solemn covenant: not that made in baptism or renewed in the supper of the lord, but another for reformation after their own way.

[41] *Anatomy of the Separatists, alias Brownists*, 1. Cf. *The Brownists Conventicle: Or an assemble of Brownists, Separatists, and Non-Conformists* (1641), 3 (mispaginated as 5).

[42] Alexander Rosse, *Gods House, or The Hovse of Prayer* (1642), sig. A2.

[43] *His Majesties Reply to the Nineteen Propositions* (Cambridge, 1642), 17, 18.

[44] Dorothy Gardiner (ed.), *The Oxinden Letters 1607–1642* (1933), 257.

It was time, Abbott appealed, not only for 'a reformation in things truly amiss' but for 'a mild and prudent eye, speedily, over Brownists, who usurp upon all the ordinances of God'.[45]

It was this rise of religious radicalism that drove Sir Edward Dering, at one time a mouthpiece for root-and-branch activism, towards a state of frightened conservatism. 'Libertinism will beget atheism', he said in a speech in October 1641, discussing 'the sad miseries of our distracted church'. 'Schismatical conventicles' had become frequent, Dering noted in November, so that 'tailors, shoemakers, braziers, feltmakers, do climb our public pulpits'. Artisan preaching was doubly disturbing, undermining social hierarchy and supplanting clerical authority. By the turn of the year Sir Edward felt threatened by 'a general increase of open libertinism, secret atheism, bold Arminianism, desperate Socinianism, stupid Anabaptism, and with these the new Chiliasts, and the willfulness of papists, strangely and strongly confirmed by these distractions.' By January 1642 he had come to fear that the entire social order was coming apart: 'all's undone, by breaking asunder that well ordered chain of government, which from the chair of Jupiter reacheth down by several golden links, even to the protection of the poorest creature that now lives among us.'[46] It was anxieties of this sort that drove so many future royalists ultimately to cleave to the King.

Sectarianism was not just a threat to traditionalists. Protestant reformers had always regarded it with horror. The Presbyterian Robert Baillie decried the 'impertinency' of 'the separatists' whom he considered an antinomian menace. When 'some of the separation' were 'found at their conventicles' in January 1641, he writes, they 'did speak disgracefully of the king, parliament and laws'. Baillie feared, not without cause, that reaction against sectarianism would rally support for the bishops.[47] In the same vein Stanley Gower, a correspondent of Sir Robert Harley, disparaged the Brownists of August 1641 as enemies who 'discourage your reformation of our Zion . . . [as] their sires and ancestors the anabaptists did hinder the reformation in the days of Luther'.[48] Richard Carter repeated the point that the schismatics 'railed against Luther also'.[49] *A Short History of the Anabaptists* reminded readers that Luther and Calvin both opposed the sects, and warned of their

---

[45] British Library, Stowe Ms. 184, ff. 27, 28v.

[46] Sir Edward Dering, *A Collection of Speeches* (1642), 92–3, 105–6, 166.

[47] David Laing (ed.), *The Letters and Journals of Robert Baillie* (3 vols., Edinburgh, 1841), i. 282, 287, 291, 293. Cf. the 'puritan' response to the antinomian crisis in David D. Hall (ed.), *The Antinomian Controversy, 1636–38: A Documentary History* (Middletown, Conn., 1968), and Como, *Blown by the Spirit*, passim.

[48] HMC, *14th Report, Manuscripts of His Grace the Duke of Portland*, iii. 79.

[49] Richard Carter, *The Schismatic Stigmatized* (1641), sig. A.

'licentiousness and rebellion'. 'God save us from a reformation wrought by a multitude misted with a frantic zeal and giddy revelations', it concluded.[50] Another 'comparative history' of the 'wild preachings and practices' of the anabaptists wished destruction on 'all the factious and seditious enemies of the church and state'.[51]

John Ley, the moderate pastor of Great Budworth, Cheshire, who was troubled on the one hand by Arminian ceremonialists, disparaged the sectaries on the other as 'the dregs of the vilest and most ignorant rabble'. 'The feeble flies of summer', he continued, 'are not more contemptible than these wretched throngs.'[52] Thomas Barrow of Kent likewise criticized the radicals for 'their new invented schismatical factions and their heretical opinions . . . For here is now not only differences between brothers but between fathers and children concerning faith and baptism. I am afraid they will shortly find out a new god also.'[53]

Cornelius Burges, John Pym's favourite preacher, warned the House of Commons on the Gunpowder anniversary in 1641 that 'matters of religion lie a-bleeding; all government and discipline of the church is laid in her grave, and all putredinous [sic] vermin of bold schismatics and frantic sectaries glory in her ashes.' Twelve months earlier Burges had cheered that Babylon was fallen and God's enemies were down. But now, after the separatist summer, and with the terrible news of rebellion in Ireland, 'we begin to fall quite back again', towards 'anarchy and confusion'.[54]

Thomas Cheshire, another embattled moderate, who described himself as a 'minister of God's holy word and sacraments', protested the onslaught against the established religion. 'When was there a greater whirlwind and tempest in the land than now is, and is there not an earthquake in this land of ours?' he cried out from the pulpit of St Paul's. Preaching on Sunday, 10 October 1641, in an attempt to hold back the cataract, Cheshire observed that 'many of our pulpits nowadays do ring of the doctrine of devils'. Profanation of the church, denigration of the clergy, condemnation of the Book of Common Prayer, and disturbance of the peace were just some of the consequences of the separatist explosion. Cheshire was not opposed to reform, and he would not have commanded such a prominent pulpit were he not in sympathy with many of the activists in Parliament, but he was

[50] *A Short History of the Anabaptists of High and Low Germany* (1642), sig. A2, 2, 54.
[51] *A Warning for England, especially London; in the famous History of the frantick Anabaptists* (1642), 1, 7, 21, 25.
[52] [John Ley], *A Discourse concerning Puritans* (1641), 65.
[53] Gardiner (ed.), *Oxinden Letters 1607–1642*, 310.
[54] Cornelius Burges, *Another Sermon Preached to the Honorable House of Commons now assembled in Parliament, November the fifth, 1641* (1641), 60, 39, preface.

adamant against the audacity and tumult of popular radicalism. Regarding attacks on surplices, for example, 'if we must forbear this vestment let us have an Hezekiah, our gracious king, with his due council to command it, not a rude Shrove-Tuesday company, and then we are well content.'[55]

SECTARIAN CONVICTIONS

Sectarianism cut to the heart of established religion, which was why so many people found it threatening. Instead of *'cor unam, via una*: one heart, one way', it posited fractious diversity.[56] Instead of a comprehensive community of Christians it fostered select gatherings, separations, and exclusions. It undercut not just three generations of English Protestantism but a millennium and a half of Christian practice. God's church had been traditionally compared to 'a field, wherein are sown tares as well as wheat; to a net, wherein are contained dead fish as well as living; and to a fold, having in it goats as well as sheep'.[57] The mixed multitude of the visible church included both the elect and the unregenerate, joined together in worship. Separatists presumed to disrupt this community by withdrawing the precious from the vile, thereby shredding Christ's seamless garment.[58] 'Oh, into what schism do we run, into what sects are we dissected? Asunder are we rent, one from the other', lamented the London conformist John Grant.[59]

Only occasionally is it is possible to hear radical sectaries speak for themselves. More often their views are refracted through the writings of their critics and enemies. Few of the correspondents and pamphleteers who wrote about Brownists and other sectaries had direct internal knowledge of those movements, and even fewer wrote of them with sympathy. The following discussion draws on separatist publications and statements made to the authorities to reconstruct a range of radical positions. Though never codified or collated, sectarian notions about the church, the ministry, worship, and salvation formed a revolutionary alternative to mainstream and puritan Protestantism.

Separatist theology was complex and challenging, but not necessarily stable or coherent. Those caught up in radical religion shared few beliefs,

---

[55] Thomas Cheshire, *A Sermon Preached in Saint Paules Church the tenth of October 1641* (1641), 12–15; Cheshire, *True Copy of that Sermon which was preached at S. Pauls*, 14.

[56] [John Grant], *Gods Deliverance of Man by Prayer* (1642), 10.

[57] Morton, *Presentment of a Schismaticke*, 7; Thomas Case, *Gods Waiting to be Gracious Unto his People* (1642), 10–11.

[58] *Turn-over and Read, And after Reading Censure* (1642), 4; *The Distractions of our Times* (1642), 2; Matthias Milward, *The Souldiers Triumph: and the Preachers Glory* (1642), 6.

[59] [Grant], *Gods Deliverance of Man by Prayer*, 10.

except perhaps the conviction that they alone were true Christians. Separatists were said to have believed that Christ had freed them, that the established church was sinful, that the elect should not worship with the reprobate, and that anyone could preach who had the gift of the spirit. Although they embraced separation, they usually denied being schismatics. They were not necessarily millenarians, not all antinomians, not necessarily proto-baptists, Seekers, or Independents. Meaningful denominational identities had yet to take shape in the ferment and flux of the early 1640s.

According to the Colchester book of examinations and depositions, the Essex tailor Richard Lee taught that his righteous assembly of Anabaptists was ruled 'by Christ's examples and precepts', while the worldly church of the diocese of London was 'governed by the renditions of men, and must have a book of canons'. Witnesses to Lee's preaching in the summer of 1640 reported that 'the whole scope of his sermon was that they were in the right way, and that salvation belonged only to them, and that God had raised a horn of salvation to break in pieces the wicked; but he hoped there was no such amongst them.' He taught that 'the ministry of the Church of England is not according to the word of God', and that 'the baptism of infants is unlawful'. Nor did Lee forget to pray for the King, asking God 'to turn his heart into the right way'. When the mayor of Colchester demanded to know by what authority Lee, a layman, presumed to preach, he answered none but the Scriptures, 'and that everyone ought to reveal that gift or light which he receives from the scriptures'. Quoting freely from the Gospel of St Luke and St Paul's Epistles to the Corinthians and Galatians, Lee further expounded his separatist position:

The Lord is pleased of his free mercy and grace to visit his people with the light of his truth before we can do anything to prevent the Lord with any moving cause in us. And if it be so, as the Lord be pleased to visit us first of his free grace and mercy, this is that that we must learn, to give to the Lord all the praise and glory of his work of our redemption. And if Christ did redeem us from that miserable condition which we are in by nature, then he do redeem us unto himself to be his servants, and we are to be governed by his righteous rules, precepts and examples, and not by canons or any other human tradition whatsoever, and not by the book of canons.[60]

Lee's outburst was triggered by Laudian attempts to impose the new 1640 canons, but his preaching appears congruent with the separatist outpouring that would follow.

In the summer of 1640 the magistracy of Essex viewed such opinions as outlandish and threatening, a challenge to the community of Colchester as

---

[60] Essex Record Office, Colchester, Book of Examinations and Depositions, 1619–1645, D/5/Sb2/7, ff. 281–281v.

well as to the Church of England. But by July 1642 it was claimed that the aldermen of Colchester themselves included 'some anabaptists, some Brownists, some Arminians, and some free-willers', although the majority still adhered to conventional parish worship.[61] Radical teaching had made rapid inroads, producing the religious fragmentation that all conservatives feared.

Puritans and conformists alike were shocked when the views of some Southwark sectarians became known, after a congregation of some sixty was apprehended in the house of Richard Sturges when they should have been in church on Sunday, 10 January 1641. They met, they told magistrates, 'to teach and edify one another in Christ', and made four extraordinary claims that fundamentally challenged the authority of the Stuart confessional state:

First, that the Act of Parliament of 35 Elizabeth for the Administration of Common Prayer in the Church was no good law, it being made by bishops. Secondly, there is no church but where the faithful are. Thirdly, the king can make no law because he is not perfect, this is, perfectly regenerate. Fourthly, the king is to be obeyed but only in civil matters.[62]

Normally such seditious and heretical views would have elicited a stiff judicial response. However, by January 1641 the mechanisms of control were breaking down. Ecclesiastical government was fast unravelling, many of the King's judges themselves had been impeached, and neither church nor state could secure discipline against a tumult of popular dissent. The House of Lords took up the issue of the Southwark schismatics on 18 January, considering their 'tumultuousness of divers persons in not suffering the common prayers, which example might breed inconveniences'. But apart from reasserting the legality of the prayer book, and admonishing the offenders to attend church, the Lords could do no more than the local magistrates to bring the sectaries to heel. In effect they were released unpunished.[63] The Bishop of Rochester, John Warner, expressed outrage that these 'anabaptists', as he called them, escaped so easily. Their leaders had openly confessed, 'but nothing [was] done unto them, not so much as to reform their opinions or [make them] come to church'. Other sectarians were released and charges against them dropped.[64]

Some of the more enterprising separatists published their own tracts or sermons, using the newly liberated medium of the press to justify or spread

---

[61] Ibid. f. 298.

[62] PRO, SP16/476/43; Bishop Warner's Diary, British Library, Harleian Ms. 6424, f. 6; *Lords Journal*, iv. 133–4.

[63] HMC, *Report on the Manuscripts of the Duke of Buccleuch and Queensberry* (The Montague papers, 2nd series, 1926), iii. 408–9; *Lords Journal*, iv. 134.

[64] Bishop Warner's Diary, British Library, Harleian Ms. 6424, ff. 6v–7.

their beliefs. The lay preacher John Spencer went into print in 1641 to assert 'the lawfulness of every man's exercising his gift as God shall call him thereunto'. The gift of prophesy and exposition, Spencer argued, was by no means confined to those who were educated, inducted, and clerically ordained. Rather, he proclaimed, the spirit of God was given to everyone, and anyone might preach who heard the call, even women. The Lord chose his messengers without regard to their status, for 'the true understanding of scripture comes not by human learning by arts and tongues, but by the spirit of God'. Spencer himself responded to the call of the holy spirit, but his attempts at public preaching bred 'amazement' and 'evil aspersion'. Critics disparaged him as a 'horse rubber', though Spencer styled himself 'Mr' and 'sometime groom to a nobleman'. He gained access to the pulpit of St Michael, Crooked Lane, on 30 March 1642, and subsequently published the core of his sermon.[65]

James Hunt, the Kentish farmer turned prophet, supplemented his public oratory with 'a book . . . concerning the overthrow of the devil and the false church'. *The Sermon and Prophecie of Mr. James Hunt* was no spoof but the authentic if idiosyncratic voice of separatism. 'Read this book', Hunt urged in 1641, expounding Christian liberty through the Scripture, the spirit, and love.[66] 'I beseech you to read my book', he repeated in 1642, as he railed against false doctrine. Hunt published several tracts with 'spiritual verses', and another sermon 'concerning the marriage of the Lamb and of the confounding of the whore of Babylon'. He attacked the common service book as full of 'false inventions', and claimed its use 'doth bring in the old Jewish religion again'. He reviled the bishops and clergy who 'have linked themselves together, as in a chain, against Christ and his elect children'. Christ, Hunt insisted, 'hath ransomed his people quite off from the old law and testament, which is the bondage of death and corruption.' It was almost a badge of pride that his efforts as 'a minister and messenger of Jesus Christ' had caused him ten times to be cast into prison.[67]

Another mouthpiece for sectarianism was Robert Coachman, who published a lengthy justification of separation in *The Cry of a Stone* (1642). Though the wicked and the godly lived side by side in the world, he argued,

---

[65] John Spencer, *A Short Treatise Concerning the Lawfullnesse of every mans exercising his gift as God shall call him thereunto* (1641), 5; *The Spiritual Warfare* (1642) by 'Mr John Spencer, sometime a groom to a nobleman'.

[66] *The Sermon and Prophecie of Mr. James Hunt* (1641), 7, 1, passim.

[67] James Hunt, *The Spirituall Verses and Prose of James Hunt: Concerning the Advancement of Christ his Glorious and Triumphing Church* (1642), 2, 3, 10, 16; idem, *These Spirituall Verses . . . Concerning the Down-Fall of Ceremonies* (1642), 7; idem, *The Sermon and Prophesie of James Hunt: Concerning the Marriage of the Lambe, and of the Confounding of the Whore of Babylon* (1642).

there was no reason for them to worship together, as they did in the Church of England. Mere reform of practice and discipline along puritan or Presybyterian lines was pointless, he thought, for 'what safety is there in amending these trifles when the body is naught?' Only separated churches measured up to Christ's yardstick of godliness. 'Any of the sons of Adam' was qualified to preach, no matter his status or education, so long as he preached God's word. Any preaching was 'as lawful in one place as another...in fairs, market-places, passage boats, fields, and dwelling houses, as in any churches or temples, provided the place be convenient and the audience silent and attentive.' Coachman made his case for the separatist lay ministry with a thick application of supporting biblical texts.[68]

Brownists had a bad press, going under 'many aspersions and calumnies, as carnal, erroneous, absurd, and the like'. But with the emergence of Congregational Independency, more separatist voices began to be heard. As one of their spokesmen said in 1641, 'the day is now dawning wherein Sion's peace and comforts shall be fulfilled.'[69] Congregational Independency was not necessarily synonymous with separatism, but its adoption would have fragmented the Church of England. Though Independency was clerical, and based in the church and the parish, it rejected hierarchy, structure, set liturgies, and centralized discipline. That Independency operated discursively at a different level than popular lay sectarianism was due to the erudition and reputation of its leaders.

The congregationalist manifesto, *A Glimpse of Sions Glory*, published anonymously in 1641 but attributed to John Goodwin, argued that Christ had given power to his church, 'not to a hierarchy, neither to a national presbytery, but to a company of saints in a congregational way'. Hierarchy would crumble and social privilege would vanish as 'God intends to make use of the common people in the great work of proclaiming his son'. This, of course, was what episcopalians and Presbyterians feared most, as a recipe for chaos. But the Congregationalist author had an answer. 'The saints of God gathered together in the church are the best commonwealths men, not seditious men, not factious, not disturbers of the state; but they are our strength in the Lord of Hosts, they are the strength of a kingdom.'[70]

The puritan celebrity Henry Burton, who had embraced Independency by the summer of 1641, asserted that 'a particular church or congregation, rightly collected and constituted, consists of none but such as are visible

---

[68] Robert Coachman, *The Cry of a Stone, or A Treatise; Shewing What is the Right Matter, Forme, and Government of the visible Church of Christ* (1642), 17, 44–5, 63. Coachman may have been the model for the weaver 'Obadiah Couchman' in *The Adamites Sermon* (1641).

[69] [John Goodwin], *A Glimpse of Sions Glory* (1641), epistle by W.K.

[70] Ibid., 5, 26.

living members of Christ the head, and visible saints under him...The church is properly a congregation of believers, called out from the rest of the world.'[71] Religious discipline, he asserted, belonged not to a bishop or archbishop but 'to the whole congregation'.[72] Ten years earlier Burton had been the voice of mainstream godliness, hammering the antinomian menace.[73] Now he was articulating a position that most moderate puritans rejected.

One of Burton's female followers, Katherine Chidley, published an eighty-page *Justification of the Independent churches of Christ* (from the same printer and in the same year as *A Glimpse of Sions Glory*). No flighty, anonymous, or surreptitious publications, these were both openly 'printed for William Larnar...to be sold at his shop at the sign of the Golden Anchor, near Paul's Chain'. Chidley wrote in direct response to the Presbyterian Thomas Edwards who published *Reasons against the Independent Government of Particular Congregations*. Whereas Edwards addressed his work to Parliament, Chidley spoke to all who would read and hear. The fact that this was a woman's work only added to its notoriety.[74]

According to Katherine Chidley, the true Christian was duty-bound to separate from the Church of England, which she equated with 'the discipline of Antichrist'. 'Separation is not a schism', she insisted, 'but obedience to God's commandment.' Every separation was also a gathering, a coming together of the faithful. Chidley dismissed the established ecclesiastical hierarchy of archbishops, bishops, deans, 'and the rest of that rabble' as 'bred in the smoke of the pit', with 'no footing' in the true word of God. True ministers, by contrast, were 'well-meaning Christians', and it made no difference whether they were 'tailors, felt-makers, button-makers, tent-makers, shepherds or ploughmen'. The true covenanted church would be 'a company of saints separated from the world, and gathered into the fellowship of the gospel'. They would be sheep separated from the goats, the precious separated from the vile, with power to admit, admonish, or cast out members according to the spirit of God.[75]

Sermons by the New England minister Samuel Eaton (not the deceased separatist button-maker), delivered at Barrow, Cheshire, in August 1641 further expounded the grounds of Independency, sometimes known as the New England way. The Book of Common Prayer was to be set aside. There would

---

[71] Henry Burton, *The Protestation Protested* (1641), sigs. B3, B3v.

[72] Henry Burton, *Englands Bondage and hope of Deliverance* (1641), 23.

[73] Henry Burton, *The Law and the Gospell Reconciled* (1631).

[74] Katherine Chidley, *Iustification of the Independent Churches of Christ* (1641); Thomas Edwards, *Reasons against the Independent Government of Particular Congregations* (1641).

[75] Chidley, *Iustification of the Independent Churches of Christ*, sigs *2, 2, 3, 5, 12, 21, 22, 23, 37, 80.

be no national or diocesan ecclesiastical organization. Every particular congregation would be absolute and independent, with a membership of covenanted saints. All ecclesiastical censures, like excommunication, were to be exercised by particular congregations within themselves.[76] This could become a respectable position, appealing to members of the gentry and middling sort who would have nothing to do with artisan sectarianism.

BRAIN-SICK CATERPILLARS

Contemporary commentary about religious radicals was overwhelmingly hostile. Much of it combined ridicule and contempt. Popular pamphlets more commonly rendered 'Brownists' and 'Anabaptists' as some kind of disease or vermin than as questing Christians seeking alternatives to the mainstream clergy-led church. The dominant discourse treated separatists as a contaminant, a folly, or a threat. Orthodox clerical authors found lay schismatics theologically objectionable, whereas reputable puritans and Presbyterians looked on them with alarm and despair. Gentlemen looked down on sectaries as socially distasteful, whereas magistrates found them unamenable to control. Common opinion rated their women as bad as their men, jumped-up, ignorant, hypocritical, and licentious. To the mainstream writers of tracts and correspondence, sectarianism represented the antinomian nightmare of an ecclesiastical polity slipping into chaos.

Hostile commentators repeatedly employed the etymological imagery of the 'swarm' of sectaries and separatists and called them 'the new crept in caterpillars of our kingdom'.[77] They used the language of infestation, tinged with Old Testament providence, to liken the proliferating sects to 'the plagues of Egypt', 'Egyptian locusts', and 'Pharaoh's frogs'.[78] Some adapted the trope of monstrosity, fathering 'monstrous shapes' on the Brownists,[79] and making them responsible for the Roundhead 'monstrous beast'.[80] Others remarked on 'those sundry sects which now are sprung up amongst us like so

[76] *Brownists Conventicle*, 4; HMC, *Fourth Report, Part 1* (1874), 55.

[77] *Anatomy of the Separatists, alias, Brownists*, 2.

[78] *His Maiesties Speciall Command under the great Seale of England ... To suppresse the Tumultuous and unlawfull Assemblies* (1641), sig. A2v; *Brownists Synagogue*, 1, 2; *The Distractions of our Times*, 2. The title of *A Swarm of Sectaries* (1641) says it all.

[79] 'George Spinola', *Rvles to Get Children By with Handsome Faces: or, Precepts for the Extemporary Sectaries* (1642), sig. A4.

[80] *The Soundheads Description of the Rovndhead* (1642), title page, 5. The Brownists were 'monsters' who would 'admit no government in church', assumed themselves 'more holy than all people', and displayed a pretended 'zeal', said the 1640 broadsheet *The Lofty Bishop, the Lazy Brownist, and the Loyall Author.*

many weeds in a pleasant garden',[81] or like 'nests of caterpillars, destroying our sweet garden roses'.[82] A broadside entitled *A Whip for the Back of a Backsliding Brownist* called them 'the cancer worms of this our English nation'.[83] Separatists were commonly associated with 'slovenliness, disorder and disproportion',[84] evoking things loathsome, noxious, and out of control.

The popular press created a sensationalist image of the Brownists as foolish, factious, and ignorant sectaries. Pamphleteers readily confused them with other groups of innovators and extremists from the early Christian eras or the continental Reformation. Hostile publications described the Brownists as 'fantastic', 'fanatic', and 'giddy-headed', 'libertines or Anabaptists'.[85] Some suggested they were mad, or symptoms of madness in a country driven to distraction. The separatists were 'false prophets' and 'frothy brained coxcombs' according to one pamphlet,[86] 'the rabble of brain-sicks who are enemies to old England's peace', according to another,[87] people with 'distempered and moon-changing brains' said a third.[88] It was a mad world of topsy turvy, declared a pamphlet of 1642, when 'every cobbler or button-maker will get into a tub, and talk to the people of divine matters', and when whores 'are in great esteem . . . and are called holy sisters.'[89]

The autumn of 1641 saw a proliferation of pamphlets that ridiculed artisan preachers, licentious Anabaptists, and ignorant Brownists, or listed and anatomized newfound heresies and sects. Schism and faction had become so acute, wrote the author of *The Diseases of the Times or, The Distempers of the Common-wealth* (most likely John Taylor), that 'the church thereby is almost turned upside down'. The author bemoans 'the strange diffusion of Brownianism' and wishes that 'instead of preaching in tubs' these sectaries would 'suddenly preach in the pillory'. Other targets for attack included 'Amsterdamian zealots' who 'can breath five hours in a text', advocates of 'feminine divinity' who would have the women wear the breeches, and lay sectarians who 'dare presume to snatch the ministerial

---

[81] *The Brownist Haeresies Confuted Their Knavery Anatomized, and their fleshly spirits painted at full* (1641), 1.

[82] 'Samoth Yarb' [Thomas Bray], *A New Sect of Religion Descryed, called Adamites: Deriving their Religion from our Father Adam* (1641), 3.

[83] *A Whip for the Back of a Backsliding Brownist* (1640?).

[84] 'Spinola', *Rvles to Get Children By with Handsome Faces*, sig. A2v.

[85] *Anatomy of the Separatists, alias, Brownists*, title page, 2.

[86] *The Brothers of the Separation. Or A true Relation of a Company of Brownists* (1641), sig. A2. The artisan separatists were 'ignorant coxcombs', according to the title page of *New Preachers, New.*   [87] Carter, *Schismatic Stigmatized*, title page.

[88] [Hall], *Survay of That Foolish, Seditious, Scandalous, Prophane Libell*, 10. 'Schismatics . . . have an itch in their brains', said John Swan, *Redde Debitum* (1640), 136.

[89] *Newes, True Newes, Laudable Newes* (1642), 4–5.

function from the mouths of the clergy'.[90] Hostile broadsheets excoriated the Brownists as an 'illegitimate sect' who would 'make a chaos of the church'.[91]

The conformist Richard Carter found the schismatics to be entirely disorderly, contrary, and disruptive. 'When we stand up reverently, they unmannerly sit on their bums. When we kneel, they either sit or loll on their elbows. When we are bare-headed, they have their bonnets and hats on their zealous noddles.'[92] At least Carter's schismatics were still coming to church. Others had broken with their parishes and set out on their own religious course.

A Discovery of 29 Sects here in London, which appeared in September 1641, purported to expose the activities of Seekers, Familists, Adamites, and Anti-Scripturians.[93] 'Almost in every domestic diocesan parish we have novelists, some Thraskites, or sabbatarians, Banisterians, Brownists, and anabaptists', claimed another pamphlet of 1641.[94] Readers encountered a fecundity of error, a profusion of sects, including naked Adamites in the suburbs of London and an offshoot of the Family of Love near Bagshot, Surrey.[95] The catalogues of sects became formulaic, with growing length but diminishing credibility, in such works as *The Divisions of the Church of England Crept in at XV Several Doores* and *Religions Lotterie, or the Churches Amazement*, both published in 1642.[96] Some of these lists were reminiscent of those bandied about by the High Commission in the mid-1630s, and rest on just as flimsy evidence. Although some pamphleteers exhibited a kind of horrified delight in listing the splinters of religious fracturing—approaching two dozen varieties by the outbreak of civil war—they also tended to lump all separatists together without regard for their theological distinction, heritage, or even plausibility. Much of this writing used derision as a way of masking fear. Even if the size of the separatist threat was exaggerated, the wave of publicity added to respectable anxieties. The author of *The Brownists Synagogue* thought the proliferation of sects a cause, not a consequence, of 'the distractions of these times'.[97]

John Taylor's prolific output provides a distinctive perspective on the separatist phenomenon. Taylor attacked 'nonconformists, schismatics,

---

[90] *The Diseases of the Times or, The Distempers of the Common-wealth* (1641?), sigs. A2, A2v, A3, A3v. [91] *The Brownists Faith and Beliefe Opened* (1641), broadsheet.
[92] Carter, *Schismatic Stigmatized*, 3.
[93] *A Discovery of 29 Sects here in London* (1641).
[94] *Brownists Conventicle*, 2.
[95] *A Description of the Sect called the Familie of Love* (1641), 1.
[96] [John Taylor], *The Divisions of the Church of England Crept in at XV Several Doores* (1642); *Religions Lotterie, or the Churches Amazement* (1642). See also Ephraim Pagitt, *Heresiography; or, a Description of the Heretickes and Sectaries of these Latter Times* (1645).
[97] *Brownists Synagogue*, 1.

separatists, and scandalous libellers' in a verse pamphlet on *Different Worships* in 1640. Deliberately confusing puritans with schismatics, his main complaint then was that 'unkneeling saucy separatists' showed insufficient respect for the ceremonies of the Book of Common Prayer. At the time Taylor wrote this the Brownists had not yet surfaced, or had not yet come to his attention, for as soon as Taylor discovered them he became their principal polemical enemy.[98]

Travelling between London and the west in the summer of 1641, Taylor encountered 'schismatics, such as Brownists, anabaptists, familists, humorists and foolists...in many places of his voyage and journey'. Amongst them was 'a blind old woman' who repeats and interprets Scripture; a pavier who 'will take upon him to mend the way'; a baker who 'will new bolt, sift, knead and mould a new religion'; a brewer's clerk who 'preaches most wonderfully in a malt-house'; and a sow gelder 'that professeth most dangerous doctrine'.[99] These were generic figures, not closely observed, through which Taylor displayed his fascination and contempt for the upstart separatist religion.

Offended and obsessed by the 'erroneous and seditious practices' of the Brownists, Taylor derided them in pamphlet after pamphlet in 1641 and 1642. They were 'wicked great bawlers', 'zealously affected children', and ignorant colluders with the papists, so he said in *The Hellish Parliament* (1641).[100] They were 'puritans' who did 'so disturb the quietness of the commonwealth, that it was now almost turned topsy-turvy', he claimed in *The Liar* (1641).[101] In *Religions Enemies* (1641) he described them as 'mutable and contentious spirits' through whom 'religion is made a hotch-potch, and as it were tossed in a blanket'.[102] Taylor's main contribution to religious sociology was *A Swarme of Sectaries, And Schismatiques: Wherein is discovered the strange preaching (or prating) of such as are by their trades Coblers, Tinkers, Pedlers, Weavers, Sow-gelders, and Chymney-Sweepers* (1641). Its illustrated title page depicted the cobbler Sam How preaching from a barrel in the upper room of the Nag's Head tavern, an image that was frequently appropriated for other publications. (See Plate 9.)

Although the dominant discourse was hostile, and some polemicists argued that Brownists were worse than papists, a few commentators were willing to hear them out. The divine and physician Aaron Streater was

---

[98] John Taylor, *Differing Worships, Or, The Oddes, betweene some Knights Service and Gods* (1640).   [99] John Taylor, *Iohn Taylors last Voyage* (1641), title page, 32.
[100] John Taylor, *The Hellish Parliament Being a Counter-Parliament* (1641), 1, 2.
[101] John Taylor, *The Liar. Or, A contradiction to those who in the titles of their Bookes affirmed them to be true, when they were false: although mine are all true, yet I terme them lyes* (1641), sig. A3.   [102] John Taylor, *Religions Enemies* (1641), title page, 6.

unusual in declaring the Brownists of his acquaintance to be harmless, loyal, and well-intentioned. 'Their religion is no bloody one', he told the Lord Mayor of London. Rather, the Brownists were well-intentioned Christians, harmless if erroneous, who deserved to be left alone.[103] The puritan Lord Brooke was also inclined to forgive the separatists their 'tang of frenzy'. 'Let us not censure such tempers', he wrote, 'but bless God for them. So far as Christ is in us, we shall love, prize, honour Christ and the least particle of his image in others.'[104]

Another publication of 1641, *The Humble Petition of the Brownists*, seems not to have been a Brownist text at all. Making a remarkable plea for religious toleration, the pamphlet solicits religious freedom for Brownists, puritans, Socinians, Arminians, Papists, Adamites, and the Family of Love, and calls on Parliament to let them all alone, so long as they submit to the state and civil laws. This argument strikes a sympathetic chord with modern readers, but nobody in 1641 believed that a free market in religion would lead to peace rather than confusion. Scholars have conjecturally identified *The Humble Petition* as the stealthy work of an English Catholic, seeking relief from the recusancy laws, or the musings of a future Leveller. Contemporaries may well have read it as a satire.[105]

BARNS AND STABLES

One of the most often repeated assertions about schismatics was that they disparaged holy spaces and preferred to conduct their meetings in taverns and barns. They made this choice in part to avoid detection, at a time when conventicles were still illegal, and when parish churches were still controlled by the established clergy. They also met in secret and secular locations to make the point that no place under heaven was more sacred than any other. A much-circulated satiric verse put words in the mouths of the city sectarians:

> For point of holiness we are not able
> To see great differences 'twixt a church and stable.
> The word of God is all one, nor can we learn
> More profit in a church than in a barn.[106]

---

[103] Aaron Streeter, *A Letter Sent to My Lord Maior* (1642), 5.

[104] Robert [Greville], Lord Brooke, *A Discourse Opening the Nature of that Episcopacie, Which is Exercised in England* (1641), 123.

[105] *The Humble Petition of the Brownists* (1641). For its authorship compare W. K. Jordan, *The Development of Religious Toleration in England* (Cambridge, Mass., 1940), 439–40, and G. E. Aylmer, 'Did the Ranters Exist?', *Past and Present*, 117 (1987), 218.

[106] Folger Shakespeare Library, Folger Ms. X. d. 20.

Pamphleteers repeated the claim that separatists would congregate in any 'field, garden, orchard, barn, kitchen or highway' that took their fancy, because 'they make no [more] reckoning of the church of God than of a barn or a stable, either of these is all alike to them.'[107] 'Our saviour chose a homely stable to be born in, and I dare avouch that his word is never the worse for being taught in a barn, a stable, or any such like place', the glover John Rogers is said to have preached to a London conventicle in August 1641.[108] 'We prophesy in the open fields as our father Adam did in the garden of Eden', explains the fictional Adamite preacher Obadiah Couchman.[109]

Fragments of information provide corroboration for some of these practices. The Bristol separatists of late 1640 talked of hiring a barn for their meetings but the proposal was not well regarded, for, according to their first historian, 'the thing of relative holiness and tincture of consecrated places was not off the people.'[110] If possible, they still preferred to do God's business in church. In London, whereas some separatist meetings took place in taverns and private houses, others resorted to woods and fields, including Highgate and Hampstead hills.[111] A group of 'rebaptists' or Anabaptists used the waters of Hackney Marsh for their immersion ceremony, claimed one publication of 1641, 'about a fortnight since'.[112] A Hampshire separatist, Edward Taylor, was presented to the Portsmouth Leet jury in April 1642 for 'saying that the church or churchyard was no holier than the common field'.[113] Another allegedly asserted 'that there was no more holiness in the church than in his kitchen'.[114]

Catering primarily to a metropolitan public familiar with London geography, the pamphlets of 1641 located Brownist conventicles in the rougher and most populous parts of the metropolis. *The Brownists Synagogue* offered a directory of urban separatism, naming Richard Rogers's congregation in Blue Anchor Alley, Jeremy Manwood's gathering in Goat

---

[107] Edward Harris, *A True Relation of a Company of Brownists, Separatists, and Nonconformists, in Monmouthshire in Wales* (1641), sig. A2; *Anatomy of the Separatists, alias, Brownists*, 5.

[108] *Brownists Conventicle*; *Brothers of the Separation*, sig. A4. The words are those of the pamphleteer.

[109] *The Adamites Sermon*, 8. For more on the Adamites, see David Cressy, *Travesties and Transgressions* (Oxford, 2000), 251–80.

[110] Roger Hayden (ed.), *The Records of a Church of Christ in Bristol, 1640–1687* (Bristol Record Society, vol. xxvii, 1974), 93.   [111] *Brownists Conventicle*, 2.

[112] *The Booke of Common Prayer, now used in the Church of England, Vindicated from the aspersion of all Schismatickes, Anabaptists, Brownists, and Seperatists* (1641), 8.

[113] Richard J. Murrell and Robert East (eds.), *Extracts from the Records in the Possession of the Municipal Corporation of the Borough of Portsmouth* (Portsmouth, 1884), 124.

[114] Cheshire, *Sermon Preached in Saint Paules Church the tenth of October 1641*, 12.

Alley, Edward Gyles in Checker Alley, the button-maker Marler in Aldersgate Street, John Tucke's convocation in Fleet Lane, Humphey Gosnold's meeting near Tower Hill, Jonas Hawkins in Chick Lane, Roger Kennet by the Royal Exchange, Edward Johnson's assembly in More Lane, John Bennet's group in Love Lane, Westminster, George Danny in the Minories, Charles Thomas in Warwick Lane, Alexander Smith's congregation in Shoreditch, and Edmund Nicholson in Seacoal Lane, besides other who kept 'no constant place'. A major separatist assembly in Houndsditch on 28 September 1641, featuring Greene the felt-maker and Spencer the coachman, heard that bishops were an 'antichristian calling', and that it was 'unseemly . . . to keep company with a reprobate'.[115]

Separatists became increasingly emboldened in the second half of 1641, meeting publicly instead of in secret, and intruding upon services in the established church. They practised both provocation and withdrawal. If schismatics did come to public worship it was as much to disrupt services and to abuse the ministers as to harangue the congregation. Critics judged them guilty on the one hand of 'sequestering themselves from the public assembly at common prayer and divine service', and on the other hand of 'opposing and tumultuous interrupting others in the performance thereof'.[116] We learn, for example, that Marler the button-maker took over the pulpit in the parish church of St Anne's Aldersgate on 8 August 1641, in the absence of the regular minister, when 'a sudden distracted mutiny among the people' permitted his intrusion.[117] A similar scuffle broke out in St George's Church, Southwark, on 12 December 1641 when Vincent the cobbler commandeered the pulpit 'and broached his Brownistical and erroneous opinions to his auditors' for over an hour. Part of Vincent's message was 'that everyone might exercise the[ir] talent according as the spirit shall enable them', a message that did not sit well with the established authorities.[118] When reports of this incident reached Cambridge they added that 'a company of anabaptists and Brownistical people went up to the minister's desk and took from him the service book and carried it in a kind of procession to the church door, and having rent it in pieces, cast it out of doors.'[119]

---

[115] *Brownists Synagogue*, 3–5.

[116] Sir Thomas Aston (ed.), *A Collection of Sundry Petitions Presented to the King's Most excellent Majestie* (1642), 12, from the Huntingdonshire petition; Northamptonshire Record Office, Finch-Hatton Ms. 2609.

[117] *A True Relation of a Combustion, Hapning at St. Anne's Church by Aldersgate* (1641), title page, 1–2.

[118] *The Coblers End, or his (Last) Sermon* (1641), title page; *His Maiesties Speciall Command under the great Seale of England*, sig. A4.

[119] Cambridge University Library, Ms. Mn. 1. 45 (Baker transcripts), 38.

MECHANICK PREACHERS AND THE SIN OF UZZAH

In the Church of England, as in most of Christian Europe, the conduct of religious services and the preaching of the word of God belonged exclusively to the tribe of Levi, to ordained ministers or priests. Early reformation notions of 'the priesthood of all believers' had little purchase in Protestant England, where lay participation in worship was mostly passive. Householders had some responsibility for domestic religious instruction, and parishioners sometimes gathered to recapitulate sermons, but it was not for them to mount pulpits or lead religious assemblies. The privileges of the pulpit depended on ordination and training as well as appropriate social status. Preaching and teaching were the preserve of professional specialists, most of whom boasted a university education. It was therefore shocking to see or hear of laymen who 'dare presume to snatch the ministerial function from the mouths of the clergy'.[120] Reports of such outrages proliferated after 1640 as lay sectarians took to preaching in public, and they grew again through the discursive amplification of print.

Hostility to artisan preaching united Laudian conservatives, Presbyterians, and moderate puritans, both clerical and lay. None of the clergy welcomed competition, and most laymen upheld the distinctive pastoral and sacramental role of the ministry.

Apologists for Congregational Independency were among the few to embrace the idea of an artisan priesthood, believing that 'God intends to make use of the common people in the great work of proclaiming the kingdom of his son.' It would be 'the vulgar multitude', not 'the priests and Levites', who would begin the work of reformation, thought John Goodwin, presumed author of *A Glimpse of Sions Glory*. But even he feared that the work would be stalled unless 'the worthies of the land' took up God's task in Parliament.[121] Among the leading Independents were renegade ministers, who made good use of their clerical training. Goodwin himself had been rector of East Rainham, Norfolk, and vicar of St Stephen Coleman Street, London, before moving deeper into Independency.

Conservatives railed against the 'presumptuous usurpation' of 'mere laics' who took upon themselves the 'holy affairs of God'.[122] It was 'not for private persons to take that upon them which belongeth not unto their place', agreed John Ball in a reasoned treatise against separation. 'When men have once begun to neglect the public exercises of religion, and to separate from the

---

[120] *Diseases of the Times*, sig. A3v.   [121] [Goodwin], *A Glimpse of Sions Glory*, 5–7.
[122] Hall, *Episcopacie by Divine Right Asserted*, 219–20.

churches of Christ, they have run from one error into another after the fond imaginations of their own seduced hearts, until they have dashed themselves on the rocks.'[123] These were blind guides, declared Thomas Morton, who thought the doctrine of cobblers and weavers 'fitter for a stage than a pulpit'.[124] The Presbyterian Edmund Calamy shared this view, declaring in 1641 'that the sin of Uzzah was the crying sin of the land, for cobblers and weavers and others of the laity intermeddling with divine offices'. Bible readers would know that Uzzah, a layman, was smitten by God when helping to transport the Ark of the Covenant, for, said the chronicler, 'none ought to carry the Ark of God but the Levites, for them has the Lord chosen . . . to minister unto him forever.'[125]

It was nothing short of 'ridiculous', thought some contemporary chroniclers, that 'illiterate people of the lowest rank' should constitute themselves as religious congregations. It was a sign of a world turned upside down for 'these tradesmen' to take up the work of preaching the gospel, 'which the prelates and great doctors had let fall'. Some joked uneasily that 'it was but a reciprocal invasion of each others' callings, that chandlers, salters, weavers, and such like preached, when the archbishop himself, instead of preaching, was daily busied by projects about leather, salt and soap.'[126]

Writers of tracts and pamphlets predictably railed against 'mechanick preaching'. Richard Carter, author of *The Schismatic Stigmatized*, attacked 'presumptuous tradesmen who dare climb up into a pulpit, and make themselves bold ambassadors of the great king of kings'. He particularly derided 'shoemakers, cobblers, tailors and butchers, glovers . . . box-makers and button-makers, coachmen and felt-makers and bottle-ale sellers' who 'astonish and amaze the poor ignorant multitude'.[127] How could such men 'educated in manuary trades' presume to 'leap from the shop-board to the pulpit', displacing the learned and painstaking clergy, asked *A Curb for Sectaries and Bold Propheciers* in 1641.[128] Other pamphlets derided those misguided laymen who 'dare presume to snatch the ministerial function from the mouths of the clergy'.[129] None should preach without lawful ordination and 'ecclesiastical authorization', insisted John Berwick in *An Antidote Against Lay-Preaching* (1642).[130] 'Let not every mechanick make his dirty

[123] John Ball, *A Friendly Triall of the Grounds Tending to Separation* (1640), sigs. A3v, Bv.

[124] Morton, *Presentment of a Schismaticke*, 24.

[125] Cambridge University Library, Ms. Mn. 1. 45 (Baker transcripts), 32; 2 Samuel 6: 3–9, I Chronicles 15: 2.

[126] Thomas May, *The History of the Parliament of England which began November the third, MDCXL* (1647), 113.   [127] Carter, *Schismatic Stigmatized*, sig. A2v, 7.

[128] *A Curb for Sectaries and Bold Propheciers* (1641), 8–9.

[129] *Diseases of the Times*, Sig. A3v.

[130] [John Berwick], *An Antidote Against Lay-Preaching* (1642), 4, 15.

shop a consecrated pulpit', pleaded another conservative writer early
in 1642.[131] It was discouraging to university-trained scholars, wrote one of
them, 'when every hat-dresser, ironmonger, cobbler and horse-collar-maker
shall pass among the multitude for as sound a divine'.[132]

Denzil Holles declared in June 1641 that if Parliament did not suppress the
'mechanical men that preached up and down the town' it might indicate that
'we intended to bring in atheism and confusion'.[133] Maurice Wynn wrote
to a kinsman soon after that 'divers [were] questioned in parliament for
preaching in divers churches, being mere lay men and without any orders'.[134]
Six months later a Welsh member of Parliament, John Griffith, remarked
'that preaching of mechanicks is one cause of our present distractions'.[135]
It was one of the ironies of 1641 that religious conservatives charged members
of Parliament with being 'illiterate mechanicks' who had no business
meddling with the affairs of the church.[136]

Punning pamphleteers recounted the tale of Samuel How, the cobbler,
'who took upon him beyond his last, the mending of souls'. How gained
notoriety in the summer of 1640 for his extempore preaching to huge audiences at the Nag's Head tavern near Coleman Street in London. One hostile
broadsheet called How a 'lump of ignorance' and a 'fantastic spirit', but he
reportedly held his own against ministers and managed to have one of his
sermons printed. 'How, the notorious predicant cobbler' appears in several
pamphlets of 1641, and the image of How preaching from a barrel in the
upper room of the Nag's Head adorns the title page of Taylor's *Swarme of
Sectaries*.[137]

How the cobbler was succeeded by 'Hunt the farmer'. Claiming to be 'a
messenger from God', the Kentish husbandman James Hunt began to
expound the Scriptures in St Paul's churchyard in 1640, and in 1641 he

---

[131] Edward Reynolds, *Evgenia's Teares for Great Brittaynes Distractions* (1642), 23.
[132] *The Distractions of our Times*, 3–4.
[133] Maija Jansson (ed.), *Proceedings in the Opening Session of the Long Parliament ... Volume
4: 19 April–5 June 1641* (Rochester, NY, 2003), 737, 741.
[134] National Library of Wales, Wynn Papers, no. 1686 (microfilm).
[135] Willson H. Coates, Anne Steele Young, and Vernon F. Snow (eds.), *The Private Journals
of the Long Parliament 3 January to 5 March 1642* (New Haven and London, 1982), 103.
[136] Jansson (ed.), *Proceedings in the Opening Session of the Long Parliament ... Vol. 4*,
412; John White, *The First Century of Scandalous, Malignant Priests* (1643), 3, 25;
A. G. Matthews, *Walker Revised. Being a Revision of John Walker's Sufferings of the Clergy
during the Grand Rebellion 1642–60* (Oxford, 1948), 44, 166.
[137] *The Coblers threed is cut* (1640), broadsheet; How's printed sermon, *The Sufficiency
of the Spirits Teaching, without Humane Learning*, was cited in *The Vindication of the Cobler*
(1640), broadsheet; *Brownists Conventicle*, 3 (mispaginated as 5); *Brownists Synagogue*, 2;
John Taylor, *A Swarme of Sectaries and Schismatiques* (1641), title page. See also Tolmie,
Triumph of the Saints, 17, 36.

attempted to preach in public at St Sepulchre's, Westminster Hall, Old Bailey, and the Old Exchange. While ecclesiastical officials described him as 'a fanatic and frantic person,' popular pamphlets ridiculed 'Prophet Hunt', and the civic authorities confined him for brief spells in Bridewell and the Lord Mayor's prison.[138]

A recirculating cast of characters drawn from the separatist fringe became immortalized in popular print. Some of them were dubiously documented, and at least two—Eaton and How—were already dead by the time they were introduced to the pamphlet-reading public. *A Curb for Sectaries and Bold Propheciers* identified Richard Farnham the weaver, James Hunt the farmer, and M. Greene the felt-maker as sectarian leaders who set themselves up against their university-educated clerical betters.[139] *The Brownists Conventicle* mentions 'Eaton the famous button-maker in St Martins, a shoemaker that dwelt between Paul's chain and Old Fish Street…one Greene a felt-maker, and a fellow who was once a serving man', among separatist preachers.[140] Another pamphlet mocked 'Greene the felt-maker, Spencer the horse-rubber, Quatermain the brewer's clerk' and 'Barebones the leather-seller' for their 'disorderly preachment, pratings and prattlings' towards the end of 1641.[141] The latter referred to the leather-seller Praisegod Barebones or Burboone, whose sermon before one hundred and fifty separatists at a house in Fleet Street on Sunday, 19 December 1641, precipitated a 'tumultuous combustion'.[142] John Taylor mentioned Spilsbery the hay merchant and Eaton the button-maker, as well as the infamous cobbler Samuel How, all notorious separatists.[143] He also invented the character of 'My-heele Mendsoale, an inspired Brownist' (perhaps based on Praisegod Barebones) who preached in a house near Bedlam in London in December 1641.[144] *The Brownists Synagogue* (1641) added Spencer the coachman and Rogers the glover to the list, as well as Hawkins the fisherman and Johnson the chandler.[145] At Diss, Norfolk, 'an apothecary turned preacher' preached the 'parliamentary faith' in the spring of 1641.[146]

Pamphleteers criticized these preachers as much for their lowly occupations as their lay status. Some of their publications dwelt more on the social origins

---

[138] *CSPD 1640*, 415; *Curb for Sectaries and Bold Propheciers*, title page; *The Sermon and Prophecie of Mr. James Hunt*; *The Discovery Of a Swarme of Seperatists* (1641), title page, sigs. A3v–A4; *New Preachers, New*, sig. A4.

[139] *Curb for Sectaries and Bold Propheciers*, title page.

[140] *Brownists Conventicle*, 3 (mispaginated as 5).   [141] *New Preachers, New*, title page.

[142] *Discovery Of a Swarme of Seperatists*, title page, sigs. A2–A2v; *New Preachers, New*, sig. A4.   [143] Taylor, *Swarme of Sectaries*, 6, 8.

[144] John Taylor, *A Tale in a Tub or, A Tub Lecture* (1641), title page.

[145] *Brownists Synagogue*, title page, 3–5.

[146] Cambridge University Library, Ms. Mn. 1. 45 (Baker transcripts), 39.

of the Brownists than their separatist beliefs. The separatists were 'mechanick persons, for the most part unlettered grooms, coachmen, feltmakers, cobblers, weavers, glovers, hawking ironmongers', sneered the 'gentleman' pamphleteer John Harris.[147] As the anatomist of 'the separatists, alias Brownists' explained, 'they hold it as lawful for artificers and laymen to preach in public, and those that are the most inferior, as cobblers, weavers, leather-sellers, box-makers, iron-mongers, felt-makers, and such mechanick fellows'.[148] They were 'sow-gelders, tinkers, felt-makers, button-makers, weavers and cobblers', mocked the waterman John Taylor, whose own social origins were equally humble.[149]

Ever the willing spokesman for the established order, Taylor protested against these workmen's usurpation of the clerical function.

> A preacher's work is not to geld a sow,
> Unseemly 'tis a judge should milk a cow.
> A cobbler to a pulpit should not mount,
> Nor can an ass cast up a true account
>   .   .   .   .   .
> If each within their limits be contained,
> Peace flourisheth, and concord is maintained
>   .   .   .   .   .
> Let tradesmen use their trades, let all men be
> Employed in what is fitting their degree
>   .   .   .   .   .
> 'Tis madness that a crew of brainless blocks
> Dares teach the learned what is orthodox.[150]

The leading separatists, so the printed record suggests, were not just uneducated artisans but actually revelled in their ignorance. Infused by the holy spirit, they were said to 'despise all ordinary calling to the ministry, all written prayers, all helps of study, all reason and good counsel'.[151] Not only were these button-makers and sow-gelders barely literate, they also rejected the learning of their clerical betters. Their hallmark, one pamphlet announced, was 'zeal joined with ignorance'.[152] Altogether unschooled, they were said to dismiss Latin as 'the language of the beast' (the Roman Antichrist),[153] and, like How the cobbler, to make a virtue of their lack of learning. Learning was for 'scribes, Pharisees, papists, Egyptians,

---

[147] John Harris, *The Puritanes Impuritie: Or the Anatomie Of a Puritane or Separatist* (1641), 4.   [148] *Anatomy of the Separatists, alias, Brownists*, 4.
[149] Taylor, *Liar*, sig. A3v.   [150] Taylor, *Swarme of Sectaries*, 2–3, 22.
[151] *A Short History of the Anabaptists*, 55.
[152] *Curb for Sectaries and Bold Propheciers*, sig. Av.
[153] *Anatomy of the Separatists, alias, Brownists*, 3.

Babylonians', How maintained, whereas Christ drew men not by learning but the Spirit.[154] Hunt the farmer similarly disparaged 'Latin tongue and Greek phrase', which served up false doctrine. 'For the deepest scholar in Cambridge school | May be taught wisdom by Christ's fool', he rhymed in his *Spiritual Verses.*[155]

The Brownist caricature would not be complete without reference to the upturned eyes, sharp noses, short hair, and pious affectation of their most prominent preachers.[156] Witness 'the town's new teacher' with his 'shop-board breeding' and 'sure election', his upturned eyes and interminable sermons, as he spread falsehood and confusion to his 'tribe', invited another verse satire of the time.[157] Thomas Cheshire attacked radical preaching as 'such hacking and hammering, as if Babel were now building, rather than the house of God'.[158] 'These are they that orate, not preach, like men raptured with their own spiritual nonsense', wrote another hostile observer in 1641.[159] In place of the orthodox rubrics and readings they framed 'a long babel-like prayer, made up with hums and haws'.[160] Brownists were derided for their lowly social status, their irregular religious practices, and their reputed moral hypocrisy. 'Inwardly Jews, though outwardly saints', they were zealous oppressing dissemblers, thought John Harris.[161] 'Yea, seeming saints', concurred another critic.[162]

Curiosity about separatist and sectarian teaching could be satisfied, in part, by the genre of the cod sermon. Several writers purported to reproduce the words of sectarian preachers, while exposing their preaching to ridicule. *The Brownist Haeresies Confuted* presents the preposterous sermonizing of a sectarian barber, inspired by the spirit but overcome by the flesh.[163] John Taylor ventriloquized the preaching voice of Samuel How in *A Swarme of Sectaries and Schismatiques* and rendered the sermon of 'My-heele Mendsoale' in *A Tale in a Tub.* He later gave us the teachings of Aminadab Blower, 'devout bellows-mender of Pimlico', who pontificated against the liturgy of common prayer.[164]

A pamphlet of 1641 entitled *The Brothers of the Separation. Or A true Relation of a Company of Brownists* purports to reconstruct a sermon

---

[154] *Vindication of the Cobler*, broadsheet.   [155] Hunt, *Spiritual Verses and Prose*, 3–4.
[156] *Anatomy of the Separatists, alias, Brownists*, 2.
[157] Bodleian Library, Ms. Rawlinson D. 398, f. 249.
[158] Cheshire, *Sermon Preached in Saint Paules Church the tenth of October 1641*, 14.
[159] *Brownists Conventicle*, 4.   [160] *Anatomy of the Separatists, alias, Brownists*, 3.
[161] Harris, *Puritanes Impuritie*, 5.   [162] *Whip for the Back of a Backsliding Brownist.*
[163] *The Brownist Haeresies Confuted Their Knavery Anatomized*, 2–4.
[164] Taylor, *Swarme of Sectaries*, 8–13; idem, *A Tale in a Tub or, A Tub Lecture*, 2–6; idem, *Some small and simple reasons, delivered in a hollow-tree* (1643).

delivered at a separatist conventicle off Whitecross Street, London, which was raided in August 1641. The preacher, John Rogers, a glover, is said to have attacked the established clergy as magpies and crows and to have praised the assembly as 'God's elect'. The anonymous pamphleteer appears equally disdainful of the preacher's social status, his foolish message, and his confused extempore preaching 'without . . . division of his text'.[165]

Thomas Bray told tales of an Adamite sermon in Moorfields in 1641 in which the preacher 'prophesied . . . the downfall of all religions except theirs, with many most blasphemous things which I am both afraid and ashamed to write'.[166] Another exposé, *The Adamites Sermon*, reported, or rather invented, 'their manner of preaching, expounding, and prophesying, as it was delivered in Marylebone Park by Obadiah Couchman, a grave weaver, dwelling in Southwark'.[167] There followed a ludicrous pastiche of sectarian ignorance, enthusiasm, and false erudition. It is a warning, or demonstration, of what can happen when the Bible is read by the unlettered. Savouring a text from *Genesis*, the preacher declares, 'No question but the prophet Genesis himself was naked when he writ these words.' There follows a tirade against idolatry, clerical garments, and crosses, a comparison of Adamite purity with the corruptions of the Church of England, and, apparently, an invitation to an orgy.[168]

Ignorant zealots make similar speeches in Richard Carter's *Schismatic Stigmatized*:

Down with all universities, colleges and schools, they do but maintain learning, an enemy to us. Down with churches, hospitals and almshouses, they do but help the widows, fatherless, blind, sick and lame, these were most of them founded by papists. Down with all these crosses in general, especially that idolatrous cross in Cheapside.[169]

Brownists are displayed as having an absurd and excessive aversion to crosses of all sorts, including 'that gilded idolatrous cross in Cheapside'.[170] One London separatist allegedly went so far as to preach in 1641 'that the king's crown should be pulled down, because it had a cross upon it'.[171] Even if actual separatists said no such thing, the perception grew that they were less mad than dangerous. The Colchester weavers Richard Farnham and John Bull were said to have adopted the identity of 'the two great prophets that

---

[165] *Brothers of the Separation*, sigs. A2v–A4v. *Brownists Synagogue*, 2, names the glover as Richard Rogers, and locates his conventicle at his house in Blue-Anchor Alley, of Whitecross Street.   [166] 'Yarb' [Bray], *A New Sect of Religion Descryed, called Adamites*, 6.
[167] *The Adamites Sermon*, title page.   [168] Ibid., 6–8.
[169] Carter, *Schismatic Stigmatized*, 13.   [170] *Brownists Conventicle*, 7.
[171] Cheshire, *Sermon Preached in Saint Paules Church the tenth of October 1641*, 12.

should come in at the end of the world', and when they died of plague in January 1642 their followers believed that they would rise again.[172]

HOLY SISTERS

The revolutionary stresses of the early 1640s touched every area of political and religious culture, including the status of women. In addition to fracturing the church and subverting its hierarchy, radical sectarians were alleged to have violated the gender order by allowing their women a public religious voice. A chorus of complaints protested the rise of she-sectaries and she-zealots, but reliable evidence about female religiosity remains slight. Just as it is difficult to discern the actual extent of the separatist movement behind the extravagant claims of the pamphlets, so it remains a problem whether women became as vocal in radical religion as is sometimes asserted. Pamphleteers sometimes depicted women among the front rank of radical sectarians, and modern historians have been inclined to agree with them.[173] The actual gendered profile of radical sectarianism may never be known, but it was clearly as deep a matter of anxiety in the past as it is a topic of interest in the present.

Women were customarily enjoined to be chaste, silent, and obedient, following St Paul's epistles to the Corinthians. 'Let them be silent as in, so of or concerning the church,' reiterated the Cambridge divine Richard Watson. It was, he thought, a mark of 'the irrational licentious practice of our times, wherein either sex of any profession crowds in a finger to the moulding of our designed reformation'.[174] Women, claimed the London preacher Matthias Milward, 'are now grown such learned doctresses that they will take upon them to teach any minister both what and how to preach'.[175] Dozens of pamphlets condemned 'she lecturers', 'she zealots', 'she divines', and 'the dangerous disease of feminine divinity'.[176] 'The holy sisters'

---

[172] *False Prophets Discovered* (1642), sigs. A3–A3v.

[173] See, for example, Henry Church, *Divine and Christian Letters* (1636), 27; Keith Thomas, 'Women and the Civil War Sects', *Past and Present*, 13 (1958), 42–62; Patricia Crawford, *Women and Religion in England, 1500–1720* (1993); Phyllis Mack, *Visionary Women: Ecstatic Prophecy in Seventeenth-Century England* (Berkeley, 1992).

[174] Richard Watson, *A Sermon Touching Schism, Lately Preached at St. Maries in Cambridge* (Cambridge, 1642), 18.

[175] Milward, *The Souldiers Triumph: and the Preachers Glory*, sig. B3v.

[176] *The Resolution of the Round-Heads to pull downe Cheap-side Crosse* (1641), sig. Av; John Taylor, *The Devil Turn'd Round-Head* (1642), 6; [Abraham Cowley], *A Satyre Against Seperatists, Or, The Conviction of Chamber-Preachers, and other Schismaticks* (1642), 3; *Antibrownitus Puritanomastix: The Speech of a Warden to the Fellowes of his Company: Touching the great affaires of the Kingdome* (1642), sig. Av; *The Diseases of the Times*, sig. A3.

expounded at separatist assemblies, delivering 'nothing but what the spirit moves', reported one publication.[177] 'When women preach and cobblers pray, | The fiends in hell make holiday', rhymed another.[178] It seemed, wrote John Taylor, that 'all the women in England were grown precise and turned preachers.'[179]

Intending to shock the reader and to ridicule the practice, the author of *The Brownists Conventicle* claimed that in some cases 'the women catechize and preach, making the back side of her groaning chair the pulpit.'[180] If men could preach from a brewer's tub, why not women from a midwife's stool? It was not only 'illiterate mechanicks' who had taken to preaching, complained Edward Reynolds, but even 'the weaker sex, who are commanded silence and not to usurp authority, have also freedom to vent their opinions.' Religion had become so disordered and fragmented, he thought, 'that every sex and sect shall have a several exposition on the text'.[181]

A stocklist of women preachers joined the notorious artisan prophets. An anonymous pamphlet of 1641 cited the verse from Corinthians enjoining women's silence in churches, and then named six women preachers, 'pleasant to be read, but horrid to be judged of'. The offenders presented here were Anne Hempstall of St Andrew Holborn, who dreamed of Anna the prophetess and preached to her houseful of gossips; Mary Bilbrow of St Giles in the Fields, wife to a bricklayer, who entertained her congregation with wine and meat; Joan Bauford of Feversham, Kent, who preached that husbands who 'crossed their wives' wills might lawfully be forsaken'; Susan May of Ashford, Kent, who declared 'that the devil was the father of the pope, the pope the father of those which did wear surplices'; Elizabeth Bancroft of Ely, Cambridgeshire, who preached, with reference to Bishop Wren, that it was fit 'to sacrifice the pope's bird upon his own altar'; and Arabella Thomas, a Welsh woman at Salisbury, who preached 'that none but such painful creatures as herself should go to heaven'.[182] The author presents these women as offensive and ridiculous, but offers no corroboration of their activities.

Richard Carter's *Schismatic Stigmatized* named a more fanciful cast of female zealots, 'our sweet sistren, as Agnes Anabaptist, Kate Catabaptist, Frank Footbaptist, Penelope Punk, Merald Makebate, Ruth Rakehell,

---

[177] *A Dialogve Betwixt Rattle-head and Round-head* (1642), sig. A3. See also 'The Holy-Sisters Character', in *A Puritane Set Forth in his Lively Colours* (1642), 6.

[178] *Lucifers Lackey, or, The Devils new Creature*, sig. A4.   [179] Taylor, *Liar*, sig. A3.

[180] *Brownists Conventicle*, 3 (mispaginated as 5).

[181] Reynolds, *Evgenia's Teares*, 10. Reynolds was the moderate conformist rector of Braunston, Northamptonshire, who became Bishop of Norwich after the Restoration.

[182] *A Discoverie of Six women preachers* (1641), title page, 1–4.

Tabitha Tattle, Pru Prattle, and that poor silly, simple, senseless, sinless, shameless, naked wretch, Alice the Adamite.'[183] Other publications recycled the same dubious information, with no specific details of the names, dates, or circumstances of female religious outspokenness. *The Anatomy of the Separatists*, published early in 1642, mentioned 'the sisters of the fraternity' and claimed that they were as guilty of schism and sedition as the brethren.[184]

The mechanick preacher John Spencer was unusual in legitimizing female preaching. He reminded readers that a woman had been instrumental in spreading the word of God among the Samaritans, and pointed out that women too could be imbued with the Holy Spirit.[185] More conventionally, Thomas Jordan's satire *A Medicine for the Times* (1641) advised how to cure a woman 'from a strange madness she hath got in expounding scripture'. The remedy was a strong dose of patriarchal discipline applied by her husband who 'is both king and bishop'.[186]

There is very little evidence to indicate whether women in London or elsewhere truly exercised religious leadership in any conventicle or congregation. The portrait in the pamphlets is a cross between a caricature and a fantasy, with more than a dose of discursive amplification. Nonetheless it seems plausible that the sectarian movement permitted some women to explore religious ideas and to experience the sway of the spirit in ways not conventionally sanctioned by the Church of England. We know that women were prominent in some parish conflicts, that women took part in conventicles, and that some women took it on themselves to subscribe the Protestation.[187] It was said that 'there were as many women as men' at the leather-seller Burboon's conventicle in Fleet Street in December 1641.[188]

One possible model for the she-separatist caricature may have been Dorothy Kelly, a grocer's wife and one of Bristol's leading Nonconformists. The widowed Mrs Kelly later married the godly minister Mr Hazzard, and became a leader (though not the preacher) of Bristol's first separatist congregation. Enemies said that the Bristol conventiclers 'met together in the night to be unclean', and the world further derided them 'as that they had women preachers among them, because there were many good women'.[189] One of their number, a Mrs Clements, justified her attendance at conventicles

[183] Carter, *Schismatic Stigmatized*, 15.

[184] *Anatomy of the Separatists, alias, Brownists*, 1, 6.

[185] Spencer, *A Short Treatise Concerning the Lawfullnesse of every mans exercising his gift*, 4.

[186] T.J. [Thomas Jordan], *A Medicine for the Times. Or, An Antidote Against Faction* (1641), sig. A2v.

[187] David Cressy, 'The Protestation Protested, 1641 and 1642', *The Historical Journal*, 45 (2002), 251–79.   [188] *Discovery Of a Swarme of Seperatists*, sig. A3.

[189] Hayden (ed.), *The Records of a Church of Christ in Bristol, 1640–1687*, 85–9.

rather than her parish church by asserting that the parson of Temple 'could preach no more than a black dog'.[190] Katherine Chidley, who was a leading metropolitan separatist as well as a controversial author, may have provided another model.[191]

Finally it was alleged, without proof, that Brownist conventicles were sites of promiscuous debauchery. Sectarian meetings in 'the conveniency of the woods, sawpits, and dark places' allowed holy brothers and sisters to engage in 'a zealous lusting'.[192] At least they allowed pamphleteers to imagine such things. Sectaries met, so popular authors reported, in 'places of excellent privacy, and free from the eyes of the sinful'.[193] It was in these 'hot, private, lusty and promiscuous meetings' that Brownists allegedly gave rise to their monstrous offspring.[194]

According to prurient caricatures, separatist prayer assemblies became orgies, their tub preachers satyrs, and the holy sisters displayed the sexual promiscuity of London whores. Indeed, it was a sign of the world turned upside down when whores 'are in great esteem...and are called holy sisters'.[195] Sectarian 'spiritual meetings, private fasts, conventicles, etc.' usurped the trade of 'the most ancient and venerable bawdy house of this most flourishing city', claimed one manuscript author. The sectaries allegedly practised 'an holy fornication', he continued. 'If the spirit do provoke or mightily stir up a brother or so towards a sister, let it be done in the fear of God, not in a set form, but the candles out; and its no sin, they must love their neighbours as themselves, especially their wives as being the weaker vessels.'[196]

Pamphlet after pamphlet dwelt on the allurements of the 'holy sisters' and the 'voluptuous wantonness' of secret sectarian conventicles.[197] When the candles go out at conventicles, claimed one satire, 'lie all the sisters down and strain lower, *procreandi causa*'.[198] Another told of 'preaching tradesmen and lay clergy women, who have coupled themselves together in a joint labour for the procreating of young saints'.[199] Yet another pamphlet depicted the lay preacher as a 'cunning lecherer', who could not wait to 'fructify' with the holy sisters.[200] The title page of *The Brownists Conventicle* shows a couple

[190] John Latimer, *The Annals of Bristol in the Seventeenth Century* (Bristol, 1900), 151.
[191] Chidley, *Iustification of the Independent Churches of Christ.*
[192] *Resolution of the Round-Heads to pull downe Cheap-side Crosse*, sigs. Av–A2.
[193] *Antibrownitus Puritanomastix*, sig. Av.
[194] 'Spinola', *Rvles to Get Children By with Handsome Faces*, sig. A4v.
[195] *Newes, True Newes, Laudable Newes*, 4–5.
[196] Huntington Library, Ms. El. 7802.
[197] *Anatomy of the Separatists, alias, Brownists*, 3.
[198] W.K., *The Devils Last Legacy: Or, A Round-headed Ironmonger, made Executor to Pluto* (1642).   [199] *Antibrownitus Puritanomastix*, sig. Av.
[200] *The Brownist Haeresies Confuted Their Knavery Anatomized*, 3–5.

embracing, the male separatist saying to his female companion, 'a little in zeal good sister Ruth'.[201] It was no fault for a Brownist to respond to 'the spirit of the flesh...provided that he doth not pollute himself with the wicked, but make use of a sister of the separation', so pamphlet readers learned.[202] Getting a 'sister' with child was no fault, John Taylor reported, provided 'a faithful brother' rather than one of the wicked had done it.[203] Taylor joked crudely about the 'zealous brethren that have stood stiffly for the cause, as the sisters can testify if they please'.[204] Other additions to this literature included references to the Adamites engaged in holy naked coupling,[205] and the promiscuous Family of Love who were believed to revere Priapus.[206] According to contemporary verse-makers the final goal of the revolutionaries was sexual: 'And when the change of government shall set our fingers free, we'll make the wanton sisters stoop, and heigh then up go we.'[207]

It was commonly claimed, though never documented, that the Brownists were 'lovers of the sisters of the scabbard'.[208] It was often joked that men attended conventicles for 'the solace of a sister' as much as for the word of the Lord.[209] Citizens' wives were said to have paired off with separatist artisans, 'merely to take down the pride of the flesh'.[210] The Brownists were alleged to 'have drawn divers honest men's wives in the night time to frequent their assemblies', enticing 'many chaste virgins to become harlots'.[211]

The Limehouse butcher, John Walters, seems to have absorbed this view, for he came before the Middlesex sessions in January 1642 'for calling Ann Cullamore and other women puritan whores, and for saying that he hoped ere long that their throats should be cut as they were in Ireland'.[212] The phrase 'puritan whore' seems incongruous, but it fits in a tradition that identified the puritans and Brownists as hypocrites and the 'holy sisters' as promiscuous sluts.[213]

---

[201] *Brownists Conventicle*, title page.   [202] *Brothers of the Separation*, sig. A3v.

[203] Taylor, *Swarme of Sectaries*, 6.

[204] Thorney Ailo [John Taylor], *A full and complete Answer against the Writer of a late Volume* (1642), 6.

[205] 'Yarb' [Bray], *A New Sect of Religion Descryed, called Adamites*, 7.

[206] *Description of the Sect called the Familie of Love*, 3.

[207] 'The Roundheads Race', in *The Distractions of our Times*, 8. Variant verses survive in manuscript collections, such as Durham University Library, Special Collections, Mickleton-Spearman Ms. MSP 9, ii. 250.

[208] *Anatomy of the Separatists, alias, Brownists*, 3. 'The sisters of the scabbard' were the prostitute partners of 'the brothers of the blade'.

[209] [Henry Peacham], *Sqvare-Caps Turned into Rovnd-Heads* (1642), 4.

[210] *Antibrownitus Puritanomastix*, sig. A4v.

[211] Harris, *A True Relation of a Company of Brownists*, sig. A2.

[212] London Metropolitan Archives, Sessions Roll, MJ/SR/904/72.

[213] Patrick Collinson, 'The Theatre Constructs Puritanism', in David L. Smith, Richard Strier, and David Bevington (eds.), *The Theatrical City: Culture, Theatre, and Politics in*

Furthering this tradition, Thomas Reade wrote facetiously from Oxford in January 1642 that

we are yet quiet here, and free from all noise but the sound of a sow-gelder's horn, which summons our zealots to their nightly devotions of psalms and repetitions, and to that religious exercise of copulation. But the horn is grown so notorious that the fraternity have resolved to change it to a warning piece . . . I have a great desire to be admitted into their congregation, but the sisters are so deformed that I have small encouragement to be reconciled to their church.[214]

The rise of radical sectarianism, whether real or imagined, fed the fear that the world was coming undone. Conservatives who shared Sir Edward Dering's alarm at licentiousness and liberty could be found in 1641 'deploring the church's anarchy' and 'grieving at fortune's malignity'.[215] Without unity and order, preached Matthias Milward in London, 'we should have as many factions as fancies, as many gospels as gossips'.[216] A chorus of complaint warned that England had become Babel, amidst 'great divisions and horrible factions'.[217] Correspondents and commentators shared the concern that 'these wicked sectaries and schismatics . . . will obey no government'.[218] Religious dissent would lead to political disorder, they foresaw, and 'overthrow the known monarchical and hierarchical state of the kingdom'.[219]

Many commentators expressed the fear that the entire social fabric was imperilled if sectarianism grew unchecked. George Morley, a canon of Christ Church, expressed deep sadness for his 'dear mother the miserably distracted Church of England', and warned of 'the greatest confusion, anarchy, and schism, that ever was seen in the church of Christ'.[220] Ephraim Udall warned of 'barbarism . . . destruction' and 'an anabaptistical liberty to do every man what he lists'.[221] Clerics in John Cosin's circle at Cambridge likewise predicted that 'barbarism and duncery would then creep in'.[222] Another described Anabaptism as 'the canker of religion and the gangrene of the state', which if left unchecked, 'will bring us in time to community of wives, community of goods, and destruction of all'.[223]

London, 1576–1649 (Cambridge, 1995), 157–69; Kristen Poole, *Radical Religion from Shakespeare to Milton: Figures of Nonconformity in Early Modern England* (Cambridge and New York, 2000).

[214] PRO, SP16/488/94.   [215] *The Stage-Players Complaint* (1641), 2.
[216] Milward, *The Souldiers Triumph: and the Preachers Glory*, 8.
[217] Huntington petition in Northamptonshire Record Office, Finch-Hatton Ms. FH/2609.
[218] PRO, SP16/486/90.
[219] Edward Browne, *Sir James Cambels Clarkes Disaster by Making Books* (1642), 6.
[220] [George Morley], *A Modest Advertisement Concerning The Present Controversie about Church-Government* (1641), 9, 20; Matthews, *Walker Revised*, 377.
[221] [Ephraim Udall], *Noli Me Tangere: Or, A Thing to be Thought On* (1642), 7, 8, 41.
[222] Cambridge University Library, Ms. Mn. 1. 45 (Baker transcripts), 30.
[223] *A Short History of the Anabaptists*, 56.

Dr Edward Layfield, the Laudian minister of All Hallows, Barking, made explicit the link between religious and social rebellion, saying, 'They are . . . like Jack Straw and Wat Tyler that speak against the ceremonies of the church.'[224] Others cited the levelling text, 'When Adam delved and Eve span | Who was then the gentleman?' and those who 'would have no man above another but all men alike and so throw down all government, learning and religion'.[225] King Charles himself invoked this fear in his response to the Nineteen Propositions, castigating the tumults of 'democracy' and the 'wild humours' of the 'common people' who would 'destroy all rights and proprieties, all distinctions of families and merit . . . in a dark, equal chaos of confusion'.[226]

Conservatives promoted the view that religious revolt was a social revolt, driving a political and constitutional revolution. Sectarianism, in this view, was the Devil's work, performed by enemies of the state. Only a restoration of religious discipline, through prayer book and episcopacy, could retrieve the situation. And only the King, who declared himself 'resolved to live and die in the protestant religion', could stand as the safeguard against chaos.[227] Shocked by their exposure to radical sectarianism, conditioned by a barrage of inflammatory pamphlets, and aroused by anti-separatist preaching, many waverers in 1642 were inclined to cleave to the King. When the King called on his judges in July 1642 'to give a stop to the over-hasty growth of anabaptism and other schisms', and to uphold 'the true protestant religion, established by law in this Church of England',[228] he was issuing a rallying cry for a traditional religious culture that had already begun to disappear. The scale of the separatist fringe may have been exaggerated, but it threatened the heart and soul of traditional religious culture.

---

[224] *Commons Journal*, ii. 35. See also *The Iust reward of Rebels, or The Life and Death of Iack Straw, and Wat Tyler* (1642).

[225] British Library, Add. Ms. 70003, ff. 236–7 (Dr Rogers's sermon in Herefordshire, April 1642); Matthews, *Walker Revised*, 195.

[226] *His Majesties Reply to the Nineteen Propositions*, 14.   [227] PRO, SP16/486/90.

[228] *The Kings Maiesties Charge Sent to all the Judges of England* (1642), 2.

11

Conservative Reactions: The Laudians Fight Back

The parliament that met in November 1640 ended the Laudian ascendancy, impeached the Archbishop of Canterbury, and fostered a campaign of parish cleansing. Almost everything the Laudians stood for—the *Book of Sports*, the 1640 Canons, the righteousness of the war with Scotland—was denounced or declared illegal. Hundreds of Laudian clerics faced investigation and censure. Dozens endured humiliation in the press. A petitioning movement struck at the institution of episcopacy, root and branch, while puritan reformers cut down rails, installed lecturers, and liberated local worship from the rigours of formalized religion. New sects emerged, or at least commanded attention, with views that conservatives deemed blasphemous, heretical, or seditious. The Laudians' 'dear mother church' with its 'beauty of holiness' was traduced, dishonoured, and despoiled. Ideals of unity and order were in ruins. By the end of 1641 a dozen bishops were imprisoned, the church courts were crippled, and parish worship became confused and conflicted. Rival factions battled for control of the pulpits, and some parishioners simply stopped going to church. Not just the Laudian ascendancy but the traditional comprehensive culture of the established Church of England seemed to be falling apart. The country was gripped by a revolution. This chapter examines conservative reactions to the disruption of religious culture in the two years before the English civil war. It shows how some Laudians fell beneath the juggernaut of renewed reformation, and how some of them stood their ground.

'Laudians' are understood here as those hyper-conformist adherents to the Book of Common Prayer and episcopacy who had flourished under Archbishop William Laud in the 1630s and whose churchmanship was enshrined in the new ecclesiastical canons of 1640. Many, at least by association, were also Arminians who rejected Calvinist predestination, and sacerdotalists who cherished the dignities of priesthood. They were linked more by style and circumstance than a checklist of beliefs and attributes, as they basked in the favour of their archbishop, their king, and their God. Most crucial was their enjoyment of patronage and preferment, their standing with those in power.[1]

No more than half the bishops in the Church of England could be construed as Laudians, but all were committed to its structures and worship. Below them were the lesser Laudians, prebendaries and chaplains, rectors and vicars, deans and archdeacons, who had supported the elaboration of ceremonialist worship, the beautification of churches, and the aggrandizement of priestly and episcopal authority. These were the ministers who had enthusiastically set their Communion tables altarwise behind newly installed rails; who forced parishioners to kneel for Communion, and insisted that women wore veils at their churchings; and who tended to identify any who disagreed with them as puritans, sectaries, or rebels. By 1641 it might be better to call them 'post-Laudians', since the Archbishop had fallen from power, but the shorthand 'Laudian' will suffice.

Although Laudians were often accused of being innovators for demanding more than the ritual requirements of the Book of Common Prayer, they were also conservatives who upheld the forms, structures, and rubrics of the national church. In this sense all Laudians were conservatives, though not all conservatives were Laudians. Many mainstream conservatives were attached to Elizabethan and Jacobean ecclesiastical traditions, embracing a prayer-book conformity and Calvinist churchmanship adapted to local conditions. During the late 1630s they mostly followed the lead of their archbishops and bishops, but were not insistent promoters of ceremonial innovations.

The opening moves of the Long Parliament shocked the conformist clerical establishment, both Laudian and mainstream. Reactions to prelatical arrogance spurred challenges to episcopacy, while objections to ceremonial excesses furthered assaults on the Book of Common Prayer. Laudians and mainstream conservatives became allies when established forms of worship and discipline came under puritan and radical assault in Parliament, in the press, and in the parishes.

Attacked by their former enemies, and with Westminster authorities against them, the Laudians employed a variety of tactics for survival and resistance. Under duress they began to fight back, using every available resource to sustain their vision of the church. Most continued to exercise their ministry (or to practise their priesthood), and continued to insist on the honour and privileges of ordination and incumbency. There was as yet no

---

[1] Peter Lake, 'The Laudian Style: Order, Uniformity and the Pursuit of the Beauty of Holiness in the 1630s', in Kennneth Fincham (ed.), *The Early Stuart Church, 1603–1642* (1993), 161–86; Anthony Milton, 'The Creation of Laudianism: A New Approach', in Thomas Cogswell, Richard Cust, and Peter Lake (eds.), *Politics, Religion and Popularity in Early Stuart Britain* (Cambridge, 2002), 162–84.

wholesale suspension, expulsion, or sequestration of 'scandalous' ministers, nor could there be until Parliament had won the civil war. Many made effective use of their pulpits (not withstanding the canard that Laudians were dumb dogs, reading priests, and indifferent or infrequent preachers). Some fought back in the press, using the same unfettered medium that benefited radicals and satirists. Conservatives spawned a proliferation of pamphlets answering pamphlets, treatises supporting episcopacy, petitions on behalf of conformity, and printed apologias for the Book of Common Prayer. Conformists, both clerical and lay, made energetic use of the media at their disposal, to uphold uniformity, to disparage radical extremism, and to warn of the consequences of religious disintegration.

The Laudian collapse was precipitous but not complete. The acute humiliation of clerical conformists in the opening months of the Long Parliament was followed by a piecemeal recovery of their voice and influence as the royalists gathered support. Some uncompromisingly defended the churchmanship of the 1630s, but others conceded that modifications might be necessary if episcopacy and the prayer book were to be safeguarded. Some took on the role of sufferers and dissidents, proudly enduring the 'pricks and thorns' of persecution.[2] Like the puritans of yesteryear, whose fortunes were now transformed, surviving Laudians identified themselves as 'godly' victims of prejudice and error. Conservative preachers and petitioners mounted a rearguard action to salvage the traditional religious order, in the course of which they articulated a new vision of the church that might for the first time be called 'Anglicanism'. At the same time their harsh denigration of their opponents and their warning of impending chaos sharpened divisions and inflamed passions that prepared the ground for civil war.

BROKEN TIMES

The meeting of the Long Parliament was catastrophic for Laudian clerics. The reversal of their influence and the shocks to their esteem were particularly acute in light of their recent advantages and expectations. Those who had been riding high were pulled down as the Laudian ascendancy crashed in ruins. Some of the victims of this process referred to their 'times of distraction', as if their age had lost its bearings or lost its mind. Dispirited clerics experienced 'broken times', 'tumultuous and disjointed times', and 'times of contradiction',[3] while

---

[2] [William Piers], *A Sermon Preached at the Tower, February 20. 1641* (1642), 6, 7.
[3] W. N. Darnell (ed.), *The Correspondence of Isaac Basire, D.D.* (1831), 40; Durham University Library, Special Collections, 'John Cosin Letterbook', 1A/31.

their lay conservative allies complained of 'this whipping time' and 'this awful parliament'.[4]

While reformers celebrated 1641 as their '*annus mirabilis*', conservatives lamented their '*annus horribilis*'. 'When was there a greater whirlwind and tempest in the land than now is, and is there not an earthquake in this land of ours?' asked Thomas Cheshire in October 1641.[5] Benjamin Spencer, the conformist minister of St Thomas, Southwark, told his congregation that 'the times were evil and dangerous, and we may fear judgement upon the land because we do not know where to go for justice.'[6] Matthew Brooke, the rector of Sudbourne, Suffolk, wrote plaintively to Matthew Wren that 'now besides all other troubles [parishioners] have deserted the holy communion, by which means I cannot compass a great part of my livelihood, and they keep away many other duties to put me to all extremities they may.'[7] Robert Abbot, the conformist vicar of Cranbrook, Kent, similarly complained of diminishing income, 'made every day less and less, by the falling of church duties about childing women, burials, marriages and the like'.[8] It was, Archdeacon Marler despaired, a time for blackcoats to tremble. 'All the clergy look for a doom', he wrote to Edward Hyde in January 1641.[9] 'Here's like to be such a purgation of black-coats', wrote Thomas Knyvett that same month, 'as if the parliament entertains all the complaints of the brethren, I know not where they will find new ones to put in.'[10]

Although Arminians, ceremonialists, and Laudian sacerdotalists were harassed and dishonoured in 1641, few of them forfeited their positions. Their principal losses were of patronage, pre-eminence, and respect. Most of the conservative clergy clung to their parishes and exercised the advantages of incumbency. In practice it was hard to dislodge them from their benefices. Parliament may have received as many as nine hundred petitions against 'scandalous' or offensive ministers, but barely a dozen were declared 'unfit for ministerial function' and ejected from their livings before the outbreak of civil war. Only later in the 1640s was there a systematic purgation of Laudians, when 'malignants' suffered sequestration.[11]

---

[4] Huntington Library, Ms. STT 748, John Farmer to his kinsman Sir Peter Temple; Bertram Schofield (ed.), *The Knyvett Letters (1620–1644)* (Norfolk Record Society, 1949), 96.

[5] Thomas Cheshire, *A Sermon Preached in Saint Paules Church the tenth of October 1641* (1641), 12–15.

[6] Benjamin Spencer, *Articles exhibited against Benjamin Spencer . . . and his answer thereunto. With his reasons of printing the same* (1642), 2–3; Maurice F. Bond (ed.), *The Manuscripts of the House of Lords, vol. xi (new series) Addenda 1514–1714* (1962), 351.

[7] G. Matthews, *Walker Revised. Being a Revision of John Walker's Sufferings of the Clergy during the Grand Rebellion 1642–60* (Oxford, 1948), 265.

[8] British Library, Stowe Ms. 184, ff. 47–47v, Abbot to Sir Edward Dering, 3 October 1641.

[9] O. Ogle and W. H. Bliss (eds.), *Calendar of the Clarendon State Papers Preserved in the Bodleian Library* (Oxford, 1872), i. 211, 217.   [10] Schofield (ed.), *Knyvett Letters*, 98–9.

[11] Clive Holmes (ed.), *The Suffolk Committees for Scandalous Ministers 1644–1646* (Suffolk Records Society, vol. xiii, 1970), 9–24.

Responding to petitions from parishioners, the House of Commons summoned dozens of so-called 'scandalous' ministers to Westminster to face reprimand as 'delinquents'. A few suffered brief spells of imprisonment in the gatehouse. The experience was costly and humiliating for them, but not fatal. Most were allowed to return to their parishes on bail, and were permitted to continue their ministry. Edward Layfield, for example, Archdeacon of Essex, vicar of All Hallows Barking, and a favoured kinsman of Archbishop Laud, was among the first to face parliamentary investigation and censure in November 1640, but he was still in his parish at the outbreak of civil war.[12] Richard Drake of Radwinter was declared unfit for the ministry in February 1641, yet he did not leave his Essex parish until 1643.[13] Hugh Reeve of Ampthill, Bedfordshire, was also deprived of his living by parliamentary order in February 1641, but he still had possession of the parsonage house over a year later.[14] It would be well worth knowing how each of the two thousand or more conformists who were ultimately ejected coped with the pressures of the immediate pre-war period, but that is beyond the scope of this study.[15] Here we can only sample the evidence from parliamentary processes, petitions, pamphlets, letters, and legal investigations.

Few fell as hard as the Arminian ceremonialist John Pocklington, who was crushed by the turn of fortune. Pocklington had flown high with royal and episcopal patronage in the late 1630s, then fell low as Parliament singled him out for humiliation. He had been a royal and episcopal chaplain, a Laudian favourite, a celebrated and controversial author, a prebendary of Windsor, and Procurator for the Chapter of Peterborough. He was the pluralist incumbent of Waresley, Huntingdonshire, and Yelden, Bedfordshire, a leading member of the 1640 Convocation, and the only cleric on the Bedfordshire judicial bench.[16] If the Laudian ascendancy had continued he might well have imagined himself deserving of a bishopric. Instead, by January 1641, he was reeling under parliamentary attack, his career in spectacular reversal.

A hostile survey of Huntingdonshire ministers described Pocklington as 'non-resident, defamed for a superstitious Arminian, and no friend of

---

[12] Matthews, *Walker Revised*, 53.

[13] Bodleian Library, Rawlinson Ms. D. 158; Matthews, *Walker Revised*, 150.

[14] HMC *5th Report* (1876), Part 1, 19.

[15] Matthews, *Walker Revised*, p. xv, counts 2,425 benefices under sequestration in the 1640s. Robert S. Bosher, *The Making of the Restoration Settlement: The Influence of the Laudians 1649–1662* (1951), 5, estimates as many as 3,600 Laudian sympathizers were harassed or expelled, from a total of 8,600 livings. Peter Heylyn, ejected from Arlesford, Hampshire, recalled being 'most despitefully reviled and persecuted with excessive both noise and violence, by such as thronged the doors of that committee', at Westminster in 1641 (Peter Heylyn, *Cosmographie* (1652), 'to the reader').

[16] Vivenne Larminie, 'John Pocklington', *Oxford Dictionary of National Biography* (2004); John Nalson, *An Impartial Collection of the Great Affairs of State* (2 vols., 1683–4), i. 355.

preaching'.[17] A Bedfordshire gentleman, John Harvey, identified Pocklington as 'a chief author and ringleader' of offensive innovations, and petitioned Parliament that he be brought to account. Like other Laudian ceremonialists, Pocklington was said to have set up Communion tables as altars, decorated them with crosses, genuflected in their presence, and refused Communion to parishioners who would not conform to these ostentatious devotions. But his main offence was the publishing of two controversial books, *Sunday No Sabbath* and *Altare Christianum*, which left puritans apoplectic.[18]

Parliament censured Pocklington in February 1641, and ordered 'all images and superstitions' he had set up to be demolished. *Altare Christianum* was to be burnt by the common hangman, with fires made in London and the two universities.[19] Edward Perkins wrote gloatingly from Oxford on 31 March 1641, 'we burnt two Pocklingtons with a great deal of solemnity.'[20] On 3 May, in a bonfire near Market Hill, Cambridge officials burnt every copy of *Altare Christianum* and *Sunday No Sabbath* they could locate within the university.[21]

Suspended from his ministry, deprived of his living, suffering emotional, spiritual, professional and financial damage, Pocklington sought to save himself from total ruin. As a former prebendary of Peterborough, he had once enjoyed the favourable lease of a small cathedral property. Pinched by necessity, he wrote a series of letters from March 1641 to March 1642 begging friends and former colleagues to help him to regain possession of the house. He even sought sympathy from the Bishop of Peterborough's wife. But John Towers, the bishop, and John Cosin, the Dean of Peterborough, mindful of their own precarious circumstances, were unwilling to help the outcast for fear 'that it will generally offend'.[22] The man who had been a golden spokesman for the ceremonialist avante-garde had become an ecclesiastical pariah. He died in November 1642 and was quietly buried at Peterborough Cathedral.

Pocklington's downfall served as a warning to others, an indication of which way the wind blew. It was apparent that the Laudian hegemony had collapsed, but by no means clear what would emerge in its place. None could tell in 1641 whether England would have a restored or modified episcopacy, an anglicized version of Scottish Presbyterianism, a New England-style Congregational Independency, or a free-for-all. All that an aspiring cleric

---

[17] Bodleian Library, Carte Ms. 103, ff. 58–65.
[18] Petition of John Harvey and answer of John Pocklington, House of Lords Record Office, Main Papers, 13 January 1641.
[19] *Lords Journal*, iv. 173; John Rushworth, *Historical Collections of Private Proceedings of State* (8 vols., 1680–1701), iv. 188.
[20] HMC, *14th Report, The Manuscripts of His Grace the Duke of Portland* (1894), iii. 75.
[21] Cambridge University Library, University Archives, V. C. Ct. I. 58, f. 43.
[22] Cambridge University Library, Peterborough Ms. 20, ff. 37–49.

could see ahead was uncertainty and dislocation. A contemporary pamphlet entitled *The Distractions of the Times* found religion so 'unordered and unsettled' that prospective ordinands were 'distracted or in a maze, not knowing how or what course they should take to live hereafter'.[23] Careers in the public ministry faced clouds of perplexity and confusion. One young scholar, James Duport, just out of Trinity College, Cambridge, delayed an important career decision in July 1641 'because I would willingly know which way church affairs would go before I absolutely accept of my lord of Lincoln's proffers.'[24]

A contemporary song entitled 'The Scholar's Complaint' or 'Alas poor scholar, whither wilt thou go?', which survives in several versions (to be sung to the tune of 'Hello my Fancy') reflects on the 'strange alterations' in religious duties, dignities, patronage, and rewards as the sun went down on Laudian ceremonialism. It satirized those ambitious young clerics whose career hopes collapsed with the crumbling of the Laudian regime. Faced with shrinking options, now that fawning conformity and ceremonial extravagance were no longer paths to preferment, the scholar of the song contemplates travel abroad or rural obscurity before settling on the relatively safe career of school-teaching.

'At great preferment I aimed', he laments, 'but now my hopes are maimed...'

> I have bowed, I have bended,
> And all in hope,
> One day to be befriended.
> I have preached, I have printed
> Whate're I hinted
> To please our English pope
> .   .   .   .
> I worshipped to the east, but the sun doth now forsake me.
> I find that I am falling, the northern winds do shake me.
> Would I'd been upright, for bowing now will break me.
> Alas, poor scholar, whither wilt thou go?[25]

One option, as always, was accommodation. While uncompromising Laudians stood their ground amidst the maelstrom of renewed reformation,

---

[23] *The Distractions of the Times* (1642), 3.

[24] Barrington Papers, British Library, Egerton Ms. 2646, f. 161. Duport eventually became a prebendary of Lincoln Cathedral and was ejected in 1650 (Matthew, *Walker Revised*, 10).

[25] [Robert Wild], *Alas poor Scholler, wither wilt thou goe* (1641), broadsheet; Mary Anne Everett Green (ed.), *The Diary of John Rous, Incumbent of Santon Downham, Suffolk, from 1625 to 1642* (Camden Society, 1856), 115–17. 'The northern winds', of course, were the triumphant Scottish covenanters. References to the flight of Windebank and Finch date the verse to late December 1640.

others cautiously adjusted their positions. Some who were renowned innovators continued to uphold church ceremonies, but others buckled under pressure. Some of the same men who had rigorously upheld altars in the late 1630s could now be seen jettisoning surplices, simplifying ceremonies, and making more flexible arrangements for Holy Communion.

Among them was John Hill, rector of Holdenby, Northamptonshire, who had formerly been a ceremonialist disciplinarian, a bower to altars, and a zealous upholder of bishops. Now, however, reported a neighbour in August 1641, 'he reproves his fellow minister for standing at the *Te Deum* . . . will not endure to see the surplice in the church . . . is so indifferent that he cares not if the communion table stand in the belfry. And upon a report that the bishops were voted down in the Lords House, and that the church was to be governed by nine laymen in every diocese, he said he was glad of it.'[26] Another was the Devonshire minister Mr Babbington, who 'had preached, when the bishops were up, against those that would not pay to the organs, but now he was turned another way' and would not say the Epistle, the Gospel, nor the common prayer. One of his parishioners called Babbington 'a whitherwitted man and a turncoat', though others supported his change of direction.[27]

The reformer Henry Burton warned members of Parliament in June 1641 that 'there are a great many ministers that are not resolved what to do, they would keep their ceremonies still, and they will wait for what the parliament will do; you may set up what religion you please, they will be of your religion still.'[28] The vicar of Bray could well have been a Caroline conformist, en route to Presbyterianism or Independency.

UPHOLDING GOD'S CHURCH

The more the established church came under attack the more vigorously some conservatives rallied to its defence. Whereas Parliament condemned the canons of 1640, and some members wanted them publicly burned, Laudian clergy upheld them as 'drawn out of scripture'.[29] John Reynolds of Houghton, Huntingdonshire, insisted that the convocation that made the new canons

---

[26] Rector since 1636, Hill was married to the niece and heir of the Laudian Dean of Arches, Sir John Lambe. The titheholder, Francis Mewce, referred to 'this ignorant unjust fellow in a cassock' as 'a turncoat', and wondered 'whither shall it be imagined he shall turn next'. He held the parish until he was sequestered in 1656 (*CSPD 1641–43*, 89), Francis Mewce to Nathaniel Tomkins, 14 August 1641; Matthews, *Walker Revised*, 279.

[27] Devon Record Office, Quarter Sessions Rolls, Q/SB, Box 46 (June 1642). This may have been Richard Babbington, formerly of Sidbury, Devon, who became a Presbyterian minister at Ingrave, Essex. [28] Henry Burton, *Englands Bondage and hope of Deliverance* (1641), 32.

[29] John White, *The First Century of Scandalous, Malignant Priests* (1643), 20.

had 'more force and authority than all parliaments'.[30] John Doughty of Lapworth, Warwickshire, told his parishioners 'there was nothing to be disliked in the new canons, and that even if St Paul had made them parliament would still condemn them.'[31]

Many Laudians were ostentatious in their orthodoxy, and proclaimed an undying loyalty to the church that had nourished them. Against parish and parliamentary reformers, Christopher Reyley, the rector of Newton Toney, Wiltshire, 'extolled the Book of Common Prayer so much that he would dare pawn his soul that there was nothing in it but that which was agreeable to the word of God'.[32] John Bradshaw, vicar of Chalfont St Peter, Buckinghamshire, declared it 'a damnable sin' to use any other prayers beside the Book of Common Prayer.[33] The moderate conservative Nathaniel Ward assured Sir Edward Dering in July 1641, 'I trust in god I shall burn at a faggot before I so far forget myself' as to 'frame my tenets to the presbyterical way'.[34]

Attacks on the organizational hierarchy of the church stiffened Laudian resistance and drove some moderate reformers to their side. While Bishop Joseph Hall expounded the belief that bishops were *jure divino*, others preached and published on the honour and worth of their calling.[35] It would be a 'miscarriage', wrote Gloucestershire petitioners, to destroy England's form of church government.[36] It was sacrilege, wrote Ephraim Udall, to tamper with episcopacy.[37] Emmanuel Uty of Chigwell went even further in teaching that the bishops were the head of the church, and that the command of the Archbishop of Canterbury was equivalent to the word of God. He allegedly told parishioners 'that he might be as well damned for not obeying the bishops' laws as God's laws', and 'that whatsoever men of holy orders

---

[30] White, *First Century of Scandalous, Malignant Priests*, 23.

[31] Matthews, *Walker Revised*, 363.

[32] British Library, Add. Ms. 22084 (reverse foliation), f. 4. He was also alleged to have said that laymen ought not to meddle with Scripture and that women should not read the Bible (Matthews, *Walker Revised*, 380).

[33] White, *First Century of Scandalous, Malignant Priests*, 8.

[34] British Library, Stowe Ms. 184, f. 41v.

[35] Joseph Hall, *Episcopacie by Divine Right Asserted* (1640); idem, *An Humble Remonstrance to the High Court of Parliament* (1641); Thomas Westfield, *A Sermon Preached in the Cathedral Church of S. Paul* (1641), 21. For the ensuing Smectymnuus controversy, named for the initials of the anti-episcopal authors Stephen Marshall, Edmund Calamy, Thomas Young, Matthew Newcomen, and William Spurstow, see Frederick L. Taft and Ashur Baizer, 'The Legion of Smec', in Douglas Bush et al. (eds.), *Complete Prose Works of John Milton, Vol. I. 1624–1642* (New Haven, 1953), 1001–8.

[36] Gloucestershire Record Office, D2510/14, Letters of John Smyth of Nibley.

[37] White, *First Century of Scandalous, Malignant Priests*, 9; Willson H. Coates, Anne Steele Young, and Vernon F. Snow (eds.), *The Private Journals of the Long Parliament 3 January to 5 March 1642* (New Haven and London, 1982), 230; [Ephraim Udall], *Noli Me Tangere. Or, A Thing to be thought on* (1642), 7–11.

speak they speak by divine inspiration'. Uty had said such things at the height of the Laudian ascendancy, but he did not back down when episcopacy came under attack.[38]

The bishops themselves provided models of dignified suffering. 'I do in all humility kiss the rod', wrote Joseph Hall from prison in January 1642, to which a correspondent replied, 'every stone is thrown at you shall turn a precious one, to deck your crown of glory'.[39] William Piers, the Bishop of Bath and Wells, likened his ordeal to the perils of St Paul. 'All the afflictions of the people of God are but pricks and thorns,' he wrote from the Tower in February 1642. 'Oh welcome, thrice welcome, these bitter sweets, these loving chastisements, these indulgent visitations, these pleasant crosses, these comfortable calamities, these wholesome miseries, these glorious trials,' with more in this vein of proud abasement.[40]

'WHEN THE MULE BREEDS I WILL DO'

Deep divisions in many parishes allowed ceremonialists to defy reforming factions and to maintain their way of worship. They became adept at delaying, modifying, thwarting, obstructing, ignoring, or countering puritan reforms, and reversing or mitigating changes to liturgical arrangements. Many continued, ostentatiously, to wear the surplice, to follow the prayer book, and to support bishops, against the objections of MPs and parishioners who wanted reforms. Laudian conservatives in the early 1640s resorted to many of the tactics that puritans had used in the 1630s, delaying, obstructing, and neglecting directives from outside the parish, while trying to deflect official pressures that would force them to comply. Since neither episcopacy nor the prayer book had yet been abolished they were strictly following the law, but by late 1641, in some areas, conformity could be construed as defiance.

Upholders of clerical and episcopal privileges rejected lay interference with their duties and resisted parliamentary orders and instructions for change. They not unreasonably countered attempts at religious reform by challenging the authority by which it was demanded. Emmanuel Uty, the vicar of Chigwell, Essex, declared that members of Parliament were illiterate mechanicks who had no business meddling with religious affairs.[41] The

---

[38] British Library, Add. Ms. 21935, f. 113; White, *First Century of Scandalous, Malignant Priests*, 2–3; Matthews, *Walker Revised*, 166.

[39] [Joseph Hall], *A Letter Lately Sent by a Reverend Bishop from the Tower to a Private Friend* (1642), 1, 12.   [40] [Piers], *Sermon Preached at the Tower*, 6, 7.

[41] Matthews, *Walker Revised*, 166; White, *First Century of Scandalous, Malignant Priests*, 3; British Library, Add. Ms. 21935, f. 113; Maija Jansson (ed.), *Proceedings in the Opening Session of the Long Parliament . . . Volume 4: 19 April–5 June 1641* (Rochester, NY, 2003), 412.

London Laudian John Clark said likewise 'that the parliament could not meddle or settle the business of the church, they being not scholars but mechanick men.'[42] 'Proud and insolent' Laudians in Surrey were said in July 1641 to 'slight all passages against them in the House of Commons'.[43] Many judged the policies emanating from Westminster to be variable and contradictory, and of questionable legal force. Conservatives appealed instead to the oaths they had taken at ordination and at visitations, and to the canons, prayer book, and statutes, which authorized their religious practices. William Ingoldsby, the rector of Watton, Hertfordshire, helpfully published *Englands Oaths. Taken by All Men of Quallity in the Church and Commonwealth*, 'for satisfaction of his parishioners'.[44]

Parliamentary efforts to redress deficient preaching and 'scandalous' worship by allowing parishioners to install lecturers not surprisingly caused further friction and resentment. Conservative incumbents were often slow to cooperate, and some refused outright to share their reading desk or pulpit. Laudians often regarded the new lecturers as intruders and treated them as enemies. Edward Partlett, the vicar of Broxbourne, Hertfordshire, for example, was among those who refused to accept the parliamentary order to admit a lecturer.[45] The minister of St Giles, Cripplegate, Timothy Hutton, was one of several who locked the church doors to prevent the appointed lecturer from preaching to the parish. It took six months of petitioning before John Sedgewick was permitted to expound without interruption.[46] At Horncastle, Lincolnshire, the vicar, Thomas Gibson, not only locked the church but hid the key in his house and 'rode early out of the town' to prevent the lecturer from speaking.[47] James Wilcock, the conformist vicar of Goudhurst, Kent, also did everything in his power to obstruct the intruded lecturer, Edward Bright, whom he described as 'a wolf in the fold, busy in my flock', and 'this master B. whom my parishioners follow in swarms'.[48] John Summerfield, vicar of Thornton, Leicestershire, once drove the lecturer, William Whatton,

---

[42] White, *First Century of Scandalous, Malignant Priests*, 25; Matthews, *Walker Revised*, 44.

[43] James Orchard Halliwell (ed.), *The Autobiography and Correspondence of Sir Simonds D'Ewes* (1845), 271.

[44] [William Ingoldsby], *Englands Oaths. Taken by All Men Of Quallity in the Church and Common-wealth of England* (1642), title page; Matthews, *Walker Revised*, 200.

[45] Matthews, *Walker Revised*, 202.

[46] *Common Journals*, ii. 294, 295, 297, 484; Matthews, *Walker Revised*, 51; White, *First Century of Scandalous, Malignant Priests*, 41.

[47] J. W. F. Hill, 'The Royalist Clergy of Lincolnshire', *Lincolnshire Architectural and Archaeological Society Reports and Papers*, new series (1940 for 1938), ii. 61.

[48] Lambert B. Larking (ed.), *Proceedings, Principally in the County of Kent, in Connection with the Parliaments Called in 1640* (Camden Society, vol. lxxx, 1862), 144–5; J.W., *A Challenge Sent to Master E. B.*, 4, 6.

'out of the church with a rapier drawn';[49] and John Bradshaw of Chalfont St Peter, Buckinghamshire, was said to have 'wished that all lecturers were hanged'.[50]

Robert Clarke, vicar of Andover, Hampshire, not only locked lecturer Richard Symonds out of the church but gave good reason for his actions. Clarke declared that 'rather than Mr Symonds should preach there, by order of parliament, he would lose his life, and his wife and children should die in prison; that the church was as much his own as his own house; and he would hold his right, let the parliament do what they would.' What Parliament did was to order once more that Symonds be allowed to preach, and to threaten the vicar with prosecution at King's Bench. Clarke eventually lost his living in the sequestrations of 1646.[51]

Some conservative clerics refused to read parliamentary orders concerning Communion rails, images, or bowing at the name of Jesus. Others gave them a supercilious or sarcastic reading to disparage the instructions from Westminster. Peter Smith, the curate of Linton, Cambridgeshire, for example, read royal declarations with a loud voice, but those of Parliament 'so softly, and after evening prayer, so as very few could understand him'.[52] Stephen Hurry of Alburgh, Norfolk, a protégé of Matthew Wren, refused to read a parliamentary order in open church, but afterwards read it carelessly in the church porch when most people had gone home.[53]

Presented in September 1641 with a parliamentary order against bowing at the name of Jesus, Benjamin Spencer, the conformist minister of St Thomas, Southwark, refused to read it, saying that for all he knew it might have 'come from a ballad monger'.[54] Conservatives at St Giles, Cripplegate, 'misused and reviled' the messenger who delivered the parliamentary order to pull down the Communion rails, and said that members of the House of Commons 'were all asses'.[55] At Deeping St James, Lincolnshire, the vicar, Christopher Smith, preached in March 1642 'that it was treason to obey any order of parliament unless it had the king's hand and seal to it'.[56] Thomas

---

[49] Bodleian Library, J. Walker Ms. c.11, f. 72.

[50] White, *First Century of Scandalous, Malignant Priests*, 8.

[51] *Commons Journals*, ii. 735; Matthews, *Walker Revised*, 180–1.

[52] Matthews, *Walker Revised*, 86.   [53] Ibid., 269.

[54] Spencer, *Articles exhibited against Benjamin Spencer*, 3. For others who refused to read Parliament's orders, see White, *First Century of Scandalous, Malignant Priests*, 9

[55] Willson Havelock Coates (ed.), *The Journal of Sir Simonds D'Ewes from the First Recess of the Long Parliament to the Withdrawal of the King from London* (New Haven and London, 1942), 17.

[56] Vernon F. Snow and Anne Steele Young (eds.), *The Private Journals of the Long Parliament 2 June to 17 September 1642* (New Haven and London, 1992), 9; Matthews, *Walker Revised*, 257. Smith, for his pains, was sent to the Gatehouse.

Carter, the master of Highgate school and reader in Highgate chapel, Middlesex, declared that 'they were mad that would read the Commons order on innovations [and] that none but fools would take the Protestation.'[57]

Parliament's Protestation of May 1641, extended nationwide in January 1642, was an anodyne declaration of support for the religious status quo. Its wording was so ambiguous that conservatives could claim it to sustain the Church of England, whereas reformers could construe it to justify the further eradication of popery.[58] Dozens of conservative incumbents nonetheless refused to subscribe the Protestation and refused to cooperate with its circulation in their parishes. Samuel Lindsell of Stratford, Suffolk, 'refused to take the Protestation and discouraged the people ... wishing them to be well advised'. Robert Sugden of Benhall took it but only 'with reservation that the church might be governed by bishops', persuading some in his parish to gloss it likewise.[59] In Cambridgeshire, Henry Downhall of Toft refused to read the Protestation 'or any other thing set out by authority of parliament'. When Mr Chandler of Oakington, reading the preamble, 'came to those words, the House of Commons, he threw it away saying what had he to do with the House of Commons'.[60] When the time came for Dr William Heywood to read the Protestation at St Giles in the Fields, he did so in a 'ridiculous, absurd and disdainful manner, with much scorn and jeering'.[61]

William Hollington, the Laudian rector of Allchurch, Worcestershire, was another 'hinderer of the taking of the Protestation', who used 'many reproachful words' against the constable who came with the Protestation, 'calling him knave, blockhead and loggerhead'.[62] At Muggleswick, Durham, the minister 'affirmed before the open assembly that the Protestation was false' and threatened ruin on those who had taken it.[63] Another Durham minister, Nathaniel Ward of Staindrop, a member of John Cosin's circle, avoided the Protestation altogether by arranging to be absent whenever it was tendered. Faced with the requirement to tender the Protestation to the rest of his parishioners early in 1642, Ward told the Durham prebendary Isaac Basire, 'when the mule breeds I will do. For no law or statute either

---

[57] Matthews, *Walker Revised*, 259.

[58] David Cressy, 'The Protestation Protested, 1641 and 1642', *The Historical Journal*, 45 (2002), 251–79.   [59] Holmes (ed.), *Suffolk Committees for Scandalous Ministers*, 69.

[60] Bodleian Library, Ms. Rawlinson D. 924, ff. 177, 184, 186, 198, 203; British Library, Add. Ms. 15672, ff. 29, 33, 47v. Richard Taylor of Aspenden and Westmill, Hertfordshire, also refused to publish the Protestation (Matthews, *Walker Revised*, 202).

[61] *The Petition and Articles Exhibited in Parliament against Doctor Heywood* (1641), 8–9.

[62] J. W. Willis Bund (ed.), *Worcestershire County Records. Division I. Documents Relating to Quarter Sessions* (Worcester, 1900), 703. Formerly a royal chaplain, Hollington was sequestered from his living in 1646.

[63] Durham University Library, Special Collections, Mickleton-Spearman Ms. MSP 9, ii. 238.

requires us to take the oath itself, or to perform such an unreasonable act'.[64]

Laudian ceremonialism was by no means a spent force, even if many of its practitioners had apparently suffered eclipse. They were battered but by no means broken. Dozens of examples can be found of ministers who used force or cajolery to thwart the process of reform. As Sir Simonds D'Ewes warned the House of Commons early in 1642, there remained many 'scandalous, loose, profane, ignorant, and popishly affected clergymen', some of whom 'have taken new heart and in divers places did again set up their tables altarwise and placed the rails before them which they had removed'.[65] Some persisted in ceremonial worship, even after the contested accoutrements were taken away. They could become sullenly obstructive and noisily uncooperative when their altar rails were forcibly removed and their Communion tables set closer to the congregation.

William Heywood stood his ground at St Giles in the Fields, notwithstanding an avalanche of criticism. Late in 1641 he still required parishioners to come up to the rails for Communion, and denied the sacrament to those who remained in their pews. 'He doth still persist in his old manner, not reforming considerable thing,' critics complained, and his elaborate altar ensemble 'stands decked continually, weekdays and all, and mewed up with the screen and rails as before'.[66] Like other Laudian diehards, Heywood refused to allow the House of Commons order 'concerning the pulling down of the rails about the communion table' to be read in his church.[67] When the churchwardens took down the rails without his permission, Heywood had them reinstalled. Eventually, in October 1641, he 'yielded to have the rails before the communion table taken away, and that the same communion table should be removed from the east end chancel, but', parishioners reported, 'some scandalous pictures yet remained.'[68] The diarist Thomas Wyatt noted, 'Dr Heywood, chaplain to the archbishop, put out of all his livings to the value of £700', but the observation was premature.[69] For as long as Heywood held his post in this prominent metropolitan parish, remnants of the Laudian programme would be preserved.[70]

---

[64] Darnell (ed.), *Correspondence of Isaac Basire*, 32, 40, checked against Latin originals in Durham University Library, Special Collections, 'John Cosin Letter Book', 1A/ 34 and 35.

[65] Coates, Young, and Snow (eds.), *Private Journals of the Long Parliament 3 January to 5 March 1642*, 137–8.

[66] *The Petition and Articles Exhibited in Parliament against Doctor Heywood* (1641), 8–9.

[67] *The Heads of Several Petitions and Complaints* (1641), 2, 4.

[68] Coates (ed.), *Journal of Sir Simonds D'Ewes from the First Recess of the Long Parliament*, 5.

[69] Bodleian Library, Ms. Top. Oxon. C. 378, 316.

[70] Heywood had enjoyed Laudian patronage, becoming rector of Laindon, Essex, in 1631, rector of St Giles in 1636, and prebendary of both Westminster and St Paul's (Matthew, *Walker Revised*, 50). The Chamberlain's accounts of December 1641 list him as a royal chaplain, PRO, LC3/1, f. 4.

Similarly in Surrey, Nicholas Andrews, rector at Guildford and vicar of Godalming, continued his ceremonialist devotions, offered prayers for the Bishop of Ely and commemoration of the dead, 'and hath lately put one from the communion because his conscience would not suffer him to kneel', an irate William Elyott informed Simonds D'Ewes in July 1641. Elyott characterized Andrews as one of the most 'popish and profane priests' in the kingdom, who would not be dislodged, 'hoping, as they say, better times'.[71] At Southwark the defiant Benjamin Spencer declared that he would continue to bow to the holy table, 'whether the rails be taken away or not'.[72] And at Ellastone, Staffordshire, when the churchwardens followed parliamentary instructions to move the Communion table away from the east-end wall, the ceremonialist vicar, John Hill, 'in contempt of the parliament', immediately set it altarwise again.[73]

Several Laudian ministers in Matthew Wren's diocese of Ely resisted parishioners who sought implementation of the parliamentary orders against idolatry and superstition. William Ling of Girton, Cambridgeshire, for example, refused to read the instruction for relocating Communion tables and taking up rails. When the churchwardens took independent action, Ling moved the table back again and obstructed the workmen engaged to level the chancel floor.[74] Cheyney Row of Orwell, Cambridgeshire, similarly threatened and bullied the churchwardens who attempted to move the Communion table and take down the rails.[75] John Hill of Coveney in the Isle of Ely dissuaded parishioners from taking down the rails, 'saying there would come a time when they might stand in need of them again'.[76] In several parishes the churchwardens were persuaded to place their dismantled rails in storage rather than consign them to the fire, rather like their Reformation-era predecessors had safeguarded images and relics. At Cerne Abbas, Dorset, for example, the churchwardens paid fourpence in 1641 for 'removing the rails about the communion table', but in 1642 they were still listed in the parish inventory.[77]

In Suffolk, within the diocese of Norwich, Alexander Clarke, the vicar of Bredfield, 'refused to let the churchwardens level the ground where the altar stood, because it was holy and consecrated, and not fit to be thrown out or

---

[71] Halliwell (ed.), *Autobiography and Correspondence of Sir Simonds D'Ewes*, 271–2. Andrews was sequestered in 1643 (Matthews, *Walker Revised*, 348). J. Evans, 'The Vicar of Godalming and his parishioners in 1640', *Surrey Archeological Collections*, 2 (1884), 210–23.

[72] Spencer, *Articles exhibited against Benjamin Spencer*, 2.

[73] Staffordshire Record Office, Q/SR/251/29, /31; Matthew, *Walker Revised*, 327.

[74] British Library, Add. Ms. 15672, ff. 29, 33, 47v.

[75] Matthew, *Walker Revised*, 86; White, *First Century of Scandalous, Malignant Priests*, 48, for similar resistance by Henry Hannington of Houghton, Kent.

[76] British Library, Add. Ms. 15672, f. 33.   [77] Dorset Record Office, mf. R/1014.

mixed with common earth'.[78] At Melton, when Parliament ordered the Communion table to be moved away from the east window the rector, William Pratt, 'commanded it to be set there again'. Likewise at Finningham, the rector, Edmund Mayor, defied the parliamentary order after the rails were removed and the table brought down, by getting help from the sexton to 'set it up again, saying there it should stand'. At Grundisburgh, after the table was 'brought down into the usual place', Edward Barton the rector 'refused to administer the sacrament'. William Proctor, the ceremonialist rector of Stradishall, observed the letter but defied the spirit of the newly approved arrangement, for 'after the rails were taken away' he substituted forms or benches and made the communicants kneel there instead.[79]

Few reacted so wildly as the minister of Waldringfield, Suffolk, Andrew Sandiland, a man 'given to superstitious and vain gestures in the church' including 'bowing towards the communion table'. Sandiland was so angry on the day that his beloved rails were pulled down that 'he came into the church porch with his pistol charged ... and threatened to dispatch the first that came out of the church.' Even after the rails had gone, he refused to administer the sacrament unless communicants knelt at their former place at the chancel steps, 'whereby some were grieven, and would not come unto the communion'.[80]

Nearby in Essex, in the diocese of London, Dr Edward Layfield of Barking, maintained his cherished religious ornaments in the face of strong local criticism, charging opponents with sacrilege when they sought to have his golden letters and images removed.[81] Robert Snell, the vicar of Matching, blocked efforts to remove a crucifix in the window over the altar when Parliament ordered the image to be removed.[82] Richard Drake of Radwinter similarly attempted to uphold clerical dignity and ceremonial worship, as antagonistic parishioners mocked and harassed him, interrupting his services and ripping his surplice. 'The insolences were so many that they seemed to tire a greater patience than mortality can attain to', Drake later recalled, but he held his ground until forced out in the civil war.[83]

---

[78] White, *First Century of Scandalous, Malignant Priests*, 16; Matthews, *Walker Revised*, 330–1. Clarke was also rector of Iken, and was sequestered from both parishes in 1643.
[79] Holmes (ed.), *Suffolk Committees for Scandalous Ministers*, 50, 64, 73, 81, 87; Matthews, *Walker Revised*, 341, 339, 326, 341.
[80] House of Lords Record Office, Main Papers, Petition of 9 February 1641. Sandiland, or a namesake, became rector of Scrayingham, Yorkshire, in late 1641 and was ejected in 1644 (Matthews, *Walker Revised*, 398). The incident with the pistol may have happened earlier in 1640.
[81] Rushworth, *Historical Collections of Private Proceedings of State*, iv. 58–9; Matthew, *Walker Revised*, 53.   [82] Matthews, *Walker Revised*, 163.
[83] Bodleian Library, Rawlinson Ms. D. 158.

Disagreements at Chelmsford developed into in a riotous assault on church windows and images, after the conformist rector, John Michaelson, refused to allow their dismantling. Attempting to regain control of the parish, Michaelson preached 'against popular tumultuous reformations', and said there could be no 'authority' in the people, nor any virtue in 'abolishing superstition with schism'. In the ensuing turmoil someone fired a bullet into the rector's study. But Michaelson too stood firm, and continued to use the prayer book and wear the surplice. He was cited before Parliament in November 1641 and summoned to appear as a delinquent, but he was still at his post in 1644 when parliamentary soldiers secured his ejection.[84]

After the Communion rails were forcibly removed at Tewin, Hertfordshire, the rector, James Montfort, put forms in their place and made parishioners kneel there for Communion.[85] Another Hertfordshire Laudian, John Montfort, the rector of Anstey and Therfield, had the churchwarden and glazier arrested for pulling down 'scandalous' pictures in the east window, although they were following the orders of Parliament.[86]

At Fornax-Pelham, 'fearing the pulling up of the rails about the communion table', the vicar, Henry Hancocks, 'walked with his sword about the churchyard in the night, saying he would rather lose his life than suffer them to be pulled up'.[87] Like Andrew Sandiland with his pistol, and others with their intemperate rhetoric, this minister was prepared to forego his clerical dignity in order to defend what he thought most precious.

HEATED AND MALICIOUS WORDS

Local Laudians had always seen the worst in their opponents and were accustomed to reviling critics of their churchmanship. They had no difficulty labelling obstructive neighbours as 'puritans' and 'sectaries' or presenting minor offenders for excommunication. They employed a rich vocabulary of vituperation to attack any who would resist their authority, demean their status, or attack their liturgical arrangements. When circumstances changed after 1640 these same conservative clerics reacted by vilifying the presumed authors of their miseries, berating reformers as dangerous zealots, bearers of parliamentary orders as madmen, members of Parliament as asses, and parish activists as vermin or dogs.

---

[84] Bruno Ryves, *Angliae Ruina* (1647), 22–6; Matthews, *Walker Revised*, 158.
[85] Matthews, *Walker Revised*, 201.
[86] Ibid., 201; White, *First Century of Scandalous, Malignant Priests*, 13.
[87] White, *First Century of Scandalous, Malignant Priests*, 17.

This heated and extravagant language was not just a venting of frustration; it also rallied opinion against puritans and radicals and worked to discredit parliamentary reforms. One of its effects was to raise tensions and sharpen divisions in increasingly polarized communities. Another was to rally support for the King against 'factious', 'seditious', and 'turbulent spirits' who were ruining both church and state.[88] Conservatives labelled their opponents as 'weak and ignorant Christians, misled and misinformed, or perverse, seditious and inconformable to the established government'.[89] If they could not prevent the work of reformers they would attempt to shout them down.

Edward Layfield denounced his enemies at Barking as 'spotted toads and venomous toads', and insisted they were 'in the state of damnation' when they tried to remove the ornaments from his church.[90] Thomas Sanders, the Laudian vicar of Caldecote, Cambridgeshire, similarly told parishioners who refused to take Communion at the rails, 'you are all damned, you are none of this congregation.'[91] A Lincolnshire minister told auditors at Stamford 'that a cursed generation of men were risen up, who went about to put down prayer and beat down the houses of God with axes and hammers'.[92] A Leicestershire minister declared, 'they were all damned that took up arms for the parliament', reading out the title page of an anti-parliamentary pamphlet to persuade parishioners to his view.[93]

At Northbourne, Kent, the ceremonialist Edward Nichols believed that complaints against him were motivated 'not for God's glory and the good of the church (for then I could have borne with it), but they violently proceed against me out of revenge, envy, hatred, malice and all uncharitable ends.'[94] John Hill, the vicar of Ellastone, Staffordshire, denounced a parishioner who subscribed a petition against him as 'puritan, roundhead and fool', and dismissed other opponents as 'young men', moved 'more out of a seeming zeal than any true knowledge'.[95]

At Burton Dasset, Warwickshire, where parishioners were preparing a petition denouncing their vicar, Robert Kenrick, as an 'idle and unworthy minister', the minister used his pulpit in February 1641 to mount a counterattack.

---

[88] British Library, Add. Ms. 36914, f. 224.
[89] I.W., *Certaine Reasons Why the Booke of Common-Prayer Being Corrected Should Continue* (1641), sigs. A2–A2v, 1, 2, 4.
[90] Rushworth, *Historical Collections of Private Proceedings of State*, iv. 58–9.
[91] Matthew, *Walker Revised*, 86.   [92] Hill, 'Royalist Clergy of Lincolnshire', 83.
[93] Bodleian Library, J. Walker Ms. c.11, ff. 56–56v, 62–4. The minister was William Parks, vicar of Belton, Leicestershire. The text in question was by the Archdeacon of Leicester, Henry Ferne, *The Resolving of Conscience . . . Whence it followeth, that the resistance now made against the higher power is unwarrantable, and according to the Apostle damnable* (Cambridge, 1642).
[94] British Library, Add. Ms. 26786, f. 107.
[95] Staffordshire Record Office, Q/SR/251/29, /31.

Kenrick chose his text from Psalm 7: 1—'Oh Lord in thee I put my trust. Save me from them that persecute me, and deliver me'—and preached against 'great and wicked men' who 'work out their malice and revenge against the godly whom they hate', no doubt making eye contact with those he had in mind. Likening such miscreants to Saul's dogs, Pharaoh's enchanters, and tormentors with bloodhounds, the vicar 'did appeal to the consciences of his hearers whether it were not so in this place amongst them'. [96] This was personal preaching with a vengeance, which helped drive either side to the extremes.

Parish harmony was no more likely at Sible Hedingham, Essex, where the ceremonialist John Jegon railed against reformers, 'terming them spirit-mongers, puritans, and people of fanatical spirits'. On the day when his beloved Communion rails came down in 1641, Jegon proclaimed 'it was pity that ever the Bible was translated into English, for now every woman and beggarly fellow think themselves able to dispute with learned divines.'[97] 'We are so glutted with the heavenly manna of divine doctrine', wrote Edward Browne in 1642, 'that now every boy or ignorant tradesman that can read his horn-book or write a scribbling character assumes himself a spirit of revelation.'[98] John Hodges, the vicar of Shakerstone, Leicestershire, concurred, 'it is a pity the common sort of people should know the word of God.'[99] Supporters of John Squire, the vicar of St Leonard, Shoreditch, who faced ruin when his Arminian practices were exposed in Parliament, denounced petitioners against him as 'men of very mean condition, schismatically affected and altogether opposite to the established government of our church'.[100] It was a common Laudian response to associate religious reform with folly, ignorance, and low social status.

Cathedral clergy, canons and prebendaries, were among the most conservative defenders of established religion, and among the most outspoken against its enemies. They were often linked in networks of support with like-minded incumbents, Oxford and Cambridge fellows, and conservative local gentry. The Laudian diehards William Bray, William Heywood, Alexander Huish, Thomas Paske, Bruno Ryves, and Samuel Lindsell all held cathedral prebends.[101] William Clarke, a canon of Chester Cathedral, included puritans among the

---

[96] Huntington Library, Ms. STTM Box 20 (25).
[97] British Library, Add. Ms. 5829, ff. 9, 10, 21–2; Matthews, *Walker Revised*, 364.
[98] Edward Browne, *Sir James Cambels Clarkes Disaster by Making Books* (1642), 4.
[99] Bodleian Library, J. Walker Ms. c.11, f. 31. Phrases like this were often ripped out of context. Cf. Daniel Whitby's rebuttal of the claim that he preached that 'the people had too much knowledge', in Daniel Whitby, *The Vindication of a True Protestant* (Oxford, 1644), 1–2.
[100] Bedfordshire and Luton Archives, St John Papers, J. 1380.
[101] Matthews, *Walker Revised*, 3–11, and passim.

'grand enemies' of the church, likening them in November 1641 to Herod and Pontius Pilate, who 'joined together for the crucifying of Christ', and charging them with seeking 'with might and main to overthrow our discipline'.[102] Cathedral ceremonialists at Exeter offered 'frowns and threats' to the reforming lecturer John Bond, calling him 'troubler, pestilent, schismatical', and accusing him 'by word and writing' of 'faction, sedition, [and] treason', so vehemently that Bond was forced to seek parliamentary protection.[103]

Similarly in Herefordshire, the reforming minister John Tombs, a protégé of Sir Robert Harley, faced abuse from his conservative enemies. 'As the cathedral men seek to sting me, so the common people exclaim much against me', he complained to his patron. By February 1642 it was reported from Leominster that there was 'no minister more hated or set against than Mr Tombs by a great number of superstitious people in this town'.[104] The cathedral men had evidently been effective in mobilizing conservative opinion.

Many Laudians blamed Parliament for their worsening circumstances, and poured scorn on the 'puritans' at Westminster.[105] These were 'words of dangerous consequence', so Parliament judged them, that denigrated 'godly' reform.[106] Laudians were among the most outspoken defenders of the Earl of Strafford, and claimed that Parliament had wrongfully caused his death. Richard Watts, vicar of Mildenhall, Suffolk, prayed publicly for the Earl and called him 'his singular good lord and master'. Theodore Beale of nearby Ash Bocking said that Strafford died unjustly, and that 'the king was therein compelled by the parliament and the parliament by the rout'. Daniel Horsmonden of Ulcomb, Kent, went so far as to say that Stafford 'was sacrificed as our saviour Christ was, to give the people content'.[107]

Another conformist minister, Richard Lloyd, was so outraged by proceedings in the House of Commons that he called the members 'a company of rogues...who went about to pull down episcopacy'. Lloyd was so angry at parliamentary preaching in 1641 that he 'vowed to pistol Dr Burges with his own hand'.[108] Another volatile conservative, Edward Jerry, allegedly cried

---

[102] Bodleian Library, Nalson Ms. 13/28–31.

[103] John Bond, *A Doore of Hope, also Holy and Loyall Activity* (1641), sig. A3. A Devonshire yeoman used more homely language in June 1642 when he called a puritan minister at Newton 'a coxcomb fool...that would not say the epistles and gospels, nor the common prayer' (Devon Record Office, Q/SB/46, 23 June 1642).

[104] British Library, Add. Ms. 70003, ff. 92, 204. Tombs would later emerge as a prominent Baptist. [105] British Library, Add. Ms. 1045, vol. v., f. 146v.

[106] Matthew, *Walker Revised*, 48, 147, and passim.

[107] Holmes (ed.) *Suffolk Committees for Scandalous Ministers*, 36, 41; White, *First Century of Scandalous, Malignant Priests*, 2, 18, 37.

[108] Maija Jansson (ed.), *Proceedings in the Opening Session of the Long Parliament...Volume 2: 21 December 1640–20 March 1641* (Rochester, NY, 2000), 478, 496–7.

out, 'a pox upon the parliament', asserting, 'that by God he would first cut the parliament's throats before they should take a course with such priests as himself'.[109] Archdeacon William Piers, the pluralist son and chaplain of the Bishop of Bath and Wells, similarly cursed members of Parliament in January 1641, 'a pox of God take them all for a company of puritanical factious fellows...and that the king should never be quiet till he had taken off twenty or more of their heads.'[110] Other Laudians denounced parliamentarians as 'mechanical men' whose views on religion were not worth considering.[111] One Kentish minister declared them 'schismastical and pragmatical fellows [who] were met together to make new laws'.[112]

George Preston, the vicar of Rothersthorpe, Northamptonshire, used more subtle means to signal his distaste for proceedings at Westminster; he came to public notice in December 1640 for naming his hogs after 'ten of the active parliament men, every hog he called by some parliament man's name'. Preston reportedly avowed that 'parliaments in England never did good...that his hogs were fit to make parliament men of, and their sty a fit place for them to sit in.' He also said of his parishioners 'that such as went from sermon to sermon were like jackdaws that hopped from twig to twig, and they did go to several churches to commit whoredom.'[113] In the same vein Benjamin Spencer of St Thomas, Southwark 'did abuse honest ministers, saying these jackdaws that formerly durst not show their faces now did appear and did shelter themselves under the eaves of the parliament'. It was Spencer who said, when presented with the parliamentary order against bowing at the name of Jesus, that for all he knew it might have 'come from a ballad monger'.[114]

Lay conservatives joined in this diatribe against parliamentary reformers. It was a churchwarden at St Giles, Cripplegate, perhaps prompted by the minister, who said that members of the House of Commons 'were all asses'.[115]

---

[109] Matthews, *Walker Revised*, 156.

[110] British Library, Add. Ms. 21935, f. 109v; Jansson (ed.), *Proceedings in the Opening Session of the Long Parliament...Vol. 2*, 105, 114; Matthews, *Walker Revised*, 317. Piers was archdeacon of Taunton, rector of Buckland St Mary, and vicar of Kingsbury Episcopi. The charge against him was supported by three witnesses, but on his knees at the bar of the House of Commons in January 1641, Piers denied it. In April he was allowed bail. He was eventually sequestered in 1646.

[111] Matthews, *Walker Revised*, 166; White, *First Century of Scandalous, Malignant Priests*, 3, 25.   [112] White, *First Century of Scandalous, Malignant Priests*, 10.

[113] British Library, Add. Ms. 1045, vol. v., f. 46v; Jansson, (ed.), *Proceedings in the Opening Session of the Long Parliament...Vol. 2*, 246; Matthews, *Walker Revised*, 283. On 22 January 1641 the Commons had him confined to the Gatehouse.

[114] Spencer, *Articles exhibited against Benjamin Spencer*, 2–3; Bond (ed.), *Manuscripts of the House of Lords, Vol. xi*, 351.

[115] Coates (ed.), *Journal of Sir Simonds D'Ewes from the First Recess of the Long Parliament*, 17.

The humorist John Taylor derided 'the hellish parliament' and its 'erroneous and seditious practices' that fostered religious schism.[116] John Werden, the principal agent for Sir Thomas Aston's petition in Cheshire, referred sarcastically to parliamentary leaders as 'our popular patriots and grandees', describing agitators against episcopacy as 'zealots' or 'seditious preachers', and labelling his opponents as 'seditious, factious, [and] dangerous'.[117] The House was sensitive to such comments and sometimes treated them as breaches of privilege.

The rhetorical sniping intensified in January 1642 following the King's disastrous attempt to arrest the five members of Parliament. John Browning, the minister of Much Easton, Essex, described by Simonds D'Ewes as 'a notable Arminian and altar-adorer', asserted that the five members were justly accused of treason, 'and that there were forty more amongst them guilty of the same crime'.[118] Soon after the King's departure from London, Thomas Paske, the Laudian subdean of Canterbury, preached not that the King had gone from his people, but 'that the people were departed from the king. They must come as Benhadad's servants did with halter[s] about their necks.'[119]

Other conservative pulpits contributed to the view that the King had been wronged, and prepared the way for a royalist reaction. Some blamed Parliament for 'all the troubles and disturbances of the kingdom'.[120] John Wood, vicar of Marden, Kent, said, 'that the parliament hath no power to do anything in the king's absence, no more than a man without a head'.[121] Thomas Chaffin, the Laudian rector of Fovant, Wiltshire, improvised an addition to the Litany, 'from all lay puritans and all lay parliamentarians good Lord deliver us.'[122] Parish leadership of this sort proved critical in 1642 in swaying opinion against Parliament's Militia Ordinance and in favour of the King's Commission of Array. Harsh and divisive language made accommodation increasingly unreachable, and may have made it easier for Englishmen to face each other in battle.

---

[116] John Taylor, *The Hellish Parliament Being a Counter-Parliament* (1641), 1.

[117] British Library, Add. Ms. 36914, ff. 206v, 210, 216, 222, 224.

[118] Coates, Young, and Snow (eds.), *Private Journals of the Long Parliament 3 January to 5 March 1642*, 241; Matthews, *Walker Revised*, 147.

[119] Coates, Young, and Snow (eds.), *Private Journals of the Long Parliament 3 January to 5 March 1642*, 223. Paske was also archdeacon of London, a prebendary of York, rector of Much Hadham, Hertfordshire, and master of Clare Hall, Cambridge. His sermon of 22 January 1642 was reported to Parliament a few days later. Benhadad was the Syrian king humbled by Israel (I Kings 20: 31–2).   [120] White, *First Century of Scandalous, Malignant Priests*, 7

[121] Ibid., 30.

[122] British Library, Add. Ms. 21935, f. 112v; Jansson (ed.), *Proceedings in the Opening Session of the Long Parliament...Vol. 2*, 257, 439, 442; Matthews, *Walker Revised*, 371. According to D'Ewes, 'the chief sense of the House was to send him to the Tower, but other urgent business diverted us for the present.'

ALL IMAGINABLE RUIN AND CONFUSION

While godly enthusiasts rejoiced in the downfall of Babylon, their conservative counterparts licked their wounds, 'deploring the church's anarchy' or 'grieving at fortune's malignity'.[123] A chorus of complaint warned that England had become Babel, amidst 'great divisions and horrible factions'.[124] It was a mobilizing cry, not just an expression of frustration, to warn of 'fraction and faction, schism and separation' in a land beset by 'miserable and remediless confusion'.[125] Puritanism led to sectarianism, and sectarianism led to chaos, in this angry and alarmist view of the world. Nobody knew for sure before 1642 that they may have been right.

Conservatives cherished order and unity, and abhorred its absence or undoing. Without unity and order, Matthias Milward preached in August 1641, 'we should have as many factions as fancies, as many gospels as gossips'.[126] The more there were signs of extremism at Westminster, the more there was turmoil in the parishes, and the more reports circulated of alleged sectarian excesses, the more conformist propagandists spread alarm at England's distempers. Laudians fed the fear that chaos was at hand, but mainstream moderate churchmen shared the concern that worse was likely to follow. One did not have to be a Laudian to be fearful of impending chaos, for the growing disorder also distressed gentlemen of moderate views, including some parliamentary reformers. Conformist clerics looking for allies among the laity found sympathies in common with worried landowners and magistrates.

It was the rising volume of radicalism in London and Kent that drove Sir Edward Dering into a deepening conservatism. Dering had earlier been identified with the puritans, but as early as Christmas 1640 he confided to his wife that all was leading to confusion. Recoiling from the imprecations of 'bold mechanicks', Sir Edward Dering condemned the 'general increase of open libertinism', which was tearing the social fabric apart. He waxed nostalgic about the traditional world in which citizens called out to him, 'God bless your worship.' But now, he wrote later in 1641, 'all's undone, by breaking asunder that well ordered chain of government, which from the chair of

---

[123] *The Stage-Players Complaint* (1641), 2

[124] Huntington petition in Northamptonshire Record Office, Finch-Hatton Ms. FH/2609.

[125] *A Defensive Vindication of the Publike Liturgy, Established Ceremonies, and Settled Patrimony, of the Church of England* (1641), 3, 7, 23, 38; I.W., *Certaine Reasons why the Book of Common-Prayer being Corrected should Continue*, 'to the reader', sig. A2v. See also Andrew Larmont's complaint against the 'giddiness' of parishioners at Claybrooke, Leicestershire, that threatened 'to subvert all order and government, and bring the church of God into confusion' (Bodleian Library, J. Walker Ms. c.11, f. 60).

[126] Matthias Milward, *The Souldiers Triumph: and the Preachers Glory* (1641), 8.

Jupiter reacheth down by several golden links, even to the protection of the poorest creature that now lives among us.' Dering was particularly unnerved by the root-and-branch petitions and by the rough artisans who promoted them. 'There is at present such an all-daring liberty, such a lewd licentiousness for venting all men's several senses (senseless senses) in religion, as never was in any age in any nation until this present parliament was met together,' he told the House of Commons in November 1641. People were saying that 'Sir Edward Dering who fought in the front, wheels about', and by January 1642 this former puritan sympathizer had become an apologist for the Church of England.[127]

It became a familiar argument in these years that criticism led to subversion, reform led to extremism, and that puritans opened the doors to antinomianism. If left unchecked, thought Joseph Hall, the result would be 'chaos . . . anarchy, and . . . all imaginable ruin and confusion'.[128] The attack on the bishops would lead to 'misery', 'confusion, anarchy, and schism', and a reign of 'barbarism and duncery', claimed other conservative clerics.[129] Bring down episcopacy, warned Huntingdonshire petitioners, and down will come monarchy, nobility, gentry, order, law, learning, and 'all true religion'.[130] The greatest danger, thought Edward Browne, lay with radicals, 'whose minds like footballs or bubbles of soap in the air are thrown and tossed to and fro with every wind of doctrine, such who under pretence of religion deride and condemn all good order in church and commonwealth, and do so labour to overthrow the known monarchical and hierarchical state of the kingdom.'[131]

Much more was at stake than a system of ecclesiastical organization. Secular authority was also at risk. 'They who despise Aaron will easily rebel against Moses also,' warned John Reading, a canon of Canterbury, at the 1641 Maidstone summer assizes.[132] Religious diversity, pamphleteers claimed, was likely 'to shake the whole foundation and to destroy both church and

---

[127] British Library, Add. Ms. 26786, ff. 25, 36, 59–60; British Library, Stowe Ms. 184, f. 43, and passim; Jansson, (ed.), *Proceedings in the Opening Session of the Long Parliament . . . Vol. 2*, 187–8; [Sir Edward Dering], *A Most Worthy Speech . . . concerning the Lyturgy of the Church of England* (1641); idem, *A Collection of Speeches* (1642), sigs. A3–A3v, 106, 166; Larking (ed.), *Proceedings, Principally in the County of Kent*, 47; Derek Hirst, 'The Defection of Sir Edward Dering, 1640–1641', *The Historical Journal*, 15 (1972), 193–208.

[128] [Joseph Hall], *A Survay of That Foolish, Seditious, Scandalous, Prophane Libell, The Protestation Protested* (1641), sig. A2v, 12.

[129] British Library, Stowe Ms. 184, f. 41v, Nathaniel Ward to Sir Edward Dering; [George Morley], *A Modest Advertisment Concerning The Present Controversie about Church-Government* (1641), 9, 20; Cambridge University Library, Ms. Mn. 1. 45 (Baker transcripts), 30.

[130] Northamptonshire Record Office, Finch-Hatton Ms. 2609.

[131] Browne, *Sir James Cambels Clarkes Disaster by Making Books*, 6.

[132] [John Reading], *A Sermon Delivered at Maidstone in Kent at the Assizes there held, August 23, 1641* (1642), 15; Matthews, *Walker Revised*, 224.

kingdom'.[133] 'No mitre, no sceptre' was a common metonymic rephrasing of the Jacobean adage, 'no bishops, no king'.[134]

Edward Layfield, the Laudian minister of All Hallows, Barking, made explicit the link between religious and social rebellion, saying, 'They are ... like Jack Straw and Wat Tyler [the leaders of medieval peasants' revolts] that speak against the ceremonies of the church.'[135] Henry Rogers, a canon of Hereford Cathedral, blamed the revolt against the King on heretical preachers with their medieval levelling text, 'When Adam delved and Eve span | Who was then the gentleman? And so ... would have no man above another but all men alike and so throw down all government, learning and religion.' King Charles's troubles, by this account, stemmed from his 'ungracious and ungrateful people ... the base rabble rout', who 'assemble themselves and will prescribe a way of government to the parliament and make laws of their own'.[136]

Laudians became adept at deploying this rhetoric, converting alarm at the fate of the Church of England into propaganda and support for the royalist cause. By this interpretation the religious revolt was a social revolt, driving a political and constitutional revolution. Only a restoration of traditional religious discipline, with prayer book, hierarchy, and episcopacy, could retrieve the situation. And only the King, who declared himself 'resolved to live and die in the protestant religion', could safeguard church and state against chaos.[137]

APPEALS TO THE MAGISTRATES

Religious politics became especially vicious and volatile between 1640 and 1642, but the public statutes governing religious behaviour remained unchanged. The Elizabethan Act of Uniformity remained in force, even if its practical provisions proved unenforceable. It was still strictly illegal to neglect or disrupt community worship, to seek sermons or services outside one's parish, or to derogate, deprave, or modify the Book of Common Prayer.[138] In former times churchwardens and incumbents reported violations to the ecclesiastical authorities, who took action ex officio to sanction offenders.[139] However, by this time the disciplinary mechanisms of the established church were in abeyance.

---

[133] *Religions Lotterie, or The Churches Amazement* (1642), title page.
[134] British Library, Harleian Ms. 4931, f. 103.   [135] *Commons Journals*, ii. 35.
[136] British Library, Add. Ms. 70003, ff. 236–7 (Dr Rogers's sermon in Herefordshire, April 1642); Matthews, *Walker Revised*, 195.   [137] PRO, SP16/486/90.
[138] *Statutes of the Realm*, 1 Eliz. cap. 2.
[139] Ronald A. Marchant, *The Church Under the Law; Justice, Administration and Discipline in the Diocese of York 1560–1640* (Cambridge, 1969); Martin Ingram, *Church Courts, Sex and Marriage in England, 1570–1640* (Cambridge, 1987).

Normally the secular magistrates sat on the sidelines, allowing the Church of England to police itself, handing out admonitions, penances, and excommunications. But as the church courts fell into disarray, this disciplinary framework ceased to be available. At the very time when the church most needed its powers of persuasion and punishment the apparatus of visitations, presentments, and investigations came to a halt. At the very moment when historians would be most grateful for the records of this process they shrink away to almost nothing. The King's proclamation of 10 December 1641 requiring 'obedience to the laws ordained for establishing of the true religion in this kingdom of England' gave comfort to Laudians and conservatives, but it did little to halt the disintegration of the church.[140]

The office side of most diocesan courts ground to a halt during 1641, hastened by the downfall of the High Commission. The gap was filled by a flurry of religious complaints before assize courts and quarter sessions, as Laudians found other ways of fighting back. The pressing of indictments 'for depraving the Book of Common Prayer' formed part of the armoury of the aggrieved conservative priest in the opening months of 1642, at a time when most of the church courts were defunct and half the bishops were in prison. A Lincolnshire yeoman, Christopher Dennys, made direct reference to this practice when he later testified against William Pavey, the Laudian rector of Mareham-le-Fen. He told the Committee for Scandalous Ministers 'that since the bishops' courts were down, so that he could not trouble those persons they call puritans there as he hath formerly often done, he [Pavey] hath caused them to be indicted at the sessions and gotten men to swear against them, whom the town and country knows to be lewd and bad persons.'[141] Sir Simonds D'Ewes observed in January 1642, 'I cannot deny that the ecclesiastical courts are reasonably quiet, but some active judges in their late circuits did very much press on the finding of indictments for the same offence.'[142]

In Staffordshire the embattled vicar of Ellastone, John Hill, sought support from the quarter sessions against his local religious enemies.[143] So too in Leicestershire Thomas Pestell referred his problems at Packington to the justices at the county sessions.[144] In Sussex, after a year or more of troubles at Horsted Parva, the Laudian rector, John Peckham, reported troublemakers to the Easter 1642 quarter sessions.[145] Another Sussex

[140] James F. Larkin (ed.), *Stuart Royal Proclamations, vol, II. Royal Proclamations of King Charles I, 1625–1646* (Oxford, 1983), 752–4.

[141] Hill, 'Royalist Clergy of Lincolnshire', 107.

[142] Coates, Young, and Snow (eds.), *Private Journals of the Long Parliament 3 January to 5 March 1642*, 138.   [143] Staffordshire Record Office, Q/SR/251/29, /31.

[144] Bodleian Library, J. Walker Ms. c.11, f. 14.

[145] East Sussex Record Office, QR/E/56/18. John Peckham, who had been rector of Little Horsted since 1623, was sequestered from his living in 1643 (Matthews, *Walker Revised*, 360).

Laudian, John Wilson of Arlington, complained to the quarter sessions in July 1642 when parishioners disputed his teaching on images and obedience. He too sought intervention from the secular magistrates to sustain his shrinking authority and to punish his local opponents.[146]

Richard Drake of Radwinter likewise sought relief from his radical parishioners, pressing charges against his tormentors at the Chelmsford assize in July 1642.[147] So too did Robert Abbot of Cranbrook, Kent, when his breakaway parishioners and their inspiring lecturer, Edward Bright, were indicted at the summer Maidstone assize for illegal attendance at conventicles.[148] In County Durham, the conservative minister of Muggleswick turned to the quarter sessions when he could no longer maintain Communion discipline.[149] Rarely do we know the outcome of these cases, but with the kingdom tumbling into civil war the issue must surely have been moot.

PRACTICAL PETITIONING

Finally, conservative clergy lent some support to the lay activist petitioners who strove to salvage, if not safeguard, episcopacy and the Book of Common Prayer. They were engaged, at least tangentially, in boosting the petitions, gathering hands, and helping to mobilize opinion. But there were good reasons for Laudians to maintain a low profile in a campaign led by conservative gentry.

One glimpse of this mobilization comes from Devon, where Robert Dove, the vicar of Ilsington, 'bestirred himself to get hands to uphold episcopacy and the government of bishops', in February 1641. One observer remarked that 'he solicited hedgers of the hedge, ploughmen of the plough, threshers in the barns; and some of them being asked what they had done, said that now they should have peace for evermore, for these notes were to conclude peace and had been sent by the governors of the church.'[150] Another comes from Cheshire, where William Clarke, a minor canon of Chester Cathedral, attacked 'grand enemies' of the church in November 1641. Urging the

[146] East Sussex Record Office, QR/E/57/60–64. John Wilson was vicar of Arlington from 1630 until his sequestration in 1643 (Matthews, *Walker Revised*, 362).

[147] Bodleian Library, Rawlinson Ms. D. 158. Drake was to have his day in court on 21 July 1642.

[148] J. S. Cockburn (ed.), *Calendar of Assize Records: Kent Indictments. Charles I* (1995), 449. Those indicted included yeomen, husbandmen, labourers, mercers, weavers, clothiers, and a barber, as well as Edward Bright, clerk.

[149] Durham University Library, Special Collections, Mickleton-Spearman Ms. other MSP 9, ii. 238.

[150] R. N. Worth (ed.), *The Buller Papers. A Series of Historical Documents Selected from the Family Records of the Bullers of Shillingham and Morval in the County of Cornwall* (privately printed, 1895), 33–4; Matthews, *Walker Revised*, 79.

congregation to renounce 'novelties, alterations and changes' emanating from Westminster, he requested them at the end of the service to 'repair to the communion table and there subscribe the petition' in favour of the Book of Common Prayer. At this point some of the godly walked out, but others lined up to subscribe (though strict ceremonialists may have wondered at this use of the holy table).[151] Hugh Barcroft, the rector of Wyberton, Lincolnshire, was likewise 'a great instrument in getting hands to the petition for the holding up of bishops in their former glory, he urged many to set their hands, telling such as scrupled at it he would open the meaning of it to them.'[152]

Laudians also set out to thwart petitions with which they disagreed. Robert Sugden, vicar of Benhall, Suffolk reacted angrily to 'a petition for the removing the popish lords and bishops out of the parliament, saying it came from a pack of puritans, and...if he had it he would rend it in pieces and burn it.'[153]

To the extent that Laudian conformists were diehard enthusiasts for ceremonial worship, who believed both prayer book and episcopacy to be congruent with the word of God, they may have found it difficult to lend wholehearted support to some of the conservative county petitions. The vision of the Church of England espoused in many of them was markedly at odds with the programme of the Laudian ascendancy. Petitioners were now willing to make tactical and rhetorical concessions in order to mitigate the present emergency, though earlier, when ceremonialists held sway, they were content to line up and kneel. They argued for episcopacy now on the grounds of its history and utility, rather than divine ordination. They recommended religious arrangements for their 'benefit and comfort', and upheld the church government that was 'most prudent and most safe'.[154] Conservative activists set out to save the prayer book, not by rigidly defending every phrase and rubric, but by conceding that it might well need some reform. Also they were not averse to distancing themselves from the Laudians, if that would help save the church. Even petitions on behalf of the established religious order criticized recent 'exorbitancies', 'abuses', and 'innovations'.[155]

---

[151] Bodleian Library, Nalson Ms. 13/28–31; Judith Maltby, *Prayer Book and People in Elizabethan and Early Stuart England* (Cambridge, 1998), 153–4.

[152] Hill, 'Royalist Clergy of Lincolnshire', 45.

[153] Holmes (ed.), *Suffolk Committees for Scandalous Ministers*, 69.

[154] Sir Thomas Aston (ed.), *A Collection of Sundry Petitions Presented to the King's Most excellent Majestie* (1642), 24, 34, and passim.

[155] Judith Maltby, 'Petitions for Episcopacy and the Book of Common Prayer on the Eve of the Civil War 1641–1642', in Stephen Taylor (ed.), *From Cranmer to Davidson: A Church of England Miscellany* (Church of England Record Society, 7, 1999), 153, 155. Cf. [Robert Sanderson], *Ad Clerum. A Sermon Preached...8 Octob. 1641* (1670), 19, which remarked of the recent ritual innovators, 'let them answer it as well as they can, it is not my business now to plead for them.'

Bedfordshire petitioners, for example, acknowledged 'the exorbitancies of ecclesiastical jurisdictions and the innovations lately obtruded upon our church', as 'great and insupportable grievances', though not enough to justify the subversion of established religion.[156] Gloucestershire petitioners praised the Church of England as 'the best constituted that any kingdom hath been blessed withal since the Apostles' times', but were willing nonetheless to correct any faults that 'of late times' had crept in, in 'these times of faulty bishops'. They asked that 'the precious may be separated from the vile', and that 'offensive' ceremonies be 'warily reformed', for the greater good of the whole.[157] Others called for 'a reformation of the abuses and punishment of offenders',[158] and a restoration of the church to 'its former purity', before 'things of ill consequence' were 'thrust into it'.[159]

Conservative pamphleteers and controversialists made a similar pitch, conceding that the Laudian regime of the late 1630s had endangered the Church of England. If there were abuses, let them be removed, if errors, let them be corrected, said Thomas Warmstry, so that the Church of England might continue as 'the pattern of the world'.[160]

'Pruning and reformation I allow, but eradication and deformation I tremble to hear of,' wrote the lay apologist for episcopacy, Sir Francis Wortley.[161] Individual bishops may have over-reached themselves, others suggested, but 'the offenders once being punished and removed, the function might remain'.[162]

As to the prayer book, the author of *A Plea for Moderation* acknowledged some defects in 'those overgrown ceremonies in the time of hierarchical power', but defended the established church against radical 'distractions'. English religion, he acknowledged, 'hath been of late dressed in too gaudy, too garish an attire', but 'libertine' extremism was now stripping her 'stark naked'. The proper remedy, this layman proposed, was reform and adjustment, not outright abolition.[163] Another lay conservative who championed the Church of England as 'the most true catholic Christian religion in the

---

[156] Maltby, 'Petitions for Episcopacy', 153.

[157] Gloucestershire Record Office, D2510/14, Letters of John Smyth of Nibley; Maltby, 'Petitions for Episcopacy', 162.

[158] Maltby, 'Petitions for Episcopacy', 124 (Huntingdonshire petition).

[159] Ibid., 126 (Somerset petition).

[160] Thomas Warmstry, *A Convocation Speech ... Against Images, Altars, crosses, the new Canons and the Oath, etc.* (1641), 2, 10; idem, *Pax Vobis of a Charme for tumultuous Spirits* (1641), title page, 14, 19, 45.

[161] Sir Francis Wortley, *ΕΛΕΥΘΕΡΩΣΙΣ ... Truth Asserted ... viz. That Episcopacie is Iure Divino* (1641), 'to the reader'.

[162] Thomas Heywood [?], *Reader, Here you'l plainly see Iudgement perverted* (1641), 2.

[163] *A Plea for Moderation* (1642), 4, 5, 6, 8.

world, both in purity of doctrine and decent orderly ceremonies', nonetheless declared himself against 'all papistical idolatry and Arminian pride in episcopacy', as was prudent in 1642.[164] Edward Reynolds of Braunston, Northamptonshire, a champion of the beauty of holiness, conceded in 1642 'that needless ceremonies have of late too much crept into the church', although he was much more offended by irreverent sectarianism.[165]

The spectre of a radical undisciplined laity frightened moderate puritans as well as orthodox clerics. The backlash against the unpoliced religious diversity of 1641 produced fresh affection for the traditional Church of England. The prospect of losing everything led to proposals for an episcopacy shorn of abuse and a prayer book that did not give offence. Now more than ever, conservatives claimed, the kingdom needed the disciplinary authority of bishops and the liturgical anchor of the Book of Common Prayer. Both might be salvaged by acknowledging their imperfections. The circumstances led some Laudian ceremonialists to make common cause with mainstream conformists against the ravages of revolution, although most would have preferred no change at all. It would not be unreasonable to ask these Anglican apologists, where was your moderation before the Long Parliament?

Rather that testifying to an enduring popular commitment to the Book of Common Prayer, many of these conservative remarks and petitions can be read as signs of desperation. Rather than revealing deep-rooted attachment to the liturgy and structures of the established church, they seem to be clutching at straws. They were part of a strategy to save the church, exhibiting not just fondness for the familiar but fear of the consequences if all were abandoned. This was a prayer-book Anglicanism driven by anxiety, a conformism shaped by fear of those 'factious spirits [that] do evidently endanger the peace of church and state'.[166]

Shocked by attacks on episcopacy and the prayer book, and by mounting religious disorders, defenders of the Church of England fought a series of rearguard actions. They continued to use all available media to press their case, through sermons, pamphlets, parliamentary speeches, and petitions. Faced with the dismemberment of their church and the abandonment of familiar forms of worship, some conservative spokesmen became willing to

---

[164] Edward Browne, *A Potent Vindication for Book-making* (1642), 8.

[165] Edward Reynolds, *Evgenia's Teares for great Brittaynes Distractions* (1642), 24.

[166] House of Lords Record Office, Main Papers, 20 December 1641. My interpretation differs from Maltby, *Prayer Book and People in Elizabethan and Early Stuart England*; eadem, 'Petitions for Episcopacy', in Taylor (ed.), *From Cranmer to Davidson*, 103–68. Cf. Peter Lake, 'Puritans, Popularity and Petitions: Local Politics in National Context, Cheshire, 1641', in Cogswell, Cust, and Lake (eds.), *Politics, Religion, and Popularity in Early Stuart Britain*, 259–89.

adjust their positions. There was some convergence of views, at least for tactical purposes, as former advocates of reform discovered virtues in the status quo, and former Laudians acknowledged the possible necessity of alteration. Only following the collapse of Laudianism, and the flows of patronage Laudians commanded, did this less strident and more pragmatic voice come to the fore. By then, of course, it was too late.[167]

---

[167] On the Laudian revival of the 1650s, see Robert S. Bosher, *The Making of the Restoration Settlement: The Influence of the Laudians 1649–1662* (1951).

PART III

THE NATIONAL CONVERSATION

12

The Press Overpressed

The period between the summoning of the Long Parliament and the outbreak of civil war saw sudden and significant changes in the writing, printing, publishing, distribution, readership, and impact of pamphlets and books. The material technology of printing barely altered, but its social and political circumstances were transformed. A revolution in communications accompanied, documented, and facilitated the revolutionary changes in politics and religion. A quickened circulation of texts contributed to an intensified national conversation.

This chapter traces the development of the press, from constraint to liberation, in the media storm that preceded the civil war. It begins by sketching the regime of constraint and censorship that prevailed before 1640 and which broke down in the opening phases of the English Revolution. A central section deals with the explosion of print and the avalanche of text that erupted when customary controls broke down. Finally, it examines attempts to roll back the revolution in print culture and to reimpose restraints, in the face of mounting complaints against libellous and scandalous publications. It prepares the way for further discussion of the opening of discourse and the expansion of the public sphere.

CONSTRAINT

Printing was a mature trade, already a century and a half old, by the time of Charles I. Around two dozen printing houses in London and the universities produced some six or seven hundred publications a year, many of them substantial texts or weighty volumes. Scores of printers, binders, publishers, and booksellers occupied stalls and shops in the vicinity of St Paul's. Others were clustered around Fleet Street and the Exchange, and in the vicinity of the court.[1]

---

[1] Peter W. M. Blayney, *The Bookshops in Paul's Cross Churchyard* (Occasional Papers of the Bibliography Society, no. 5, 1990), 5.

The industry operated under a double set of controls, with the monopolistic Company of Stationers safeguarding commercial privileges and profit, and the chaplains of the Archbishop of Canterbury and the Bishop of London watching out for heresy, nonconformity, and sedition. John Milton would refer to these licensers derisively as 'our inquisiturient bishops and the attendant minorites their chaplains'.[2] The book trade was further subject to surveillance by the Privy Council, Star Chamber, and Court of High Commission. Informers reported infringements and snitched on illicit publications. The licensing system imposed prior restraint to ensure conformity, and to prevent certain works from being published; a regime of corrective censorship sought after-market punishment for offensive publications, whether licensed or not. Writers took greater risks than printers, as the authorities distinguished between mundane artisanal production and the more dangerous authorial voice.

One of the most notorious sufferers in the early part of Charles I' s reign was Alexander Leighton, whose *Appeal to the Parliament; or Sion's Plea Against the Prelates* (1628) cost him a beating, branding, pillorying, fining, and ten years imprisonment. Leighton was made 'a theatre of misery to men and angels', he later protested, for 'nothing but a book'. The severity of Leighton's punishment, and the renewed attention it received in Parliament in 1640, helped focus animosity against the Laudian bishops.[3] 'See the strange alteration of these times', wrote the London minister Henry Burton in the late 1620s, when the bishops 'gave liberty to popish Arminian books to be published, and restraint to their opposites.' Whereas Edward Elton's Calvinist 'book of the commandments' was burned at Paul's Cross, John Cosin's Arminian book of devotions, which Burton thought 'popish and worthy the fire', was sponsored through three editions.[4]

---

[2] Sheila Lambert, 'The Printers and the Government, 1604–1640' in Robin Myers and Michael Harris (eds.), *Aspects of Printing from 1600* (Oxford, 1987), 9; Michael Treadwell, 'Lists of Master Printers: The Size of the London Printing Trade, 1637–1723', in Myers and Harris (eds.), *Aspects of Printing from 1600*, 143–6; John Milton, *Areopagitica; A Speech of Mr. John Milton For the Liberty of Unlicenc'd Printing* (1644), 9.

[3] Maija Jansson (ed.), *Proceedings in the Opening Session of the Long Parliament . . . Volume 1: 3 November–19 December 1640* (Rochester, NY, 2000), 58, 63, 66. Leighton's *Appeal to the Parliament* was published in Amsterdam in 1628 and republished in London in 1640 or 1641. His sufferings are summarized in Alexander Leighton, *An Epitome or Briefe Discoverie, From the Beginning to the Ending, of the many and great Troubles that Dr. Leighton suffered* (1646), 90. See also Stephen Foster, *Notes from the Caroline Underground: Alexander Leighton, the Puritan Triumvirate, and the Laudian Reaction to Nonconformity* (Hamden, Conn. 1978).

[4] Henry Burton, *A Tryall of Private Devotions* (1628), sigs. A, A2; Edward Elton, *Gods Holy Mind Touching Matters Morall* (1625); John Cosin, *A Collection of Private Devotions* (1627). The Arminian Richard Montague expressed satisfaction to John Cosin in 1625 at 'what a goodly fire our Sabbatarian heretics made at the Cross', adding, 'it is well the books made a fire, though not all, I doubt' (George Ornsby (ed.), *The Correspondence of John Cosin*, 2 vols. (Surtees Society, Durham, 1869), i. 59, 61).

Burton himself would become a celebrity victim of Laudian censorship, alongside the physician John Bastwick and the lawyer William Prynne. All three suffered pain, degradation, and prolonged incarceration for publications that the authorities deemed scandalous, libellous, or seditious. Their books were burned before them in public while they stood in the pillory in 1637, each had his ears severed, and Prynne was branded on his face with the letters 'S.L' (for 'seditious libel', though he insisted they stood for *'stigmata Laudis'*). One of Prynne's printers, William Jones, was 'deprived of his calling', and another, John Wharton, appeared five times before Star Chamber and was held in the Fleet prison. One of those who informed against him, John Chilliburne, was rewarded by being made a licenser of ballads.[5]

State control was further tightened with the Star Chamber decree of 1637, which came out just a month after the sentence against Prynne. Most of the master Stationers supported this order, which strengthened their monopoly and their right to search for infringements. The decree not only ordained that no book could be published without licence, but also that books already licensed should not be reprinted unless their licence was renewed. A new edition of Foxe's *Acts and Monuments* fell foul of this provision, and imported copies of Lewis Bayly's *Practice of Piety*, which had already gone through thirty-six editions, were kept off the market. Disputes in the wake of the decree more often concerned rights and ownership than controversial content, but stationers could be forced to close their shops for selling banned books by Burton, Bastwick, and Prynne.[6]

In 1640, when it became safe to say such things, petitioners to Parliament complained of godly authors who were punished and good books 'denied the press'. The City Petition of December 1640, popularly known as 'the root and branch petition', charged the prelates with 'the hindering of godly books to be printed, the blotting out or perverting those which they suffer, all or most of that which strikes either at popery or Arminianism, the adding of what or where pleaseth them, and the restraint of reprinting books formerly

---

[5] *CSPD 1640–41*, 327. Petition of Hannah Reynolds on behalf of her father, John Wharton, Lambeth Palace Library, Ms. Misc. 943, 733. The same John Chilliburne was involved in the entrapment of John Lilburne for producing and importing forbidden books (*A Coppy of a Letter Written by John Lilburne* (1640), 10).

[6] *A Decree of Starre-Chamber, Concerning Printing* (1637); John Rushworth, *Historical Collections of Private Proceedings of State* (8 vols., 1680–1701), ii. 450, 463, 616; Cyprian Blagden, 'The Stationers' Company in the Civil War Period', *The Library*, 5th ser., 13 (1958), 7; Sheila Lambert, 'State Control of the Press in Theory and Practice: The Role of the Stationers' Company before 1640', in Robin Myers and Michael Harris (eds.), *Censorship and the Control of Print in England and France 1600–1910* (Winchester, 1992), 22; Joseph Black, ' "Pikes and Protestations": Scottish Texts in England, 1639–40', *Publishing History*, 42 (1997), 5, for the case of the stationer John Bartlett.

licensed, without relicensing'. 'Lascivious, idle and unprofitable books' had been permitted, it claimed, along with 'popish' and 'dangerous' works, whereas works of godliness (presumably puritan criticism and Calvinist theology) had been suppressed.[7] Other petitions protested that under the prelatical regime of the 1630s, 'many books of orthodox divines have been mangled, corrupted, or suppressed' while lascivious and superstitious texts enjoyed free circulation.[8] Daniel Featley's sermons were said to have been 'castrated' or 'gelt' by the expunging of thirty pages, including 'masculine' passages against images that had passed scrutiny under the previous archbishop. William Fenner's books 'were denied the press', and only appeared after his death in 1640.[9] The Commons committee on religion heard in November 1640 how 'truth is suppressed', and 'the most learned labours of our ancient and best divines' had been 'corrected and defaced' by 'our late imprimaturs'.[10]

Further elaboration of these charges appears in complaints on behalf of William Jones, 'a man of learning and integrity', whose *Commentary upon the Epistles to Philemon and to the Hebrews* (1635) was so altered by the licenser, Dr Samuel Baker, as to misrepresent the author's intentions. Sir Edward Dering, chair of the House of Commons committee that later took up Jones's case, declared in February 1641, 'by this card you may see what compass the great directors and correctors of our church do sail, and to what port they are making'. The licenser had evidently 'dashed and altered' some five or six hundred lines of Jones's text, blotting out 'sound doctrine' and substituting phrases 'to the advantage of our Roman adversaries'. Whereas the author had advocated 'a serious contemplation of the sabbath', the licensers had 'expunged' words incompatible with 'the Book of Sports, much

---

[7] *The First and Large Petition Of the Citie of London . . . For a Reformation in Church-government, as also for the abolishment of Episcopacie* (1641), 5–6.

[8] Petition of Suffolk ministers, January 1641; Maija Jansson (ed.), *Proceedings in the Opening Session of the Long Parliament . . . Volume 2: 21 December 1640–20 March 1641* (Rochester, NY, 2000), 211.

[9] William Prynne, *Canterburies Doome* (1646), 108, 254; British Library, Add. Ms. 26786, f. 4; Lambert B. Larking (ed.), *Proceedings, Principally in the County of Kent* (Camden Society, first series, vol. lxxv, 1862), 84; Jansson (ed.), *Proceedings in the Opening Session of the Long Parliament . . . Vol. 1*, 410–11. Maurice F. Bond (ed.), *The Manuscripts of the House of Lords, vol. xi (new series) Addenda 1514–1714* (1962), 420; Arnold Hunt, 'Licensing and Religious Censorship in Early Modern England', in Andrew Hadfield (ed.), *Literature and Censorship in Renaissance England* (Basingstoke and New York, 2001), 140–2. Daniel Featley, himself a licenser, published *Clavis Mystica: A Key Opening divers Difficult and Mysterious texts of Holy Scripture* in 1636, and testified at Archbishop Laud's trial about its expurgation. William Fenner was a puritan minister at Rochford, Essex. None of his sermons appeared in print before his death in 1640, although *A Divine Message to the Elect Soul* and *Christ's Alarm to Drowsie Saints* went through several editions in the 1640s and 1650s.

[10] [Sir Edward Dering], *Three Speeches of Sir Edward Dearings* (1641), 10–12; Larking (ed.), *Proceedings, Principally in the County of Kent*, 82–6.

of the same date'. And in perhaps the most egregious example, where Jones had written in his commentary on Hebrews 3: 14, 'we have begun in sound and pure religion, let us not end in popery', Baker had changed the last phrase to read 'let us not end in profaneness'. Jones's commentaries were indeed licensed for print, but, Dering claimed, with 'the life, the vigour, and, as it were, the eyes of them picked out'. Investors in this publication complained to the committee that 'Baker so abused the copy of it, [it] is worth little and cost them £400.'[11]

Another of the 'godly books' hindered from publication during the Laudian ascendancy was Francis Rous on *Catholick Charitie*, a Calvinist response to Christopher Potter's 1633 Arminian publication, *Want of Charitie Justly Charged* and the Romist treatise *Charity Mistaken*. When Rous eventually published this work in 1641, with a licence from the Bishop of London's chaplain dated 2 December 1640, he explained that though 'it came to birth' some years earlier 'there was no strength to deliver' against 'the judgement of those times'. A manuscript version circulated privately, perhaps reaching Rous's stepbrother John Pym, but the tract could not be printed until the politics of religion changed.[12] William Hinde's *Faithfull Remonstrance of the Holy Life and Happy Death of John Bruen* was said to have languished unpublished for a decade, 'suffering more than an ostracism, before it could be admitted to speak in the language of the press' in 1641.[13] Simonds D'Ewes likewise noted in the preface to *The Primitive Practice for Preserving Truth* (1645) that he penned it 'about eight years since' (i.e., 1637) but made no attempt to publish it when 'the press was then only open to matters of a contrary subject'.[14] John Vicars complained privately in 1636 that printing was 'nowadays prohibited' to God's people, 'especially if their writings have any least tang or tincture of opposition to Arminianism, yea or even to popery

---

[11] Lambeth Palace Library, Ms. Misc. 943, 735–7; Jansson (ed.), *Proceedings in the Opening Session of the Long Parliament . . . Vol. 2*, 525; Larking (ed.), *Proceedings, Principally in the County of Kent*, 89; Prynne, *Canterburies Doome*, 255. Jones was the minister of East Burgholt, Suffolk, and died in 1636. Some of his earlier work had been published by his namesake William Jones of Red Cross Street, who had also been one of the printers of Prynne's *Histrio-Mastix*. The 1635 edition of Jones's *Commentary* is an expensively produced folio of over 700 pages, and its backers may have been more concerned at its failure to sell than because the licensers had tampered with its content.

[12] Francis Rous, *Catholick Charitie* (1641), sig. A2. I owe this reference to Sears McGee, who is completing a major study of Rous and his circle. Other works written earlier but not publishable before 1641 include John Ley, *A Letter (Against the erection of an Altar) Written Iune 29, 1635* (1641), and John Eaton, *The Honey-Combe of Free Justification* (1642).

[13] William Hinde, *A Faithfull Remonstrance of the Holy Life and Happy Death of John Bruen* (1641), sig. A6.

[14] Simonds D'Ewes, *The Primitive Practice for Preserving Truth* (1645), sig. A3. I am grateful to Sears McGee for this reference.

itself.'[15] Even the publisher of the authorized *Foreign Occurrences* complained that 'the licenser...would not oftentimes let pass apparent truth, and in other things oftentimes so cross and alter, which made us almost weary of printing.'[16]

Recent scholarship has emphasized the limitations of Caroline censorship, depicting the regime as more capricious than oppressive. Revisionist and post-revisionist historians have pointed to cracks and loopholes that writers could exploit, and coded references they could use to transmit dangerous ideas.[17] As many as a third of all publications, mostly deemed lightweight or harmless, may have passed unregistered and unlicensed. Despite efforts by the authorities to tighten control, lazy, inattentive, or inconsistent licensing allowed potentially 'transgressive' texts to leak into the marketplace. Sometimes, if one licenser proved obdurate, another would oblige. Licensers admitted slackness, and favour to friends. Occasionally a stationer might independently restore the passages that the licenser had 'expunged and purged'.[18]

Readers could also turn to illicit or unauthorized publications, produced clandestinely or smuggled in from the Low Countries or Scotland. Although it was sometimes said that 'England's *Imprimatur* is worse than Italy's *Index Expurgatorius*', writers and publishers knew ways around both. 'Factious and malicious pamphlets' occasionally appeared despite official prohibition,

---

[15] Frederick S. Boas (ed.), *The Diary of Thomas Crosfield* (1935), 89.

[16] [Nathaniel Butter and Nicholas Bourne], *The Continuation of the Forraine Occurents*, no. 48 (11 January 1640/1), in Joad Raymond, *Pamphlets and Pamphleteering in Early Modern Britain* (Cambridge, 2003), 150.

[17] Annabel Patterson, *Censorship and Interpretation: The Conditions of Writing and Reading in Early Modern England* (Madison, 1984); Lambert, 'The Printers and the Government, 1604–1640', 1–29; Lambert, 'State Control of the Press in Theory and Practice', 1–32; A. B. Worden, 'Literature and Political Censorship in Early Modern England', in A. C. Duke and C. A. Tamse (eds.), *Too Mighty to be Free: Censorship and the Press in Britain and the Netherlands* (Zutphen, 1987), 45–62; Michael Mendle, 'De Facto Freedom, De Facto Authority: Press and Parliament, 1640–1643', *The Historical Journal*, 38 (1995), 307–32; Cyndia Susan Clegg, *Press Censorship in Elizabethan England* (Cambridge, 1997); eadem, *Press Censorship in Jacobean England* (Cambridge, 2001); Anthony Milton, 'Licensing, Censorship, and Religious Orthodoxy in Early Stuart England', *Historical Journal*, 41 (1998), 625–52; Debora Shuger, 'Civility and Censorship in Early Modern England', in Robert C. Post (ed.), *Censorship and Silencing: Practices of Cultural Regulation* (Los Angeles, 1998), 89–110; Andrew Hadfield, 'The Politics of Early Modern Censorship', in idem (ed.), *Literature and Censorship in Renaissance England*, 1–13.

[18] Nicholas Oakes appeared before Star Chamber in 1639 for reinserting 'some popish and unsound passages' in Francis de Sales, *An Introduction to a Devout Life*, which the licenser had removed. Copies of the book were burned in Smithfield market (James F. Larkin, *Stuart Royal Proclamations...1625–1646* (Oxford, 1983), 557–8). Dr Bray later excused himself for licensing books by the Arminian John Pocklington, 'the which he said passed his hands by a careless overview of them upon his good opinion of the author' (British Library, Add. Ms. 21935, f. 113; Larking (ed.), *Proceedings, Principally in the County of Kent*, 83–4).

often with government agents in pursuit.[19] Scottish propaganda in the late 1630s was said to have come out 'by owl-light in little books or ballads to be sold in the streets'.[20] Other controversial texts circulated privately in manuscript, while anonymous authors contributed libels and placards, pasquils and squibs, to a semi-public literary underground.

William Prynne's career is an extreme but telling example of a gadfly who continued to publish despite the most harsh impositions. Prynne's *Histrio-Mastix* (1633), the anti-theatrical diatribe that drew down the wrath of the court, was actually licensed and legitimately printed. The licenser, Thomas Buckner, a holdover appointee of the late Archbishop Abbott, apparently glanced at just 64 of Prynne's 1,006 pages, and found nothing amiss; he subsequently faced investigation and punishment, along with Prynne's printers and publishers. The Star Chamber judges deemed *Histrio-Mastix* to be 'monstrous', and in 1634 condemned the author to be put in the pillory, to have his ears cut off, and to suffer 'perpetual imprisonment', amongst other punishments and degradations. Prynne's book was the first to be burned in England by the common hangman. None of this stopped Prynne from writing, and several of the inflammatory pamphlets he composed while imprisoned in the Tower were secretly printed abroad. One of Prynne's most outrageous works, the anti-espiscopal *News from Ipswich*, was printed in Scotland and came out in three editions in 1636 under the pseudonym Matthew White. Archbishop Laud acquired two copies from the Bishop of Exeter, 'which were sent thither to a stationer with blank covers'. When Star Chamber condemned Prynne to even more severe punishment in June 1637, alongside Bastwick and Burton, it stipulated that he be deprived of 'pen, ink or paper' and have no other books but the Bible, the prayer book, and conformable books of devotion. Prynne published nothing more until his triumphant rehabilitation as one of the 'holy martyrs' at the end of 1640.[21]

Few authors suffered the mutilations or incarcerations of Leighton, Burton, Bastwick, and Prynne, although several experienced frustration and inhibition. No printer or stationer endured physical disfigurement, although raids and disruption of trade were not uncommon. The Caroline system was not monolithic, but it limited press production, encouraged self-censorship, and constrained the market in opinion and ideas. The pressures were usually more subtle than savage. Whereas some authors withheld their works or chose not to put pen to paper, others accepted the licensers' excisions and alterations as

---

[19] *CSPD 1640–41*, 530; Larkin, *Stuart Royal Proclamations . . . 1625–1646*, 703–5.
[20] D.L., *The Scots Scouts Discoverie by Their London Intelligencer* (1642), 30.
[21] Lambeth Palace Library, Ms. Misc. 943, 270; Rushworth, *Historical Collections*, ii. appendix, 69.

conditions for going into press. As in other areas of English public life, conformist rigidities became especially demanding in the later 1630s.

Most of the works deemed 'seditious' before 1640 were printed abroad, beyond the reach of episcopal licensing and outside the Stationers' jurisdiction. An unknown number emerged illicitly from shadowy English presses. 'Seditious pamphlets . . . are spreading everywhere', Archbishop Laud complained in 1639, when he sought the Bishop of Chester's help to locate 'the author or spreader' of publications friendly to the Scots.[22] Laud also worked through the English ambassador at The Hague to seek Dutch assistance against publications by 'the fierce faction at Amsterdam', with only limited success.[23]

Bibles printed in Holland, and other books printed without the Stationers' authority, were officially forbidden, though that did not prevent a lively traffic in such publications. In May 1640 a Norwich bookseller, Abraham Attfen, who acknowledged 'receiving and vending' books from overseas, promised 'not to meddle again' with such contraband products.[24] An intercepted shipment of Bibles, prayer books, and psalm books, brought out of the Low Countries, was still being held by parliamentary authority in the spring of 1642, when the Stationers still hoped to exercise their privileges.[25]

Local magistrates generally cooperated in the suppression of illicit publications, not by energetically looking for them but by reporting such items to the central authorities as came to their attention. In April 1639 a Cambridgeshire yeoman, Henry Lawrence of Pampisford, surprised local justices by coming forward with two illicit Scottish publications, *The Late Proceedings* of 1637 and *The Protestation of the Covenanters* of 1638. They had been left behind in his house, he said, by 'one Mr Davy', a London shopkeeper from Fleet Street, who was a suitor to his daughter, and Lawrence thought the pamphlets should be handed in. It is not clear whether the yeoman's report came from a sense of duty, a desire to be rid of potentially incriminating items, or because he wished to thwart his daughter's suitor. But the case throws interesting light onto informal distribution networks and the operation of post-publication censorship. The magistrates, John Millecent and Michael Dalton, reported their discovery to Secretary Windebank, who referred the matter to the Attorney General John Bankes.[26]

---

[22] Staffordshire Record Office, Correspondence of Bishop Bridgeman, D. 1287/18/2, f. 182.
[23] E. G. W. Bill, *Catalogue of Manuscripts in Lambeth Palace Library, Mss. 2341–3119* (1983), 65.
[24] *CSPD 1640*, 411. Attfen was cited before the High Commission and questioned by the King's printers.
[25] Vernon F. Snow and Anne Steele Young (eds.), *The Private Journals of the Long Parliament 7 March to 1 June March 1642* (New Haven and London, 1987), 129; [Michael Sparke?], *Scintilla, or A Light Broken into darke Warehouses* (1641), 3.
[26] Bodleian Library, Ms. Bankes 65/2, f. 94.

The security of the regime depended on control of the written word. But the clandestine circulation of Scottish books and ballads, and their occasional discovery in the hands of English countrymen and soldiers, shows that security was sometimes breached. 'There hath been such a number of ballad-makers and pamphlet writers employed this year', many of them pro-Scottish or anti-prelatical, observed an anonymous publication from the time of the second Bishops' War.[27] Underground printing became more ambitious, and there was a growing traffic in illicit imports. One copy of the *Information . . . from the Scottish Nation* was found beneath a stone in Braintree churchyard when troops bound for Scotland were quartered nearby.[28] Another clandestine pamphlet passed from a Suffolk clothier into the hands of a recent military recruit.[29] In April 1640 the Council identified Captain Audley, 'dwelling in Bloomsbury, near the cherry garden', as 'a spreader of libels and Scottish pamphlets'.[30] More Scottish imprints were available from a distributor who 'lurks about Grays Inn in a satin doublet, with his man Primacombe following him with a cloak bag full of books'. In September an informer, John Highland, told Archbishop Laud that 'there are thirty in the city have joined together to maintain a press to print seditious and libellous books.'[31]

Facing a national emergency in 1640 with the war with Scotland, the government intensified its crackdown on unauthorized texts, whether popish, Presbyterian or, sectarian. The new Laudian canons threatened excommunication against 'the makers, importers, printers, and publishers or dispensers of any book, writing, or scandalous pamphlet, devised against the discipline of the Church of England',[32] and the Privy Council (of which Laud was a leading member) ordered all 'libellous and seditious pamphlets and discourses sent from Scotland' to be destroyed, lest they 'raise mutiny and sedition in the kingdom'.[33] Prohibited works were ordered burned by the hangman in Smithfield Market, and Londoners were treated to several such fires in the months before the Long Parliament. Since the burning of

---

[27] *Vox Borealis, or The Northern Discoverie* [1641, written 1640], sig. Bv; C. H. Firth, 'Ballads on the Bishops' Wars, 1638–40', *Scottish Historical Review*, 3 (1906), 261.

[28] *CSPD 1640*, 622.   [29] Ibid., 635, 638; PRO, SP16/465/43.   [30] *CSPD 1640*, 27.

[31] *CSPD 1640–41*, 40. This may have been the so-called Cloppenburg press, perhaps brought over from Amsterdam by Richard Overton. See A. F. Johnson, 'The "Cloppenburg" Press, 1640, 1641', *The Library*, 5th ser., 13 (1958), 280–2. I am grateful to David Como for discussion of this point.

[32] William Laud, 'Constitutions and Canons Ecclesiastical', in *The Works of the most Reverend Father in God, William Laud, D.D.*, 7 vols., ed. W. Scott and J. Bliss (Oxford, 1847–60), v. 620–2.

[33] Larkin (ed.), *Stuart Royal Proclamation . . . 1625–1646*, 703–5; British Library, Add. Ms. 11045, vol. v., f., 108; Firth, 'Ballads on the Bishops' Wars', 257–73; *Vox Borealis*, sig. B3.

Histrio-Mastix in 1634 this had become a ritualized, theatricalized process, with trumpeters announcing the arrival of the hangman who brandished his ropes above the fire.[34]

The crackdown affected readers as well as writers, encompassing the owners, makers, and distributors of forbidden texts. In April 1640, for example, the High Commission went after a Wiltshire man, Obadiah Blisset of Marlborough, 'for writing to Joan Beckham alias Mason for some prohibited books, which he denied on oath having received'.[35] In May the Privy Council proceeded against Mary Silvester, a laundry maid to the Spanish ambassador, who kept a cache of Catholic publications for distribution.[36] In July the High Commission authorized searches for 'heretical books' and 'seditious writings' as well as 'printing presses employed in the printing of any such'.[37] In August London booksellers faced censure for possessing manuscript copies of 'The Queries of the Clergy of the Diocese of London' and 'Demands of the Ministers in Kent and Northamptonshire', which challenged the Laudian canons.[38] In September the Council authorized raids on private houses to seize 'scandalous books printed and divulged to the prejudice of the government'.[39] The home of the preacher Cornelius Burges was among those ransacked for incriminating texts.[40] At least one of the Paul's churchyard booksellers fell foul of the authorities at this time, and was only released from the Fleet prison on the eve of the Long Parliament.[41] Copies of John Williams's *Holy Table Name and Thing* (1637) were also confiscated from booksellers in 1640, notwithstanding that this work by the disgraced Bishop of Lincoln had previously been licensed to be printed and sold.[42]

LIBERATION

Everything changed with the collapse of the King's military, financial, and political strategies in the summer and autumn of 1640. A prideful but inept regime was brought down by an unnecessary and ill-managed war. By September 1640 a Scottish army occupied north-east England. By November a new parliament began to flex its muscles at Westminster. Episcopacy was

---

[34] PRO, PC2/52, ff. 246, 276; *A Second Discovery by the Northern Scout* (1642), 9.
[35] *CSPD 1640*, 406.   [36] Ibid. 176; PRO, SP16/455/131; PRO, PC2/52, f. 246v.
[37] *CSPD 1640*, 441.   [38] Ibid. 619–20.
[39] British Library, Add. Ms. 11045, vol. v., f. 118,   [40] PRO, PC2/52, f. 369.
[41] *Privy Council Registers* (facsimile of PRO, PC2/53) (1968), xii. 16, 40. Luke Faune, at the sign of the Brazen Serpent in Paul's churchyard, was imprisoned for three weeks in October 1640. His previous publications included Richard Sibbes, *The Bruised Reed* (1635 and 1638).
[42] *CSPD 1640*, 154. See also C. E. Welch, 'The Downfall of Bishop Williams', *Transactions of the Leicestershire Archaeological and Historical Society*, 40 (1964–5), 42–58.

under challenge, root and branch; the Archbishop of Canterbury and the Earl of Strafford were under arrest; the ship-money judges were impeached; and leading state officials had fled into exile.

Even without any official ordinance, law, or proclamation, the character of the book trade began to change. An outpouring of grievances accompanied the opening of the parliamentary session. Petitioners complained of authors who had been punished and books that had been gutted or suppressed. The House of Commons established a committee to examine 'all abuses in print-ing, licensing, importing, and suppressing of books of all sorts', including 'denying of licenses to some book and expunging several passages' out of others. Chaired by Sir Edward Dering, the committee was empowered to send for all parties, witnesses, papers, records, books, and manuscripts.[43] The officials responsible for the Laudian 'restraint of the press' were now themselves subject to investigation, while the victims of censorship enjoyed celebrity status. The cases of Leighton, Burton, Bastwick, and Prynne were reviewed and the judgments against them reversed. The episcopal licensers were stripped of their functions, and nobody took their place.[44]

The Stationers' monopoly broke down, along with other court-backed monopoly projects. Well before the abolition of Star Chamber in July 1641, writers, printers, and publishers became aware of new opportunities and new freedoms, and took advantage of the abandonment of regulation.[45] Although some historians have identified the collapse of censorship with the fall of Star Chamber, Clarendon correctly dates the rise of the untrammelled press to the first few weeks of the Long Parliament when all 'unruly and mutinous spirit[s]' were let loose. Printed papers circulated alongside manu-script libels, 'and the presses [were] at liberty for the publishing the most invective, seditious, and scurrilous pamphlets that their wit and malice could invent'.[46] Like many features of this transformation, the change took effect earlier than most scholars have conjectured.

---

[43] Jansson (ed.), *Proceedings in the Opening Session of the Long Parliament . . . Vol. 1*, 260; Jansson (ed.), *Proceedings in the Opening Session of the Long Parliament . . . Vol. 2*, 428, 437; Mendle, 'De Facto Freedom', 314.

[44] British Library, Add. Ms. 26786, ff. 4v, 10v; Add. Ms. 21925, ff. 112v–113; Larking (ed.), *Proceedings, Principally in the County of Kent*, 94. Dr Bray, who had licensed Pocklington's work, was forced in March 1641 to make a recantation. A few of the licensing chaplains continued to make themselves available, but printers and publishers were no longer compelled to resort to them.

[45] Sharon Achinstein, 'Texts in Conflict: The Press and the Civil War', in N. H. Keeble (ed.), *Cambridge Companion to Writing of the English Revolution* (Cambridge, 2001), 57.

[46] Edward Hyde, Earl of Clarendon, *The History of the Rebellion and Civil Wars in England Begun in the Year 1641*, ed. W. Dunn Macray (6 vols., Oxford, 1888), i. 264, 269; Frederick Seaton Siebert, *Freedom of the Press in England 1476–1776: The Rise and Decline of Government Controls* (Urbana, Ill., 1952), 166–70; Cyprian Blagden, 'The Stationers' Company in the Civil War Period', *The Library*, 5th ser., 13 (1958), 8.

The explosion of print in the opening years of the Long Parliament was one of the most revolutionary features of the English Revolution. The quantity, character, and impact of these publications constituted an unprecedented media storm. From just six or seven hundred known items a year in the 1630s, the numbers of known publications rose dramatically to almost nine hundred in 1640, over two thousand in 1641, and over four thousand in 1642. There were more items published in 1641 than in any year in the previous history of English printing (2,177 in the English Short-Title Catalogue, of which the bookseller George Thomason collected 721). More appeared in 1642 than at any time again before the eighteenth century (4,188 in ESTC, including 2,134 in Thomason).[47] If anyone doubts there was revolution in mid-Stuart England they have only to look at these peaks. If printing itself was revolutionary, this was a revolution within the revolution[48] (see Figure 1). The surge in the number of publications points to a pent-up demand as well as a new abundance of supply—a convergence of output, audience, and opportunity—in a culture suddenly freed from restraint. As one godly author remarked when he went into print for the first time in 1641, 'the stone that made the stoppage of the well of Haran is now removed and the flocks of Laban may drink freely.'[49]

The numbers of print-shops almost doubled in the 1640s, though many of the upstarts had short professional lives. The London print trade expanded from around twenty-four shops with fifty presses early in 1640 to more than forty shops and some seventy presses by 1649.[50] Because the supply of paper was relatively inelastic, and typesets were not readily cloned, the material

[47] Figures from the online 'English-Short Title Catalogue', September 2003; Alain Veylit, 'Some Statistics on the Number of Surviving Printed Titles for Great Britain and Dependencies from the Beginnings of Print in England to the year 1800', http://www.cbsr.ucr.edu/ESTCStatistics.html; G. K. Fortescue (ed.), *Catalogue of the Pamphlets, Books, Newspapers, and Manuscripts Collected by George Thomason, 1640–1661* (2 vols., 1908), i., p. xxi. The effect of Thomason's collecting should not be underestimated, though he had only a third of the publications of 1641 and half of those of 1642. For similar figures based on the Wing catalogue, see D. F. McKenzie, 'The London Book Trade in 1644', in John Horden (ed.), *Bibliographia: Lectures 1975–1988 by Recipients of the Marc Fitch Prize for Bibliography* (Oxford, 1992), 152; John Barnard and D. F. McKenzie (eds.), *Cambridge History of the Book in Britain*, iv. (Cambridge, 2002); Joad Raymond, *Pamphlets and Pamphleteering in Early Modern Britain* (Cambridge, 2003), 163–70, 194–5.

[48] Marshall McLuhan, *The Gutenberg Galaxy; the Making of Typographic Man* (Toronto, 1962); Elizabeth L. Eisenstein, *The Printing Revolution in Early Modern Europe* (Cambridge, 1983); Achinstein, 'Texts in Conflict', in Keeble (ed.), *Cambridge Companion to Writing of the English Revolution*, 50–4.

[49] Hinde, *Faithfull Remonstrance of the Holy Life and Happy Death of John Bruen*, sig. A6, invoking Genesis 29: 2–10.

[50] Lambert, 'The Printers and the Government, 1604–1640', 9; Treadwell, 'Lists of Master Printers', 143–6; Marjorie Plant, *The English Book Trade: An Economic History of the Making and Sale of Books* (1939), 83.

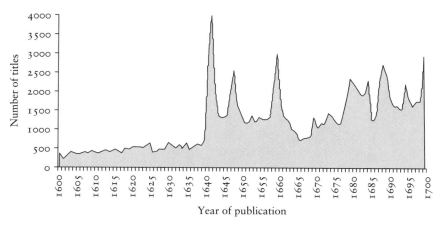

FIGURE 1. Surviving titles, 1600–1700

change in the amount of ink on paper may have been less dramatic. Rather, there was a proliferation of small cheap pamphlets, as printers switched from substantial productions to more slender and more saleable items.[51] Very little is known about provincial printing, but some of the anonymous productions that bear no imprint may have come from mobile or hidden presses. When 'three carts with printers things' turned up at Stafford in 1641 the mayor ordered that they be watched.[52] When the court left London in 1642 it was followed by printers who set up royalist presses at Shrewsbury, York, and Oxford.

The number of publications grew rapidly, as 'thread-bare scribblers', journeymen printers, and 'wandering book-sellers' expanded their market.[53] Observers remarked on the upsurge of 'unlicensed printers, upstart book-sellers, trotting mercuries, and bawling hawkers', who were offering texts in the streets. 'Wandering stationers' added to the cries of London, 'come buy a new book, a new book, newly come forth.'[54] Formerly those seeking books would turn to the stationers' stalls around St Paul's and the Exchange, but

[51] All printing paper was imported. Paper for pamphlets cost four or five shillings a ream (Raymond, *Pamphlets and Pamphleteering in Early Modern Britain*, 72–3). On the output of sheets, as opposed to a revolution in content, see McKenzie, 'London Book Trade in 1644', 135–7; Lambert, 'State Control of the press in Theory and practice', 22.

[52] Staffordshire Record Office, Stafford Borough Accounts 1528–1660, D 1323/E/1, f. 261.

[53] John Taylor, *The Whole Life and Progresse of Henry Walker the Ironmonger* (1642), 2–3.

[54] *The Downefall of Temporizing Poets* (1641), title page, 2. *A Description Of the Passage of Thomas late Earle of Strafford over the River of Styx* (1641), n.f.

now, in addition to those outlets, readers could wait for vendors to come to them. When parishioners of St Thomas, Southwark, wanted a copy of a parliamentary order against bowing at the name of Jesus they bought one from a ballad-monger or 'one that sold pamphlets about the streets', and demanded that their minister read it.[55]

One pamphleteer, Henry Walker, ironmonger, religious radical, and enterprising self-publisher, passed out copies of his work on the streets and on 5 January 1642 even attempted to present one to the King. According to his rival John Taylor, Walker 'contrived with a printer ... to write and print a perilous petition to his majesty, and borrowed the printer's wife's bible, out of which he took his theme out of the first of *Kings* 12:16, part of the verse, "to your tents oh Israel". There was writing and printing all night, and all the next day those libels were scattered, and when his majesty had dined [at Guildhall] and had taken coach to return to Whitehall, Walker stood watching the king's coming by amongst the drapers in Paul's churchyard, and having one of his pamphlets in his hand meaning to have delivered it to his majesty, but could not come at him by reason of the press of people, insomuch as Walker (most saucily and impudently) threw it over the folks heads into his majesty's coach.' Prompted by the King's failed attempt to arrest the five members of Parliament, the text, rather menacingly, alluded to the deposition of King Rehoboam.[56] King Charles himself was rattled by 'those many scandalous pamphlets and printed papers which are scattered with such great license throughout the kingdom,' though he thought it beneath his 'royal dignity' to take note of them.[57]

The collapse of episcopal licensing released a welter of voices—official, contestant, subaltern, satiric—and an unprecedented surge of information, news, and opinion. Jests and libels that had previously circulated clandestinely in taverns now appeared on the shelves of reputable booksellers. The subversive 'literary underground' went public.[58] 'Roaring ballad-singers' sold their wares to enterprising printers.[59] Satirists published puns and jests on the

---

[55] Benjamin Spencer, *Articles exhibited against Benjamin Spencer ... and his answer thereunto. With his reasons of printing the same* (1643), 5.

[56] Taylor, *Whole Life and Progress of Henry Walker the Ironmonger*, 4; Ernest Sirluck, 'To your tents, O Israel: A lost pamphlet', *Huntington Library Quarterly*, 19 (1955–6), 301–5. Walker had previously printed *The Churches Purity* (1641), a fifteen-page attack on the Church of England, dedicated to King Charles.

[57] J. P. Kenyon (ed.), *The Stuart Constitution 1603–1688* (2nd ed., Cambridge, 1986), 220n, from the King's declaration of 26 May 1642 concerning Hull.

[58] Alastair Bellany, 'Libels in Action: Ritual, Subversion and the English Literary Underground, 1603–1642', in Tim Harris (ed.), *The Politics of the Excluded, c.1500–1850* (Basingstoke, 2001), 116–17.

[59] *Mercuries Message Defended* (1641), 3, 10; *A Presse full of Pamphlets* (1642), sigs. A2v–A4.

names of Finch, Wren, Duck, and Lambe, Laudian canons, and episcopal
sees. Many of these publications had illustrated title pages, designed to draw
the readers' attention. Savage cartoons accompanied stiletto squibs against
Laud and his minions, showing Laud suffering nightmares, Laud in a shipwreck, Laud in a halter, Laud dining on his victims' ears, and the Archbishop
exploding or vomiting the recent church canons.[60] Several had a prurient
appeal, depicting 'the brothers of the blade' and 'the sisters of the scabbard'
(the vagina sisters) from the London *demi monde*, or exposing the absurdities
(and privities) of the naked Adamites.[61]

By 1641, almost anyone could publish almost anything (though rabid
anti-monarchical sentiments were still unlikely to find a printer). The old
regime of licensing gave way to a revolutionary culture of licence, in which
authors and printers explored previously forbidden areas. Writings of the
1630s that could not have passed the Laudian licensers now appeared openly in
print. Foxe's *Book of Martyrs* came out in new editions, alongside uncensored
reprints of *Leicester's Commonwealth*.[62] Reprints of the Elizabethan
Marprelate Tracts made Martin and Margery Marprelate familiar figures in
the renewed attack on the bishops. Henry Burton's *Divine Tragedy* and
William Prynne's *Newes from Ipswich*, two of the most subversive underground texts in the Caroline culture wars, could now be openly reissued,
along with Leighton's *Appeal to the Parliament*. These latter, when they first
appeared, were dangerous protests against the misdirection of the Church of
England; by the time of their republication in 1641 they were part of the
triumph of reformers who were remaking the religious and political world.

Theology tinged with sacrilege, politics laced with sedition, and sensational,
scatological, and even pornographic publications jostled for attention on the

---

[60] *Canterbvries Amazement* (1641); Thomas Stirry, *A Rot Among the Bishops, or, A Terrible
Tempest in the Sea of Canterbury* (1641); *The Bishops Mittimvs to goe to Bedlam* (1641); *The
Bishops Potion* (1641); *A New Play Called Canterburie His Change of Diot* (1641); *The Black
Box of Roome* (1641). Visual and verbal puns alluding to current affairs suggest an audience of
city wits as well as educated artisans. Religious radicals were treated with comparable satire,
though the King himself remained off-limits. See also [Abraham Cowley], *A Satyre Against
Seperatists, Or, The Conviction of Chamber-Preachers, and other Schismaticks* (1642), 4.

[61] *The Brothers of the Blade Answerable to the Sisters of the Scaberd* (1641); *The Sisters of the
Scabards Holiday* (1641); *A Nest of Serpents Discovered. Or, A knot of old Heretiques revived,
Called the Adamites. Wherein their original, increase, and several ridiculous tenets are plainly laid
open* (1641); 'Samoth Yarb' [Thomas Bray], *A New Sect of Religion Descryed, called Adamites:
Deriving their Religion from our Father Adam* (1641); *The Adamites Sermon* (1641).

[62] In October 1641 the Privy Council attempted to suppress a new edition of *Leicester's
Commonwealth*, 'a book unfit to be divulged' (though written fifty years earlier) that the current Earl of Leicester found offensive, but they were powerless to prevent its printing or
distribution (*CSPD 1641–43*, 136). In November 1641 William Prynne presented a copy of the
reprinted *Book of Martyrs* to the church at his birthplace, Swainswick, Somerset (Bodleian
Library, Oxford, Tanner Ms. 69, f. 1).

bookshelves. Here was the beginning of 'the world turned upside down', not after but preceding the civil war.[63] The press became a medium for building or destroying reputations, commentary on affairs of the moment, and the promotion of controversial ideas. Petitions to the King and Parliament publicized themselves and answered each other in print. Printed accounts of recent events created the genre of contemporary history. Parliament itself took to printing, and by the end of the year readers could look forward to competing diurnals or digests of weekly news.[64]

In May 1641, soon after the execution of the Earl of Strafford, a correspondent reported, 'everything sells that comes in print under his name; therefore he is every day apparelled with one idle pamphlet or other bearing the affection of the true author, either in favour of him or against him.'[65] Over a hundred publications in 1641 dealt directly with the Earl of Strafford. Almost as many commented on the downfall of Archbishop Laud.[66] None of these would have passed the controls of the ancien regime. One pamphlet of 1641 imagined a dialogue between the exiled Secretary Windebank and former Lord Keeper Finch with one of them saying, 'there have been more impressions of several kinds of lamentable ballads and pamphlets made upon us two than ever was of *The Practice of Piety* or *Crums of Comfort*.'[67] Another remarked on 'the multitudes of paper sheets sent from the press' with the sales cry, 'come buy a book concerning little Will'.[68]

Some authors remained anonymous, although there was now no penalty for illicit publication. John Milton's 1641 pamphlet *Of Reformation*, for example, did not include the author's name. Others hid behind absurd and transparent anagrams, John Taylor passing himself as Thorny Ailo, Thomas Bray writing as Samoth Yarb, Henry Walker as Levek Hunarry, and Henry Peacham impersonating Ryhen Pameach. 'What liberty is here', remarked

---

[63] Christopher Hill, *The World Turned Upside Down* (1972), locates the beginning of the ferment about 1647. Cf. Keith Thomas, 'The Meaning of Literacy in Early Modern England', in Gerd Baumann (ed.), *The Written Word: Literacy in Transition* (Oxford, 1986), 120: 'In the 1640s, *with the civil war*, all controls seemed to have lapsed and the result was an extraordinary output of heterodox ideas' (my emphasis).

[64] *The Heads of Severall Proceedings in this Present Parliament, from the 22 of November to the 29* (1641), has been heralded as 'something quite revolutionary' because of its openly printed presentation of current domestic news (Joad Raymond (ed.), *Making the News: An Anthology of the Newsbooks of Revolutionary England 1641–1660* (Moreton-in-Marsh, 1993), 2–3).

[65] HMC, *12th Report, The Manuscripts of the Earl Cowper...Preserved at Melbourne Hall, Derbyshire* (1888), ii. 282.

[66] Figures from ESTC. Eighty-six publications of 1641 featured Strafford in their title, 116 had Strafford as subject. The equivalent figures for Laud were 19 and 65.

[67] *Times Alteration* (1641), broadsheet. On best-sellers, see I. M. Green, *Print and Protestantism in Early Modern England* (Oxford, 2000).

[68] *The Deputies Ghost: Or An Apparition to the Lord of Canterbury in the Tower* (1641), broadsheet.

Robert Baillie in December 1640, 'when such books dare bear the names of author, printer and seller.'[69]

Works appeared openly, brazenly, anonymously, and pseudonymously. The imprint information on the title page could be true, false, veiled, or simply not given. Some omitted details about their publication, claiming simply to be 'printed in this year of hope, 1641', or 'printed in the year, when prelates fall is neere'.[70] At least two publications—John Taylor's *Swarme of Sectaries and Schismatiques* and the anonymous *Downfall of Temporizing Poets*— announced themselves as 'printed merrily, and may be read unhappily, betwixt hawke and buzzard, 1641'. Another pamphlet—*Vox Borealis*— claimed to be 'printed by Margery Mar-prelate, in Thwackcoat lane, at the sign of the crab-tree cudgel, without any privilege of the Cater-caps, the year coming on', 1641. *A Dreame, or Newes from Hell*, revealing fantastic popish designs against the parliament, was said to be printed 'in Sicilia on the back-side of the Cyclopean mountains', although it was almost certainly produced in London.[71]

When a pamphlet like *The Schismatic Stigmatized* (1641) declared on its title page that it was written by Richard Carter, and printed by John Okes, for Francis Coles, to be sold at his shop in the Old Bailey in London, certain claims were made for its authorship and its authority, its provenance and its production. By contrast, when a pamphlet announced no more than that it was printed in 1641, it left no apparent traces for readers (or authorities) to pursue. Some items claimed to be 'published by authority' but that phrase was rendered almost meaningless by the collapse of episcopal licensing and the collapse of the Stationers' monopoly. The phrase could signal conformity to church and state, it could lay claim to the authority of Parliament, or it could simply be an advertising slogan or a joke.

Hundreds of pamphlets announced themselves as carriers of news, with titles that helped to shape readers' responses. As printed news became controversial and abundant, writers parodied its forms, playing on popular appetites for information. They promised news in print that was current and timely, the 'last and best', as well as news 'true' and 'certain', 'extraordinary'

---

[69] David Laing (ed.), *The Letters and Journals of Robert Baillie* (3 vols., Edinburgh, 1841), i. 286.

[70] Richard Dey, *Two Looks over Lincolne* (1641); *Canterburies Tooles* (1641). See also *Wrens Anatomy*, 'printed in the yeare, that Wren ceased to domineere, 1641'; *Reader Here you plainly see Iudgement perverted*, 'printed in the happy yeare of Grace, 1641'; and *The Manner of the Impeachment of the XII Bishops*, 'printed in the new yeare of the bishops feare, Ano Dom. 1642'.

[71] Some of these may have been printed in Amsterdam, where Richard Overton ran an energetic subversive press. For the attribution of *A Dreame* to the London printers Fossett and Alsop, see 'Renewed Attempts at Control' later in this chapter.

or 'strange', 'laudable', 'lamentable', 'joyful' or 'welcome'. Printed publications dispersed partisan accounts of what had happened recently, 'of late'. (Further discussion of the circulation of news is reserved for the following chapter.)

Contemporaries marvelled at the explosion of print, though not all were delighted by its consequences. The Scot Robert Baillie expressed amazement that 'all things now are printed [in London]. There is a world of pamphlets here.'[72] An anonymous author of 1641 complained of 'so many idle scandalous pamphlets daily cast abroad to the great vexation of each other and trouble to the whole realm'.[73] Swamped by 'many thousand reams of... songs, rhymes and ballads', the poet George Wither remarked in 1641 that, 'these times do swarm with pamphlets, which be far more dangerous than mortal poison'.[74] 'I know not what this parliament may produce', William Montague wrote to his father towards the end of 1641, 'for the present I am sure it produceth many printed pamphlets.'[75]

Readers and consumers of the press remarked on its sudden abundance. Pedlars carried copies to the country, and correspondents enclosed pamphlets with their letters, 'for your entertainment at spare hours' or 'to make you a little merry withal'.[76] The London wood-turner Nehemiah Wallington became so addicted to the popular press that 'finding so many of these little pamphlets of weekly news about my house I thought they were so many thieves that had stole away my money before I was aware of them'.[77] The Suffolk minister John Rous felt similarly overwhelmed by the 'multitudes of books and papers, unto which God in mercy put an end'.[78] There was so much 'foul ink besquittered and besquirted' in 'roguish pamphlets', claimed John Taylor, that they covered all England with their 'lies'. By 1642, he said, there was enough unlicensed print to paper the whole kingdom.[79] Another wit claimed that the outpouring of paper was fit only for 'Sir Ajax his office', the privy.[80]

Fascinated with the novelty of their own achievement, authors engaged in ironic, self-reflexive commentary on the freedom of the press. Pamphlets

[72] Laing (ed.), *Letters and Journals of Robert Baillie*, i. 300.
[73] *The Humble Petition of the Brownists* (1641), 5.
[74] [George Wither], *A Prophesie Written Long Since for the Yeare 1641* (1641), 9–10.
[75] HMC, *Report on the Manuscripts of the Duke of Buccleuch and Queensberry...at Montague House* (1899), 289. [76] *CSPD 1641–43*, 253, 273.
[77] British Library, Add. Ms. 14827, 6 February 1642.
[78] Mary Ann Everett Green (ed.), *Diary of John Rous Incumbent of Santon Downham, Suffolk, from 1625 to 1642* (Camden Society, 1856), 121.
[79] John Taylor, *A Reply as true as Steele, To a Rusty, Rayling, Ridiculous, Lying Libell* (1641), 1; John Taylor, *A Cluster of Coxcombes* (1642), 7.
[80] *Mercuries Message Defended*, 10.

spoke to pamphlets, with such titles as *The Diseases of the Times* (John Taylor, 1641) answering *A Medicine for the Times* (Thomas Jordan, 1641), and *A Swarm of Sectaries and Schismatics* (John Taylor) precipitating *An Answer* (by Henry Walker) and *A Reply as true as Steele* (Taylor again). A flood of 'fabulous pamphlets' followed the Irish rebellion, prompting one author to publish *No Pamphlet, Bvt a Detestation Against all such Pamphlets* to set the record straight.[81]

Pamphleteers themselves remarked on the 'numerous rabble of pestiferous pamphlets' that 'pestered' and cluttered the kingdom, and complained of 'the too many unlicked lumps that the press hath too lately spewed forth'.[82] 'The press is over-pressed', complained Martin Parker, who railed at the waste of paper 'by these calumnious idle pamphleteers'.[83] It had become a 'paper age', railed Edward Browne, 'wherein many strive to vent the froth of their inventions into the press, so that lying and scandalous pamphlets fly about the city in every corner, and prove vendible ware'.[84] Writing in April 1642, the pamphleteer–poet John Bond complained of 'the innumerable multitude of pamphlets which have been surreptitiously inserted above this twelve months and half to the ignominious scandal of the state'.[85] Another pamphlet entitled *A Presse Full of Pamphlets* remarked on the novel 'diversity of prints . . . fraught with libellous and scandalous sentences' that were flooding the streets of the metropolis 'in this last remarkable year of printing'. Printers were to blame, the author proclaimed, 'in publishing every pamphlet that comes to their press'. There was never a parliament so abused, he continued, since printing 'exposed [their proceedings] to the view of all men'.[86]

'Book-selling is grown hugely in request', wrote the Lincolnshire gentleman John Ogle in February 1642, offering facetiously to take up that trade if he could find no more honourable employment.[87] 'Booksellers are increased tenfold in number within these two years', wrote John Taylor in

---

[81] *No Pamphlet, Bvt a Detestation Against all such Pamphlets As are Printed, Concerning the Irish Rebellion* (1642), sig. A2; cf. Henry Ferne, *The Resolving of Conscience* (Cambridge, 1642), 45: 'the distress of Ireland by the help of wicked pamphlets hath been used as a great engine to weaken the king's reputation with his people.' See also Ethan Howard Shagan, 'Constructing Discord: Ideology, Propaganda, and English Responses to the Irish Rebellion of 1641', *Journal of British Studies*, 36 (1997), 4–24.

[82] I.W., *Certaine Affirmations In defence of the pulling down of Communion Rails . . . answered* (1641), sig. B; Martin Parker, *The Poets Blind mans bough* (1641), title page; *The Soundheads Description of the Roundhead* (1642), 2.

[83] Parker, *Poets Blind mans bough*, sig. B4v.

[84] [Edward Browne], *A Paradox Useful for the Times* (1642), sig. A3v.

[85] John Bond, *The Poets Recantation* (1642), 1.

[86] *A Presse Full of Pamphlets*, title page, sigs. A, Av, A3. See also A. D. T. Cromartie, 'The Printing of Parliamentary Speeches November 1640–July 1642', *The Historical Journal*, 33 (1990), 23–44. [87] Bodleian Library, Carte Ms. 2, f. 328.

1642.[88] The entire book trade experienced a surge of business, but established vendors lamented the loss of their monopoly. The collapse of guild authority worked 'to the mighty impeachment and detriment of the worshipful brotherhood of the Stationers', so John Taylor claimed, for 'the bread hath been eaten out of their mouths by those vagrants, commonly called mercuries and hawkers.'[89] In 1641, one author remarked, 'the printing and selling of such books hath been a means to help many a poor man in London these dead times of trading.'[90] Another observed, 'there are men mercuries and women mercuries and boy mercuries, mercuries of all sexes, sorts and sizes, and these are they that carry up and down their pasquils and vent them unto shops.'[91] When three such mercuries were 'taken in the streets with pamphlets' in June 1642 and were briefly committed to Bridewell, one was found to be aged fourteen, one was a vagrant from Gloucestershire, and the third was described as 'an abusive fellow'.[92]

Publications, of course, were commodities as well as texts. Broadsheets could be bought for a penny, eight-page pamphlets for a penny or twopence, little more than the cost of a drink.[93] John Ogle wrote derisively of 'Mr. Pym's twopenny speeches'.[94] More substantial productions might cost a shilling or more, depending on their size or their demand. Sir Edward Dering's controversial collection of speeches sold for fourteen pence early in 1642, though parliamentary attempts at suppression more than doubled its value on the street.[95] Manuscript newsbooks or 'separates' in the 1630s had cost their subscribers from sixpence to three shillings, or as much as twenty pounds per annum; by contrast, printed diurnals of the early 1640s cost no more than a couple of pennies, and reached a much wider audience.[96]

It is hard to discover how readers responded, but a sprinkling of evidence indicates some of the impact of cheap print. Participants in alehouse arguments

---

[88] Taylor, *Cluster of Coxcombes*, 7.

[89] Taylor, *Whole Life and Progresse of Henry Walker the Ironmonger*, 3.

[90] *Sions Charity Towards Her Foes in Misery* (1641), 4.

[91] *Description Of the Passage of Thomas late Earle of Strafford.*

[92] Corporation of London Record Office, Bridewell and Bethlem, Court of Governors Minutes, 19 April, 17 June 1642. I am grateful to Paul Griffiths for directing me to this source.

[93] Henry Peacham, *The Worth of a Peny. Or, A Caution to keep Money* (1641), 28. A dozen pamphlets from this period purchased by the Kentish clergyman George Stancombe, now in the Folger Shakespeare Library, record the price paid, usually one or two pennies.

[94] 'How finely it will become my countenance to sell one of Mr. Pym's twopenny speeches according to the manner of the new trumpet' (Bodleian Library, Carte Ms. 2, f. 328).

[95] Willson H. Coates, Anne Steele Young, and Vernon F. Snow (eds.), *The Private Journals of the Long Parliament 3 January to 5 March 1642* (New Haven and London, 1982), 255.

[96] For the price of newsletters, Richard Cust, 'News and Politics in Early Seventeenth-Century England', *Past and Present*, 112 (1986), 60–90; Esther S. Cope and Willson H. Coates (eds.), *Proceedings of the Short Parliament of 1640* (Camden Society 4th ser., vol. xix, 1977), 35.

could be found citing or brandishing the latest publications in support of their political opinions. Responding to the question, 'what news?' for example, an Exeter grocer 'drew a paper or writing out of his pocket and read the same' to a Devonshire yeoman, including 'some passages about parliament' and warnings of 'troubles in the north'.[97] All sorts of publications reached Thomas Wyatt in his Oxfordshire parish of Ducklington. Among them were printed editions of the Earl of Strafford's speeches as well as parliamentary business and sermons. In July 1641 he noted, 'infinite pasquils and base abusive ballads and trifling pamphlets came forth daily'. One of them, 'a book printed in Edinburgh entitled *The Government and Order of the Church of Scotland*', commended the Presbyterian system, which Wyatt thought 'no good order, but a Babylonish confusion'.[98] Readers also read and argued over pamphlets while standing in stationers' shops. One such altercation between a citizen, a gentleman, and a minister came to the attention of the House of Commons.[99]

Radical pamphlets also appeared in church. At Isleworth, Middlesex, the Laudian vicar William Grant complained that Gilbert Barrell, attorney, 'commonly brings pamphlets to church and reads them in time of divine service'. On Sunday, 2 May 1641, Barrell interrupted Grant's sermon 'by laughing and jeering in his face on the sudden, and immediately after that reading of a pamphlet, and refusing and denying openly to lay it aside'.[100] A more challenging incident occurred at Radwinter, Essex, in March 1642 when a parishioner, George Traps, interrupted divine service and 'came to the reading desk and threw to the curate a base pamphlet called *An Answer of the Roundheads to the Rattleheads*, saying, there is reading work for you, read that'.[101]

As England's political situation deteriorated, as the regime fell further apart, conservatives blamed the kingdom's distempers on the outpourings of an unbridled press. Thomas Wiseman, for example, identified 'the liberty of the press' as the leading factor that 'poisoned the obedience of his majesty's subjects'.[102] Lord Cholmondley expressed amazement 'that people are so insistently audacious to put to print so notorious lies'.[103] 'What calumniations are vented, printed, uncensured, unpunished', cried the London conformist

[97] Devon Record Office, Exeter Quarter Sessions Book, 1630–1642, f. 391.

[98] Diary of Thomas Wyatt, Bodleian Library, Ms. Top. Oxon. C. 378, 316, 318, 320.

[99] *Commons Journals*, ii. 661. They were arguing about *The Declaration or Resolution of the County of Hereford* (1642).

[100] William Grant, *The Vindication of the Vicar of Isleworth, in the County of Middlesex. From a scandalous pamphlet* (1641), 17, 19. Cf. *The Petition of the Inhabitants of Isleworth . . . against William Grant* (1641).

[101] Bodleian Library, Ms. Rawlinson D. 80, ff. 17–17v; Ms. Rawlinson D. 158, ff. 43–4.

[102] *CSPD 1641–43*, 255.

[103] Cholmondley to Sir Thomas Aston, 10 April 1641, British Library, Add. Ms. 36914, f. 212.

John Grant.[104] Edward Browne charged 'your lying diurnals, your absurd passages, your diabolical news from heaven, your horrible, terrible, and fearful tidings, and such like', with 'filling people's minds full of jealousies both against king and parliament'.[105] Thomas Fuller, author of *The Holy State* and *The Profane State* (1642), found himself in a time of tempest, 'wherein the press, like an unruly horse, hath cast off his bridle of being licensed', and serious books were 'hooted at by a flock of pamphlets'.[106] Preaching in Lincolnshire in October 1641, Robert Sanderson worried that the proliferation of 'base and unworthy pamphlets' would cause such a 'stink' in God's nostrils that he would 'grow weary . . . and forsake' England.[107] Most of these protests were in the form of print answering print.

The 'malice and mischief' of 'pestiferous pamphlets' was such, John Taylor complained, that 'neither religion, church, king, peers, priests or people have escaped railing, libelling, and transcendent traducing'.[108] Pamphlets and invectives spread 'false distrusts and jealousies, mad tumults, libels, base reports and lies'.[109] Author after author lamented the impact of 'the numberless pamphlets of these distracted times' on 'the ignorant, misjudging and ill affected multitude', although, tellingly, they expressed their concern in print.[110]

Petitioners on behalf of the established religion blamed 'the contents of many printed pamphlets swarming at London and over all countries' for undermining episcopacy and the Book of Common Prayer. Petitioners from Kent were especially troubled by 'those scandalous and ill-affected pamphlets which do fly abroad in such swarms'.[111] Joseph Hall blamed the throng of 'slanderous libels, bitter pasquins, and railing pamphlets', put out by 'furious and malignant spirits', for the breakdown of religious orthodoxy.[112] Petitioners from Somerset in December 1641 demanded 'punishment of those who under a veil of religion publish pamphlets conducing to confusion and rebellion'.[113]

---

[104] [John Grant], *Gods Deliverance of Man by Prayer* (1642), 9.

[105] [Browne] *Paradox Useful for the Times*, sig. A.

[106] Thomas Fuller, *The Holy State* (1642), sig. A2.

[107] [Robert Sanderson], *Ad Clerum. A Sermon Preached . . . 8 Octob. 1641* (1670), 19.

[108] Taylor, *Cluster of Coxcombes*, 7.

[109] John Taylor, *A Delicate, Dainty, Damnable Dialogue, Between the Devill and a Jesuite* (1642), sig. A2. Cf. *CSPD 1640–41*, 440.

[110] Edward Reynolds, *Evgenia's Teares for Great Brittaynes Distractions* (1642), 38.

[111] Sir Thomas Aston (ed.), *A Collection of Sundry Petitions Presented to the King's Most excellent Majestie* (1642), 11, 14, 39.

[112] [Joseph Hall], *An Humble Remonstrance to the High Court of Parliament* (1640), 1, 6–7. This came out in January 1641.

[113] House of Lords Record Office, Main Papers, 10 December 1641.

RENEWED ATTEMPTS AT CONTROL

Parliamentary authorities attempted to restrain this outpouring, but it was like trying to bridle a dragon or cap a volcano. Whereas enthusiasts like John Vicars and Thomas Mocket applauded the 'setting our printing presses open' as one of the 'unparalleled mercies' of the age,[114] others sought to bring the monster under control. Even John Milton, who associated the end of licensing with 'the breaking forth of light', countenanced some suppression of 'scandalous, seditious and libellous books'.[115] Most reformers wanted a godly press, not a free one, and certainly not one that affronted their policies or God's honour. Hence their delight in the burning of their enemies' books, as in the gloating report from Oxford in March 1641, 'we burnt two Pocklingtons with a great deal of solemnity'.[116] Lord Digby's speech sympathetic to the Earl of Strafford was burned publicly in July 1641, and a similar fate befell Sir Edward Dering's speeches six months later.[117] John Pym's charge against Archbishop Laud in this regard was not just that he had prevented godly works from being printed, but that he had approved the licensing of books 'full of falsehood, of scandals, such as have been more worthy to be burnt by the hand of the hangman in Smithfield'.[118]

Throughout 1641 and into 1642, in the year and half before the start of civil war, a chorus of complaint demanded that the press be restored to discipline. Some of this may have been stimulated by the Stationers' Company, who sought the reinstatement of their 'immunities and privileges'. But it was also driven by a politics of censure and recrimination, in an increasingly fractious political culture.[119] Parliamentarians could be just as offended as Laudian councillors at unregulated commentary and opinion, but they were never as successful at stemming the tide. The crucial mechanisms of control had been surrendered, and the Commons never had the weapons or authority of the Privy Council and the prerogative courts.

---

[114] John Vicars, *Jehovah-Jireh. God in the Movnt. Or, Englands Parliamentarie-Chronicle* (1644), 42. Thomas Mocket, *The National Covenant* (1642), sig. A2.

[115] Milton, *Areopagitica*, 4.   [116] British Library, Add. Ms. 70003, f. 82.

[117] *CSPD 1641–43*, 53.

[118] [John Pym], *The Speech of Declaration of John Pymm, Esquire, To the Lords ... Against William Laud* (1641), 29.

[119] Blagdon, 'The Stationers' Company in the Civil War Period', 1–17; Mendle, 'De Facto Freedom', 318–22; Jason Peacy, *Politicians and Pamphleteers: Propaganda during the English Civil Wars and Interregnum* (2004), 136–44; *To the Right Honorable, the Knights, Citizens and Burgesses, now Assembled in the High Court of Parliament. The Petition of the Master and Workmen Printers of London* (1642?), broadsheet.

In February 1641 the Scottish commissioners, who had cheered the reversal of Laudian policies, now demanded 'that all scandalous papers and libels printed against them might be burnt'.[120] Moderate reformers proposed 'that all pamphlets might be stayed from the press, which take upon them . . . to propound models and forms of [church] government'.[121]

Early in March the House of Lords authorized the Stationers to proceed against the printers and vendors of such unlicensed pamphlets as *The Black Box of Rome* and *The Dreame, or Newes from Hell*, and set up a committee to pursue the matter.[122] The committee was particularly interested in the source of the 'copy', or manuscript original, which might reveal the identity of anonymous authors. Under investigation, the stationer John Hamon confessed that 'he sold a book called *The Dreame, or Newes from Hell*. It was printed by Fawcett and Alsop, who had the copy from Pecham, a minister.' Another bookseller, Thomas Bates, acknowledged selling *The Dreame, or Newes from Hell*, which he said he obtained from [Giles] Calvert, a book-binder, who confessed it was printed by Fawcett. 'But being asked from whom he had the copy, told us, he had it from one of the city, but refused to tell his name.' Bernard Alsop, who printed several 'unlawfull books' including *The Black Box of Rome*, claimed to have received his copies from two book-binders 'who undertook to save him harmless'. One of the searchers affirmed 'that he found in [Henry] Walker's house at the least one hundred pamphlets called *The Lord of Canterbury's Dreame* and these were printed in [Thomas] Fawcett's house. The said Walker confesses he did disperse pamphlets called *The Prelates Pride* and verses made of the Lord Finch and of Bishop Wren, and these he told us he made himself.' In all, the inquiry named eight printers and twelve distributors of books and pamphlets, but could do little more than threaten them with discipline. The printer John Wells and the stationer Stephen Bulkeley, 'being sent for by the committee, refused to come'.[123]

A few days later on 12 March 1641 a group of leading divines, including the parliamentary preachers Edmund Calamy and Stephen Marshall, wrote to the Lords regarding licensing for the press. They repeated the puritan complaint that in recent years, under the bishops' licensers, many 'dangerous' books had been published, while 'divers godly treatises' had been 'either

---

[120] Jansson (ed.), *Proceedings in the Opening Session of the Long Parliament . . . Vol. 2*, 420.

[121] *Vnitie, Trvth and Reason* (1641), 13.

[122] Bishop Warner's Diary, British Library, Harleian Ms. 6424, f. 47v; House of Lords Record Office, Main Papers, 4 March 1641.

[123] House of Lords Record Office. Main Papers, 4 March 1641 See also the parliamentary complaint against John Turner for printing *The Saints Belief* in May 1641, and *The Lord Strafford's Defence* in June 1641 (Jansson (ed.), *Proceedings in the Opening Session of the Long Parliament . . . Vol. 4*, 433, 737, 744).

wholly rejected and suppressed, or so mangled by leaving out many most material passages, sometimes whole leaves or sheets together, that they have been made in a great part unserviceable.' Their purpose, however, was not to celebrate the end of episcopal licensing but to institute a new regime of control in its place. They urged the Lords that

the power of licensing books for the press may be committed to such orthodox and godly men, as may take special care for the suppressing of all such dangerous and poisoned treatises as tend to error and ungodliness, and for the allowing of those that contain only sound and wholesome doctrine, or other matters profitable for public use.

The eighteen clerics who subscribed this request seem to have imagined themselves as ideal censors, and at least eight of them were later nominated to the Westminster Assembly.[124]

The House of Commons also attempted to inhibit printing. 'Many printers were punished, and a strict order made that no pamphlets or journals nor any parliamentary proceedings should be printed, but by special order of the House,' William Montague told his father on 28 March 1641, 'you may see the fruits of this order by the paucity of books which I send.'[125] However, the freeze was short-lived, and parliamentary attention only made the offending publications more vendible. In June, angered by unauthorized printing of their proceedings, Parliament ordered the Stationers 'to prevent the printing of such pamphlets and speeches, and that no books shall be printed without licence'.[126] But again they were unable to staunch the flood.

In September 1641 supporters of a bill to reintroduce licensing rehearsed the 'dangers' and 'inconveniences' of an unregulated press.

If printing in England be not under good rule and government, every libelling spirit will have free liberty to traduce the proceedings of the state, every malicious spirit may then with ease revile whomsoever he pleaseth to account his adversary, yea, every pernicious heretic may have opportunity to poison the minds of weak minded men with wicked errors.

Indeed, some thought, that was exactly what had happened. 'A loose press' would allow 'the fancies of every idle brain' to be cried about the streets, exacerbating the kingdom's 'deplorable distractions'. The bill proposed that

---

[124] House of Lords Record Office, Main Papers, 12 March 1641. The subscribers were Simeon Ash, John Barry, Richard Bernard, Robert Bettes, Nathaniel Bugge, Edward Calamy, Thomas Edwards, John (?) Heyrick, Thomas Hedges, William Janeway, John Ley, Stephen Marshall, Henry Paynter, William Rathbone, Lazarus Seaman, Edmund Staunton, George Walker, and John White.

[125] HMC, *Report on the Manuscripts of the Duke of Buccleuch and Queensberry* 294–5.

[126] Rushworth, *Historical Collections*, iv. 282; *Commons Journals*, ii. 168.

nothing should be printed without licence, that imported books should be prohibited, and home-produced 'libels and loose pamphlets' should be restrained, rather as they had been in the 1630s. It projected a licensing board of 'grave, learned and well-affected divines', nominated by the state (almost all Presbyterians), and it sought to restore the Company of Stationers' privileges.[127] Similar proposals against 'the abusive printing of pamphlets and libellous books' recurred in the next six months but none made headway through the parliamentary process.[128] A proposal from the House of Lords in December 1641 restricting the sale of certain works 'to nobility, gentry and scholars, but not to women', proved equally impractical.[129]

The House of Commons repeatedly took offence at 'false and scandalous pamphlets' and determined 'to find out the printers and authors'.[130] Members complained of 'the exorbitancy of the press', and demanded action against such authors, printers, and publishers as could be identified.[131] But, Sir Simonds D'Ewes observed, 'if we only enquire after the contrivers or publishers of such libels and make not some public determination against them, we shall never suppress them.'[132] The committee for printing was empowered to 'examine these abuses . . . and to consider of some way for the preventing thereof', but the pressure of events prevented effective action.[133] When Parliament attempted to persuade the Company of Stationers to discipline its own members the printer Richard Hearne threatened to kill the master if he set foot in his house.[134] Another proposal in January 1642 'that no printer shall print any book without naming the author' predictably came to nothing.[135]

---

[127] *CSPD 1641–43*, 129; PRO, SP16/484/57. Parliament eventually passed an ordinance regulating printing in June 1643.

[128] Willson Havelock Coates (ed.), *The Journal of Sir Simonds D'Ewes from the First Recess of the Long Parliament to the Withdrawal of the King from London* (New Haven and London, 1942), 191, 192, 318–19; Snow and Young (eds.), *Private Journals of the Long Parliament 7 March to 1 June March 1642*, 34, 314; House of Lords Record Office, Main Papers, 9 December 1641, 5 April 1642; HMC, *5th* Report, 16; *Lords Journals*, iv. 700.

[129] *CSPD 1641–43*, 86. The works in question were thought to be favourable to Roman Catholicism.

[130] Snow and Young (eds.), *Private Journals of the Long Parliament 7 March to 1 June March 1642*, 55, 77, 97.

[131] Coates (ed.), *Journal of Sir Simonds D'Ewes from the First Recess of the Long Parliament to the Withdrawal of the King from London*, 30; Coates, Young, and Snow (eds.), *Private Journals of the Long Parliament 3 January to 5 March 1642*, 120.

[132] Snow and Young (eds.), *Private Journals of the Long Parliament 7 March to 1 June March 1642*, 98.

[133] Coates (ed.), *Journal of Sir Simonds D'Ewes from the First Recess of the Long Parliament to the Withdrawal of the King from London*, 191, 192.

[134] Siebert, *Freedom of the Press*, 174; *Commons Journals*, ii. 268–9; *Lords Journals*, iv. 180, 182, 398.

[135] Coates, Young, and Snow (eds.), *Private Journals of the Long Parliament 3 January to 5 March 1642*, 216, 222.

Parliament summoned several printers to Westminster as 'delinquents', including George Dexter, printer of *The Apprentices Advice to the XII Bishops*, who said he feared 'he should be undone'.[136] The speaker could order delinquents to be held in the Gatehouse, and require that they to stand at the bar of the House for reprimand.[137] But many authors and publishers remained anonymous, and there was no means to force them to dance to Parliament's tune. Sir Simonds D'Ewes recommended the pillory and the whip 'to make these men examples for a terror to the rest', but it was not a terror to be taken seriously.[138] No author from this time had cause to fear the loss of his ears.

Other works singled out for investigation included 'a false letter printed . . . to his majesty touching the state of the kingdom',[139] 'a letter of news out of Ireland very scandalous to the Scots', and various satirical pamphlets deemed 'extreme scandalous against the parliament'.[140] All enjoyed wide circulation. Petitioners also complained in vain at 'the unpunished printing of many licentious and scandalous pamphlets', including rumours about the Queen.[141] Deeply offended by *New Orders of the Parliament of Roundheads* and *The Speech of a Warden to the Fellows of His Company Touching the Great Affairs of the Kingdom*, the Commons demanded of the Stationers how they 'justified the printing of the one and selling of the other'. The stationer Stephen Bulkeley was summoned to Westminster as a delinquent but instead fled to the King at York, taking his printing equipment with him.[142]

Attempts at censorship only drew attention to controversial works and stimulated demand. As John Milton observed, citing Francis Bacon, 'it raises them and invests them with reputation'.[143] 'The stir' of suppression made copies 'much more inquired after' and turned some of them into best-sellers.[144] In December 1641, on the same day that the King issued a proclamation to

---

[136] Ibid., 96, 100, 103.

[137] Ibid., 161, 165. Printers or publishers who were designated 'delinquent' and subjected to parliamentary sanction between January and June 1642 included Bernard Alsop, John Bennet, Stephen Bulkley, Gregory Dexter, Gregory Dixon, Thomas Fawcett, John Frank, William Gaye, John Greensmith, John Thomas, William Umfreville, Robert Wood, and John Wright.

[138] Ibid., 165–6.   [139] Ibid., 230.

[140] Vernon F. Snow and Anne Steele Young (eds.), *The Private Journals of the Long Parliament 2 June to 17 September 1642* (New Haven and London, 1992), 37, 42, 53, 77, 78.

[141] *To the Right Honourable the House of Peers Now Assembled in Parliament. The humble Petition of many thousands of Courtiers, Citizens, Gentlemens and Trades-mens wives, inhabiting within the Cities of London and Westminster, concerning the staying of the Queenes intended voyage into Holland* (1641), broadsheet.

[142] Snow and Young (eds.), *Private Journals of the Long Parliament 2 June to 17 September 1642*, 78. See also Lawrence Hanson, 'The King's Printer at York and Shrewsbury 1642–3', *The Library*, 4th ser., 23 (1943), 129–31.   [143] Milton, *Areopagitica*, 26.

[144] Clegg, *Press Censorship in Jacobean England*, 89, 219; Featley, *Cygnea Cantio*, 40.

uphold the established form of worship, Matthew Symons was committed for publishing Lewis Hughes's *Certain Grievances or Errors of the Service Book*. But censorship could not be restored at that time, any more than the Church of England could be saved, and the book went through five editions within a year.[145] Sir Edward Dering's *Collection of Speeches* likewise became a desirable item after Parliament condemned it as 'a most scandalous, seditious, and vainglorious book'. Dering himself marvelled in January 1642, 'there are above forty-five hundred . . . sold and more in printing; never anything sold like that.' Some in Parliament believed that Dering had even sought permission from the Bishop of London's chaplain to have his book published '*cum privilegio*', but the author denied this.[146]

Sir Simonds D'Ewes counselled the Commons against a public burning of Dering's speeches, 'because that might make the book to be inquired after by many who would else never hear of it', and that is exactly what happened. Oliver Cromwell moved that the books be destroyed on Friday, 4 February, but the authorities could not lay their hands on sufficient copies and 'there wanted books of Sir Edward Dering's to burn'. Only after diligent search over the weekend did they round up enough copies for the hangman to make a decent fire.[147] 'The book I could have bought for fourteen pence last night, but now a crown cannot buy it', wrote Henry Oxinden to his cousin. D'Ewes thought the burning might drive the price to fourteen shillings and 'hasten a new impression'.[148] Dering was expelled from Parliament and his printer made to stand in the pillory, but nothing could stop the appearance of a new edition. As Dering himself protested to his persecutors, 'you have burnt my book, and thereby raised the price, and raised the desires of such as would have it. Alas, the burning of my book cannot confute me, nor silence me in the way I go.' And in this he was absolutely right.[149]

In August 1642, as civil war seemed imminent, the parliamentary committee on printing proposed again to suppress 'such scandalous pamphlets as were printed to the scandal of the state and parliament', and again they were unable to implement their will. This order, as D'Ewes said, would have

---

[145] Larkin (ed.), *Stuart Royal Proclamations . . . 1625–1646*, 754n.

[146] Coates, Young, and Snow (eds.), *Private Journals of the Long Parliament 3 January to 5 March 1642*, 253, 261.   [147] Ibid., 264, 268, 283.

[148] Dorothy Gardiner (ed.), *The Oxinden Letters 1607–1642* (1933), 287; Coates, Young, and Snow (eds.), *Private Journals of the Long Parliament 3 January to 5 March 1642*, 255.

[149] Coates, Young, and Snow (eds.), *Private Journals of the Long Parliament 3 January to 5 March 1642*, 248, 253–5, 261, 264, 268, 283; Centre for Kentish Studies, Dering Mss. U. 350/C2/96; Larking (ed.), *Proceedings, Principally in the County of Kent*, p. xlii; Bodleian Library, Ms. Rawlinson D. 141 ('England's Memorable Accidents'), 19; Gardiner (ed.), *Oxinden Letters 1607–1642*, 287; *A Collection of Speeches made by Sir Edward Dering, Knight and Baronet, in matter of Religion* (1642).

re-established the Stationers' monopoly with 'all that illegal and tyrannical power which they did put in practice before the beginning of this parliament, by virtue of the king's letters patent and by colour of certain orders made at the Council table and the Star Chamber'. Such a proposal, members agreed, would have 'dangerous consequences', so instead of effectively regulating the press at this time of crisis they did nothing but express their displeasure.[150] All they could do, as they had done intermittently for the past year and a half, was to grumble *ex post facto*, burn a few books, and subject a few printers to minor harassment. There would be no ordinance for licensing until June 1643, and even that, as John Milton acknowledged, was 'easily eluded'.[151]

'Paper bullets' flew thick and fast by the summer of 1642, as each side objected to the 'scandal' and 'disgrace' of the other's publications. Parliament continued to burn texts it found objectionable and to sanction printers as 'delinquents', while the royalist press at York and Oxford ridiculed the posturings at Westminster.[152] Neither could put the genie back in the bottle, and neither would give up the propaganda advantage of its own scandalous and libellous press. It is no surprise that 1642 yielded the highest number of publications in early modern history, for the war was fought in print as well as on the battlefield. The two sides took to arms amidst a cacophony of protestations and remonstrances, diurnals and declarations that became the commonplace of rancorous conversations. Avid readers rapidly absorbed the latest prints and diurnals, becoming addicted to news and opinion. 'Loose' and 'libellous' it may have been, but the press proved irrepressible, providing fuel and commentary for a long revolution.

---

[150] Snow and Young (eds.), *Private Journals of the Long Parliament 2 June to 17 September 1642*, 314.

[151] C. H. Firth and R. S. Rait (eds.), *Acts and Ordinances of the Interregnum, 1642–1660* (3 vols., 1911), i. 184–7; Milton, *Areopagitica*, 17.

[152] Snow and Young (eds.), *Private Journals of the Long Parliament 2 June to 17 September 1642*, 37, 42, 53, 77, 78.

13

News of High Distractions

The media storm of the early 1640s saturated England with an onslaught of news. An extraordinary sequence of events gave rise to a remarkable series of narratives and a novel abundance of public intelligence. People not only lived through such episodes as the fall of the Earl of Strafford and the breakdown between King and Parliament but read about them, heard about them, and re-imagined them in the telling. The rebellions in Scotland and Ireland, the fracturing of the Church of England, and the unravelling of the government of Charles I stimulated an insatiable appetite for news and information. The news could be exhilarating or depressing, giving rise to optimism or despair. Information and misinformation both helped to shape opinion, so that the loyalties and alignments that developed between 1640 and 1642 were buoyed up by a raft of news. This chapter examines the currency, circulation, and quality of news in the opening stages of the English Revolution.

Living through 'tumultuous and disjointed times', many people knew not what to believe. Their hunger for news was fed by rumour, report, and gossip. Information flowed intermittently, sometimes abundantly, at other times stinted. It assumed a variety of forms including oral reports, half-heard rumour, scribal correspondence, and printed publications. News of the nation's affairs spread quickly among the literate elite and percolated across the social order. Opinion passed from debating chambers to private parlours, from the magistrate's bench to the ale-bench, onto the streets, and into the wind.

Country correspondents actively solicited metropolitan information. 'At this distance I would willingly know as much as I might, having no other entertainment here but of pains, trouble and business', wrote the Earl of Bridgewater to his London agent in August 1640.[1] Humbler enquirers greeted travellers with the standard question, 'What news?'

---

[1] Huntington Library, Ms. El. 6565.

SCRIBAL INTELLIGENCE

The gentle and aristocratic families who composed the traditional 'political nation' traditionally drew on privileged connections to stay well informed about public and national affairs. Leading landowners and those connected to them wrote regular letters linking kinsmen in London and the provinces, sons at the universities and Inns of Court, office-holders, magistrates, clerics, men of business, and their wives. These circuits of gentle correspondence formed a primary network for the transmission of news. The sitting of Parliament was always a stimulus to correspondence, an occasion for sharing information; its prolongation after November 1640 created conditions for an expanded stream of correspondence. Men with business at Westminster wrote frequently to their associates, neighbours, families, and friends. The letters they received in return contained religious encouragement, domestic gossip, local news, and information about the administration of their estates. The cost of carriage per letter was usually a penny or twopence.[2]

London news could reach all parts of the metropolis within hours of its happening. The same news could cover the country within days, depending on the quality of the roads, the carriers, the horses, and the weather. Official correspondence typically took two days to travel between London and the Welsh marches, three or four days to reach the north. Private letters might take several days longer, depending on the availability of carriers. The Wynn family letters, for example, often took five days to go between north Wales and London.[3]

Many leading families had for a decade or more subscribed to manuscript newsletters to keep them abreast of public affairs. Professional newswriters in London, backed by teams of scriveners, sent weekly or fortnightly compendia of scribal intelligence to their provincial and aristocratic clientele. Among those whose productions survive are some of Thomas Jenyson's letters to Sir Roland St John and Edward Rossingham's newsletters for Viscount Scudamore. John Castle similarly supplied the Earl of Bridgewater, William Hawkins kept the Earl of Leicester abreast of developments, John Dillingham wrote diligently to Lord Montague of Boughton, and

[2] In April 1640 Thomas Temple wrote from London to his mother in Warwickshire, 'I sent a letter to you the last week and the carrier would not carry it because the porter would not lay out 2d. for the carriage' (Huntington Library, Ms. STT 2218).
[3] Huntington Library, Mss. El. 6558, 6568, 6581, 7350; National Library of Wales, Wynn Papers, no. 1666 (microfilm). One letter from Bridgewater House left Charing Cross at 7pm on 14 October 1640, reached St Albans after 1am, was at Stony Stratford by 9am on the 15th, at Daventry by 3pm, cleared Coventry past 7pm, and was received at Ludlow Castle at 7am on 16 October.

William Perkins corresponded regularly with the Earl of Cork. These letters were rich with news both domestic and foreign, including appointments, disappointments, and the doings of the great at court, but they did not come cheap. Manuscript 'separates' cost between sixpence and three shillings each, an expense that limited their circulation.[4] 'Captain Rossingham sets so high a rate upon his news... he writes not under twenty pounds per annum,' observed Robert Crane in May 1640.[5]

Some of this scribal journalism continued up to the time of the civil war, but after 1640 it was increasingly supplemented by news in print. The drama of events and the freeing of the press added to the torrent of information. Letters to the provinces transmitted metropolitan publications to a growing network of readers. Surviving correspondence comments frequently on the traffic in news and print.

The Kentish squire Henry Oxinden, for example, belonged to an active circle of readers, and shared the latest printed items with kinsmen and friends. Letters, pamphlets, books, and papers circulated easily among them, linking town and country.[6] Oxinden's brother-in-law Thomas Barrow distinguished 'news not in print' from the novel products of the press, but dispatched both in abundance from London to Kent.[7]

Others in Kent read and discussed reports of proceedings in Parliament. John Elmeston wrote from Cranbrook on 1 December 1640 to tell Sir Edward Dering of 'the common rejoicing of all well affected people hereabouts for your worthy speaking and doing in this present parliament.... We were much affected with the report and view of your first speech.' Correspondents remarked on 'the tidings and sight' of Dering's speeches, which originally circulated in manuscript and in 1641 were among the first to be rendered in print.[8]

Writing from Northamptonshire in March 1641, Sir Roland St John thanked his London cousin Hugh Floyde 'for the books and letters of news, which to us in the country is of great contentment'.[9] Baynham Throckmorton and Thomas Smyth similarly shared journals and news that came to Bristol and Ashton Court.[10] John Willoughby's London relations

---

[4] Ian Atherton, ' "The Itch Grown a Disease": Manuscript Transmission of News in the Seventeenth Century', in Joad Raymond (ed.), *News, Newspapers, and Society in Early Modern Britain* (1999), 39–65; Richard Cust, 'News and Politics in Early Seventeenth-Century England', *Past and Present*, 112 (1986), 64; Esther S. Cope and Willson H. Coates (eds.), *Proceedings of the Short Parliament of 1640* (Camden Society, 4th ser., vol. xix, 1977), 35.

[5] Bodleian Library, Oxford, Tanner Ms. 65, f. 78.

[6] Dorothy Gardiner (ed.), *The Oxinden Letters 1607–1642* (1933), passim.

[7] Ibid., 310.   [8] Centre for Kentish Studies, Maidstone, Dering Mss. U. 350/C2/86.

[9] Bedfordshire and Luton Archives, St John Papers, J. 1378.

[10] J. H. Bettey (ed.), *Calendar of the Correspondence of the Smyth Family of Ashton Court 1548–1642* (Bristol Record Society, vol. xxxv, 1982), 172–3.

supplied him in Devon with 'the newest news', pamphlets, and copies of manuscript libels in verse.[11] Robert Appleton informed a kinsman in Suffolk in July 1641, 'I have sent you down some eight small things from the press.'[12] Francis Newport sent packets of pamphlets to Sir Richard Leveson commenting, 'these I send you are all pertinent and necessary for your knowledge.' Early in 1642 he had only 'ill news, the times afford no better'.[13] Sir Giles Mompesson and Edward Hyde also exchanged weekly 'journals' of public affairs.[14] Philip Morton wrote from London to his father in Cheshire on 3 June 1641, enclosing 'a petition which came out in print about three days since; I pray when you have read it send it to my brother Morton with his letter.' Six months later Morton was sending 'diurnal occurrences', commending one sent on 25 January 1642 as 'the truest copy that came forth'.[15] 'I have enclosed some printed news', wrote Robert Nelson to Lady Temple on 11 January 1642, reporting the King's departure from London.[16]

The Wynn family similarly sent correspondence and texts back and forth between North Wales and London. Enclosing a royal speech and a parliamentary remonstrance with one letter in January 1641, Thomas Spicer suggested to Richard Wynn that 'when he is weary of reading it, then may he recreate himself after supper upon this thing like a book.'[17] A postscript to one of Owen Wynn's letters to his uncle in March 1641 adds 'for news, I refer you to the enclosed diurnals'.[18] Robert Wynn sent 'the enclosed pamphlets' to kinsman Richard Griffith in March 1642, advising him that 'the latest news you may perceive by the diurnals'.[19]

Metropolitan correspondents influenced country opinion by their selection of reading matter and their comments upon it. 'I send you herewith divers printed books of several styles, all which I leave for your entertainment at spare hours', wrote Sidney Bere to Sir John Pennington in January 1642.[20] Richard Fitch added to Pennington's library in February, enclosing Pym's latest speech and 'another scurrilous pamphlet which this day came forth, to make you a little merry withal'.[21] Sir John Coke used almost the same words to commend 'several printed papers' he sent to his father in March 1642, 'to entertain you withal'.[22] 'Out of these prints you may feel how the pulse of the

---

[11] W. C. Trevelyan and C. E. Trevelyan (eds.), *The Trevelyan Papers, Part III* (Camden Society, no. 105, 1872), 192, 202, 208, 216.   [12] Bodleian Library, Oxford, Tanner Ms. 66, f. 110.

[13] Staffordshire Record Office, Leveson Letter Book, D. 868/2/33 and 34.

[14] Folger Shakespeare Library, Ms. X. c. 23.

[15] British Library, Add. Ms. 33936, ff. 235, 253–4.

[16] Huntington Library, Ms. HM 46431.

[17] National Library of Wales, Wynn Papers, no. 1674 (microfilm).

[18] National Library of Wales, Llanfair-Brynodel letters, C31.

[19] Ibid., C34, Robert Wynne to Richard Griffith, 19 March 1642.

[20] *CSPD 1641–43*, 253.   [21] Ibid., 273.

[22] HMC, *12th Report, The Manuscripts of the Earl Cowper . . . Preserved at Melbourne Hall, Derbyshire* (1888), ii. 305, 310.

king and kingdom beats, both highly distempered', wrote Thomas Knyvett to his mother in May 1642.[23]

Sometimes printed news ran ahead of scribal communications. Information could travel faster than some correspondents could write. Describing the King's visit to Cambridge in March 1642, Joseph Beaumont wrote to his father, 'What he did there and what he did at Newmarket, printed papers I suppose have already told you.'[24] Writing to Sir Richard Leveson in June 1642, Edward Littleton commented, 'Were not the news in print I should write more largely.'[25] Pamphlets printed on 9 June and 5 August reported 'horrible news' that took place just a few days earlier.[26]

On other occasions the news was too fresh, too complex, or too confusing to be summarized in hurriedly written letters. Oral, scribal, and printed forms of communication would have to be combined. Correspondents commonly dispatched their scribblings 'in haste', 'most hastily', or 'with all possible speed', and invited their readers to learn more from the bearer or courier.[27] At Ludlow, the Earl of Bridgewater supplemented his 'intelligence' by 'what I shall receive by Tom Long the carrier'.[28] Writing from London to Cornwall in the summer of 1640, Francis Sawle advised Jonathan Rashleigh, 'as for news, John Langdon will acquaint you with all that is going'. In another letter he wrote, 'as for news, we have more than is good, and many flying reports.... More news you will have shortly, I pray God send good or none.'[29] Reporting the outbreak of hostilities in the summer of 1642, Thomas Salisbury told Thomas Bulkely, 'the manner I leave to the relation of the bearer to whom I read the news, it being too long to transcribe'.[30]

Correspondents learned to be careful what they committed to paper. The alerts and alarms of the early 1640s made some writers exceptionally cautious. Several surviving letters contain tantalizing hints about information deliberately withheld. Writing to the Earl of Rutland about the situation at York, for example, Thomas Gower remarked, 'many things I could tell worth your hearing, but dare not write; they are fitter to be told than written.'[31]

---

[23] Bertram Schofield (ed.), *The Knyvett Letters (1620–1644)* (Norfolk Record Society, 1949), 107.

[24] Charles Henry Cooper, *Annals of Cambridge* (4 vols., Cambridge, 1842–52), iii. 322.

[25] Staffordshire Record Office, Leveson Letter Book, D. 868/3, 19.

[26] [Adam Jones], *Horrible Newes from Leicester. Being the Copie of a Letter sent from thence the 6 of Iune* (1642); *An Extract of a Letter from Yorke. Dated on Friday night, August 5* (1642).

[27] For example, National Library of Wales, Llanfair-Brynodel letters, C26–9, Thomas Glynn to Griffith Jones and John Griffith, September–October 1640.

[28] Huntington Library, Ms. El. 6569.

[29] Cornwall Record Office, DD R(S)/1/1039, 1040.

[30] National Library of Wales, Wynn Papers, no. 1711 (microfilm).

[31] HMC, *The Manuscripts of His Grace the Duke of Rutland, G.C.B., Preserved at Belvoir Castle* (1888), i. 522.

John Barry affected ignorance of political affairs in a letter to Sir Philip Percival in March 1641, 'considering how dangerous it is to write truth in this age'.[32] Handwriting could be more dangerous than printing, so Henry Herbert maintained in November 1641, explaining to Viscount Scudamore why he had put so little news in his letter.[33]

Anxieties about the security of correspondence became more acute in 1642 after the King's departure from London. 'Everybody had need be careful what they write for fear of interception', warned Sir John Coke in January 1642, hoping that a 'feigned' hand would mask his scribal identity.[34] Sidney Bere was similarly cautious that same month, 'in a time so distracted and wherein is so little assurance into what hands letters may fall'.[35] Sir Philip Percival's correspondents in February 1642 warned that they could not 'safely write what we believe'.[36] Writing in April 1642, after the King's exclusion from Hull, Thomas Knyvett told his wife, 'I know how my heart stands, but 'tis not safe to write any opinion of these high distractions.'[37] 'There is no safety in writing anything', the Earl of Manchester warned Lord Montague in May.[38] A letter from Lord Montague in June 1642 is endorsed with the memo, 'I sent word to my son William to burn this.'[39] Who knows how many letters from this time went up in flames?

Usually the post was secure, but in tumultuous times it could not be guaranteed. Early in October 1641 'the post was robbed' on the road north from London and some government correspondence was taken by 'fellows with vizards on their faces'. Thomas Wiseman, who suspected that the robbers were disbanded soldiers, remarked, 'such an insolency has not been known before'.[40]

By 1642 any bundle of news might be deemed suspicious, and ordinary travellers became swept up in the national panic. An Essex clergyman, Edward Cherry, fell foul of a magisterial investigation in January 1642 when his correspondence with a kinsman who was an officer in the army aroused suspicions. Potentially incriminating material came to light at a roadblock between Hatfield and Boreham and was turned over to the watch.[41] A package

---

[32] HMC, *Report on the Manuscripts of the Earl of Egmont* (1905), vol. i., part 1, 128.

[33] PRO, C115/107/8521.

[34] HMC, *12th Report, The Manuscripts of the Earl Cowper*, ii. 305.

[35] *CSPD 1614–43*, 253.

[36] HMC, *Report on the Manuscripts of the Earl of Egmont*, vol. i., part 1, 163.

[37] Schofield (ed.), *The Knyvett Letters (1620–1644)*, 100–1.

[38] HMC, *Report on the Manuscripts of the Duke of Buccleuch and Queensberry . . . at Montague House* (1899), 299.

[39] HMC, *Report on the Manuscripts of the Duke of Buccleuch and Queensberry* (The Montague papers, 2nd series, 1926), iii. 414.

[40] *CSPD 1641–43*, 134; *Privy Council Registers* (1968), xii. 183, 189.

[41] British Library, Add. Ms. 34253, ff. 7–12.

of seven letters from Kent to a recusant in Norfolk was broken open and its contents read before the mayor of Norwich in June 1642, but being found to contain 'no matters of any public concernment but only private business', the papers were returned to their carrier.[42] Another letter allegedly revealing a plot against Scotland only came to light when found quilted into the courier's saddle.[43] Sir John Hotham's correspondence with Parliament would have reached Westminster sooner, he explained in May 1642, had not the courier from Hull 'been stayed by the way and his letters taken from him'.[44] More letters between Yorkshire and Westminster were delayed in July 1642 as parliamentary couriers had to dodge marauding Cavaliers.[45] To safeguard their secrecy, letters containing sensitive political or military information employed numerical or alphabetical ciphers rather than plain text.[46]

FALSE AND UNCERTAIN NEWS

Whether handwritten or printed, the news was not necessarily reliable. The jumble of gossip, rumour, truth, and falsehood challenged anyone who was seeking certainty. Scribal communication was idiosyncratic, but the news was not necessarily more trustworthy for being published in print. Correspondents lamented the confusion of the news, and satirists made fun of its admixture with falsehoods. Contemporaries knew too well that 'false news follows true at the heels, and often outslips it'.[47] 'I never knew reports so false and uncertain', complained Robert Hobart in December 1640.[48] 'The general news is, nobody knows what to make of this world', claimed the author of 'Pigg's Corranto' in 1640.[49]

Participants in the news culture experienced scarcity and abundance, and swung between falsehood and certainty as well as optimism and despair. Too

---

[42] Norfolk Record Office, Norwich Mayor's Court Book, 1634–1646, f. 353v.

[43] Bedfordshire and Luton Archives, St John Papers, J. 1384.

[44] Vernon F. Snow and Anne Steele Young (eds.), *The Private Journals of the Long Parliament 7 March to 1 June March 1642* (New Haven and London, 1987), 222; University of Hull, Brynmor Jones Library, Hotham Papers, DDHO/1/2.

[45] University of Hull, Brynmor Jones Library, Hotham Papers, DDHO/1/7.

[46] [John Wilkins], *Mercury, or the Secret and Swift Messenger: Shewing How a Man may with Privacy and Speed communicate his Thoughts to a Friend at any distance* (1641). For an application of cypher, see Mary Anne Everett Green (ed.), *Letters of Queen Henrietta Maria* (1857), 46, 54.

[47] Quoted from a sermon of 1623, in Adam Fox, *Oral and Literate Culture in England 1500–1700* (Oxford, 2000), 334.   [48] Bodleian Library, Oxford, Tanner Ms. 65, f. 217.

[49] 'Pigg's Corranto', Durham University Library, Special Collections, Mickleton-Spearman Ms. MSP/9, ii. 133; PRO, SP16/475/16.

often the news was inadequate, contradictory, or depressing. Henry Herbert complained in November 1641 of 'the variety of tidings that, like waves at sea in a storm, one begets another and without beginning or ending'.[50] Edward Partheriche told correspondents in Kent who asked for 'the news of these sad times' that the news was 'so uncertain and hath so many changes and that on a sudden, as what was believed and published for news and truth this hour the next is changed and utterly false'.[51] 'The news from Ireland is uncertain, some say good, more bad, but what none', Robert Jager complained in February 1642.[52] 'There was no news stirring worth your knowledge, at present there is none that is good', Robert Wynn told correspondents in Wales in March 1642.[53] Even the highest men in the land, like privy councillors Archbishop Laud and the Earl of Bridgewater, confessed in their correspondence of 1640, 'I know not what to believe.'[54] If political leaders of this stature faced confusion, is it any wonder that others were bewildered by the uncertainties of public affairs?

Despite the accelerated flow of information, correspondents complained repeatedly about the dearth or uncertainty of the news. 'Intelligence of all news in the northern parts' was 'so various that I know not what to write', confessed Richard Harrison to the Earl of Bridgewater in September 1640. 'If this day I have one thing, tomorrow I shall perhaps have the contrary, so that no certainty can be related.'[55] John Castle had similar trouble sorting out 'verity or falsehood' following the fall of Newcastle. Robert Woodford of Northampton, who was normally well informed about national affairs, conceded in September 1640 that news concerning the Scots was 'very uncertain, and what the event will be the Lord alone knoweth'.[56] 'Many talk but little certainty' noted Thomas Wyatt in his diary at this time.[57]

The summoning of a new parliament in the autumn of 1640 also produced contradictory information. Writing to Henry Oxinden in October, the London merchant Thomas Barrow commented, 'I dare not persuade you to

---

[50] PRO, C115/107/8521.

[51] East Kent Archives, Sandwich Borough Muniments, Mayor's Letter Book 1639–44, Sa/C1, f. 77, 27 January 1642. Partheriche was a Member of Parliament for the Cinque Port of Sandwich.

[52] East Kent Archives, Sandwich Borough Muniments, Mayor's Letter Book 1641–83, Sa/C4, f. 3.

[53] National Library of Wales, Llanfair-Brynodel letters, C34, Robert Wynn to Richard Griffith, 19 March 1642.

[54] Laud to Bishop Morton, Durham University Library, Special Collections, Mickleton-Spearman Ms. MSP/46, f. 143; Huntington Library, Ms. El. 7848, 10 August 1640.

[55] Huntington Library, Ms. El. 6572.

[56] Ibid., Ms. El. 7858, 26 September 1640; Robert Woodford's diary, New College, Oxford, Ms. 9502, 8 September 1640.

[57] Diary of Thomas Wyatt, Bodleian Library, Ms. Top. Oxon. C. 378, 310.

believe the truth of this enclosed paper, but you may read and suspend your judgement.'[58] Edward Hyde's Wiltshire correspondent Archdeacon Thomas Marler desired in December 1640, 'to know the certainty', but all he had was 'parliament news in riddles'.[59]

The correspondence of 1641 reflected the fast-moving revolutionary crisis, but recipients hungered for better information. 'I take very little for certainty', Lady Brilliana Harley told her husband, except what she heard from her closest kin. Attempting to sift 'rumours' from 'intelligence', she longed 'exceedingly . . . to hear the truth of things'.[60] The Scottish commissioner Robert Baillie shrewdly took much of the flow of news 'for clatters'.[61] Edmund Percival admitted to being overwhelmed by the flow of news. 'As for news', he wrote to his cousin early in 1641, 'there are so many different reports of our parliamentary proceedings that I cannot deliver you any certainty of anything.'[62]

Readers in the country were frustrated by 'weekly reports' that 'admit of contradictions the week following'.[63] Edward Perkins wrote to Robert Harley from Oxford at the end of March 1641, 'we are tortured with the diversities of relations'.[64] The news of the execution of the Earl of Strafford 'will come to you so many ways that I do not trust this for your first intelligence', wrote Viscountess Falkland to Lady Hastings in May. 'The manner of it is so differently related that I believe your ladyship will find very little truth amongst a great deal of falsehood.'[65]

'News is very scant, but what I know you shall share of', wrote William Thomas to his cousin in Wales in September 1641. He offered scraps about the Scots, the King, the army and the parliament, as well as titbits about the queen mother and the incidence of plague, before apologizing, 'other news I have none'.[66] Confessing no 'certainty' about the news, another London correspondent in October 1641 opined that there were 'as many opinions as

---

[58] Gardiner (ed.), *Oxinden Letters 1607–1642*, 184.

[59] Bodleian Library, Ms. Clarendon 19, no. 1460.

[60] British Library, Add. Ms. 70110, f. 60; Add. Ms. 70003, f. 78, misdated in HMC, *14th Report, The Manuscripts of His Grace the Duke of Portland* (1894), iii. 75. For similar correspondence with her son Edward, see Thomas Taylor Lewis (ed.), *Letters of the Lady Brilliana Harley* (Camden Society, vol. lviii, 1854), 95, 118, 129, 136, 157, 158.

[61] David Laing (ed.), *The Letters and Journals of Robert Baillie* (3 vols., Edinburgh, 1841), i. 269. Milton also uses the word 'clatter' in *Of Reformation* (1641), 26.

[62] HMC, *Report on the Manuscripts of the Earl of Egmont*, vol. i., part 1, 125.

[63] Trevelyan and Trevelyan (eds.), *Trevelyan Papers, Part III*, 208.

[64] HMC, *14th Report, The Manuscripts of His Grace the Duke of Portland*, iii. 75.

[65] Huntington Library, Ms. Hastings Correspondence, HA 1271.

[66] National Library of Wales, Llanfair-Brynodel letters, C33, William Thomas to Richard Griffith, 4 September 1641.

there are faces'.[67] Early in December Sir John Coke wrote, 'the news out of Ireland is worse and worse, all like to be lost.'[68]

Though increasingly momentous, the news of 1642 was no more certain, and no more reassuring. In January 1642 a correspondent in Chester wrote that the 'news is so bad that it almost made me sick to read it'.[69] Thomas Stockdale advised Lord Fairfax about the flurry of rumours in February 1642, 'which when they have been searched after, they fly before the pursuer as a shadow and at length vanish into air'.[70] In March 1642, complained Sir John Coke, 'so many false reports are spread abroad that a man knows not what to believe'.[71] In May Thomas Knyvett noted 'many ... things are fluttering up and down, more false than true'.[72]

Pamphlet writers took up the theme of malicious and mendacious misinformation. 'Why then, oh why, are lies and falsehoods spread? | Shall men by lying earn their daily bread?' asked the pamphleteer-poet Martin Parker.[73] John Taylor, who was not himself beyond making things up, observed how lies went forth as 'true tales', while incredible falsehoods circulated as truth.[74] With so many 'extreme and incredible lies' in print, claimed John Bond, it was a hard task 'to distinguish betwixt the lies and real books'.[75] Responding to just such a packet of pamphlets in April 1641, Viscount Cholmondley wondered that people were so 'audacious to put to print so notorious lies'.[76] The Fleet Street writer John Dillingham forwarded the latest diurnal to Lord Montague in February 1642 with the comment, 'you will find not above three lies, but many truths left out.'[77]

The potentially dangerous consequence of the appetite for news is indicated by a cautionary tale that appears in a pamphlet of 1641. It concerns a young gentlewoman of Pirford, Surrey, who, 'holding prattle with one of her father's men, one day began to question him about the new sects of religion which were so much talked of, enquiring what news he heard of any of them.'

[67] HMC, *Report on the Manuscripts of Lord Montague of Beaulieu* (1900), 131. The remark anticipates comments about the diversity of opinions in *Heads of all Fashions* (1642).

[68] HMC, *12th Report, The Manuscripts of the Earl Cowper*, ii. 296.

[69] HMC, *Report on the Manuscripts of Lord Montague of Beaulieu*, 146. The unidentified author was responding to John Dillingham's reports from London.

[70] G. W. Johnson (ed.), *The Fairfax Correspondence. Memoirs of the Reign of Charles the First* (2 vols., 1848), ii. 375.

[71] HMC, *12th Report, The Manuscripts of the Earl Cowper*, ii. 305, 310.

[72] Schofield (ed.), *Knyvett Letters (1620–1644)*, 103.

[73] Martin Parker, *The Poets Blind mans bough* (1641), sig. B.

[74] John Taylor, *The Liar. Or, A contradiction to those who in the titles of their Bookes affirmed them to be true, when they were false: although mine are all true, yet I terme them lyes* (1641), sig. A4.

[75] John Bond, *The Poets Knavery Discouered, in all their lying Pamphlets* (1641 or 1642), title page.   [76] British Library, Add. Ms. 36914, f. 212.

[77] HMC, *Report on the Manuscripts of Lord Montague of Beaulieu*, 147.

This proved a dangerous enquiry, according to the pamphlet, for her curiosity led to her entanglement in orgies of the Family of Love.[78] It was similar openness to novelty and suggestion, other pamphlets suggested, that drew weak souls to other sectarian excesses, like the Adamites.[79]

Abundance of news did not necessarily make people better informed or better prepared to make judgements about public affairs. It did, however, provide plenty to talk about. Ripples and rivulets of information spread news and commentary to all parts of the kingdom, so that by the outbreak of civil war all parts of the country could be drawn into the national conversation.

---

[78] *A Description of the Sect called the Familie of Love* (1641), 1.

[79] *A Nest of Serpents Discovered. Or, A knot of old Heretiques revived, Called the Adamites. Wherein their original, increase, and several ridiculous tenets are plainly laid open* (1641); 'Samoth Yarb' [Thomas Bray] *A New Sect of Religion Descryed, called Adamites: Deriving their Religion from our Father Adam* (1641); *The Adamites Sermon* (1641).

14

Discourse, Opinion, and the Making of a Revolutionary Culture

One of the most difficult tasks of the early modern historian is to capture the voices of ordinary political conversation. It requires a double effort of imagination, first to acknowledge that citizens and subjects were talking and listening to each other in the past, and secondly to attempt to retrieve what they said. Politics, by this time, was no longer the preserve of the 'political nation', nor was all discourse embodied in text. This chapter sets out to eavesdrop on the arguments in streets and taverns, and to suggest some of the ways in which the energized culture of news and opinion became mobilized at the onset of the English Revolution.

Most conversations went unrecorded, of course, but fragments survive from a few that were reported to the authorities or otherwise found their way into the historical record. The Privy Council attempted to police the bounds of discourse, at least until its own authority crumbled, and county magistrates sought to curb speech that was disorderly, scandalous, or seditious. Correspondents and pamphleteers also made mention of public discussion. The following examples help bring to life some of the lost conversations of early revolutionary England. They illustrate some of the vehemence of popular politics and the partisan vigour of debate, away from the more polished interactions at Westminster and in the press.

SPHERES OF DISCOURSE

There is abundant evidence, from a variety of sources, of the vitality of politicized public conversation before, during, and after the English Revolution. Alongside the high politics of the court and council the political culture of

Tudor and Stuart England fostered the beginnings of a precocious 'public sphere'. This term, associated with the German philosopher Jürgen Habermas, has come to signify an arena of informed and critical engagement with national political affairs, in which people acted more as citizens than as subjects. It differentiates a proto-democratic future from a somewhat mythologized past in which political discourse belonged exclusively to an elite. Classically located in eighteenth-century England in the culture of the coffee house, many of the characteristics of the public sphere have been discerned in other societies elsewhere and earlier. Whether they match the criteria of their prime theoretician is of little immediate interest. There is no need here to follow those scholars who have been drawn more to theoretical ingenuity than to uncovering the past.[1]

A popular audience for news and opinion emerged much sooner in England than is often imagined. Specialists in earlier and earlier eras have noted signs of its birth. We can now see that the expanding 'public sphere' of the later Stuart era was prefigured in the social and civic discourse of the mid-seventeenth century. The energized popular politics that surrounded the civil war had antecedents in the 1620s. An earlier generation in the 1590s found stimulus in Elizabethan print and polemic. Ordinary people in the reign of Henry VIII expressed critical opinions about the nationally important topics of the Reformation.[2] One of the purposes of this chapter is to show how this long tradition of discursive citizenship was revitalized and transformed in the years between 1640 and 1642.

Long before coffee houses first appeared in the 1650s, English men and women obtained their news and shared their views in a variety of public and semi-public locations. People talked wherever they met, and every place of public resort was potentially a site for conversation. Friends and strangers conventionally greeted each other with the question, 'What news?' They exchanged gossip, rumour, news, and views in lanes and highways, urban squares and village greens. The church porch, the parish pump, the market cross, or whipping post or pillory were nodal points in the flow of information, and obvious sites for posting printed broadsheets or handwritten libels. The staples of news in the early modern metropolis included Westminster and St Paul's, Cheapside and the Exchange, the docks and the court. Many of the

---

[1] Jürgen Habermas, *The Structural Transformation of the Public Sphere* (Cambridge, Mass., 1989).

[2] See, for example, Steve Pincus, ' "Coffee politicians does create": Coffeehouses and Restoration Political Culture', *Journal of Modern History*, 67 (1995), 807–34; Joad Raymond, 'The Newspaper, Public Opinion, and the Public Sphere in the Seventeenth Century', in idem, *News, Newspapers and Society in Early Modern Britain* (1999), 109–40; Alexandra Halasz, *The Marketplace of Print: Pamphlets and the Public Sphere in Early Modern England* (Cambridge, 1997); Ethan Shagan, *Popular Politics and the English Reformation* (Cambridge, 2003).

subversive writings that scandalized the early Stuart authorities first appeared on public thresholds (places of entry and egress, half indoors and half out), on walls, gates or doorways, or entrances to churches, churchyards, or shops.

Above all, news and opinion circulated in places of refreshment and entertainment, wherever alcohol and fellowship loosened tongues. Travellers especially were carriers of news and their places of tippling, victualling, and lodging formed the nexus of the national conversation. Exchanges were especially vigorous on occasions of public assemblies, holidays, markets, fairs, quarter sessions, assizes, and ecclesiastical visitations, where clerics and gentry, plebians and countrymen, frequently mingled together. Every church day was potentially a day of gossip.

By the later sixteenth century alehouses, inns, and taverns had become places to read as well as to talk. Both printed and scribal publications found their way into the company of drinkers, where ballads, bills, and broadsheets commonly adorned the walls.[3] As we know from recent research into manuscript libels, such settings were also conducive to writing, or at least to the collective composition of scandalous satirical verse. Libels circulated, so witnesses claimed, 'in divers alehouses, taverns and other open and public places'.[4] Pot poets and scribblers composed and shared their work amidst the clatter and conviviality of the common drinking board.

The Elizabethan George Puttenham observed that texts were both made and displayed in places of 'common resort, where it was allowed every man might come, or be sitting to chat and prate, as now in our taverns and common tabling houses, where many merry heads meet, and scribble with ink and chalk'. Such writings might be found on tables, walls, or windows, and some were 'put in paper and in books, and used as ordinary missives'.[5]

Contemporaries marvelled, and moralized, at the proliferation of 'alehouses and tippling houses' that invited 'citizens of most sorts and ranks' to socialize over food and drink.[6] Lord Keeper Egerton complained in 1599 about the increasing numbers who, 'at ordinaries and common tables, where they have scarce money to pay for their dinner, enter politique discourses of princes, kingdoms and estates and of councils and councillors, censuring every one according to their own discontented and malicious humours without regard of religion, conscience or honesty'.[7] Affairs of state could not be

---

[3] Tessa Watt, *Cheap Print and Popular Piety, 1550–1640* (Cambridge, 1991); Peter Clark, *The English Alehouse: A Social History, 1200–1830* (1983); *A Health to all Vintners, Beer-brewers and Ale-tonners* (1642), broadside.

[4] Adam Fox, *Oral and Literate Culture in England 1500–1700* (Oxford, 2000), 321.

[5] George Puttenham, *The Arte of English Poesie* (1589), 44.

[6] Richard Rawlidge, *A Monster Late Found Out and Discovered* (1628), 8.

[7] Fox, *Oral and Literate Culture*, 340, citing PRO, SP12/273/35.

confined to the class of statesmen. Although early modern monarchs were protective of the *arcana imperii*, and members of the traditional elite felt political discourse belonged to themselves alone, they could not prevent intrusions by the masses. Commenting early in Charles I's reign on the commercialized flow of discourse and opinion, John Taylor remarked on the variety of written materials available in 'taverns, ordinaries, inns, bowling-greens and alleys, ale-houses, tobacco-shops, highways and water passages', a variety to which his own prolific output contributed.[8]

Much of the conversation in early modern drinking establishments was no doubt apolitical and unthreatening. But the quickening crisis that began with the Scottish wars in the late 1630s drew many more citizens into the arena of controversy. It was hard to ignore news about the insolencies of the army or the prospects of Parliament, hard to resist rumour about Catholic machinations or outrages in Ireland. Opinions varied in 1640 about the fate of the bishops and the future of the church, and everyone seemed to have a point of view. The level of discourse grew louder, its content more fractious, as the kingdom drew closer to civil war. The greeting, 'What news?', elicited increasingly troubled responses in 1641 and 1642 as the news grew worse and worse.

Writing to Sir John Pennington in December 1641, Thomas Smith reported 'much discourse in court, parliament and city, nay, and country too, and much discontent in all of them', as passion corrupted judgement.[9] 'Religion is now become the common discourse and table talk in every tavern and ale-house, where a man shall hardly find five together in one mind, and yet everyone presumes he is in the right', reported John Taylor about that time.[10] Religion had become 'the ordinary discourse at our very commons and ordinaries', echoed another pamphlet of 1642.[11] The very pamphlets that contained these remarks could be found on the boards and walls of inns and taverns. Participants in alehouse arguments about politics and religion cited, brandished, or sought to discredit the cheap publications that poured off the newly liberated press. 'Wine, beer and tobacco' nourished both the writing and consumption of news, observed one of these pamphlets in spring 1642, as the alcohol quickened tempers and loosened tongues.[12]

'Discord hath made men's tongues wrangle and jangle', as 'arguments and discourses' overflowed 'in taverns and other meeting places', claimed

---

[8] John Taylor, *Wit and Mirth* (1626), title page; Bernard Capp, *The World of John Taylor, the Water-Poet, 1578–1653* (Oxford, 1994).   [9] *CSPD 1641–43*, 206.

[10] John Taylor, *Religions Enemies* (1641), 6. The title pages depicts religion as a book tossed in the blanket of tumultuous disputation.

[11] *The Anatomy of the Separatists, alias, Brownists, the factious Brethren in these Times* (1642), 1.   [12] *A Presse Full of Pamphlets* (1642), sig. A3.

A Remonstrance of Londons Occurrences. 'Matters of consequence' at Whitehall and Westminster became topics of heated public debate. 'There was never such a confusing of babbling and pro and conning...at bake-houses, barbers' shops, and ale-houses', as disputants talked politics and religion. 'Common people', ignorant people, and even women were now talking above themselves, about 'the whole estate of this kingdom'.[13]

Another pamphlet from 1642 evoked the animation and discursive bustle of the pre-war metropolitan crowd. It described how 'people flock to lectures in towns...some scoffing, some comparing, some flattering, asking, doubting, some swearing...some calling, jeering, cursing...some scorning, shunning, dreading, some disdaining'.[14] Whether attending midweek sermons or socializing at the alehouse, these townsmen were anything but passive. They belonged to an engaged and energized public, diverse in their viewpoints and ready to hear more.

WORDS IN ACTION

Fragments of evidence bring us closer to some of these conversations. We can sometimes see the circumstances of arguments and altercations, even if we cannot always hear the words. Phrases and utterances are adduced and reproduced in a variety of testimonies, complaints, and recollections.

Much of the libelling against Archbishop Laud in the late 1630s originated and circulated in drinking establishments. It was a Southwark drinker who proclaimed that 'the pope of Lambeth...doth pluck the royal crown off his majesty's head and trample it under his feet, and did whip his majesty's arse with his own rod'. Drinkers at the Three Cranes in Chancery Lane drank healths to the destruction and confusion of the Archbishop in July 1640.[15] Inns and taverns also gave cover to incipient sectarian activities. When the notorious separatist John Canne stayed at the Dolphin Inn at Bristol in the summer of 1640, he 'taught them the way of the Lord more perfectly and settled them in church order', leaving behind copies of his writings, and recruiting auditors for his sermon the following Sunday.[16]

---

[13] *A Remonstrance of Londons Occurences* (1642), sigs. A2–A2v, A4–A4v, title page.
[14] [William Lilly], *Lilli's propheticall history of this yeares accidence, 1642* (1642), 7–8.
[15] PRO, SP16/248/93; 250/58; 327/140; 372/109; *CSPD 1639*, 43, 260, 300; *CSPD 1640*, 474, 487.
[16] Roger Hayden (ed.), *The Records of a Church of Christ in Bristol, 1640–1687* (Bristol Record Society, vol. xxvii, 1974), 90–1.

In London 'the Nag's head tavern near Coleman Street' was a centre of Brownist activity. Samuel How, the radical sectarian shoemaker, gained notoriety in the summer of 1640 for his extempore sermons at the tavern.[17] Tub preaching was often tavern preaching, before radicals gained access to more reputable pulpits.

The Scottish war of 1640 occasioned lively debate among soldiers and civilians. When the Suffolk clothier Edward Cole encountered a conscripted soldier at the White Hart inn at Bocking, Essex, he offered him a clandestine book, most likely a pamphlet from Edinburgh, intending, so the Council believed, 'to persuade the soldiers not to fight against the Scots'.[18] The same issue gave rise to a violent scene at the Green Dragon in Bishopsgate, London, when two clothiers from Essex got into a fight with an army officer over whether the Scots were rebels or good Christians. Tankards flew and diners scattered as the officer, Captain Watts, drew his sword and derided other drinkers as puritans.[19]

In May 1640 at Lutterworth Fair a Northamptonshire yeoman proclaimed that the King was about to 'bring his forces back from Scotland upon the city of London', and spread rumours that 'the best men of the kingdom' (he named Lords Saye and Brooke and the Earl of Warwick) were already 'imprisoned by the king'. Although the news was false, it drew ordinary people into agitated conversation about the great affairs of the kingdom.[20] A short time later in Staffordshire, John Sheppard of Comberford alarmed fellow drinkers by saying that 'he cared not for the king nor his laws'. Warned by his companions 'of the heinousness of the said words, [Sheppard] wept and said he had but a life to lose and he could but lose it, and that his life lay in their hands'. One of those present reported the speech to a bailiff who in turn informed a magistrate, who indicted the offender at the midsummer sessions 'for contemptuous words against the king's majesty'. A sober and repentant Sheppard disowned his words and insisted that he lived 'without any detection of ill-loyalty to the king or duty to his country and neighbours', and the court, it seems, was prepared to give him the benefit of the doubt.[21]

Similar indiscretions scandalized a Yorkshire alehouse one Sunday in January 1641, though the speaker, who said the King 'was worthy to be hanged', later denied his words, as if the alcohol, not the subject, had done the talking.[22] Comparable words of sedition became common in the year

---

[17] *The Coblers threed is cut* (1640), broadsheet; *The Vindication of the Cobler* (1640), broadsheet; John Taylor, *A Swarme of Sectaries, And Schismatiques* (1641), title page; Murray Tolmie, *The Triumph of the Saints: The Separate Churches of London 1616–1649* (Cambridge, 1977), 17, 36. [18] *CSPD 1640*, 635, 638; PRO, SP16/465/43. [19] *CSPD 1640–41*, 31; PRO, SP16/466/13. [20] PRO, SP16/458/110. [21] Staffordshire Record Office, Q/SO/5/16; Q/SR/243/6–11. [22] PRO, ASSI 45/1/3/47.

before the civil war, though such sentiments rarely appeared in print. Print culture generally maintained the fiction of a benign but ill-led monarch, whereas subjects spoke more rashly in their cups. Drinkers at an unlicensed alehouse at Pleshey, Essex, in September 1641 heard Joan Allen say to a justice of the peace that 'she knew not the king, nor cared not for him, nor for the said Sir Francis, nor would she obey his authority'.[23] In April 1642 the keeper of a Westminster victualling house 'uttered many base and scandalous words against his majesty's justices of the peace, saying that he does not care a fart nor turd for them all'.[24]

Drinkers at an inn in Trowbridge, Wiltshire, early in 1641 showered 'uncivil words' on Jasper Heiley, a royal messenger, and the innkeeper and others 'threw a chamber pot full of filthiness upon him' when they 'understood that [he] was his majesty's servant'. The unfortunate messenger fared no better when he reached his lodging in Bristol, where he was once again 'violently assaulted and abused'. Local authorities offered no assistance, so all Heiley could do was report these outrages to his masters at Whitehall.[25] Provincial inns had become dangerous places for wearers of the royal livery.

In May 1641, the Wentworth family papers disclose, 'a discourse happened' at the Cross Keys tavern in the Strand, on the outskirts of London, on the afternoon of the execution of the Earl of Strafford. Several gentlemen were deep in discourse with the tavern master and his brother about the manner in which the earl met his death.

One said he died an atheist, another a puritan, a third a papist. Mr. Harris said, I would he had died as good a catholic as he did a protestant; whereupon Mr Lambert interrupted them and said, why trouble you us with this damned fellow? He is as surely damned, said he, as I will break this glass (having then a glass full of sack in his hand) and therewithal threw the glass to the top of the room, and it struck against the ceiling and roof and fell against the wall and so to the floor, and broke not; which amazed Mr Lambert and the whole company, all of them having ever since (as occasion hath been offered) readily testified this story's truth, to the honourable memory of the said earl.

The main point of the story is the unbroken glass, a feat of providence that suggested that the earl had gone to glory. But it also testifies to the intensity of interest in religious and political affairs that spilt over from Whitehall and Westminster to the Cross Keys tavern.[26]

---

[23] Essex Record Office, Quarter Sessions Rolls, Q/SR/314/130.

[24] London Metropolitan Archives, Sessions Roll, MJ/SR/909/102.

[25] PRO, SP16.487/80, 487/81.

[26] Sheffield Archives, Wentworth Woodhouse Muniments, Strafford Papers 40/61. The named drinkers included Edmund Lambert, John Harris, and Richard Lloyd. A similar providential episode involving an apparently unbreakable glass is reported in Thomas Fuller, *The*

By the end of 1641 London's drinking establishments had become lively debating chambers, where gentlemen, artisans, and shopkeepers discussed pamphlets, speeches, and petitions. The arguments sometimes led to shouting and shoving, as when the minister Richard Lloyd could not contain his anger at parliamentary proceedings and started a brawl in a Westminster tavern.[27] London's advanced literacy generally facilitated this process, though one did not have to be able to read or write to join in the conversation, or the brawl.[28] Writing home from the metropolis the Kentish squire Henry Oxinden reported, 'the best pastime I find here is at the ordinary, where we have variety of humours, discourse and opinions.'[29]

The Maidenhead in Ave Maria Lane, the Hen and Chickens in Paternoster Row, the Swan in Dowgate, and the White Lion tavern in Canning Street became active centres for petitioning and pressure points for the gathering of hands. In December 1641 William Hobson, mercer, accused citizens who refused to sign the petition against episcopacy as being 'neither good Christians nor honest men, not well affected to the commonwealth'. John Greensmith, tobacconist, warned a neighbouring druggist, 'you are like to have your throat cut', if he refused to subscribe against bishops.[30] Similar pressures applied in favour of conservative petitions.[31] Thousands of Londoners set hands to the petition to exclude 'popish lords and bishops' from the House of Lords, though their activity was interrupted 'by ill-affected persons'.[32] Arguments also raged in provincial towns like Maidstone, where tavern drinkers debated the merits of a Kentish petition after the gentry at quarter sessions had disavowed it.[33] Court records from Exeter likewise reveal yeomen and tradesmen 'sitting together and speaking of the troubles of the times'.[34] The Ram at Cirencester and the Red Lion at Kettering were similar sites of gathering, discourse, and contestation.[35]

History of the Worthies of England (1662), second pagination, 86. See also Alexandra Walsham, *Providence in Early Modern England* (Oxford, 1999), 333.

[27] Maija Jansson (ed.), *Proceedings in the Opening Session of the Long Parliament...* *Volume 2: 21 December 1640–20 March 1641* (Rochester, NY, 2000), 478.

[28] David Cressy, *Literacy and the Social Order: Reading and Writing in Tudor and Stuart England* (Cambridge, 1980).

[29] Dorothy Gardiner (ed.), *The Oxinden Letters 1670–1642* (1933), 155.

[30] *CSPD 1641–43*, 193, 197; PRO, SP16/486/30, 33, 45.

[31] R. N. Worth (ed.), *The Buller Papers. A Series of Historical Documents Selected from the Family Records of the Bullers of Shillingham and Morval in the County of Cornwall* (privately printed, 1895), 33–4; J. W. F. Hill, 'The Royalist Clergy of Lincolnshire', *Lincolnshire Architectural and Archaeological Society Reports and Papers*, new series, 2 (1940 for 1938), 45.

[32] *The Citizens of London's Humble Petition* (1641), sigs. A3, A4.

[33] Vernon F. Snow and Anne Steele Young (eds.), *The Private Journals of the Long Parliament 7 March to 1 June March 1642* (New Haven and London, 1987), 203.

[34] Devon Record Office, Exeter Quarter Sessions Book, 1642–1660, f. 6v.

[35] Gloucestershire Record Office, Gloucester, D2510/15, Letters of John Smyth of Nibley; Bedfordshire and Luton Archives, St John Papers, J. 1389.

It is hard to generalize from such fragments, but a strong impression emerges of plentiful opportunities for people to form political opinions and to develop viewpoints, allegiances, and beliefs. News, rumour, and opinion circulated freely, so that by October 1641 a London correspondent could claim that there were 'as many opinions are there are faces'.[36] The flow of information was unregulated, unchannelled, and potentially dangerous. 'Opinion' ruled the world, speaking 'distractedly and out of ignorant malice', claimed a characteristically opinionated and malicious pamphleteer.[37] 'Fame', said another, was a many-headed monster, proclaiming news 'both true and new'.[38] 'Lovers of their own opinion', a conservative writer lamented, were 'likely to resolve the world again into its first chaos, and make it a Babel not of languages but sects.'[39]

---

[36] HMC, *Report on the Manuscripts of Lord Montague of Beaulieu* (1900), 131.
[37] [Henry Peacham], *Sqvare-Caps Turned into Rovnd-Heads* (1642), 3.
[38] *Heads of all Fashions* (1642), 3.
[39] Edward Reynolds, *Evgenia's Teares for great Brittaynes Distractions* (1642), 9.

15

Libels, Satire, and Derision

Every stage of the national political drama was mirrored in unofficial commentary. The new-found freedom of printing by no means ended the flow of manuscript libels and pasquils. Indeed, the passions and controversies of the period may have given life to many more ephemeral scribal publications. The tradition of popular libelling, especially fertile in the 1620s, was revitalized with unprecedented vigour, velocity, and venom. Energized by the crisis of 1640, the authors of 'railing rhymes and vaunting verse' moved rapidly from attacks on individual targets to more general engagement with public affairs. By early in 1641, in ways not possible before the collapse of censorship, satirical, scandalous, and subversive texts could be written and possessed without peril, and could be marketed openly by hawkers and booksellers.[1] This chapter examines some of these lesser-known materials that helped stir anxiety and unease in England's times of distraction.

The Bishops' Wars against the Scots generated songs both favourable and hostile to the 'blue caps', the popular name for the Covenanting soldiers.[2] The collapse of episcopal authority in late 1640 produced cascades of derisory verse. Another chorus of improvised balladry accompanied the rise of the radical sectarians in 1641. More railing rhymes criticized parliamentary excesses and the reign of 'King Pym'. The formal petitions, protestations, and remonstrances that came before Parliament in the year and half before the civil war had their counterpart in songs, squibs, and satires. Most, no

---

[1] Alastair Bellany, ' "Rayling Rymes and Vaunting Verse": Libellous Politics in Early Stuart England', in Kevin Sharpe and Peter Lake (eds.), *Culture and Politics in Early Stuart England* (Stanford, 1993), 285–310, 367–71; Adam Fox, 'Ballads, Libels and Popular Ridicule in Jacobean England', *Past and Present*, 145 (1994), 47–83; Pauline Croft, 'Libels, Popular Literacy, and Public Opinion in Early Modern England', *Historical Research*, 68 (1995), 266–85; Tom Cogswell, 'Underground Verse and the Transformation of Early Stuart Political Culture', *Huntington Library Quarterly*, 60 (1997), 303–26. Andrew McRae, 'The Literary Culture of Early Stuart Libelling', *Modern Philology*, 97 (2002), 364–92; idem, *Literature, Satire and the Early Stuart State* (Cambridge, 2004).

[2] C. H. Firth, 'Ballads on the Bishops' Wars, 1638–40', *Scottish Historical Review*, 3 (1906), 257–73.

doubt, were instantly forgotten, but several circulated in manuscript and a few passed into print. They offered light entertainment amidst the distempers of the crisis, while inviting their audiences into complicity with dangerous or disreputable opinions.

Topical satire became inseparable from the public conversation in the early 1640s. With the general exception of the King and his family, no target was immune from derision. Profane ballads were 'cried up and down the streets' in London.[3] Entertainers at Norwich performed 'pupping [puppet] plays' on contemporary themes.[4] A gentleman who repeated 'two staves of a song that was sung at Newmarket at the last Assizes', apparently in mockery of Parliament, was briefly confined in the Fleet prison.[5] 'Scandalous' songs 'written on paper' were performed in West Country taverns, in derision of the leaders at Westminster.[6] When diners in London called for 'a song of mirth' in May 1642 they were treated to 'a scurrilous rude song in disgrace and disparagement of the parliament'.[7]

Versions of some of these songs survive among the manuscripts of gentle families who collected them. Correspondents circulated copies of libels and verses as well as pamphlets 'to entertain you' or 'to make you a little merry withal'.[8] Not everyone followed the instructions of the Countess of Lindsey who sent the latest libels to Lord Montague in March 1642, 'which when you have read I pray commit to the fire'.[9] The Suffolk cleric John Rous rhymed in his notebook at the end of 1640, 'I hate these following railing rhymes | Yet keep them for precedent of the times.'[10] Sir Humphrey Mildmay, who liked to laugh 'heartily at the puritans', was pleased to find 'laughing matter' in his correspondence late in 1640.[11] John Werden enclosed 'papers of verses' with a letter to Sir Thomas Aston in April 1641 to show that 'we have poets as well as madmen in our town'.[12] In July 1641 Sir John Lenthall was convinced that his 'credit' was diminished by 'scandalous, libellous' singing. He wrote to Sir Peter Temple,

These rogues in the common gaol do so abuse us both, as that I am infinitely perplexed to hear them. Every night they sing a scandalous libellous song of you and

---

[3] British Library, Add. Ms. 70002, f. 299 (Stanley Gower to Edward Harley, 26 June 1640).

[4] Norfolk Record Office, Norwich Mayor's Court Book, 1634–1646, f. 327.

[5] Henry Wingfield's petition, British Library, Egerton Ms. 2651, f. 100.

[6] Devon Record Office, Exeter Quarter Sessions Book, 1630–1642, f. 400; Exeter Quarter Sessions Book, 1642–1660, f. 7v.   [7] Bodleian Library, Ms. Tanner 63, f. 40.

[8] HMC, *12th Report, The Manuscripts of the Earl Cowper...Preserved at Melbourne Hall, Derbyshire*, (1888), ii. 305, 310; CSPD 1641–43, 273.

[9] HMC, *Report on the Manuscripts of the Duke of Buccleuch and Queensberry...at Montague House* (1899), 291.

[10] Mary Anne Everett Green (ed.), *The Diary of John Rous, Incumbent of Santon Downham, Suffolk, from 1625 to 1642* (Camden Society, 1856), 109.

[11] British Library, Harley Ms. 454, ff. 32, 36.   [12] British Library, Add. Ms. 36914, f. 211.

me to which multitudes of people stand and harken. I am fearful to go by the prison, they do so abuse us both, and threaten to pull down both our houses.[13]

In this case we do not know the words but we can be sure they hit their mark.

'Certain seditious verses' by Peter Maxfield of Meir, Staffordshire, stung hard enough in April 1642 for their author to be called before the House of Commons, then summoned to the Shropshire assizes. The fiddlers responsible for a scurrilous song against Parliament in June 1642 were sent to the house of correction.[14] Nobody charged the men at Westminster with having a sense of humour.

In August 1642 a servant in Devonshire was prosecuted for carrying 'a scandalous song' to a scrivener 'to be written out or copied'. Allegedly performed in the Bear tavern in Exeter, the song ridiculed Lord Kimbolton and the five members of Parliament that the King had attempted to arrest the previous January. Unfortunately the Exeter Sessions records do not preserve the words of the song, but they reveal something of its transmission. The servant, William Tuck, claimed that he had the song from one Randall who lodged in his master's house and desired him to get it copied. John Collop, a musician from Dorset, denied singing the song in Edward Wood's house, but confessed that 'he hath seen the like before this time both in Bath and [Exeter] and was offered copies thereof'. He denied singing the offending song in the tavern, but conceded that 'Edward Seymour, esquire, delivered him a song, written on paper, and desired him to sing it', but the words he could not now remember.[15] Another Devonshire man, Andrew Holeman, had been bound over a few months earlier for 'transcribing and publishing of a scandalous libel'.[16]

Libellous texts blended laughter with anger. Their satire tended to be more juvenile than Juvenalian, more contemptuous than amused. The jokes were often scathing and scatological, their commentary snarling and savage. Perhaps it was better to laugh than to cry. While some verses veered into fantasy and absurdity, others offered a sexualized rhetoric of promiscuity, disease, and dirt. Whereas some satires reflected a submerged radicalism and an eagerness for reform, others gave voice to thwarted conservatives outraged at the turning of the world. Jesting proved an indirect way for authors to challenge the dominant regime, whether Laudian in the 1630s or parliamentarian in the 1640s. Before November 1640 political libels often targeted the bishops or criticized the Scottish war; after the rise of the Long Parliament they were as likely to satirize sectarian radicals, 'roundheads', 'prickears', or 'King Pym'.

---

[13] Huntington Library, Stowe-Temple Ms. STT 1345.
[14] *Commons Journals*, ii. 544, 604.
[15] Devon Record Office, Exeter Quarter Sessions Book, 1642–1660, f. 7v.
[16] Devon Record Office, Exeter Quarter Sessions Book, 1630–1642, f. 400.

The authors of underground texts, so far as we can tell, were a mixture of excluded elements, alehouse scribblers and city wits, impromptu journalists and budding pamphleteers. A few were established poets or minor play-wrights. Others were runaway scholars from Oxford and Cambridge who 'came up to London to write scurrilous pamphlets for half a crown a piece'.[17] The drinking houses around Fleet Street, Fetter Lane, and the Inns of Court even then were home to hacks who for the price of a couple of dinners would compose insulting verses or fabricate pastiches of parliamentary speeches or petitions.[18] Some of the satires had literary pretensions, to be appreciated for their cleverness as well as their point of view.[19]

Behind the veil of anonymity these manuscript squibs could raise questions, tweak noses, and draw attention to absurdities, in a flow of mock petitions, dialogues, and verse. Many of these efforts hit home, so that even the targets of satirical verse took note. The texts of some of the most vicious attacks on William Laud survive in the Archbishop's own papers. Satires against the doings of Parliament were reported and sometimes cited in the House of Commons.

The Scottish war produced a variety of songs and verses, including this one that appeared in print:

> O good King Charles, blame not my pen,
> Spare your purse, and save your men,
> Give Laud to the Scots, and hang up Wren,
> The echo answered still, amen.[20]

An eight-page squib entitled 'the Devil's letter' circulated in manuscript in September 1640, purportedly written by Lucifer to congratulate the Pope on the confusions besetting England. It identified the bishops as the Devil's children, blamed the lawyers for spreading 'debate', congratulated the Scots for making rebellion, and generally applauded the discontent and division gripping the land. The Catholic triumph would soon be complete, aided by a French invasion. The only thing the Devil feared that might thwart his counter-reformation plans was the summoning of an English parliament, an event that was imminently expected.[21]

A widely circulated verse of late 1640 began by announcing, 'the state lay sick, very sick', and imagined the bishops, the Scots, papists, puritans, sectarians, and parliamentarians as doctors offering glisters and emetics,

---

[17] *Mercuries Message Defended* (1642?), 10.

[18] Willson H. Coates, Anne Steele Young, and Vernon F. Snow (eds.), *The Private Journals of the Long Parliament 3 January to 5 March 1642* (New Haven and London, 1982), 165–6, 283, 326, 328, 329.　　[19] McRae, 'The Literary Culture of Early Stuart Libelling', 375–97.

[20] D.L., *The Scots Scouts Discoveries by their London Intelligencer* (1642), 12.

[21] PRO, SP16/466/60.

mandrakes and opium, in pursuit of absurd and desperate cures. One diagnosis attributed England's ills to 'a surfeit contracted by too much ease'. Another identified the black-clad 'magpies, blackbirds, jackdaws and rooks' of the cathedrals as the principal cause of the disease, and Parliament as its only cure: 'The only physic good for a weak state | is a parliament, so it comes not too late.'[22]

Another venomous verse implicated Laud and Strafford in a 'devilish plot' to enslave English Protestants and to divide the King from his subjects:

> Lordless Will of Lambeth Strand
> And Black Tom Tyrant of Ireland
> Like Fox and Wolf did lurk.
> With many a rook and magpies
> To pick out good King Charles his eyes
> And then be Pope and Turk.

Once again, the state lay sick, this time suffering from 'pox and flux and stone'. But recovery now seemed likely as 'plot and pride begins to fall', with Parliament and the Scots cooperating as physicians.[23]

Dozens of acerbic libels targeted Archbishop Laud. One that appeared both in manuscript and in print began

> U.R.I.C. [you are I see] poor Canterbury in tottering state
> A.P.O.P.E. some say you'll be, tis now too late.[24]

Another delighted that 'Canterbury...will prove a man may fall from grace and never rise again.'[25] A plethora of attacks on the Archbishop accompanied his arrest and impeachment, ridiculing his 'graceless grace' and threatening little Will with 'a headman or halter'.[26]

Caroline functionaries with animal and bird names attracted streams of punning ridicule. A menacing verse from 1641 linked Laud and Strafford to Lord Keeper Finch, Bishop Matthew Wren, and the ecclesiastical judges Arthur Duck and Sir John Lambe, and wished confusion to them all:

> A bishop's head, a deputy's breast, a Finch's tongue, a Wren from's nest
> Will set the devil on foot.

---

[22] PRO, SP16/473/113; Huntington Library, Ms. El. 8847; British Library, Harley Ms. 4931, ff. 84–86v; Bodleian Library, Ms. Tanner 306, d. 158. George Thomason collected another version entitled 'A satyre upon the state of things this parliament', transcribed in British Library E. 205, dated 'about December 1640'.   [23] PRO, SP16/487/48.

[24] Folger Shakespeare Library, Folger Ms. V.b. 303, p. 257. For a printed version see *On Wings of Feare, Finch Flies Away. Alas Poore Will, Hee's forc'd to stay* (1641), broadsheet.

[25] Ibid., 313.

[26] Examples include *Canterburies Amazement* (1641); *Canterburies Conscience Convicted* (1641); *Canterburies Dreame* (1641); *Canterburies Pilgrimage* (1641); *Canterburies Potion* (1641); and *Canterburies Tooles* (1641); Huntington Library, Ms. El. 8847.

He is like to have a dainty dish at once both flesh and fowl and fish
And Duck and Lamb to boot.
But this I say though your lewd life did fill both church and state with strife
And trample on the crown.
A blessed martyr you will die for church's good, she riseth high
When such as you fall down.[27]

Another observed that 'the little Wren that soared so high thought on his wings away to fly like Finch', but was now ensnared in the 'subtle whirlwind' of parliamentary vengeance.[28] Printed pamphlets made visual jokes and wordplay at the expense of the unfortunately-named Wren, Finch, Duck and Lambe, showing them flying through the air or perched on masts or steeples. A broadsheet entitled *On Wings of Feare, Finch Flies Away* depicted the former Lord Keeper with wings, and imagined others as running or flying. A pamphlet entitled *Old Newes Newly Revived* depicted both Keeper Finch and Secretary Windebank airborne over the Channel[29] (see Plate 10). A mocking ballad observed, 'there's many hath catched the running disease'.[30] Another pamphlet thick with schoolboy Latin declared, 'The country shakes, as frightened Ducks *ab aqua*, | Fly gaggling homewards *quicquid, quoquo quaqua*.'[31] 'The Duck's wings will be plucked, and Lamb begins to be out of season', observed other broadsheets of 1641.[32]

Petitioners to the November parliament met with mockery as well as approbation from the city wits. A jesting manuscript entitled 'Alderman Wiseacre's speech' enjoyed wide circulation in December 1640. Alternatively called 'the ballad against the city petitions', it satirized the London movement against episcopacy and the 'root and branch' petition delivered to Parliament on 11 December. Over four pages of crudely crafted verse, it derided the petitioners for their low social position and ridiculed them for the naïveté of their religious demands. Although their petitions were 'plentifully wrought with understanding hands', it claimed, many of the subscribers were barely literate. 'What though some could not write, yet I dare promise | They

---

[27] Huntington Library, inside Hastings Ms. 39466. For comments on 'all the jests…upon the names of Laud, Duck, Wren and Lamb, Cannons and Bishops' seas', see also [Abraham Cowley], *A Satyre Against Seperatists, Or, The Conviction of Chamber-Preachers, and other Schismaticks* (1642), 4.   [28] Huntington Library, Ms. inside Hastings Ms. 39466.
[29] *On Wings of Feare, Finch Flies Away*, broadsheet; *Old Newes Newly Revived* (1641), title page.
[30] *Good Admonition. Or, Keep thy head on thy shoulders, And I will keepe mine* (1641). The 'running disease' was also the 'French pox' or 'the running of the reins', discussed in *Articles Ministred By His Majesties Commissioners…against John Gwin* (1641), sig. A3v, and Richard Bunworth, *A New Discovery of the French Disease and Running of the Reins* (1662). I owe this observation to Jaimie Sassone.
[31] [William Lilly], *Lilli's propheticall history of this yeares accidence* (1642), 5.
[32] *Times Alteration* (1641); *The Organs Eccho* (1641).

have made a G for John and S for Thomas.' Their spokesmen, Aldermen Wiseacre and Woodcock (based on Aldermen John Wollaston and John Warner), led a chorus of shopkeepers and shoemakers, weavers and draymen, tailors and bakers, and 'yeomen of the bristle' who plied their trade with brushes and brooms. Londoners of every guild and trade were represented: 'tinkers, turners, carriers, upholsterers, saddlers, cutlers, barbers, farriers, fishmongers, painters, fullers, dyers, coachmen, perfumers, blacksmiths, joiners, butchers, ropemen, and millions more of good souls as last week attended on saints Burton, Prynne and Bastwick', whose rapturous welcome to London began on 28 November 1640.[33]

Each verse punned on the attributes of a particular trade, so that the chandlers who dealt in candles wished for amendment of 'the blinding light of the church', the haberdashers who sold clothing wished the church 'new dressed', the bakers called for episcopal wealth to be pared like a pie-crust, and the shoemakers hoped 'religion will turn right at last'. Regarding the bishops, said Alderman Wiseacre,

> That anti-christian calling doth so grieve us
> That we beseech your goodness to relieve us.
> For such they are the great abominations
> The frogs and locusts of the Revelations.
> Sound each of them, you'll find a pope in's belly
> As plain as you can smell a turd from jelly.

Episcopacy would soon yield to Presbyterianism,

> When some of us whom they may think church gelders
> Shall rule the roost and be appointed elders.

Nor would the religious revolution stop there, as sectarians and independents rejected the structures and traditions of the church:

> For point of holiness we are not able
> To see great differences twixt a church and stable.
> The word of God is all one, nor can we learn
> More profit in a church than in a barn;
> And much more fruitfully do we receive it
> Than some well-tutored twenty-nobles Levite
> Shall mounted on a stock demurely utter
> Sweet pleasing words as soft as oil or butter.[34]

---

[33] I have compared PRO, SP16/473/48, Folger Shakespeare Library, Folger Ms. X. d. 20, and Northamptonshire Record Office, Finch-Hatton Ms. FH 593 and have quoted from all three versions.   [34] Folger Shakespeare Library, Folger Ms. X. d. 20.

A popular song from the end of 1640 similarly satirized those radicals who were destroying the social order along with the framework of episcopacy. With repeated reference to things coming down, and the whooping refrain of 'up go we', it catches the spirit of revolutionary transformation. Deans and bishops, popery and ceremony, arts and learning, all were coming down, and good times were coming in. The hierarchy of nobles and gentry was next in line, 'and heigh then up go we'. The 'we' of these verses presumably includes both parliamentary root-and-branchers and the artisan iconoclasts who were cheering them from the streets. Like the 'ballad against the city petitions', the song invites admiration for its own cleverness, incorporating anticlericalism, anti-intellectualism, iconoclasm, licentiousness, uncouthness, and insubordination. But whether it condemns or encourages those activities is hard to judge. Presumably it was performed as well as read. For its wit, venom, and pseudo-revolutionary zeal, the song deserves to be better known:[35]

> Know then my brethren deaneries clear and all the clouds are gone—a
> The righteous now shall flourish and good days are coming in—a.
> Come then my brethren and be glad and each rejoice with me—a.
> Lawn sleeves and rochets shall go down, and Heigh then up go we—a.
>
> We'll break the windows which the whore of Babylon hath pented—a
> And when the papist saints are down then Burton shall be sainted.
> Then neither cross nor crucifix shall stand for men to see—a.
> Rome's trash and trumpery shall go down, and Heigh then up go we—a.
>
> Whate'er the popish hands hath built our hammers shall undo.
> We'll break their pipes and burn their copes and pull down churches too.
> We'll exercise within the groves and teach beneath the tree—a.
> We'll make a pulpit of a cart, and Heigh then up go we—a.
>
> We'll down with universities where learning is professed,
> Because they practice and maintain the language of the beast.
> We'll drive the doctors out of doors and arts what ere they be—a.
> We'll cry all arts and learning down, and Heigh then up go we—a.
>
> If once the antichristian crew be pressed and overthrown
> We'll teach the nobles how to crouch and keep the gentry down.
> Good manners have an ill report and turns to pride we see—a.
> We therefore cry good manners down, and Heigh then up go we—a.

---

[35] Durham University Library, Special Collections, Mickleton-Spearman Ms. MSP 9, ii. 249–50. An expanded version appears in *Rump: Or an Exact Collection of the Choyceset Poems and Songs Relating to the Late Times* (2 vols., 1662), i. 14–16.

The name of the Lord shall be abhorred for every one a brother.
No reason is in church or state one man shall rule another.
And when the change of government shall set our fingers free—a.
We'll make the wanton sisters stoop, and Heigh then up go we—a.

A generation later some still remembered the vaunting cry of 'up go we' as the revolutionary catchphrase that preceded the civil war.[36]

Several verses from 1641 and 1642 ridiculed the devotional style of the 'sanctified crew' of radical upstart preachers, with their eyes turned up, their hands held out, loud sighs, and extempore prayers. The poet was scathing about their meetings, where anyone could preach, 'and a weaver can teach things I fear past his reach'. He had nothing but contempt for those who were 'led by the spirit' instead of the Book of Common Prayer:

> See, see what strange sects now there be
> Of unheard of purity, when the devil's turned saint.
> Next the anabaptist
> And the Bedlam Brownist
> Yea and nay separatist
> Who all power will resist
> Might they do what they list
> And supreme head of none
> Cause the Romanists have one.[37]

By 1641 the principal target of libels and satires had shifted from over-mighty prelates to overreaching parliamentarians. Wits and penmen complained of the ascendant King Pym, rather than the imprisoned Archbishop Laud. Satires, libels, and placards appeared in public places, outside the Houses of Parliament or pasted on posts at the Exchange, as well as in the ephemeral press. In April 1641, for example, a manuscript appeared in public listing the Earl of Strafford's enemies under the heading, 'The Anabaptists, Jews, or Brownists of the House of Commons'.[38] Another manuscript libel in August 1641 asked, 'Whether the subjects must rule the king, or the king the subjects?' and 'Whether we have as much skill in building up as pulling down?'[39]

Disbanded soldiers may have shared the responsibility with conservative citizens for some of 'the most pestilent libels spread abroad against the

---

[36] *The Whig's Exaltation; a Pleasant New Song* (1682). See also *The Whig Rampant; Or, Exaltation* (1682), which used the same chorus to satirize 'the good old cause'.

[37] Durham University Library, Special Collections, Mickleton-Spearman Ms. MSP 9, ii. 250–1. See also the verse on 'the town's new teacher', discussed in Chapter 10 (Bodleian Library, Ms. Rawlinson D. 398, f. 249). [38] *CSPD 1640–41*, 560.

[39] *CSPD 1641–43*, 113.

precise Lords and Commons' that appeared in October 1641. Thomas Smith wrote on 26 October that 'libels in abundance are thrown up and down in abuse of the best in parliament, but I dare not name them; if the authors be found they will be severely punished.'[40] The Venetian ambassador reported libels in London and Yorkshire expressing 'a universal dissatisfaction with the efforts of the Parliament'. In November 'fresh bills [were] posted up in public places against the puritans and their leaders'.[41]

One such libel 'set upon a post in the street or on the parliament's door' was given the title, 'a new play called A King or No King, acted by the House of Commons'.[42] A manuscript ballad of 1642 entitled 'Roundheads all in a row, to the tune of cuckolds all in a row' opened with those words, 'a king or no king', and concluded by declaring Parliament and the citizens traitors.[43] Other manuscript verses in wide circulation charged Parliament with knavery, blasphemy, sedition, and treason.[44]

'The Protestation of the Protestants', a savage swipe at the parliamentary leaders, circulated in manuscript in the early autumn of 1641 and survives in several copies. It evoked and belittled the parliamentary Protestation of May 1641, and laid claim to the title of 'protestants' only for adherents of the established Church of England. The earls of Essex, Bedford, and Suffolk and a dozen more nobles were named as 'a pack of half-witted lords, having no capacity of being remarkable for anything in the state but betraying the honour and privileges of the nobility, under the tutoring of Lord Saye the anabaptist'. Commoners tarred with this brush included Pym, Hampden, and half a dozen more members of Parliament, 'Pennington and Venn, two bankrupt citizens; Perd and White, two principal pettifoggers; Vane the secretary and St. John the solicitor, both Judases: all Brownists'. It charged that 'all promiscuously have conspired together against the king's crown and posterity, and have subverted our religion to be merely arbitrary, have prostituted the honour of England, have beggared the nation to enrich the Scots, have protected the ignorant and licentious sectaries and schismatics to stir up sedition and bring in atheism, and have discountenanced all reverend ministers, and have endeavoured to take away the common prayer book.' Then came a defiant resolution that foreshadowed that winter's troubles

Know all the world that we the gentry, soldiers, and all the true protestants do protest against the foresaid persons as enemies to God, traitors to the king, church and state, and desire this our protestation to be recorded in parliament, and demand justice

---

[40] Ibid., 134. [41] *CSP Venetian*, 1640–42, 225, 236.
[42] Cambridge University Library, Ms. Mn. 1. 45 (Baker transcripts), 29.
[43] Folger Shakespeare Library, Folger Ms. V.b. 303, p. 323.
[44] Huntington Library, Ms. El. 8776, El. 8777.

against these incendiaries of the disaffection betwixt the king and his people, and that they may be forthwith banished the kingdom or to be delivered up to be torn in pieces by the loyal subjects of a religious king whom God preserve from such conspirators.[45]

The proto-Cavaliers who originated this prose libel may have been hard-pressed to find a printer during the reign of 'King Pym', but they had no trouble ensuring its circulation in manuscript. The authors deliberately threw their opponents' terminology back at them, identifying the authors of Parliament's Protestation as 'incendiaries', the word used earlier by the Scots to denounce Strafford and Laud. The vigour of some of these underground texts may partially derive from their authors' exclusion from more orthodox modes of discourse.

Attacks on the parliamentary leadership continued in such libels as 'Mr. Pym's Picture' (from late 1641 or early 1642), which depicts him as powerful enough to inspire fear in the Devil: 'He struck so high as to pull bishops down | And in the mitre to control the crown.'[46] Another much copied verse asked poignantly,

> Is there no God, let it be put to the vote.
> Is there no king but Pym, as some men dote.
> Is there no church, be it so we are content
> So it be done by act of parliament.
> Is there no God, no king, no church, 'tis well
> If they can find at last there is no hell.

Some versions continued:

> Is there no God, why does Saye the Commons fool.
> Is there a king, why then does Pym bear rule.
> Is there a church, why are the members rent
> And not made up again by parliament.
> Is there a God, a king, a church, 'tis even
> Is just they should enact there is a heaven,
> Unless that God, the king, hell, heaven, all
> Like Strafford by one Pym must stand or fall.[47]

---

[45] Bodleian Library, Ms. Rawlinson D. 843, f. 48; HMC, *Calendar of the Manuscripts of the Most Honourable The Marquess of Salisbury Preserved at Hatfield House, part 24, Addenda 1605–1668* (1976), 277. Another copy is in Northamptonshire Record Office, Finch-Hatton Ms. FH 3814. They are dated 'the day of the nine lords protestation against the common prayer book'. See *Lords Journals*, iv. 398.

[46] Folger Shakespeare Library, Folger Ms. V.b. 303, p. 316; Huntington Library, Ms. El. 8841.

[47] Huntington Library, Mss. HM 46532, El. 8807, El. 8809; Bodleian Library, Ms. Rawlinson D. 317B, f. 209; *Rump*, i. 64.

In a somewhat different vein the mock heroic poem about Alderman Atkins provided scatological amusement while simultaneously belittling the parliamentary preparations for war in late spring 1642. This elaborate libel celebrated 'that renowned, valiant and prime colonel of the new militia for the city of London that beshit himself on the general training day May the 10th 1642':

> Stout man at custard and a son of Mars
> But oh the foul disaster of his arse
> .   .   .   .   .   .
>
> Wielding his truncheon like a weaver's beam
> And yet beshit his hose in every seam
> .   .   .   .
>
> When eight thousand men discharged their muskets, he discharged too.

Although Thomas Atkins became a parliamentary treasurer, Lord Mayor of London, and a leading Independent, he never lived down this moment of spectacular incontinence, which reverberated in verse for almost twenty years.[48]

More railing rhymes from the first half of 1642 blamed Parliament for England's miseries. One set the charge in the form of a financial account:

> So much to purchase peace with the Scot
> And so much to make war at home
> Whilst we defend we know not what
> And fight against we know not whom
> .   .   .   .   .   .
>
> So much for fears and jealousies
> Though without sense or reason.
> So much for lies, so much for spies
> So much laid out in treason
> .   .   .   .   .   .
>
> So much to him that writes short-hand
> For taking their long-winded speeches.
> And so much to that Alderman
> That wronged in their defence his breeches
> .   .   .   .   .   .

---

[48] Folger Shakespeare Library, Folger Ms.V.b. 303, pp. 319–20; Huntington Library, Ms. El. 8795; *Rump*, i. 136–7. Thomas Atkins, a puritan cloth merchant, was one of the four aldermen imprisoned in May 1640 for not cooperating with the forced loan. In 1642 he was elected to the Militia Committee and became a colonel of the London trained bands (Valerie Pearl, *London and the Outbreak of the Puritan Revolution* (Oxford, 1961), 312).

So much to Burton and to Burges
For boldly preaching strange seditions.
So much for either when he forges
His neighbour's hand to their petition.[49]

Another manuscript verse circulating in the summer of 1642 offered a
reward for the recovery of 'law, wit and reason, which hath been lost twenty-
one months', from the opening of the Long Parliament. Using the form of the
town crier who cried lost and found, it enquired 'if any man hath found law
in a declaration strayed from Westminster commons, after a strange fashion,
from the first of December', that is, from the day the Grand Remonstrance
was presented to the king.[50] Royalists as well as radicals were saying, 'there is
no law now.'

Anti-parliamentary sentiment found fuller expression in a celebrated
set of verses that scorned those politicians who had overthrown the old
constitution. It survives in several versions and repays reading at length:

To make Charles a great king and give him no power,
To honour him much and obey him not an hour,
To provide for the subject and take away the Tower,
To vote all things sweet be they never so sour,
This is the new order of the land
And the land's new order.

To secure the subjects lives, liberties and estates
By an arbitrary power if so please the fates,
To take away taxes by imposing greater rates,
And so make us a plaster by breaking our pates,
This is . . .

   .   .   .   .

To sit and consult for ever and a day,
To countenance treason in a parliamentary way,
To quiet the land by tumultuous fray,
New plots to devise and them to betray,
This is . . .

   .   .   .   .

To free all men's votes by the 'prentices' force,
To make one petition serve all countries by course
May make Pym as great as his mother's great horse

---

[49] 'The Parliament's Account', Bodleian Library, Rawlinson Ms. D. 398, f. 234; Durham
University Library, Special Collections, Mickleton-Spearman Ms. MSP 9, ii. 256; Huntington
Library, Ms. El. 8882. The first line puns peace and pease; the man who notoriously soiled his
breeches was Alderman Atkins, the butt of much anti-parliamentary humour.
[50] Huntington Library, Ms. El. 8886.

Which Will gave Agnes, though his meaning was worse,
This is ...

.   .   .   .

To make God's house clear, yet shit in the pews,
To revere all evil, yet turn churches to stews,
To make up a union twixt anabaps, Brownists and Jews,
To settle our trades by selling of news,
This is ...

.   .   .   .

God send these zealots to heaven in a string
Who else to confusion church and kingdom will bring,
Who say the lord's prayer is a popish thing,
Who pray for themselves, yet quite leave out the king.
This is the new order of the land
And the land's new order.[51]

The solemn events of 1642 produced a chorus of sardonic levity and derision. One text presenting itself as 'the humble petition of the poets' appeared soon after the King's attempt to arrest the five members. Whereas other petitions to the House of Commons claimed to come from the bottom of their subscribers' souls, this one avowed that it came 'from the depths and bottom of our bowls'. The privilege of poetic licence, its authors claimed, gave poets alone the power 'to change age into youth, turn nonsense to sense, and falsehood to truth, in brief to make good whatever is fault'. It was the poets' business to tackle tyrants and monsters, to make and unmake kings. Now the House of Commons had violated this privilege by encroaching on the poets' domain. Parliament's recent attempts at reformation, it said, were 'but poems in prose', but unlike the output of the professional poets, the petitioners suggested, 'yours wants the rhythm, the wit and the sense'. As for lying, 'the most noble part of a poet', Parliament possessed that skill in abundance. 'If poverty be a part of our trade, | So far the whole kingdom poets you have made.' In reducing the crown to want and dependency, 'you have made King Charles himself a poet.'[52]

The partisan descent towards war of mid-1642 produced more flurries of manuscript commentary and verse. Yet another mock petition blamed Parliament for creating a topsy-turvy world in which subjects were freed of their liberties, and burglary by the authorities replaced the rule of law.

---

[51] Folger Shakespeare Library, Folger Ms. V.b. 303, pp. 317–18; Huntington Library, Ms. El. 8879, El. 8880; Durham University Library, Special Collections, Mickleton-Spearman Ms. MSP 9, ii. 243; Bodleian Library, Ms. Rawlinson D. 398, f. 250; *Rump*, i. 13–14. Modern readers may imagine this song performed with the phrasing of Bob Dylan, 'Its Alright Ma (I'm Only Bleeding)'.

[52] Bodleian Library, Rawlinson Ms. D. 398, f. 233; Durham University Library, Special Collections, Mickleton-Spearman Ms. MSP 9, ii. 255; *Rump*, i. 22–3.

Parliament, the author claimed, was given to 'voting impossibles', for 'we know your legislative power can raise the fundamental laws and privileges of parliament above the Ten Commandments'. Parliament had emptied citizens' counters 'in defence of the property of the subject', and encouraged subjects 'to rebel against the king for his good'. Now peace was 'strangled . . . when his Pymship played at backwards with the king's message', and England faced the horror and absurdity of war. 'Go on then ye triumphing round-heads, gird your swords to your thighs, ye mighty worthies, rebel stoutly in the Lord's cause.' This was a Cavalier nightmare vision of the world turned upside down.[53]

The preposterous notion of the world turned upside down extended to the workings of the cosmos as well as the commonwealth. Another satiric poem entitled 'the man in the moon's almanack', written, so it said, in the 'unhappy year of grace' 1642, matched sublunary changes with revolutionary disturbances in the heavens. This too is worth quoting in full for its invocation of the topsy-turvy turning of the social, religious, and political sphere.

> The Man in the Moon's Almanack—1642
>
> Since the Star Chamber is pulled down
> And *Primum Mobile* removed
> He that affirms the world ith' moon
> Says no more than may be proved.
>
> For change below
> Encreaseth so
> That mortal eye
> Cannot descry
> Here then or there more certainty.
>
> If you enquire of Charles his wain
> It hangs but loosely on its wheels.
> An *Ignis Fatuus* hath or'ta'en
> Thee, and ghosts it at the heels.
>
> The dog star now
> From his clear brow
> Dares to detract
> And for that act
> Boasts admiration to attract.
>
> The claret drinker in the moon
> For fashion's sake falls drinking sack

---

[53] Huntington Library, Ms. El. 7802.

Changeth his liquor, and that done
Writes to the world this almanack.

The lower house
Is grown so cross
That it is bent
By most's consent
To deal each sign new regiment.

Pisces you rule the head and face
And Aries you the feet.
Aquarius in the neck take place
Taurus for legs thought very neat.

No holy days
For saints just praise
No fasting shall
On the eves fall
Good Friday is a festival.

A new found admiration
Rakes up in ashes Ember weeks
No such thing as Rogation
I'th calendar a wiseman seeks.

Nay farther yet
I'th north they sit
Warmer by far
And all days are
As bad as the canicular.

Out of the Terms blot Hilary
As well as Michaelmas cut short.
Be it full sea in each good eye
For that's indeed the fittest sport.

Good Christmas Day
Is swept away
By a strange tide
Yet lest you chide
Virgo in Lent may be a Bride.
1642 Unhappy year of grace.[54]

Almost every line is laden with topical references. There had been recent speculation about extraterrestrial life and publications about the man in the moon, but the Moon here may well be the name of a drinking establishment,

---

[54] Bodleian Library, Ms. Rawlinson D. 398, ff. 237b–238.

the place where the poem was penned.[55] The prerogative court of Star Chamber, abolished in 1641, was named for the star-painted ceiling in the room it once occupied. Charles's wain was a popular name for the constellation of the plough or dipper, though a wain was also a wheeled farm wagon. An *Ignis fatuus* was a fool's fire, a manifestation of phosphorescence, a will o' the wisp. Canicular days were the hot dog days of August, under the influence of the dog star. The signs of the zodiac, by tradition, each had their 'regiment' or domain, which were here out of order. Aries ruled the head and Pisces the feet, but here their positions were reversed. The properties of Aquarius and Taurus were similarly inverted.[56] Time itself and the progression of the year were also out of kilter. The old customs of the ecclesiastical year had long been contested by puritans, and were now being violated, ignored, or swept away.

Laughter, it has been suggested, directs attention to areas of structural ambiguity, exposing the tensions and anxieties of the past.[57] Humour, in this light, provided a means of coping with the absurdities and anomalies of a culture under stress. The jesting could serve both radical and conservative ends, with some of the derision subverting the established order and some of it setting a disordered world to rights. The libelling and satire from this period of revolution testifies to the creativity, wit, and attentiveness that drew people deeper into the national conversation.

[55] 'Domingo Gonsalves' [Francis Godwin], *The Man in the Moone, or a Discourse of a Voyage Thither* (1638); John Wilkins, *The Discovery of a World in the Moone* (1638); idem, *A Discourse Concerning a New World & Another Planet* (1640). David Underdown, *A Freeborn People: Politics and the Nation in Seventeenth-Century England* (Oxford, 1996), 95–9, discusses the scurrilous and subversive serial of 1649–50 entitled 'The Man in the Moon'. For London taverns named for 'The Man in the Moon' see John Taylor, *Taylors Travels and Circular Perambulation* (1636), sig. A3v, and idem, *A Preter-Pluperfect Spick and Span* (Oxford, 1643), 12, the latter a centre for 'drink, smoke, and talk'.

[56] Samuel Ashwell, *A New Almanacke and Prognostication for the yeare of our Lord God, 1642* (1642), 'The Anatomie'.

[57] Keith Thomas, 'The Place of Laughter in Tudor and Stuart England', *TLS*, 21 January 1977, 77–81.

16

The Social Order Threatened

It was not just religious turmoil and the spectre of sectarianism that persuaded many leaders of opinion that their world was descending into chaos. The revolutionary crisis also subjected the social order to extraordinary stress. Traditional gradations of hierarchy and deference appeared to founder amidst a sea of insubordination, as customary arrangements of status, rank, and office were tested to their limits. Evidence suggested that gentility no longer commanded respect, magistracy had difficulty projecting authority, and the clergy suffered intolerable indignities. Alienated parishioners exhibited contempt for the weakened Caroline state, and crude popular antagonism even touched the majesty and power of the King. Moderate gentlemen might well conclude that 'a great calamity' was upon them, as England became 'a theatre of distractions'.[1]

The political and constitutional earthquakes that shook England's central government between 1640 and 1642 set off aftershocks across provincial and parochial jurisdictions.[2] Disturbances to the social equilibrium, partly triggered by public events, contributed in turn to the anxieties of the governing elite. Many social leaders experienced insolence and refractoriness that threatened their privileged positions. Many magnified the threat in their minds and imagined that relations would rapidly get worse. In the last resort they feared a social levelling that jeopardized all rights and property, and a descent into anarchy that would leave their religion and culture in ruins.

---

[1] Sir John Temple to Sir John Coke, HMC, *12th Report, The Manuscripts of the Earl Cowper...Preserved at Melbourne Hall, Derbyshire* (1888), ii. 286; Endymion Porter to Sir Edward Nicholas, British Library, Nicholas Papers, Egerton Ms. 2533, f. 207. For similar concerns, see 'Sir Roger Twysden's Journal', *Archaeologia Cantiana*, 2 (1859), 176; British Library, Nicholas Papers, Egerton Ms. 2533, ff. 141, 143v, 157v; *CSPD 1641–43*, 104, 126.

[2] This, indeed, was the image used in the 1649 best-seller *Eikon Basilike*, which found the 'mischiefs' that followed the convening of the Long Parliament 'like an earthquake, shaking the very foundation of all'. Between November 1640 and January 1642, it recalled, 'the confluence and clamours of the vulgar' had passed 'all boundaries of laws and reverence to authority', bringing 'confusion and ruin upon church and state' ([John Gauden], *Eikon Basilike* (1649), ch. 4).

This chapter examines some of the strains in the social fabric and the challenges to the social order that accompanied the revolutionary disturbances of the early 1640s. It begins by reviewing the normal or normative state of affairs and the conservative ideology that sustained it. Frictions and stresses were not uncommon, but normally they could be smoothed or contained. Discussion then turns to some of the disruptive elements that menaced the social order—vagrants who were always marginal to society, poachers who disregarded gamekeepers, citizens who refused to perform their duties, and tenants who withheld their rents. A central section examines verbal taunts and insults that undermined customary relationships and transgressive behaviour that sabotaged established authority. Examples include commoners who disparaged gentility, parishioners who abused the constables, defendants who spoke ill of magistrates, and subjects who uttered sedition. None of these disturbances was entirely new, nor did they constitute a social revolution, but their concentration and vehemence in the opening years of the Long Parliament contributed to the revolutionary ferment. The deterioration in civility did not cause the civil war, but it fostered a climate of anxiety and alarm in which people made catastrophic political errors.

GOOD ORDER AND OBEDIENCE

Without a police force, extensive bureaucracy, or intrusive coercive apparatus, English society operated on trust. The social fabric was generally flexible and cohesive, stitched together by intangible threads. Social relationships were governed by customary understandings of rank and status, hierarchy and deference. They were further modulated by protocols of gender and authority, duty and obligation. An array of social indicators inscribed the virtues of birth, blood, and breeding. Local social dealings were also shaped by notions of neighbourliness and reputation that buttressed the realities of wealth and power. Everyone knew, in principle, that age outranked youth, that women were subordinate to men, and that 'men of quality' took precedence over 'the common sort'. Magistrates commanded respect according to their gentility, rank, and office, as well as their power to impose the penalties of the law. Laymen deferred to clerics, and subjects bowed to the authority of the Crown. Humble status enjoined practical humility, reflecting lowly esteem as well as limited resources. The system was not altogether toothless, but its operation depended on a broad cultural consensus. Participants learned the languages and gestures of social differentiation, including bowing, hat honour, and when to say 'sir' or 'sirrah'.[3]

---

[3] Cf. the 'hot words' between the Earl of Warwick and the Bishop of Lincoln in December 1641 when one 'saying "Sir" ' was mistaken to have said "Sirrah" '. HMC, *Report on the Manuscripts of*

The conservative ideologies that sustained this system were deep-rooted, and found repeated expression in contemporary commentary. Generations of English men and women had grown up on the catechisms, homilies, and biblical citations that attributed hierarchal authority to the will of God. The standard approved catechism expanded the biblical commandment to 'honour thy father and thy mother' to include obedience to all in command, including magistrates and ministers of the church.[4] The Tudor Homilies, frequently reprinted, enjoined 'good order and obedience' on 'every degree of people in their vocation, calling and office', teaching 'kings and princes . . . inferiors and subjects, priests and laymen, masters and servants, fathers and children, husbands and wives, rich and poor' that 'every one have need of other. . . . For where there is no right order, there reigneth all abuse, carnal liberty, enormity, sin, and babylonical confusion.'[5] The speech Shakespeare gives to Ulysses in *Troilus and Cressida*, observing 'degree, priority and place, insisture, course, proportion, season, form, office and custom', was a particularly elegant rephrasing of this central conservative idea: 'take but degree away, untune that string, and hark, what discord follows.'[6]

Social relations in practice were never so orderly or uncontested as theorists would have wished. The social fabric was always at risk of fraying, and was constantly in need of maintenance. The consensual fiction of 'the great chain of being' masked a much rougher realm of frictions and transgressions. Most magistrates would at some time have heard words spoken 'in contempt of authority and government'.[7] Many clergymen too experienced abuse of their person and their office.[8] A chronically obstreperous underclass often taunted the traditional hierarchical order. On occasion the English seemed to be an ungovernable people, but it is more appropriate to say that most knew their place, although they sometimes succumbed to a looseness of tongue.[9]

the *Duke of Buccleuch and Queensberry . . . at Montague House* (1899), 289. For normal operations of this ordered society, see Cynthia B. Herrup, *The Common Peace: Participation and the Criminal Law in Seventeenth-Century England* (Cambridge, 1987); Susan Amussen, *An Ordered Society: Gender and Class in Early Modern England* (Oxford, 1988); Paul Griffiths, Adam Fox, and Steve Hindle (eds.), *The Experience of Authority in Early Modern England* (1996); Michael J. Braddick and John Walter (eds.), *Negotiating Power in Early Modern Society: Order, Hierarchy, and Subordination in Britain and Ireland* (Cambridge, 2001).

[4] G. E. Corrie (ed.), *A Catechism Written in Latin by Alexander Nowell, Dean of St. Paul's, Together with the Same Catechism Translated into English by Thomas Norton* (Parker Society, Cambridge, 1853), 130.

[5] *Certaine Sermons or Homilies Appointed to be Read in Churches* (1623), 69. Further editions appeared in 1635 and 1640. [6] William Shakespeare, *Troilus and Cressida*, I. iii.

[7] Cheshire Record Office, QJF/69/1, f. 57.

[8] David Cressy, *Travesties and Transgressions in Tudor and Stuart England* (Oxford, 2000), 138–61.

[9] John Brewer and John Styles (eds.), *An Ungovernable People: The English and Their Law in the Seventeenth and Eighteenth Centuries* (1980); John Morrill and John Walter, 'Order and Disorder in the English Revolution', in John Morrill (ed.), *The Nature of the English Revolution*

English men and women of all social ranks could be rude and disorderly, especially if money was demanded of them or they were flush with drink.

A Hertfordshire man, for example, told a Jacobean official, 'thou art a Jack dog, and I am as good a man as thyself', and referred to a constable as 'a scurvy knave also and busy fellow'.[10] A Yorkshire labourer declared, 'I care not for the constable or the king', and a village blacksmith embellished this by saying, 'the devil go with the king and all the proud pack of them, what care I.'[11] A Cambridge man told a local official to 'kiss mine arse',[12] whereas a Yorkshire yeoman contemptuously declared, 'I care not a fart for Sir Francis Wortley's warrants.'[13] A Nottinghamshire labourer made the old joke that a particular magistrate 'was sometimes a Justice of Peace and sometimes a just ass'.[14]

These utterances were all drawn from early Stuart court records, before the crisis of the 1640s. Similar words might be heard at the best of times. Although they expressed insolence and insubordination, they did not necessarily endanger the social fabric. Magistrates found them annoying rather than threatening, and offenders usually apologized and submitted to correction. Most could be disciplined by a warning, community pressures, or binding over to keep the peace. Egregious troublemakers might be fined, whipped, stocked, or confined to the house of correction. The frown of authority was usually sufficient to repair social relations and restore the bounds of hierarchy.

Commentators warned repeatedly of the consequences if order and deference unravelled. The liberty and confusion foretold in the Homilies had always to be kept at bay. 'Sovereignty and subjection' went hand in hand, said Viscount Wentworth in his capacity as Lord President of the North, 'the authority of a king is the keystone which closeth up the arch of order and government . . . which once shaken, infirmed, all the frame falls together into a confused heap.'[15] It was the business of judges, said Lord Chief Justice Finch, 'to break the insolencies of the vulgar before it approach too nigh the royal throne'.[16] The people, in this view, were inherently unstable, and needed

---

(1993), 359–91. For the subleties of social subversion see James C. Scott, *Weapons of the Weak: Everyday Forms of Peasant Resistance* (New Haven, 1985), and idem., *Domination and the Arts of Resistance: Hidden Transcripts* (New Haven, 1990).

[10] William Le Hardy (ed.), *Hertfordshire County Records. Calendar to the Sessions Books . . . 1619 to 1657*, (Hertford, 1928), v. 42.

[11] Maurice Ashley, *Life in Stuart England* (1964), 21, 22.

[12] Cambridge University Library, Ms. EDR LA/5a, f. 33.

[13] John Lister (ed.), *West Riding Sessions Records. Vol. II. Orders, 1611–1642. Indictments, 1637–1642* (Yorkshire Archaeological Society, vol. liii, 1915), 160.

[14] H. Hampton Copnoll, *Nottinghamshire County Records. Notes and Extracts from the Nottinghamshire County Records of the Seventeenth Century* (Nottingham, 1915), 25.

[15] J. P. Kenyon, *The Stuart Constitution* (2nd. edn., Cambridge, 1986), 16.

[16] 'Notes taken from the Lord Keeper Finch his speech', in William Drake's Journal, Huntington Library Ms, HM 55603.

constantly to be kept under discipline; only the diligence of magistrates and monarchs prevented slippage into confusion and chaos. 'The common people...have neither constancy nor gratitude', and deserved neither love not trust, Lord Conway remarked in 1640.[17] As Henry King, the dean of Rochester, explained that spring in a sermon on the King's accession day, 'the people are as an inundation of water, like the waves for number and for noise, and would resemble the wild disorder of a wrought sea...did not the king in his authority limit their incessant motion.' The King, social theory agreed, was 'the state's pilot, and his law the compass', without which the state would be adrift.[18]

The events of 1640–2 exacerbated conservative anxieties. Gentlemen of both royalist and parliamentary persuasions shared similar social concerns. Some of the most forceful reiterations of conventional social ideology were triggered by alarm that the social fabric was indeed unravelling. The Lambeth disturbances, the insolencies of the northern army, the street agitation around Westminster, and a host of parish turmoils provided indications of a social structure in disarray. So too did the verbal affronts to gentility and magisterial office. The populace, it seemed, had become rowdier, and the established authorities less effective. Myriad examples pointed to the collapse of customary deference, the breakdown of local order, and the erosion of social controls. The system had not disintegrated, but it was certainly fraying at the edges.

Ill humours among 'the common multitude' in 1640 prompted John Swan's production of a patriarchalist tract, 'in confutation of all disobedient and factious kind of people who are enemies both to the church and state'. Swan's *Redde Debitum. Or, A Discourse in Defence of Three Chiefe Fatherhoods* expounded a profoundly conservative view of the world, with admixtures of observation, anachronism, and wishful thinking. It was a world in which churchmen acted as 'spiritual parents', magistrates as 'political parents', and kings as 'nursing fathers' of their country. The operating principle of society, in this view, was that 'the wise, the noble, the mighty, must govern the foolish, ignorant, and weak, suppress the stubborn, and bridle the obstinate. For thus doth order maintain the brittle fabric of the world from ruin.'[19] Unfortunately for Swan and his ilk, this world of benevolent,

---

[17] *CSPD 1640*, 190; British Library, Add. Ms. 70002, f. 295 (Lord Conway to George Garrard, 20 May 1640).

[18] Henry King, *A Sermon Preached at St Pauls March 27. 1640*, in Mary Hobbs (ed.), *The Sermons of Henry King (1592–1669)* (Cranbury, NJ, and Aldershot, 1992), 222–3.

[19] John Swan, *Redde Debitum. Or, A Discourse in defence of three chiefe Fatherhoods* (1640), title page, sig. A2v, 6–11, 18–19. The treatise was reprinted in 1641. Swan was curate at Duxford, Cambridgeshire.

hierarchical patriarchy seemed to be turning upside down. Similar concerns run through the pamphlet debates of 1641. Shocked by 'stirs and discords... betwixt superiors and inferiors', one pamphlet suggested that all would be well again if normal hierarchical relations were restored between masters and servants, parents and children, husbands and wives, and the King and his subjects.[20] Another cited a dozen passages of Scripture justifying 'the duty of inferiors to the superiors', in order to prove that 'God's word doth not allow or countenance mutinies, unlawful assemblies, or rebellions against government'.[21]

The period from the spring of 1640 to the summer 1642 saw an extraordinary upsurge of hostility to established authority. Insubordination became more vocal, non-cooperation became more belligerent. The fiction of hierarchical harmony became exposed and undermined as customary displays of deference and respect were set aside. These years saw an outpouring of scorn against magistrates and constables, and an overflow of derision directed at the clergy, nobility, and gentry. Recalcitrance seemed to be contagious. Hundreds of people were cited for refusing to assist the constables, refusing to serve on watches, or refusing to pay assessments. Few were effectively punished. Refractory behaviour in town and country included parishioners who refused to pay church rates, soldiers who refused to obey their officers, and tenants who refused to pay their rents. Local courts faced streams of offenders who refused to submit to authority: apprentices disobeying their masters, artisans resisting constables, and vagrant hordes disregarding the discipline of the watch.[22] Commentators may have magnified these threats and exaggerated the danger, but their alarm itself was part of reality.

WANDERERS

There was nothing novel in the vagrant threat, but it contributed to heightened anxieties. England was teeming with ragged drifters, discharged soldiers and deserters, women with children, wanderers from Ireland, victims of losses, carriers of confusion, and bearers of tales. The company of the road included victims of economic collapse, the unemployable and mentally ill, refugees from wars and rebellions, runaways and wounded veterans, masterless men and abandoned women, as well as criminals, tricksters, tinkers,

---

[20] E.F., *Newes From Heaven Both Good and True* (1641), sig. A2.

[21] I.W., *Certaine Affirmations In defence of the pulling down of Communion Rails... answered* (1641), 3, 15.

[22] Corporation of London, Bridewell and Bethlem, Court of Governors' Minutes, 1640–1642, passim.

peddlers, and carriers of messages and goods. They did not belong to the communities through which they passed, and were, in every sense, out of place. A stack of Elizabethan statutes charged local magistrates with the punishment of vagabonds, rogues, and sturdy beggars. They also authorized relief to legitimate travellers, and encouraged them to keep moving on.[23]

Even in the best of times the mobility and marginality of England's wanderers posed a threat to good order, and at times of social, economic, and military disturbance the problem was especially severe. Early in the Scottish war, 'at this time when lewd practices are daily multiplied and seditious tongues are busy, and the country...more subject to rapine and spoil than at other times', Hampshire magistrates ordered a special watch for 'malefactors and lewd people...rogues, vagrants and wanderers, night riders and walkers, or such as continue longer than ordinary in inns, taverns or victualing houses'.[24] Vagrants were suspected of petty thievery, pilferage, and the snatching of livestock, food, and clothes. They were also blamed for the spreading of disease and the spreading of rumours and fears. Devon magistrates in October 1640 ordered the watch 'to apprehend all suspicious and wandering persons' who might be carriers of infection.[25] Their concern was not unreasonable, since plague had returned that summer.

Four members of the Banister family found wandering in Middlesex and 'vageing' as 'counterfeit Egyptians' were whipped in August 1640 and sent back to their parish of origin in Cornwall.[26] Other wanderers on the West Country roads included veterans discharged from the European wars with their destitute dependants. One party examined at Tavistock in January 1641 acknowledged 'they have eaten a great many cats' but denied stealing any: 'the two cats which they eat yesterday at Lamerton they had from some children'. They were journeying from Derbyshire to Cornwall and were apprehended on the edge of Dartmoor, no place for anyone in winter.[27] Another group, wandering near Exeter in June 1642, included Cornishmen returning from continental service with their entourage of wives, children, and dogs. The magistrates took note that 'the men being armed with swords seemed to be very dangerous and desperate and a terror to the country people where they came, using also a canting language and eating cats like Egyptians [i.e., gypsies] which render them more suspicious.'[28] Within a few

---

[23] *Statutes of the Realm*, 14 Eliz. I c. 5; 39 Eliz. I c. 4; 43 Eliz. I c. 2.

[24] Hampshire Record Office, Jervoise of Herriard Ms. 44 M69/G3/220.

[25] Devon Record Office, Quarter Sessions Order Book 1640–51, Q/S 1/8, n.f.

[26] London Metropolitan Archives, Sessions Books, MJ/SBB/11 and 12 (calendar 10360.t.1, 41, 49).   [27] Devon Record Office, Quarter Sessions Rolls, Q/SB, Box 44/59.

[28] Ibid., Box 46. The law was especially strict on so-called Egyptians, 22 Henry VIII c. 10, 1 and 2 Philip and Mary c. 4, 5 Eliz. I c. 20.

months they would have opportunities to serve in the English army of their choice.

A swarm of wanderers plagued Hertfordshire in the spring of 1641. Neighbours complained of 'a constant meeting, concourse and lodging of vagrant persons' in the vicinity of Sawbridgeworth, Guilston, and Widford. Their numbers ranging from twenty to sixty, they found refuge in various private barns. Richard Haynes, husbandman of Much Hadham, was identified as 'a common harbourer of rogues' who 'suffereth their victuals to be... dressed and their clothes to be... washed in his dwelling house'. Rather like Springlove in 1641's hit comedy, *A Jovial Crew*, Haynes had an affinity for the wandering poor. One wonders whether Richard Brome used this episode as the basis for his play. When the constables moved to apprehend them, neighbours complained, the beggars fled to neighbouring parishes, 'and so have escaped apprehension, and do molest the country thereabout intolerably contrary to the laws'. Although Haynes was frequently cited for his offence, he was never effectively punished.[29] Magistrates in Cheshire in October 1641 likewise took note of 'the great number of rogues and vagabonds and sturdy beggars wandering and lurking in the country, to the great trouble and terror of the same', and ordered the constables to discover who lodged or harboured them.[30]

The Irish rebellion of 1641 added to the wanderers on England's roads. Even before the October uprising, England was accustomed to the movements of poor and suspicious travellers out of Ireland. They used the lesser ports of north Cornwall, Devon, and Somerset as well as the major gateways of London, Bristol, and Chester. Theophilus Jule, late of Artcullum (Arklow?), County Wexford, was among a group travelling through north Devon in December 1641 who were stopped by local magistrates. He explained that they were fleeing the Irish rebels, and were dependent on the good will of relatives in England.[31] Mary Crowe and her children were among the 'poor distressed protestants' who sought relief in Hertfordshire in April 1642, being driven out of Ireland 'by the misery of that place'.[32] Around this time the constables of Upton, Nottinghamshire, shared fourpence between 'three Irish people which were stripped and had

---

[29] Hertfordshire Record Office, QSB 2B, f. 25. Haynes had been in trouble for the same offence in 1636 and would be indicted again 'for harbouring rogues and vagabonds' in 1648 (Le Hardy (ed.), *Hertfordshire County Records. Calendar to the Sessions Books...1619 to 1657*, v. 222, 292–3, 383). Richard Brome, *The Jovial Crew*, was performed in 1641, published in 1652, and revived at the Restoration.

[30] Cheshire Record Office, Quarter Sessions Books 1640–1643, QJB 1/6, f. 46.

[31] Devon Record Office, Quarter Sessions Rolls, Q/SB, Box 45.

[32] Hertfordshire Record Office, QSB 2B, f. 34v.

lost all their goods, which had a pass'.[33] Two Irishmen travelling through Wiltshire that spring could not give a satisfactory account of themselves, and being deemed 'dangerous rogues' rather than Protestant refugees, they were detained in the Devizes house of correction.[34] Other wanderers out of Ireland passed through East Anglia. A mother and child were given a pass to move on from Norwich in May 1642, and more suspicious vagrant Irish women showed up in June. The city attempted to rid itself of such vagrants who could give 'no good account of their travelling up and down'.[35]

The vagrant problem was insoluble, and economic, military, and religious disturbances only made it worse. It was partially in response to these problems that King Charles charged his judges in July 1642, 'that rogues, vagabonds and other disorderly people might be apprehended, dealt with and punished according to the laws', because they exacerbated 'the distempers of the present times'.[36]

DERELICTION OF DUTIES

Although county and parochial government continued to function through these years of 'distemper', it was hamstrung by resistance and insubordination. Borough sessions and quarter sessions still met as scheduled, but they could no longer count on the cooperation that normally supported their efforts. Petty recalcitrance, neglect of court orders, and refusal to pay rates and subsidies did not in themselves constitute a revolution; even at the best of times it was difficult to secure full compliance. But accumulating evidence points to arrears uncollected, officials unpaid, offices unfilled, roads and bridges unrepaired, and nuisances unabated in the years 1640–2. Both the material infrastructure and the community glue that maintained it seemed to be falling apart.[37] Ship money became uncollectable, even before Parliament declared it illegal.[38] Thousands refused to pay for coating and conducting the

[33] Martyn Bennett (ed.), *A Nottinghamshire Village in War and Peace: The Accounts of the Constables of Upton 1640–1660* (Thoroton Society Record Series, vol. xxxix, Nottingham, 1995), 8.

[34] Wiltshire Record Office, Quarter Sessions Great Roll, A1/110 Easter 1642, 158.

[35] Norfolk Record Office, Norwich Mayor's Court Book, 1634–1646, ff. 327, 346, 347, 349v.

[36] *The Kings Maiesties Charge Sent to all the Judges of England* (1642), 3–4.

[37] Devon Record Office, Quarter Session Order Book, Q/S 1/8; Herefordshire Record Office, Quarter Sessions, BG 11/5/3; Essex Record Office, Quarter Sessions Rolls, Q/SR/310/67.

[38] *CSPD 1640*, 8, 105, 126, 146, 220, 229, 230, 244, 245, 253, 264, 269, 315, 444, 466, 488; PRO, PC2/52, ff. 264v, 290–2; PRO, SP16/458/110.

1640 northern army. The sinews of power became severed when subjects withheld their money.[39]

Although the crisis of the kingdom stimulated many people to greater interest in public affairs, it allowed others to shirk their responsibilities. Presentments to the Westminster sessions in October 1641, for example, cited dozens of men who no longer attended church, who refused to do watch and ward, and who reneged on their parish duties and fiscal obligations.[40] As far as their civic role was concerned, some of these citizens had gone on strike. The London authorities at the end of 1641 complained of 'the great disrespect of magistracy and contempt of government' exhibited by citizens and householders. The orders of the Common Council were disregarded, there was 'great neglect in appearance of the trained bands', civic duties and customary obligations seemingly went by the board.[41] Local constables too were cited for failing to keep watch, refusing to apprehend criminals, neglecting to collect rates, and otherwise 'not attending and exercising their office' during periods of mounting lawlessness. When magistrates in Kent remarked in October 1640 that 'such contempts as these and the like are very dangerous of evil consequence, tending much to the neglect of his majesty's service', they could not know how prescient were their remarks.[42]

Hundreds of parishioners were cited at quarter sessions in these years for refusing to perform customary work on the highways or otherwise perform their community duties. In Cheshire the ways between Nantwich and Acton had become greatly decayed and unpassable in winter, but the inhabitants would not fulfil their obligations.[43] Others refused to work with their oxen at Beaubridge causeway, or to give any time to repairs.[44] Highway surveyors were unable to assemble work gangs, and tired judges all over the country noted similar deficiencies.[45] The failure to repair the roads around Writtle, Essex, in 1640 was especially serious, 'the time then being very troublesome in regard of pressing of soldiers'.[46] Highway repairs were impossible, said the inhabitants of South Otterington, Yorkshire, in October 1641, 'forasmuch as the country hath been very sore oppressed and put to great charge by reason of soldiers billeted in most parts of the North

[39] PRO, SP16/459/47; SP16/459/54 and 55; SP16/245/94; SP/461/103. See also Joan Kent, *The English Village Constable 1580–1642: A Social and Administrative Study* (Oxford, 1986), 242–6.

[40] London Metropolitan Archives, Sessions Roll, MJ/SR/897/137.

[41] *A Common Councell, Held at Guild-hall, In the City of London, the 31 of December 1641* (1641), 9.   [42] Centre for Kentish Studies, Q/SO WI, f. 115.

[43] Cheshire Record Office, QJB 1/6, f. 19v; QJB 2/6, ff. 4, 7–20, 28v, 32, and passim.

[44] Cheshire Record Office, QJF 69/2, f. 18; QJF 70/2, f. 24.

[45] Durham Record Office, Quarter Sessions Order Book 1640–43, Q/S/OB 3, 24, 25, 29; Essex Record Office, Q/Sba2/43; Wiltshire Record Office, Quarter Sessions Great Roll, A1/110 Trinity 1642, 133.   [46] Essex Record Office, Q/Sba2/43.

Riding'.[47] The military traffic of men and carts put additional stress on the transport infrastructure, at a time when diarists were reporting some of the wettest weather in memory.[48]

In Hertfordshire the highway from Hitchin into Bedfordshire became 'greatly annoyed', but men of all ranks refused to lend their labour or their draught teams to repairs.[49] Thirty-five parishioners of Hailsham, Sussex, were cited for defaults in July 1641, having not performed their several days of 'working in the king's highways according to the statute'.[50] In Lincolnshire the road infrastructure had become 'much neglected', noted petitioners in January 1642, because those responsible for its upkeep were now 'more careless than otherwise they would have been'. Statutory penalties applied in such circumstances, but the courts had little success in securing compliance.[51] Not all was mud and decay, however, as the Sussex authorities reported in October 1641: the bad ways at Witham were now 'very well and sufficiently mended and repaired in very good and sufficient manner'.[52] Whether they would last through another winter was yet to be seen.

RENTS IN ARREARS

Relations between landlords and tenants became more than usually strained as the English economy slowed and the prolonged political crisis kept many gentlemen away from their estates. 'It is a very dead time here, no money stirring, rents are very hard to be got', Charles Seagrave reported from Leicestershire in November 1640. Lady Day rents on the Hastings estates were severely in arrears, and Michaelmas rent was 'yet to be got'.[53] Viscount Scudamore's agents in Gloucestershire observed in February 1641 that 'we found a kind of unwillingness in tenants to disburse your monies'.[54] Wiltshire gentlemen complained in March 1641 that the slowdown in trade 'makes tenants want money to pay their landlords rent'.[55] Maurice Wynn remarked on the 'deadness of trading' in London that month, when a creeping economic paralysis compounded the political crisis.[56] 'Last year's rent' remained unpaid,

---

[47] J. C. Atkinson (ed.), *Quarter Sessions Records [1634–47]* (North Riding Record Society, vol. iv, 1886), 214.

[48] Diary of Thomas Wyatt, Bodleian Library, Ms. Top. Oxon. C. 378, 306; Diary of Sir Humphrey Mildmay, British Library, Harleian Ms. 454; *CSPD 1641–43*, 128.

[49] Hertfordshire Record Office, QS MB 2/326, /406, and passim.

[50] East Sussex Record Office, QR/E/53/19. *Statutes of the Realm*, 22 Henry VIII, c. 5.

[51] Lincolnshire Archives, LQ.S/A/10/138.   [52] East Sussex Record Office, QR/E/54/8.

[53] Huntington Library, Ms. HA 10728.   [54] PRO, C115/98/7225.

[55] British Library, Stowe Ms. 184, f. 31.

[56] National Library of Wales, Wynn Papers, no. 1680 (microfilm).

and arrears of forty-seven pounds were compounding because the tenant
'refuseth to pay'.[57]

Sir Robert Harley's Herefordshire tenants would 'pay no rent' in 1641 or 1642
while their landlord was away in London for the parliament. Brilliana Harley's
letters to her husband complain over and again that 'the tenants have paid no
money', necessitating tighter budgeting. By February 1642 she was suggesting,
'if they will pay their rents no better than they do, it is better for you to take
other tenants'.[58] Sir Edward Dering suffered similar problems, and wrote to his
wife in July 1641 to 'ask the overseers for the rent of Marketman. If I have no
rents sent up, I do not know how I can come down' from London to Kent.[59]

Arrears were so severe and cash so short that some landlords threatened
distraint of cattle and other punitive measures. 'If I receive not my rent I shall
be prejudiced beyond your imagination', John Ryves warned Sir Peter Temple
in September 1641.[60] Temple's Dorset tenants would not pay their rent, and
were further behind in May 1642.[61] Agents for the Earl of Bridgewater's
estates experienced similar difficulties.[62] Henry Oxinden's tenants in Kent
were also 'backward in paying their rents'.[63] An audit of the Neville family's
estate in Berkshire between Lady Day and Michaelmas 1641 found twelve out
of nineteen tenants 'not paid' or 'will not pay'.[64] Arrears of rent from the Earl
of Arundel's Sheffield and Hallamshire properties approached six hundred
pounds in the year ending Lady Day 1642, more than twice the shortfall of
the previous two years.[65] From Cornwall in spring 1642 came reports of
'refractory men' who had grown 'very remiss and backward' in their payment
of tithes and dues.[66]

Ecclesiastical tenants proved particularly recalcitrant. Bishop Bridgeman's
estate steward in the diocese of Chester expressed frustration in October 1641
over 'refusers' whose rent was behind, though 'demanded three or four times
over'.[67] Robert Bidgood, a tenant of the bishop of Exeter, took advantage of

---

[57] National Library of Wales, Wynn Papers, nos. 1681, 1684 (microfilm).

[58] British Library, Add. Ms. 70003, ff. 87, 180v, 188v, 192v, 200, 209, 217; Add. Ms. 70110, f. 62;
Thomas Taylor Lewis (ed.), *Letters of the Lady Brilliana Harley* (Camden Society, vol. lviii, 1854),
134, 139, 147.   [59] Centre for Kentish Studies, Maidstone, Dering, Mss. U. 350/C2/94.

[60] Huntington Library, Ms. STT 1761.   [61] Huntington Library, Ms. STT 2041.

[62] Huntington Library, Ms. El. 7337.

[63] Dorothy Gardiner (ed.), *The Oxinden and Peyton Letters 1642–1670* (1937), 9.

[64] Berkshire Record Office, Neville Papers, D/EN F8/1/6.

[65] Sheffield Archives, Wentworth Woodhouse Muniments, Bright Papers, 'A Book of
Proffites' 1642, showing revenues totalling £7,466; David Hey, *A History of Sheffield* (1998),
41–2. Though agent for a conservative peer, Stephen Bright belonged to one of the leading
puritan families of south Yorkshire, and was brother to the vicar of Sheffield.

[66] Judith Maltby, 'Petitions for Episcopacy and the Book of Common Prayer on the Eve
of the Civil War 1641–1642', in Stephen Taylor (ed.), *From Cranmer to Davidson* (Church of
England Record Society, vol. vii, 1999), 150.

[67] Staffordshire Record Office, Correspondence of Bishop Bridgeman, D. 1287/18/2, f. 208a.

his grace's troubles to withhold his rent of four pounds a year. A quarter session court in January 1642 ordered him to make good his arrears.[68] Rent collecting was especially difficult in the diocese of Durham in areas under Scottish occupation. The Covenanters discouraged payments to the Dean and Chapter or anyone associated with them, who were 'enemies to this cause and expedition'. Instead, cathedral tenants were supposed to contribute 'towards the relief and maintenance of this army'.[69] The political troubles of episcopacy had local economic consequences, though the bishops were not the only landlords to experience stresses.

Nor was withholding rent the only way for tenants and dependants to frustrate their masters. The Wynn estates in north Wales suffered depredation in March 1641 when 'the poor weir-men' took to unauthorized felling of trees.[70] In Somerset Florence Smyth complained of the difficulty of keeping the labourers, threshers, and mowers in 'awe' while her husband was away on parliamentary business. On 24 June 1641 she wrote to Thomas Smyth that the 'clowns' failed to help in a planned round-up of cattle. On 1 July she wrote that 'the wild rascals cannot be gotten out of the alehouse, be the weather never so fair, for this fine day I could not get a swath cut by them.'[71] Thomas Smyth himself complained in February 1642 of the 'increased disorders of all my people', who were taking advantage of his absence from Ashton Court. The Ashton tenants showed disrespect, thought Smyth, 'by doing eye-service and having it their purpose to return to their vomit again as soon as ever my back is turned about from them'.[72] 'Wood-stealers . . . who care not for justices' warrants' caused similar problems on Edward Phelips's Montacute estate while he was busy at Westminster.[73] These difficulties may reflect the usual problems of an absent master, as well as the bloody-mindedness of English labourers. However, the frequency and intensity of remarks of this sort points to a deepening challenge to authority during the revolutions of 1641.

POACHING AND TUMULTS

Poaching, though illegal, was endemic in early modern England. It was a crime that involved trespass and theft, and its targets included private parks

---

[68] Devon Record Office, Quarter Session Order Book 1640–1651, Q/S 1/8, n.f.

[69] Huntington Library, Ms. El. 7738, orders of the Scottish army, 14 September 1640.

[70] National Library of Wales, *Calendar of Wynne (of Gwydir) Papers, 1515–1690* (Aberystwyth, 1926), 271.

[71] J. H. Bettey (ed.), *Calendar of the Correspondence of the Smyth Family of Ashton Court 1548–1642* (Bristol Record Society, vol. xxxv, 1982), 174.

[72] Ibid., 177, checked against Bristol Record Office, Smith papers, 36074/156 b.

[73] Somerset Record Office, Phelips Ms. DD/PH/229/8.

and royal forests. Deer-stealers and rabbit-takers risked punishment in pursuit of illicit venison and conies, and they may also have enjoyed the thrill of outwitting keepers and estate owners.[74] Some of the poachers themselves were of gentle or yeoman status. Fragmentary evidence suggests that poachers became bolder in the early 1640s, as law and order deteriorated. The unpaid rangers and keepers of the royal parks also took to rewarding themselves with the King's deer, explaining, to the satisfaction of one pamphleteer of 1642, 'the miracle of so great store of venison to be sold at the cooks' shops about London this year'.[75]

It was almost a licence to poach in July 1640 when the Berkshire grand jury complained of 'the innumerable increase of deer' in Windsor forest, 'which if they shall go on as fast in ten years will neither leave food nor room for any other creature'.[76] Raids on the royal forest at Windsor were so severe in September 1641 that the House of Commons wrote to local magistrates, 'requiring them to take care that the deer in his majesty's forests be not destroyed, and to repress all tumults'. But poaching and tumults continued. In February 1642 the Earl of Holland reported that 'the people of the country in a riotous and tumultuous manner have lately killed a hundred of his majesty's fallow deer, and besides red deer, and do threaten to pull down the pales' about the New Lodge at Windsor. This occurred soon after the King himself had left Windsor castle. Depredations continued all spring and summer, impervious to all authority.[77] One poacher at Swinley Walk, Berkshire, bragged in May 1642 that 'he cared neither for king nor parliament' and broke free after shooting the constable's horse.[78]

Hertfordshire poachers with dogs, ferrets, and nets broke into Hatfield park in September 1640, taking the Earl of Salisbury's rabbits.[79] The Earl of Pembroke's deer suffered depredations in January 1641.[80] Lady Geratt lost deer from her enclosed grounds in Lancashire in April.[81] Across the Pennines at Pontefract, Yorkshire judges heard cases involving the poaching of hares and red deer.[82] A tanner and a yeoman were among those charged with breaking

[74] Roger B. Manning, *Hunters and Poachers: A Social and Cultural History of Unlawful Hunting in England, 1485–1640* (Oxford, 1993); Dan Beaver, ' "Bragging and Daring Words": Honour, Property and the Symbolism of the Hunt in Stowe, 1590–1642', in Braddick and Walter (eds.), *Negotiating Power in Early Modern Society*, 149–65.

[75] *A Deep Sigh Breath'd Through the Lodgings at White-Hall, Deploring the absence of the Court, And the Miseries of the Pallace* (1642), sig. A3v.   [76] *CSPD 1640*, 466.

[77] Robert Richard Tighe and James Edward Davis (eds.), *Annals of Windsor* (2 vols., 1858), ii 160–7; HMC *5th Report* (1876), 9; *Lords Journals*, iv. 602.   [78] HMC *5th Report*, 24.

[79] Hertfordshire Record Office, QS MB 2/337.

[80] Wiltshire Record Office, Quarter Sessions Great Roll, A1/110 Hilary 1640, 117.

[81] Lancashire Record Office, QSB/1/1/244/7 and 8.

[82] Lister (ed.), *West Riding Sessions Records. Vol. II.*, 189.

into Sir Francis Wortley's park 'and there killing a doe with a handgun charged with powder and shot'. The poaching began in July 1640 but it took six months for Sir Francis to bring the offenders to court, where he himself presided.[83] The same park was hit again in October 1641 by large bands of hunters, none of whom could be arrested.[84] Poachers who took deer belonging to the Earl of Cumberland were still at large a year after the alleged incident.[85] Sir William Saville's park was violated in August 1641 when a labourer and a cobbler took their greyhounds after the baronet's bucks. The cobbler, Robert Wilkinson, was brought to justice two months later and threatened with three months in York castle gaol unless he paid five pounds damages.[86]

Deer-stealers in Sussex took advantage of the sanctions against Roman Catholics by poaching in Sir Richard Weston's grounds. Thomas Bishop boasted that he had killed four deer in one night in July 1641, and that 'Sir Richard Weston being a recusant convicted he could have no remedy by law for it.' Bishop and his company had also taken deer from the park of Mr Thomas Middleton, who was no recusant but a magistrate and member of Parliament. One of the poachers who drew his sword at the keeper was subsequently committed to prison, but Thomas Bishop, the only one of the offenders of gentle rank, escaped serious punishment.[87] Elsewhere in Sussex, in June 1642 six men disguised in vizards and caps entered the park of John Busbridge, esquire, with greyhounds to hunt his deer and rabbits.[88] Reports also circulated of violent confrontations with poachers in Berkshire, and of the mass slaughter of three hundred deer in Oxfordshire.[89]

Young men of Roxwell, Essex, faced magistrates in May 1641 for breaking into Writtle park and stealing Lord Petre's deer. Though bloodstains, a greyhound, and a gun were found in John Crossingham's house, neither he nor any of the others would admit any knowledge of the incident.[90] Other yeomen poachers in Essex went after the deer of Sir Richard Wiseman.[91] Waltham Forest in south-east Essex became a battleground between gamekeepers and poachers. Benjamin Kesar of West Ham, a repeat offender, was cited before magistrates in January 1642 for battling one of the King's keepers while illegally hunting deer.[92] In the spring of 1642 especially assertive poachers announced that 'they came for venison, and venison they would have, and there was no law settled at this time, [and] laughed at the warrant of the Earl of Carlisle.'[93] These poachers belonged to a band of some

---

[83] Ibid., 264.   [84] Ibid., 355–6.   [85] Ibid., 293.   [86] Ibid., 321, 329.
[87] East Sussex Record Office, QR/E/53/78 and 131.
[88] East Sussex Record Office, Lewes, QR/E/59.
[89] HMC, *5th Report*, 21, 24.   [90] Essex Record Office, Q/SR/312/30,/96,/135; Q/Sba2/42.
[91] Essex Record Office, Quarter Sessions Rolls, Q/SR/315/36.
[92] Essex Record Office, Q/Sba2/45.   [93] HMC *5th Report*, 20; *Lords Journals*, v. 37.

forty or fifty men from several parishes, including gentlemen, labourers, a turner, a butcher, and a local minister. Armed with guns and dogs, and contemptuous of royal and aristocratic authority, they brought down does, bucks, stags, and others forbidden game. The depredations began in the Maytide festivity and extended to midsummer 1642. Some of these offenders discovered that there was indeed law, when they were indicted for riot at the Chelmsford Michaelmas quarter sessions. However, the matter was unresolved, for by this time civil war had started and both poachers and magistrates had more pressing concerns.[94]

ABUSE OF CONSTABLES

Constables served as agents for magisterial authority. They delivered writs, collected taxes, arrested malefactors, and raided illegal alehouses. Generally they upheld the King's peace and enforced the King's laws. Usually they came from the leading ranks of local society and acted as village headmen, mediating between the localities and county government. Some were drawn from the minor gentry. In fulfilling the expanding range of duties imposed upon them by the early modern state, constables relied on their own social status as well as the authority of their commission. Parishioners were supposed to obey their instructions and come to their assistance, and normally they paid them appropriate respect.[95] It was therefore troubling to see constabulary authority undermined. Parish constables were among the first to encounter 'the audacious height of disobedience' that the conservative pamphleteer John Taylor identified among 'the diseases of the times or the distempers of the commonwealth'.[96] The slighting of local authority enfeebled the body politic.

No doubt parish constables were accustomed to a degree of banter and non-cooperation. Drunken offenders were notoriously loose-tongued, and others hurled offensive words in anger. Baiting the constables may have provided anti-social parishioners with a kind of spectator sport. We have no register or barometer of invective for the early modern period, so cannot compare incivilities in different periods. But a strong impression emerges that local community relations around 1640 were especially fraught. County and borough sessions records from 1640 to 1642 are filled with reports of violence and abuse, not all of which could be remedied. Constables from all regions suffered wounds and indignities as neighbours scoffed at their

---

[94] Essex Record Office, Q/SR/317/77, /94; Q/SR/318/33–40.

[95] Kent, *English Village Constable 1580–1642*, 263.

[96] John Taylor, *The Diseases of the Times or, The Distempers of the Common-wealth* (1641?), sig. A3v.

authority and flouted the law.[97] A cascade of abuse and resistance prevented them from 'doing the king's service'.[98] Offenders called constables such names as 'saucy boy', 'knave', 'jackanapes', 'rag manners', 'blockhead', 'simple skinned rogue', and 'goodman goose'.[99] Petty offenders refused to come quietly, troublemakers rejected justices' warrants,[100] and order became harder to maintain. Rescues from constabulary custody became more violent and more common.[101] Taken in isolation, these incidents may be regarded as trivial, but taken together they fuelled the impression that the social fabric was coming undone.

A Hertfordshire man, Thomas Collis, gave the constables 'reproachful speeches' in July 1640 and told them 'he would knock out our brains if [they] came near his door'.[102] In Worcestershire Richard Calloe, a yeoman, railed at constable Paul Rumney in November 1640, saying he would not be ruled 'by a chafing, shittering and busting baddam'. The incident occurred outside Suckley Church when the constable demanded money for setting forth soldiers. The citation deemed Calloe's outburst especially offensive because this constable was 'accounted, reputed and taken to be a gentleman, and to be descended and come of good parentage'. The yeoman had broken social decorum, reneged on his financial obligation, abused an official, and disgraced a gentlemen, and since the offence took place in a churchyard, he 'did abuse the sacred ground'. Attempts to prosecute the case in the Worcester consistory court came to nothing, as that court, like all church courts, was rapidly losing authority. The quarter sessions intervened in an attempt to restore harmony, ordering the parties to find sureties for peaceable behaviour towards each other.[103]

---

[97] Essex Record Office, Quarter Sessions Rolls, Q/SR/309/17; London Metropolitan Archives, Sessions Books, MJ/SBB; Wiltshire Record Office, Quarter Sessions Great Roll, A1/110 Michaelmas 1640, 46–7; Gloucestershire Record Office, Sessions Orders 1633–1671, GBR/G3/SO2, 24 September 1641; Lancashire Record Office, QSB/1/264/8–11. See also Borthwick Institute, archdeaconry of Cleveland acts, C/V/CB 3, ff. 7, 7v, 8, 26v, and passim.

[98] Bristol Record Office, Quarter Sessions Minute Book 1634–47, JQS/M/3, f. 171; Norfolk Record Office, Norwich Mayor's Court Book, 1634–1646, f. 323.

[99] Norfolk Record Office, Norwich Mayor's Court Book, 1639–1644, NCR/16a/20, ff. 278v, 284, 344v; Devon Record Office, Exeter Quarter Sessions Book, 1630–1642, f. 395v.

[100] Norfolk Record Office, Norwich Mayor's Court Book, 1634–1646, f. 323.

[101] The constable of Houndsditch was roughed up and his coat torn during the attempted rescue of Robert Cobbett in January 1642 (London Metropolitan Archives, Sessions Roll, MJ/SR/905/92). When authorities attempted to serve James Hunt of Hereford with a warrant in May 1642 he 'took an iron broach or spit in his hands and ran at the constable and did rescue himself away, wounding one constable' (Herefordshire Record Office, Quarter Sessions, BG 11/5/35, 18 May 1642).

[102] Hertfordshire Record Office, Hertford Borough Records, vol. ix, 1617–1740, no. 159.

[103] Worcestershire Record Office, BA 2102/9, pp. 447, 503; J. W. Willis Bund (ed.), *Worcestershire County Records. Division 1. Document Relating to Quarter Sessions. Calendar of the QuarterSessions Papers. Vol. 1. 1591–1643* (Worcester, 1900), 691.

In Devonshire two silkweavers were fined at Exeter in January 1641, 'for assaulting and abusing of Ezechiel Wood, a constable'.[104] Also in January the constable of Walgherton, Cheshire, 'who is the king's sworn officer', complained that Alexander Seckerson assaulted and abused him 'in the execution of his office, and to the ill example and encouragement to others'.[105] In February, when the constables of Bristol attempted to hold Thomas Philpott, a wire-drawer, for his 'drunkenness and lewd living', he threatened to kill them 'and tore the band off one of their necks'.[106] When they attempted to summon Thomas Ward, a smith, before the mayor, Ward 'had his hammer and iron in his hand and threatened to run at the constables'.[107] Following another 'mutiny' in Bristol High Street, a gathering of artisans and shopkeepers refused to disperse and ended up throwing stones at the constables.[108] In March 1641 Richard Coulthurst of Chipping, Lancashire, threatened to run at the constable with his knife if he pursued him for unlawful drinking.[109] John Lightbourne, a webster, threatened the constable of Bolton with a sword, and would not be silenced even after being sat in the stocks.[110] A West Riding yeoman told a constable in May that he was 'bankrupt, roguish and knavish'.[111] Another yeoman in London threw the constable of east Smithfield down some stairs, 'saying he had better commission than the said constable had'.[112] Similar altercations were recorded from the West Country to East Anglia.[113]

Not surprisingly, in these circumstances, it became harder to find men to take on local office. Hundreds of eligible candidates refused to become constables.[114] William Pennard, husbandman, of Cowley, Middlesex, flatly refused to take the constable's oath in December 1640 despite 'being lawfully elected by the inhabitants…according to the ancient custom of the parish'.[115] At Exeter in January 1641 it was difficult to find anyone willing to undertake the task. Thomas Ford and Samuel Clarke, both merchants,

---

[104] Devonshire Record Office, City of Exeter Quarter Session Book 63, 1630–1642, f. 345.
[105] Cheshire Record Office, QJF 69/4, 74. Seckerson was not quickly punished, for the same citation came up four months later (QJF 70/1, f. 29).
[106] Bristol Record Office, Quarter Sessions Minute Book 1634–47, JQS/M/3, f. 163v.
[107] Ibid.   [108] Ibid., ff. 176v–177.   [109] Lancashire Record Office, QSB/1/245/36.
[110] Lancashire Record Office, QSB/1/251/53.
[111] Lister (ed.), *West Riding Sessions Records. Vol. II*, 332.
[112] London Metropolitan Archives, Sessions Roll, MJ/SR/893/50.
[113] Staffordshire Record Office, Q/SR/247/6; Essex Record Office, Quarter Sessions Rolls, Q/SR/313/29, Q/SR/314/59; Devon Record Office, Quarter Session Order Book 1640–1651, Q/S 1/8, n.f.
[114] Cheshire Record Office, QJB 1/6, 20; Durham Record Office, Quarter Sessions Order Book 1640–43, Q/S/OB 3, 26, 32, 36; Lancashire Record Office, QSB/1/233/32; Kent, *English Village Constable*, 76–7.
[115] London Metropolitan Archives, Sessions Roll, MJ/SR/883/40.

refused the oath of a constable, despite the insistence of the justices.[116] Ralph Welford told the justices at the Durham Quarter Sessions in July 1642, 'that do what they would he would not be high constable, let them bind him over if they would to appear at the Assize.'[117] Why would anyone want such a job at such a time, when neighbours were more likely to offer abuse than assistance?

ABUSE OF MAGISTRATES

Constables came mainly from the local community, and may have carried little more social weight than some of the people they were trying to control. Disobedience of the kind documented here may have been common, although it appears to have become more widespread and more reckless after the collapse of the Short Parliament. Magistrates, by contrast, belonged to the gentry, and were accustomed to commanding respect. The abuse of men of this rank was a much more serious offence, impugning the King's justice as well as the honour of the gentlemen who administered it. Borough mayors and aldermen also exercised magisterial authority, and suffered similar affronts.

A spate of 'mistermful' speeches against magistrates broke out in 1640 as commoners spoke abusively to those set in authority over them. The records of borough courts and quarter sessions reveal a flood of indecent words and expressions of defiance.[118] In January 1641 the Lancashire widow Margery Barker called one of the aldermen of Liverpool an 'old dog', and her son asserted, 'I care not a fart for the mayor and aldermen.'[119] John Pratt, a Southampton shoemaker, similarly raged against local governors in March, saying, 'a plague of God confound all assessors and the devil in hell confound him that pays a penny.' Of the borough aldermen, Pratt declared, 'I care not a fart for them, if I were a mile out of town I were as good a man as the best of them.' As for the justices, 'he would call them knaves again to their faces... with above thirty imprecations and horrible oaths.'[120]

In April 1641 a Westminster yeoman, Richard Dalton, told one of the Middlesex magistrates 'that he was a silly justice and did not know what

---

[116] Devon Record Office, Quarter Sessions Order Book, 1630–1642, 346, 348.

[117] Durham Record Office, Quarter Sessions Order Book 1640–43, Q/S/OB 3, 32.

[118] Essex Record Office, Quarter Sessions Rolls, Q/SR/310/54; Wiltshire Record Office, Quarter Sessions Great Roll, A1/110 Michaelmas 1640, 21; Lancashire Record Office, QSO/2/16, 13 January 1641.

[119] George Chandler, *Liverpool Under Charles I* (Liverpool, 1965), 276.

[120] R. C. Anderson (ed.), *The Book of Examinations and Depositions 1622–1644* (Southampton Record Society, 1936), 18.

for'.[121] In the same month a Devon yeoman, Thomas Maunder, declared loudly that the mayor and sheriff of Exeter were both 'loggerheads' and 'mump-heads', and the subsidy assessors 'fools and knaves'.[122] Edward Blackmore, another yeoman visiting Exeter later in the year, said 'that he did not care a fart for the mayor and justices of this city'.[123] In May Thomas Constable, a wooden heel maker of Winwick, Lancashire, told local magistrates, 'that he careth not for binding to good behaviour no more than geese or ducks which he pulled from the ground and spurned with his foot'.[124]

The Shropshire magistrate, Sir Gilbert Cornwall, faced both verbal and physical assault when he attempted to break up a disturbance at a house in Ludlow around midsummer 1641. Thomas Pringle and his wife pulled the justice by the hair and wrestled him to the ground, proclaiming that Thomas 'was as good a man as the said Sir Gilbert'.[125] A cheese-monger from St Giles in the Fields, George Harwood, told the Middlesex magistrate, Mr. Roberts, that 'he did not care for him and . . . did bid Mr. Roberts to commit him if he dared.'[126] The same sessions heard that a Westminster carpenter, Thomas Kingston, made 'most uncivil speeches against my Lord of Lincoln, and wishing all justices of peace in England to be hanged'.[127] When John Fulcher of Tibbenham, Norfolk, was summoned to appear at Norwich at mid-summer he said 'he would not come, and dissuaded others not to appear at sessions.'[128]

In September 1641 a minor altercation took on seditious overtones when Joan Allen of Pleshey, Essex, raised her voice against the authorities. She had already threatened the justices with a pitchfork, and was renowned as some-one who 'is not to be contained in any order'. On 25 September the church-wardens and constables raided her house 'to prevent the great abuse of the sabbath from surfeiting and drunkenness and other most luxurious rioting'. When Sir Francis Cooke advised her 'that he was one of the king's justices of peace, and in authority to see good rule and order to be kept by the king's authority, she the said Joan Allen answered, she knew not the king, nor cared not for him, nor for the said Sir Francis, nor would she obey his authority.' These were dangerous words, for which the justices wanted exemplary punishment. On the Earl of Warwick's order Joan Allen was held in prison

---

[121] London Metropolitan Archives, Sessions Books, MJ/SBB/18 (calendar 10360.t.1, 69).
[122] Devon Record Office, Exeter Quarter Sessions Order Book, 1630–1642, ff. 355v, 356, 358.
[123] Ibid., f. 381v.
[124] Lancashire Record Office, QSB/1/246/30–2. Constable's original offence was to say that all men of reason tread down the surplice and other ceremonies.
[125] Shropshire Record Office, Ludlow Borough Quarter Sessions, LB 11/4/68/3.
[126] London Metropolitan Archives, Sessions Books, MJ/SBB/22 (calendar 10360.t.1, 97).
[127] Ibid., MJ/SR/894/45; MJ/SBB/21 (calendar 10360.t.1, 91).
[128] Norfolk Record Office, Quarter Sessions Book 1629–44, C/S1/6, n.f.

for a month, then whipped for her 'most reproachful' speeches, and sent back home to her husband.[129]

Disruptive words continued into the autumn, when Francis Porter, a tanner, of Gainsborough, abused a Lincolnshire justice 'in very base terms of contempt'.[130] A Staffordshire man, Francis Barrett, offended magistrates in October 1641 by saying 'that he cared not a fart for Sir John Persall, with other disgraceful languages'.[131] Also in October, the Shrewsbury artisan George Prees uttered 'opprobrious and disgraceful speeches' against the wardens of the company of clothworkers, saying 'that he did not care a fart for their authority' and that 'warden Jones is but twopenny Dick'.[132] Another Shropshire artisan, Richard Butler, used 'base words' against the sessions court, saying that the mayor of Shrewsbury 'was a forsworn man because he did not maintain justice as he ought to do, and not worth so much money as will pay for the carriage of a ton of coals'.[133]

Towards the end of the year John Rowbuck of Furby, Lincolnshire, 'did openly say that Sir William Quadring, knight, was and is a poor foolish justice', and utterly refused to pay his assessments. His neighbour Stephen Wright told the magistrates that 'if they did their worst they could cause him but to be whipped, and what cared he for that?'[134] Ordinary people were supposed to care, and were supposed to bow to authority, but in 1641 authority seems to have lost its edge. More abusive language was heard in 1642 as the political crisis deepened. In April it was reported that opponents of fen drainage in Lincolnshire, who pulled down houses on newly drained land, 'will not be appeased by justices nor by the sheriff'.[135] The keeper of a Westminster victualling house that month 'uttered many base and scandalous words against his majesty's justices of the peace, saying that he does not care a fart nor turd for them all'.[136]

Dozens of incidents show anger directed at the instruments of magisterial authority, combining recalcitrance, scatology, and sedition. In London in May 1640, in the wake of the Lambeth disturbances, a crowd of citizens manhandled the provost marshall, who was armed with a privy council warrant, and called him 'rogue and many other abusive names' when he attempted to arrest a suspected prostitute. In the midst of the mêlée Thomas Homer, a bookbinder, took the warrant in his hands and said, 'I care not a fart for it.' And being reminded of the King's proclamation against tumultuous persons,

---

[129] Essex Record Office, Quarter Sessions Rolls, Q/SR/314/130.
[130] Lincolnshire Archives, LQS/A/10/26. [131] Staffordshire Record Office, Q/SO/5/80.
[132] Shropshire Record Office, Shrewsbury Borough Records, 3365/2240, no. 31.
[133] Ibid., no. 28. [134] Lincolnshire Archives, LQS/A/10/136.
[135] Bodleian Library, Ms. Tanner 63, f. 17 (Richard Dugard to Dr Ward, 16 April 1642).
[136] London Metropolitan Archives, Sessions Roll, MJ/SR/909/102.

he exploded, 'tumultuous persons, God bless them, God prosper them, let them get on with that I say.'[137] In November 1640 a Middlesex butcher, William Spencer, vehemently rejected magisterial authority when he threw Mr Reynold's warrant in the ditch, 'saying he cared not for it, nor for any justice's warrant'.[138] Further undermining traditional authority in December, John Hatten refused to execute the lawful warrant of a justice of the peace, he being headborough of Mile-End.[139] In December 1641 the authorities at Newgate were forced to use smoke to quell a riot when condemned prisoners refused to go quietly to their executions unless seven Jesuits also in custody died with them.[140]

In Herefordshire the special bailiffs of the Council of the Marches, who were armed with 'the king's majesty's letters', found their authority trampled upon and their safety imperilled. When bailiff John Prichard attempted to arrest James Jenkins in July 1641, Jenkins not only resisted 'in a fierce and violent manner' but ripped up the letters, saying 'he would wipe his tail with them'. Armed with iron spits, fire shovels, and other improvised weapons, Jenkins and his friends then beat off the bailiff and his assistant, stripping Prichard naked, so that he was forced 'to borrow a sheet from an old woman to wrap about [his] middle to hide and cover [his] privities'.[141] Another incident occurred in September 1641 when Thomas Pugh, gentleman, tried to serve papers on Thomas Probert, who laughed and jeered 'in a scornful and disdainful manner', tore up the royal letters, 'and said he would not give a turd for the council's process'.[142] Similarly at Norwich, when the alderman magistrates attempted to serve a warrant in July 1642 on the brewer Thomas Copping, he told them 'that he cared no more for it than for the wind which came from his backside, and that now it was read he might wipe his backside with it'.[143]

SEDITIOUS WORDS

Some of the commoners who derided the constables and insulted the magistrates were foolish or reckless enough to disparage the authority of

---

[137] PRO, SP16/455/7 and 8. Charged again with saying 'God bless them all and God speed them all and let them go forward,' Homer tried to excuse himself by saying that he meant the word to apply to the Council and justices, not to the rioters or rebels.

[138] London Metropolitan Archives, Sessions Roll, MJ/SR/885/70.

[139] Ibid., MJ/SR/886/47.

[140] *His Maiesties Speciall Command under the great Seale of England . . . To suppresse the Tumultuous and unlawfull Assemblies* (1641), sig. A4v.

[141] Huntington Library, Ms. El. 7560. For similar incidents in September 1641, see Huntington Library, Mss. El. 7561 and 7562.   [142] Huntington Library, Ms. El. 7563.

[143] Norfolk Record Office, Norwich Mayor's Court Book, 1634–1646, f. 354.

the King. This did not necessarily make them parliamentarians, any more than cursing against Parliament made one a royalist, but it signalled a disruption of carefully maintained cultural patterns. 'Behold what infamous aspersions are daily cast on the superior magistrates', expostulated John Taylor in 1641, 'yea, some are so peremptory that they dare even detract from the king's imperial throne and diadem. If this disease, so ignominious, shameful and contagious, continueth incorrigible, it will exulcerate the whole kingdom beside.'[144] Royal authority was to the nation 'as the head, eye, or soul is to the body', wrote another conservative commentator in 1641, 'take away the life and senses, and what remains but a useless and senseless carcass?'[145]

Most of the examples that follow reveal a belligerent hostility to royal authority rather than an articulate ideological opposition to monarchy. Some expressed anger at aspects of King Charles's rule or his religion. Even if some of these statements were lubricated by alcohol, they represent a deconsecration of majesty and a demystification of power that traditionalists found deeply alarming. Cursing the King, drunk or sober, made it easier to take up arms against him.

In May 1640 the Court of Great Sessions at Chester heard of 'certain speeches given out by Matthew Scott tending to rebellion against his majesty'. Like the 'seditious words concerning the king's majesty and the state of this realm' heard at the next session, they were probably sentiments favourable to the Scots.[146] Peter Steebeman of St Martin's in the Fields appeared before Middlesex magistrates in June 'for certain uncivil words spoken... against his majesty',[147] though the actual words went unrecorded. Nor do we know the content of the 'very foul speeches against his majesty' uttered by Abraham Somner, a labourer from Hailsham, Sussex, in August 1641. Somner was pursued as a fugitive, described as 'a man of tall stature, about forty years of age, yellow haired and of slender body', but he could not be brought to justice and his words were not entered into the record.[148]

We can only guess at the sentiments expressed by London rioters in December 1641 who were charged with 'vilifying the king's proclamations'.[149] Nor do we know what John Coates said that sent him to Bridewell in July 1642 'for speaking scandalous words against his majesty'.[150] When two

---

[144] Taylor, *Diseases of the Times*, sig. A3v.
[145] I.W., *Certaine Affirmations In defence of the pulling down of Communion Rails*, 3, 15, 23.
[146] Public Record Office, Chester Court of Great Sessions, CHES 24/125/4.
[147] London Metropolitan Archives, Sessions Roll, MJ/SR/875/19.
[148] East Kent Archives, Sandwich Borough Muniments, Mayor's Letter Book 1639–44, Sa/C1, f. 63. [149] London Metropolitan Archives, Sessions Roll, MJ/SR/904/21.
[150] Corporation of London, Bridewell, and Bethlem, Court of Governors' Minutes, 15 July 1642.

Devonshire men, James Knapman and John Southmeade, were presented at the Exeter Assizes in August 1642 for 'scandalous words spoken of the king's majesty and the parliament and the Book of Common Prayer' they were bound over to appear at the next assize. Their wait turned out to be longer than expected, for there were no more assizes in Exeter until August 1646.[151]

Seditious and contemptuous speech against the Crown became bolder and more vociferous as the crisis of the kingdom deepened. In January 1641 Judith Castle appeared before Middlesex magistrates charged with bidding her husband to go and kill the King. She confessed that 'out of her distemper [she] spoke such words because she wished the death of her husband, and she is very sorry that she spoke such words'.[152] Again, it appears that she was allowed to go home. Francis Cornwall, clerk, was not so lucky, for after saying publicly at Loose, Kent, in June 1641, 'that if the king enjoined the Book of Common Prayer or any other testimonies or discipline that were not expressly delivered in God's words, we ought not to obey him', he was sentenced at Maidstone Assizes to a year's imprisonment.[153] A Wiltshire man, William Saie, also found himself in the house of correction at the end of 1641 for saying that the King 'did not regard his subjects, for if he regarded his subjects' he would not allow the kingdom to 'run ruinate as it is'.[154]

A crucially damaging charge against the King was that he had failed to protect the Protestant religion. A related complaint was that he was unduly influenced by his Catholic Queen. Daring libellers alleged that 'the king was a Scot, the queen was French, and their children were Germans . . . alluding to Mr Jermyn, who was supposed to be too familiar with the queen'.[155] Scandalous remarks of this sort had been directed against every early modern monarch, but some of the loose talk of the early 1640s alleged that King Charles was an apostate as well as a cuckold.

Protesters in London at the time of the Lambeth disturbances in May 1640 proclaimed that 'the king goes to mass with the queen'.[156] Thomas Stafford, a drinker in a Yorkshire alehouse, declared, 'God a mercy good Scot', one Sunday in January 1641, saying that 'the king and queen was at mass

---

[151] J. S. Cockburn (ed.), *Western Circuit Assize Orders 1629–1648: A Calendar* (Camden Society, 4th series, 17, 1976), 234.

[152] London Metropolitan Archives, Sessions Books, MJ/SBB/15 (calendar 10360.t.1, 61).

[153] J. S. Cockburn (ed.), *Calendar of Assize Records: Kent Indictments. Charles I* (1995), 420, 438.

[154] Wiltshire Record Office, Quarter Sessions Great Roll, A1/110 Hilary 1642, 199.

[155] Cambridge University Library, Ms. Mn. 1. 45 (Baker transcripts), 36. Henry Jermyn was Henrietta Maria's vice-chamberlain, master of horse, and later her bodyguard. He was created Earl of St Albans at the Restoration.

[156] Alleged words of Mrs Chickelworth, reported to Archbishop Laud 21 May 1640, *CSPD 1640*, 193.

together, and that such a king was worthy to be hanged'. Defending himself before the East Riding Assizes, Stafford wisely denied speaking 'any such words against the king and queen'.[157] When Edward Fairbrother, a glazier of Gravesend, Kent, said openly in February 1642 that 'King Charles...is a papist' his seditious words cost him a fine of forty pounds and imprisonment at the King's pleasure, although it is not clear that the sentence was actually carried out.[158]

Public disputes about the King's religion came to the attention of the East Sussex Quarter Sessions when John Peckham, the Laudian rector of Horsted Parva, reported trouble with his parishioners. By the time the minister reported these exchanges to magistrates at the Easter 1642 sessions his own authority had become as problematic as the King's. Peckham said that when talking with Thomas Shore early in 1641 'concerning prayers for the king's majesty', Shore enquired of the King, 'of what religion is he. . . . I know not of what religion he is or whether he be of any.' Six months later, around mid-summer 1641, the rector had to remind one of the churchwardens, Thomas Prowl, that it was 'against his majesty's laws' not to turn in his accounts. 'Whereupon the said Thomas Prowl replied these words: what care we for his majesty's laws and statutes?' When Peckham asked him, 'what, do you not care for his majesty's laws and statutes, his answer was thereunto, no not we.' The majesty of kingship had become badly tarnished if Sussex villagers could so forget their duty.[159]

By spring 1642, when the King had virtually lost command of his kingdom, some parishioners became even bolder in expressing contempt for the monarch. On 27 March 1642, the anniversary of King Charles's accession and the start of the eighteenth year of his reign, a Yorkshire tanner, Thomas Godsey of Selby, declared openly in church, 'I care not for the king nor his laws.' This was no alehouse indiscretion, but a poignant and public repudiation of royal authority. The scandal was reported to the West Riding sessions at Pontefract, but the offender failed to appear.[160]

By the summer the constitutional and political crisis was the centre of many parish conversations. One such exchange at Knaresborough, Yorkshire, moved onto dangerous ground in June 1642 when Francis Gifford asked, 'what should befall if the king did not keep the laws and his oath?' His neighbour

---

[157] PRO, ASSI 45/1/3/47.

[158] Cockburn (ed.), *Calendar of Assize Records: Kent Indictments. Charles I*, 424.

[159] East Sussex Record Office, QR/E/56/18. John Peckham, who had been rector of Little Horsted since 1623, was sequestered from his living in 1643 (John White, *The First Century of Scandalous, Malignant Priests* (1643); A. G. Matthews, *Walker Revised. Being a Revision of John Walker's Sufferings of the Clergy during the Grand Rebellion 1642–60* (Oxford, 1948), 360).

[160] Lister (ed.), *West Riding Sessions Records. Vol. II*, 367.

John Troutbeck answered, 'he might be deposed for ought he knew.' Troutbeck also said 'that the king's majesty was half French and half German', though he claimed he was so drunk at the time that he barely knew what he was saying. Within three days of their utterance these words were referred to magistrates at the Northern Assize, but the pressure of events prevented their effective prosecution.[161] (See, Chapter 18, for more seditious words from the summer of 1642.)

HIERARCHY UNHINGED

Concern that social certainties were crumbling surfaced at parliamentary elections in the spring and autumn of 1640. Elections were usually consensual affairs, based on elite agreement, but those of the 1640s were especially combative and fraught, when many more than usual were contested.[162] Traditionalists in some constituencies expressed alarm that 'the great number of the commonalty' should outweigh aristocratic interests.[163] It was scandalous, some said, that 'fellows without shirts' (England's *sans culottes*) should 'challenge as good a voice' as Lord William Maynard.[164] Sir Edward Dering's agent in Kent complained in October 1640 that the electors of Maidstone were as inclined to listen to 'any cobbler or tinker as to a gentleman'.[165] At Sandwich, when the 'voices of the better sort' were overwhelmed by 'the meanest sort of people', the defeated Lord Grandison grumbled that the new members were returned 'by the unruly multitude, sore against our wills'.[166]

In the face of perceived insolencies and threats, defenders of the traditional order reasserted their attachment to hierarchy and deference. Their complaints in the early 1640s addressed a social system under stress. 'A gentleman of good quality and of an ancient family', one such insisted, automatically deserved deference and respect, whereas he seemed to be receiving neither.[167] It was 'sauciness', wrote another, for any 'base fellow' to

---

[161] PRO, ASSI 45/1/4/57–8.

[162] *CSPD 1640*, 2, 333; Bodleian Library, Ms. Rawlinson D. 141 ('England's Memorable Accidents'), 7; Derek Hirst, *The Representative of the People? Voters and Voting in England under the Early Stuarts* (Cambridge, 1975), 111, 139, 147–50; Mark Kishlansky, *Parliamentary Selection: Social and Political Choice in Early Modern England* (Cambridge, 1986), 108–10.

[163] Berkshire Record Office, Reading Corporation Minutes 1636–1761, 109; J. M. Guilding (ed.), *Reading Records. Diary of the Corporation, Vol. III (1630–1640)* (1896), 507.

[164] William Maynard to Sir Thomas Barrington, 19 March 1640, HMC, *7th Report* (1879), 549.

[165] British Library, Add. Ms. 26786, f. 11.

[166] East Kent Archives, Sandwich Borough Muniments, Mayor's Letter Book 1639–44, Sa/C1, ff. 38–38v, 52v. The winners had 179 and 100 voices, Lord Grandison only 87.

[167] Centre for Kentish Studies, Q/SO WI (Quarter Sessions, October 1640), f. 120v.

speak disparagingly of his 'betters'.[168] It was 'scandalous', said a third, that common 'rogues' should sing libellous songs in abuse of gentlemen.[169] Other victims of upstart temerity took offense when a yeoman gave a gentleman the lie or called him 'cozening knave'.[170] They regarded it as a gross violation of decorum—more than ordinary disorder among women—for a common miller's wife to abuse 'a gentlewoman of good quality, threatening to slit her nose and break her face'.[171] Upholders of gentility deemed it inappropriate for a clothier to be 'liberal of his language on matters above him',[172] and unfit that 'rascally fellows' below the rank of gentleman should carry swords.[173]

Sponsors of conservative petitions similarly appealed to traditional social values. Sir Thomas Aston expressed particular pride that his petition of March 1641 was subscribed by 'the best of the gentry, with divers freeholders and inhabitants of good rank', whereas the rival petition represented men 'of mean condition'. While Aston's signatories represented 'all his majesty's well-affected subjects', his opponents were 'turbulent spirits' distinguished by their vulgarity, their malice, and their error.[174] Aston's compendium of pro-episcopal petitions printed in May 1642 similarly drew attention to the social credentials of the subscribers, whose quality mattered more than the 'noise and number' of their opponents. How preposterous, he wrote, in a classic formulation of disdain, 'that old women without spectacles can discover popish plots, young men and 'prentices assume to regulate the rebellion in Ireland, seamen and mariners reform the house of peers, poor men, porters, and labourers spy out a malignant party and discipline them, the country clouted-shoe renew the decayed trade of the city, the cobbler patch up a religion.' Aston's disgust was not just that his world was spinning rapidly out of control, but that the changes were driven by people of the lowest sort.[175]

Turbulence in the social hierarchy had enormous political consequences, prompting more reactionary formulations. Socially conservative commentators condemned the bold speaking of 'men of mean condition' and their irruption into public life. Stung by challenges to their status and authority,

---

[168] National Library of Wales, Great Sessions 4, Flintshire Gaol Files 983/2/5.

[169] Huntington Library, Stowe-Temple Ms. STT 1345.

[170] Devon Record Office, Okehampton Sessions Book, 1639–1648, 3248A/3/3. London Metropolitan Archives, Sessions Books, MJ/SBB/17 (calendar 10360.t.1, 64).

[171] London Metropolitan Archives, Sessions Roll, MJ/SR/895/172.   [172] *CSPD 1640*, 583.

[173] Cheshire Record Office, Cause Papers, EDC 5/1640/68; Public Record Office, CHES 24/126/3. Cf. [G.A.], *Pallas Armata. The Gentlemans Armorie* (1639), sig. A2.

[174] British Library, Add. Ms. 36914, ff. 201, 224. Cf. the claims of 'all men of good rank and quality' in *The Petition of the Citizens of London ... with their desires for Iustice to be executed upon the Earle of Strafford* (1641).

[175] Sir Thomas Aston (ed.), *A Collection of Sundry Petitions Presented to the King's Most excellent Majestie* (1642), sigs. A2, A2v, 4, 14, 23, 33, 36, 41, 43, 46, 67.

aristocrats insisted that only 'the better sort' should fill public offices, and that 'men of the meaner sort' and 'men of the inferior quality' should keep their place.[176] People of lowlier status, gentlemen claimed, had no business meddling with the business of the realm. The work of healing the kingdom belonged to magistrates and ministers, not common tradesmen, insisted the preacher Thomas Warmstry. 'Study to be quiet, and do your own business', he enjoined Londoners in 1641, 'live uprightly and honestly in your trades and callings, and...keep yourselves within your limits.'[177] It was not for 'the base rabble rout' to 'prescribe a way of government to the parliament and make laws of their own', preached Henry Rogers at Hereford in April 1642.[178] 'Study to be quiet', repeated the London minister Ephraim Udall. 'Follow your own plough, and meddle not in things that belong not to your calling', he advised auditors in July 1642. Otherwise there would be 'strife and contentions, and great and hateful thoughts of heart that prepare men unto civil war'.[179]

LIBERTINE LEVELLING

Underlying many of these concerns was the fear that worse was to follow. Alarmists read the demeaning of gentility, the scorning of warrants, and the disparagement of magistracy, as indicators of a descent into anarchy. They saw the expansion of the political arena as a diminution of gentry power. Although in fact there was no social revolution, pessimists predicted that a catastrophic collapse of hierarchy and deference was at hand.

'The times look very black', wrote a correspondent from Essex in August 1640, ''tis stark naught' and 'the laws everywhere broken'.[180] A poem that circulated at the end of 1640 prophesied that the 'poison' of disobedience that undid 'the bonds of nations and of nature' would produce 'a monstrous body that will have no head'.[181] Some observers blamed the parliament for creating expectations 'that everyone might do what he list'.[182] Conservative petitioners where aghast that 'many do what seemeth good in their own eyes only, as if there were no king nor government in this our Israel.'[183] 'All government,

---

[176] Bedfordshire and Luton Archives, St John Papers, J. 1390.
[177] Thomas Warmstry, *Pax Vobis or A Charme for Tumultuous Spirits* (1641), title page, 10–11, 17, 30.   [178] British Library, Add. Ms. 70003, ff. 236–7.
[179] Ephraim Udall, *The Good of Peace and Ill of Warre* (1642), 28, 29.
[180] HMC, *9th Report* (1884), Part II, Appendix, 432.
[181] Durham University Library, Special Collections, Mickleton-Spearman Ms. MSP/9, ii. 122.
[182] Cambridge University Library, Ms. Mn. 1. 45 (Baker transcripts), 39.
[183] Aston (ed.), *A Collection of Sundry Petitions Presented to the King's Most excellent Majestie*, 45.

learning and religion', were imperilled, warned one conservative preacher, now that 'the base rabble rout' had overawed Parliament to 'make laws of their own'.[184]

A chorus of pessimism warned of barbarism, anarchy, confusion, and collapse. The ultimate aim of the people, Edmund Waller warned Parliament, was to make things 'flat and level' and to institute 'an equal division of lands and goods'. Having attempted 'an equality in things ecclesiastical', their next demand would be 'the like equality in things temporal'. The nightmare prospect included 'community of wives, community of goods, and destruction of all'.[185]

Concerns of this sort intensified in the first half of 1642 among political leaders who disagreed on everything else. A pamphlet entitled *Englands Warning-Piece* warned of the dangers ahead, 'for then would the laws be cast off, the magistrates despised, the liberty of the subject turned into the licentiousness of rebels, and all things strangely metamorphosed into a confused chaos'. Some people believed that this process of disintegration had already started, and many believed it to be inevitable if civil war should happen.[186]

Conservative preachers attacked religious sectaries and social levellers who 'would have no man above another but all men alike and so throw down all government, learning and religion'. The spectres of medieval peasant rebels walked abroad with their levelling refrain, 'When Adam delved and Eve span | Who was then the gentleman?'[187] Pamphleteers reminded readers of Jack Straw and Wat Tyler, 'who for their rebellion and disobedience to their king and country, were suddenly slain, and all their tumultuous rout overcome'.[188] King Charles himself invoked this motif in his response to the Nineteen Propositions in June 1642, castigating the tumults of 'democracy' and the 'wild humours' of the 'common people', who would 'destroy all rights and proprieties, all distinctions of families and merit...in a dark,

---

[184] British Library, Add. Ms. 70003, ff. 236–7 (Dr Rogers's sermon in Herefordshire, April 1642).

[185] Edmund Waller, *A Speech...Concerning Episcopacie* (1641), 4–6; [Ephraim Udall], *Noli Me Tangere: Or, A Thing to be Thought On* (1642), 7, 8, 41; *A Short History of the Anabaptists* (1642), 56.

[186] Thomas Morton, *Englands Warning-Piece* (1642), 5; Vernon F. Snow and Anne Steele Young (eds.), *The Private Journals of the Long Parliament 2 June to 17 September 1642* (New Haven and London, 1992), 45.

[187] British Library, Add. Ms. 70003, ff. 236–7 (Dr Rogers's sermon in Herefordshire, April 1642). See also *The Iust Reward of Rebels, or The Life and Death of Iack Straw, and Wat Tyler* (1642).

[188] *Iust reward of Rebels, or The Life and Death of Iack Straw, and Wat Tyler*, title page. Wye Saltonstall, *Englands Complaint: Against Her Adjoyning Neighbours the Scots* (1640), sig. A6v, recalled that the 'rude mechanick rebels' led by Wat Tyler, Jack Straw, and Jack Cade had all been scattered and confounded.

equal chaos of confusion, and the long line of our many noble ancestors in a Jack Cade or Wat Tyler'.[189] There would be no Leveller movement until several years later, but radical social notions were already spreading terror and provoking alarm before the civil war began.[190]

Ultimately, the English revolution involved no class war, no struggle of one social sector against another. There would be no objective repositioning or revolutionary rearrangement of social and economic resources, no permanent or purposeful reconstruction of the social order. Nonetheless the revolutionary ferment aroused multiple affronts to power and privilege, expressed through insults and non-cooperation, insubordination and recalcitrance, the weapons of the weak. The threat of the vulgar rising above themselves, the agitations of the 'furious multitude', and the apparent disintegration of customary social relationships helped to mobilize many of the gentry who ultimately sided with the King. The fear of social levelling, as much as the fear of religious fragmentation, boosted support for the royalist cause and constructed the King as the anchor of stability. These fears and stresses may also have stimulated new thinking about the social foundations of sovereignty by such varied theorists as Henry Parker, James Harrington, and Thomas Hobbes.[191]

[189] Charles I's reply to the Nineteen Propositions, 18 June 1642, in J. P. Kenyon (ed.), *The Stuart Constitution 1603–1688* (2nd. edn., Cambridge, 1986), 18–20.

[190] David Wootton, 'From Rebellion to Revolution: The Crisis of the Winter of 1642/3 and the Origins of Civil War Radicalism', *English Historical Review,* 105 (1990), 668.

[191] C. B. Macpherson, *The Political Theory of Possessive Individualism: Hobbes to Locke* (Oxford, 1962); Michael Mendle, *Henry Parker and the English Civil War: The Political Thought of the Public's 'Privado'* (Cambridge, 1995); Arihiro Fukuda, *Sovereignty and the Sword: Harrington, Hobbes, and Mixed Government in the English Civil Wars* (Oxford and New York, 1997).

PART IV

THE ONSET OF CIVIL WAR

17

Tumults and Commotions

The beat of popular disturbance built to a crescendo between the spring of 1640 and the winter of 1641. Increasingly raucous and self-confident crowds clogged the metropolitan streets and engaged in noisy debate. The 'probationary tumult' of May 1640 became the 'tumultuous riot and outrage' of the autumn. The protesters who had gathered around 'Captain Club' and 'Captain Mend-all' in the aftermath of the Short Parliament grew in agitational experience with their assaults on the High Commission and their mass petitioning at Westminster.[1] In November they were cheering for the puritan martyrs, then demanding the end of episcopacy. In May 1641 they were adamant against the Earl of Strafford, then exercised against popish plots. The violent stirs of December drew together concerns about the Irish rebellion, the Grand Remonstrance, and the undue influence of popish lords and bishops. By January 1642 they were shouting for the privileges of Parliament, and making menacing gestures against the King. It was the 'noise and tumults' of 'the many-mouthed rout' that eventually drove King Charles from London.[2]

Some members of Parliament commended the citizenship of the citizens, whose interest in justice and reformation temporarily coincided with their own. Sir Simonds D'Ewes expressed gladness in 1641 'that the meanest of the people were sensible both of the danger and safety of the kingdom', and were willing to risk themselves in the breach.[3] But traditional authorities regarded these upstart crowds as 'insolent' and 'seditious', and used words like 'mutiny' and 'insurrection' to describe their irruption.[4] Conservative critics were especially disdainful of humbler citizens who thought their own voices

---

[1] [Hamon L'Estrange], *The Reign of King Charles. An History Disposed into Annals . . . with a reply to some late observations* (1656), 191. See Chapters 5 and 7.

[2] *Abraham Cowley. The Civil War*, ed. Allan Pritchard (Toronto, 1973), 77. Cowley's poem was composed in 1643.

[3] Willson Havelock Coates (ed.), *The Journal of Sir Simonds D'Ewes from the First Recess of the Long Parliament to the Withdrawal of the King from London* (New Haven and London, 1942), 338, 356.

[4] *Privy Council Registers* (facsimile of PRO, PC2/53) (1968), xii. 36, 42.

worthy of attention, and they were alarmed by the disorderly and intimidating manner in which the mob demanded to be heard. In raising the rabble in support of their proceedings, parliamentary leaders had roused a monster they were unable to control. Their tumults were among 'the ills of democracy', the King declared, a symptom of a polity out of balance.[5]

Early historians of this period saw the pre-civil war commotions as signs of social and political breakdown. The Earl of Clarendon's account of this period is little more than a tirade against the 'insolencies' of the 'disorderly rabble', when 'seditious preachers' propelled 'the meaner people' into 'tumults' in the precincts of Westminster.[6] *Eikon Basilike* of 1649, ostensibly Charles I's own history of the crisis, regarded the tumults in the first year of the Long Parliament as 'ominously presaging all these mischiefs which have followed'. More terrifying than any storm, the vulgar clamours were 'like an earthquake, shaking the very foundation of all'.[7] Other conservative historians charged parliamentary leaders with orchestrating or manipulating the mob.

The popular agitation that preceded the civil war is a well-known part of the story. Substantial scholarly investigations have illuminated the arousal of the urban populace, their links to radical religion, and the interaction of the crowd with opposition leaders in Parliament. High political histories tend to treat the mob as a sideshow, a backdrop to the drama at Westminster, whereas populist accounts allow the people more agency.[8] This chapter reviews the tumults and commotions that accompanied the breakdown of the traditional order and the rise of citizen militancy. It highlights the volatility of the metropolitan crowd and the multiple registers of the popular urban voice.

TUMULTUOUS STIRRINGS

The first major crowd event of the Long Parliament occurred on 28 November 1640, when Londoners turned out in force to welcome the returning puritan

---

[5] *His Majesties Reply to the Nineteen Propositions* (1642), 12.

[6] Edward Hyde, Earl of Clarendon, *The History of the Rebellion and Civil Wars in England Begun in the Year 1641*, ed. W. Dunn Macray (6 vols., Oxford, 1888), i. 448–53; O. Ogle and W. H. Bliss (eds.), *Calendar of the Clarendon State Papers Preserved in the Bodleian Library* (Oxford, 1872), i. 256.

[7] [John Gauden], *Eikon Basilike* (1649), ch. 4 'Upon the Insolency of the Tumults'.

[8] Valerie Pearl, *London and the Outbreak of the Puritan Revolution* (Oxford, 1961); Brian Manning, *The English People and the English* Revolution (1976); Anthony Fletcher, *The Outbreak of the English Civil War* (1981); Conrad Russell, *The Fall of the British Monarchies 1637–1642* (Oxford, 1991); Keith Lindley, *Popular Politics and Religion in Civil War London* (1997).

martyrs, Henry Burton and William Prynne. Their passage into the city had elements of a triumphant royal entry, accompanied by bonfires and bells. 'This day Burton and Prynne came to town, met upon the way with a number of coaches, and multitudes of people on horseback, with rosemary branches, and the streets and windows full of people to see them coming in', wrote Viscount Montague.[9] Even the weather showed them favour, with a warm November sun pushing back the clouds and mists as if to symbolize the lifting of the Laudian gloom.[10]

Most accounts of this day emphasize the large numbers and reputable quality of the people who welcomed the returning martyrs. Everyone refers to a multitude. The Venetian ambassador reported 'three hundred horse ... a hundred coaches and countless number of the common people'.[11] The Scottish commissioner Robert Baillie estimated up to three hundred coaches, and as many as four thousand horse, as well as 'a world of foot, everyone with their rosemary branch'. The Northamptonshire puritan Robert Woodford counted a hundred coaches and up to two thousand horsemen, as well as throngs of standers by.[12] This was London's best, on their best behaviour, to celebrate the overturning of the Laudian regime. The Earl of Strafford had gone to the Tower just three days earlier, and charges were already building against the Archbishop. The crowd was an ally and witness to the good proceedings at Westminster. Its mood was not contestatory but festive.

Two weeks later Londoners presented their petition for 'reformation in church government' and the abolition of episcopacy, root and branch. Allegedly subscribed by fifteen thousand Londoners (and satirized in the ballad of Alderman Wiseacre), the petition was escorted to Parliament on 11 December by a thousand or more supporters and brought in by the most reputable of them. The deferential demeanour of the petitioners belied the revolutionary content of their petition. They came 'in their best apparel ... without tumult ... in a very modest way', and having completed

---

[9] Bastwick came home a week or so later to similar crowds and acclaim. HMC, *Report on the Manuscripts of the Duke of Buccleuch and Queensberry* (The Montague papers, 2nd, series, 1926), iii. 395; New College Oxford, Ms. 9502, 'Robert Woodforde's Diary,' 28 November 1640; HMC, *Report on the Manuscripts of the Right Honourable Viscount De L'Isle ... Vol. VI. Sidney Papers, 1626–1698* (1966), 346; HMC, *The Manuscripts of Lord Kenyon* (1894), 60; HMC, *Manuscripts of S. H. Le Fleming, Esq. Of Rydal Hall* (1890), 18.

[10] William Prynne, *A New Discovery of the Prelates Tyranny* (1641), 114–15; Henry Burton, *A Narrative of the Life of Henry Burton* (1643), 41. Rosemary was the herb of remembrance.

[11] Allen B. Hinds (ed.), *Calendar of State Papers and Manuscripts, Relating to English Affairs, Existing in the Archives and Collections of Venice, Vol. 25, 1640–1642* (1924), 103.

[12] David Laing (ed.), *Letters and Journals of Robert Baillie* (3 vols., Edinburgh), i. 277; New College, Oxford, 'Robert Woodforde's Diary', 28 November 1640.

their business they 'forthwith retired to their dwellings'. Their purpose was to present their proposal for discussion, not to highjack the political process.[13]

By May 1641, however, the dynamics, ambition, and composition of the crowd had changed. Leading London aldermen no longer controlled the turnout, and civic leaders could no longer discipline the citizens. Much of the traditional awe for authority had already dissipated. Reputable artisan householders were joined in the streets by journeymen, apprentices, and some of their sisters and wives, demanding 'justice' against the Earl of Strafford. The incendiary earl's attainder was almost complete when rumour swept London of a plot to save him from the axe. Ten thousand or more Londoners took to the streets on Monday, 3 May, occupying Westminster Palace Yard and obstructing access to Parliament. Members of the House of Lords had a particularly uncomfortable time. Correspondents reported 'great tumults and disorders, especially about Westminster'. 'The town has been in an uproar, tumultuously seeking of justice and speedy execution', observed John Barry. The tumultuous press of citizens crying 'justice' and 'execution' 'did much distract' the lords of Parliament, reported Maurice Wynn.[14] The humbler sorts of people 'who do not rule' had gatecrashed the political arena, and Westminster politics would never be the same.

Eyewitnesses to the demonstration, Eusby Andrews (a barrister at law) and Francis Littleton (a servant to the King), asked the veteran radical John Lilburne 'the meaning of the numbers of people then gathered together'. It was apparent that crowds had meanings, even if their message was not self-evident. In this case the meaning lay in the numbers and temper of the people, who were willing to take up arms in the streets. Lilburne allegedly answered that 'they came for justice, and were about the number of six or seven thousand, and that there would be forty or fifty thousand the next day; and that they came then with their cloaks, but that the next day would come

[13] Maija Jansson (ed.), *Proceedings in the Opening Session of the Long Parliament... Volume 1: 3 November–19 December 1640* (Rochester, NY, 2000), 564, 568, 571–5; [Nathaniel Fiennes], *A Speech of the Honorable Nathaniel Fiennes* (1641), 1–3; *Popular Politics and Religion in Civil War London* (1997), 14–16. The manuscript petition was soon printed as *The First and Large Petition of the Citie of London and Other Inhabitants Thereabouts: For a Reformation in Church-Government* (1641). For the satire see PRO, SP16/473/48; Folger Shakespeare Library, Folger Ms. X. d. 20; Northamptonshire Record Office, Finch-Hatton Ms. FH 593; and Chapter 15 of this book.

[14] Bulstrode Whitelocke, *Memorials of the English Affairs* (4 vols., Oxford, 1853), i. 130; HMC, *Report on the Manuscripts of Lord Montague of Beaulieu* (1900), 129–30; HMC, *Report on the Manuscripts of the Earl of Egmont* (1905), vol. i, part 1, 134; Earl of Monmouth to Earl of Middlesex, HMC, *4th Report* (1874), Appendix, 295; National Library of Wales, Wynn Papers, nos. 1684, 1685 (microfilm); *The Petition of the Citizens of London... with their desires for Iustice to be executed upon the Earle of Strafford* (1641).

with their swords by their sides and armed.' Andrews then asked, 'what would be the end of this business, or what their meaning was in so doing; to which Lilburne answered, there was a report or rumour that they will either have the Deputy or the king.'[15] These were seditious words, verging on treason, and Lilburne was brought to answer for them before the House of Lords. However, to Bishop Warner's disgust, the offender was 'utterly and freely discharged'. The lords may have sensed an element of entrapment, and may have doubted whether Lilburne actually said the words attributed to him, but it seems most likely that they did not want to make another popular political martyr.[16]

As Lilburne predicted (or was said to have said), the crowds reassembled on 4 May, this time equipped with weaponry. The Earl of Monmouth was horrified that the citizens returned to Whitehall and Westminster, 'in like sort and number, but in a worser manner, for then they had swords and staves', all polite deference set aside. Sir Francis Godolphin reported their menacing return, 'in great numbers, with swords and clubs, demanding justice against my lord of Strafford'.[17] Swords traditionally were gentlemen's weapons, markers of superior status, so their flaunting by artisans represented a social challenge as well as a risk of violence. For a dependent apprentice to heft a sword was doubly presumptuous, and a threat to the safety of the kingdom.

A rare opportunity to hear more-or-less directly from an armed member of the crowd occurs in a report made to London magistrates later in 1641. An informant, John Michaelson, recounted that he was with John Cole and others at the Spread Eagle in Gracechurch Street late on the night of 24 November, two days after the passage of the Grand Remonstrance. Cole, 'a lusty young man' apprenticed to a haberdasher in Distaff Lane, was 'then newly come from the palace yard in Westminster where he with a thousand more had been that evening, all armed with swords'. Michaelson says he asked Cole, 'the reason why they would, or how they durst adventure in that unlawful way, to gather themselves together to put fears and jealousies in the parliament, and told him it was not allowable by the laws of God or of the land, and asked him what warrant they had for this disorderly act.' Cole in reply said, 'that they were sent for by some parliament men', adding that 'his master was

---

[15] HMC, *10th Report* (1887), Appendix, Part 6, 141; 'A Diary of ye Lords in Parliament' [Bishop Warner], Hertfordshire Record Office, XII.B. 37, f. 67. The examinations taken after this incident were printed in *An Original Account* (1641; E. 241), 215–34.

[16] 'A Diary of ye Lords in Parliament' [Bishop Warner], Hertfordshire Record Office, XII.B.37, f. 67.

[17] Earl of Monmouth to Earl of Middlesex, HMC *4th Report* (1874), Appendix, 295; Cornwall Record Office, DD RP/1/11.

a constable who gave him a sword and bad him go, and he believed that the masters of the other apprentices that were with him gave them the like direction, and that he would not have done so unless some warrant or direction had come from some parliament men.' Asked to what end they went, Cole explained 'that they heard there was a division in the lower house, and that the best-affected party was like to be overpowered by the other, and their direction and intention was to assist them when they should be called for; but finding that they agreed well and came peaceably away together, he and his fellows came quietly away.' One of the magistrates observed that this citizen activism, 'if I mistake not, comes near to high treason'. The apprentices were armed, with their masters' support, on behalf of 'the best-affected party' who feared that votes in Parliament would not go their way, a menacing intrusion into public affairs.[18] John Cole's November evening out would be practise for the wilder disturbances of December.

WINTER TUMULTS

The year 1641 closed with more violence and disorder in London, more recrimination and division at Westminster, and tumults in parishes throughout the country. The situation was not completely out of hand, accommodation not entirely given over, but political discourse was increasingly shadowed by animosity and violence. King Charles had returned to London on 25 November after settling the peace with Scotland, but he failed to capitalize on the 'expressions of love and loyalty' shown at his homecoming.[19] Men of moderation might have rallied to their monarch, but a cauldron of fears and alarms prevented unanimity. The metropolitan crowds were far from united, though vigorously aroused by the Grand Remonstrance, the fate of episcopacy, and the Catholic uprising in Ireland. Faction and division, anxiety and alarm, permeated every gathering and conversation.

December saw the social, political, religious, and constitutional elements of the crisis combine in a month of brawls and mêlées. The 'root and branch' movement against episcopacy gathered new strength as agitators made violent

---

[18] Bodleian Library, Nalson Ms. 13/33. Another young Londoner, John Thurth, faced discipline at Bridewell that week 'for attempting to steal a sword' (Corporation of London Record Office, Bridewell and Bethlem, Court of Governors' Minutes, 26 November 1641). For more on citizens with swords, see Coates (ed.), *Journal of Sir Simonds D'Ewes from the First Recess of the Long Parliament to the Withdrawal of the King from London*, 211, 214, 216; *CSPD 1641–43*, 188.

[19] John Taylor, *Englands Comfort and Londons Joy* (1641), 5, 7; *Ovatio Carolina: The Triumph of King Charles... Upon his Safe and Happy Return from Scotland* (1641); *Evcharistica Oxoniensia* (Oxford, 1641).

efforts to strip bishops of their votes in Parliament and to bar their entry to the House of Lords. Londoners were heard baying against bishops with even more vehemence and venom than they had directed against the Earl of Strafford. Streams of citizens were seen 'flocking to the house of parliament... crying aloud, no bishops, no bishops, calling them the limbs of antichrist'.[20] Apprentices 'rudely' blocked the waterside and prevented bishops from landing at Westminster.[21] 'The meaner sort of Londoners took to the streets shouting that 'they would have no bishops in parliament house nor popish lords'.[22] But the citizens were also shouting against each other, some in support of religious radicalism and some vehemently against it. Many followed John Pym, but others were against him. The city, like the parliament, was divided, 'every day at great heats'.[23]

'We are running to ruin', wrote William Montague on 2 December. 'The citizens grow very tumultuous, and flock by troops daily to the parliament... and there they never cease yawling and crying, "no bishops, no bishops".' The demonstrators came with 'offensive words' backed up with staves and swords. The trained bands seemed powerless to disperse them. 'The citizens slight muskets charged with powder', Montague continued, 'I myself saw the guard attempt to drive the citizens forth, but the citizens blustered and would not stir an inch.' Rank and status had no pull. 'I saw and heard my Lord of Dorset entreat them with his hat in his hand, and yet the scoundrels would not move. I think this would provoke authority to the height of rigour, but now that is condemned and trampled on.'[24] A few days earlier Dorset had urged his musketeers to fire on the crowd 'and the pikemen to run them through', when they overwhelmed the Court of Requests with petitions. Members of Parliament could not agree whether these petitioners were 'loyal' or 'tumultuous', or whether the greater threat to liberty came from the streets of London or from the Earl of Dorset.[25] More crowds invested Westminster in the days that followed, and the trained bands struggled to clear them from Parliament's doors.[26]

---

[20] HMC, *Report on the Manuscripts of the Duke of Buccleuch and Queensberry... at Montague House* (1899), 287.

[21] HMC, *Report on the Manuscripts of Lord Montague of Beaulieu*, 138.

[22] Diary of Thomas Wyatt, Bodleian Library, Ms. Top. Oxon. C. 378, 326.

[23] *CSPD 1641–43*, 202.

[24] HMC, *Report on the Manuscripts of the Duke of Buccleuch and Queensbery*, 287; Dorothy Gardiner (ed.), *The Oxinden Letters 1607–1642* (1933), 258.

[25] Coates (ed.), *Journal of Sir Simonds D'Ewes from the First Recess of the Long Parliament to the Withdrawal of the King from London*, 211, 226, 230.

[26] *His Maiesties Speciall Command under the great Seale of England... To suppresse the Tumultuous and unlawfull Assemblies* (1641), sig. A3v; *Lucifers Lackey, or, The Devils new Creature* (1641), sig. A3v.

Sir John Bramston thought that the constitutional process had been overwhelmed by 'tumults and affronts'. Mob action, street violence, and vociferous intimidation reduced civic and political life to chaos, he recalled, with 'the people of London and the suburbs running into tumults, crying in the streets, "no bishops, no magpies, no popish lords" and the like.' Members of the trained bands displayed their weapons,

with [the] Protestation fastened to their pikes or their hats. The seamen and watermen, fitting up barges and other vessels filled with armed men, came by water before Whitehall, whilst the broad place before the Banquetting House and up to Charing Cross was full of the rabble armed, so that his majesty seemed to be besieged in his own house, both by land and water. The bishops [were] assaulted as they went up the stairs to the Lords' house, and their gowns torn.[27]

This was a description of an insurgency, not a debate.

Just as there were strains and contradictions in Parliament's claim to be the representative body of the kingdom, so there were questions about who truly represented London. The mayor and common council claimed to speak for the City, but the citizens and sectaries who took to the streets asserted themselves as the true representatives of the metropolis.[28] Radicals gained dominance in the December Common Council elections, 'my Lord Mayor having no more sway than Perkins the tailor, Riley the boddice-maker, or Nicholson the chandler', as one disgusted conservative complained. Perhaps it was only fitting that in the disturbances of early January 1642 'the Lord Mayor had his chain torn from his neck by a zealous sister'.[29]

Whereas some politicians were horrified by this eruption of common people onto the public stage, others were ready to welcome them as allies. Citizen activists could be 'our surest friend', thought Sir Simonds D'Ewes, so long as they stood up for Parliament against papist designs and arbitrary power. They were mobilized in support of 'the best-affected party', and provided a human shield against catholic or cavalier attacks.[30] But some of them had other fish to fry, or rallied to a different drum.

The composition of these politicized crowds remains uncertain. They were mostly male, mostly young, and probably well-complemented with apprentices. But some of their masters were there too, with other reputable artisans, as well as the London riff-raff, rural runaways, and discharged soldiers.

---

[27] *The Autobiography of Sir John Bramston, K.B., of Skreens, in the Hundred of Chelmsford* (Camden Society, 32, 1845), 81–2.   [28] *CSPD 1641–43*, 192.
[29] *A Letter from Mercurius Civicus to Mercurius Rusticus* (Oxford?, 1643), 18, 22. On the change in City government, see Pearl, *London and the Outbreak of the Puritan Revolution*, 125–40. Sir Richard Gurnay was Lord Mayor in 1641–2.
[30] Coates (ed.), *Journal of Sir Simonds D'Ewes from the First Recess of the Long Parliament to the Withdrawal of the King from London*, 338, 356.

Observers usually called them 'apprentices', though the astute Thomas Wyatt referred to 'a disorderly multitude under the name of apprentices'.[31] The astrologer William Lilly, who may himself have gone along with the crowd, described them as 'most of them men of mean or a middle quality ... but set on by some of better quality .... In general they were very honest men and well-meaning,' though 'some particular fools ... got in amongst them, greatly to the disadvantage of the more sober. They were modest in their apparel, but not in languages.'[32] Sir Simonds D'Ewes shrewdly recognized that 'the citizens are not all the sons of one mother nor of one mind, and we know not how in this case they may be divided among themselves.'[33] Writing a year later a conservative Londoner identified the protestors as 'citizens and their wives', and gave his opinion that 'the women ... have hugged their husbands into this rebellion'.[34]

Stung by the ferocity of popular disorders, the King commanded the London authorities on 9 December to repress all 'tumults, riots, routs or unlawful assemblies'.[35] The following day he issued a proclamation in support of 'the true religion in this kingdom', upholding episcopacy, the prayer book, 'and the peace and tranquillity of the church'.[36] The sheriffs arranged a show of force to maintain order, though members of Parliament could not be sure whether it was to intimidate them or protect them. A newsletter of 10 December reported, 'there came near two hundred men with halberds to Westminster, but it was not known who sent them, nor for what end.' Some members 'took offence' when the Lord Keeper established 'a guard of three to four hundred men about parliament', ostensibly for public security.[37]

On the following Saturday, 11 December, a delegation of four hundred leading Londoners, many riding in coaches, delivered a petition to Parliament expressing their 'great terrors, fears and distractions', and urging the removal of 'popish lords and bishops' from the House of Lords. The petition was said to be 'subscribed with the names of above twenty thousand',

[31] Diary of Thomas Wyatt, Bodleian Library, Ms. Top. Oxon. C. 378, 328.

[32] William Lilly, *Monarchy or No Monarchy in England* (1651), 106.

[33] Coates (ed.), *Journal of Sir Simonds D'Ewes from the First Recess of the Long Parliament to the Withdrawal of the King from London*, 366.

[34] *Letter from Mercurius Civicus to Mercurius Rusticus* 12, 13.

[35] *His Maiesties Speciall Command under the great Seale of England ... To suppresse the Tumultuous and unlawfull Assemblies*, sigs. A2–A2v.

[36] James F. Larkin (ed.), *Stuart Royal Proclamations, vol. II. Royal Proclamations of King Charles I, 1625–1646* (Oxford, 1983), 752–4

[37] HMC, *Report on the Manuscripts of Lord Montague of Beaulieu*, 134; Coates (ed.), *Journal of Sir Simonds D'Ewes from the First Recess of the Long Parliament to the Withdrawal of the King from London*, 256–6, 268, 270, 275; *Commons Journal*, ii. 340; Russell, *Fall of the British Monarchies*, 433–4.

though it faced 'some interruption . . . by ill-affected persons'.[38] One of them, Justice Long, was committed to the Tower 'for affronting the citizens of London in bringing [the petition] to the Parliament'.[39] There was so much 'tumultuous noise' in Parliament, Lord Newark complained on 14 December, that he could neither speak nor hear.[40] The rumbles continued through the rest of month, amidst 'foul' and 'very boisterous weather'.[41]

TWELVE DAYS OF CHRISTMAS

The character of the commotions changed towards the end of December. Observers remarked on 'the multitude of gentry and soldiers who flock to the court . . . armed with swords and pistols'.[42] Some of these discharged veterans gained reputations for their hard drinking bravado, and were beginning to be known as 'Cavaliers'. The level of violence rose with the arrival of 'troopers that were disbanded in the north', who 'now wanting employment were ready to fall on any to gain the king's favour'.[43] John Dillingham reported that around Christmastide these soldiers 'offer[ed] their majesties to untie the knot', adding ominously, 'what was meant you may judge'.[44]

The streets of the metropolis were filled with armed assemblies, seemingly answerable to none but themselves. Artisans and apprentices took to the streets, ostensibly to protect the parliament, while the soldiers and gentlemen camped at Whitehall gate in order to protect the court. Observers reported confrontations shaped by class as well as faction and religion, with sword-wielding 'gentlemen' fighting humbler 'citizens' armed with cudgels and stones (although some, as we have seen, had edged weapons). Thomas Smith observed at the end of December that 'such jealousies and discontents are daily raised by the malignant party between the king and people, that we talk now of nothing but drawing of swords, and a war between the protestants and papists, which God forbid.'[45] Gentlemen advised each other to 'provide weapons, get muskets, powder and shot'. One writer reported from London at the end of December, 'there is great ado made for arms, and in vain, for there is not any muskets or other guns to be bought, nor iron to make them

---

[38] *The Citizens of London's Humble Petition* (1641), sigs. A3, A4.
[39] Bodleian Library, Ms. Rawlinson D. 141 ('England's Memorable Accidents'), 16.
[40] Ibid.
[41] *CSPD 1641–43*, 206, 210; PRO, SP16/486/111; *The Atachment Examination and Confession of a French-man upon Christmas Day* (1641). [42] *CSPD 1641–43*, 242.
[43] Lismore Mss., vol. 22, National Register of Archives, vol. 20594/15, 916.
[44] HMC, *Report on the Manuscripts of Lord Montague of Beaulieu*, 137–8. Significantly, the offer was made to 'their majesties', both King and Queen. [45] *CSPD 1641–43*, 215.

of, so great is the fears of the people here.' Another reported, 'there is now nothing sought for so much as guns and trimming up of old ones.'[46]

Cavalier influence may have persuaded the King to appoint the notorious Colonel Thomas Lunsford to be Lieutenant of the Tower. This sensitive office controlled London's armoury and ordnance, and the citizens reacted noisily in protest. Lunsford's appointment on 23 December 'begat so general discontent that his majesty was pleased to remove him after two or three days', wrote one letter-writer.[47] It was a reminder of the King's ineptitude and weakness, and also of the political weight of the mob.

The Christmas holidays, like Maytide, were traditionally a season of festive exuberance, excess, and semi-licensed misrule. The Christmas of 1641 was exceptionally boisterous and bitter. Writing to Sir John Pennington on 30 December, Sidney Bere observed that

since the holidays began here have been such rude assemblies and multitudes of the baser sort of people that every day threatened a desperate confusion, nor are we yet free of those fears.... These distempers have so increased by such little skirmishes that now the train bands keep watch everywhere, all the courtiers are commanded to wear swords, and a corps-de-garde is built within the rails by Whitehall; all which fills every one with fears and apprehensions of greater evils.[48]

Robert Slingsby remarked the same day,

I cannot say we have had a merry Christmas, but the maddest one that ever I saw.... I never saw the court so full of gentlemen; every one comes thither with his sword. This day five hundred gentlemen of the Inns of Court came to offer their services to the king... the citizens for the most part shut up their shops, and all gentlemen provide themselves with arms as in time of open hostility. Both factions talk very big, and it is a wonder there is no more blood yet spilt, seeing how earnest both sides are. There is no doubt but if the king do not comply with the Commons in all things they desire, a sudden civil war must ensue, which every day we see approaches nearer.[49] (See Plate 11.)

Christmas Day passed relatively peaceably, but more fights broke out around Westminster Hall on Monday, 27 December. Thousands of apprentices flocked to Westminster to demand answers to another anti-episcopal petition. They were met by Capt. David Hyde and his men who set about them with swords. In one bout, it was reported, the gentlemen came off

---

[46] HMC, *Report on the Manuscripts of Lord Montague of Beaulieu*, 137, 139.

[47] Sidney Bere to Sir John Penington, *CSPD 1641–43*, 216. Lunsford was also made a Gentleman of the Privy Chamber and was soon rewarded with a knighthood (PRO, LC3/1, f. 25v).

[48] *CSPD 1641–43*, 216.   [49] Ibid., 217.

worst when 'the citizens ... fought like enraged lions'. The dean's house at Westminster Abbey, occupied by servants of John Williams, the newly promoted Archbishop of York, became a flashpoint of anti-episcopal frenzy. The next day the gentlemen-soldiers and their allies had their revenge, when some thirty or forty of them charged out of the Abbey church, 'and fell pell mell, with swords and pistols upon [the citizens] and hurt many of them. ... In the afternoon the said soldiers issued out of Whitehall and cut and hacked the apprentices that were passing to Westminster.' In response the citizens threatened a strike that would bring the city to a standstill, offering 'to shut up shops and desist from trade'.[50]

Belatedly and ineffectually, the government sought to restore order by issuing a proclamation on 28 December 'against riotous assemblies in London and Westminster'.[51] It might as well have ordered the Thames to reverse its flow. The King ordered the Lord Mayor to use maximum force against these riotous assemblies, even

> to kill and slay such of them as shall persist in their tumultuous and seditious ways and disorders; for however we are very unwilling and sorry to use such extremity against any of our subjects, yet since we are by their disorder constrained, we have thought it better that so strict and severe a course be taken against some disorderly persons than that there should happen an inconvenience to our good people in general, which such insolencies do threaten.[52]

Henry Hastings, Earl of Huntingdon, described the continuing violence in a vivid letter to his son:

> to let you know of the latest occurrences here. Upon Tuesday last [28 December 1641] the apprentices assaulted my lord Archbishop of York's house at Westminster, and were led by Sir Richard Wiseman, and came into the minster to pull down the tombs and organs; but his servants shot so fast as drove them away and Sir Richard is dangerously wounded. Had it not been for my lord of Dover and my lord Faulconbridge that rescued him, he [Archbishop Williams] had been pulled in pieces, but he had no harm, only his tippet torn off. Upon Wednesday ten thousand prentices were betwixt York House and Charing Cross with halberds, staffs, and some with swords. They stood so thick that we had much ado to pass with our coaches, and though it were a dark night their innumerable number of links made it as light as day. They cried 'no bishops, no popish lords,' looked in our coaches [to see] where any bishops were therein, that we went in great danger.[53]

---

[50] Lismore Mss., vol. 22, National Register of Archives, vol. 20594/15, 916; HMC, *Report on the Manuscripts of Lord Montague of Beaulieu*, 138–9.

[51] Larkin (ed.), *Stuart Royal Proclamations ... 1625–1646*, 755–6.

[52] *CSPD 1641–43*, 214; PRO, SP16/486/99.

[53] Huntington Library, Ms. Hastings Correspondence, HA 5554.

Wiseman eventually died of his wounds, an early casualty in these new bishops' wars.[54]

Other observers described the 'uproars and disorders' of running battles around Whitehall and Westminster, with violent clashes between soldiers and citizens. One affray outside the court gates on the afternoon of 29 December brought some two hundred 'people who went by the name of apprentices' into collision with the gentlemen Cavaliers who were mounting guard. What began as a relatively orderly demonstration, with cries of 'down with the bishops, hang up the popish lords', degenerated into violence when some of the gentlemen began taunting the crowd. Several of the demonstrators retaliated by throwing clods of dirt (one account says 'clots of ice', suggesting snowballs), and very soon the gentlemen were beating about the crowd, 'many swords being drawn on either side'. The citizens came off worst, suffering several wounds, although one of the gentlemen was hit in the forehead. This was a minor incident, not a major confrontation, but it was symptomatic of the stresses that were fracturing the metropolitan community.[55]

Amidst the confusion, a few ringleaders were identified and subsequently interrogated. Some may have been urged into action by parliamentary zealots, but others were militant on their own account. John Noy was committed by the Middlesex justices for 'speaking of dangerous words in bringing four or five hundred men to pull down Whitehall and Westminster'. Edward Grigg may have been less politically minded, being charged 'that with other apprentices [he] did in most riotous and disorderly manner break down the windows of George Cross, vintner, and there carry away plate and certain parcels of goods'.[56] An apprentice bricklayer and an apprentice weaver were taken prisoner after threatening to pull down the Lord Mayor's house, but were set free 'by strong hands and force in Cheapside' when the sheriffs attempted to convey them to Newgate.[57] One of the constables of St Martin in the Fields sought compensation from Parliament after he was cut in the leg by sword-wielding apprentices who broke into the Mermaid tavern to release other rioters who were held prisoners.[58]

---

[54] *Londons Teares, upon the never too much to be lamented death of... Sr. Richard Wiseman* (1642), broadsheet.

[55] PRO, SP16/486/103, 104, 105, 113, 114. Reviewing this history eighteen years later, Peter Heylyn recalled that some in the crowd called out 'that the king was not fit to live, other that the prince would govern better; all of them with one voice, that they would have no porter's lodge between them and the king, and would come at him when they pleased, using some other threatening words, as if they meant to open the gate' (Peter Heylyn, *Examen Historicum: Or A Discovery and Examination of the Mistakes, Falsities, and Defects in Some Modern Histories* (1659), part 2, 131). [56] London Metropolitan Archives, Sessions Roll, MJ/SR/903/55.

[57] Bodleian Library, Ms. Clarendon 20, no. 1546; Ogle and Bliss (eds.), *Calendar of the Clarendon State Papers Preserved in the Bodleian Library*, i. 222.

[58] HMC, *5th Report*, 4; *Commons Journals*, ii. 382.

In response to this pattern of outrages, which impeded their passage to Parliament, a dozen bishops subscribed a protest on 29 December complaining that they had been 'violently menaced, affronted and assaulted by multitudes of people', who prevented them sitting at Westminster. The bishops asserted the illegality of any proceedings from which they had been excluded, saying in effect, 'no bishops, no parliament'. The following evening all twelve were 'brought upon their knees' before the bar, and impeached for high treason.[59] Laud's diary provides a succinct account of these developments.

The Archbishop of York and eleven bishops more [were] sent to the Tower for high treason, for delivering a petition as a protestation into the House, that this was not a free parliament, since they could not come to vote there as they were bound without danger to their lives.[60]

John Warner, the Bishop of Rochester, wrote of 'tumultuous assemblies and affronts' on the day his twelve brother bishops were kept from the House and impeached.[61] Their trial dragged on through the spring, when most of them were freed on bail, so long as they promised not to go to York.[62]

The political volatility at the start of the new year was matched by the violence of the weather. Snowfall followed thunderstorms over Christmas, and 2 January saw torrential rain and flooding. It was in this disturbed climate that the King devised a plan that would make or break his fortunes. In an act of rare boldness that proved disastrously counter-productive, King Charles sought to regain the initiative by arresting his leading parliamentary opponents. Charges of treason were drawn up against Sir Arthur Haselrig, John Hampden, Denzil Holles, John Pym, and William Strode, and their principal ally among the peers, Viscount Mandeville. In a famous scene on 4 January 1642 the King entered the House of Commons, backed by military force, to arrest the five members, but found to his surprise that 'all my birds are flown'.[63] It was, as so often for this King, an ill-advised act, incompetently executed.

London reacted with panic and indignation. The King's ill-judged attempt to arrest the five members, and his crude disregard for the privileges of Parliament, left observers like the preacher Simeon Ash with a 'sinking

[59] John Rushworth, *Historical Collections of Private Proceedings of State* (8 vols., 1680–1701), iv. 466–7; *Commons Journals*, ii. 362; *Lords Journals*, iv. 496; *The Manner of the Impeachment of the XII Bishops* (1642), sigs. A2v, A3v.

[60] William Laud, 'Devotions, Diary and History', in *The Works of the Most Reverend Father in God, William Laud, D.D.*, ed. James Bliss and William Scott (7 vols., Oxford, 1847–60), iii. 243.   [61] Bishop Warner's Diary, British Library, Harleian Ms. 6424, f. 99.

[62] *Commons Journals*, ii. 44; *Lords Journal*, v. 6, 45.

[63] HMC, *Report on the Manuscripts of Lord Montague of Beaulieu*, 141; Coates (ed.), *Journal of Sir Simonds D'Ewes from the First Recess of the Long Parliament to the Withdrawal of the King from London*, 381.

heart... in this day of our deep danger and exceeding, exceeding great fear'.[64] It was, John Vicars observed, 'a day of terror and wonder'.[65] That night both city and court were tense, 'everyone possessed with strange fears and imaginations'.[66] If there really was a Cavalier–papist conspiracy, this surely was when it would emerge.

The next day London exploded in uproar. The missing members had found refuge in the City, and the rest of the Commons adjourned there to Guildhall. Citizens were determined to welcome and protect them. When the King entered the City on 5 January, John Dillingham reports, he 'had the worst day in London... that ever he had'. It was a chilling and threatening reception—some might say treasonous—a far cry from the rapturous welcome the King had received six weeks earlier on his return from Scotland. The normally respectful crowd shouted 'privilege of parliament' and 'prayed God to turn the heart of the king, shutting up all their shops and standing at their doors with swords and halberds'.[67] At the King's meeting with the Lord Mayor and Alderman, some of the common councilmen chanted, 'parliament, privileges of parliament', while a smaller group cried 'God bless the king'. 'These two continued both at once a good while, I know not which was the loudest', remarked Robert Slingsby.[68]

As on previous occasions of controversy and tension, the City was awash with libels, but now, for the first time, they directly targeted the monarch.[69] Thomas Wiseman described King Charles 'returning to Whitehall, the rude multitude followed him, crying "privileges of parliament, privileges of parliament", whereat the good king was somewhat moved, and I believe was glad when he was home.'[70] Demonstrators brandished copies of the Protestation, and some were thrown into the King's coach.[71] This was the occasion when the ironmonger Henry Walker lobbed the King a copy of his insurrectionary pamphlet, 'To your tents, oh Israel', commending the deposition of King Rehoboam.[72]

---

[64] Simeon Ash, *A Support For the Sinking Heart in Times of Distresse. Or A sermon preached in London, to uphold hope and allay feare, January 4th. Which was a day of great trouble and deepe danger in the City* (1642), 11.

[65] John Vicars, *God in the Mount. Or, Englands Remembrancer* (1641), 71.

[66] *CSPD 1641–43*, 244.

[67] HMC, *Report on the Manuscripts of Lord Montague of Beaulieu*, 141.

[68] *CSPD 1641–43*, 243.

[69] Robert Slingsby noted 'many libels printed against the king' (ibid.).   [70] Ibid., 241.

[71] Coates (ed.), *Journal of Sir Simonds D'Ewes from the First Recess of the Long Parliament to the Withdrawal of the King from London*, 387.

[72] John Taylor, *The Whole Life and Progresse of Henry Walker the Ironmonger* (1642), 4; Ernest Sirluck, '*To your tents, O Israel*: A lost pamphlet', *Huntington Library Quarterly*, 19 (1955–6), 301–5. Walker's notorious exploit was also memorialized in *Letter from Mercurius Civicus to Mercurius Rusticus*, 13, and Lilly, *Monarchy or No Monarchy*, 109.

Tumults and disorders intensified after this disloyal epiphany. The crowds quickly swelled, amid all too predictable cries that 'the papists were arising', as the City braced for the King's revenge. [73] Citizens and apprentices took to the streets with whatever weapons they could find, answerable to none but themselves. The trained bands were out, but whether to control the mob or join it could not readily be determined. The threat posed to order by these 'thousands of men... in arms... without any lawful authority' was a leading factor in the King's decision to remove his family from London.[74]

The night of Thursday, 6 January, Twelfth Night in the traditional festive calendar, was a night of turmoil and fear. To the London wood-turner Nehemiah Wallington it was a night

I desire might never be forgotten. For in the dead time of night there was a great bouncing at every man's door to be up in their arms presently and to stand on his guard, both in the City and suburbs, for we heard, as we lay in our beds, a great cry in the streets that there were horse and foot coming against the city. So that the gates were shut and the cullices let down and the chains put across the corners of our streets, and every man ready in his arms. And women and children did then arise and fear and trembling entered on all.[75]

Rumours spread quickly of popish plots and royalist conspiracies, none of them immediately validated. 'The City and suburbs were almost wholly raised', reported Simonds D'Ewes, 'so as within little more than an hour's space there were about forty thousand men in complete arms, and near an hundred thousand more that had halberds, swords, clubs and the like.'[76] Makeshift barricades blocked the streets to impede the expected Cavaliers.[77]

Writing to Sir John Pennington later that night, Thomas Wiseman remarked, 'what these distempers will produce the God of Heaven knows, but it is feared they cannot otherwise end than in blood.... Thus you see the changes of the times, wherein I pray God preserve our gracious king and send us peace at home, whatever we have abroad.'[78] Another letter to Pennington dated 6 January reported, 'all things are now in so great distraction here that there is no thinking of doing anything, but everybody are providing for their own safety, as if everything were inclinable to ruin.'[79] Other correspondents wrote of the 'heavy news' from London, and God's 'heavy judgement... upon

---

[73] *A Conspiracie of the Twelve Bishops in the Tower* (1641), sig. A3v.

[74] *Privy Council Registers*, xii. 210.   [75] British Library, Add. Ms. 21935.

[76] Coates (ed.), *Journal of Sir Simonds D'Ewes from the First Recess of the Long Parliament to the Withdrawal of the King from London*, 392.

[77] *Letter from Mercurius Civicus to Mercurius Rusticus*, 13.

[78] *CSPD 1641–43*, 241.   [79] Ibid.

this nation'.[80] Clarendon too recognized these events as a turning point, remarking in his *History* 'how great a change there appeared to be in the countenance and minds of all sorts of people, in town and country, upon these late proceedings of the king'.[81] King Charles had managed to turn a mob into a movement, turning the bulk of the metropolis at least temporarily against him.

[80] G. W. Johnson (ed.), *The Fairfax Correspondence. Memoirs of the Reign of Charles the First* (2 vols., 1848), ii. 297; HMC, *12th Report, The Manuscripts of the Earl Cowper... Preserved at Melbourne Hall, Derbyshire* (1888), ii. 303.

[81] Clarendon, *History of the Rebellion*, i. 505.

18

∾✦∽

Death's Harbinger: The Drift to Civil War

King Charles left London on 10 January 1642, his majesty in shreds, his regime in tatters, after failing to mount a coup against the leaders of Parliament. It was said that if he stayed in his capital 'the King had like to have been torn in pieces by the citizens'.[1] Unable to dissolve the assembly, it seemed that he had set out to dissolve himself. The contrast could not have been greater with the resplendent monarch of just a few years earlier, who had ruled in majesty over a settled and fortunate realm.[2]

Uncounselled and barely attended, Charles Stuart's departure from London had some of the qualities of King Lear going out onto the heath. Sympathizers pitied 'a King so fleeting and so friendless . . . so poor he cannot feed them that follow him'.[3] The royal entourage was a shambles, no longer a household or a court. At Windsor they found none of the bedding made ready. At Cambridge the King's ragtag followers behaved as if they had not had enough to eat. When the King left Cambridge some of the townswomen followed his coach, shouting out to him to 'return to his Parliament or they

---

[1] Bodleian Library, Ms. Tanner 63, f.83, 'scandalous words' of Ellis Coleman, June 1642.

[2] John Booker's almanac prognostication for March 1642 made grimly ironic reading after the King had lost his lustre: 'The prince of planets, Sol, day's glorious eye, | Mounted on's throne, rules in full majesty, | And crowns this year with happiness throughout. | And as King Charles is compassed round about | With dukes, earls, lords, knights, esquires, gentlemen | In courtly sort, stars are Sol's royal train.' John Booker, *MDCXLII. Almanack et Prognosticon* (1642), 'March'.

[3] Sir Edward Dering to his wife, January 1642, British Library, Add. Ms. 26785, f. 59v. Clarendon depicted the King 'in a most disconsolate, perplexed condition, in more need of comfort and counsel' than ever before. He had fallen 'from a height and greatness that his enemies feared, to such a lowness that his own servants durst hardly avow the waiting on him' (Edward Hyde, Earl of Clarendon, *The History of the Rebellion and Civil Wars in England Begun in the Year 1641*, ed. W. Dunn Macray (6 vols., Oxford, 1888), i. 507, 524, 526).

should be undone'.[4] He arrived at York with only thirty-nine gentlemen and
seventeen guards, a fraction of the courtly establishment that normally
attended the monarch. The final indignity came at Hull on 23 April,
St George's day, when the garrison commander, Sir John Hotham, refused
him entry. Bargaining with his own lieutenant to enter his own stronghold,
the King 'offered to enter only with thirty men, as few as he could do with his
dignity', but to no avail.[5] King Charles withdrew to York, nursing his dishonour and calling 'heaven and earth to record his revenge'.[6] One thinks again
of the enraged King Lear threatening, 'I will do such things, what they are yet
I know not.'[7]

At this time King and Parliament were not yet in arms—nor was
it inevitable that war should break out later that summer. However,
England's social, political, and religious environment was already
completely transformed. The King had become a supplicant in his own
kingdom, and some of his subjects could say openly, 'I care not [a fart] for the
King nor his laws.'[8] He had lost his war with Scotland, sacrificed his Deputy
in Ireland, and had yielded unprecedented swathes of the royal prerogative.
How this isolated and humiliated monarch attracted a following capable of
fighting a civil war is a sizeable problem for historians to ponder. For by May
he had a following, by August he had an army, and in October 1642 he came
close to winning the civil war at the battle of Edgehill, 'every inch a King'.[9]
Indeed, the most difficult problem is not why Charles I lost the support of his
kingdom or why his regime cracked; it is why so many of his previously critical
subjects ultimately came over to his side, and why they resorted to arms.[10] Part
of the answer must be that England was already caught up in a revolution that
produced fear and panic among a deeply divided governing class.

---

[4] Charles Henry Cooper, *Annals of Cambridge* (4 vols, Cambridge, 1642–52), iii. 322–3.
Edward Walker, *Iter Carolinum* (1660), 1–3, lists the King's peregrinations, showing thirty
changes of lodging between leaving London in January and setting up his standard at
Nottingham in August 1642. See also the Lord Steward's Creditors Book, PRO, LS8/1, for the
movements of the court.
[5] Francis Newport to Sir Richard Leveson, 26 April 1642, Staffordshire Record Office,
Leveson Letter Book, D. 868/3/15. Hotham had been appointed in January 1642 with orders not
to give up the town or magazine of Hull 'without the king's authority, signified unto him by the
lords and commons house of parliament'. I. E. Ryder, 'The Seizure of Hull and its Magazine,
January 1642', *Yorkshire Archaeological Journal*, 61 (1989), 141.
[6] Cornwall Record Office, DD R(S)/1/1059. John Harris to Jonathan Rashleigh, 12 May 1642.
[7] William Shakespeare, *King Lear*, II. iv.
[8] John Lister (ed.), *West Riding Sessions Records. Vol. II. Orders, 1611–1642. Indictments,
1637–1642* (Yorkshire Archaeological Society, vol. liii, 1915), 367.   [9] *King Lear*, IV. vi.
[10] Cf. Conrad Russell, *The Fall of the British Monarchies 1637–1642* (Oxford, 1991), 526: 'It
is the English Royalists, not the English Parliamentarians, who are the peculiarity we should be
attempting to explain.'

This chapter follows the unfolding of the crisis from January to August 1642. It attempts to illuminate the temper of the times as the polity slipped closer to civil war. Among its themes are the sharpening of partisan opinion, the forlorn quest for accommodation, and the militarization of a society already gripped by revolution.

WESTMINSTER TO HULL

The King's precipitous departure left London in Parliamentary hands. A near-catastrophe for the Commons turned into a nervous political triumph. When the threatened members moved back to Westminster on 11 January, from their temporary refuge in the City, they were escorted by the trained bands and hundreds of armed citizens, with cartloads of powder and shot. Many of the marchers displayed the Protestation on their hats, pikes, or spears, in support of 'the privileges of Parliament'. The Thames was 'furnished with five hundred sailors in boats and barges with cannons in them', with volleys firing on the river and crowds cheering on shore. Correspondents described the assembly of 'four thousand well armed men with flying colours, and four thousand more . . . expected the next day following; abundance of boats well manned lay between Durham House and the Parliament Stairs.'[11] It was a formidable show of force, and perhaps a wise precaution, since nobody knew what forces King Charles could still command.

The following weeks saw flares of alarm, especially outside of London. An unsanctioned and premature rising was forestalled on 12 January 1642 when the recently knighted Colonel Lunsford raised the royal standard at Kingston upon Thames and invited the King's supporters to declare themselves. This royalist 'hurly burly', which involved several hundred horsemen, ended with Lunsford under arrest and his henchmen retreating towards Windsor.[12] The King was too weak to pose an immediate threat, but his resources and intentions remained unknown. Rumour told of bands of Cavaliers and cartloads of weapons making their way to Windsor, as well as recusants ready to rise, but a Mr Gydgeman, returning from Windsor on

---

[11] *CSPD 1641–43*, 252, 254; Huntington Library, Ms. HM 4643; Bodleian Library, Carte Ms. 2, f. 298; Bodleian Library, Oxford, Tanner Ms. 66, ff. 234, 242; John Vicars, *God in the Mount. Or, Englands Remembrancer* (1641), 77.

[12] Bodleian Library, Carte Ms. 2, f. 298; HMC *5th Report* (1876), 4; Willson H. Coates, Anne Steele Young, and Vernon F. Snow (eds.), *The Private Journals of the Long Parliament 3 January to 5 March 1642* (New Haven and London, 1982), 40; *Commons Journals*, ii. 373, 389; *Lords Journals*, iv. 515; *A True Relation of the Late Hurliburly at Kingston* (1642).

14 January could reassure Londoners, 'that he never saw so thin a court, and that he saw not forty horse'.[13]

Most of the major towns and cities looked urgently to defend themselves, against whom they could not be sure. Neither King nor Parliament yet had an army, though both had enemies as well as friends. The opening months of 1642 saw a widespread furnishing and refurbishing of weapons, strengthening of walls, and setting of overnight watches as the country braced for trouble. Provincial cities protected their perimeters, set chains at gates and bridges, inspected their gunpowder and ordnance, and put their men into training. In London, it was reported, 'every house abounds with ammunition'.[14]

At Norwich, after inspecting the city's arms in January 1642 'to see whether they be...for service', the captains of the trained bands were given enough money to remedy their decay and defects.[15] At Great Yarmouth the night watch was equipped with a dozen muskets. Gates were secured, fortifications repaired, and weapons made siege-ready, 'in regard of the present troubles and dangers of the time'.[16] Ipswich undertook similar preparations, trimming its weapons, readying its powder, and cleaning the borough swords.[17] Other cities mustered soldiers and mounted watches in light of 'the imminent dangers we may expect from these miserable times'.[18] Northampton put twenty men on night watch and set chains at its bridges, 'in regard of these dangerous times'.[19] Salisbury, which did not previously have a night watch, now set one up.[20] Coastal towns in Sussex drew stores of gunpowder from the county magazine at Lewes.[21] Local preparations almost exhausted the nation's stock of gunpowder, so to ease supplies Parliament

---

[13] British Library, Add. Ms. 14827, f. 4. On the same day a Mr Bagshaw told the House of Common he had seen four hundred horsemen and forty officers at Windsor (*Commons Journals*, ii. 379).

[14] Josias Berners to John Hobart, 10 January 1642, Bodleian Library, Oxford, Tanner Ms. 66, f. 234v.

[15] Norfolk Record Office, Norwich Mayor's Court Book, 1634–1646, ff. 335v, 336v.

[16] Norfolk Record Office, Great Yarmouth Assembly Book, 1625–1642, Y/C19/6, ff. 498v–501v.   [17] Suffolk Record Office, Ipswich Chamberlain's Accounts, C/3/3/2/67.

[18] Cooper, *Annals of Cambridge*, iii. 319; Gloucestershire Record Office, Sessions Orders 1633–1671, GBR/G3/SO2, 24 January 1642; Gloucester Council Minutes, 1632–1656, GBR/B3/2, 3 February 1642; G. W. Johnson (ed.), *The Fairfax Correspondence. Memoirs of the Reign of Charles the First* (2 vols., 1848), ii. 344, 362; S. C. Ratcliff and H. C. Johnson (eds.), *Warwick County Records, Vol. II. Quarter Sessions Order Book, Michaelmas, 1637, to Epiphany, 1650* (Warwick, 1936), 116; Helen Stocks and W. H. Stevenson (eds.), *Records of the Borough of Leicestershire...1603–1688* (Cambridge, 1923), 309.

[19] Northamptonshire Record Office, Northampton Town Assembly Book, 3/2, f. 66; Christopher A. Markham and J. Charles Cox (eds.), *The Records of the Borough of Northampton* (2 vols., Northampton, 1898), ii. 434.

[20] Wiltshire Record Office, Salisbury Borough Ledger, 1640–1723, 23/1/4, f. 6v.

[21] East Sussex Record Office, QR/E/56/116.

relaxed restrictions on the saltpetre men and encouraged them to dig wherever necessary.[22]

Watchful authorities sparked occasional panic. There were scares at Chester in January 1642 when city officials intercepted 'Colonel Butler, an Irish gentleman of great experience in military affairs and in religion a papist', who was presumed to be offering his services to the King.[23] Another scare ensued in Essex towards the end of January when a letter mysteriously found on the highway was turned over to the watch. Dated 22 January, the letter was written by Edward Cherry, the curate of St Osyth and parson of Much Holland, to one Captain Appleton, wishing him good success 'in that most pious and religious service you are in'. The letter referred somewhat guardedly to the captain's 'high employment' but offered no explanation as to what that might be. Nervous magistrates feared some kind of royalist–papist–army plot, but eventually they accepted that the letter was no more than an exchange of greetings between kinsmen. Captain Appleton turned out to be Cherry's wife's uncle, an officer with the King at Windsor, 'employed in the service of Ireland against the rebels there'. The incident reveals the heightened fear of plotting after the King's departure from London, made all the more alarming by this letter's origin in a part of Essex reputed to be a recusant stronghold.[24]

Printed news and letters spread both information and alarm. 'These distracted times put us all in great disorders', wrote Lady Sussex in mid-January, 'I hope we shall not be killed yet.'[25] Events, thought Sir Simonds D'Ewes, were '*malum augurium*, an ill presage of greater troubles', for 'if there be any further misunderstanding between us and his majesty the flame may grow higher'.[26] A newsletter of late January reported 'fears and distractions' in Yorkshire and London, and expressed the concern 'that the people cannot in all probability be kept from rising'. John Dillingham predicted, with reference to the King, that 'unless there be some yielding to the House of Commons, all will suddenly be set on fire'.[27] It was about this time, in response to the question 'What news?' that the Exeter grocer George Marye 'drew a paper or writing out of his pocket and read the same' to a Devonshire yeoman, including 'some passages about Parliament', warnings of 'troubles in the north', and the prophecy that conditions would soon be 'as bad and worse in England than ever was heard in Ireland'.[28]

[22] Commons order of 12 April 1642, Bodleian Library, Ms. Tanner 63, f. 4.

[23] British Library, Add. Ms. 34253, f. 5. Chester officials asked the Earl of Northumberland how they should handle 'persons evil-affected to the state'.   [24] Ibid., ff. 7–12.

[25] HMC, *7th Report* (1879), 436.

[26] Coates, Young, and Snow (eds.), *Private Journals of the Long Parliament 3 January to 5 March 1642*, 112–13.

[27] HMC, *Report on the Manuscripts of Lord Montague of Beaulieu* (1900), 145.

[28] Devon Record Office, Exeter Quarter Sessions Book, 1630–1642, 391.

It was hardly surprising that Londoners were woken early in February by cries of 'arm, arm, arm together, a mutiny and tumult', which proved to be a false alarm.[29] The City experienced a sharp economic downturn, with 'neither buying nor selling nor almost any commerce or trade'.[30] Families around the City and Westminster complained of the 'utter cessation and decay of all our trading' following the breakup of the court.[31] The King's abandoned lodgings at Whitehall fell quickly 'from majesty to muckery', one visitor remarking on 'the raw scent of moist walls, and all as silent as midnight'.[32]

By mid-February 1642 the King had arrived at Dover, where he saw Henrietta Maria take ship for Holland. The Queen sought refuge with her European relations, taking the crown jewels with her in order to purchase arms.[33] Now more forlorn and friendless than ever, the King and a small band of followers began their dispirited journey to the north.

Joining Prince Charles at Cambridge on 15 March, the King found a mixed reception. The university authorities made their usual 'vehement acclamations of *vivat rex*'. However, the sheriff of Cambridgeshire failed to appear and the town provided none of the honourable attendance customary at a royal visit. At a hastily prepared buffet at St. John's College, the small royal entourage crammed and pocketed food for the journey. 'Return unto your Parliament and so unto your people' was the popular cry from the streets.[34] There could be no cure for England's ills 'till our great King return *Londinium versus*', echoed a more Latinate pamphlet.[35]

When King Charles entered York a few days later he found the bare shadow of a civic reception. Many of the aldermen made excuses why they

---

[29] Corporation of London, Bridewell and Bethlem, Court of Governors Minutes, 4 February 1642. One of those responsible, a wanderer from Derbyshire, excused himself by saying he was drunk.

[30] *To the Right Honorable, the High Court of Parliament; The Humble Petition of many hundreds of distressed Women, Trades-mens Wives, and Widdowes* (1642), broadsheet; Coates, Young, and Snow (eds.), *Private Journals of the Long Parliament 3 January to 5 March 1642*, 112–13.

[31] *To the Right Honourable the House of Peers Now Assembled in Parliament. The humble Petition of many thousands of Courtiers, Citizens, Gentlemens and Trades-mens wives, inhabiting within the Cities of London and Westminster, concerning the staying of the Queenes intended voyage into Holland* (1641[i.e., 1642]), broadsheet.

[32] *A Deep Sigh Breath'd Through the Lodgings at White-Hall, Deploring the absence of the Court, And the Miseries of the Pallace* (1642), sigs. A3, A4v.

[33] Ostensibly the Queen went into Holland to accompany her daughter who was married to the Prince of Orange, but Archbishop Laud noted, 'The true cause was the present discontents here' (in *The Works of the Most Reverend Father in God, William Laud, D.D.*, ed. James Bliss and Willam Scott (7 vols., Oxford, 1847–60), iii. 243).

[34] Cooper, *Annals of Cambridge*, iii. 322–3; Cambridge University Library, Ms. Mn. 4, 57.

[35] *Vox Populi: or the Peoples Humble Discovery, of Their own Loyaltie* (1642), 5; [William Lilly], *Lilli's propheticall history of this yeares accidence, 1642* (1642), 8.

should not turn out to greet their monarch—their horse was lame, their dwelling was too remote, they had other pressing occasions. One group of townsmen petitioned the King to be reconciled with his Parliament, but another offered a more loyal welcome and the mayor, Edmund Cooper, was knighted that day after dinner.[36] When petitioners from Lincolnshire came to York at the end of March to ask the King 'to reside nearer the Parliament', a crowd composed of 'sundry of the meaner sort of the town, to the number of about eighty', invaded their lodgings to protest against 'their attempt to draw his majesty from them'. The 'meaner sort' of York may have been drawn to the mystique of kingship, but they also recognized the business advantage of the presence of the court.[37]

In the weeks and months that followed supporters of the King drifted towards York, where 'at least a good face of a court' was established. The city soon became 'a sanctuary to all those that despise the Parliament'.[38] Sir Hugh Cholmley expressed concern that 'there was few about the King but soldiers of fortune, and such as were no friend to the public peace.'[39] Prince James, the Duke of York, joined his father and brother on 16 April, the city honouring him with a horse and an ornate saddle. The aldermen who refused to wait on the King were threatened with punishment, but the city could still only manage a meagre assembly.[40] Writing that same day from Wrexham to the Earl of Bridgewater, Richard Lloyd declared, 'the present condition of affairs are the worst that have been since the beginning of the Parliament.'[41] 'We are reduced to the very brink and ruin and desolation', despaired William Drake, who saw little hope of relief from 'this dark and gloomy cloud that hath lately lowered so black upon this kingdom'.[42]

On 23 April, instead of meeting in state with the order of St George,[43] King Charles decided to enter the northern garrison town of Hull, some forty miles from York, where the young Duke of York was being entertained with visiting dignitaries. Hull was a military bastion, a strategic fortress and armoury, where most of the munitions for the Scottish war had been stockpiled. The prize included some fifty cannon, nine hundred barrels of

[36] York City Archives, Corporation House Book, 1638–1650, B/36, ff. 69–72.

[37] Bodleian Library, Ms. Tanner 63, f. 17, Richard Dugard to Dr Ward, 16 April 1642.

[38] Clarendon, *History of the Rebellion*, ii. 74; *A Letter Sent By a Yorkshire Gentleman, to a friend in London* (1642), 4.

[39] Jack Binns (ed.), *The Memoirs and Memorials of Sir Hugh Cholmley of Whitby 1600–1657* (Yorkshire Archaeological Society Record Series, vol. cliii, 2000), 103.

[40] York City Archives, Corporation House Book, 1638–1650, B/36, ff. 69–72; Chamberlain's Book of accounts, 1640–1645, C/23, ff. 27–27v.

[41] Huntington Library, Ms. El. 7557, 16 April 1642.

[42] Huntington Library, Ms. HM. 55603, ff. 43v–44.

[43] Diary of Thomas Wyatt, Bodleian Library, Ms. Top. Oxon. C. 378, 331.

gunpowder, and more than seven thousand muskets, which Parliament planned to move to London. Parliament had recently made Sir John Hotham governor of Hull, with instructions to admit none but by authority from Westminster.[44]

When King Charles appeared before the gates of Hull on the morning of 23 April Sir John Hotham denied him entry. The King had with him two or three hundred attendants, mostly Yorkshire gentry, who were witnesses to his humiliation. The King began to bargain, like Lear with his heartless daughters. 'Sir John Hotham denied him, then he offered to enter only with thirty men, as few as he could do with his dignity. That Hotham denied too, expostulating with the King upon the walls a long time.'[45] Hotham's final offer was for the King to reduce his train to just twelve. Pleading in the rain with one of his own subjects, negotiating over numbers, and patently failing to prevail, the King was publicly dishonoured, his authority exposed as a shadow.[46]

The affront at Hull was deeply wounding, leaving the King 'full of trouble and indignation' and burdening him 'with infinite perplexity of mind', so Clarendon remembered.[47] It was 'a great disgrace . . . to his royal progeny', including the nine-year-old Prince James who witnessed the affair.[48] Safely back at York, after an overnight stay at Beverley, King Charles appealed to the gentlemen of Yorkshire to defend his person and to repair his damaged honour.[49] A letter sent to Cornwall described how the King demanded 'satisfaction' and 'vindication', and 'called heaven and earth to record his revenge against Hotham's treason, as he calls it'.[50]

The situation became darker and more combustible after the dramatic stand-off. Hotham's deed set England talking, with many warning of impending war. Sir John's denial of the King's entry into Hull could be seen as a necessary safeguarding of vital munitions, or a monumental affront to the King's prerogative and honour. Parliament commended Hotham, and

---

[44] Ian Ryder, 'The Seizure of Hull and its Magazine, January 1642', *Yorkshire Archaeological Journal*, 61 (1989), 139–48.

[45] Francis Newport to Sir Richard Leveson, 26 April 1642, Staffordshire Record Office, Leveson Letter Book, D. 868/3/15.

[46] Basil N. Reckitt, *Charles 1 and Hull 1639–1645* (1952), 26–32; Bulstrode Whitelocke, *Memorials of the English Affairs* (4 vols., Oxford, 1853), i. 168; Vernon F. Snow and Anne Steele Young (eds.), *The Private Journals of the Long Parliament 7 March to 1 June 1642* (New Haven and London, 1987), 222, 228; University of Hull, Brynmor Jones Library, Hotham Papers, DDHO/1/34; Bodleian Library, Oxford, Tanner Ms. 63, f. 27v.

[47] Clarendon, *History of the Rebellion*, ii. 48, 50.

[48] *The King of Denmarks Resolution Concerning Charles King of Great Britain* (1642), sig. A2v.

[49] Staffordshire Record Office, Leveson Letter Book, D.868/3/16; York City Archives, Corporation House Book, 1638–1650, B/36, f. 72.

[50] Cornwall Record Office, DD R(S)/1/1059, John Harris to Jonathan Rashleigh, 12 May 1642.

disbursed £2,000 'forthwith' for the garrison at Hull, whereas the King proclaimed him a traitor.[51] Disparaging Charles's message to Parliament after the encounter at Hull, Sir Henry Ludlow said, rather rashly, 'that he that writ it did not deserve to be King of England'.[52] One of Nehemiah Wallington's correspondents warned that any hostile retaliation by the King would 'kindle such a fire in England as will never be quenched'.[53] 'The ball is now banded to the height. What the issue will be God above knows', wrote Thomas Knyvett on 28 April, 'all people murmur, and it cannot be expected but must come to actual distraction.' A few days later Knyvett wrote again to his wife of the 'threatening storm' that looked likely to end in 'a deluge of blood', as 'perplexities and vexations increase'. There now seemed 'not a tittle of hope of accommodation, so that we can foresee nothing but a public phlebotomy, if God in mercy doth not in time cast out these evil spirits amongst us'.[54]

The gloom and despair was almost palpable as spring moved into summer. 'Each hour produceth new fantasies, every day new follies', lamented Edward Reynolds, as the kingdom was battered by 'this deluge of distempers'.[55] Mary Eure wrote to her nephew Ralph Verney on 7 May 1642, 'here in the north, we are like so many frighted people. For my part if I hear but a door creak I take it to be a drum, and am ready to run out.'[56] Roger Hill confided to his wife on 21 May 1642, 'we fly higher every day and we have good cause to prepare against a day of trial'. It now appeared 'that the King intends to make war against his Parliament'.[57] 'We are like to have civil wars here if God turn not things unto the best', despaired the London lawyer Thomas Michael on 24 May.[58] 'God put an end to these distractions', wrote John Hampden to Sir John Hotham, as he pondered what means there were 'to quench the fire by'[59] (see Plate 12).

'In God I trust, we shall lose no blood', wrote Henry Manney in June 1642, but his hopes were slim as 'the distractions not only continues but grows more formidable'.[60] Thomas Barrow wrote similarly that same month, 'we

---

[51] *Commons Journals*, ii. 542–3; University of Hull, Brynmor Jones Library, Hotham Papers, DDHO/1/74; National Library of Wales, Pitchford Mss. Correspondence C/1/98, Richard Brown to Sir Francis Ottley, 3 May 1642.

[52] Staffordshire Record Office, Leveson Letter Book, D.868/3/18.

[53] British Library, Sloan Ms. 922, f. 130v.

[54] Bertram Schofield (ed.), *The Knyvett Letters (1620–1644)* (Norfolk Record Society, 1949), 100–3, 105.

[55] Edward Reynolds, *Evgenia's Teares for great Brittaynes Distractions* (1642), 2, 8, 20, 36.

[56] HMC, *7th Report*, 438.

[57] Buckinghamshire Record Office, Hill Family Letters (Transcripts) D 192/8/2b.

[58] National Library of Wales, Wynn Papers no. 1709 (microfilm).

[59] University of Hull, Brynmor Jones Library, Hotham Papers, DDHO/1/2, John Hampden to Sir John Hotham, 17 May (1642, year inferred).

[60] HMC, *Report on the Manuscripts of Lord Montague of Beaulieu*, 154.

are all in the way to be a miserable people, for here is nothing but distractions, the which makes me fear will bring us to confusion.'[61] The kingdom had fallen into a 'dark and inextricable labyrinth', wrote the Earl of Dorset towards the end of June, though he hoped that a way might be found 'to lead us all forth. . . . Let not fears prevail above hope.'[62] The worst threat now came not from the Scots, or foreigners, or papists, but from inside England. These were 'times of extreme danger', claimed a midsummer pamphlet as 'fears, jealousies and perplexities' compounded England's 'manifold distempers'.[63] The King's reply to the Nineteen Propositions similarly cited 'the noise of fears and jealousies'.[64] 'Oh times, oh manners, what strange times are we fallen into', sighed another classically read author, as he raged at 'the black web of all our weavings' that entangled England in darkness and ruin.[65]

FOR KING AND PARLIAMENT

There could be no civil war without armies, and at this point neither side could command one. Nor were the divisions in the country clear cut enough to constitute 'sides'. Opinions hardened during the spring and summer of 1642, but most people, if pressed, would say that they were for both King and Parliament. They would 'talk of the King, and then of the Parliament, as it happens and chances, and conclude with prayers for both'.[66] A report from Northamptonshire allowed that when the King rides by the people cry ' "For King Charles," but presently, when his royal majesty is gone, they stand for the Parliament'.[67] Only extremists could be labelled royalists or parliamentarians before the issue came to arms.

Debate raged furiously across the country all year, fed by pamphlets and rumour. Local discussion at assizes and quarter sessions mirrored the divisions at Westminster. Towns and villages were in turmoil, parishes divided, and congregations split over the rift in public affairs. Popular discourse was never so animated by arguments, collisions, conversations, and confrontations. Fuelled by alcohol or anger, some contestants were ready to back their opinions with force. Rival groups came to blows in the

---

[61] Dorothy Gardiner (ed.), *The Oxinden Letters 1607–1642* (1933), 303.
[62] HMC, *Calendar of the Manuscripts of the Most Honourable The Marquess of Salisbury Preserved at Hatfield House, part 24, Addenda 1605–1668* (1976) 372.
[63] *An Appeale to the World in These Times of Extreame Danger* (1642), 1.
[64] *His Majesties Answer to the Nineteen Propositions* (Cambridge, 1642), 3.
[65] *Englands Tears and Lamentations for her lost Friend Peace* (1642), sigs. Av, A2.
[66] *A Remonstrance of Londons Occurrences* (1642), sig. A2v.
[67] *His Majesties Proceedings . . . from the 16 of August to the 23* (1642), 4.

streets of Hereford on Candlemas day (2 February), for example, and other communities experienced partisan affrays.[68]

Town meetings became fractious and rowdy. Communal civility seems to have broken down. The borough of Northampton struggled to restore decorum in April 1642 after members of the Assembly jumped up in their seats, spoke out of turn, and made noises to drown out others.[69] At Ipswich the borough court complained in May 1642 of 'much disorder . . . by many persons speaking together in a tumultuous manner, in such wise as the court cannot take any notice of what is spoken'.[70] At Canterbury residents of the parish of St Mary Magdalene lamented in June 1642 that 'there are such divisions grown up' about Parliament and the King 'that we can hardly look upon one another in charity'.[71]

Spring 1642 saw growing numbers of late-night assemblies in drinking establishments and private houses, where conversation turned on the affairs of the kingdom. These meetings had something of the flavour of secular or political conventicles. When one such gathering at Plymouth was broken up by the watch close to midnight on 29 April it disgorged a clergyman, a merchant, a vintner, and customs officials, who had been discussing a recent petition to Parliament from Cornwall. John Smith, the rector of St Ewe, told the watchmen that 'though the times were now for them, yet he knew the times would shortly alter', perceptively forecasting a shift of balance away from Parliament in favour of the King.[72]

Some of the remarks overheard in inns were vehemently hostile to Parliament. Others were contemptuous of the King. Westminster leaders grew sensitive to popular opinion, and sought to expose and to punish promoters of malignant or scandalous invective. One gets the impression of a rising volume and a quickening intensity, as citizens became more forthright or more reckless in their views.

In March 1642, a Cambridge physician, Thomas Shawberry, spoke rashly while drinking at the Spread-Eagle tavern in London, calling the Parliamentary leader 'King Pym' and 'rascal', and threatening to 'cut him in pieces if he had him'. Called by the Commons to account for his words, Shawberry said he was drunk and knew not what he said, but his utterance

---

[68] Herefordshire Record Office, Quarter Sessions, BG 11/5/35. The second circulation of the Protestation provided multiple occasions for discord as well as displays of consensus. See also Thomas Taylor Lewis (ed.), *Letters of the Lady Brilliana Harley* (Camden Society, vol. lviii, 1854), 167, 170.
[69] Markham and Cox (eds.), *Records of the Borough of Northampton*, ii. 20.
[70] Suffolk Record Office, Ipswich General Court Minute Book, 1609–1643, C/2/2/3/2, f. 315.
[71] HMC *5th Report*, 33; *Lords Journal*, v. 221.
[72] Bodleian Library, Ms. Tanner 63, ff. 21–6; A. G. Matthews, *Walker Revised. Being a Revision of John Walker's Sufferings of the Clergy during the Grand Rebellion 1642–60* (Oxford, 1948), 100.

cost him a stay in the gatehouse and a fine of a hundred pounds.[73] Also in March, Col. Francis Edmunds, an Irish-born Catholic and a quintessential Cavalier, proclaimed in the Balcony tavern in Covent Garden 'that he hoped that the King would now . . . maintain his prerogative by force of arms, and that if he knew where Mr. Pym, Mr. Hampden, and Mr. Strode were to be found, he would ease the King of further trouble by them'. He too paid for these words with a month in parliamentary custody.[74]

By this time, while the King was floundering in Yorkshire, Parliament was acting with increased boldness, performing 'acts of sovereignty' befitting an executive power.[75] On 5 March 1642 it passed the Militia Ordinance, which put the military resources of the country into hands of its own choosing. Members spent much of the next few months trying to justify and implement this revolutionary measure. It was undertaken, they said, 'for the safety and defence of the kingdom', or '*pro salute regis et populi*'.[76] On its own authority, Parliament took control of the strategic bastions and armouries at the Tower of London, Portsmouth, and Hull, denying these resources to the King. If Ireland was to be subdued and England made secure it would be done by parliamentary ordinance.

Enunciating constitutional theory that would have been unthinkable a year or two earlier, Parliament projected itself as the representative of all the people and as an emergency caretaker government. The Nineteen Propositions of June 1642 instructed the King that Parliament was 'your majesty's great and supreme council', the proper place to determine 'the great affairs of the kingdom'.[77] Westminster propagandists repeated the claim that 'parliament is the foundation and basis of government, and consequently of the peace and happiness of the kingdom'.[78]

These were 'times of extreme danger', claimed a parliamentary pamphlet of midsummer 1642, as 'illegal demands of the king' compounded England's 'manifold distempers'. If King Charles himself was not directly at fault, the responsibility lay with 'the evil counsels and wicked designs of those who under his majesty threaten to carry all before them'.[79] Parliamentarians

[73] Snow and Young (eds.), *Private Journals of the Long Parliament 7 March to 1 June 1642*, 39, 42, 43; *Commons Journals*, ii. 478.

[74] Snow and Young (eds.), *Private Journals of the Long Parliament 7 March to 1 June 1642*, 8, 9. [75] Clarendon, *History of the Rebellion*, i. 517.

[76] C. H. Firth and R. S. Rait, *Acts and Ordinances of the Interregnum* (3 vols., 1911), i. 1–5; *Questions resolved, and propositions tending to accommodation and agreement* (1642), sig. A3v.

[77] *Nineteen Propositions Made By both Houses of Parliament . . . With His Majesties Answer thereto* (Cambridge, 1642), 2.

[78] *An Appeale to the World in These Times of Extreame Danger* (1642), 1.

[79] Ibid. William Prynne, *A Soveraigne Antidote to Prevent, Appease, and Determine our Unnaturall and Destructive Civill Wars* (1642), sig. A1, charged the King 'seduced through pernicious counsellors', with preparing to wage 'a causeless, groundless civil war'.

could claim that they alone stood for the King's honour, God's glory, and the laws and liberties of England, against a disgraced regime that represented 'the tyranny of an arbitrary government'.[80] If the papists about the King had their way, warned one letter-writer, it would 'put a period to all parliaments, and so by consequence destroy our religion, liberty, and property'.[81]

The King, by contrast, claimed that Parliament was erecting 'an upstart authority' and that its agents were guilty of treason. Their intent, he claimed in his reply to the Nineteen Propositions, was to bring down 'our just, ancient, regal power'.[82] Although most of Parliament was against him and the capital had become untenable, King Charles still had substantial assets. Most important was the intangible advantage of kingship. Kings of England, even if disliked and mistrusted, commanded deep reserves of loyalty and respect. Kingship was among the powers ordained by God, and monarchs were answerable only to their creator. The canons of 1640 had upheld the 'divine right' of Kings to 'rule and command in their several dominions all persons of what rank or estate soever', and many people still believed this.[83]

Whereas conservative clergymen upheld royal authority, there were many among the gentry who thought it a matter of honour to serve their sovereign. Many commoners too clung to the royal mystique. The King was defender of the faith, the preserver of hierarchy, the embodiment of order and tradition. He was also, however, a growing target of opprobrium. 'Poor King', wrote Thomas Knyvett from London in May 1642, 'he grows still in more contempt and slight here every day. . . . And no wonder, when the reverence and worship of the King of Kings comes to be construed superstitious and idolatrous.'[84]

At the beginning of summer at Exeter some citizens were speaking 'seditious words against puritans and Roundheads', while others spoke ill of the King. A tailor and an embroiderer complained to the Exeter Quarter Sessions that Richard Bennett, a local goldsmith, spoke 'scandalous words of the Parliament' in July 1642, saying 'that Mr. Pym was a traitor . . . with other reproachful terms of the said Mr. Pym.'[85] Similar 'words against Mr. Pym' came from drinkers at Southampton. James Chapman, a pewterer from Petworth, Sussex, asserted in July 1642 that Pym 'was a traitor and a knave and he would maintain it, and that he would be hanged or did hope to see

[80] *A Declaration of The Valiant Resolution of the Famous Prentices of London* (1642), 5.

[81] *Letter Sent By a Yorkshire Gentleman, to a friend in London*, 5. Parliament's ordinance of 9 June 1642 'for bringing in plate, money and horses' likewise charged the malignants about the King with intending 'the destroying of our religion, laws, liberty, and propriety' (Firth and Rait, *Acts and Ordinances of the Interregnum*, i. 7).

[82] *His Majesties Answer to the Nineteen Propositions*, 2, 6.

[83] *Constitutions and Canons Ecclesiastical . . . 1640* (1640), sig. B4v.

[84] Schofield (ed.), *The Knyvett Letters (1620–1644)*, 103.

[85] Devon Record Office, Exeter Quarter Sessions Book, 1642–1660, ff. 1v, 5v.

him hanged within some short time'.[86] An anonymous satire of 1642 contrasted the oppressive regime of Pym's Parliament with 'the simple time when there was law', as if law had now gone missing.[87]

Conservative clergymen used their pulpits to bolster their support for the King. Preaching after King Charles's departure from London, the rector of Rotherby, Leicestershire, Francis Needham, warned parishioners of the King's 'enemies . . . that would take the King's crown off his head and set it on their own'.[88] John Wood, the Laudian vicar of Marden, Kent, preached 'that the parliament hath no power to do anything in the King's absence, no more than a man without a head'.[89] John Squire, the vicar of Shoreditch, 'compared his majesty to the man that went from Jerusalem to Jericho, and fell among thieves that wounded him of his honour, robbed him of his castles and hearts of his people'. The inference was obvious, in disparagement of Parliament.[90] The Herefordshire cleric Henry Rogers likened King Charles to the biblical King David. Both Kings had been forced to flee their capital by 'an ungracious and ungrateful people'. But whereas David fled Jerusalem with an entourage of six hundred, Charles left London with 'scarce his own servants with him'. The sermon ended with a prayer to 'confound all those Shimites that curse the King and esteem no more of him than of a dead dog, that would carry the church of God down to the ground'.[91]

'Judge whether I am to obey God or man', John Gwin, vicar of Cople, Bedfordshire, challenged parishioners when rejecting a parliamentary declaration in favour of directives from the King. 'By God's word I am commanded to obey the King; I find no such command for the parliament.'[92] Henry Ferne, Archdeacon of Leicester, likewise made it the duty of every divine 'to urge obedience, honour, and subjection' to the King's authority. 'The King is the *higher power* according to St. Paul, *the supreme* according to St. Peter, *the Father of the Commonwealth*', he argued in his influential treatise on *The Resolving of Conscience*.[93]

[86] R. C. Anderson (ed.), *The Book of Examinations and Depositions 1622–1644* (Southampton Record Society, 1936), 39. See also ill words about the parliament, reported to the House of Lords (*Lords Journal*, v. 156–7, 180, 220, 226, 241).

[87] Huntington Library, Ms. El. 7802, p. 1.

[88] Bodleian Library, J. Walker Ms. c. 11, f. 43.

[89] John White, *The First Century of Scandalous, Malignant Priests* (1643), 30.

[90] Ibid., 25.

[91] British Library, Add. Ms. 70003, ff. 236–7. The Puritan John Tombs collected notes on Rogers's sermon and forwarded them via Stanley Gower to Sir Robert Harley. The biblical Shimei cursed and threw stones at King David (II Samuel 16: 5–13).

[92] *Commons Journal*, ii. 691; Matthews, *Walker Revised*, 65.

[93] Henry Ferne, *The Resolving of Conscience* (Cambridge, 1642), epistle (original italics). The treatise was reprinted at London and York. A copy survives in the papers of Sir John Hotham, Hull University Library, DDHO/2/10.

Preaching in London on the anniversary of King Charles's accession (27 March 1642), the Oxford cleric Richard Gardyner reminded auditors that the King was the Lord's anointed, and 'it is by him that we move in our proper sphere'. Without a king, he said, 'our meetings would be mutinies, our pulpits cockpits, authority would lose its authority . . . the honourable would be levelled with the base, the prudent with the child, all would be amassed and huddled up in an unjust parity.' Even a bad king was better than no king at all.[94] These were conventional teachings, but they were particularly poignant at a time when the King had apparently abandoned his capital, and a large part of the populace had apparently abandoned their King. 'Touch not mine anointed' became the most commonly cited conservative text, along with the injunction to 'give Caesar his due'.[95] It was on this same 'crownation day' anniversary when the Yorkshire tanner Thomas Godsey declared publicly in Selby church, 'I care not for the king nor his laws.'[96]

Other reported conversations from June 1642 illuminate the strains in popular allegiance. Debate at Grantham, Lincolnshire, grew heated when one disputant declared for both King and Parliament, but said if pressed he would be for the King with all his heart. William Clarke, a local apothecary, immediately protested, 'thou hast a rotten, stinking heart within thee, for if thou wilt be for the King thou must be for the papists.' Further examined by local justices, Clarke apparently suggested that the Prince of Wales or the Duke of York should be crowned in the King's absence. Horrified officials referred the matter to Parliament, which side-stepped it to King's Bench.[97]

At Salisbury around the same time, an apothecary and a paper-maker were heard talking 'at the door of one widow Howell', when conversation turned to the likelihood of war. Henry Whately, the paper-maker, said rather rashly that 'if there were civil wars the first that he would pitch upon would be John Braxton', a local adversary. On matters of allegiance, Whately insisted that 'he for his part would be for the king', whereas Thomas Stevens, the apothecary, said that he would be 'for the king and the parliament'. Whately then declared that 'he did not care a pin for the parliament, saying they were a company of rebels'. Examined before the mayor and justices of Salisbury, he

---

[94] Richard Gardyner, *A Sermon . . . on the Day of his Majesty's Happy Inauguration* (1642), 9, 10.

[95] For example, William Sclater, *Papisto-Mastix, or Deborah's Prayer against God's Enemies* (1642), 39; Reynolds, *Evgenia's Teares*, 44; John Taylor, *A Plea for Prerogative: Or, Give Caesar his due* (1642), title page; *The Soveraignty of Kings* (1642).

[96] Lister (ed.), *West Riding Sessions Records. Vol. II*, liii. 367.

[97] Vernon F. Snow and Anne Steele Young (eds.), *The Private Journals of the Long Parliament 2 June to 17 September 1642* (New Haven and London, 1992), 136–7.

tried to excuse himself by saying he was drunk at the time, but added, 'they were a company of fools that would not hold with the king'.[98]

Taking an opposite line, Simon Zeager, a tanner from Minehead, Somerset, scandalized the company at an Exeter inn by blaming the King for maintaining popery and supporting the Irish rebels. A goldsmith who was present denounced Zeager's 'very seditious and traitorous words of the king's most excellent majesty', and claimed that the rest of those drinking wished no more than 'a happy union between his majesty and the parliament'.[99] Words like these would accompany the combatants into civil war.

Similar questions about royal authority and the duties of the subject exercised the villagers of Arlington, Sussex, where arguments about religion and politics overflowed from the church, to the alehouse, to the street. Parishioners were 'earnest in discourse' and deeply divided on fundamental matters of allegiance, and some of their words were reported to the East Sussex Quarter Sessions.[100] After church on Sunday, 3 July 1642, the vicar, John Wilson, continued conversation with neighbours, including tailors, husbandmen, and servants, at the house of John Foster, yeoman. One witness said that they 'were talking of the king and parliament'. Another reported they were 'earnest in discourse of the scriptures'. In fact, the two topics were inseparable.

According to witnesses, 'there happening to be speeches said about the king and parliament disagreeing', the conversation turned to questions of obedience. Mr Wilson said they should obey the King, even if he 'commanded images to be set up in the church to be worshipped, we ought to follow it'. But Samuel Andrews, a tailor, took the opposing line, 'that if a Christian king commanded laws contrary to God's laws he ought not to be obeyed'. Wilson insisted that Christians should 'honour a Christian king', but Andrews daringly replied that 'perhaps he did not deserve so much honour'. When the minister played his trump card, 'urging that the king was God's anointed, Andrews answered and said that he was not God's anointed, for God did not anoint him'.

The discussion then turned to the King's law-making capacity. John Wilson insisted that 'the king had power to make what laws he thought best for the good ordering of the commonwealth'. Pressed by Samuel Andrews to explain how this should be done, he replied that 'it was not to be disputed by them, but yet he thought the safest way were to observe the same course that had always been taken, namely by the king and two houses of parliament'.

---

[98] Bodleian Library, Ms. Tanner 63, ff. 66–7.
[99] Devon Record Office, Exeter Quarter Sessions Book, 1642–1660, f. 6v.
[100] East Sussex Record Office, QR/E/57/60–4.

To reinforce this view, Wilson quoted 'some text of scripture to prove that Moses had power from God to make laws, and that the Apostles yielded obedience to the heathen emperors. Whereupon the said Andrews replied, better to yield obedience to one of them than him. And the said Andrews further said the king had no more power from God to make laws.'

This was a remarkable exchange, not just for its subject matter, which touched on principles of constitutional law, but also for its pitting of a village artisan against a university-trained minister. When another tailor, Thomas Sicklemore, joined the debate, the vicar berated him as 'a rebellious fellow because he would not come to his church'. Sicklemore replied, 'that he could not profitably come thither', to which John Wilson expostulated, 'it is no marvel that thou art a rebel; the parliament are rebels and do rebel against the king, setting forth laws contrary to his will'. The conversation ended in rancour, with Wilson saying 'that the parliament did raise arms against the king'.[101]

Exchanges like these, the parish equivalents of the elite debate on Parliament's Militia Ordinance and the King's Commission of Array, testify to deep cracks in popular allegiance and severe tarnishing of the royal majesty. For artisans to dispute with ministers about royal sovereignty and Christian obedience was almost unprecedented. Under pressure of events, some citizens voiced sentiments that would not previously have crossed their minds, and others recoiled from such thoughts in horror. When Edward Jude, the rector of Hunsdon, Hertfordshire, reminded parishioners of their obligations to the monarch in the summer of 1642, one of them protested, with breathtaking incision, 'what speak you of the king, he is nothing but words?'[102]

---

[101] The apparent purpose of these depositions was not to punish the tailors but to paint John Wilson in the most unfavourable light. He was indicted as a common barrator, though the case was removed from the court by a *certiorari*. A Laudian ceremonialist, Wilson had served as vicar since 1630 and was sequestered in 1643. John White, *First Century of Scandalous Malignant Priests*, 1, claimed that Wilson had attempted buggery, and taught that 'baptism utterly taketh away original sin'. See also Anthony Fletcher, *A County Community in Peace and War: Sussex 1600–1660* (1976), 256–7, and R. C. Redwood (ed,), *Quarter Sessions Order Book 1642–1649* (Sussex Record Society, vol. liv, 1954), pp. xxii, 16.

[102] Hertfordshire Record Office, Ms. 46351. The rector was Edward Jude, who was charged in 1643 with vilifying Parliament. Comparable 'words of high concernment' were reported to Norfolk justices in the opening years of the civil war. Arguing with other women late in 1642, Rachel Mercy of Fakenham declared 'that she cared not, for there is no king, no laws, no justice', adding that 'there was no king…because the king was not where he should be'. In 1643 Thomas Theodrick of Fincham, glover, said that 'the King is no King, he is a bastard, and was crowned with a leaden crown', to which Francis Hubbert, yeoman, responded 'that those words were bloody words, wishing him to take heed what he spake' (Norfolk Record Office, Quarter Sessions Rolls, C/S3/34/3 and 4).

THE FAILURE OF ACCOMMODATION

Nobody wanted war. It was inconceivable, wrote the Kentish conservative Sir Roger Twysden, that a kingdom without an enemy abroad and 'in firm peace at home' should descend so quickly into civil combustion.[103] It was shocking to contemplate the end of the long domestic peace that distinguished England from less fortunate European nations.

'Look upon the Empire of Germany, what a havoc and desolation has the sanguine hand of war made there', wrote the author of *Englands Doxologie* at the time of the peace with Scotland.

View our neighbour nation of France. Behold that grand monarch of Spain. Take a survey of the Netherlands, and those passages between the States and the House of Austria. Consider these premises, and you will easily conclude the ruin and devastation that direful war hath been the cause of in these latter times. Other great kingdoms have lamentably suffered, only this little island is secure.[104]

It was unthinkable, wrote the author of *Englands Present Distractions*, that 'this land flowing with milk and honey' should be 'converted into a wilderness'. How horrible for England, 'the darling and delight of Europe', to be drawn into the 'dance of death' that was sweeping the continent from Germany to Spain.[105] Other propagandists cited the horrors of France and Germany, ancient Rome, or contemporary Ireland, to warn of the miseries of civil combustions.[106]

'I pray God keep us from the misery that other nations have suffered by war', wrote Lady Sussex to Sir Ralph Verney in January 1642.[107] 'God grant this kingdom not to a general combustion', prayed Edward Reynolds months later. 'Albion cliffs are yet free from those crimson stains which have so deeply dyed thy eastern neighbours.'[108]

Once started, a civil war would have horrific consequences. It would signify, Lord Mandeville avowed, 'the dissolution of this government'.[109]

---

[103] 'Sir Roger Twysden's Journal', *Archaeologia Cantiana*, 1 (1858), 199.

[104] J.L., *Englands Doxologie* (1641), 1–4.

[105] H.G., *Englands Present Distractions. Paralleld with those of Spaine, and other forraigne Countries* (1642), 3, 8.

[106] Thomas Morton, *Englands Warning-Piece: Shewing the Nature, Danger, and ill Effects of Civill-Warre* (1642); *A Warning for England, Especially for London* (1642); H.P., *The Manifold Miseries of Civill Warre and Discord in a Kingdom* (1642); *Englands Tears and Lamentations for her lost Friend Peace*; Ephraim Udall, *The Good of Peace and Ill of Warre* (1642), 38.   [107] HMC, *7th Report* (1879), 436.

[108] Reynolds, *Evgenia's Teares*, 23, 29.

[109] Snow and Young (eds.), *Private Journals of the Long Parliament 7 March to 1 June March 1642*, 349.

Other speechmakers warned of the social consequences of the impending catastrophe. Edward Waller warned in June 1642 that a civil war 'would destroy the law, which did put a difference between man and man, and so in the issue must come to a parity and confusion'. Sir Simonds D'Ewes agreed that 'if . . . civil war should ensue, the law would be destroyed'. Cicero had taught him that 'the laws stand mute in war'.[110] Civil war would be the end of civil society, thought the bishop of Durham, Thomas Morton, 'for then would the laws be cast off, the magistrates despised, the liberty of subjects turned into the licentiousness of rebels, and all things strangely metamorphised into a confused chaos.'[111]

Other Cassandras dwelt on the social cost of conflict. The drift to war, they feared, was a drift towards levelling confusion and anarchy. We stood 'at the pit's brink, ready to plunge ourselves into an ocean of troubles and miseries', warned Bulstrode Whitelocke in the debate upon the Militia bill. If civil war came, he continued, 'we must surrender up our laws, liberties, properties and lives into the hands of insolent mercenaries.' The danger was not just loss of life, but that 'the ignoble will rule the noble, and baseness will be preferred before virtue, profaneness before piety.'[112] Simonds D'Ewes advised similarly, 'there is no doubt that all right and property, all *meum* and *tuam*, must cease in civil wars; and we know not what advantage the meaner sort also may take to divide the spoils of the rich and noble amongst them.'[113]

Writers and speakers on all sides of the political debate warned of 'the near approaching of our unspeakable miseries and calamities'.[114] 'We are at the very brink of combustion and confusion', declared Sir Benjamin Rudyerd in July 1642. 'If blood once begin to touch blood, we shall presently fall into a certain misery.'[115] Every effort was needed, wrote the Londoner John Price, to avoid the 'imminent calamities' of war and the 'universal desolation which like a meteor hangs over us'.[116]

Every effort indeed was needed to secure 'reconcilement' and 'accommodation'. These were among the most used words in 1642, as politicians sought a way back from the precipice and statesmen struggled to avoid civil war.

---

[110] Snow and Young (eds.), *The Private Journals of the Long Parliament 2 June to 17 September 1642*, 44.   [111] Morton, *Englands Warning-Piece*, 5.
[112] [Bulstrode Whitelock], *Memorials of The English Affairs* (1682), 57; idem, *Memorials of the English Affairs* (4 vols., Oxford, 1853), i. 176–7; Ruth Spalding (ed.), *The Diary of Bulstrode Whitelock, 1605–1675* (Oxford, 1990), 132.
[113] Snow and Young (eds.), *Private Journals of the Long Parliament 2 June to 17 September 1642*, 44–5.
[114] John Digby, *A Speech by the Right Honorable, Iohn Earl of Bristoll, in the High Court of Parliament: May 20, 1642. Concerning an accommodation* (1642), 3.
[115] Benjamin Rudyerd, *A Worthy Speech . . . July the ninth, 1642* (1642), 1, 4.
[116] [John Price], *Some Few and Short Considerations on the Present Distempers* (1642), 3, 6.

King Charles himself evoked this discourse in January when he wrote of 'his fatherly care of all his people' and his hopes for 'a happy and blessed accommodation'.[117] Leading figures in the King's camp and at Westminster trumpeted the need for accommodation, so long as they were not the ones who had to back down. Queen Henrietta Maria, however, thought accommodation 'unsupportable'. Her manipulative letters from Holland pressured King Charles against accommodation, and made him promise never to yield to his enemies behind her back.[118]

In May the House of Lords established a committee, 'to consider how there might be an accommodation between the king and his people, for the good, happiness, and safety of both king and kingdom'. However, as Clarendon wryly observed, 'this temper of accommodation troubled them not long'.[119] There were more 'overtures of accommodation' in July, but, Sir Gilbert Pickering told Roland St John, 'most men think they smell the air of peace, yet provide for war'.[120] 'This is not the way for peace', wrote Lady Denbigh to her son Lord Feilding, 'to imbroil the whole Christian world in wars, and then to declare it for religion and make God a party to these woeful affairs.'[121]

Frantic petitioners addressed both houses of Parliament and the King. Petitioners from Exeter in July 1642 appealed for 'the closing up the present breaches of this distracted...kingdom', and pressed for 'a compliance' between the king and parliament. They wanted what everyone wanted, 'the unity of King and Parliament, unity in religion, unity in loyal affections to his majesty', which would preserve the kingdom in 'peace and charity'. How this accommodation could be achieved was not specified, but they left no doubt that without peace 'this time of public calamity' would degenerate into further 'lamentable distractions and convulsions'.[122]

Offering terms from Parliament in July 1642 the Earl of Holland urged King Charles 'to remember his father's motto, blessed are the peacemakers'. The King replied that he would rather lose his life than 'lose his rights', and observers concluded there could be 'no answer of peace' from that quarter.[123] The printed *Propositions of Accommodation for the composing of the present Differences* of that month used the Irenic language of 'reconcilement',

[117] Coates, Young, and Snow (eds.), *Private Journals of the Long Parliament 3 January to 5 March 1642*, 125.
[118] Mary Anne Everett Green, *Letters of Queen Henrietta Maria* (1857), 58–9, 61, 70, 118–19.
[119] Clarendon, *History of the Rebellion*, ii. 119.
[120] Bedfordshire and Luton Archives, St John Papers, J. 1410; *Lords Journals*, v. 208.
[121] HMC, *4th Report* (1874), 259.
[122] Devon Record Office, Quarter Session Order Book, Q/S 1/8, 12 July 1642.
[123] *Advertisements from Yorke and Beverly* (1642), 1.

'concurrence', and 'accommodation'. But, like many declarations of this period, it was less an olive branch than an ultimatum. 'All distractions and misapprehensions' could be ended, it declared, but only by placing the militia under parliamentary supervision.[124] The Propositions repeatedly expressed desires for a 'happy concurrence' while offering terms that no English monarch could accept.

GEARING FOR WAR

Bulstrode Whitelocke's observation on the eve of the civil war is justifiably regarded as classic:

> It is strange to note how we have insensibly slid into this beginning of a civil war, by one unexpected accident after another, as waves of the sea which have brought us thus far, and we scarce know how, but from paper combats, by declarations, remonstrances, protestations, votes, messages, answers and replies, we are now come to the question of raising forces and naming a general and officers of the army.[125]

As spring passed to summer in 1642 the English polity moved piecemeal to a warlike footing.

While Parliament promoted the Militia Ordinance, the King's supporters upheld traditional royal authority through the Commission of Array. The two instruments were mutually opposed and incompatible, so that Henry Oxinden told his cousin in July 1642, 'methinks my condition betwixt the Commission of Array and the ordinance of parliament is like his that is between Scylla and Charybdis' (between a lethal rock and a devouring whirlpool).[126] It did not help that the Commission of Array was in Latin, and was based on Plantagenet principles. Clashes occurred when rival agents arrived in towns to make proclamations, to secure local munitions, and or to enlist support for their cause.[127]

The militarization of English towns continued, as local grandees and warlords manoeuvred for advantage. The summer saw increased mobilization, along with bullying, intimidation, and occasional acts of violence. Both King

---

[124] *Propositions of Accommodation For the composing of the present Differences between His Majestie and the Parliament* (1642), broadsheet, printed 9 July.

[125] [Whitelock], *Memorials of The English Affairs*, 57. There is no evidence that these actual words were spoken in the course of the militia debate in February 1642, but Whitlocke's speech on that topic is mentioned in Spalding (ed.), *Diary of Bulstrode Whitelock*, 132.

[126] Gardiner (ed.), *Oxinden Letters 1607–1642*, 312.

[127] HMC, *5th Report*, 32–43; HMC, *Tenth Report, Appendix, Part IV* (1885, reissued 1906), 24. A translation of the Commission of Array is in Joyce Lee Malcolm, *Caesar's Due: Loyalty and King Charles 1642–1646* (1983), 232–3.

and Parliament lined up supporters, but there was no enthusiastic rush to take sides. The London trained bands went through their paces, and the King began to attract soldiers to York. Observers remarked on 'the great number of ordnance' arriving in York, 'thank the crown jewels of the crown'.[128]

On 3 June King Charles rallied the freeholders of Yorkshire on Haworth Moor. Many of them offered loyal sentiments, crying 'God bless the King', but others called on God to 'unite the king and parliament, and turn the king's heart'. The crowd was far from unanimous, with jostling over pamphlets and petitions.[129] A month later the King ordered twelve thousand men of the northern trained bands to turn out, 'yet not one in sixty appeared', so one unfriendly observer remarked.[130]

Friends of the parliament urged them to take counter measures. 'If you dare not night and day arm, arm, and prepare yourselves to preserve the peace of the kingdom you will be over-run before you be aware', warned one pro-Parliamentary writer in July who had observed the build-up of weaponry at York.[131] 'Look to the arms of your trained bands betimes, or it will be too late', urged another letter printed in early August.[132]

The material preparations for war continued all through the spring and summer, alongside attempts to avoid it. The London cutlers and gunsmiths worked overtime to supply swords, muskets, and carbines.[133] Gentry families as well as towns continued to build up their stocks of weapons. Rival forces intercepted or interdicted armaments they thought might be used against them. Bulstrode Whitlocke, who had already acquired carbines, gunpowder, bullets, and swords, added pikes, pistols, and good horses to his personal armoury, as he and his neighbours 'began to arm and to provide for their own defence'.[134] Lady Sussex reported 'great fear at St. Albans' and a haste to buy weaponry for self-defence.[135] Lord Coventry sent chest-loads of muskets into Buckinghamshire.[136] Sir Edward Verney instructed his steward in July 1642, 'I pray have the carbines at home in readiness for the defence of the house if need be, and have powder and bullets ready.'[137] In some places common people too were acquiring weapons. London apprentices were sporting

---

[128] *Advertisements from Yorke and Beverly*, 2.
[129] *Letter Sent By a Yorkshire Gentleman, to a friend in London*; Bodleian Library, Oxford, Tanner Ms. 63, f. 43.
[130] *An Extract of a Letter from Yorke. Dated on Friday night, August 5* (1642), 1.
[131] *Advertisements from Yorke and Beverly*, 3.
[132] *Extract of a Letter from Yorke*, 3.
[133] Ordinary swords cost 7s. 6d., swords for horsemen 10s. Muskets cost 16s. 6d. apiece wholesale, carbines 22s. to 30s. A pair of pistols cost 56s. Bodleian Library, Oxford, Tanner Ms. 63, ff. 5, 1, 14, 15.   [134] Spalding (ed.), *Diary of Bulstrode Whitelock*, 121, 132.
[135] HMC, *7th Report*, 436.   [136] *Commons Journal*, ii. 607, 609.
[137] HMC, *7th Report*, 439.

swords, and artisans around Bristol 'had gotten divers clubs very lately' when they stirred up a 'commotion' in April.[138]

Borough records from the summer of 1642 reveal a frenzy of preparation. Worcester repaired its walls in June and authorized sixty pounds 'for arms for the public use and defence of this city', to be disbursed 'with all convenient speed'.[139] Gloucester moved ordnance onto its walls, set chains across its gates, and readied gunpowder, bullets, and match in anticipation of a siege.[140] Leicester put chains and posts across its gates and bridge, 'for the safeguarding and strengthening of those parts of the town'.[141] Salisbury dug trenches, set up chains, and ordered all householders to join in the watch, 'in regard of the eminent danger the kingdom now standeth in'.[142] Norwich ordered a double watch throughout the city in July 1642 'in regard of the great distractions and dangers of this kingdom'.[143] Decayed gunpowder in the city magazine was exchanged for powder 'of the new and best sort'.[144]

The summer saw further military preparations at Devizes, the county town of Wiltshire, where the corporation stocked powder and match, and acquired some artillery pieces from Bristol. There were orders 'for chaining and blocking up the town's end at several times', and 'for beating of a drum for volunteers'. Perhaps anticipating problems, the town paid five shillings in 1642 'for the making of a new gallows'.[145] At Cambridge the mayor's budget was increased by fifty pounds in August 1642 to cover extra expenses 'in these extraordinary dangerous times'.[146] Oliver Cromwell sent arms to Cambridge and began to prepare a Cambridge militia. A musket could be had for about one pound, and men of both town and gown began to brandish weapons in an informal process of militarization. Some of these men saw action even before the civil war started, when Cromwell seized the Cambridge college silver that was being smuggled out of the town to the King.[147] On 15 August the Common Council of Bristol ordered walls and gates to be repaired and chains to be installed, 'in readiness for the safety of this city'.[148] If there was to be a war, as now seemed certain, everyone knew that Bristol would be a

---

[138] Bristol Record Office, Quarter Sessions Minute Book 1634–47, JQS/M/3, f. 192.

[139] Shelagh Bond (ed.), *The Chamber Order Book of Worcester, 1602–1650* (Worcester Historical Society, new series, vol. viii, 1974), 352–4.

[140] Gloucestershire Record Office, Sessions Orders 1633–1671, GBR/G3/SO2, GBR/B3/2.

[141] Stocks and Stevenson (eds.), *Records of the Borough of Leicestershire . . . 1603–1688*, 313.

[142] Wiltshire Record Office, Salisbury Borough Ledger, 1640–1723, 23/1/4, f. 9.

[143] Norfolk Record Office, Norwich Mayor's Court Book, 1634–1646, f. 355v

[144] Ibid., f. 357.

[145] Wiltshire Record Office, Devizes General Entry Book, 1572–1660, ff. 165–165v.

[146] Cambridgeshire Record Office, Cambridge Corporation Common Day Book, vol. vii (1610–1646), 358.   [147] Cooper, *Annals of Cambridge*, iii. 326–7.

[148] Bristol Record Office, Common Council Proceedings, vol. iii (1627–42), 123.

target and a prize. Newcastle, still recovering from the Scottish occupation, began to rearm its citizens in August 1642.[149]

In several places these preparations were put to the test. 'A desperate combat' erupted at Leicester on market day, 4 June 1642, after royal and parliamentary agents clashed at the Angel tavern. Nobody was killed on this occasion, but swords were drawn and combatants engaged in 'sharp and uncivil words'.[150]

A more serious clash occurred at Manchester, where Lord Strange had gone to secure the powder magazine for the King. The townsmen 'put themselves in arms' and held his lordship at bay. Street battles broke out on 4 and 5 July when Lord Strange returned to take the magazine by force. In the resulting exchange of gunfire, according to a report sent to Parliament, twenty-seven of Lord Strange's men were killed and eleven men of Manchester.[151] Another report made no mention of the musketeers killing anyone, 'but the rain being so great put out most of their matches'.[152]

Following this skirmish, some observers thought the civil war had already started. But even now, it was not too late to avert catastrophe. 'God in his great mercy stop the sword from going any further', prayed a correspondent in Lancashire, 'as it is but a little way drawn, so lord I beseech thee sheath it again.'[153]

East Yorkshire was already braced for combat. 'Here is no other sound but war', observed a Yorkshire writer on 1 August. Cavalier forces conducted a desultory siege of Hull, and there were skirmishes between the besiegers and the garrison. One raid and counter-raid involved more than a hundred men at arms.[154] Other quasi-military actions occurred at Portsmouth, Warwick, Coventry, and elsewhere, involving little more than musketry and menaces. In Kent parliamentary troops occupied the blockhouse at Gravesend and stood guard at Chatham castle and Rochester bridge.[155] Other parliamentary volunteers marched through Middlesex and Buckinghamshire in early August, leaving a trail of burnt books, shredded surplices, and shattered Communion rails.[156]

---

[149] Newcastle upon Tyne Records Committee, *Extracts from the Newcastle Upon Tyne Council Minute Book 1639–1656* (Newcastle, 1920), 15.

[150] [Adam Jones], *Horrible Newes from Leicester. Being the Copie of a Letter sent from thence the 6 of Iune* (1642).

[151] *Severall Letters From the Committees in Severall Counties* (1642), 2; *The Beginning of Civil-Warres in England, or, A Skirmish between the Lord Strange, and the Inhabitants of Manchester* (1642); Huntington Library, Ms. El. 7762.

[152] *A Very True and Credible Relation of the Severall Passages at Manchester* (1642), sig. A3.

[153] *Beginning of Civil-Wares in England*, sig. A4e.

[154] *Some Speciall Passages from Hull, Anlaby, and Yorke* (1642), 3–5.

[155] *Special Passages From Divers Parts of the kingdome . . . From Tuesday, the 16. of August, to Tuesday, the 23* (1642), 9–11, 14–15.

[156] Nehemiah Wallington to George Willingham, 16 August 1642, *CSPD 1641–43*, 371–3.

The textbooks used to tell us that civil war broke out in England on 22 August 1642, when King Charles I raised his standard at Nottingham. But amidst the confusions of that summer it was not clear when the fighting actually began. England had already experienced military violence for a month or more, but there would be no major battle until after harvest in the autumn. The raising of the standard outside Nottingham castle was a formal ceremonial gesture, as medieval as the Commission of Array. It did not immediately change anything. By one account, the King's standard unfurled before a crowd of a couple of thousand, 'who came more to see the manner of the thing than any ways to offer assistance to his majesty'.[157] Even after this heraldic declaration of war there were some in the King's camp who hoped 'for a fair treaty and accommodation of peace, and that all differences and mistakes might be ended'.[158] They found themselves in a war that nobody wanted, but nobody knew how to avoid.

---

[157] *A True and Exact Relation of the Manner of his Maiesties setting up of his Standard at Nottingham* (1642), sig. A4.   [158] Ibid., sig. A4v.

Postscript: Why the English Revolution Matters

The revolution that convulsed England between 1640 and 1642 took many more forms across the following twenty years. The telling of it generated many more stories. Half a decade of military campaigning turned makeshift civilian armies into professionalized fighting forces. The effort to raise men and matériel put unprecedented pressure on the kingdom's financial and economic resources. As many as 85,000 died in combat, 23,000 in 1643 alone.[1] A second civil war in 1648 was shorter and nastier than the first. New political circumstances stimulated new political thinking about the nature and locus of sovereignty, about relations between King and Parliament, and whether a king was even necessary. Parliamentary Presbyterians abolished episcopacy and the prayer book, effectively dismantling the Church of England. They also abolished the Court of Wards and Liveries and put an end to feudal tenure. Parliamentary soldiers and their artisan allies developed the proto-democratic ideas of the Levellers. Radicalized army officers took independent political action, subjecting England to a succession of military coups. In January 1649 the King went on trial, and to near-universal astonishment he was executed. The very institution of kingship was abolished, along with the House of Lords, and England became a republican Commonwealth.

The Diggers emerged soon after the Regicide, proclaiming communal ownership of the land. Ranters took religious radicalism to extremes, proclaiming their merging with God and their own freedom from sin. Seekers, Fifth Monarchists, Muggletonians, and Quakers contributed to the religious ferment of the 1650s, while Baptists and Independents built congregations, Anglicans went underground, and Oliver Cromwell even made arrangements to welcome back the Jews.

As leader of the Commonwealth's armed forces, and then as Lord Protector, Cromwell exercised power over a forcibly unified British state. The compromises and complexities of Cromwellian government both extended and undermined the revolution. Cromwell's death in 1658 brought it crashing to an end. The counter-coup that engineered the Restoration brought back the

---

[1] Charles Carlton, *Going to the Wars: The Experience of the British Civil Wars 1638–1651* (1992), 204.

trappings of monarchy and episcopacy, but left unresolved the legacy of 'the good old cause'. Revolutions within the revolution released energies and inspired ideas that could not readily be extinguished. Despite counter-revolutionary pressures for indemnity and oblivion, the revolution that began in 1641 was one from which there was no going back.

Readers who have come this far, or who have turned to this point, may be contemplating whether the effort is worth the reward. A similar challenge might be posed to any scholarly enterprise, which every scholar should bear in mind. Why does the English Revolution matter? A wide range of answers comes to mind, beginning with the claim that the subject is intrinsically interesting. England's historical experience is rich with incident, and the drama commands attention. The surviving sources are richer and more var-ied than for any other early modern society. The sheer weight and quality of historiographical investment in this period compels our regard, and the effort involved in sifting the material and reconstructing the story is intellec-tually and aesthetically gratifying. It is good to teach, and good to think with. This may all be true, but it is only a beginning.

An earlier generation of historians made high claims for the centrality and significance of this English Revolution. More recent writers on the subject tend to be more circumspect and more modest. It may be useful to review some of the best known justifications before returning to the central claims of this book.

Most stark and forthright was Christopher Hill's declaration, in his first major publication on the subject, that 'the revolution of 1640–9' was 'per-haps the most important event that has yet happened in English history'. Setting forth the Marxist belief that in mid-Stuart England 'an old order that was essentially feudal was destroyed by violence, a new and capitalist social order created in its place', Hill made claims for the significance of this revolu-tion 'for us at the present day'. His was a history of praxis and engagement, providing background and inspiration for the modern struggle to establish socialism.[2] A quarter of a century later, in *The World Turned Upside Down*, the transformation from feudalism was less visible, but Hill still saw the revo-lution as 'the greatest upheaval that has yet occurred in Britain'. It was to be celebrated now for its 'glorious flux' that set in train 'the colossal transfor-mations which ushered England into the modern world'.[3]

Hill was by no means alone in these assessments. His cold-war contemporary Perez Zagorin claimed that the English Revolution possessed 'world-wide'

---

[2] Christopher Hill, *The English Revolution 1640: Three Essays* (1948), 6, 9, 10.
[3] Christopher Hill, *The World Turned Upside Down* (1972, 1991 edn.), 13, 14, 384.

significance, especially for its 'libertarian ideas which...figure in the struggles of the present day'.[4] Lawrence Stone agreed that the ideas emanating from the English Revolution were of lasting importance—'ideas of liberty not liberties, equality not privilege, fraternity not deference'. Anticipating the French contribution by almost a century and half, these ideas from mid-seventeenth-century England made this 'the first "Great Revolution" in the history of the world, and therefore an event of fundamental importance in the evolution of Western civilization'.[5]

Other historians have seen the English Revolution as the birthplace of modernity, or at least the incubator of modernization. By undermining the mystique of monarchy and stimulating discussion of such previously unthinkable ideas as popular sovereignty and religious toleration, the revolution gave rise to liberal, democratic, and pluralistic political theories. Its two decades of political, constitutional, military, and religious upheaval were accompanied by an explosion of printed material and an outpouring of original thought that turned the world upside down. Its reverberations could be felt in England in 1688, in America in 1776, and in France in 1789.

It is easy to slip into hyperbole, easy to claim too much. The chains of future connection are not always clear. Incidents and outcomes are not necessarily commensurate. Legacies become detached from the history that gave rise to them. Nor is posterity the best measure for the historical significance of any epoch. An alternative approach, one which most historians in fact practise, is to consider the impact of past change on the generations who lived through it. Our history might tell us how it felt to live though extraordinary disruptions, and how the experience of revolution changed people's minds, or changed their lives. We can choose to be more concerned with how the English Revolution unfolded than what it led to. The true significance of the revolution then might lie in the processes and media and recovered conversations of the age of Charles I that put early modern England to the test. The revolution exposed the stresses of post-Reformation society, revealing which institutions worked well, and which did not.

Nobody in 1642 could tell what would befall them in the next decade, or in the next few months, any more than we ourselves know what lies ahead. The revolution that gave shape to seventeenth-century history was

---

[4] Perez Zagorin, 'The English Revolution 1640–1660', *Journal of World History*, 2 (1955), 671, reproduced in idem, *The English Revolution: Politics, Events, Ideas* (Aldershot and Brookfield, Vt., 1998), 28.

[5] Lawrence Stone, *The Causes of the English Revolution 1529–1642* (1972, 1996 edn.), 146, 147. See also Lawrence Stone, 'The Results of the English Revolutions of the Seventeenth Century', in J. G. A. Pocock (ed.), *Three British Revolutions, 1641, 1688, 1776* (Princeton, 1980), 23–108.

unimaginable before it happened. Yet even before the outbreak of civil war English society had been exposed to a buffeting of revolutionary proportions. Caroline England was beset by political, constitutional, religious, and cultural revolution, and its fulcrum was 1641. That this revolution was flawed and incomplete, unstable and contradictory, makes it no less revolutionary, and goes some way to explaining what followed. The experience was all the more shocking because it occurred in a culture that prized order, continuity, and decorum, and was averse to innovation.

An earthquake of cosmic proportions rocked English society between the spring of 1640 and the summer of 1642. These were some of its shocks and repercussions:

- a military mobilization in 1640 greater than any since 1588, with none of the national cohesion induced by the Elizabethan Spanish threat, followed in 1642 by renewed mobilization, this time of English forces geared up to fight each other;

- the experience of military disorders and insubordination, with parts of northern England exposed for the first time to English and Scottish standing armies, and citizen soldiers at far geographical remove from their places of origin;

- a revolution in the relations of England, Scotland, and Ireland, with King Charles losing his ability to govern all three kingdoms—Scotland in rebellion, Ireland in religious revolt, and constitutional challenges in England;

- a questioning of royal authority, sacrifice of the royal prerogative, and the effective end of the royal supremacy in matters ecclesiastical;

- the rapid demystification of majesty and the undermining of sacred kingship, from public affronts to the King's honour to the King's displacement from his court;

- the overthrow of the King's principal advisors, including the Earl of Strafford executed, Windebank and Finch in exile, the ship money judges discredited, Archbishop Laud imprisoned, another dozen bishops impeached, and eventually Queen Henrietta Maria forced abroad—no wonder the King was uncounselled and pitied as friendless;

- the rapid rise of Parliament as the self-conscious representative of the people, promoted to near-permanence through the legislation of 1641, capable of executive action, with expanded notions of parliamentary privilege, and novel claims that royal councillors and officers should be subject to parliamentary approval;

- if not the end, then at least the death throes of the *arcana imperii*, the exposure of the kingdom's business to all interested parties, and the opening of public affairs to the general public, including women and 'the people who do not rule';
- the emergence of partisan political conflict, in which issues and ideologies transcended the traditional social cohesion of the elite;
- the exercise of lay popular voices, never completely mute, as some of the King's subjects asserted themselves as citizens, and citizens of London demanded to be heard at Westminster; outdoor politics, the politicization of discourse, and tumultuous petitioning by freeholders, artisans, and women;
- a transformation in the content, output, circumstances, and control of the popular press, inviting readers to react with laughter, anger, approval, or indignation to printed commentary and news; a reading revolution that built its own audience and turned occasional readers of texts into avid consumers of print, within an energized public sphere;
- local and national changes in religious culture that discredited the arrangements of the Laudian ascendancy, defanged the instruments of ecclesiastical discipline, and destabilized the long-established Church of England; community worship became contested and contentious as parishioners pursued new paths as wayfaring Christians, becoming swept up, in William Haller's memorable phrase, by 'a cyclonic shattering storm of the spirit';[6]
- a sense in some quarters that there was 'no law now', that customary constraints and protections had been compromised, and that magisterial authority could no longer effectively assert itself;
- multiple transgressions, some more imagined than real, involving lay intrusions on the domain of the clergy, lowly intrusions on the domains of the elite, the rascality rubbing against magistracy, the city clashing with the court, the street with institutions of government, and women encroaching on the territories of men;
- widespread and widely reported affronts to gentility and authority, erosions of hierarchy and deference, and verbal social challenges from an irascible and obstreperous underclass;
- a widely experienced fear or dread that dangers loomed and cataclysm was around the corner, as secure and stable structures of the polity appeared to crumble.

[6] William Haller, *Liberty and Reformation in the Puritan Revolution* (New York, 1963), p. xiv.

None of these developments was complete or irreversible, nor could contemporaries know where they might lead. All they could tell, as the revolution rocked around them, was that they were in a labyrinth, an earthquake, or a storm. These linked processes, and the disruptive contradictions within them, made the years 1640 to 1642 years of shaking and of prayer. The simultaneity, concatenation, and cumulative, compounding effect of these disturbances gave them their ferocious intensity. This was the revolution before the Revolution, the revolution that led to civil war.

Chronology

1640

March
27 Fri   Accession Day (16th year of King Charles)

April
13 Mon   Parliament meets

May
5 Tue   Parliament dissolved
11 Mon   Attack on Laud's house at Lambeth
29 Fri   Convocation completes new Canons

June
13 Sat   King Charles endorses new Canons
17 Wed   Mutiny at Farringdon, Berkshire

July
8 Wed   Mutiny at Wellington, Somerset
18 Sat   Public fast against plague and other judgements

August
20 Thur   Scots cross border, King Charles sets out for York
28 Fri   Battle of Newburn
30 Sun   Scots occupy Newcastle

September
24 Thur   Great Council of Peers at York

October
1 Thur   London churchwardens refuse new oath
21 Wed   Anglo-Scottish Treaty of Ripon
22 Thur   Riot at High Commission
30 Fri   King Charles returns to London

November
1 Sun   High Commission records destroyed
3 Tue   Opening of Parliament
5 Thur   Gunpowder Treason Day
7 Sat   Pym's speech to Commons
11 Wed   Strafford impeached

16 Mon   Scottish commissioners in London
17 Tue   Fast day sermons by Burges and Marshall
25 Wed   Strafford to Tower
28 Sat   Burton and Prynne return to London

December
9 Wed   Commons debate on new church canons
10 Thur   Secretary of State Windebank flees to France
11 Fri   'Root and Branch' petition presented to Commons
16 Wed   Canons of 1640 voted illegal
18 Fri   Archbishop Laud impeached
22 Tue   Lord Keeper Finch flees to the Hague

1641
January
16 Sat   Lords order upholding established worship
21 Thur   Commons debates on religion
23 Sat   Commons order against religious images

February
8 Mon   Commons debate on 'Root and Branch' petition
16 Tue   Triennial Act

March
1 Mon   Archbishop Laud to the Tower
22 Mon   Strafford's trial begins
27 Sat   Accession Day (17th year of King Charles)

April
21 Wed   London petition for 'justice' against Strafford
            Commons votes attainder (204:59)

May
1 Sat   May Day. King says that he cannot condemn Stafford for treason
2 Sun   Marriage of William of Orange and Princess Mary
3 Mon   Tumultuous crowds at Westminster
            Protestation in Parliament
5 Wed   Pym reveals army plot
10 Mon   King signs Strafford Attainder Act
            Act Against Dissolution
12 Wed   Strafford executed
31 Mon   Stork seen on House of Commons

June
20 Sun   Burton preaches on the Protestation
23 Wed   Commons reads bill for scandalous ministers

July

5 Mon   Star Chamber and High Commission abolished; Bishop Matthew Wren impeached

August

7 Sat   Ship money declared illegal
10 Tue   King Charles sets out for Scotland
14 Sat   Charles at Edinburgh
16 Mon   Plague in Westminster
28 Sat   Riot at French ambassador's house

September

1 Wed   Commons resolution against superstition and innovation in church affairs
7 Tue   Peace with Scotland; Public thanksgiving
9 Thur   Commons order against idolatry and superstition and Lords order supporting established worship, both to be printed
               Parliamentary recess
18 Sat   Northern army disbanded

October

12 Tue   'Incident' plot foiled in Scotland
20 Wed   Parliament resumes, trained bands guard Westminster
23 Sat   Irish rebellion begins

November

1 Mon   News of Irish rebellion reaches London
5 Fri   Gunpowder Treason Day; Cornelius Burges preaches to Commons
8 Mon   Grand Remonstrance introduced in Commons
15 Mon   Catholic scares, news of second army plot
22 Mon   Grand Remonstrance passed (159:148)
25 Thur   King Charles returns to London from Scotland
28 Sun   Armed citizens at Westminster

December

1 Wed   Grand Remonstrance presented to the king
7 Tue   Militia Bill in Parliament
9 Thur   Writs to suppress unlawful assemblies
10 Fri   Proclamation in support of established religion
11 Sat   London citizens petition against bishops
15 Wed   Commons vote to print Grand Remonstrance (135: 83)
21 Tue   London Common Council election
23 Thur   London apprentices petition; Colonel Lunsford appointed Lieutenant of the Tower
26 Sun   Lunsford removed as Lieutenant of the Tower
27 Mon   Crowds jostle bishops; mêlée at Westminster
28 Tue   Armed citizens and apprentices at Westminster

29 Wed	Riots and strong night watch at Westminster
30 Thur	Twelve bishops impeached and sent to Tower
31 Fri	Armed citizens face armed guards at Whitehall

1642
January

2 Sun	Torrential rains
3 Mon	Impeachment of five MPs plus Lord Mandeville (later Earl of Manchester)
4 Tue	King Charles attempts to seize five MPs
5 Wed	Commons adjourn as committee to Guildhall; Charles in City
6 Thur	Twelfth Night
10 Mon	King Charles and family leave London, to Hampton Court
11 Tue	MPs return to Westminster
13 Thur	King Charles at Windsor
25 Tue	London petitions against bishops and popish lords

February

5 Sat	Bishops excluded from House of Lords (Royal assent 13 Feb.)
9 Wed	King Charles at Hampton Court
11 Fri	King Charles at Greenwich
14 Mon	King Charles at Canterbury
23 Wed	Queen Henrietta Maria sails from Dover, with crown jewels
26 Sat	King Charles at Greenwich

March

5 Sat	Militia Ordinance
9 Wed	King Charles at Newmarket
15 Tue	King Charles at Cambridge
19 Sat	King Charles at York (with only 39 gentlemen and 17 guards)
27 Sun	Accession Day (18th year of Charles)

April

| 23 Sat | St George's Day; King Charles denied entry to Hull |

May

10 Tue	London trained bands mustered in Finsbury Fields
12 Thur	King Charles summons gentry in arms to York
17 Tue	Lord Keeper sends Great Seal to York

June

2 Thur	Nineteen Propositions presented to King
11 Sat	Commissions of Array
18 Sat	King answers Nineteen Propositions

July
4 Mon   Mêlée at Manchester

August
10 Wed   Cromwell intercepts Cambridge plate
15 Mon   Cromwell seizes Cambridge magazine
22 Mon   Royal standard raised at Nottingham

Index